Why Do You Need This New Edition?

6 good reasons why you should buy this new edition of *The West: A Narrative History*

1. This edition is closely tied to the innovative website, the New MyHistoryLab, which helps you save time and improve results as you study history (www.myhistorylab.com). MyHistoryLab icons connect the main narrative in each chapter of the book to a powerful array of MyHistoryLab resources, including primary source documents, analytical video segments, interactive maps, and more. A MyHistoryLab Connections feature now appears at the end of each chapter, capping off the study resources for the chapter. The New MyHistoryLab also includes both eBook and Audio Book versions of *The West: A Narrative History*, Third Edition, so that you can read or listen to your textbook any time you have access to the Internet.

2. New with this Third Edition: *The West: A Narrative History* now uses the latest release of the New MyHistoryLab, which offers the most advanced Study Plan ever. You get personalized Study Plans for each chapter, with content arranged from less complex thinking— like remembering facts—to more complex critical thinking—like understanding connections in history and analyzing primary sources. Assessments and learning applications in the Study Plan link you directly to *The West: A Narrative History* eBook for reading and review.

3. Key Questions, which begin each chapter and focus on a prominent theme in the chapter, have been replaced or revised in over a third of the chapters in the book.

4. The Review Questions found at the end of each chapter in the second edition have been replaced in the third edition with a list of Activities that encourage students to complete mini-projects on key chapter topics.

5. A short list of Further Readings appears at the end of each chapter in the third edition, comprised of books that might intrigue an undergraduate to read further on the topics discussed in each chapter.

6. The final chapter, Chapter 26, has been revised and expanded to include coverage up to 2012.

PEARSON

The West

volume 2: since 1400

The West
A Narrative History
third edition

A. Daniel Frankforter
The Pennsylvania State University

William M. Spellman
University of North Carolina, Asheville

PEARSON

Boston   Columbus   Indianapolis   New York   San Francisco   Upper Saddle River
Amsterdam   Cape Town   Dubai   London   Madrid   Milan   Munich   Paris   Montréal   Toronto
Delhi   Mexico City   São Paulo   Sydney   Hong Kong   Seoul   Singapore   Taipei   Tokyo

Editorial Director: Craig Campanella
Editor-in-Chief: Dickson Musslewhite
Executive Editor: Jeff Lasser
Editorial Project Manager: Rob DeGeorge
Editorial Assistant: Julia Feltus
Director of Marketing: Brandy Dawson
Senior Marketing Manager: Maureen E.
   Prado Roberts
Marketing Coordinator: Samantha Bennett
Senior Managing Editor: Ann Marie McCarthy
Senior Project Manager: Denise Forlow
Senior Manufacturing and Operations Manager
   for Arts & Sciences: Mary Fischer
Operations Specialist: Christina Amato
Senior Art Director: Maria Lange

Cover Designer: Red Kite Project
Director of Media and Assessment: Brian Hyland
Media Project Manager: Amanda Smith
Digital Media Editor: Alison Lorber
Cover Art: Vario Images GmbH & Co. KG/
   Alamy—Befreiungshalle, Kelheim, Germany
AV Project Manager: Mirella Signoretto
Project Coordination, Editorial Services,
   Art Rendering, and Text Design:
   Electronic Publishing Services Inc., NYC
Electronic Page Makeup: TexTech
Printer/Binder: R.R. Donnelley/Harrisonburg
Cover Printer: R.R. Donnelley/Harrisonburg
Text Font: Minion Pro

Credits and acknowledgments borrowed from other sources and reproduced, with permission, in this textbook appear on the appropriate page within the text or on pages 827–829.

Library of Congress Cataloging-in-Publication Data

Frankforter, A. Daniel.
   The West : a narrative history / A. Daniel Frankforter and William M. Spellman. — 3rd ed.
      p. cm.
   Includes bibliographical references and index.
   ISBN 978-0-205-18095-0
   1. Civilization, Western—History.   I. Spellman, W. M.   II. Title.
   CB245.F7 2011
   909'.09821—dc23

2011038697

10 9 8 7 6 5 4 3 2

Combined Volume
ISBN 10: 0-205-18095-7
ISBN 13: 978-0-205-18095-0
Instructor's Review Copy
ISBN 10: 0-205-22744-9
ISBN 13: 978-0-205-22744-0
Instructor's Review Copy (B/W)
ISBN 10: 0-205-88861-5
ISBN 13: 978-0-205-88861-0
Volume 1
ISBN 10: 0-205-18093-0
ISBN 13: 978-0-205-18093-6

Books a la carte Volume 1
ISBN 10: 0-205-24107-7
ISBN 13: 978-0-205-24107-1
Volume 2
ISBN 10: 0-205-18091-4
ISBN 13: 978-0-205-18091-2
Books a la carte Volume 2
ISBN 10: 0-205-24109-3
ISBN 13: 978-0-205-24109-5

BRIEF CONTENTS

CONTENTS

PART FIVE The Revolutionary Impulse   418

14 The Early Modern State   421

15 New World Views: Europe's Scientific Revolution   451

PART SEVEN Europe in Crisis:
1914–1945 646

PART EIGHT The Postwar Western Community: 1945–2012   736

DOCUMENTS

Note: The following documents are referenced in the margins of the text and are available at **www.myhistorylab.com**

MAPS

KEY QUESTIONS

PREFACE

Students at American colleges and universities are—regardless of their ethnic backgrounds—immersed in a culture deeply indebted to Europe and the Mediterranean region. Other parts of the globe have made undoubted contributions to the formation of what is a nation of immigrants, but these influences are adapted to the values and institutions of a trans-Atlantic civilization that, for want of a better term, is invariably described as "Western." Despite this, most students begin their undergraduate careers with very little knowledge of the deeper roots of the American past. Those who come from American public schools have repeatedly been taught something of their national history, but they have seldom had more than a cursory introduction to the historical processes that shaped their nation's "Western way of life." Their lack of understanding of its origins makes it difficult for them to situate the American experience in a global context. Having an inadequate knowledge of themselves, they are hampered in their efforts to comprehend others. Far from narrowing their perspective, a course in Western civilization that helps American students grasp how and why they have come to be what they are equips them to understand how and why other peoples have developed differently. Such understanding is essential if students are to comprehend the logic of other cultures, acknowledge their integrity, and be prepared to innovate creative responses to their conflicts.

The West: A Narrative History is not a reduced version of a larger book, but a fully realized "brief history" in its own right. It was conceived and developed to provide an efficient introduction to the history of "the West" defined in the broadest terms. It treats all the major cultures that trace at least some of their ancestry to the ancient Mediterranean world. The text consistently reminds its readers that the West owes a great debt to regions of the world that are today not commonly regarded as "Western."

This concern distinguishes *The West: A Narrative History* from many of the textbooks currently available for teaching courses in Western civilization. Many books begin with brief treatments of ancient Mesopotamia and Egypt and then largely abandon the Middle East. When they reach the medieval period, they mention the rise of Islam but leave students under the impression that Islam is an alien, non-Western phenomenon. This obscures the fact that Christians and Muslims built on the same cultural foundations—Hebraic religion and Hellenistic thought. Both claimed portions of Rome's "western" empire, and both borrowed significantly from the civilizations of India and the East. The importance of the help that the Muslim world gave medieval Europe in reclaiming its legacy from the ancient era is often slighted, and with the rise of the Ottoman Empire Islam usually disappears from the narrative (except for brief references to later European encroachments on Ottoman territory).

Such skewed treatment of Western history poorly prepares students to understand the current international situation and its mounting tensions between an "East" and a "West." The peace of the world may depend on Western civilization's Euro-American and Middle Eastern heirs acquiring an understanding of their history of interaction and an appreciation of what they have in common.

Ultimately, a book—particularly a history textbook—has to be a "good read" if it is going to achieve the goal of forming and informing its audience. It needs to grab the interest of those who begin by scanning through it, for only if it piques their interest can it hope to seduce them into an extended reading of its contents. *The West: A Narrative History* attempts to do this by telling a good and compelling human story.

New to This Edition

- This edition is closely tied to the innovative website, the New MyHistoryLab, which helps you save time and improve results as you study history (www. myhistorylab.com). MyHistoryLab icons connect the main narrative in each chapter of the book to a powerful array of MyHistoryLab resources, including primary source documents, analytical video segments, interactive maps, and more. A MyHistoryLab Connections feature now appears at the end of each chapter, capping off the study resources for the chapter. The New MyHistoryLab also includes both eBook and Audio Book versions of *The West: A Narrative History*, Third Edition, so that you can read or listen to your textbook any time you have access to the Internet.

- New with this Third Edition: *The West: A Narrative History* now uses the latest release of the New MyHistoryLab, which offers the most advanced Study Plan ever. You get personalized Study Plans for each chapter, with content arranged from less complex thinking—like remembering facts—to more complex critical thinking—like understanding connections in history and analyzing primary sources. Assessments and learning applications in the Study Plan link you directly to *The West: A Narrative History* eBook for reading and review.

- Key Questions, which begin each chapter and focus on a prominent theme in the chapter, have been replaced or revised in over a third of the chapters in the book.

- The authors carefully revised the text in a myriad of places to make explanations clearer, more complete, and easier for students to follow.

- The authors reorganized the outline in places (note, in particular, the treatment of the Middle East in Chapter 11) to improve the flow.

- The People in Context feature in Chapter 12 now focuses on Isabella d'Este as well as Elisabetta Gonzaga. The People in Context feature in Chapter 9 has been rewritten to highlight the significance of the work of Hroswitha of Gandersheim.

- The Review Questions found at the end of each chapter in the second edition have been replaced in the third edition with a list of Activities that suggest ways for students to study, analyze, and master the chapter's subjects.

- A short list of Further Readings appears at the end of each chapter in the third edition, comprised of books that might intrigue an undergraduate to read further on some aspects of the history discussed in the chapter.

- The final chapter, Chapter 26, has been revised and expanded to include coverage up to 2012.

The Instructor's Resource Center

Instructors using this text can visit the Instructor's Resource Center online at www.pearsonhighered.com/irc in order to download text-specific materials, such as the Instructor's Resource Manual, Test Item File, MyTest, and PowerPoint presentations.

Download Resources

Many products in our catalog have instructor resources available for download.
Here's how to access them!

1. **Find your book or product in our catalog.**
   Enter the author's last name and a key word from the title:

Frankforter	**and**	The West

   `Go`

2. **On the product page, click on the "Resources" tab.** If there is no Resources tab, there are no resources available for that product.

3. **Click the "View Downloadable Files" link below any resource.** If this link does not appear below a particular listing, there are no downloadable resources for that product.

4. **Click on the name of the file you want to download.** If you are not already logged in, you will be prompted to log in at this time.

5. **Save the file to your computer.** If the file is compressed (.zip or .sit), extract the files within the archive. Now you're ready to use the file!

Acknowledgments

The only names that appear prominently on books are those of their authors. However, all books—particularly textbooks—are communal projects to which many people contribute their skills and expertise. The authors wish to acknowledge the debt they owe to all who have assisted them in bringing this project to completion, particularly the following individuals. Jeff Lasser, executive editor at Pearson, sponsored this edition of the text. He deserves credit for many aspects of its design and its special features. Credit for the book's attractive appearance belongs to Maria Lange, senior art director. Julia Feltus, editorial assistant, took on many daunting assignments with grace and aplomb, while production editors Amy Pavelich and Denise Forlow brought all the strands together to create the volume you hold in your hands.

A useful, accurate textbook owes much to the scholars who agree to review its contents from the perspective of their fields of specialization. Their willingness to take time from their own research and writing to enhance the value and utility of a textbook is a service to their profession that rarely receives the acknowledgment it deserves. Their contributions to this project are hardly repaid by this brief expression of gratitude: Wayne Ackerson, Salisbury University; John Cox, Florida Gulf Coast University; Ross Huxoll, University of Nebraska—Kearney; Preston Jones, John Brown University; James Martin, Campbell University; Michael Pascale, SUNY at Suffolk, Farmingdale College; Jonathan S. Perry, University of South Florida; and Walter Roberts, Ohio University.

MyHistoryLab™   MyHistoryLab™

MyHistoryLab (www.myhistorylab.com)

MyHistoryLab delivers proven results in helping individual students succeed. Its automatically graded assessments, personalized study plan, and interactive eText provide engaging experiences that personalize, stimulate, and measure learning for each student. And, it comes from a trusted partner with educational expertise and a deep commitment to helping students, instructors, and departments achieve their goals.

Annotated Instructor's eText Housed in the instructor's space within MyHistoryLab, the *Annotated Instructor's eText for The West: A Narrative History,* Third Edition, leverages the powerful Pearson eText platform to make it easier than ever for teachers to access subject-specific resources for class preparation, providing access to the resources below:	**CourseSmart** www.coursemart.com CourseSmart is an exciting new choice for students looking to save money. As an alternative to purchasing the printed textbook, students can purchase an electronic version of the same content. With a CourseSmart eTextbook, students can search the text, make notes online, print out reading assignments that incorporate lecture notes, and bookmark important passages for later review.
The Instructor's Resource Manual Available at the Instructor's Resource Center, at www.pearsonhighered.com/irc, the Instructor's Resource Manual contains a chapter summary, a chapter outline with references to the MyHistoryLab resources cited in the text, learning objectives from the text, lecture topics, class discussion topics, and the MyHistoryLab Connections feature found at the end of each chapter in the text.	*Books à la Carte* The Books à la Carte edition offers a convenient, two-hole-punched, loose-leaf version of the traditional text at a discounted price—allowing students to take only what they need to class. Books à la Carte editions are available both with and without access to MyHistoryLab.
The Test Item File Available in Word and PDF formats at the Instructor's Resource Center at www.pearsonhighered.com/irc, the Test Item File contains a diverse set of over 2,100 multiple choice, short answer, essay, identification, and map-based questions, supporting a variety of assessment strategies. The large pool of multiple-choice questions for each chapter includes factual, conceptual, and analytical questions, so that instructors may assess students on basic information as well as critical thinking. The Test Item File is also available at www.pearsonmytest.com. MyTest is a powerful assessment generation program that helps instructors easily create and print quizzes and exams. Questions and tests can be authored online, allowing instructors ultimate flexibility to access existing questions and edit, create, and store using simple drag-and-drop and Word-like controls.	Titles from the renowned **Penguin Classics** series can be bundled with *The West: A Narrative History*, Third Edition, for a nominal charge. Please contact your Pearson sales representative for details.

SUPPLEMENTS FOR QUALIFIED COLLEGE ADOPTERS	SUPPLEMENTS FOR STUDENTS
PowerPoint Presentations Available at the Instructor's Resource Center, at www.pearsonhighered.com/irc, the PowerPoint slides to accompany *The West: A Narrative History*, Third Edition, include a lecture outline for each chapter and full-color illustrations and maps from the textbook. All images from the textbook have captions from the book that provide background information about the image.	***Library of World Biography Series*** www.pearsonhighered.com/educator/series/Library-of-World-Biography/10492.page Each interpretive biography in the Library of World Biography Series focuses on a person whose actions and ideas either significantly influenced world events or whose life reflects important themes and developments in global history. Titles from the series can be bundled with *The West: A Narrative History*, Third Edition, for a nominal charge. Please contact your Pearson sales representative for details.
	The Prentice Hall Atlas of Western Civilization, Second Edition Produced in collaboration with Dorling Kindersley, the leader in cartographic publishing, the updated second edition of *The Prentice Hall Atlas of Western Civilization* applies the most innovative cartographic techniques to present western civilization in all of its complexity and diversity. Copies of the atlas can be bundled with *The West: A Narrative History*, Third Edition, for a nominal charge. Contact your Pearson sales representative for details. (ISBN 0-13-604246-5)
	***A Short Guide to Writing about History*, Seventh Edition** Written by Richard Marius, late of Harvard University, and Melvin E. Page, Eastern Tennessee State University, this engaging and practical text helps students get beyond merely compiling dates and facts. Covering both brief essays and the documented resource paper, the text explores the writing and researching processes, identifies different modes of historical writing, including argument, and concludes with guidelines for improving style. (ISBN 0-13-205-67370-8)

NOTE ON DATES AND SPELLING

Dates

Human beings have tried numerous strategies to orient themselves in the featureless sea of time. For much of history the heavens have served as their primary clock and calendar. The Bible claims that the Creator placed two "lights" in the sky, one to rule the day and the other the night. This sounds simpler than it turns out to be in practice, for the two lights travel in cycles that are difficult to coordinate. Earth's journey around the sun, which produces its annual seasons, takes 365.2424 days. The moon's waxing and waning transit of Earth takes 29.53059 days. A year can be divided into 12 months by charting the phases of the moon. But the lunar year passes weeks faster than its solar partner, which causes months to drift from one season into another.

As ancient peoples improved accuracy in measuring the movements of the heavenly bodies, they devised a variety of increasingly sophisticated methods for computing calendars that better synchronized months and seasons. The **Egyptians** favored a year divided into 12 equal, 30-day-long months to which they annually added five days to complete the year. This still fell about six hours short of the actual length of the solar year, and as the centuries passed, those six hours accumulated, causing months to slide away from their seasons. The **Babylonians** devised a calendar based on cycles of 19 years—a combination of seven years of 13 months and 12 years of 12 months. This was close, but still short enough to fall behind by several weeks each century. Julius Caesar drew on the best astronomical information of his day and decreed a year of 12 months (some 30 and others 31 days long) with an additional "leap" day added every four years. This **Julian Calendar** was an improvement, but there was still a small discrepancy that eventually made a noticeable difference. In 1582 Pope Gregory XIII ordered a leap of 11 days (by creating an abbreviated October in which the fifteenth day immediately followed the fourth) to synchronize months and seasons and added another refinement to calendar calculations. In the **Gregorian Calendar**, leap years were to occur every four years but be omitted for years that marked centuries divisible by 400 (e.g., 2000 C.E.). This, the calendar most widely used today, is still several seconds out of sync.

Not only did ancient calendars differ on how to calculate years in terms of months and supplemental days, but there was also no consensus on when a year began. The cycle of seasons disposed people to look on spring, the season of rebirth, as the appropriate time to declare a new start. Therefore, in the northern hemisphere, March was often favored as the first month of the year. A memory of this survives in the names still used for some months: September, October, November, December—seventh, eighth, ninth, and tenth months (counting from March). About a century and a half before the birth of Christ the Romans decided to begin their year on January 1, the date on which their chief executives (the consuls) took office. The custom lapsed in many places during the Middle Ages and did not begin to win general acceptance until about 300 years ago.

The lack of a universal standard for measuring years and of agreement on when the year began made life difficult for ancient record keepers. A common strategy for dating things was to associate an event with some memorable person or unusual development. For example: "This happened in the eighth year of the reign of King Sed, 17 years after the great famine." Greeks and Romans sometimes created "**eponymous**" offices and named each year for the person who held that office that year. For example: "In the year of the *praetor maximus* Livius Aurelianus." This system required public records offices to keep long and growing lists of names.

The current convention for charting a path through time is to choose a fixed point from which to count the passage of years. The Jewish calendar begins with the traditional date for the Creation of the world—calculated from information provided by the genealogies recorded in the Hebrew Scriptures. The Muslim calendar begins with an event in the Prophet Muhammad's life, the act that marked the birth of the *umma*, the community of Islam. After Christianity became their society's dominant faith, Europe's scholars began to reference what they believed was the date of Jesus' birth as the pivot point of history. **Dionysius Exiguous** (c. 500–560) is said to have first suggested this. About a century and a half later, his system was popularized by the best historian of the day, an English monk named **Bede** (672–735). The result was the convention of designating years as either B.C. ("Before Christ") or A.D. (*anno Domini*, "In the year of the Lord")—e.g., "457 B.C." (457 years "Before Christ") or A.D. 457 ("In the year of the Lord 457"). Writers who wish to be sensitive to the fact that not all their readers may share the Christian faith now use B.C.E. and C.E., which can be read as "Before the Common [or Christian] Era" and the "Common [or Christian] Era."

These dating conventions mean that years are counted down from the most remote eras to the birth of Christ and up to the present time from the birth of Christ. Thus, in the pre-Christian (or pre-Common) era events become more recent as numbers grow smaller (i.e., 132 B.C.E. is earlier than 32 B.C.E.) and in the post-Christian (or Common) era events become more recent as numbers grow larger (i.e., 32 C.E. is earlier than 132 C.E.). Counting back from the birth of Christ, the third century B.C.E. would begin in 299 and end in 200 (i.e., the third century B.C.E. is the 200s). Counting forward from the birth of Christ, the twelfth century would begin in 1100 and end in 1199 (i.e., the 1100s).

Spelling

Human beings can make a wide range of sounds, and they have used their extensive vocalization skills to construct a myriad of different languages. Some are fairly monotone. Others are almost musical, using differences in pitch to indicate meanings. Some favor soft, mellifluous sounds, while others emphasize harsher noises. There are even languages that employ percussive clicks that non-native speakers may find impossible to master.

Writing systems invent symbols to represent the sounds of speech. But because not all languages use the same sounds, it can be difficult to write a given language using a symbol system that has been developed for a different one. Letters may have to be combined in odd ways to suggest unique sounds (e.g., "kw"), "diacritical" marks may be added to indicate how a sound should be made (e.g., á, ä, or â), or entirely new symbols may have to be invented to supplement those that normally suffice. An added complication derives from the fact that a number of ancient languages were written only with consonants. Readers were expected to infer vowel sounds for themselves from context. A modern scholar who wishes to transliterate words from these languages using letters familiar to readers of English must make educated guesses about how these long silent tongues were once pronounced. For instance, the seventeenth-century English translators of the Bible thought that the Hebrew consonants for God's name should be supplied with vowels and read as "Jehovah," but many biblical scholars now prefer "Yahweh." The two English terms render the same word in Hebrew, but they do not look or sound much alike.

Linguists have devised rules to promote consistency in moving from one writing system to another, but different traditions and customs have prevailed at different times and in different academic environments. For instance, because "c" in English can be pronounced like "s" or "k," a Greek name that begins with a hard consonant (a *kappa*) might be spelled with either a "c" or a "k." British scholars might prefer one spelling of the name while Americans choose another. Classicists may favor one and historians another. Students need to be prepared to be flexible when they confront variant spellings in different texts.

ABOUT THE AUTHORS

A. Daniel Frankforter is Emeritus Professor of History at the Pennsylvania State University, where he has taught for over four decades. His undergraduate work was in the history of ideas and philosophy at Franklin and Marshall College. He earned a Master of Divinity degree from Drew University, did graduate work at Columbia University and the University of Göttingen, and completed master's and doctoral degrees in medieval history and religious studies at Penn State. His research interests are in English ecclesiastical history, the evolving status of women in medieval Europe, and textual criticism. His articles on these topics have appeared in such journals as *Manuscripta, Church History, The British Studies Monitor, The Catholic Historical Review, The American Benedictine Review, The International Journal of Women's Studies,* and *The Journal of Women's History.* His books include *A History of the Christian Movement: An Essay on the Development of Christian Institutions* (Nelson-Hall, (1978), *Civilization and Survival* (University Press of America, 1988), *The Shakespeare Name Dictionary* (Garland, 1995) (with J. Madison Davis), *The Medieval Millennium: An Introduction* (Prentice Hall, 2003, 1999), *The Western Heritage,* brief edition (Prentice Hall 2005, 2002, 1999, 1996) (with Donald Kagan, Stephen Ozment, and Frank Turner), *The Heritage of World Civilizations,* brief third edition (Pearson, Prentice Hall, 2007) (with Albert Craig, William Graham, Donald Kagan, Stephen Ozment, and Frank Turner), an edition and translation of Poullain de la Barre's *De L'Égalité des deux Sexes* (Edwin Mellen, 1989), and *Stones for Bread: A Critique of Contemporary Worship* (Westminster John Knox, 2001). His most recent work is *Word of God/ Words of Men: The Use and Abuse of Scripture* (Circle Books, 2011). Over the course of his career he has developed 15 courses dealing with aspects of the ancient and medieval periods of Western civilization, the Judeo-Christian tradition, and gender issues. His service in the classroom has been acknowledged by the Penn State Behrend Excellence in Teaching Award and the prestigious Amoco Foundation Award for Excellence in Teaching Performance.

William M. Spellman is Professor of History at the University of North Carolina, Asheville and Director of the Council of Public Liberal Arts Colleges, a consortium of 26 institutions in the United States and Canada. He is a graduate of Suffolk University, Boston, and holds a PhD from the Maxwell School of Citizenship and Public Affairs at Syracuse University. He is the author of *John Locke and The Problem of Depravity* (Oxford, 1988); *The Latitudinarians and the Church of England* (Georgia, 1993); *John Locke* (Macmillan, 1995); *European Political Thought, 1600–1700* (Macmillan, 1997); *Monarchies, 1000–2000* (Reaktion, 2000); *The Global Community: Migration and the Making of the Modern World* (Sutton, 2002); *A Concise History of the World Since 1945* (Palgrave, 2006); *Uncertain Identity: International Migration Since 1945* (Reaktion, 2008); and *A Short History of Western Political Thought* (Palgrave, 2011).

INTRODUCTION

The Nature of History

History is not a natural phenomenon—something like gravity or the cycle of a plant's life. People "make" history in two ways: (1) by their actions in the present, and (2) by what they think about the past. Without the former, of course, there would be no past for historians to study. However, the present is important to historians not only because it becomes the past, but because it influences how they interpret the past. Each of us comes into a world that we did not make, and each of us is forced to live in circumstances that we, as individuals, cannot entirely control. A desire to understand the fore-ordained conditions that provide the context for our lives is often what makes us curious about the past. We want to know the origins of the problems, institutions, and values that are important to us—and even when we study remote eras or cultures that have no immediate or obvious ties with our world, we tend to interpret them in light of what matters to us—our interests, convictions, and life experiences.

Before people begin seriously to study history, they sometimes assume that the story of the past is a simple, straightforward, objective narration of dates, facts, and figures—and that, like most things that leave little room for imagination and intuition, it is "cut and (literally) dried." History can, of course, be badly written and taught so as to meet the lowest of expectations. But because historians write about the past from the perspective of the present, their work often has the potential to stir up controversy and evoke strong emotional responses. It can have a deeply personal dimension for both its writer and its reader. Curiosity about ourselves plays a role in determining what we choose to read and what we are drawn to research. We are tempted to identify ourselves and our issues with figures and events from the past, and we are inclined to sit in judgment on what previous generations have thought and done. The past may be, as novelist L. P. Hartley wrote, "a foreign country . . . where they do things differently," but even the most rigorously scientific researchers cannot entirely escape observing it through lenses shaped by their educations and backgrounds.

The influence of the present on perceptions of the past makes any given historian's work a source of information on two sometimes widely separated eras—the one the historian writes about and the one the historian writes in. For example: **Edward Gibbon**'s *The Decline and Fall of the Roman Empire* is one of the most famous (if not one of the most read) works by an English historian. This immensely detailed description of Rome's decline rests on a mountain of evidence that Gibbon mined from the physical and literary remains of the ancient world. But it is also thoroughly imbued with the intellectual assumptions of Gibbon's own eighteenth century (Europe's "**Age of Enlightenment**"). Gibbon ended his long narrative with a short and succinct summary of its thesis: "In the preceding volumes of this History I have described the triumph of barbarism and religion. . . ."[1] Most European intellectuals of Gibbon's

---

[1]Edward Gibbon, *The Decline and Fall of the Roman Empire*, vol. II (Chicago: Encyclopedia Britannica, Inc., 1952), p. 592.

generation believed that reason held the key to understanding and solving all of humanity's problems and that rational thinking would inevitably spread—advancing science and sweeping away every trace of supernaturalism. Rome, Gibbon argued, had been brought down by the opposite trend. It fell victim to the growth and convergence of two kinds of irrationality: ignorance and superstition—by which Gibbon meant the barbarism of German tribes and the faith of Christians.

Gibbon's argument appeared convincing at the time, and his study seemed destined to become the last word on its subject. But a century later the story of Rome's fall looked quite different to Russian-born and educated historian **Michael Ivanovich Rostovtzeff** (1870–1952). He lived at a time when the theories of **Karl Marx** had great influence. Marx believed that economic activities and class struggles were the engines that drove historical evolution, and in mid-life Rostovtzeff had witnessed an event that seemed to support Marx's theses. A popular revolution overthrew Russia's inept tsar and aristocracy and established a classless, but brutally oppressive society in the historian's homeland. Something similar, Rostovtzeff believed, had happened to bring down first the Roman Republic and then the Roman Empire. He wrote:

> But so long as Rome was fighting for pre-eminence in the ancient world, the division of classes within the state remained in the background or at least did not cause bloodshed. As soon, however, as she became mistress of the world, the power of "the best men," the *optimates* or aristocracy, was assailed by the citizens in general. Their war-cry was a better and juster distribution of property, and a more democratic form of government. For eighty years this bloody conflict lasted, and the aristocracy came out of it defeated and demoralized. . . . The development of these states of mind—apathy in the rich and discontent among the poor—was at first slow and secret. But suddenly became acute, when the empire was forced, after nearly two centuries of peace and tranquility, to defend itself against enemies from without. The time called for a great display of enthusiasm. But the rich could not be roused from their indifference; and the poor, seeing the helplessness and weakness of their betters, and deprived of all share in their idle and indolent contentment, were filled with hatred and envy.[2]

The reasons Rostovtzeff gives for Rome's fall in the fifth century might serve almost as well as an explanation for the decline of tsarist Russia in the early twentieth. The fact that what seems important to historians in their own day often looms large in their view of the past does not mean that historians have no objectivity and simply write themselves into their narratives. It does, however, help us understand why history is never definitively written but is always in the process of being revised and rewritten. As time passes, newly evolving social contexts create new perspectives from which to view the past, and new perspectives suggest new ways of framing questions. Because people tend to see what they look for and ignore things they do not value, new questions prompt new discoveries. The modern feminist movement illustrates this dynamic. For centuries historians thought they could adequately explain the past by focusing only on the activities of men—and usually only a very few "great men." By

---

[2]Michael Rostovtzeff, *Rome* (NY: Oxford U. Press, 1960), pp. 321 & 323.

demonstrating the importance of women to contemporary societies, feminism alerted historians to the necessity of understanding their activities in earlier periods. If the present could not adequately be understood without examining the roles of women, neither could the past. This realization has resulted in the discovery of information that has caused many narratives to be rewritten.

The involvements, commitments, and loyalties that individuals embrace as fundamental to their identities can make them passionate about the past. They may, for instance, come to resent injustices that have been done to a specific category of people and write history to vindicate the importance of that group—to reveal its previously ignored contributions and to accord it what they regard as its due dignity. An Irish-American author, who is proud of his lineage, writes a book to explain *How the Irish Saved Civilization* (Thomas Cahill, 1995). Or an advocate for the peoples of the "developing world" writes to correct what he regards as a deliberate effort to conceal their historical significance (Martin Bernal, *Black Athena: The Afroasiatic Roots of Classical Civilization*, 1987). Advocacy for a cause is not necessarily bad. But if passions run too high, the attempt to write history in service of a cause can distort, abuse, or even fabricate the past. Much history has been written to justify or convict, to claim credit for or to excuse, to vindicate or to shame one party or another. Such works can be fun to read, but their entertainment value should not get in the way of the primary reason for studying history: to understand the past.

The Divisions of History

To create a context for events it is useful to try to grasp human history as a whole, but good general surveys rest on a myriad of specialized studies. There are political histories, gender histories, economic histories, intellectual histories, national histories, and numerous other approaches to narrating the past. Different scholars have different preferences and vigorously debate the merits of their respective approaches—different ways to develop narratives about the past.

One of the hotter arguments concerns the legitimacy or usefulness of studying "Western" civilization. Some scholars insist that to do so is to endorse a tradition of historiography that unfairly exalts European societies over the cultures of other peoples. The current international political climate has made their conviction especially strong. Hatred of "the West" (the European and American so-called first world) is emerging as the major political problem of the twenty-first century. It has motivated both appalling acts of terrorism and a violent defensive reaction—a "war on terrorism." The world—especially the academic world—seems increasingly to be divided between extreme critics (e.g., post-colonialists and post-modernists) and extreme defenders (e.g., Eurocentrists) of "the West." Each tars the other's position with a broad brush that makes fair and useful conversation difficult.

The sins alleged to be the legacy of Western civilization are many: colonial exploitation, slavery, sexism, racism, heartless capitalist manipulation, wasteful consumerism, and environmental degradation. There is no denying that Europeans, Americans, and their cultural kin have been guilty of these things, but it is less certain that all of these transgressions against humanity are innately or uniquely "western." A kind of racism based on differences in human physical features was uncritically accepted by many eighteenth- and nineteenth-century Europeans, but many peoples around the world and throughout history have drawn sharp lines between themselves and groups with characteristics (e.g., linguistic, cultural, and physical) that allegedly marked them as "other" and therefore inferior. Imperialism, slavery, and abuse of women long predate the rise of European powers and can be found in many cultures around the globe. As for capitalism, China may have preceded Europe in its invention, and environmental degradation began with the invention of agriculture and the technologies that supported Earth's first civilizations. What the West may not always get due credit for is its effort to promote the moral sensitivities, the self-critical attitudes, and the rational and scientific discourses that have been used to combat imperialism, slavery, sexism, racism, abusive capitalism, and ecological devastation.

Some students may be surprised to learn that courses in Western civilization are a relatively new development and that they are an American invention. They first appeared in the early twentieth century and were designed to lay a foundation on which to build a coherent college education. Their content was profoundly influenced by the political environment of the first half of the twentieth century—particularly the two World Wars. Americans and their European allies fought these bloody struggles in the belief that they were sacrificing themselves to save the world from tyranny. Wars create extreme conditions that can degrade patriotism into chauvinism, and scholars are not

The arrogance with which some Western nations have dealt with weaker countries is illustrated by this magazine cover from 1911. It asserts that the people of Morocco should yield gratefully to paternalistic dominance by France and the imposition of France's concept of civilized life. Abraham Lincoln's Emancipation Proclamation, however, is an icon for more enlightened behavior by Western powers, which have been in the forefront of movements to end social evils such as slavery.

immune to their effects. At times Western civilization has been taught in ways that implied that it was the only true civilization—the goal toward which all other peoples should aspire and the standard by which their lives should be judged. The triumphalism that accompanied this view of the West encouraged the belief that the West was innately superior and self-generating—that it owed little or nothing to inventions and ideas borrowed from others. Its alleged native genius supposedly gave it a right to world leadership if not world domination.

The study of history is almost inevitably corrupted by the prejudicial assumptions and ethical blind spots of each generation that undertakes it. This is certainly true of the way in which Western civilization has sometimes been studied and taught. But things change, and the heirs of a tradition are free to correct the errors of earlier practitioners. Some people insist, however, that the whole enterprise is ill conceived and should be abandoned. They claim that the current environment of globalization makes a focus on Western civilization obsolete and that world history should take its place. Others argue, however, that exploration of the world might best begin with careful examination of one's own culture. Students at American colleges and universities are—regardless of their more or less distant ethnic backgrounds—products of a society that is deeply indebted to Europe and the Mediterranean region. Other parts of the globe have made significant contributions to the identity of their largely immigrant nation, but these have been integrated into core values and institutions long characterized as "Western."

Many students bring some knowledge of their nation's political and social history to college, but they have had few opportunities to consider that history in a larger context. One approach that they might take to broaden their understanding is to situate the American experience in the older European-Mediterranean tradition. This involves exploring that tradition's indebtedness to, and relations with, other regions of the world. Study of one's own culture need not always lead back to oneself. It can serve as intellectual preparation for the challenge of searching out meaningful patterns in the flurry of information generated by an increasingly complex global community.

Where Is "the West"?

One problem with the study of Western civilization is the slippery nature of the term *west*. It is difficult to define or pin down just what historians mean when they speak about "the West." "West" is, after all, a direction, not a place. Dictionaries define it as the opposite of Earth's rotation (the English word *west* has a root meaning "evening"). This makes "the west" relative to the point of view of the person who watches the sun set. Because such a shifting standard is of no assistance for global navigation, geographers have arbitrarily fixed a line—the "prime meridian," running north-south through an observatory in Greenwich, England—to separate east from west. Technically most of the British Isles, a small portion of France, Spain, and a bit of the African continent are in "the west" while the rest of Europe and Africa are in "the east." This definition of the west may help sailors, but it is not very useful for historians.

At first glance it might seem odd that books dealing with Western civilization begin in the Middle East and only slowly work their way (following the sun) across the Mediterranean to Europe and the Atlantic. But *west* and *east* are not simply geographical terms. They have always also had cultural implications. The Bible's Book of Genesis begins the human story in a garden that God plants "in the east"—the place where the sun rises being the appropriate metaphor for the absolute beginning. Similarly, the west has long been associated with death and ending. For these reasons, graves and places of worship (including medieval Christian churches) have often been oriented to the path of the sun.

The antagonism that developed between Christians and Muslims during the European Middle Ages created a "West" that was Christendom, the portion of Europe under Christian control. For the explorers of the sixteenth century "the West" was the "New World." For nineteenth-century Americans "the West" became a frontier, a wild land to be explored and tamed. During the Cold War of the second half of the twentieth century, "the West" indicated a political alliance—a block of states that opposed a communist "East." Most people today think of "the West" as referring to countries whose cultures are, or once were, closely linked with those of Western Europe. This "West" spans the globe, for it includes Europe, the United States, Canada, New Zealand, and Australia. But does it also apply to the Catholic, Spanish- and Portuguese-speaking nations of South America? Does it include English-speaking South Africa? Should it include Russia? Does it describe Turkey, a majority Muslim state that is a member of NATO and an associate member of the European Union? Should it now include modern China because China has passionately embraced the "western" ideologies of capitalism and Marxism?

Confusion about the definition of "the West" today is not solely due to the ways in which European and American influences have spread in the modern era. It also reflects the complexity of the historical origin of the civilization with which these nations are associated. "The West" did not give birth to itself. It is the child of many parents, and it has always existed in the context of diverse cultures exchanging goods and ideas over immense distances. The modern world has been compared with a "global village," but to greater and lesser degrees "the West" has always been part of a global community. Its foundations were laid in the Middle East, which from the earliest eras was in contact with the Far East. The Hellenic Greeks were deeply involved (and sometimes in awe of) their eastern neighbors. Alexander sought to build a state encompassing all the peoples from the Aegean to the Indus valley, and his achievement was the cultural foundation on which the Romans built. Islam opened new channels of communication between Europe and India, and the European explorers who founded the colonial empires of the Early Modern Era flooded their homelands with transforming foreign influences. Western peoples may too rarely acknowledge—or even be aware of—their debts to other civilizations, and at times they have drawn sharp distinctions between themselves and cultures they denigrate as alien. But "the West" has usually remained open to learning from those with whom it comes in contact, and this goes a long way toward explaining the vitality and creativity of its civilization.

What Is Civilization?

If the definition of *western* creates problems for courses in Western civilization, so does the definition of *civilization*. The word's Latin root (*civis*) means "citizen," the resident of a city (*civitas*), and the common assumption is that urban institutions are central to civilizations. Civilizations are also said to be characterized by bureaucratic governments, stratified social systems, long-distance trade, and specialized technologies such as metal working and writing. Descriptions of this kind are, however, not all that informative, for they merely assert that civilization appears when people begin to do what are thought of as civilized things. They do not explain what makes a behavior civilized, and the lists of civilized behaviors they propose are not definitive. This approach to defining civilization also begs the question of which and how many civilized attributes a people must manifest in order to be considered civilized. The Inca of ancient Peru, for example, had urban institutions, monumental architecture, and metal working, but no writing system. Did the absence of literacy mean they were not civilized?

Civilization is a tricky term, for its use sometimes implies a judgment about a society. There are ethical and aesthetic dimensions to civilized living. Despite romantic myths about "noble savages," people with civilized lifestyles have often been regarded (or have regarded themselves) as more fully developed human beings than those who have not made the progress that civilization allegedly represents. Not to be civilized is to be primitive, backward, or even barbaric—all descriptors charged with negative feelings.

Cultural relativists challenge the assumption that one society can legitimately be judged by the standards of another. They particularly object to the long tradition of historical writing that assumes the superiority of "Western" (European-based) civilization, but it seems unduly contentious to question the value of civilization itself. The humane values identified by great thinkers from many of the world's civilizations would seem to provide a scorecard by which all societies can justly be evaluated. If torture, slavery, human sacrifice, and cannibalism are authentic, indigenous practices of a society, does that validate them—or are there ethical lines that no one, in the name of common humanity, should cross? There are, of course, costs to civilization that have to be weighed against its benefits, and a painful gap often yawns between the problems that civilization causes and the technologies it invents to deal with its effects. Civilization also offers no surefire way to prevent people from behaving barbarously, and it has in fact often helped human beings magnify the effects of their baser impulses.

Arguments about the relative merits of "complex civilizations" versus "simple cultures" might benefit from contemplating what both forms of social organization have in common. They are best understood not as contradictory ways of life, but as points on a single continuum. Civilization is simply an elaborate form of the cultural behavior that is an innate characteristic of human beings and (to a lesser degree) the higher primates. The goal of that behavior is the preservation and enhancement of life. How that goal is best achieved depends very much on the context in which a population operates. The most achievable outcome for the global community may not be the triumph of a single civilization, but the establishment of diverse ways of life, each honoring an agreement on how to define and foster humane values.

The West

Michelangelo's *David* This photo is of a replica of one of the most famous statues from the era of the Italian Renaissance, Michelangelo's *David*. When the priceless original was moved indoors, the replica took its place on Florence's Piazza della Signoria.

12 | Renaissance and Exploration

((•−[Hear the Audio   Chapter 12 at MyHistoryLab.com

LEARNING OBJECTIVES

What set the stage for Italy's Renaissance? • What were the novel achievements of the Renaissance? • How did northern Europe assimilate the Renaissance? • How was the Muslim world transformed by the Ottoman Turks? • What prompted Europeans to undertake global exploration, and what was the result?

God gives man the power to have whatever he wants and become whatever he decides to be. All that animals will ever have they have at birth (i.e., from their mothers' wombs). Angels, at the moment of Creation (or shortly thereafter), became what they will forever be. But when man appeared, God the Father bestowed on him all of life's possibilities. Therefore whatever each individual cultivates will mature and bear the fruit that gives him his unique being.

—Giovanni Pico della Mirandola, *Oration on the Dignity of Man*

KEY QUESTION

Does respect for history inspire or retard change?

Giovanni Pico della Mirandola had high ambitions for himself and for all humanity. The youngest son of the ruler of a tiny state in Italy's Po valley, he studied at the universities of Bologna, Padua, and Paris. Pico believed that the insights of major thinkers from all the ancient Western civilizations—Greek, Latin, Hebrew, and Arabic—could be woven into a single coherent system of thought, and, at the young age of 23, he set out to prove this by proposing some 900 theses. When the church condemned 13 of his propositions as heresies, Pico fled to France. After a powerful patron interceded for him, he was allowed to return to Italy to live out the remainder of his short life in Florence, the capital of the Renaissance.

Pico's celebration of human potential—his faith in the power of people to shape their own destinies—signaled a shift in European intellectual history. Early medieval thinkers, such as **Augustine of Hippo** (354–430), claimed that sin rendered human nature impotent and turned the world into a worthless realm doomed to extinction. Medieval theologians often denigrated life on Earth as something from which to be rescued by God's grace. There was much in both pagan philosophy and sacred literature to support their view, but Renaissance optimists like Pico argued that these thinkers had missed a more fundamental truth. The Bible's Creator-God had declared His Creation good, imparted His image to His human creatures, and ordered them to populate and subdue His world. God's prime directive was a command that humanity share in the divine work of perfecting Creation—themselves included.

Pico was not alone in proclaiming the "dignity" and "excellence" of humanity. The architect **Leon Battista Alberti** (1404–1472) spoke for many of his contemporaries when he asserted that "man can do everything that he sets his mind to." Theirs, Pico, Alberti, and others argued, was not a groundless faith but a truth taught by Scripture and affirmed by the Greek and Roman sages. What made the pioneers of Italy's Renaissance "modern" men and set them apart from their medieval predecessors was not a new discovery, but a recovery of ancient wisdom.

Some clergy and conservative scholars of the Renaissance era urged caution. They warned that it was a mistake to put too much trust in human virtue, rationality, and self-sufficiency, for they found little historical evidence to support the kind of confidence in human nature that Pico and Alberti preached. In light of humanity's dubious record, bold challenges to the status quo were, they insisted, unwise.

Western civilization has repeatedly reengaged its own history. Sometimes the past has served as a "dead hand," a legacy that limits what people permit themselves to think and do. This sort of reverence for the past inspires a kind of cultural fundamentalism, a conviction that it is dangerous to question established ideas or institutions. People who live in turbulent times may find this sort of idolization of the past attractive. Although it stifles innovation and retards development, it seems to promise safety. Sometimes, however, challenging situations prompt a surge of interest in a particular historical era, and the past prompts people to think about the present in new ways. Instead of encouraging them to try to turn back the clock, this use of history encourages them to adapt, reform, and grow. Either way, their perception of history shapes their future. ▓

The Context for the Renaissance

The Renaissance is a controversial period for historians. They debate when it began, how it should be defined, and even its importance. Some scholars stress the Renaissance's role in ending the medieval era and launching the modern world. Others emphasize its continuity with the Middle Ages and note that its effects were limited. There is, however, widespread agreement that its origin can be traced to medieval Italy's unique urban institutions.

Formation of City-States in Italy   The commercial activity that flourished during the High Middle Ages scattered towns across the map of Europe, but city life flourished more vigorously in Italy than elsewhere. Most of Europe's trade via Mediterranean routes passed through Italy's ports and generated employment for large urban populations. By 1400, four of Europe's five largest cities (**Genoa, Florence, Milan,** and **Venice**) were to be found in Italy. Only **Paris** (at about 80,000) was their equal. Italy had about 20 cities in the second rank with populations of about 25,000. In the rest of Europe, there were only four.

Size and number were not all that made Italy's cities noteworthy. In most parts of Europe a city's jurisdiction ended at its walls, and a city was an isolated island of special political privilege operating inside a larger governmental entity such as a kingdom or the domain of a noble. Italy's cities, however, acquired power over the lands around them and became **city-states.** The territory a town controlled was often small. Its farthest frontier might be only a day's ride from its urban center. But wealth from trade and industry gave some Italian city-states influence comparable with that of the much larger countries that were forming in northern Europe.

🔍 **View** the **Map**

Northern Italy in the Mid-Fifteenth Century

on **MyHistoryLab.com**

Geography—a mix of mountains, valleys, and plains—encouraged the political division of the Italian peninsula. Some of Italy's city-states had once been *civitates* of Rome's empire. Others owed their origin to medieval Italy's unique political and economic situations. The division of the Carolingian Empire in the ninth century had established kings who attempted to unify France and Germany. But no king or native dynasty appeared to provide an anchor for the formation of an Italian state. One major Italian power was even dedicated to preventing such a development. Rome's bishop, the pope, ruled a portion of Italy called the **Papal States.** He was therefore embroiled in Europe's politics as one of its secular heads of state. But he also claimed spiritual jurisdiction over all Christians—i.e., over all other rulers and their subjects. If a secular monarch had succeeded in uniting Italy, the pope would have come under that monarch's control and lost all credibility as the head of a universal church. Consequently, the papacy was convinced that the only way to preserve the church was to prevent Italy's political unification. (Popes today are still the heads of a state—the 105-acre **Vatican City**—that is independent of Italy's government, for example.)

For much of the medieval period, it was Germans and not Italians who tried to establish monarchy in Italy. Germany's kings repeatedly assumed the imperial title and claimed that, as Roman emperors, they had authority over Italy. When the Germans invaded, Italy's landed magnates had no native king behind whom to rally in defense of their estates. But they did have support from another quarter. The urban communities that flourished as trade began to revive in the eleventh and twelfth centuries shared the nobility's opposition to German domination. In addition to this common political objective, town and country also had the same economic interests. Townspeople bought food and raw materials (for Italy's thriving cloth industry) from the nobles' rural estates, and nobles bought products manufactured and imported by towns. As self-interest brought urban and rural leaders closer together, nobles moved into town, intermarried with bourgeois families, and integrated into urban life. When the intermingling of the families and properties of merchants and landowners spread the town's authority over the countryside, the town became a city-state.

Many of Italy's city-states began as **communes**—associations of tradespeople who voluntarily banded together for mutual benefit. A commune was often governed by a town council (of a hundred or more members) assisted by a pair of executive officers. Checks and balances and short terms in office were instituted to prevent individuals or political parties from monopolizing power, but these strategies were not invariably effective. Family and clan groups competed for dominance. They built fortified towers inside towns and sallied forth to battle one another in the streets.

Trade and merchant **guilds** and various kinds of fraternities also jockeyed for advantage. Consequently, a commune's leaders were engaged in a never-ending struggle to persuade its numerous factions to work together. If a hopeless stalemate developed, it became common (by the second half of the twelfth century) for a town to suspend its constitution and temporarily turn itself over to a *podestà*. A *podestà* was an outsider who was empowered to govern a town for a limited period of time. Because a *podestà* was a neutral stranger, warring parties could trust him to arbitrate their disputes fairly and get their community back on track. The danger, of course, was that a *podestà* might make his lordship permanent. This happened frequently, for republics were far less efficient and less able to defend themselves than states ruled by autocrats. Sometimes the autocrats openly reveled in their power, as did the **Visconti** and **Sforza** dukes who ruled Milan. Sometimes they masqueraded behind a republican facade, as did Florence's **Medici** family. The exception was the "**Serene Republic**" of Venice, which was governed by a small number of families who alone had hereditary right to political office. A constitution that headed off suicidal factional fighting among these families and an adequate distribution of wealth, however, prevented the kind of internal upheaval that brought strongmen to power in many of Italy's states.

Italy's Political Development   The Italian peninsula was divided into political zones of different types (see Map 12–1). A kingdom centered on **Naples** governed the southern portion of the peninsula. Its rulers won and lost Sicily several times and occasionally crossed the Adriatic to try to conquer portions of the Balkans. The popes' realm, the **Papal States,** spanned the center of Italy and extended up the Adriatic coast into the former Byzantine exarchate of Ravenna. It was a large, but inherently unstable, entity. Entrenched aristocratic families fought among themselves for control of the papacy, and popes, who were often elderly men with short reigns, had difficulty maintaining order. Northern Italy was divided among major and minor city-states that experimented with different kinds of governments. Some (primarily Venice, Florence, Genoa, Lucca, Pisa, and Siena) called themselves republics. Others (Milan, Ferrara, Mantua, and Modena) were duchies. Functionally, all were oligarchies dominated in different ways by wealthy minorities.

International trade gave the Italian city-states more wealth and influence than small territories might be expected to possess. **Milan,** a large northern duchy, lacked access to the sea but controlled approaches to vital passes through the Alps. **Genoa,** Milan's western neighbor, was a small coastal republic controlled by a powerful merchant oligarchy. It had a large navy and was one of Italy's richest ports. **Venice,** a city built on lagoons and islands at the top of the Adriatic, was Genoa's chief competitor for Mediterranean trade. Its wealth derived from its commercial ties with Constantinople and the Byzantine Empire. Venice, like Genoa, was formally a republic and functionally an oligarchy. With the exception of Venice, factionalism plagued the Italian city-states—none more than Florence, the cultural capital of the Renaissance.

Florence was an inland town on the Arno River that traded through the port of **Pisa** (which it conquered in 1406). Its wealth, which derived from textile manufacturing, banking, and international finance, was immense, but unevenly distributed. A few Florentine families amassed huge fortunes and used them to fight among themselves. Lesser persons were drawn into their disputes, and unruly factions formed behind the major contestants. Social and economic conditions periodically increased the volatility of the

MAP 12–1 Renaissance Italy This map simplifies the complicated political geography of Italy during the era of the Renaissance. The boundaries of its states shifted with their military fortunes, and the alliances and leagues they formed and dissolved frequently altered the configuration of the political landscape.

QUESTION: Did the political division of Italy reflect the peninsula's geography?

situation. Well over half the city's residents were wage laborers whose economic condition was perilous. Their employment depended on the wildly fluctuating international cloth market. When it boomed, the laborers worked. When the market crashed from overproduction or was otherwise disrupted, they starved. The great plague that spread across Europe in 1347 created a major crisis. It may have reduced the city's population by more than a third in a few months. Florence, along with the rest of the world, was thrown into economic confusion. By 1350 Florence's first banks, those of the Riccardi, Frescobaldi, Peruzzi, and Bardi families, had all failed—due in large part to the refusal of some of Europe's kings to repay their loans. The city's government was unprepared to deal with the situation. Urban governments were controlled by trade and merchant guilds that looked out for the interests of the propertied classes. Humble laborers had no representation. In 1378 poverty and frustration, with an unresponsive political system, triggered a rebellion by the city's wool workers. Their so-called **Ciompi Revolt** was put down, and political infighting among the great families continued.

A new era began in 1434 with the ascendancy of **Cosimo de Medici** (1389–1464). The bank his father, Giovanni de Medici (1360–1429), founded laid the foundation for the staggering fortune that Cosimo used to oust his opponents and bring the Florentine republic under his control. After **Francesco Sforza**, a *condottiere* (commander of a mercenary army), came to power in Milan in 1450, Cosimo ended a war with the Milanese duchy. This was followed in 1454 by a treaty (the **Peace of Lodi**) that established a balance of power among Italy's greater states: Florence and Milan on one side and Venice and Naples on the other.

Florence owed its cultural as well as its political influence to Cosimo de Medici, for he began his family's custom of providing patronage for scholars and artists. His grandson, **Lorenzo "the Magnificent"** (1449–1492), attached some of the period's greatest artists (e.g., the young **Michelangelo**) to his household. Medieval artists often labored in anonymity as humble craftsmen, but the Medici broke with tradition and treated the artists and intellectuals they supported more as honored guests than as servants. The Renaissance highly esteemed talented individuals, no matter what their origin, and the princes who competed for their services believed that their own reputations were enhanced by the genius of the people they attracted to their courts.

The Italian cities' willingness to agree to the Peace of Lodi in 1454 may have owed something to an event that occurred in May of 1453. **Constantinople** fell to the **Ottoman Turks,** who had previously moved into the Aegean, Greece, and the Balkans. They were eventually to occupy Hungary, besiege Austria, attempt a direct assault on Italy, and replace Venice as the dominant naval power in the eastern Mediterranean. The fear they inspired was ultimately, however, not great enough to persuade the Italian states to cease their squabbling and form a united front. In 1494 the papacy joined Naples and Florence in an alliance aimed at Milan, and Milan responded by seeking aid from France. The armies of King **Charles VIII** (r. 1483–1498) swiftly swept through Italy, and the French laid claim to Naples. The Pope and Venice then appealed to Germany's Holy Roman Emperor for help, and what had begun as a contest among Italy's city-states spread to include France, Germany, and Spain. The event that is sometimes seen as marking the end of the Renaissance was a sack of the city of Rome by German forces in 1527 (see Chapter 13).

Italy's troubles during this period prompted the composition of one of the most influential books ever written about politics: *The Prince* by Florentine historian **Niccolò Machiavelli** (1469–1527). *The Prince* purports to be a primer for the instruction of a young Medici heir in the arts of government. The lesson Machiavelli draws from history is that a ruler should allow nothing—religion, morality, law, or conscience—to stand in the way of the pursuit of

[📖] Read the Document

Excerpts from The Prince *(1519), Machiavelli*

on **MyHistoryLab.com**

power. The "Machiavellian methods" the book bluntly advocates (manipulation, brutality, hypocrisy, and treachery) are so extreme in their ruthlessness and amorality that some readers believe that Machiavelli intended his essay as a joke. It is likely, however, that Italy's turbulent history convinced the Florentine scholar that nothing mattered more than maintaining order.

In 1516 (three years after *The Prince* appeared), Machiavelli's English contemporary, **Thomas More,** published a witty satire that was similarly pessimistic in its assessment of politics. More called his book and the mythical society it described Utopia (Greek for "No-place"). More's Utopians behaved completely rationally. The contrast between their customs and those of More's contemporaries revealed that Europeans clearly did not follow the dictates of reason. Like Machiavelli, More was acutely aware of the painful gap between what human beings are and what they might aspire to be.

> **Read** the **Document**
>
> *Excerpts from* Utopia *(1516), Sir Thomas More*
>
> on **MyHistoryLab.com**

Italy's Economy and the Renaissance   The leaders of the Renaissance broke with the ascetic, world-denying ideals of the Middle Ages by stressing the nobility of human existence and the legitimacy of earthly pleasures. They gloried in the creation of beautiful things, the possession of rare objects, esoteric scholarship, courtly refinements, and various forms of conspicuous consumption. All of this was supported and encouraged by the great wealth that accumulated in Italy. Much of that wealth came from Italy's dominance of trade between Europe and the Middle East. Profits from this commerce provided capital to fund banks, and Italy's bankers multiplied their wealth by becoming Europe's leading financiers, industrialists, and (what today would be called) venture capitalists.

Much of the wealth that Italians earned stayed in Italy, for they had to spend little of it abroad. Italy had sufficient raw materials to supply its home industries, enough agricultural production to feed its population, and monopolies on the manufacture of many (but certainly not all) of the luxury goods its people consumed. Even more money entered Italian markets with invading German, French, and Spanish armies, and the papal treasury in Rome siphoned funds from every corner of Europe.

Political fragmentation prevented any one ruler or government from monopolizing these resources. Wealth was always concentrated in the hands of small elites, but Italy's chronic instability—shifting political fortunes, economic crashes, and onslaughts of plague—kept society open and provided opportunities for some social mobility. Italy, in short, had an ideal environment for the growth of an entrepreneurial middle class of pioneering capitalists who respected talent, industry, and ambition. The Renaissance was, in many ways, an affirmation of the politically engaged, family-oriented, secular lifestyle of a prosperous, powerful, and self-aware bourgeoisie.

The Culture of the Renaissance

Most people today associate Italy's Renaissance with the arts—sculpture, painting, and architecture. But the Renaissance was above all a literary movement devoted to the study of ancient Greek and Latin texts. Its scholars searched out forgotten manuscripts, and they found some long-disregarded works in Europe's libraries. (Cicero's letters and Tacitus' histories were significant additions to the Latin corpus.) A surge in Greek studies also made texts by Homer and Plato widely available to Western Europeans. But the Renaissance owed less to the discovery of new documents than to the development of a new way of reading familiar ones. Medieval scholars had long mined classical literature for ideas they could use to bolster their Christian worldview. But Renaissance scholars valued this pagan literature for its own sake and did their best to grasp the original intent of its authors. As they read, they were excited to discover what they claimed was a description of an ancient way of life that confirmed the legitimacy and superiority of their own.

Most historical eras are named by later generations looking back at the past, for it usually takes time for the significance of events to become clear. But the Renaissance was an era named by the people who lived it. The poet and scholar **Petrarch** (1304–1374) witnessed a world convulsed by plague, war, and the breakdown of the church. But instead of predicting gloom, he claimed that his generation was on the brink of a glorious new age—that it was emerging from a long dark period during which civilization had languished. Petrarch defined civilization as the way of life pioneered by the ancient Greeks and Romans, and he believed that this was what was being reborn in Italy's city-states—communities that he assumed resembled ancient Athens and Rome. For Petrarch, the previous thousand years had been "the middle ages," a period of loss, cultural retreat, and retrenchment that separated the ancient from the modern worlds—the eras of true civilization.

The Humanist Agenda   The intellectual leaders of the Renaissance were called **humanists,** for they advocated the study of humanity (*studia humanitatis*). This should not be taken to imply that they embraced what some Americans have called "secular humanism," an atheistic ideology. That the Renaissance was far from a secular movement is obvious from the abundance of religious paintings from the era that are to be found today in the collections of major museums. The humanists did, however, value the material world and secular life more highly than many of their medieval predecessors.

Renaissance humanists were often professional scholars who specialized in rhetoric—in techniques of artful literary composition derived from the works of ancient poets or of orators such as Cicero and Seneca. Their more traditional faculty colleagues, the scholastic dialecticians who worshiped Aristotle, had little concern for aesthetics. They believed that language should be developed as a scientific instrument for rigorously logical thinking. The humanists were by no means irrational, but they believed that people were more than reasoning machines. Logic and detached contemplation were not enough. Truth needed to engage human emotion to inspire complete conviction. Feelings and intuition also helped an individual engage productively with the world.

The humanists' philosophy of life affirmed the values of Italy's urban classes, which contrasted vividly with those of the ascetic monks who set the medieval standards. Humanists believed that people should marry, have families, shoulder political responsibilities, develop their individual talents, and enjoy the beauties and pleasures

☐●┤Read the **Document**

Letters to Cicero, *Petrarch*

on **MyHistoryLab.com**

of the material world. They maintained that a fully human life was packed with action and achievement and that a fully developed human being was a multifaceted individual who was interested in everything and able to do all things well. This was more than a theory; it was a reasonably accurate description of some of the giants of the Renaissance.

Poets and Prose Writers   Early signs of the Renaissance appear in the work of the poet **Dante Alighieri** (1265–1321) and emerge more clearly in the writings of two of his fellow Florentines of the next generation: the aforementioned Petrarch and Boccaccio (1313–1375). All three, as was the medieval custom, wrote in Latin when addressing the scholarly community, but their fame derives in large part from what they wrote in Italian. Humanists were enthusiastic students of the classical languages, but they understood that Latin and Greek had been the speech of ordinary people in the ancient world. They concluded therefore that poets and serious thinkers should be able to use the vernacular tongues common to the modern era.

Dante's thought had deep medieval roots, but he lived like a Renaissance intellectual. Most medieval scholars took clerical orders, but not Dante. He married, had a family, and pursued a political career. He became a professional man of letters after his party's fall from power forced him to leave Florence and spend the rest of his life in exile.

Among Dante's Latin works was a treatise (*De vulgari eloquentia*) that urged scholars to break with tradition and write in the vernacular so that a wider audience might profit from their work. Dante practiced what he preached—with phenomenal success. About 1293, while he was still living in Florence, he finished *La Vita Nuova* (*The New Life*), a cycle of lyric poems and prose narratives celebrating his passion for a woman called **Beatrice.** She was not his wife or mistress, but a woman whom he adored from afar (like a medieval courtly lover) as the feminine ideal. His masterwork was a huge poem written during his years in exile. He called it *Comedia*, not because it was funny, but because—unlike a tragedy—it was a story with a happy ending. **The Divine Comedy**, the title Dante's readers gave his poem, purports to describe a dream in which the poet journeys through Hell and Purgatory to Heaven, where he is granted a vision of God. Dante's guide during the first stages of his trip is the pagan Roman poet **Virgil** (70–19 B.C.E.).

Read the **Document**

The Divine Comedy, *Dante*

on **MyHistoryLab.com**

Because medieval scholars interpreted one of Virgil's poems as a prediction of Christ's birth, Virgil served Dante as a symbol for the truths that reason can intuit without the help of faith. Because reason does not require Scripture or revelation to grasp society's need for laws that enforce justice, Virgil can lead Dante through the realms where sinners are punished—Hell and Purgatory. But because reason cannot grasp the mysteries of divine grace, Virgil turns back at the gates of Heaven, and Beatrice, Dante's love, then appears to lead him into Paradise. *The Divine Comedy*'s cosmology and theology are medieval, but its respect for the dignity of human nature and human love hints at the emerging Renaissance. Dante has a higher opinion of some of the sinners whose punishments he describes in Hell than of spiritless people who go to their graves having done nothing very bad, but also nothing notable or good.

Petrarch studied at a university, was ordained a priest, and sought ecclesiastical stipends to support his work. At first glance, therefore, his scholarly career looks more conventional than Dante's, but the two men had much in common. Although he did not marry, Petrarch formed an attachment with a woman and lived as a family man raising a son and daughter. He shared Dante's interest in the poetry of courtly love, and his equivalent of Dante's Beatrice was an unidentified woman whom he called Laura. The sonnets she inspired him to write in Italian are his most popular compositions.

The Renaissance shines more clearly in Petrarch's work than Dante's primarily because of the role Petrarch played in sparking the Renaissance's passion for classical literature. He has been called "the father of humanism." Petrarch believed that intellectual darkness had descended on Europe after Rome's fall, but that the light of civilization was being rekindled for his generation. Progress, he argued, required an educational reform based on a curriculum that polished literary skills (e.g., Latin grammar, rhetoric, and poetry) and inspired moral edification (e.g., Roman history and Greek philosophy). He urged scholars to comb through libraries for forgotten works by ancient authors, and he believed that he and his contemporaries could train themselves to pick up where these giants of the past had left off. He encouraged the use of classical Latin rather than the ecclesiastical Latin that had evolved during the Middle Ages. His most ambitious attempt to honor the classical tradition was a poem entitled *Africa*, a Latin epic on the life of the Roman republican general, Scipio Africanus (237–183 B.C.E.). It dealt with the struggles leading to the Roman Republic's victory over Carthage in the Punic Wars. In 1341 the people of Rome gathered on the Capitoline Hill to award Petrarch the ancient symbol of achievement, a crown of laurel. Petrarch's love for the classics persuaded him that fame was a noble pursuit, but it did not override his Christian concern for the sin of pride. He took his pagan trophy to the Vatican and dedicated it to God. The Romans who honored Petrarch were less deferential to traditional religious authority. Six years later (1347) they rose up, took control of the city from the pope, and tried (unsuccessfully) to revive Petrarch's beloved Roman Republic.

Boccaccio, the out-of-wedlock son of a Florentine banker, was Petrarch's devoted disciple. Petrarch's influence persuaded Boccaccio to abandon the poetry and storytelling of his youth and take up classical studies. He wrote a number of books in Latin that served his contemporaries as useful compendia of information culled from ancient sources. The most popular of these were a genealogical encyclopedia of the pagan gods and collections of biographies of famous men and women. His better known compositions, however, are his earlier vernacular works, the most famous of which is a collection of bawdy and serious tales entitled **Decameron** (a combination of Greek words for *ten* and *day*). It is a fictive record of a hundred stories that ten young Florentine men and women allegedly told to entertain themselves while they hid from the plague in the comfort of a luxurious country house. Like Dante and Petrarch, Boccaccio's poetry was inspired by love for a woman. But

[●] Read the Document

Decameron: The Tale of the
Three Rings, *Boccaccio*

on **MyHistoryLab.com**

The *Decameron* This illustration decorates a page of Giovanni Boccaccio's *Decameron* and depicts the context Boccaccio asks his readers to imagine for the work. The Black Death is ravaging Florence (which is depicted by the urban environment and burials taking place on the left). To escape contagion, a group of young nobles have taken refuge in a delightful garden in the countryside (depicted on the right) where they entertain themselves by telling tales.

unlike Dante and probably Petrarch, he had an intimate relationship with Fiammetta, the lady whom he idolized. When she deserted him, he poured out his anguish in verse. The personal material he revealed in these poems illustrates his humanist's confidence that the emotions and interior life of the individual are worthy of study and documentation.

Boccaccio's contemporary, the English author **Geoffrey Chaucer** (c. 1340–1400), shared this faith. Chaucer, like many of the great Renaissance artists and scholars, was a son of the middle classes with a background in business and experience in politics. He is not usually thought of as a Renaissance figure, but he read Italian and modeled some of his poems on Boccaccio's work. Italy's Renaissance would not have spread so readily to the rest of Europe if cultures north of the Alps had not, on their own, been evolving similar values and interests. Chaucer's most popular work, ***The Canterbury***

Donatello's *David* Cosimo de Medici, the banker and leader of Florence, built a magnificent palace for his family, and in 1430 commissioned the sculptor Donatello to create a statue for its courtyard. Donatello's subject was the biblical account of the fight between David and Goliath. He represented David as a very young man, nude except for elaborate boots, and standing over the head of his slaughtered enemy. Donatello's *David*, the first free-standing nude human form to be sculpted since the end of the Roman era, is sometimes said to be the first true Renaissance sculpture. *Bargello National Museum, Florence/Canali PhotoBank, Milan/SuperStock*

Tales, describes a company of pilgrims en route to the shrine of St. Thomas Becket at Canterbury. Chaucer introduces each pilgrim and then narrates the stories each tells to amuse the others. In this way the book resembles Boccaccio's *Decameron*. The characters in *The Canterbury Tales* are not the kinds of abstract or allegorical types found in much medieval literature. They are unique, memorable persons, and Chaucer bestows individuality on his pilgrims by matching his descriptions of them with the natures of the stories he has them tell.

Sculptors   Vernacular literature spread the Renaissance beyond the narrow circle of humanist scholars, but literature was not the only thing that helped the Renaissance extend its influence. Artists and architects created urban environments that exposed ordinary men and women to the spirit of the new age.

Artifacts of Roman civilization were more abundant in late medieval Italy than they are today, and their influence on Italy's sculptors was apparent as early as the thirteenth century. Real bodies seem to exist beneath the classical robes with which the sculptors **Nicola Pisano** (c. 1220–1284) and his son **Giovanni** (c. 1250–1320) draped their figures. Renaissance artists did not, however, simply copy ancient models. They combined the idealism of classical art with a new realism that reflected the humanists' emphasis on the worth of the individual. Many ancient statues have a detached, timeless quality that renders them static, but Renaissance sculptures have a unique, characteristic vibrancy. Medieval sculptors had thought of statuary as architectural ornament and subordinated it to the lines of the buildings it decorated. But **Donatello** (1386–1466), a Florentine artist, created statues that, like those in the ancient world, were meant to stand alone and be viewed in the round. They were so natural and imbued with life that some people found them shocking. The early work of **Michelangelo** (1475–1564), particularly the gigantic *David* he created to stand in front of Florence's town hall, represents the humanist ideals of the Renaissance at their purest. *David's* heroic nudity proclaims the glory of an idealized human body, but the statue's proportions were not dictated by slavish imitation of nature or some mathematical theory about ideal form. The statue's outsized head and hands impart tension to its design, and the intense look on David's face hints at the youth's thoughts as he contemplated his unequal contest with the giant, Goliath (I Samuel 17).

Church of St. Andrea   The facade of the Church of St. Andrea, Mantova, Italy, illustrates the conventions of Renaissance architecture: classical motifs, symmetry, and abstract geometrical forms. It was designed about 1470 by Leon Battista Alberti.

Architects   The Gothic style that originated in France in the twelfth century had some influence in Italy, but the Mediterranean region clung to the older Romanesque tradition and the elements of classical style that it preserved. The Renaissance's architects drew both inspiration and, unfortunately, building materials from Italy's abundant Roman ruins. Marble, columns, bronze ornaments, and simple bricks were plundered from the remains of ancient buildings for use in new structures. A book on architecture by **Vitruvius,** a first-century B.C.E. Roman engineer, that came to light in the fifteenth century also helped spread knowledge of the principles underlying classical designs.

The first of the great Renaissance architects was **Filippo Brunelleschi** (1377–1446). The dome he designed for Florence's cathedral is an engineering marvel that still dominates the city's skyline. Brunelleschi intensively studied Roman buildings, but, like the sculptors of the Renaissance, he did not merely copy his models. He admired their symmetry, simplicity, and proportions, and he used the standard elements (pillars and round arches) of their design. But the way in which he manipulated and integrated these things mated classical stability with Renaissance energy.

PEOPLE IN CONTEXT   Isabella d'Este and Elisabetta Gonzaga (1472–1526)

Feminist historians have pointed out that the Renaissance did not affect men and women in the same way. The respect the period accorded talent and achievement opened doors for some men. But the classical Greek and Roman societies the Renaissance admired were thoroughly patriarchal, and this shaped the humanists' view of family life. It gave new currency to the ancient belief that women should be confined to the domestic sphere and subordinated to the male heads of their households. In most poor and middle-class families economic reality had more to do with the status of women than humanist ideology. Women in these ranks had to do whatever was needed to support their families, but the wealthy upper classes could afford either to limit or indulge the ambitions of their women.

Elisabetta Gonzaga, a daughter of the ruling family of Mantua, became the model for the official feminine ideal. At the age of 16, she wed Guidobaldo da Montefeltro, the duke of Urbino. He was a friend of humanists, an art collector, and the owner of one of the larger libraries in Italy. As the duchess of Urbino, Elisabetta presided over a court famous for its refinement and elegance.

The Studio of Isabella d'Este in the Ducal Palace at Mantua   Isabella's quarters in the palace at Mantua housed a small museum of works by leading artists of her era. And the apartment was decorated with images that celebrated her role as patron of the arts and arbiter of taste. This door panel is an allegory of music, an art of which Isabella was a noted practitioner.

One of the ornaments of her court was **Baldassare Castiglione** (1478–1529), a distinguished diplomat. Near the end of his life, Castiglione drew on his extensive experience in aristocratic circles to write *The Book of the Courtier*, a kind of guidebook to the upper reaches of Renaissance society. The volume was translated into numerous languages and remained a best seller for over a century. It set the standard for polite society and made Elisabetta famous.

The Book of the Courtier purports to be an account of a conversation on the subject of the nature of gentility that took place in Elisabetta's salon. Not surprisingly, it comes to the conclusion that the hostess is the ideal Renaissance lady. She is praised for her education—for a knowledge of literature, art, and music that ensures that cultured men find her conversation worthy of their time. But her special vocation as a woman is to keep her court running smoothly and, by her charm and elegant behavior, elevate its tone. The physical activities in which men indulge—riding, hunting, and warfare—are beneath her. She attends to the domestic sphere and serves the wider world by civilizing the men who run it.

A feminine ideal of a very different nature was, however, modeled by Elizabetta's sister-in-law, **Isabella d'Este** (1474–1539). Despite the limited role that women were expected to play in public life, a surprising number of them became heads of state in the sixteenth century. Isabella, the marchesa of Mantua and "the First Lady of the World" (as a prominent politician dubbed her) was one of these. Her father, the king of Naples, arranged her marriage (at age 16) to **Francesco Gonzaga**, marquis of Mantua and commander-in-chief of the armies of the Republic of Venice. She bore her husband eight children, but her activities extended far beyond maternal duties. She translated Greek and Latin texts and carried on a voluminous correspondence with leading political and cultural figures. As a *condottiero* (the head of a company of mercenaries), her husband was often abroad on military campaign. During his absences she presided in Mantua, and, when he was captured in 1509 and imprisoned for three years, she assumed control, commanded armies, presided over diplomatic conferences, and skillfully kept an invading French army at bay. Her reputation cast such a shadow over her husband's record that, when he returned, their marriage broke down. After his death in 1519, she ruled Mantua as regent for her son, the heir. She founded a school for girls, turned Mantua into a major cultural center, and negotiated its recognition as a duchy. Following a disagreement with her son, she relocated to Rome where she won appointment as a cardinal for another of her boys. She finished her brilliant career as ruler of the town of Solarlo in the Papal States. ■

QUESTION: To what extent can a society's theories about gender roles be assumed to govern how its people behave?

The most ambitious of the Renaissance's building projects was the reconstruction of Europe's largest church, St. Peter's at the **Vatican.** The first St. Peter's was a basilican church that Emperor Constantine built for the popes in the fourth century. By the fifteenth century it had deteriorated so badly that Pope **Nicholas V** (r. 1447–1455) proposed replacing it with an entirely new building. The work dragged on for two centuries and involved over a dozen architects, the most important of whom were **Donato Bramante** (1444–1514),

> **Read** the **Document**
>
> Life of Michelangelo, *Georgio Vasari*
>
> on **MyHistoryLab.com**

Michelangelo (1475–1564), and **Gianlorenzo Bernini** (1598–1680). Michelangelo was not only a superb sculptor, but also a brilliant architect, an extraordinary painter, and a competent poet. The frescoes he created for the vault and altar wall of the Vatican's **Sistine Chapel** (named for its builder, Pope **Sixtus IV**, r. 1471–1484) are a miracle of design and execution.

Painters   Unlike sculptors and architects, Renaissance painters had few ancient examples of their art to study. They were inspired by classical sculpture. But to imitate it, they had to invent techniques to represent three-dimensional figures on the two-dimensional surfaces of their paintings.

The Creation of Adam   Although Michelangelo preferred to work as a sculptor, Pope Julius II persuaded him to undertake the execution of frescoes for the ceiling of the Vatican's Sistine chapel. Over a period of four years (1508–1512) the sculptor turned painter created one of the greater monuments of Western civilization. His design featured nine major panels illustrating texts from the Book of Genesis. Three deal with the origin of the universe, three with Adam and Eve, and three with the story of Noah (i.e., the consequence for the Creation of Adam and Eve's sinful rebellion).

Medieval artists thought of paintings as pages of text. They drew flat figures against blank backgrounds and suggested depth and distance simply by placing some figures in front of others. They often combined different scenes from a story in the same composition. A single painting of the Virgin Mary might, for instance, depict the Annunciation, the birth of Jesus, and the Virgin's ascent to heaven. Its overall design could be aesthetically pleasing, but its meaning only became clear when its elements were separated and read like words on a page. Renaissance paintings were less like pages and more like windows. They framed a scene—a realistic view of a three-dimensional world into which a spectator could imagine stepping.

The Florentine painter **Cimabue** (c. 1240–1302) worked in a style that was heavily influenced by Byzantine frescoes and mosaics, but he anticipated the Renaissance by experimenting with ways to suggest three-dimensional space and by giving the faces of his subjects individuality and emotional intensity. **Giotto di Bondone** (1267–1337), his student, had greater success in achieving these objectives. His human subjects manifest strong feelings and move in real space—like actors in theatrical scenes. The plague that began to spread through Europe in 1348 may explain why Giotto (like his younger contemporary, the poet Dante) had no immediate successor. Eventually, however, a Florentine called **Masaccio** (1401–1428) picked up where Giotto left off, and an extraordinary number of great artists appeared over the course of the next few generations.

Research into how to represent **perspective** (that is, create the illusion of three-dimensional space) began with the study of vision and a search for mathematical

Perspective This painting by **Piero della Francesca** was executed for the ducal palace in Urbino, Italy. It represents an idealized city-scape and illustrates how Renaissance artists created the illusion of space and depth. The rigor of the composition compels viewers to see the scene from the artist's perspective and is consistent with the humanist's vision of a rationally ordered world. *Piero della Francesca (c. 1420–1492). Italian (Piero della Francesca?). View of an Ideal City. Galleria Nazionale delle Marche, Urbino, Italy. Photo credit: Scala/Art Resource, NY*

formulae that would describe how light enters the eye. Brunelleschi's analyses of architectural spaces led to the discovery that if lines are traced along the profiles of buildings and extended as far as possible, they all converge at a single point on the horizon. Renaissance artists quickly began to orient their compositions around this so-called **vanishing point.** Another architect, **Leon Battista Alberti,** worked out and published the mathematics governing the projection lines that meet at a vanishing point.

Renaissance painters added a new medium to their art. Medieval and early Renaissance painters usually worked in **tempera**—that is, with pigments mixed with a binder such as egg yolk. They painted on wooden boards or walls covered with a damp plaster that absorbed colors. Tempera was a restrictive medium, however, for it dried quickly and its colors did not blend well. Northern European painters were the first to discover that these difficulties could be overcome by mixing their pigments with oils. Oils dried slowly, and translucent **oil-based paints** could be applied in multiple layers to produce an infinite variety of intense, glowing colors. There is literary evidence for oil painting as early as the twelfth century, but the first great practitioners of the art were the Netherlanders, **Hubert** (c. 1366–1426) and **Jan van Eyck** (c. 1390–1441) and **Dirk Bouts** (1415–1475). They filled their pictures with a wealth of detail—precisely describing the physical world and representing the gleam or texture of all kinds of materials. Northerners also pioneered **landscape painting.** Medieval artists had sometimes sketched landscapes as background for human activities, but the respect that Renaissance humanists had for the material world made that world a fit subject for study and description in its own right.

Artists working in Venice introduced oil painting to Italy in the late fifteenth century, along with a second northern invention: the use of a canvas on stretchers as a surface for a painting. This expanded the market for art by reducing the cost of pictures and improving their portability. The church's dominance of patronage declined as the prospering urban classes began to commission paintings, and artists found plenty of work producing decorative objects to satisfy the Renaissance's taste for luxury and self-promotion. The era's renewed respect for the individual created an especially strong market for a kind of art that had languished during the medieval era: the portrait.

Leading Artists and Authors of Italy's Renaissance

ca. 1220 Nicola Pisano	1284
1240 Cimabue	1302
1250 Giovanni Pisano	1320
1265 Dante	1321
1267 Giotto	1337
1295 Andrea Pisano	1348
1304 Petrarch	1374
1313 Boccaccio	1375
1377 Brunelleschi	1446
1378 Ghiberti	1455
1386 Donatello	1466
1395 Fra Angelico	1455
1399 Della Robbia	1482
1400 Jacopo Bellini	1470
1401 Masaccio	1428
1406 Filippo Lippi	1469
1407 Lorenzo Valla	1457
1415 Piero della Francesca	1492
1429 Gentile Bellini	1507
1430 Giovanni Bellini	1516
1431 Mantegna	1506
1435 Verrocchio	1488
1444 Bramante	1514
1445 Botticelli	1510
1452 da Vinci	1519
1457 Filippino Lippi	1504
1469 Machiavelli	1527
1475 Michelangelo	1564
1475 Giorgione	1510
1483 Raphael	1520
1485 Titian	1576
1500 Cellini	1571
1518 Palladio	1580

The Adoration of the Lamb   This is the center panel of a very large, elaborate altarpiece begun by Jan van Eyck and finished in 1432 by his brother Hubert. The whole assemblage consists of 24 panels. This one represents Christ, the Lamb of God, on an altar, the place where Catholic doctrine holds that the elements of the mass become his body and blood. The Holy Spirit, in the form of a dove, hovers above him, and the fountain of new life that he brings stands in the foreground. Angels surround the altar and beyond them are groups of worshippers representing the faithful witness of saints, martyrs, and scholars. The themes and symbols are traditionally medieval, but the precise realism of the painting's style reflects the influence of the Northern Renaissance.

The Northern Renaissance

Germany and the Politics of the Holy Roman Empire   **Frederick II,** the Hohenstaufen emperor, had largely ignored Germany while he struggled vainly to win control of Italy. After his death and the extermination of his dynasty, the German nobles were slow
to seat a new king. Their throne remained vacant from
1254 to 1274. In the interim, the country's hundreds of
political entities enjoyed independence. Some regions
were governed as hereditary duchies, some were ruled

View the **Map**

Renaissance Europe, c. 1500
on **MyHistoryLab.com**

by the church, and many were tiny baronies or urban republics and oligarchies. The most original political organization that emerged to counter the confusion of the era was a powerful league of cities.

The German merchants who operated in the Baltic region compensated for the absence of a royal protector by forming a corporation (*Hanse*) and working together to defend themselves. The cities that established the **Hanseatic League** in 1359 did not occupy contiguous territories, but the army and navy they maintained policed the land and sea routes that connected them. At the league's peak, it had about 170 members and exercised a virtual monopoly over Baltic and North Sea commerce. The league dominated the Scandinavian kingdoms, and England and France treated the Hanse as if it were a sovereign state. The development of

Atlantic trade routes eventually eroded its economic clout, but it survived into the seventeenth century.

A development with more significance for Germany's future occurred on the country's eastern borderlands. In 1248, when the family that ruled Austria died out, the duchy of **Austria** should have returned to its overlord, Frederick II. However, he was too preoccupied with wars in Italy to assert his claim. A year after Frederick II died, **Ottokar II** (r. 1253–1278), heir to the kingdom of **Bohemia** (the region around Prague), annexed Austria. So long as Germany had no king, there was no one to challenge his usurpation of lands that doubled the size of his kingdom.

The situation changed in 1273 when Pope **Gregory X** (r. 1271–1276) persuaded the German barons to end the squabbling over their vacant throne by electing a king. They chose a minor nobleman, **Rudolf of Habsburg** (r. 1273–1291), in the belief that he would pose no threat to their independence. Because Rudolf's barons feared the powerful king of Bohemia more than their new Habsburg leader, they agreed to help Rudolf reclaim the duchy of Austria for the crown. When the Bohemians withdrew, Rudolf left his tiny ancestral barony on the Aar River east of the Swiss city of Bern and moved his family to Vienna. The Habsburgs reigned there until 1918, when World War I brought their regime to its end.

The German monarchy was elective, and the nobles' preference for weak rulers turned them against the rapidly rising Habsburg family. After Rudolf's death, the electors transferred the royal title to less consequential men. However, in 1310 their efforts to ensure the weakness of their king were confounded when history repeated itself. Ottokar of Bohemia's family died out, and the Bohemians offered their throne to the son of Germany's king, **Henry VII** (r. 1308–1313). Henry's family, the **Luxemburgs,** then followed the example set by the Habsburgs and relocated to their new central European domain. In 1347 **Charles IV** (r. 1347–1378), the Luxemburg ruler of Bohemia, was elected Germany's Holy Roman Emperor, and in 1356 he issued a decree designed to guarantee that his descendants would keep the imperial title. Charles's **Golden Bull** (from *bullum*, the seal that ratifies a document) helped to stabilize Germany by limiting participation in imperial elections to the heads of seven great principalities (four secular lords and three archbishops). This established a rough balance of power among the German magnates and ended the pope's meddling in Germany's affairs. Because Charles recognized the independence of the seven **Electors,** they felt safe in allowing the crown to remain with the Luxemburg family.

In 1440 the Luxemburgs died out, and the throne passed to the Habsburgs with whom they had intermarried. By then, the imperial title was largely an empty honor, and the Habsburgs were far less interested in Germany and Italy than in the empire they were building in central Europe. On their eastern frontier, they faced the rising power with whom the Italians were also attempting to come to terms in the late fifteenth century: the Ottoman Turks.

The Arts   Political confusion was no more antithetical to cultural progress north of the Alps than it was to regions south of the mountains. But a vibrant medieval tradition lingered in the north that affected how northerners appropriated aspects of

Italy's Renaissance. Gothic architecture was far from dead in the late fifteenth century, particularly in England where a refined and delicate **"Perpendicular Gothic"** style flourished. The minutely detailed realism that characterized the work of northern oil painters (such as Hubert and Jan van Eyck) owed more to the tradition of medieval manuscript illumination than to Renaissance classicism.

Albrecht Dürer (1471–1528) was the first major northern artist to take a serious interest in Italy's Renaissance. He was a citizen of Nuremberg, an independent German city that had extensive commercial ties with Italy. Many of Italy's Renaissance artists were trained in the shops of goldsmiths. Dürer's father was a goldsmith, and Dürer practiced one of the goldsmith's arts: engraving. His interest, however, was not in ornamenting objects, but in the artistic potential of one of the most revolutionary inventions of the era. About 1455 **Johannes Gutenberg** had perfected the

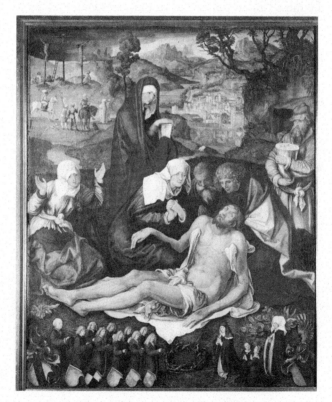

Lamentation for Christ Albrecht Dürer created this interpretation of the "deposition" (i.e., removal of Christ from the cross) on commission from the Holzschuher and Gruber families, whose members and heraldic emblems appear as the small figures at the base of the painting. Although Dürer was a Renaissance artist, the painting honors many medieval conventions. It refers to several episodes in the story of its subject. An empty cross flanked by the two thieves crucified with Christ appears in the distance as does the mouth of the tomb in which Jesus is to be buried. Mary Magdalene and Joseph of Arimathea carry ointments for the preparation of the corpse. Jesus' Mother is present, as are St. John and Nicodemus, figures often represented as lowering Christ from the cross.

printing press. Dürer made a name for himself not only as a painter but as an engraver of plates for printing pictures. His multiple trips to Italy were probably motivated by his desire, as a draftsman, to study Italian artists' techniques for drawing in perspective. Dürer immersed himself in the rapidly growing literature dealing with the laws of perspective, and his reading of classical authors and study of ancient statuary convinced him that art should be informed by a close, scientific study of nature. He filled files with detailed sketches of plants, animals, and people and worked these elements into superbly executed woodcuts and engravings. Prints from his blocks and plates were inexpensive enough that, for the first time in history, people of modest means could purchase the work of a major artist. The printing press encouraged the growth of literacy in early modern Europe and helped spread the art and literature of the Renaissance to an ever widening spectrum of European society.

Northerners went to Italy to study the Renaissance firsthand, but some Italian artists also emigrated to northern regions. **Leonardo da Vinci** (1452–1519), whose *Mona Lisa* may be the most famous portrait of all time, was employed by King **Francis I** (r. 1515–1547) of France. Francis's political aspirations probably explain why he was the first of northern Europe's kings to become a patron of the Renaissance. Whenever the Germans withdrew from Italy, the French were tempted to move in. After the death of Frederick II and his heirs, **Charles of Anjou** (brother of France's King Louis IX) had seized the kingdoms of Naples and Sicily. Sicily rebelled and broke free in 1282, and the French eventually lost their grip on Naples. But in 1525 Francis launched a new war in the hope that acquisition of Italian territory would enable him to counter the growing power of the Habsburgs. He failed

View the **Closer Look**

Leonardo Plots the Perfect Man

on **MyHistoryLab.com**

The Last Supper   Leonardo da Vinci's depiction of the Last Supper Jesus shared with his disciples is one of the most famous (and most studied) paintings from the period of Italy's Renaissance. It was completed about 1498 and its theme may have been suggested by its location—the wall of a monastery refectory (i.e., dining hall). Triangular designs organize the painting. They give the disciples' spontaneous, shocked reactions to Christ's prediction of his betrayal a look of stable, eternal timelessness.

spectacularly, but even futile military ventures were culturally significant. They sent hordes of foreign soldiers into Italy who absorbed aspects of its culture, which they subsequently mediated to their homelands.

Northern Humanism   The environment of northern Europe shaped the kind of interest that northerners took in the Renaissance. Northern Europe had few inspiring Roman ruins to remind people of the grandeurs of classical civilization. Unlike Italy's powerful urban communities, its towns did not see themselves as successors to the classical world's famous city-states, and it was not the pagan past that drew northern scholars to the work of Italy's humanists. The northerners were intrigued by another of the ancient civilization's legacies: the Bible and the church.

The northern Renaissance was energized by a religious revival—the **Modern Devotion**—that originated in the Netherlands in the fourteenth century (see Chapter 11). It championed an intensely personal and private form of mystical piety. **Thomas à Kempis** (c. 1380–1471), a Catholic monk, captured the spirit of the movement in an enduring devotional classic entitled *The Imitation of Christ.* The Modern Devotion also inspired the foundation of quasi-monastic organizations dedicated to charitable work and education. The schools maintained by the most famous of these, the **Brethren of the Common Life,** were noteworthy for the training they provided in the ancient languages. Italy's humanists had pursued the study of classical Latin and Greek in order to better understand the civilization of ancient Rome and Greece. The northern humanists sought the same linguistic competence, but applied it to the study of the Bible.

Desiderius Erasmus (1466–1536), the most prominent of the northern humanists, was the illegitimate son of a learned priest. His father developed an interest in humanism while visiting Italy, and he had Erasmus educated by the Brethren of the Common Life. Erasmus followed his father into the church, the traditional career path for a medieval scholar. He became a monk and was ordained a priest, but soon realized that this had been a mistake. He found monastic life stultifying, and he was no happier when his superiors sent him to study theology at the University of Paris. The medieval scholasticism that still held sway in Paris repulsed Erasmus and drove him into the humanists' camp.

Erasmus's greatest achievement was a superior edition of the Greek New Testament based on a critical analysis of some of the ancient Greek sources. Scholars used it to improve the accuracy of Latin and vernacular translations. Erasmus was, however, much more than an arid philologist whose studies were ends in themselves. Like others of the Renaissance period, he believed that intellectuals should not keep their work to themselves, but rather should use it to benefit the masses. The understanding of early Christianity that he acquired from his close examination of the Scriptures awoke his appetite for religious reform. He urged the church to jettison much of the baggage it had accumulated during the Middle Ages and revert to the simplicity of the New Testament era. Authentic Christianity, he believed, was a charitable and selfless way of life guided by a personal experience of God. The

[◉] **Read** the **Document**

Satire by Erasmus: Pope Julius Excluded from Heaven

on **MyHistoryLab.com**

best way to restore and build faith, he argued, was to give ordinary people a Bible they could read for themselves. He had little sympathy for clergy who wanted to keep their congregations ignorant and subservient. One of his most popular books, *Praise of Folly*, was a social satire that targeted the clergy. Erasmus was such an outspoken critic of medieval Catholicism that his contemporaries joked that he laid the "egg" that the Protestant reformers hatched. When the **Reformation** broke out, however, Erasmus—like his friend, the English humanist **Thomas More** (1478–1535)—was unwilling to leave the Catholic Church. Erasmus agreed with the **Protestants** that the church should be reformed to bring it in line with the New Testament model. But as a humanist, he preferred a more tempered and rational faith than the leading Reformers preached (see Chapter 13). Up until this point, historically prominent individuals, such as these men, have been known to the modern world almost always only as names. But, thanks to the artists of the Renaissance, many of those names now have faces associated with them. The leading portrait painter of the era, **Hans Holbein** the Younger (c. 1497–1543), produced intriguing images of Erasmus, More, and others that invite speculation about their interior lives.

The Middle East: The Ottoman Empire

The states that the **Seljuk Turks** had established in the Middle East in the eleventh century were undermined by the **Mongol** invasion in the thirteenth century. As they crumbled, other Turks who were pushed west by the Mongol advance took their place. The **Ottoman Turks** were named for Osman (r. 1299–1326), a chief who settled them in Asia Minor close to the Byzantine city of Nicaea. In 1301 he defeated a Byzantine army, and he and his successors steadily detached territory both from Constantinople's crumbling empire and from neighboring Turkish chiefdoms. The Ottomans' location on the frontier of the Byzantine Empire allowed them to recruit men for a popular holy war with Islam's Christian opponents. In 1331 they took Nicaea. By 1340 they had brought most of Asia Minor under their control. In 1354 a contender for the Byzantine throne, who wanted their help, allowed them to establish a base at Gallipoli, a fortress commanding a choke point on the channel that links the Black and Aegean Seas. From there they moved into the Balkans and began to encircle Constantinople. In 1389 they defeated the Serbs at the first battle of Kosovo, and a year later the remaining parts of Asia Minor and Syria as far east as the Euphrates submitted to them.

Expansion of Ottoman Power   In 1402 **Timur the Lame** (Tamerlane), the greatest Mongol conqueror since Genghis Khan (see Chapter 11), routed an Ottoman army and killed the sultan Bayezid I (r. 1389–1402). However, the Mongols soon turned their attention elsewhere and left the Ottomans to fight among themselves. A decade of confusion ensued until **Mehmed I** (r. 1413–1421) finally won the upper hand and began to restore Ottoman unity and territory. His son, **Murad II** (r. 1421–1451), conquered Greece and the Balkans

☐▶ Read the Document

A Contemporary Describes Timur, *Ibn Khaldun*

on **MyHistoryLab.com**

and pushed into Hungary. The defeats he gave the Hungarians at the battle of Varna in 1444 and at the second battle of Kosovo in 1448 crippled the Christian state and opened the way for the Ottomans to drive deep into Catholic territory.

Murad's son, **Mehmed II, "the Conqueror"** (r. 1451–1481), secured the Ottomans' position by winning a prize that had eluded Muslim armies for nearly 800 years. On May 29, 1453, the 20-year-old Turkish sultan took the city of **Constantinople**—with the help of some European technology. In 1452 a Hungarian gunsmith offered to construct a huge cannon for the last Byzantine emperor, **Constantine XI** (r. 1448–1453). When Constantine failed to raise the money for the project, the Hungarian approached the

Read the Document

Description of the Ottoman Emperor Mehmed II

on **MyHistoryLab.com**

Ottomans, who commissioned several pieces of artillery. The largest was a 26-foot-long cannon that fired missiles weighing 800 pounds. With weapons like this, it took only a few weeks to pound the impoverished and depopulated capital of eastern Christendom into submission. Venice and Genoa might have helped Constantinople, but they did not want to do anything to risk harming good commercial relations with the Ottomans.

The Turks renamed Constantinople **Istanbul** and turned its great church, the *Hagia Sophia*, into a mosque. The loss of the last major Christian outpost in the Middle East was a shock to Europe, but it had little practical significance. Constantinople had ceased to protect the eastern frontiers of Christendom, and its new Muslim rulers had no intention of severing its mutually profitable commercial ties with Europe. Italy actually profited from the disaster that befell Constantinople. Greek scholars fleeing the Ottomans sought refuge in Italy, and their linguistic expertise and libraries were important resources for the Renaissance. Cultural influences also flowed in the opposite direction. Mehmed employed Italian artists and architects. Despite Islam's occasional hostility to representational art, he sat for portraits by one of Italy's great Renaissance painters, **Gentile Bellini** (1429–1507).

Several things contributed to the Ottomans' success. For one, they did not divide their conquests to provide domains for all a ruler's sons. The **sultanate** passed intact to only one heir (not inevitably the eldest), and to ensure safety and stability his brothers were killed. Mehmed II formalized this tradition as the Ottoman law of fratricide. Unique customs also governed how sultans sired their heirs. Their marriages were celibate, and they had their children by concubines. Once a concubine had borne a son, the sultan ended relations with her. This motivated her to focus on the care and preparation of her son to be the winner in the life-and-death struggle for succession to the throne. The relationship that this built between a woman and her son meant that a sultan's mother could become an extremely powerful influence on his government. Once the Ottoman royal house settled in Constantinople and built its lavish residence, the Topkapi Palace, its princes were confined to quarters and raised in luxurious seclusion. This, of course, meant that heirs came to the throne with very little experience of the world. In 1603 concern for the survival of the dynasty ended the practice of executing its princes, and it became customary for the throne to pass to the eldest Ottoman heir—often the brother of the previous sultan.

Mehmed II This portrait of the conqueror of Constantinople is ascribed to the Italian Renaissance artist, **Gentile Bellini**. The classical style of the arch with which the painter has framed his subject may seem somewhat at odds with Mehmed's eastern dress and appearance, but he obviously would not have thought so. Islam had claims of its own to the classical legacy of Greece and Rome, and the Ottomans were well informed about developments in Italian politics and art.

The Ottoman Empire had an extremely diverse population. Although the Ottomans were Muslims, they were exposed to multiple religious influences, for there were different kinds of Islam just as there were different kinds of Christianity. Given that the Ottomans first expanded into Byzantine territory, more of their subjects may initially have been Greek Orthodox Christians than Muslims. Many of the former preferred Muslim rule to domination by the Latin Catholics who had staked claims to Byzantine lands after the Fourth Crusade sacked Constantinople in 1204 (see Chapter 11). Europe's Christians viewed eastern Christians as near heretics and pressed them to submit to the papal church. The Ottomans, by contrast were tolerant of both Christians and Jews. They continued the long-standing Muslim practice of according "the people of the book" a kind of second-class citizenship. Christians and Jews paid special taxes, but were protected and allowed a limited degree of autonomy. Among the taxes they paid, however, was a unique kind of human tribute. Christian boys were taken at a young age, converted to Islam, and educated for special military and governmental service in the corps of **Janissaries** ("new troops"). **Murad I** (r. 1362–1389) was said to have founded the Janissaries to counter the influence of the Turkish cavalry. The horse soldiers were supported by grants of land, which gave them a degree of independence from the sultan, but Janissaries were the sultan's slaves. Slave armies had a long history in the Middle East. The Seljuk and Mamluk regimes had been founded by formerly enslaved soldiers. The trust the Ottoman sultan placed in the Janissaries led to their occupying many of the posts in his government. The result was a Muslim empire largely managed by recent converts from Christian families.

Mehmed and his successors did not concentrate all their attention on European targets, for they had much to do in the divided Muslim world. In 1502 Shah **Ismail I** (r. 1502–1524) founded the **Safavid Empire** in Persia (Iran). Religion complicated the situation, for the Ottomans were Sunni Muslims, and the Safavids were

Shi'ites (see Chapter 7). Each empire regarded the other as heretical, and each tried to purge its territory of inhabitants who professed its opponent's faith. In 1514 **Selim I** (r. 1512–1520), the Ottoman ruler, routed a Safavid army and took control of Egypt and the Muslim holy cities of Mecca and Medina. This brought the Arab homeland into the Ottoman Empire, and in 1517 Selim was hailed as caliph, a title implying religious as well as governmental authority (see Map 12–2).

The Ottoman Empire reached a peak of power and magnificence during the reign of Selim's successor, **Süleyman** (r. 1520–1566). His domain extended east into Iraq and north and west to Hungary and up the Danube valley to the walls of Vienna (which he besieged in 1529). In 1522 he drove the Knights of St. John from the island of Rhodes and established the dominance of his navy in the eastern Mediterranean. The Ottoman juggernaut rolled on without serious reverses until 1565, when a great armada failed to take the island of Malta south of Sicily.

[●] **Read** the **Document**

An Ambassador's Report on the Ottoman Empire, *Ogier Ghiselin de Busberq (1555)*

on **MyHistoryLab.com**

Ottoman Civilization The civilization of the Ottoman Empire was shaped by the Turks' devotion to Islamic religious law (**Shariah**). Muslims believe the Qur'an literally records God's words. As such, it is a source of immutable laws for human conduct. All such laws are, in theory, already revealed in the life and teachings of the Prophet Muhammad. Additions to the law are therefore impossible, but religious scholars can interpret the law to deal with new situations. The Ottoman ruler's function was not to make law but to apply this divine law with the help of **muftis** (religious jurists). Islam has no priests, for it has no sacraments. Its religious leaders, like Jewish rabbis, are specialists in the interpretation of sacred texts and laws. Muslim faith in a definitive code of divine laws did not stifle change, but it did make change problematic. New things had to be justified as extensions of established Islamic principles.

Contrary to what might be expected, the Ottomans' concern for Muslim orthodoxy did not lead to intolerance. The Ottoman Empire was, in fact, far more religiously tolerant than most contemporary European states. The empire had many Jewish, Christian, and even some Shi'ite Muslim subjects, and there were variations within its official Sunni faith. Muslims who found the legalism and formal liturgies of their state religion emotionally unfulfilling turned to **Sufism.** Sufis were mystics who used music, song, poetry, and dance to cultivate ecstatic trances and visions.

Culturally, the Ottoman Empire was sandwiched between two quite different peoples: the Shi'ite Safavids in the east and the Catholic Europeans in the west. Although both were enemies, both influenced the Ottomans. Protection and promotion of commercial relations was a priority of Istanbul's government, and the empire allowed Europeans to establish residency in its ports and to travel within its boundaries. Few Muslims, however, toured Europe. The empire's trade outposts in Europe were usually manned by its Jewish or Christian subjects.

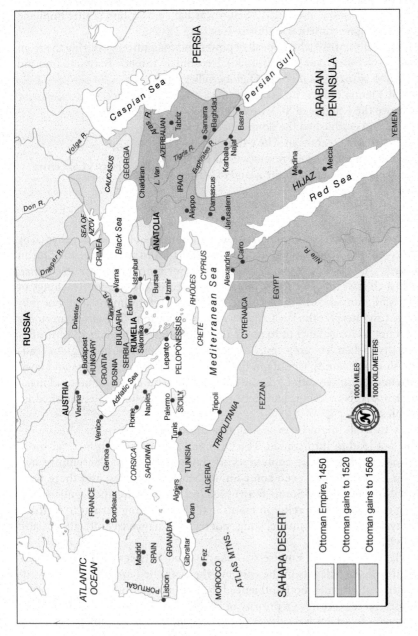

MAP 12–2 The Ottoman Empire After the conquest of Constantinople, the Ottoman sultan maintained, as his Byzantine predecessors had, that he stood in a line of rulers that began with Rome's emperors. The lands he controlled included and exceeded those of the ancient eastern Roman Empire.

QUESTION: In terms of territory and culture, was the Ottoman Empire a "western" or an "eastern" state?

The Ottoman Empire survived into the twentieth century. Its longevity is proof of its ability to evolve and adapt, but whether such adaptation should be viewed as success or decline depends very much on one's perspective. As early as the seventeenth century, some Turkish historians judged their empire to be weakening. The fault, they claimed, lay with sultans who allowed unworthy favorites and corrupt servants to usurp their authority. For whatever reason, the power of the central government, if not the empire, had begun to fade by the late sixteenth century.

In 1571 the Ottoman navy suffered a major defeat in a battle off **Lepanto** in the Gulf of Corinth. Although the fleet was rebuilt, the nature of naval warfare changed. The era of great armadas battling for control of Mediterranean trade came to an end as the European states shifted their attention to the Atlantic and global exploration. Faster kinds of ships, designed for the oceans, replaced heavy galleys. Without policing by powerful navies, the Mediterranean was overrun by pirates, privateers, and enterprising buccaneers. Ottoman merchants faced competition of a different kind in the Red Sea and Indian Ocean where Portuguese traders began to establish bases.

The Ottomans continued military activity on some fronts. In 1669 they took over Crete, and in 1683 they staged their final assault on Vienna. But the strain of fighting wars on two fronts (Europe and Persia) sapped the empire's resources. Manpower shortages lowered standards of training, and even the discipline of the elite Janissaries suffered. Warlords appeared in the provinces, raised private armies, and compelled Istanbul to grant them greater degrees of autonomy. The sultan's government scrambled to meet expenses and resorted to tax farming. The weakening of centralized government did not, however, lead to the fall of the empire. Local governments strengthened and assumed greater responsibility for maintaining peace, prosperity, and stability. Rebellious factions did not seek the overthrow of the empire but only greater freedom to operate within it.

Europe and Atlantic Exploration

The rise of the Ottoman Empire meant that once again Western Europe was under siege from the east. By the late sixteenth century, however, the anxiety this initially created was receding (except perhaps in central Europe, which was directly threatened by Ottoman armies). Europeans had discovered that the Atlantic was not, as their ancestors assumed, an impassable obstacle at their backs. For the first time in history, they shifted their attention from the Mediterranean and the Middle East to the Atlantic and to a much larger world than they had ever imagined might exist.

A long tradition of technological and scientific invention lay behind the ships, weapons, and tools that equipped Europeans to embark on the adventures that spread the influence of their civilization around the globe. Many of the inventions that enabled them to explore and to transform their world were made by eastern peoples and diffused across the Eurasian continents. New farming tools and techniques had appeared early in the medieval era. By the eleventh century, the horse's potential for use on the farm and on the battlefield was being fully realized for the first time. The Romans had watermills, but medieval people may have improved on them with ideas from the Chinese. Medieval Europe's inventors also harnessed the winds and tides and invented crankshafts and camshafts to improve on machines driven by these powers of nature. They built sawmills to make lumber and water-powered hammers to pulverize ore and full cloth. By the fourteenth century, water-powered bellows—which the Chinese had developed as early as the first century C.E.—were easing the work of ore smelting and forging.

Some societies resist learning from others, but medieval Europeans readily appropriated (and improved on) ideas from many sources. They learned papermaking from the Muslims, and then created a product that competed successfully on the world market. The Chinese or Koreans pioneered printing with inked blocks of wood. The earliest Chinese printed book dates to the ninth century, but block printing of texts was an arduous task. Europeans, on the other hand, tinkered with inks, papers, metal casting methods, and die cutting, until finally Johannes Gutenberg put them all together with a press like those used to crush grapes and olives. The result was an economical means of printing with moveable type and a revolution in European literacy. There may have been only about 100,000 books in all of Europe in 1450, but by 1500, there were probably 9 million. Gutenberg may have been preceded in the invention of movable type by the Chinese. But if so, the Chinese did not find the innovation as useful as did Europeans—perhaps because Europe's languages could be printed with a handful of letters, while the Chinese script employed thousands of characters.

The Chinese invented gunpowder, perhaps as early as the ninth century, and they may have cast the first metal cannon in the late thirteenth century. These weapons appeared in Europe in the early fourteenth century and soon led to the vastly improved armaments with which Europeans built and maintained colonial empires. A Chinese astronomer of the eleventh century is believed to have constructed a mechanical clock, but his invention (like the model steam turbines built by the Hellenistic Greeks) had little impact on his world. Yet, when the clock appeared in Europe at the start of the fourteenth century, it revolutionized human behavior. Once time could be accurately measured, the activities of whole communities could be coordinated and work planned with unprecedented efficiency. Towns all across Europe financed construction of clock towers as a public service. The Chinese discovered the properties of magnetized needles and used them as compasses. Compasses and the astrolabe (an ancient Greek invention for making celestial measurements that was improved by medieval Muslims) made voyages easier for sailors. By the thirteenth century, Europeans had ships that relied entirely on sails (not oars). By the fourteenth, they had large vessels with multiple masts and lateen rigging—a Muslim invention that permitted a ship to sail against the wind. By the fifteenth century, a host of innovations that improved sailcloth, rope, carpentry, metals, and navigational instruments contributed to the creation of the ships that enabled Europeans to undertake global exploration.

Portuguese Explorations   The tiny Iberian state of Portugal pioneered European Atlantic exploration. It was highly motivated, for its only access to the

Mediterranean (the center of the medieval world's trade network) was through the Straits of Gibraltar, which were controlled by Spanish and Muslim competitors. In 1415 Prince **Henry "the Navigator"** (1394–1460), third son of Portugal's king, John I (r. 1385–1433), earned his knight's spurs in a battle that won Portugal the Muslim port of **Ceuta** on the African coast opposite Gibraltar. Henry's subsequent military campaigns were inconsequential, but his sponsorship of voyages of Atlantic exploration paid huge dividends.

The Portuguese initially worked their way down the Atlantic coast of Africa, searching for the source of the gold that Muslim caravans brought across the Sahara Desert from Africa's interior. By 1432, the Portuguese had discovered the Atlantic islands: the **Canaries, Azores,** and **Madeiras.** When these proved suitable for growing sugar, the nearby African continent was raided for slaves to work the island sugar plantations. (A few slaves were to be found in Renaissance Europe employed as household servants, but it was in regions where plantation systems were profitable that slavery truly flourished.) Successive expeditions inched farther and farther down the African coast until **Bartolomeu Dias** (c. 1450–1500) rounded the southern tip of the African continent in 1488. In 1498 **Vasco da Gama** (c. 1460–1524) explored the east coast of Africa and, with the help of Muslim sailors, charted a sea route across the Indian Ocean that linked Portugal to the port of **Calicut.** News of his return with a cargo of spices (particularly pepper) sent shock waves through the markets of Europe. By importing directly from India, the Portuguese could undercut the prices charged by merchants who used the older overland routes. The Portuguese wasted no time in exploiting their advantage. They dispatched a fleet of ships, negotiated access to Indian ports, and then pushed farther east to Indonesia, China, and Japan.

> **Read** the **Document**
>
> *Accounts of Duarte Barbosa's Journeys to Africa and India*
>
> on **MyHistoryLab.com**

However, Vasco da Gama was not the first to sail around the African continent. An ancient Carthaginian may have done so, and Arab and Chinese vessels had worked their way down the eastern coast of Africa and into the Atlantic before the Portuguese charted the continent's western coast. One of the puzzles of world history is why Europeans rather than Chinese exploited the sea route between the West and the Far East. The third emperor of the **Ming dynasty** (1386–1644) built ships that were many times larger than any that his European contemporaries were capable of constructing, and between 1405 and 1433, he dispatched fleets of 60 or more vessels to Africa's eastern coast. His successors, however, disbanded the fleet, and China ceased to explore. What the Chinese had learned of the outside world evidently did not intrigue them, and they may have concluded that the costs of exploration outweighed its potential profits. China did not withdraw from trade and contact with other cultures. But it preferred foreigners to bring their goods to its markets, and to bolster the emperor's claim to govern with the authority of a heavenly mandate, foreign trade was officially recorded as tribute.

Spanish Explorations   Italy, with centuries of seafaring experience to draw on, produced excellent navigators and cartographers, some of whom were eager to take part in the Atlantic adventure. About 1478 **Christopher Columbus** (1451–1506), a Genoese sailor and map maker, emigrated to Portugal, where he married the daughter of a ship's captain who had sailed for Prince Henry.

Columbus's study of the geographical information available in his day led him to grossly underestimate the size of the globe. Otherwise, he never would have proposed trying to reach the Far East by sailing west across the Atlantic. Had the Americas and certain Pacific islands not been where they are, no ship of Columbus's day could have survived a journey directly from Europe to the other side of the world. Columbus tried to persuade the Portuguese government to fund an expedition to prove his theory that the shortest route to the Far East lay west. However, Portugal decided that its African explorations, which were just beginning to pay off, were a better investment.

Columbus considered going to France next, but he finally decided to try his luck at the Spanish court. **Spain** was a new nation, which had been formed in 1469 by the marriage of Queen **Isabella I** of Castile and King **Ferdinand V** of Aragon (joint reign, 1474–1504). The royal couple was intrigued by Columbus's proposal, but the time was not propitious for a new project. In 1484 Ferdinand and Isabella had set out to conquer **Granada,** Spain's sole remaining Muslim state. Until that costly campaign was resolved, they were not prepared to take on anything else. Granada finally surrendered on January 2, 1492. Thereafter, things moved quickly. Columbus received his commission on April 17, set sail with a fleet of three small ships on August 3, and 70 days later planted Spain's standard on what was probably one of the Bahamian islands—although he was certain that it was not far from Japan. Columbus

[ ] Read the Document

The Letters of Columbus to Ferdinand and Isabel

on **MyHistoryLab.com**

Watch the Video

So Why Did Columbus Sail Across the Atlantic Anyway?

on **MyHistoryLab.com**

had been lucky. By striking south to avoid the Portuguese, he had discovered the prevailing winds that offered the easiest passage across the Atlantic.

Columbus's largest ship ran aground in the Caribbean, and he was forced to leave half his crew (44 men) behind when he hastened back to Spain to announce that he had reached outlying portions of India and contacted **"Indians."** He received a hero's welcome, a title of nobility, and a much larger fleet for a return to what he claimed, until the end of his days, was the perimeter of Asia. The four expeditions Columbus led explored the Caribbean and the coast of Central America, but they never found the passage to Japan that their admiral was certain had to be in the vicinity.

England occupied the extreme western end of the lengthy medieval trade routes that linked Europe with the Far East. The shorter Atlantic passage that Columbus claimed to have found promised to be an economic godsend for England. News of his discoveries therefore persuaded King **Henry VII** (r. 1485–1509) to fund an expedition by another Genoese explorer, whose anglicized name was **John Cabot** (1450–1498). In 1497 Cabot reached islands off the coast of Canada and returned to England to inform the king that he had made contact with Asia somewhere north of Japan. A second voyage in 1498 took Cabot as far south as Labrador. England's financiers contemplated

European Fantasies of the New World   This woodcut was executed about 1500, and it may be the earliest European representation of peoples from what Europeans thought of as the "new" world. It depicts these peoples as barbarous cannibals.

more expeditions, but because Cabot had found nothing of value aside from some furs, investors and plans were slow to materialize.

In 1500 a Portuguese fleet bound for India via the African route went off course and sighted a land its leader named **Brazil** (for a species of tree that grew there). A year later, the Portuguese dispatched a follow-up expedition piloted by **Amerigo Vespucci** (1454–1512), one of Columbus's associates. Vespucci was among the first to suggest that what the Europeans were exploring was not the outer edge of Asia, but a **"New World"**—new to Europeans that is, but obviously not to its indigenous peoples. The geographers who used his reports labeled the continent whose outline was emerging on their maps "the discoveries of Amerigo" (**"America"**). Any lingering doubts about the place America occupied on the globe were resolved in 1522 when the remnants of a Spanish fleet that had set out under the command of **Ferdinand Magellan** (1480–1521) completed the first circumnavigation of the Earth (see Map 12–3).

Columbus never found the gold he promised his Spanish sponsors, but in 1519 the longed-for wealth finally began to flow. **Hernán Cortés** (1485–1547) invaded Mexico and looted the treasures of the **Aztec Empire.** Ten years later **Francisco Pizarro** (c. 1475–1541) overthrew the New World's other major civilization, the empire of Peru's **Inca.** Small companies of Spanish soldiers subdued large native populations with surprising ease, for the invaders had advantages that more than compensated for their inferior numbers. Their weapons were vastly

Read the **Document**

Smallpox Epidemic in Mexico, 1520

on **MyHistoryLab.com**

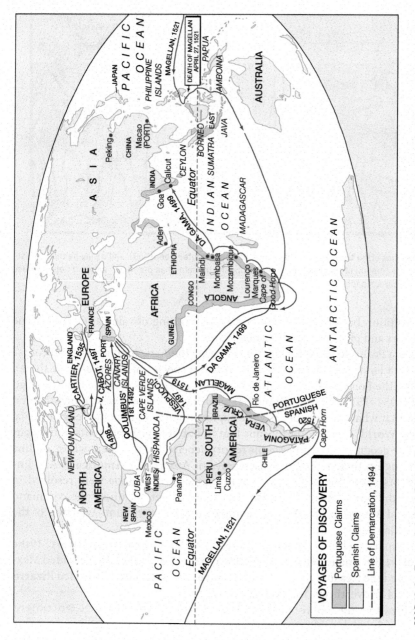

MAP 12–3 Europe's Initial Global Explorations This map shows the routes taken by the Portuguese, Spanish, English, and French explorers as they ventured into the Atlantic and beyond.

QUESTION: How might Europeans' increasing preoccupation with global exploration have affected relations between Christians and Muslims?

superior, and they had horses—animals that were new to the Americas, which had no comparable indigenous species. Native armies had never before confronted anything as formidable as a force of mounted warriors with guns. But an unplanned development further tipped the scales in favor of the Europeans. Without intending it, they became practitioners of germ warfare. Migration and trade among the peoples of Asia, Africa, and Europe had exposed the inhabitants of these regions to many diseases. Over time, their descendants evolved the ability to minimize the effects of what gradually became routine infections. Lack of similar exposure meant that the peoples of the Western Hemisphere had different immune systems that left them defenseless against diseases that were minor childhood afflictions for Europeans. Smallpox, chicken pox, measles, and other illnesses swept ahead of the European invaders and cleared the way for their conquests. Native populations were quickly reduced to such a low level that the European entrepreneurs who established plantations and mines in the New World had

Read the **Document**

Bartolome de Las Casas Argues for Amerindian Rights

on **MyHistoryLab.com**

to reconstitute its workforce by importing slaves from Africa—people who shared the Old World immunities. The brutality with which Columbus and later explorers treated Native Americans might seem incompatible with their sincere desire to baptize these people and recognize them as fellow Christians. Some European missionaries did indeed protest the abuse of indigenous peoples, but the profits from slave labor in mining and plantation agriculture proved too tempting even for the church to forego.

In 1494 Pope Alexander VI presumed, as Christ's vicar on Earth, to draw a longitudinal line that divided the globe into Portuguese and Spanish spheres of influence. Territories east of his "**Line of Demarcation**" (which ran through Brazil) were declared Portuguese, and anything to the west was said to be Spain's property. Other European nations with access to the Atlantic refused to be restrained by the papal decree. Three years after the pope's proclamation, John Cabot staked England's claim to a portion of the New World, and in 1534 France sent out the first of its explorers, **Jacques Cartier** (1491–1557). He made four trips to a land he thought the natives called **Canada** (the word they were using actually meant *village*). Cartier searched for a waterway through the Americas to the Far East and a rumored North American kingdom that was said to be as rich in gold

View the **Map**

European Empires

on **MyHistoryLab.com**

as Mexico's Aztec Empire. Although Cartier found neither, France sent out more explorers and added the Mississippi watershed and some Caribbean islands to the American territories it claimed. In 1595 tiny Holland established bases in the East Indies to compete with the Portuguese. England and France eventually followed. As Europeans moved out into the world, they built colonial empires that spread their civilization around the globe. The human community is still struggling to come to terms with the consequences.

KEY
QUESTION
REVISITED

Does respect for
history inspire or
retard change?

A handful of European explorers needed only a few decades to change the course of world history. They cleared the way for Europe's civilization and the political and economic power of its colonial empires to transform life for peoples around the globe. Europeans were as profoundly affected as any of the indigenous peoples their colonizers encountered. The gold, silver, and raw materials that poured into Europe greatly expanded its economy. Luxury consumables, such as sugar, rice, and spices, became much more affordable. The new plants that explorers brought back for cultivation in Europe revolutionized society at every level. Europeans tasted maize, squash, and tomatoes for the first time and discovered the pleasures of tobacco and chocolate. They eagerly took to coffee, an Ethiopian beverage that spread through the Muslim world in the fifteenth century. Tea from the Far East likewise entered the European market in the sixteenth century. The potato, which was indigenous to Peru and Chile, flourished in Europe's cool, wet climate and began to replace wheat as the staple food of the poor. This eased famines and encouraged population growth. The national cuisines for which European countries are famous today feature foods, drinks, and flavors that were unknown to Europeans until relatively recently.

The New World's creation of a new Europe caused Europeans some anxiety. The flood of information that suddenly became available to them about peoples, places, and things whose existence they had not previously suspected posed immense challenges. For the first time, they became aware of viable alternatives to their way of life, and this forced them to rethink the fundamental assumptions of their civilization and religion. There was no hint in their histories and religious traditions of what they were about to discover, but they were accustomed to adapting to unanticipated developments. Their late medieval Renaissance sought the rebirth of the past not as a refuge but as a foundation on which to continue to build. The Classical era that intrigued the humanists of the Renaissance had been (as their own period in history was becoming) an age of exploration, discovery, and empire building. The classical culture from which the Renaissance drew inspiration had pushed back the frontiers of science, art, and philosophy. It had experimented with new forms of government, argued over values and morality, and integrated diverse cultures. It had forged ahead in the confidence that the human mind was capable of dealing with whatever challenges it encountered, for the world was humankind's legitimate domain. The Classical world taught the people of the Renaissance how to proceed with the grand project of, as Pico della Mirandola might have said, perfecting humanity. The past was only the beginning.

Not everyone, however, responded to the upheavals of the late medieval era with the optimistic confidence of the Renaissance humanists. Change is costly. What one person counts as gain another experiences as threat or loss. The usual rationale for resisting change is to insist that life's essential truths are those inherited from the past—customs, institutions, and values that have endured the tests of time. The responsible thing to do therefore is to cling firmly to tradition and reject anything that might question or undermine established practices. There is wisdom in urging caution lest a mere appetite for novelty forfeit a

◉ Watch the Video
The World in 1491
on **MyHistoryLab.com**

legacy of valuable lessons hard won by earlier generations. But it is also true that excessive reverence for the past stifles curiosity about the world, limits imagination, and undercuts the will to experiment and explore. If this is allowed to happen, a society stagnates and drifts toward irrelevance. What people do with their past determines their future.

Key Terms

guilds, *p. 342*

podestà, *p. 342*

condottiere, *p. 344*

studia humanitatis, p. 346

perspective, *p. 354*

Hanseatic League, *p. 357*

muftis, *p. 365*

Modern Devotion, *p. 361*

Line of Demarcation, *p. 373*

Activities

1. List the names (bold print) of the Renaissance artists and authors in this chapter and associate something of significance with each one.

2. Explain why Renaissance humanism developed in the environment of the Italian city-state.

3. Explain the features shared by the different arts of the Italian Renaissance—sculpture, architecture, and painting—that identify them as products of the Renaissance.

4. Explain how and why the Renaissance movement changed as it spread into northern Europe.

5. What impact did the rise of the Ottoman Empire have on Islam and on relations between Christians and Muslims?

6. List the ways in which the lives of Europeans were altered by their global explorations.

Further Reading

John Paoletti and Gary M. Radke, *Art in Renaissance Italy* (2005), an art history textbook that has received good reviews for general readability.

Peter Murray, *The Architecture of the Italian Renaissance* (1997), an inexpensive, but amply illustrated, and accessible introduction to Renaissance architecture and engineering.

Susie Nash, *Northern Renaissance Art* (2009), an introduction to the Renaissance arts of northern Europe that makes a strong case for their originality.

Suraiya Faroqhi, *Subjects of the Sultan: Culture and Daily Life in the Ottoman Empire* (2005), a social history of the Ottomans with primary emphasis on their arts.

Jared Diamond, *Guns, Germs, and Steel: The Fates of Human Societies* (2005), a widely read and debated thesis proposing explanations for the ways in which global societies have responded to their environments and to contacts with one another.

MyHistoryLab **Connections**

Visit **MyHistoryLab.com** *for a customized Study Plan that will help you build your knowledge of* Renaissance and Exploration.

Questions for Analysis

1. What was Dante's vision of Paradise?

Read the **Document** Dante, *The Divine Comedy*, p. 347

2. How was Leonardo's work influenced by the culture of Rome?

View the **Closer Look** Leonardo Plots the Perfect Man, p. 360

3. What seems to be Erasmus's criticism of Pope Julius?

Read the **Document** Satire by Erasmus: *Pope Julius Excluded from Heaven*, p. 361

4. Why was Columbus interested in finding a new trade route?

Watch the **Video** So Why Did Columbus Sail Across the Atlantic Anyway?, p. 370

5. What are some of the ways in which environmental factors influence history?

Watch the **Video** The World in 1491, p. 374

Other Resources from This Chapter

View the **Map** Northern Italy in the Mid-Fifteenth Century, p. 341

Read the **Document** Excerpts from *The Prince* (1519), Machiavelli, p. 344

Read the **Document** Excerpts from *Utopia* (1516), Sir Thomas More, p. 345

Read the **Document** *Letters to Cicero*, Petrarch, p. 346

Read the **Document** *Decameron: The Tale of the Three Rings*, Boccaccio, p. 348

Read the **Document** *Life of Michelangelo*, Georgio Vasari, p. 353

View the **Map** Renaissance Europe, c. 1500, p. 357

Read the **Document** *A Contemporary Describes Timur*, Ibn Khaldun, p. 362

Read the **Document** Description of the Ottoman Emporer Mehmed II, p. 363

Read the **Document** *An Ambassador's Report on the Ottoman Empire*, Ogier Ghiselin de Busbecq (1555), p. 365

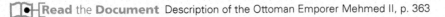

Read the **Document** Accounts of Duarte Barbosa's Journeys to Africa and India, p. 369

Read the **Document** The Letters of Columbus to Ferdinand and Isabel, p. 370

Read the **Document** Smallpox Epidemic in Mexico, 1520, p. 371

View the **Map** European Empires, p. 373

Read the **Document** Bartolome de Las Casas Argues for Amerindian Rights, p. 373

Queen Elizabeth I England's first Queen Elizabeth (1533–1603) struggled to navigate the currents of an era made turbulent by religious and political struggles. She was about 47 when she sat for this portrait by the Italian painter **Federico Zuccari** (c. 1542–1609).

13 Reformation, Religious Wars, and National Conflicts

((•─[Hear the Audio   Chapter 13 at MyHistoryLab.com

LEARNING OBJECTIVES

What role did Martin Luther play in launching the Reformation?   •   How did the Reformation in Switzerland differ from the similar movement in Germany?   •   How did the Catholic Church respond to the Protestant Reformation?   •   What was the military situation on the continent in the Reformation era?   •   To what extent did England embrace the Protestant Reformation?   •   How were long-standing foreign and domestic conflicts resolved in England, Spain, and France?   •   What was the outcome of the "the Wars of Religion"?

Why should we tear the world apart arguing over obscure things which are incomprehensible or arguable or useless? The world is filed with anger, hostility, and strife.

—Desiderius Erasmus, *Sponge to Wipe Away the Aspersions of Hutten*

KEY QUESTION

How should conflicts over values and ideologies be managed?

The humanist scholar **Erasmus** (c. 1466–1536) was dismayed to witness the unintended fruits of his labors. His manuscript studies had revealed errors in the traditional Latin text of the Bible, and his witty satires had lampooned corrupt clergy. But his intent had been to promote reform, not rebellion. He expected people to behave reasonably—to welcome the opportunity he gave them to transcend religious disputes by correcting misinformation and abuses.

What he witnessed instead was an escalation of controversy and a rush to war—all in the name of religion. Wars are not rare in human history, but a congruence of forces (e.g., rivalries among rulers, the class struggles of an emerging capitalistic economy, diverse belief systems, and a host of cultural changes) made conflict especially abundant in sixteenth- and seventeenth-century Europe. People in almost every era have grievances that could prompt them to go to war, but they do not always act on these or always find the same things worth fighting over. It is important to try to understand therefore how an issue becomes a grievance worth the sacrifice of life itself. What history suggests is that what causes a conflict and what justifies it to those who fight it may not be the same thing. When this is not understood, attempts at mediation fail and battles drag on. This was one thing that made the sixteenth and seventeenth centuries the **Age of Religious Wars.**

At the start of the sixteenth century, the Protestant Reformation challenged the papacy's claim to monopolistic authority over the practice of the Christian faith in Europe. Confronted for the first time with religious pluralism, Europeans reacted violently. Wars flared as they took up arms to champion one variety of Christian faith in opposition to another. Catholics usually fought Protestants, but occasionally some Protestants sided with some Catholics against other Catholics or other kinds of Protestants. The religious convictions that people proudly claimed as justification for war were obviously not their only motives.

Most people have consciences that require them to justify violent acts. They prefer to think that when they commit mayhem, they do so for a noble purpose. If a personal advantage can also be obtained, that is only a pleasant and well-deserved reward for their willingness to champion a righteous cause. The most exalted of motivations is fidelity to an absolute—to God, to country, or to a concept of civilization itself. Although the West's major religions—Judaism, Christianity, and Islam—urge people to live together in love and peace, they have often inspired hatred and slaughter. Secular ideologies, such as communism, fascism, nationalism, and democracy, have done the same. It is reasonable therefore to ask whether faith (in either a sacred or secular ideal) is a cause for war, a pretext for war, a precondition for war, or a preventative of war. A culture endorses a set of values (secular and/or religious) to provide its people with a context that gives meaning to, and rallies support for, its way of life. And even a highly civilized society can resort to barbarism to promote and defend what it regards as its noblest principles. History offers many examples of the tragedies that result when people fail to understand the moral ambiguity inherent in upholding moral ideals. ■

The Lutheran Reformation

The Reformation sprang from ground tilled by the humanists of Italy's Renaissance. The humanists believed that the West's authentic civilization had declined over the centuries, but that its original nature could be restored by studying its ancient texts. The Reformation's supporters shared the humanists' belief that ancient wisdom would correct the errors of the recent past. But their enthusiasm was not for paganism's classical culture. It was for the "authentic" or "apostolic" Christianity described in the New Testament. The humanist movement had also largely been confined to an intellectually elite segment of society whereas the Reformation became a mass movement—the sort of thing that was not possible before the invention of the printing press. The press created the modern world—a place where debates among scholars and leaders are referred to the court of public opinion.

Luther   **Martin Luther** (1483–1546), the man whose personal religious struggle became a catalyst for the Protestant Reformation, was not destined by birth or education to lead a rebellion. Until middle age, he led a very conventional life, and he never abandoned a certain fundamental conservativism. Although he claimed peasant origins, his father was actually an upwardly mobile member of the middle class who could afford to give his son a good education. Luther completed his arts degree at the University of Erfurt in 1505 and then began to study law in preparation for a secular career. But growing anxiety for the state of his soul eventually led him to do what highly motivated medieval Christians had been doing for centuries. He turned his back on the world, dropped out of school, and entered a monastery. He completed the novitiate, took the vows of an Augustinian monk, and in May 1507 was ordained a priest. He earned a doctorate in theology, and his order sent him to teach at the University of Wittenberg in Saxony.

Luther was well into his thirties before anything caused him to question his medieval Catholic faith. He had been taught to think of himself as a sinner destined for judgment by a righteous and angry God. Fear of God and of eternal punishment had driven him to take monastic vows, but the fasts, prayers, and disciplines of the monastic life failed to bring him an assurance of salvation. Sometime after 1512, however, he had a kind of conversion experience—a burst of insight prompted by reading the letters of the Apostle Paul (particularly Paul's Epistle to the Romans). Paul, according to the New Testament's Book of Acts, had not wanted to become a Christian and was actively persecuting the church when God suddenly intervened, bestowed faith upon him, and made him a Christian. Luther concluded that what had been true for Paul was true for all people. They did not earn salvation by doing good works; salvation was a gift God freely gave them while they were still sinners. It could not be earned, and human beings could not comprehend God's motives in bestowing it.

Luther's resolution of his personal crisis of faith did not turn him into a reformer or a critic of the church, for he did not believe that he had discovered anything revolutionary. He had only understood what was plainly laid out for everyone in the Bible. Therefore he settled back into his routine as a college professor and might never have been heard of had it not been for a chance encounter in 1517 with a Dominican friar named **Johann Tetzel** (c. 1465–1519).

In 1514 an ambitious German clergyman, Albert of Brandenburg, sought a favor from the pope. At the age of 23, Albert was already bishop of two dioceses, but now he wanted a third: the archdiocese of Mainz, one of Germany's most important sees. Pope **Leo X** (r. 1513–1521) agreed to sell Albert the office and to license a sale of indulgences in Germany (by men like Tetzel) to help raise the money to pay for it. An **indulgence** was a dispensation from the need to do penance for one's sins. Church doctrine held that while God freely forgave the guilt of sin, sinners still owed compensation for the moral damage caused by their sin. The souls of the dead who had not fully atoned for their sins in life were sent to **Purgatory** (not to Hell from which there was no release) to complete their penances before being admitted to Heaven. Originally, the church granted indulgences as an act of mercy or as a reward for self-sacrificial service. An indulgence would release a Christian from a penance that proved too severe or protect a crusader who died fighting for the faith in a foreign land where he had no opportunity to receive absolution from a priest. In 1343, however, a pope opened the way for indulgences to be granted with unprecedented liberality. He declared that the church possessed an infinite "treasury of merit," a vast spiritual reservoir of grace, that it could draw on to pay the debts of individual sinners—both dead and alive. The temptation for the church was then to begin to grant indulgences from this inexhaustible source for more and more reasons. When it showed its gratitude to generous donors by dispensing them from the penalties of their sins, it opened itself to the charge that it was selling salvation.

The Sale of Indulgences The printing press made it possible for Protestant Reformers to take their case to the people, and woodcut prints, such as this one, were major propaganda tools. The scene represents the practice of the church that first roused Martin Luther to action. It depicts a richly mounted cardinal overseeing cash sales of spiritual goods in the form of the church's dispensations from the consequences of sin.

View the **Closer Look**

A Saint at Peace in the Grasp of Temptation

on **MyHistoryLab.com**

Martin Luther certainly believed that Johann Tetzel was doing this, for Tetzel devised a thoroughly modern marketing campaign to peddle Pope Leo's indulgences. He dispatched advance men to whip up customer interest. He organized parades with banners and songs, and composed what may be history's first advertising jingle: "When a coin in my coffer rings, a soul from Purgatory springs!" Luther's understanding of the Christian faith rested not only on the tradition of the church but on his study of the New Testament. He believed that Tetzel, by claiming to be able to sell what God freely gave, was committing fraud and endangering souls. He also believed that it was his duty as a pastor to expose Tetzel, whom he assumed was operating on his own initiative without sanction from the church. Following medieval scholastic tradition, he proposed debating **ninety-five theses** relating to indulgences. Tradition holds that he nailed them to the door of his Wittenberg church. If he did, this was not an attack on the church. Church doors served as community bulletin boards, and all sorts of notices were posted on them. The fact that Luther wrote his 95 propositions in Latin suggests that they were intended for his fellow scholars and not meant to rouse the populace.

Read the **Document**

Martin Luther's Ninety-Five Theses

on **MyHistoryLab.com**

When the debate Luther stirred up began to hurt the sale of indulgences, Archbishop Albert asked the pope to silence the annoying monk. The pope was willing, but there was a complication. Luther's overlord was **Frederick the Wise,** the Elector of Saxony (r. 1486–1525), one of the princes who had the power to bestow the title of Holy Roman Emperor. Frederick was no proto-Protestant. (He had one of the largest collections of holy relics in Europe.) He was, however, not about to let the pope compromise his sovereignty by intervening in his territory. Frederick took Luther under his wing, and Luther unexpectedly found himself in a theological dispute that was also a high-stakes political struggle.

The Political Context   In June 1519 the election of the Habsburg heir, **Charles V** (r. 1519–1556), as Holy Roman Emperor created a situation that gave men like Frederick reason to be protective of their sovereignty. The domain the nineteen-year-old emperor inherited included Austria, Hungary, Bohemia, the Netherlands, Spain, Sicily, Sardinia, the Kingdom of Naples, and nominal overlordship of Germany and Italy (see Map 13–1). Charles posed a threat to every ruler in Europe, and Germany's lords were particularly worried about maintaining their autonomy. The Reformation provided them with an excellent rationale for opposing any attempt the Catholic emperor might make to exercise jurisdiction over them.

MAP 13-1   The Empire of Charles V   Charles's empire was the product of a series of carefully plotted dynastic marriages that made him the heir to lands scattered across Europe.

QUESTION: Does a viable empire have to consist of contiguous territories?

In 1521 Charles summoned Luther to appear before a **Diet** (Germany's equivalent of England's Parliament and France's Estates General) in the city of **Worms.** Luther had never intended to break with the church, but a series of pamphlets he wrote to explain his position questioned some traditional beliefs and practices Luther articulated three "**Protestant Principles.**" The first was that salvation is by faith alone—that it is a gift from God that cannot be earned by human effort. The second was that the Bible (not the pope or the tradition of the church) is the primary authority a Christian must obey. And the third maintained that every Christian has a direct relationship with God that does not depend on the church and mediation by its priests. When the church ordered Luther to recant these claims, he refused. To do so, he insisted, would be to violate his conscience, the highest court to which he believed each individual is ultimately accountable.

The emperor and the diet condemned Luther as a heretic, but Frederick the Wise saved him by spiriting him away to a remote castle. He passed his time in hiding by translating the New Testament into German. His insistence at Worms that private conscience and the Bible were the highest authorities to which a person should be held accountable implied that ordinary men and women were entitled to have Bibles they could read for themselves. Vernacular translations of the Scriptures already existed, but most were based on the Vulgate, the Latin translation of the Greek text that Saint Jerome had made in the early fifth century. The Renaissance humanists had labored to recover and improve the accuracy of the ancient texts that were the primary sources of Western civilization, and Luther built on their work. He based his translation on the best Greek text then available—the edition that Erasmus published in 1516. Luther's German New Testament appeared in print in 1522 and was an instant success. Within a decade, nearly 200,000 copies were sold. A companion volume containing the Old Testament did not appear until 1534, for its preparation required delving into Hebrew manuscripts with the assistance of other scholars. The popularity of Luther's German Bible had a tremendous impact on the development of a German literary language.

During Luther's absence from the public stage, the Reformation proceeded without him and took an alarming course. Luther's opponents had warned him that his insistence on the autonomy of each individual's conscience threatened the breakdown of society by undermining respect for authority. Luther feared that they might be right, for some of his self-proclaimed followers began to vandalize churches and monasteries, seize their property, and make radical changes in traditional religious practices.

In the spring of 1524 the situation threatened to spin completely out of control. A **Peasants Revolt** spontaneously erupted in southwestern Germany. It found leaders among the professional mercenaries who were for hire in the region and rapidly spread. The authorities were caught off guard, for many of their regular troops had been committed to campaigns in Italy. Early in 1525 negotiators proposed a multiple-point plan for restoring order. The peasants wanted the abolition of serfdom and burdensome dues and taxes, but they also wanted the right to choose their own clergy. Luther had justified his rebellion against the church by an appeal to Scripture, and the peasants seized on his arguments to ground their revolt against

[●]**Read** the **Document**

Germany: Peasants' Demands in Manifesto

on **MyHistoryLab.com**

Peasants' War This page is a "broad sheet" from the sixteenth century. It lists various monasteries and castles in the Black Forest region that were looted by rebellious peasants. The woodcut print at the center of the page depicts a peasant armed with a flail, a weapon derived from a farm implement used for threshing.

an oppressive religiously sanctioned social order. They even offered to submit their demands to Luther and a board of mediators and relinquish any that were proven to be contrary to Scripture.

The uprising was initially restrained, but became increasingly violent as it spread. A particularly radical faction materialized around **Thomas Müntzer,** a university-educated man whom Luther had recommended for a pastorate. Müntzer challenged the authority of scholars (like Luther) by claiming that the inspiration of the Holy Spirit could reveal truths to simple people that exceeded those derived from the study of Scripture. He urged his followers to seize control of towns, drive out their opponents, and establish communities governed by leaders who were directly inspired by God. Müntzer believed in the imminence of the **Apocalypse** and saw the bloody struggles of the era as signs of the strife that was prophesied to herald Christ's return. Luther initially tried to steer a middle course between the peasants and Germany's princes, but he became alarmed

Read the Document

Against the Robbing and Murdering Hordes of Peasants

on **MyHistoryLab.com**

as the increasing radicalism of Müntzer and the rebels threatened to undermine support for the Reformation. In 1525 he published an intemperately worded pamphlet, *Against the Robbing and Murdering Hordes of Peasants,* that urged the German nobles to "smite, slay, and stab" the peasants—claiming that nothing is more "devilish than a rebellious man." Luther insisted that God had created princes to maintain order and that they were justified in doing whatever was necessary to stamp out rebellion. As the princes' troops began to return from Italy in mid-1525, they quickly put down the divided and poorly led rebels. Müntzer was executed, and thousands of peasants were hunted down and killed.

Luther's fundamental instincts were conservative. He feared disorder, and there was much about the medieval church to which he was emotionally attached. Seeing no other option, he concluded that heads of state, whom he believed were charged by God with maintaining order in society, had a duty to decide what kind of religion they would tolerate and to use force to require their subjects either to conform or to emigrate. Luther filled the void of leadership he had created when he repudiated the pope by endorsing a government-controlled **state church.**

Luther had inadvertently unleashed disorder and instability on the world. As he aged and struggled with illness, he became increasingly intolerant of opposition and persisting theological arguments. He refused to compromise with other Reformers, and he turned against the **Jews,** who he had once hoped would convert to his renewed version of Christianity. In 1543 he published a series of harshly worded pamphlets, with such titles as *The Jews and Their Lies,* that have caused some people to brand him, fairly or unfairly, as an anti-Semite.

The power to suppress rebellion that Luther said God gave to secular leaders might have been claimed by Charles V to squelch the Reformation had crises on other fronts not distracted him. However, a decade passed before Charles could give his full attention to events in Germany. In the interim, **Lutheranism** spread widely, particularly in urban areas. Its empowerment of the individual appealed to humanist scholars and their students at universities, and these men scattered across Germany preaching and leading public discussions of Luther's call to return to the religious practices described in the

Martin Luther The printing press made leading figures of the Reformation, such as Martin Luther, the first media stars. This likeness of the reformer is from the workshop of **Lucas Cranach the Elder** (1472–1553), painter to the court of Luther's protector, Duke Frederick of Saxony. It may have been executed about 1529. Oil portraits were sometimes copied in engravings or woodcuts to produce inexpensive prints for distribution to the masses.

New Testament. Luther had artistic talents, and the **hymns** he composed and set to popular tunes were effective instruments for proselytizing the masses. He authored a flood of pamphlets that poured off the new presses, which also issued woodcut prints and cartoons—a new form of highly effective propaganda. Some rulers were attracted to Protestantism by the excuse the Reformation provided for confiscating church property and taking control of the clergy. In the 1530s, the king of Sweden— the dominant Scandinavian monarch—established Lutheranism as his country's official religion, and Denmark and Norway soon followed suit.

In 1530 Charles convened a Diet at Augsburg and gave the Lutherans a year in which to return to the Catholic faith or face dire consequences. This prompted some of the Lutheran states to form the **Schmalkaldic League,** a military alliance named for the town where its leaders met. Civil war was averted when problems elsewhere in Charles's sprawling empire prevented him from acting on his threat. He was not able to return to Germany until 1546. A year later, he defeated the armies of the Schmal- kaldic League, but Catholic France helped the Lutherans recover. Catholic rulers were no more eager for Charles to unite and control Germany than were their Lutheran colleagues.

Charles finally concluded that his huge empire could not be governed by one person. He retired in 1556 and divided his domain between his brother **Ferdinand** (r. 1558–1564) and his son **Philip II** (r. 1556–1598). Ferdinand was assigned Austria and the Habsburg's lands in central Europe and Philip the family's western possessions (Spain, the Netherlands, and the growing estates in the New Word). In 1555 another Diet that met at Augsburg arranged a truce between Lutherans and Catholics. On the assumption that people of different faiths could not live together, it decreed that each prince should decide for himself whether his state would be Catholic or Protestant. His subjects would then have the option to accept his choice or move to a place where their faith was legal. The **Peace of Augsburg** lasted until 1618, but by polarizing Germany, it set the stage for one of Europe's most devastating conflicts, the **Thirty Years' War** (1618–1648).

The Swiss Reformation

Martin Luther was neither the first nor the only person to challenge the authority of the papacy on the basis of a reading of the Scriptures. **Peter Waldo** had done so in the twelfth century. A group of Franciscan friars, the **Spirituals,** had taken a similar stance in the thirteenth century. The English theologian, **John Wyclif,** had followed suit in the fourteenth century, and his writings inspired the Bohemian scholar, **John Hus,** to launch a successful reform movement in the early fifteenth century. It was, however, one thing for the church's critics to agree that Christians should be guided by Scripture and another for them to agree on what the Scriptures said. Luther's conservative practice was to allow traditional customs that were not mentioned in the New Testament to continue in use so long as they did not contradict Scripture. However, an independent reform movement that began in Switzerland was more radical. It insisted on wiping the slate clean and restoring only what the Bible mandated, but even this rigorous approach failed to produce a consensus among its supporters.

Zwingli **Ulrich Zwingli** (1484–1531), the first major figure of the Swiss Reformation, became a reformer thanks in large part to the humanist education that prepared him for the Catholic priesthood. Like the great humanist biblical scholar Erasmus, he believed that the study of the New Testament would disperse medieval superstitions and bring about the moral regeneration of Christian society. Zwingli was a powerful orator, and his gifts served him well when, in 1519, he was assigned to fill the pulpit of the chief church in the Swiss city of Zurich.

Zwingli persuaded his congregation to embrace reform by explicating biblical texts in his sermons. His study of the New Testament led him to question traditional customs (e.g., priestly celibacy) that had no scriptural basis. He also concluded that churches should be purged of art and musical instruments, for there was no New Testament precedent for the presence or use of such things. Zwingli could also find no support for the Catholic doctrine of transubstantiation. He argued that the **Eucharist,** the ritual meal that Jesus directed his disciples to celebrate, was not a sacrament (a divine mystery in which people literally partook of the body and blood of Christ) but only a symbol, a ritual commemoration that reminded the faithful of Christ's work. Luther passionately disagreed, and his opposition to Zwingli hampered the efforts of Protestant leaders from both camps to cooperate against their common opponents. In 1529 **Philip of Hesse** (r. 1509–1567), the leader of the Lutheran princes, arranged a meeting between Luther and Zwingli. Charles V was preparing to attack Germany's Lutherans. (They had begun by then to be called **Protestants** because of their protestations against Charles's policies.) Philip hoped that a united front would strengthen the Protestant cause, but it was not to be. Luther insisted that Christ's flesh and blood were in some sense truly present in the Eucharist, and he was appalled by Zwingli's reduction of the central Christian mystery to a mere symbol. Swiss and German Protestants declined to work together, and in 1531 Zwingli died in a war with Swiss Catholics. Luther did not lament his passing.

The Anabaptists Luther considered Zwingli a radical, but some of Zwingli's fellow Swiss did not think that he was radical enough. Zwingli convinced them that the Bible was the sole standard governing faith, but they were frustrated by his cautious approach to enforcing its precepts. In 1523 they took matters into their own hands and alarmed the authorities by smashing religious art and demanding an immediate end to the Roman mass. When they met resistance, they withdrew from society into communities of their own. They called themselves the **Swiss Brethren,** but their opponents dubbed them **Anabaptists** (Rebaptizers). They insisted on baptizing adult converts who had been baptized as children because they considered infant baptism to be unbiblical and therefore invalid.

The Anabaptists advocated separating from society and establishing elite communities of "saints" governed solely by Scripture. Their eagerness to recreate biblical societies led some of them to endorse practices, such as polygamy and communal ownership of property, that are in the Bible but that were out of step with the widely held convictions of their contemporaries. A literal reading of the Bible's apocalyptic passages also convinced some Anabaptists that the end of the world was at hand, and this prompted more radical behavior. In 1534 a group of Anabaptists seized the

German city of **Münster** and purged it of everyone who did not profess their faith. Lutherans and Catholics joined forces to retake the city and to stamp out the Anabaptist movement. This caused some Anabaptists to moderate their conduct, to give up hope of mastering the world, and to retreat to parts of Europe where they could live unmolested. Some (the **Mennonites, Hutterites,** and **Amish**) eventually emigrated to North America and established communities that have remained faithful to what their founders taught was the godly way of life.

Calvin and the Reform Tradition   Lutheranism did not spread as widely as the brand of Protestantism named for **John Calvin** (1509–1564), a Frenchman who eventually settled in Geneva. Like Luther, Calvin was the son of a family newly risen to the middle class, raised a Catholic, and educated for the priesthood. At the University of Paris, he made the acquaintance of humanists, but in 1528 his father ordered him to give up his theological studies and enter the law school at the University of Orléans. Unlike Luther, he completed his degree, and legal training shaped his work as a theologian and reformer.

On May 21, 1534, at the age of 25, Calvin took a step that radically altered his circumstances. Having been persuaded of the truth of Protestantism by an experience that he described as a burst of insight, he resigned the posts in the Catholic Church that provided his income. His change of mind owed much to humanism, but he did not share the humanists' optimism about human nature. Like Luther, the Apostle Paul, and the early Latin theologian Augustine of Hippo, he believed that human beings were captive to sin and lost unless God intervened to save them.

Calvin was a subject of the French monarch, **Francis I** (r. 1515–1547). Francis was a patron of the Renaissance and had sympathy for aspects of humanism, but he had no motive for backing the humanists' push for radical church reform. The papacy had ceded the French king virtual control over the Catholic Church in France, and Francis did not want anyone to interfere with an institution that had become one of the instruments of his power. In October 1534, after militant reformers plastered Paris with posters attacking the mass, the king struck hard at suspected Protestants.

Calvin fled and found asylum in the Swiss city of Basel, and there, in August 1535, he published a rigorously rational explication of Protestant faith, *The Institutes of the Christian Religion*. The book was immediately popular and influential. Luther was a brilliant polemicist who dashed off thoughts in response to specific situations. This resulted in some gaps and inconsistencies in his writings that make their interpretation difficult. Calvin, however, was a systematic thinker who, in lawyerly fashion, developed a complete, succinct, and tightly reasoned case for Protestantism. Catholics, with centuries of scholarship to draw on, were well-prepared for theological debates; Calvin leveled the playing field by providing Protestants with cogent arguments for their beliefs.

Calvin and Luther agreed that the Bible was the sole guide to faith and that salvation was entirely a gift from God. Both endorsed **predestination**—the idea that humans could not affect God's decision about their ultimate fate. But they differed on the

Read the **Document**

Calvin on Predestination

on **MyHistoryLab.com**

implications of this principle. Luther believed that God's laws were meant to convince people of the depth of their sin and the impossibility of earning salvation by their own efforts. Once they accepted that salvation was God's gift, they were freed from all concern for themselves and therefore able to do truly good works. Luther worried that if the church imposed rules governing behavior, people would slip back into thinking that obedience to these rules would earn them salvation. Calvin disagreed. He claimed that God's law was eternally valid. Although it did not earn anyone salvation, it was still binding on everyone (the damned as well as the saved) simply because it was God's law. It had to be enforced because God is God and all human beings, as His creatures, owe Him obedience.

Catholics insisted that the Protestant doctrine of salvation by faith undercut the motive for moral striving. Why, they asked, should anyone be good if good deeds are not rewarded? Contrary to Catholic expectation, however, Calvinist doctrine did not turn Calvinists into libertines. It tended instead to produce dour moralists and ascetics—people who embraced the "**Protestant work ethic,**" the sober lifestyle of the pleasure-averse laborers who, some scholars claim, have been major contributors to the success of the West's capitalist economy. The **Calvinists'** behavior makes some sense when viewed from a psychological perspective. If people believe that the most important decision that could ever be made about their lives has already been made, they will want desperately to know what this decision is. Calvin warned that no one could be certain that he or she is among the "elect" whom God had chosen for salvation. But it was reasonable to assume that those whom God had saved would do God's will. After all, the Bible promised that "you will know them by their fruits" (Matthew 7:16). The desire to assure themselves that they were saved encouraged Calvinists to be disciplined and introspective. To see into their own hearts, they began to compile diaries in which they recorded their deeds and analyzed their motives.

In 1527 the people of **Geneva** expelled their Catholic bishop, and in 1534 they invited Calvin to reorganize their churches. The rigorous discipline he imposed was not popular, and the town's governing councils refused fully to empower the Consistory, a board of clergy and lay elders that Calvin set up to police public morals. Calvin was dismissed in 1538, but in 1541 Geneva recalled him and submitted to his reform program. With Calvin in charge, Geneva quickly became a haven for Protestant refugees from every corner of Europe. About 5,000 of them entered the city between 1549 and 1559—a huge number for a town that originally had about 12,000 inhabitants. When it was safe for them to go home, the Calvinism they absorbed in Geneva went with them. **John Knox** (1513–1572), Scotland's reformer, claimed that Geneva was "the most perfect school of Christ that ever was in the earth since the days of the Apostles."

The lessons people learned in Calvin's "school" extended beyond the practice of faith to the realm of politics. Luther endorsed a state church established by secular authority. However, **Reform** (Calvinist) congregations followed what they believed was the custom of the early Christians. They elected councils

View the **Closer Look**

Baroque and Plain Church: Architectural Reflections of Belief

on **MyHistoryLab.com**

Read the **Document**

John Calvin, Ecclesiastical Ordinances

on **MyHistoryLab.com**

of **presbyters** ("elders"), consisting of both clergy and laity, to lead them. The bodies of representatives that ran their churches increased pressure on their states to establish similar forms of popular government.

The emphasis that Calvin placed on individual conscience and participatory decision making did not lead him (any more than it had Luther) to sanction rebellion against authority. He drove those who opposed him from Geneva and even burned a Spanish refugee, **Michael Servetus** (1511–1553), at the stake for denying the doctrine of the Trinity and the divinity of Christ. However, when the shoe was on the other foot and Calvinists were the persecuted rather than the persecutors, they readily rationalized revolution—as the kings of England and France discovered (see Map 13–2).

MAP 13-2 Religious Diversity in Post-Reformation Europe By the middle of the sixteenth century the region that medieval people thought of as **Christendom** was no longer united in allegiance to a single church. This affected the policies of the states that were emerging in many parts of the continent.

QUESTION: Does the map suggest any explanation for how Protestantism spread?

The Catholic Reformation

At the start of the Reformation, most of Europe's Christians belonged to a church that was—at least in their frame of reference—literally **catholic** ("universal"). But within a few years of Luther's excommunication, the church headed by Rome's pope was **Catholic** only in name and struggling to defend traditions and institutions that had long been taken for granted. Its response to the Protestant challenge has been characterized as a Counter-Reformation. It would, however, be more accurate to call it a **Catholic Reformation,** for it was more than a reaction to the rise of Protestantism. It owed much to a reform movement that was active within the church before Martin Luther spoke out. In 1517, the year in which Luther attacked indulgences, an organization called the **Oratory of Divine Love** was founded in Rome to promote religious renewal among both clergy and laity. Its influential members advocated reform, but they faced a serious obstacle in the Renaissance papacy.

The Renaissance Popes   In the years leading up to the Reformation, the papacy was preoccupied with rebuilding its power. The Great Schism (1378–1417) had lessened respect for popes, and the Conciliarist movement had questioned the basis for their authority (see Chapter 12). Secular governments were also limiting a pope's right to operate within the boundaries of the emerging territorial states. The popes responded to these challenges abroad by building up their home base, the Papal States. Many of the popes were members of the aristocratic families that jockeyed for power in Italy, and they were well-schooled in the use of the tools wielded by Renaissance politicians: bribery, deception, assassination, and war. Their eager participation in Italy's convoluted politics made it difficult to distinguish them from the secular lords with whom they contended.

Popes, like the Renaissance's secular rulers, used patronage of the arts to bolster their image, and therefore their power. Pope **Nicholas V** (r. 1447–1455), the founder of the Vatican library, launched a program for reconstructing Rome that continued for generations. The city filled with buildings designed to bestow majesty on the papacy. Churches multiplied. Cardinals erected lavish palaces, and the old Vatican basilica, which Emperor Constantine had given to Rome's bishops, was pulled down to make way for construction of what was intended to be the grandest ecclesiastical building in Christendom. Kings embarked on similar programs of conspicuous display to nurture similar claims to status and respect, but behavior acceptable for a secular ruler was less so for a spiritual leader. The schemes popes devised to fund their pursuit of power earned them a reputation for greed and worldliness.

The most disreputable popes had few aspirations beyond living like kings and enriching their relatives. **Sixtus IV** (r. 1471–1484) concentrated on the wars that raged among the Italian states and was even implicated in a plot to assassinate the Medici family during mass in Florence's cathedral. The ironically named **Innocent VII** (r. 1484–1492) had 16 children, whom he richly rewarded from the spoils of the papal office. **Alexander VI** (r. 1492–1503) won the papacy by bribing the cardinals and used the church's wealth to fund wars that he hoped would carve out an Italian duchy for his son, **Cesare Borgia** (1476–1507). **Julius II** (r. 1503–1513) was determined—as he made clear by the name he chose when he became pope—to emulate the conquests of Julius Caesar. He donned armor and personally led troops in battle. But he was also a knowledgeable patron of the arts who commissioned **Raphael** to decorate the papal apartments and **Michelangelo** the Sistine Chapel. It fell to a Medici prince, **Leo X** (r. 1513–1521), to deal with Martin Luther. Not surprisingly, the aristocratic Italian pope failed to take the ranting of an obscure German monk seriously.

The papacy did not begin to mount a serious offensive against Protestantism until the reign of **Paul III** (r. 1534–1549). Paul appointed reforming cardinals and established a commission to draw up a plan for renewing the church. In 1537 his agents issued a report that documented many of the abuses of ecclesiastical authority of which Protestants complained. Three years later, Paul authorized the establishment of the **Society of Jesus** (the **Jesuits**), a religious order dedicated to serving the papacy and winning converts for the church. In 1542 he gave the Court of **Inquisition** authority to hunt down heretics everywhere in Europe, and in 1545 he convened the body that was primarily responsible for defining the faith and practice of the post-Reformation Catholic Church, the **Council of Trent.**

The Council of Trent relied on the Society of Jesus for help in implementing the Catholic Reformation. The Jesuits were founded by **Ignatius Loyola** (1491–1556), a Basque soldier who discovered his spiritual vocation while recuperating from a war injury. The order accepted only the most gifted men, and it subjected candidates for admission to a twelve-year-long course of study and testing that prepared them for the church's toughest assignments. Jesuits reversed gains the Reformation initially made in southern Germany, Poland, and Hungary. They spread the Catholic religion to the Americas, the East Indies, Japan, and China, and they founded hundreds of schools, colleges, and universities to provide Catholics with a firm intellectual grounding in their faith.

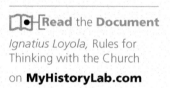

Read the Document

Ignatius Loyola, Rules for Thinking with the Church

on **MyHistoryLab.com**

The Council of Trent, which met intermittently from 1545 to 1563, set the Catholic Church on the path that it has (with some adjustments) followed ever since. The council affirmed that faith was based not only on Scripture, as Protestants claimed, but also on the traditions of the church. It rejected the idea that salvation was by faith alone and asserted the importance of good works. It reaffirmed transubstantiation as the explanation for the mystery of the Eucharist and asserted that each mass was an offering of Christ's sacrifice on the cross. The council's decrees were not meant to invite a dialogue that would lead to compromise and reconciliation with Protestants. They were intended to strengthen the Catholic cause by making it perfectly clear where the church stood in opposition to Protestantism. Having decided on its position, the church vigorously defended it. The

Read the Document

The Counter-Reformation Council of Trent

on **MyHistoryLab.com**

Inquisition weeded out dissenters, and in 1559 the papacy imposed censorship. It forbade the reading of vernacular translations of the Bible and published an **Index of Prohibited Books.** So strict were the Index's standards that it condemned works by Erasmus, the loyal humanist biblical scholar who opposed the Reformation.

The success of the Reformation should not be assumed to imply that sixteenth-century Catholicism was a moribund faith. While the Reformation spread in some parts of Europe, elsewhere a surge of enthusiasm for monastic vocations and passionate, mystical piety reflected renewed devotion to traditional religious life.

Commitment to the defense and advancement of Catholicism was strongest in Spain, where Ferdinand and Isabella, "the Catholic kings," presided over the last phase in the long Iberian crusade. They celebrated their conquest of Granada, Spain's last Islamic state, by banishing Jews as well as Muslims from Spain and by establishing an Inquisition that mercilessly policed the Catholic orthodoxy of their subjects. Spain's inquisitors were so alert to any whiff of heterodoxy that they briefly incarcerated the Jesuit's founder, Ignatius Loyola, and cast a wary eye on **Teresa of Ávila** (1515–1582), a Carmelite nun who was the era's leading mystic. Loyola's *Spiritual Exercises* and the works of Teresa and her disciple, **John of the Cross** (1542–1591), have become classics of Christian mystical literature. All three of these influential authors were eventually canonized (i.e., declared saints).

The Habsburg-Valois Wars

The Protestant and Catholic reformers did not work in a social vacuum. Because it was widely assumed that peoples of different faiths could not live together in the same state, allegiance to a religion was assumed to imply loyalty (or opposition) to a government and the faith that government endorsed. This made religious and political issues inseparable, but it did not ensure that a shared religion would be enough to guarantee political cooperation. Internal conflicts raged in both the Catholic and Protestant camps.

The collapse of the German monarchy that followed the death of the Hohenstaufen emperor **Frederick II** in 1250 (see Chapter 12) had cleared the way for France to move into Italy. **Charles of Anjou,** brother of Louis IX of France, conquered the **Kingdom of Naples** and founded a dynasty that survived until 1435. In 1494 King **Charles VIII** of France (r. 1483–1498) led an army into Italy to reclaim Naples for France, but a league of Italian states defeated him. In 1499 his successor, **Louis XII** (r. 1499–1515), occupied the duchy of Milan. However, by 1512 the French had once again been forced to retreat from Italy.

The election of Charles V (a Catholic) as Holy Roman Emperor in 1519 made control of Italian territory a high priority for France's (Catholic) king, **Francis I** (r. 1515–1547). Charles held lands on every side of France, and Francis hoped that by occupying Italy he could avoid encirclement by the Habsburg Empire (see Map 13–1). Francis's first campaign ended in 1525 with his defeat and capture by Charles. No sooner was the king freed, however, than he began a second war that also ended disastrously—particularly for his ally, Pope **Clement VII** (r. 1523–1534). In May 1527 Charles's imperial army broke out of control and sacked Rome—making the pope a virtual prisoner. Francis still refused to give up. In 1533 he strengthened his ties with the pope, who was eager to get out from under Charles's thumb. Francis arranged for Clement's niece, **Catherine de Medicis** (1519–1589), to marry his heir, **Henry II** (r. 1547–1559). Francis then shocked Europe by establishing diplomatic relations with the Ottoman sultan, **Süleyman the Magnificent** (r. 1520–1566), who had occupied most of Hungary and besieged Habsburg Vienna in 1529 with 200,000 men. Süleyman attacked Vienna again in 1532, and Francis wanted him to keep pressure on Charles V while the French navy assisted the Turkish fleet against the Habsburgs in the Mediterranean.

Francis began a third war with Charles in 1535. Fighting erupted in Italy, southern France, and the Habsburg Netherlands and dragged on until 1538. A fourth war broke out in 1542. Francis invaded Spain, and Charles thrust into France nearly to the gates of Paris. But by 1544 mutual exhaustion forced the opponents to agree to a truce. Both men were dead by the time the **Treaty of Câteau-Cambrésis** established peace between France and Spain in 1559.

England's Ambivalent Reformation

Apart from the Scandinavian states, England was the only major country to break with the papacy. Its decision to do so owed more to politics than to religion. As nation-states consolidated in the late medieval era, their governments increasingly regarded the papacy as a foreign power whose intervention in their affairs had to be curtailed. In the mid-fourteenth century, the English Parliament limited the pope's authority to fill offices in the English church and hear appeals from English courts. In 1438 the **Pragmatic Sanction of Bourges** declared that the French clergy (actually their king) would choose the bishops who headed the French church. Even the Court of Inquisition that the papacy established to root out heretics in Spain in 1477 was used to consolidate the government of Spain's rulers, Ferdinand and Isabella. The decision to break with the papacy and make England a nominally Protestant country was similarly driven by a plan to serve the kingdom by ensuring the future of its **Tudor dynasty** (1485–1603).

Henry VIII   England's civil war, the **War of the Roses,** ended in 1485, when Henry Tudor, a Welsh noble, defeated **Richard III,** the last Plantagenet king, and ascended the throne (see Chapter 11). England did not yield easily to its new ruler, **Henry VII** (r. 1485–1509). He spent much of his reign suppressing rebellions, but his clemency, intelligent government, and sound fiscal policies laid a solid foundation for his Tudor dynasty.

England had long cultivated alliances with the Spanish kingdoms against France, and in 1501 Henry reaffirmed this foreign policy. He obtained the hand of **Catherine of Aragon** (1485–1536), daughter of Spain's Ferdinand and Isabella, for **Arthur** (1486–1502), his son and heir. When Arthur died less than

Henry VIII   This portrait of the Tudor monarch who launched the English Reformation is by one of the leading portrait painters of his generation, Hans Holbein. It depicts the aging king in the elaborate costume favored by royalty in the era of the Renaissance.

six months after the wedding, Henry decided to maintain the tie with Spain by obtaining papal permission for Catherine to wed his new heir, his second son, the future **Henry VIII** (r. 1509–1547). A dispensation from canon law was required, for a biblical text (Leviticus 20:21) forbade a marriage between a man and his brother's widow.

Catherine endured many pregnancies, but only one of her children survived, a daughter named **Mary.** Henry doubted that England would accept a female heir to his throne and feared that after his death, the country would lapse back into the civil war from which it had recently emerged. He believed that the security of his kingdom depended on his having a son. When Catherine, who had not had a pregnancy in seven years, turned 40 in 1525, Henry—who was 34—decided that his only hope for a son lay in taking a younger wife.

Henry hoped that the pope would void his marriage on the principle that God had rendered sterile a marriage that the Bible had forbidden. The church had a long history of finding reasons to dissolve inconvenient marriages for influential people, but **Clement VII,** the pope to whom Henry appealed, was in no position to oblige England's king. Catherine opposed Henry's petition, and her nephew, **Charles V**— whose troops had recently sacked Rome—dominated Italy. When the pope prolonged the negotiations to buy time, Henry turned to Parliament for help in pressuring Rome. Parliament obliged by enacting a series of laws that began to sever ties between England and the papacy.

Events came to a head in 1533. Henry had fallen in love with **Anne Boleyn** (1504–1536), the daughter of one of his courtiers. Near the close of 1532 Anne became pregnant. Henry, who was desperate to assure the legitimacy of her child, secretly wed her in January 1533. In May his compliant archbishop of Canterbury, **Thomas Cranmer** (1489–1556), declared that he had never been validly married to Catherine and that Anne was therefore his legal wife. To the king's great disappointment, Anne then bore him another daughter, **Elizabeth.**

In 1534 the pope came to Catherine's defense and declared her to be Henry's legitimate wife. Parliament responded by passing the **Act of Supremacy,** which severed ties with the papacy and recognized the king as the head of England's church. The break with Rome was not motivated by any royal attraction to Protestantism. Henry had made his antipathy to the Reformation clear in 1521 by (allegedly) writing a book attacking Luther. The pope had been so grateful for Henry's support that he had awarded him the title: "Defender of the Faith." England's monarchs still list this among their honors although the faith they defend has changed.

A few prominent individuals, most famously the humanist **Thomas More** (the king's former chancellor), refused to swear allegiance to the new church and were executed. Although some historians believe that anticlericalism was on the rise in England, most of Henry's subjects considered themselves Catholics. In 1536, when Henry began to suppress England's monasteries and confiscate their vast properties, there was a rebellion (the **Pilgrimage of Grace**) in the north of England. This was not, however, solely motivated by religious concerns. It was in part a reaction by the numerous tenants who lived on monastic estates to Henry's disruption of their lives. The strongest support for reforming England's church came from the merchant class,

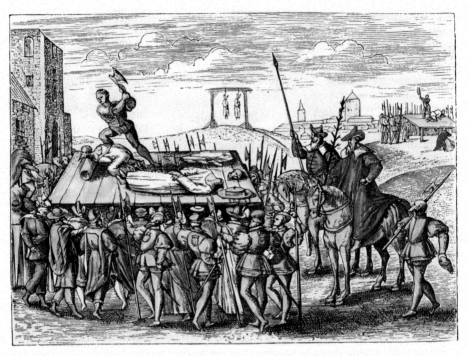

English Reformation This colored woodcut depicts the beheading of prominent Catholics (e.g., Thomas More, John Fisher, and the Countess of Salisbury) who refused to accept the Act of Supremacy (1534) that severed England's ties with the papacy and acknowledged King Henry VIII as the head of the Church of England.

which had close commercial ties with those parts of Europe where Protestantism was spreading. This segment of English society was well represented in the Parliaments that met in 1536, 1537, 1538, 1539, and 1543 to draw up regulations for the new church. But apart from suppressing monasteries and endorsing the use of vernacular Scriptures, Henry made few concessions to Protestantism. The **Anglican Church** (i.e., English) over which the king presided was to be nationalized, but not to depart significantly from its Roman Catholic predecessor. It was to be ruled by bishops (whom the king appointed) and staffed by a celibate clergy who celebrated seven sacraments, and continued most medieval liturgical practices.

The king had risked much to marry Anne, and when her second pregnancy miscarried, he lost faith in her. He accused her of adultery, beheaded her, and took a third wife, **Jane Seymour** (1509–1537). On October 12, 1537, she died not long after giving birth to the long-sought male heir, the future **Edward VI.** Henry's next bride, a German Lutheran named **Anne of Cleves** (1515–1557), was chosen to forge an alliance between England and Germany's Lutheran princes. **Thomas Cromwell** (c. 1485–1540), Henry's chief minister, had argued that this would dissuade France and Spain from heeding the pope's call for a crusade against England. But Henry found Anne so unattractive that their (unconsummated?) marriage was annulled. In 1540 he wed **Catherine Howard,** a sprightly young niece of the duke of Norfolk. Her flagrant promiscuity with young men at court prompted her execution in 1542. A few months later, Henry married his sixth wife, **Catherine Parr** (1512–1548), a sensible widow with strong Protestant sympathies. She provided her aging husband with domestic comforts and took charge of the education of his children.

The Tudor Succession   When Henry died in January 1547, his 9-year-old-son, **Edward VI** (r. 1547–1553), ascended the throne. Edward was afflicted with chronic ill health but was intellectually precocious and (thanks to his stepmother and the Lutheran tutors she provided) a sincere Protestant. The chief monument of his brief reign was a new liturgy for the Anglican Church, *The Book of Common Prayer.* It tried to reconcile the various religious factions that were developing in England by taking ambiguous stands on contentious issues.

The course of the English Reformation was nearly reversed when the young king died. His father's will named his half-sister Mary, Catherine of Aragon's Catholic daughter, next in line to the throne. Edward's Protestant advisors persuaded the dying boy to disinherit Mary, but the English people refused to accept this and rallied to her side.

Mary I (r. 1553–1558) shared her Spanish mother's conservative Catholic faith and was eager to restore England's allegiance to the papacy. She imprisoned some prominent Protestant clergy at the start of her reign but preferred to rid England of Protestants by urging them to reconvert or emigrate. Hundreds fled to the Netherlands, Germany, and Switzerland. There, under the influence of Calvinism, some became **Puritans**—sober, but passionate, Protestants who were filled with contempt for Catholicism and dedicated to "purifying" England's church of every taint of "papism."

Mary's first Parliament revoked some of her brother's religious legislation but balked at restoring England's monasteries. This would have necessitated the return of their confiscated lands, many of which had been acquired by members of Parliament. The thing that alarmed Parliament most about its new queen was not her religion but her intended marriage. Mary was 37 years old, and she was desperate to bear an heir who would guarantee a Catholic succession to the English throne. The mate she chose was Charles V's son, **Philip II,** heir to Spain and the western half of the Habsburg Empire. Premarital agreements could limit the rights of the queen's husband over her kingdom, but not those of any child she and her spouse might have. It would have inherited both their thrones and made England, the weaker country, a Spanish dependency.

Four months after she became queen, Mary swept Parliament's objections aside and married Philip by proxy. Nine months later Philip arrived in England to meet a bride who was 11 years his senior. With Philip's encouragement, Mary sought formal reconciliation with Rome, which was granted on November 30, 1554.

Fear of Spain undercut popular support for Mary, and this encouraged her Protestant opponents. She reacted by searching out and executing Protestant sympathizers. She may have burned about 280 men and women at the stake (the standard punishment for heretics), which caused later Protestant historians to blacken her reputation. Some scholars point out that she was responsible for fewer deaths than her successor, her

Protestant sister Elizabeth, but Elizabeth's record as an executioner accumulated over a much longer reign.

After less than a year of marriage, Philip left England. He did not give Mary a child, but he did draw her into the Habsburgs' wars with France. This misadventure cost England its last continental possession—the French port of Calais. Mary, isolated and disillusioned, lost touch with reality. When she died on November 17, 1558, Elizabeth—Mary's halfsister and the daughter of Anne Boleyn, whose marriage to Henry VIII had humiliated Mary and her mother—claimed her throne.

☐●☐ **Read** the **Document**

British Religious Turmoil: The Execution of Archbishop Cranmer

on **MyHistoryLab.com**

Convergence of Foreign and Domestic Politics: England, Spain, and France

The religious diversity the Reformation engendered greatly complicated political life in Europe. Protestant and Catholic factions struggled for dominance over some countries. And subjects who differed with the religion of their ruler were suspected of treason, particularly when wars erupted between Catholic and Protestant states.

Elizabeth's Compromises   In 1558 **John Knox** (c. 1505–1572), a Protestant exile from Scotland who found refuge in Geneva, published *The First Blast of the Trumpet Against the Monstrous Regiment of Women*. Knox blamed the ills of his generation on the women who, contrary (he claimed) to the laws of God and nature, were presuming to govern kingdoms. Mary Tudor, an ardent opponent of Protestantism, ruled England. In addition, **Mary of Guise** (1515–1560), a daughter of a powerful French Catholic family, governed Scotland as regent for her daughter, **Mary Stuart** (r. 1542–1567). What Knox considered a bad situation was destined, from his point of view, to get worse. France soon came under the thumb of its queen mother, Catherine de Medicis, and in 1558 England's throne passed to its second female heir. There were, however, no more blasts from Knox's trumpet, for timing made his book something of an embarrassment for his Protestant allies. The *First Blast* was intended to deafen a Protestant enemy, Mary Tudor, but it grated on the ears of Europe's most important Protestant monarch, her sister **Elizabeth I** (r. 1558–1603).

Because Catholics did not recognize the validity of the marriage between Henry VIII and Anne Boleyn, they believed that Elizabeth's birth was illegitimate and that she therefore had no right to England's throne. But political objectives could trump religious scruples, and Europe's Catholic powers did not immediately attack the new queen. The pope held out hope for her conversion, and Philip II, Mary's widower, considered proposing to her. Elizabeth's position was precarious. England was nearly surrounded by Catholic states, and there was a Catholic claimant to her throne: Mary Stuart, a granddaughter of a sister of Henry VIII's who had married the king of Scotland. She was Scotland's hereditary queen and, as spouse of France's short-lived King **Francis II** (r. 1559–1560), briefly queen of France. Religious tensions were also increasing among Elizabeth's subjects. Some opposed her father's Reformation, and some—particularly the radicalized Puritans who returned to England from exile after Mary Tudor's death—believed that his Reformation had not gone far enough.

Elizabeth survived by making it difficult for everyone to figure out where she stood. She was adept at depriving potential opponents of clear targets and keeping alive their hopes for reconciliation. She flirted with, but never committed to, the many men who sought her hand in marriage. She endorsed some Catholic practices and some Protestant ideas. Gradually, she eased her country toward a "settlement" of religion— a church with a Catholic hierarchical structure and ritual and a partially Protestant theology. This did not end religious conflict in England, but it postponed a showdown until the 1630s.

[●] Read the Document

Elizabeth I, Religious Acts of Uniformity

on **MyHistoryLab.com**

Philip II and Spain's Golden Age

Elizabeth hoped to maintain England's alliance with Spain against France, but Spain's ruler had other plans. **Philip II** (r. 1556–1598) inherited the western half of Charles V's empire: Spain, Spain's New World possessions, and the Habsburg Netherlands (modern Belgium, Holland, and Luxembourg). Control of the commercially rich Netherlands and a steady flow of gold and silver from America gave Philip great resources, and he was willing to spend whatever it took to bring more of Europe under his control.

The weakest point in Philip's empire was the **Netherlands,** a small but highly urbanized and wealthy country whose independent townspeople were notoriously difficult to govern. The Netherlands was a loose collection of culturally diverse regions. Its ten southern provinces were French or Flemish, and the seven northern ones were linked by the Rhine River to Germany and Switzerland. Protestant influences (predominantly Calvinistic) spread to the Netherlands and there, as elsewhere, appealed to urban populations. Townspeople had, throughout the Middle Ages, been predisposed to self-government, and they responded enthusiastically to Luther's defense of the rights of the individual and Calvin's arguments for representative institutions. Philip concluded therefore that to strengthen his hold over the highly urbanized provinces, he had to purge them of Protestants. This, predictably, only increased the determination of some Netherlanders to resist Spanish domination.

In 1567, after lesser measures had failed, Philip sent an army into the Netherlands to enforce religious conformity. This heavy-handed action roused nationalistic passions, and a resistance movement formed around a native nobleman, **William of Orange** (1533–1584). William tried to unite all the provinces, but religious disputes doomed his efforts. In 1579 the largely Franco-Catholic southern provinces sided with Spain, while the north's more easily defended Dutch-speaking provinces formed a Protestant alliance (the **United Provinces**) and continued the fight for independence. Because the United Provinces received help from England's Protestant queen, Philip planned to subdue both these enemies with a single campaign. Developments seemed to favor his success. William of Orange was assassinated in 1584. A pro-Spanish faction won ascendancy at the French court, and a plot unfolded in England to place Mary Stuart on Elizabeth's throne.

England's Henry VIII had tried to win **Mary Stuart**'s hand for his son and successor, Edward. But the Scots, who had long relied on France's help to maintain

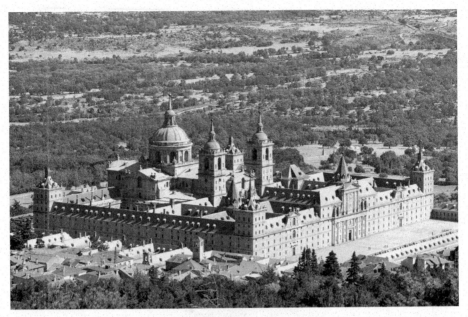

El Escorial The greatest monument from Spain's Golden Age is the huge palace-monastery complex that Philip II erected in honor of St. Lawrence, El Escorial. The structure reflects the wealth, power, and ardent faith of its builder. Philip's austere quarters were placed next to its great church and featured a window through which the king, who was sometimes bedridden, could witness the celebration of mass.

their independence from England, preferred that their queen wed the heir to the French throne. As a young child, Mary (1542–1567) was sent to France to be educated for her future role as its queen. Her mother, Mary of Guise (a member of an extremely powerful and ardently Catholic French noble family), governed Scotland as her regent. Although some Scots favored the French alliance, others feared French dominance. In 1559 a cadre of nobles, with an agenda that mixed religion and politics, overthrew Mary of Guise and recalled a native son, **John Knox,** from exile in Geneva. Knox, a former Catholic priest who had embraced Calvinism, was charged with reforming Scotland's church. A year later, Mary Stuart's husband, Francis II, died. The young widow of the French king was then sent back to Scotland to govern a country she had not seen since early childhood. Mary, who was accustomed to the luxury and sophistication of the elegant French court, was ill-prepared for life in a much poorer and less urbane society. Her manner (and gender) offended men like Knox, and she was soon at odds with powerful members of her court. She worsened her situation by conducting an affair with—and ultimately marrying—the man suspected of killing her second husband, a great-grandson of England's Henry VII. In 1566 she gave birth to a son (Scotland's **James VI** and England's future **James I**), and a year later she was compelled to abdicate her throne to him. She then fled to England to ask for help, despite the fact that she was a potential rival for its Protestant queen's throne. Elizabeth was uncertain what to do with her. Not wanting to kill her or trusting what she might do if she were free, the English queen kept Mary in confinement for 20 years. Rumors of plots to overthrow Elizabeth and enthrone Mary persisted and multiplied, and in 1587

Mary, Queen of Scots This portrait is the work of **Nicholas Hilliard** (1547–1619), the leading painter of miniatures at the court of Elizabeth I. A number of prominent figures from the Elizabethan age, including the queen herself, had likenesses drafted by Hilliard.

evidence for Mary's involvement in one of Philip II's schemes persuaded Elizabeth to order her beheading.

Elizabeth had good reason to fear for her throne, for Philip was assembling a great fleet for an invasion of England. His plan was to sail to the Netherlands with an army, pick up additional troops there, and then cross the channel to England. Various setbacks delayed the departure of the so-called **Spanish Armada** until the summer of 1588, and then the expedition was undone by a combination of bad planning, worse weather, and the skills of English sailors. After the Armada's destruction, Philip continued to threaten England, but his resources were diminishing as his problems were multiplying. The struggle in the Netherlands continued, and in 1589 he attacked France. The English monarchy also devised an effective way to undermine him. It licensed privateers (government-authorized and privately funded pirates) to raid Spanish shipping. The queen herself invested in these highly profitable ventures, over a hundred of which sailed in some years. England did not yet have a navy, but the island nation anticipated its future as a major sea power.

Read the Document

Reports on the Spanish Armada

on **MyHistoryLab.com**

After Philip's death in 1598, Spain entered a long period of gradual decline. The gold and silver that Spaniards had extracted from the Americas had not been invested in building a productive domestic economy. Instead, the bullion had flowed

The Maids of Honor   This painting by Diego Velázquez is one of the greatest masterworks of the baroque period. Baroque artists reveled in complexity and exuberant demonstrations of technical proficiency. Velázquez designed this painting so as to make its subject ambiguous. At first the picture seems to focus on the princess and her attendants. But off to one side the painter himself appears working at his easel and looking out at something beyond her. Over his shoulder is a mirror reflecting what he sees, King Philip IV and his second wife. Viewers are left to puzzle out for themselves the message that Velázquez intended.

through Spain to fund Philip's numerous wars. The church controlled about half the land in Spain and supported a huge number of clergy. Most of the rest of the country was in the hands of an entrenched aristocracy that clung to its medieval prerogatives. Portraits of Spain's grandees by the artist **El Greco** (c. 1541–1614) proclaim their sense of entitlement, and the paintings by **Velázquez** (1599–1660), a generation later, suggest a royal court that had drifted into the realm of fantasy. In addition to major artists, Spain's Golden Age also framed the career of its greatest writer: **Miguel de Cervantes Saavedra** (1547–1616). Cervantes' groundbreaking novel, *Don Quixote*, affectionately lampooned his countrymen's romantic devotion to an archaic way of life that was dooming them to irrelevance.

◉—Watch the **Video**

The Columbian Exchange

on **MyHistoryLab.com**

◉—Watch the **Video**

The Art of El Greco

on **MyHistoryLab.com**

▯◉▯Read the **Document**

Miguel de Cervantes, Don Quixote *excerpt*

on **MyHistoryLab.com**

France's Wars of Religion

Spain was not Elizabeth's only concern. A war between Catholic and Protestant factions raged in France for much of her reign and complicated her foreign policy. In France, as elsewhere, the Reformation attracted people who were critical of established authority and who saw religious change as part of a broader program of reform. Many of these came from the professional and middle classes and the lower nobility—educated people who chafed under the restraints of institutions that they regarded as outmoded. France's Protestants were Calvinists called **Huguenots.** Scholars are uncertain of the origin of their name.

For most of the sixteenth century, France's royal government left much to be desired. Francis I used the French Catholic Church as a source of political patronage and squandered his country's resources in futile wars with his Habsburg rival, Charles V. Francis's son, Henry II (r. 1547–1559), achieved little before an accident in a tournament ended his life and delivered France into the hands of his Italian wife, **Catherine de Medicis** (1519–1589). Catherine was the power behind a throne that passed in succession to three of their sons. **Francis II** (r. 1559–1560) survived his father for only a year. He was succeeded by his 10-year-old brother, **Charles IX** (r. 1560–1574). The third brother, **Henry III** (r. 1574–1589), was an adult when he became king, but debauchery guided his conduct more than mature judgment.

It was all that Catherine could do simply to preserve her husband's **Valois dynasty,** for France was less a unified kingdom than a league of powerful principalities. Whenever its kings were weak, aristocratic factions led by great noblemen fought for dominance at court. During the sixteenth century, religious differences defined the opposing camps. The Catholic party was led by the dukes and cardinals of the **Guise family** and the Protestants by the **Bourbons,** a cadet branch of the royal house. In 1562 the duke of Guise began a war with the Protestants by slaughtering 70 Huguenots whom he surprised at worship. In 1572 Catherine's attempt to reconcile France's Catholic and Protestant factions backfired and led to a mass murder that shocked Europe. The French aristocracy gathered in Paris for the wedding of Catherine's daughter, Margaret, to **Henry of Navarre,** the Bourbon head of the Huguenot faction. The marriage was intended to bring Catholics and Protestants together, but on the eve of the ceremony someone tried to assassinate one of the Huguenot leaders. Fear of Protestant reprisals prompted the crown to act quickly and with great force. Early on the morning of August 24, the feast of St. Bartholomew, the king's army fell on the unsuspecting Huguenots. The slaughter spread to other cities, and some 70,000 Protestants may have perished before the purge ended. The **St. Bartholomew's Day Massacre** poisoned relationships between Protestants and Catholics throughout Europe and diminished hope that the faiths could ever trust each other enough to coexist peacefully.

📖 Read the Document
France: Massacre of St. Bartholomew
on **MyHistoryLab.com**

Spain and England encouraged civil war in France by providing aid to the combatants, and the bloodshed continued until 1589, when a monk extinguished the Valois dynasty by assassinating Henry III. This cleared the way to the throne for the Bourbon heir, the Protestant Henry of Navarre, France's King **Henry IV** (r. 1589–1610). After a prolonged struggle, Henry concluded that his largely Catholic country would not accept a Protestant king, and he converted—allegedly quipping, "Paris is worth a mass." Henry IV, a nominal Catholic with Protestant credentials, had enough credibility with both sides to

📖 Read the Document
The Edict of Nantes, 1598
on **MyHistoryLab.com**

declare a truce between them. In 1598 he issued the **Edict of Nantes,** which acknowledged France to be a Catholic country but designated places where Huguenots could
worship and ceded some towns to their control. Since 1555, a similar arrangement
(the **Peace of Augsburg**) had maintained order in Germany, but events there were
about to demonstrate that segregation was not a permanent solution for religious
differences.

The Final Religious Upheavals

By the end of Elizabeth's reign (1603), a lull was developing in Europe's conflicts.
England was fairly secure. Spain's struggles in the Netherlands were winding down,
and France was recovering from its long internal bloodletting. There were, however,
problems on the horizon. Despite all the killing, Europe's population had increased by
about 40 percent during the sixteenth century. The gold and silver that had flooded in
from the New World had caused inflation to soar. Widespread poverty and unstable
economies inspired riots and rebellions. Governments strained to control their subjects, and some failed conspicuously.

The Thirty Years' War   By separating Germany's Lutherans and Catholics,
the Peace of Augsburg diminished opportunities for the two faith communities to
develop strategies for coexistence. Some people were also determined to undermine
Augsburg's truce. The Jesuits reclaimed much of southern Germany for the Catholics.
The Calvinists, who were rivals of the Lutherans and who had not been accorded legal
recognition in the Augsburg agreement, were equally aggressive in their recruiting.
In 1608 the Calvinist ruler of the Palatinate (southwestern Germany), **Frederick IV**
(r. 1592–1610), established the **Protestant Union,** an alliance of Protestant states.
Duke **Maximilian of Bavaria** (1573–1651) countered by recruiting members for what
was called the **Catholic League.** France, England, and Holland supported Frederick,
and the Habsburgs—both Spanish and Austrian—backed Maximilian.

The only thing needed for war to break out in this polarized environment
was an incident to trigger hostilities. That was provided by a colorful event that
took place in Prague in 1618 in the wake of the ascension to the Bohemian throne
of the Austrian archduke Ferdinand (1578–1637), the Catholic heir to the Holy
Roman Empire (as **Ferdinand II**). The kingdom of Bohemia had accommodated
religious heterodoxy at least since the early fifteenth century, when the followers
of John Hus fought for and won a degree of independence from the papacy (see
Chapter 11). Bohemia had subsequently provided refuge for Anabaptists, and
Calvinism had spread in some aristocratic circles. The Jesuit-educated Ferdinand,
however, had no sympathy with his new kingdom's
tradition of tolerance, and he broke pledges he
had made to his Protestant subjects by mandating
their return to Catholicism. The Bohemian nobles
reacted to the orders he sent them by tossing his
messengers out a window onto a dung heap. Ferdinand regarded this **"Defenestration of Prague"** as

Read the **Document**

*Description of the Beginning
of the Thirty Years' War,*
John Rushworth
on **MyHistoryLab.com**

PEOPLE IN CONTEXT   William Shakespeare (1564–1616)

Literature flourished in Elizabethan England as never before, and the period's greatest author was, as one of his contemporaries put it, "not of an age, but for all time." He might have added "and for all cultures," for **William Shakespeare**'s plays have been translated into many tongues, staged as operas and Broadway musicals, and produced as commercially successful films. Given their fame, it is surprising that so little is known about their author.

Shakespeare, for all his talent, seems to have led a fairly conventional life. John Shakespeare, his father, was a glove maker, money lender, and commodity trader in the town of **Stratford-on-Avon.** He and his wife, Mary Arden, had eight children. Will, the eldest of their four sons, was born in a terrifying year in which about 250 of Stratford's 800 inhabitants died of the plague. John served a term as mayor of Stratford and applied for a coat-of-arms to bolster his social aspirations. But by the time Will reached the age of 11, his father was suffering serious financial reverses and could do little to help his son make a start in life.

Shakespeare's formal education appears to have been in Stratford's free school. Unlike other famous playwrights of his generation, there is no evidence that he studied at one of England's universities. His modest schooling has caused some to doubt that he could have written the works ascribed to him. Various more distinguished individuals (including noblemen and rival poets) have been proposed as writers for whom he fronted.

Although his works have been minutely combed for clues to the identity of an anonymous author, there is no convincing evidence that Shakespeare did not write the plays and poems his contemporaries credited to him. His plays testify to his familiarity with the major classic authors (Ovid, Plutarch, Seneca, etc.) but do not suggest that he was unusually well read. Genius such as he displayed is not unprecedented, but it usually seems inexplicable.

At the age of 18 Shakespeare married **Anne Hathaway,** a woman eight years his senior. Six months after the wedding, their daughter **Susanna** was baptized, and three years later they had twins—a boy and a girl. No one knows how young Shakespeare supported his family or what drew him to London and the theater in the late 1580s.

William Shakespeare   This portrait of William Shakespeare is from an engraving that was made for a 1623 edition of his work.

Somehow he learned to act and to write plays, and by 1592 his work was attracting envious notice from his competitors. By 1597, he was rich enough to purchase the second largest house in Stratford, and by 1599, he was part-owner of a new London theater called "**The Globe.**"

Shakespeare's family may have secretly clung to the old Catholic faith, but Shakespeare was no propagandist or overt advocate for any cause. He was a professional playwright whose goal was to please his audiences without overtly taking sides in contentious political or religious debates. He dealt with universal themes of perennial human concern: love, jealousy, ambition, deceit, treason, and the meaning of life. He wrote to make a living, and when he could afford to (in 1613), he laid down his pen and devoted the rest of his life to managing his business interests. He appears to have given little thought to preserving his work for posterity. He died on April 23, 1616, and seven years passed before a group of admirers gathered up scattered manuscripts of his plays and edited them for publication.

Shakespeare wrote exclusively for his own company of actors at the rate of about two plays a year. He is credited today with about 40 plays as well as 154 sonnets and several longer poems. His theatrical works span the genre: comedies, tragedies, histories, romances, and fantasies. The great characters he created for the stage—Romeo, Juliet, Hamlet, Macbeth, Lear, Othello, Falstaff, and many others—have become prototypes in world literature. Lines from his plays (e.g., "Neither a borrower nor a lender be," *Hamlet*) are commonplace quotations that are sometimes mistaken for verses from Scripture. It is likely no other single author has had more influence on the development of the English language and its literary canon.

QUESTION: Does Shakespeare's work support the common assumption that artists reflect the dominant values and concerns of the eras in which they live?

a declaration of war and prepared to invade Bohemia. The Bohemians responded by turning to the son and successor of Frederick IV of the Palatinate, **Frederick V** (r. 1610–1632), for help. The German states quickly chose sides—not allowing their religious preferences to stand in the way of their political interests. Some Lutherans, who despised Calvinists, supported Ferdinand. Some Catholics, who did not want the Catholic Habsburgs to grow stronger, sided with Frederick.

In the first phase of the war, the Catholic forces swept through Germany and routed Frederick, but that only widened the conflict. The possibility of a Germany united under a Catholic monarch so alarmed Germany's neighbors that they intervened on the Protestant side. Denmark was the first to attack, but its campaign foundered and enabled the Catholics to seize additional ports on the Baltic. That, however, brought Sweden into the fray. In 1630 Sweden's great warrior king, **Gustavus Adolphus** (r. 1611–1632), forced Ferdinand to retreat from northern Germany. Catholic France then allied with Lutheran Sweden. After Gustavus Adolphus was killed in battle, France assumed leadership of the war against the Catholic emperor. France was governed by **Cardinal Richelieu** (1585–1642), chief minister for Henry IV's son, **Louis XIII** (r. 1610–1643). Richelieu was a sincere Catholic and a "prince" of the papal establishment, but

Treaty of Westphalia   The Thirty Years' War was a generation-long conflict that devastated Germany and left it a divided country. But the Treaty of Westphalia that concluded hostilities was an occasion for resolving other conflicts as well. On January 30, 1648, the Spanish and the Dutch (depicted here) concluded the Treaty of Münster which ended the war between them, begun 80 years earlier by Philip II, and which recognized the independence of Holland.

he put the interests of his country above those of his church. Given that the last thing France wanted was to confront a unified Germany along its eastern frontier, Richelieu had little choice but to help Germany's Protestants fend off their Catholic emperor. The intervention of foreign powers turned Germany into an international killing ground. By the time the war ended, battles, raids, plagues, massacres, and famines had resulted in the deaths of about eight million people, roughly 40 percent of Germany's population.

The **Peace of Westphalia** that concluded the war in 1648 ensured that Germany would remain an impotent collection of hundreds of tiny states and that the **Holy Roman Empire** would be an empire only in name. The victors rewarded themselves with bits of German territory, and the Habsburg defeat cleared the way for the Swiss cantons and the Dutch Republic to be recognized as independent states. Germany's collapse and Spain's decline also meant that France now had a chance to dominate the continent (see Map 13–3).

Read the **Document**

The Peace of Westphalia

on **MyHistoryLab.com**

England's Civil War

By the time Westphalia brought the continent's religious wars to an end, a conflict between **Puritans** and **Anglicans** was raging in England. England's religious factions had different political visions for both their country's church and its government. The Puritans wanted a church consisting of

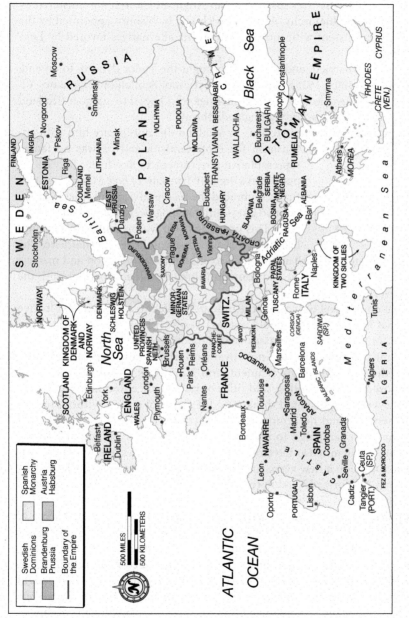

MAP 13-3 Europe After the Peace of Westphalia The Treaty of Westphalia redrew the map of Europe. France and Sweden acquired additional territory. The United Provinces and the Swiss cantons were recognized as independent states, and Germany's political fragmentation was assured to continue.

QUESTION: To what extent were the political borders that the treaty drew on the map of Europe determined by geography and to what extent by cultural and linguistic differences?

self-governing congregations overseen by a national synod to which congregations elected representatives. The secular equivalent for this ecclesiastical organization was a monarchy headed by a king who ruled in consort with Parliament. Elizabeth and her successors understood the political implications of Protestant church order, which was one reason why they insisted on an Anglican Church administered by the traditional Catholic hierarchy. A state church run by bishops appointed by the crown was more consistent with monarchy than the alternatives favored by England's Protestants.

Elizabeth never married, and her death brought the Tudor dynasty to an end. Her heir, **James I** (r. 1603–1625), was Mary Stuart's son, Scotland's King James VI. Ironically, centuries of war waged by English kings who hoped to conquer Scotland ended with Scotland's king ascending England's throne.

James' experience with Presbyterians in Scotland did not inspire him with enthusiasm for Protestantism, and he was no fan of representative government in any form. In 1598 he published a book, *A True Law of Free Monarchies,* that firmly embraced the medieval principle that God appointed kings and that kings were accountable only to God. This was out of step with recent trends in English history that had strengthened **Parliament.** The Tudor dynasty had needed Parliament's help to effect the Reformation and manage its consequences, and Parliament had come to think of itself as a partner with the monarch in governing England.

□□□□Read the Document

James I, The Divine Right of Kings

on **MyHistoryLab.com**

Parliament could meet only when the monarch called it, and what kept it alive was the fact that England's kings could not levy taxes without the approval of the representatives of the tax-paying classes who composed Parliament. To avoid calling a Parliament that might try to limit royal authority, a king had to find other ways to meet the expenses of government, and James was inventive at devising these. He imposed customs duties, sold titles of nobility, licensed monopolies for a fee, and did everything he could think of to fill the royal coffers without resorting to Parliament. He had no sympathy with any aspect of Puritanism and even sponsored a national campaign to encourage the recreations, games, and sports that the Puritans condemned as frivolous and ungodly pastimes. His major concession was to commission a new vernacular translation of the Scriptures. The result was the eloquent Authorized Version (or as it is popularly known, the **King James Version**) of the Bible.

James's policies and dissolute court were so offensive to Puritans that some of them gave up hope for England's reformation and decided to make fresh starts elsewhere. In 1593 a small group of radical Puritan separatists left London for the Netherlands, and in 1620 they emigrated again to found a colony called **Plymouth** in North America. They were the vanguard of a much larger migration that eventually brought thousands of more mainstream Puritans to New England and the islands of the West Indies. As it turned out, they were somewhat premature in anticipating the decline of the Puritan cause in their homeland.

James's son and successor, **Charles I** (r. 1625–1649), shared his father's determination to rule without interference from his subjects. After a Parliament early

Leaders of the Reformations and the Wars of Religion

RELIGIOUS LEADERS	POLITICAL LEADERS	EVENTS
Luther (1483–1546)	Charles V (1519–1556)	Diet of Worms (1521)
Leo X (1513–1521)	Süleyman (1520–1566)	
Zwingli (1484–1531)	Francis I (1515–1547)	Habsburg-Valois Wars (1521–1544)
Clement VII (1523–1534)	Henry VIII (1509–1547)	
Calvin (1509–1564)	Catherine of Aragon (1485–1536)	English Reformation (1534)
		Geneva reformed (1541)
Ignatius Loyola (1491–1556)	Edward VI (1547–1553)	Peace of Augsburg (1555)
Paul III (1534–1549)	Mary Tudor (1553–1558)	Council of Trent (1545–1563)
Knox (1505–1572)	Philip II (1556–1598)	Scotland reformed (1559)
Theresa of Avila (1515–1582)	Elizabeth I (1558–1603)	Spanish Armada (1588)
	Mary Stuart (1542–1567)	
	Catherine de Medicis (1485–1536)	French Wars of Religion (1562–1589)
	Henry IV (1594–1610)	Edict of Nantes (1598)
	James I (1603–1625)	
	Frederick V (1596–1632)	
	Ferdinand II (1578–1637)	Thirty Years' War (1618–1648)
	Gustavus Adolphus (1611–1632)	
	Richelieu (1585–1642)	
	Charles I (1625–1649)	English Civil War (1642–1646)
	Cromwell (1599–1658)	English Republic (1649–1660)

in his reign forced him to acknowledge that he had no unilateral right to levy taxes, he avoided convening another session for eleven years (1629–1640). He was even less willing than his father to compromise with Protestants, and the Puritans suspected him of being a Catholic at heart. His French wife enjoyed the privilege of hearing mass at court, and his archbishop of Canterbury, **William Laud,** had his support in promoting liturgical reforms that Puritans regarded as a reversion to Roman worship.

Puritans who criticized him in print or from their pulpits were dragged into court, speedily convicted, and harshly punished. What precipitated his fall, however, was not his quarrel with England's Puritans but his determination to force Scotland's church to conform to Anglican practice. In 1637 Charles ordered Scotland's Presbyterian clergy to use the Anglican prayer book. When the Scots refused, Charles took up arms against them. The small army he was able to raise without Parliament's assistance failed to do anything but goad the Scots into invading England (1640). This forced Charles to call a Parliament, but that only worsened his situation. When Parliament insisted that he carry out extensive governmental reforms before they granted new tax levies, he dissolved the meeting (the "**Short Parliament**"). A few months later, a victory by the Scots forced him to reconvene Parliament. This meeting passed a law to the effect that a parliamentary session could only be ended by vote of its members. Given that no resolution for adjournment was passed for the next 20 years, this opened the "**Long Parliament.**" The Long Parliament moved rapidly to curtail the power of the king. It dismissed his archbishop, punished some of his councilors, repealed his taxes, and decreed that in future the king had to convene Parliaments at regular intervals. Charles believed that Parliament was vastly overstepping its boundaries and curtailing his royal prerogatives. The reforms it demanded were in fact similar to those that later limited the powers of the throne and established Parliament as the dominant body in Britain's government. In 1642 the exasperated king made the mistake of ordering his soldiers to disperse Parliament. When Parliament's leaders resisted and London rose to support them, the king began to rally royalist forces in the counties of the west and north.

This was the prelude to a civil war that raged for four years (1642–1646). Its turning point came in 1645 when Parliament commissioned the **New Model Army,** a reorganized military recruited from committed Protestants called "**Roundheads.**" (Their closely cropped hair contrasted with the flowing locks of the king's courtiers, the "**Cavaliers.**") Unlike earlier armies, the New Model Army was commanded not by aristocrats, but by experienced officers promoted for merit. Its men were strictly disciplined, passionate about their cause, and respected for their moral rectitude. They routed armies larger than their own and did not indulge in the rape and pillage that had traditionally been the prerogatives of victorious soldiers. Parliament was also fortunate in finding a brilliant military strategist among its members. **Oliver Cromwell** (1599–1658), a member of the **House of Commons,** was an obscure individual from the ranks of the country gentry. He raised a company of cavalrymen whose spirit and discipline spread through the parliamentary forces, and he quickly rose in the chain of command.

Oliver Cromwell   This unfinished miniature is a likeness of the enigmatic Puritan leader, Oliver Cromwell. He allegedly had a religious experience in his youth that convinced him that he was one of God's elect—a man destined to serve God in unique ways. His confidence in his calling may explain the forceful means he often employed to impose his will on others.

The king's army was broken at the **Battle of Naseby** in June 1645, but Charles eluded capture and survived as a fugitive in his own country for a year. In May 1646 he surrendered to the Scots who held him for eight months before turning him over to the English.

Parliament was better at winning wars than governing England. Its victory only cleared the way for its numerous religious factions to begin to fight among themselves. A rift also opened between politicians and soldiers when Parliament attempted precipitously to trim the budget by disbanding the army. Parliament's Presbyterian majority was more conservative than many of its soldiers. A faction known as the **Levelers** demanded that the current Parliament be dissolved and that every adult male citizen be given the right to vote for a new Parliament that would govern without restraint by a king or **House of Lords.** Freedom of religion was also to be guaranteed.

In November of 1647 the king escaped, and the war flared up again. This reenergized the army and forfeited whatever respect the soldiers still had for the monarchy. The army recaptured the king, occupied London, and purged Parliament of its Presbyterian majority. The much reduced "**Rump Parliament**" then convicted the king of treason and—on January 30, 1649—beheaded him. The monarchy was declared at an end, and England was henceforward to be governed as a republic. In reality, Cromwell became the new head of state. His support derived in large part from his ability as a military leader to restore order to a country that was desperate for stability. He stuck to a Puritan middle path—suppressing both the radical Levelers and the Anglo-Catholics. He dealt harshly with critics and opponents and mounted new

"TAKE AWAY THAT BAUBLE!" CROMWELL DISSOLVING PARLIAMENT, 1654.

Cromwell Dissolves the Rump Parliament Oliver Cromwell found that it was easier to overthrow a monarchy than to establish a republic in its place. He first tried reducing the size of England's Parliament. But when infighting among different groups frustrated efforts to create a workable government and state church, he dispensed with an elected assembly and ruled with the support of his army. This engraving is how an artist imagined the scene that took place on April 20, 1653, when Cromwell and 40 of his soldiers forcefully dispersed Parliament and established Cromwell in sole power as England's "Lord Protector."

📖 Read the Document

Cromwell Abolishes the English Monarchy

on **MyHistoryLab.com**

military campaigns. He put down revolts in Ireland, brought Scotland back under England's control, and waged war at sea with the Dutch. The taxes he imposed were more onerous than those that Charles had levied, and in 1653 this prompted Parliament to consider disbanding his army. He prevented this by sending in soldiers to disband the Rump Parliament. Cromwell intended to rule in cooperation with a Parliament, but whenever debates in the meetings he subsequently convened grew too radical for his tastes, he sent their delegates home. He leaned heavily on the army to stay in power, and in May of 1657 he assumed a title: **Lord Protector**—a king by a new name. He survived for another year, dying on September 3, 1658.

Cromwell's son, **Richard,** briefly assumed his father's office, but he was unable to maintain control of a divided army and a country that had been disillusioned by both republican and Puritan extremism. A period of confusion ensued in which civil war again threatened. Finally, a powerful general arranged for the election of a new Parliament. In April of 1660 it invited Charles I's son, **Charles II** (r. 1660–1685), to return from exile in France and restore the monarchy and the Anglican Church. England embraced its former institutions, but the Puritan revolution had not been a complete failure. Mindful of Charles I's fate, England's kings moderated claims to absolute authority and conceded Parliament a permanent role in government. Britain's "constitutional" monarchy was not yet complete, but it was nearing the final stages in its development.

KEY QUESTION REVISITED

How should conflicts over values and ideologies be managed?

During the sixteenth and seventeenth centuries, Europeans tried to resolve power struggles of various kinds. Emerging states jousted for advantage, and there were tugs of war between supporters of local and centralized government within states. Nobles resisted the growing power of kings, and commoners challenged aristocratic privilege. Social and economic classes and rural and urban areas were in conflict. The two traditions that had long struggled to determine Europe's future—imperial unity and religious homogeneity versus political fragmentation and cultural diversity—faced off on numerous battlefields.

Religious convictions, both sincere and opportunistic, provided moral justification for decisions to shed blood that was to be spilled for many other reasons as well. The ethical context for the wars of the Reformation era was more complex than for the religious wars of earlier generations. Unlike Europe's crusades, which were wars of foreign aggression waged in the name of European Christianity against what was thought to be a hostile, competing faith and culture, Europe's "wars of religion" were civil wars within Christendom. Their partisans held a variety of opinions on what was the true and what was a perverted form of Christian faith. And their religious ideals were mixed with commitments for reforming political and class systems.

German princes pursued political advantages by embracing or opposing the Reformation. Fear of the Catholic Habsburg emperor drove some into the Protestant camp, while the expectation of help from him kept others loyal to the papacy. In France, religion split an aristocracy that had a long history of division within its own ranks. And in England, more openly than in other countries, politics drove the decision to break with Rome and then politics prolonged the lingering quarrel over how real that break should be.

Opportunism aside, religious and political values were inevitably intertwined, for religious faith helped people understand what gave legitimacy to systems of government and justice. Protestantism's faith in the primacy of God's relationship with each individual elevated the worth of the individual and argued for the autonomy of conscience. These values implied a divine sanction for some form of popular government. Catholics, who believed that all authority originated with God, understood [the right to rule to be a divine mandate bestowed on persons of His choice. This conviction gave legitimacy to monarchy and hierarchical systems of government. Partisans from both camps faced the same dangerous temptation—to equate particular human institutions with absolute truths.

Key Terms

indulgence, *p. 381*
diet, *p. 384*
Peace of Augsburg, *p. 387*
Thirty Years' War, *p. 387*
Predestination, *p. 389*
Reform (Calvinist
   Protestantism), *p. 390*

Oratory of Divine Love, *p. 392*
Inquisition, *p. 393*
Council of Trent, *p. 393*
Pragmatic Sanction
   of Bourges, *p. 395*
Act of Supremacy, *p. 396*
Puritan, *p. 398*

Spanish Armada, *p. 402*
St. Bartholomew's Day
   Massacre, *p. 404*
Edict of Nantes, *p. 405*
Peace of Westphalia, *p. 408*
New Model Army, *p. 412*

Activities

1. List the key principles that distinguish Protestantism from Catholicism and explain how Luther arrived at each of them.

2. Identify the different kinds of Protestants that emerged as the Reformation unfolded and explain the theological and political differences among them.

3. Identify the stages that the Reformation went through in England and decide whether religion or politics had the greater influence on the outcome.

4. Did the challenge mounted by the Protestant Reformation weaken or strengthen the papacy?

5. Outline an essay in which you argue which of Europe's many wars in this period could most accurately be described as a "war of religion."

6. What impact did the conflicts of this period have on efforts to consolidate governmental authority in Spain, France, Germany, and England?

Further Reading

Martin E. Marty, *Martin Luther: A Life* (2008), an introduction (by a popular and prolific American religious scholar) to one of the major figures of this period which focuses on his private life.

Antonia Fraser, *The Wives of Henry VIII* (1993), a survey of the aspect of Henry's reign that has attracted most attention by a historian who has a following among general readers.

C. V. Wedgwood and Anthony Grafton, *The Thirty Years' War* (2005), a survey of one of the major campaigns in European history—for the military history enthusiast.

Neil Hanson, *The Confident Hope of a Miracle: The True Story of the Spanish Armada* (2006), a description of a famous event in military history that delves into the cultural and technological background of the venture.

Alison Weir, *The Life of Elizabeth I* (1999), one of many books on England's famous queen, but especially useful for debunking myths and providing glimpses into the era's court life.

MyHistoryLab **Connections**

Visit **MyHistoryLab.com** *for a customized Study Plan that will help you build your knowledge of* Reformation, Religious Wars, and National Conflicts.

Questions for Analysis

1. What is Martin Schongauer saying about the power of faith in his depiction of St. Anthony?

[View the **Closer Look** A Saint at Peace in the Grasp of Temptation, p. 382

2. Why does Martin Luther object so strongly to the selling of indulgences?

[Read the **Document** Martin Luther's Ninety-Five Theses, p. 382

3. What was the impact of the silver trade on world economies in the sixteenth century?

[Watch the **Video** The Columbian Exchange, p. 403

4. How does Cervantes depict Don Quixote?

[Read the **Document** Miguel de Cervantes, *Don Quixote*, excerpt, p. 403

5. According to Rushworth, how did the Thirty Years' War begin?

[Read the **Document** Description of the Beginning of the Thirty Years' War, John Rushworth, p. 405

Other Resources from This Chapter

[Read the **Document** Germany: Peasants' Demands in Manifesto, p. 384

[Read the **Document** Against the Robbing and Murdering Hordes of Peasants, p. 385

[●] Read the Document Calvin on Predestination, p. 389

[◉] View the Closer Look Baroque and Plain Church: Architectural Reflections of Belief, p. 390

[●] Read the Document John Calvin, *Ecclesiastical Ordinances*, p. 390

[●] Read the Document Ignatius Loyola, *Rules for Thinking with the Church*, p. 393

[●] Read the Document   The Counter-Reformation Council of Trent, p. 393

[●] Read the Document British Religious Turmoil: The Execution of Archbishop Cranmer, p. 399

[●] Read the Document Elizabeth I, *Religious Acts of Uniformity*, 1559, p. 400

[●] Read the Document Reports on the Spanish Armada, p. 402

[◉] Watch the Video The Art of El Greco, p. 403

[●] Read the Document France: Massacre of St. Bartholomew, p. 404

[●] Read the Document The Edict of Nantes, 1598, p. 404

[●] Read the Document The Peace of Westphalia, p. 408

[●] Read the Document James I, *The Divine Right of Kings*, p. 410

[●] Read the Document Cromwell Abolishes the English Monarchy, p. 414

PART FIVE

The Revolutionary Impulse

Joseph Wright of Derby, *An Experiment on a Bird in the Air Pump, 1768*

During the seventeenth and eighteenth centuries, Europeans were confronted with un-precedented challenges to conventional political thought and practice, to their picture of the physical universe, and to established social and religious values. In politics, ambitious monarchs consolidated their power through the expansion of royal bureaucracies and the formation of large standing armies. In both its absolutist and constitutional forms, monar-chy made important strides toward the enhancement of state authority.

For almost two millennia, the accepted understanding of the cosmos placed humans at the center of God's creation. This Earth-centered and hierarchical **cosmology** was embraced by church authorities as reflecting the centrality of the human drama in creation. By 1700 this model of physical creation had been replaced by a sun-centered and mathe-matically ordered cosmos. Leading eighteenth-century thinkers extended the principles of order and rationality at the heart of the Scientific Revolution to new areas. Calls for reform were predicated on a new assumption: if the physical world operated according to natural laws, then comparable laws could be discovered and implemented in the social, religious, economic, and political spheres. A colonial political revolt in Britain's American empire in 1776 set the stage for a sweeping revolution in France in 1789. In both settings the institution of monarchy was eventually rejected, and efforts to build civil society anew on the basis of assumed laws of nature were carried forward.

T I M E L I N E

	ENVIRONMENT AND TECHNOLOGY	SOCIETY AND CULTURE	POLITICS
1543	1543 Copernicus, *On the Revolutions of the Heavenly Orbs*	1611 King James Bible	1643–1715 Reign of Louis XIV
	1543 Vesalius, *On the Fabric of the Human Body*	1633 Trial of Galileo 1637 Descartes, *Discourse on Method*	1642–1649 Civil War in England
1650	1609–1619 Kepler's laws of planetary motion	1662 English Royal Society founded	1660 Restoration of English monarchy
	1610 Galileo, *Starry Messenger*	1666 French *Academie des Sciences* founded	1688 Revolution in England
	1620 Bacon, *Novum Organum*	1690 Locke, *Essay Concerning Human Understanding*	1689–1725 Reign of Peter the Great
			1690 Locke, *Two Treatises of Government*
1700	1687 *Mathematical Principles of Natural Philosophy*	1751 *Encyclopedia* 1764 Beccaria, *Of Crimes and Punishments*	1740–1786 Reign of Frederick the Great 1762–1796 Reign of Catherine the Great
1776	1700 European population reaches 100 million	1700–1750 Height of Baroque Music	1776 American Revolution
	1712 First steam engine	1776 Smith, *Wealth of Nations*	1789 French Revolution
	1733 Flying shuttle invented	1791 Death of Mozart at age 35	1792 *Vindication of the Rights of Woman*
	1760 Spinning jenny invented		1793 France becomes a republic
	1780s–1850s Britain becomes first industrial nation		
	1800 European population reaches 190 million		
1815			

William and Mary Detail from the Painted Hall in Greenwich, England, showing the resplendent English monarchs King William III (1650–1702) and Queen Mary II (1662–1694). William and Mary assumed the English throne in the bloodless "Glorious Revolution."

14 The Early Modern State

((•⃝─Hear the Audio Chapter 14 at MyHistoryLab.com

LEARNING OBJECTIVES

How stratified was Early Modern European Society? • How did political theory shape Europe's emerging state system? • What were the main features of French absolutism? • What was the English alternative to absolutism? • How did the causes and conduct of warfare change in the seventeenth century? • What were the key elements of Russian and Prussian absolutism? • What were the factors leading to the relative decline of some states?

A well conducted government must have an underlying concept so well integrated that it could be likened to a system of philosophy. All actions taken must be well reasoned, and all financial, political, and military matters must flow towards one goal, which is the strengthening of the state and the furthering of its power. However, such a system can flow but from a single brain, and this must be that of the sovereign.

—Frederick II

KEY QUESTION

How do political systems reflect the structure of social and economic life?

Frederick II (r. 1740–1786) of Prussia, also known as Frederick the Great, viewed himself as one of a new breed of European monarchs. In his *Political Testament*, written in 1752, he observed that a king must be the "first servant of the state" and not an arbitrary ruler. Still, as the previously quoted passage indicates, Frederick refused to acknowledge that his subjects had any right to help formulate state policy. "Just as it would have been impossible for Newton to arrive at his system of attractions if he had worked in harness with Leibnitz and Descartes, so a system of politics cannot be arrived at and continued if it has not sprung from a single brain." For Frederick, and for many of his royal contemporaries, absolute monarchy was necessitated by the flaws inherent in human nature. The leading Protestant reformers had reminded their followers that sinfulness and disobedience lay at the core of the human predicament. Apologists for absolutism maintained that social order and political harmony were impossible without the steady hand of divine-right rulers. In the wake of the Protestant Reformation, as political leaders claimed greater autonomy from Rome, the theory of absolutism found fertile ground in an intellectual climate that emphasized human frailty.

During the approximately 200 years from 1600 to the French Revolution that began in 1789, Europe's social structure, family traditions, and behavioral patterns remained largely unchanged, but some countries saw the stirring of new values and practices. Just as the hierarchy that had characterized the physical universe was challenged by Copernicus, Galileo, Kepler, and Newton, so too did Europe's hierarchical social and political structures come under increased scrutiny. In mid-seventeenth-century England, the old model of rulership under king, priest, and noble was temporarily upset during a protracted civil war, while in England's North American colonial empire a combination of environmental and geographical factors aborted efforts to transfer Europe's hierarchical social and political order to a new setting.

Monarchy was restored in England in 1660 after a troubled 11-year experiment in quasi-republican government, and in France a powerful form of centralized rule was forged under the leadership of King Louis XIV (r. 1643–1715). However, the experience of government without a king in England, the emergence of elected assemblies in Britain's North American colonies, and the acceleration of new forms of economic activity brought about by overseas exploration and colonization contributed to the emergence of a new and dynamic society in Western Europe. It was a society where material wealth began to displace hereditary status, titles, and landholding as the key measure of political power. By the last quarter of the eighteenth century, challenges to political absolutism reflected the emergence of a more confident picture of human nature and human potential. Individuals were assumed to possess certain rights that could not be abridged by either civil or religious authorities. ▪

Society in Early Modern Europe

Status and Authority   For centuries European society had been divided into *estates* or status groups. Most people identified themselves with membership in occupational, religious, and regional groups that looked to the past for guidance in determining how to conduct life. The notion of individual rights, especially individual rights against public authority, was largely absent. Corporate assumptions—the well-being of the community before the advancement of the individual—informed the texture of everyday life. As late as the mid-eighteenth century most of Europe's population lived in rural settings, worked the land for subsistence, and rarely traveled more than a few miles from their place of birth. Society's natural leaders were identified by their lineage, not by their talents. Even leaders of popular revolts against high taxes and brutal landlords accepted the hierarchical social order and its traditional leaders. Indeed, most rebels called for a restoration of traditional practices and relationships, not a fundamental change in the economic and social fabric of life.

Aristocracy   Historians often refer to the period between 1650 and the third quarter of the eighteenth century as the *ancien régime* (Old Regime). Europe's aristocrats, a tiny fraction of the overall population, continued to dominate the political, religious, economic, and social life of the continent even though the growth of overseas trade and urban commerce was producing fundamental economic changes. Members of the titled aristocracy (dukes, marquises, counts, barons, etc.) considered themselves to be the natural leaders of society, their wealth derived from rents on lands worked by serfs or heavily taxed free peasants. Titled aristocrats were privileged subjects of the crown, serving as local political and military leaders, responsible for maintaining good order in the countryside, and monopolizing leadership positions within the established churches. In most European countries, aristocrats enjoyed a political voice at the national level through their residence at court or their membership in a parliament, diet, or assembly. In England, for example, the aristocracy consisted of a mere 400 families, but they enjoyed exclusive control over the upper chamber of Parliament, the House of Lords. In France, where there were 400,000 nobles out of a population of almost 20 million, the aristocracy exercised political influence through their monopoly over high positions in the church, the military, the courts, and the bureaucracy.

The fiscal privileges the aristocracy enjoyed were enormous. In France they were exempted from paying the *taille* or land tax, nor could they be obliged, as the peasants were, to contribute to the *corvée* (forced labor) on public works projects. Polish nobles were exempted from taxes after 1741, while various exemptions were available to the aristocratic class in the German states, Russia, Austria, and Hungary. Holding the exclusive right to bear arms, members of the aristocracy were expected to come to the aid of the poor who lived around their estates because status was thought to entail responsibility to one's inferiors. However, compassion for the poor was combined with wide-ranging power and legal discretion. Polish nobles held the power of life and death over their serfs, while in Prussia, Russia, England, and France manorial courts placed enormous judicial power in the hands of aristocrats. In return for humane treatment, the poor were expected to show deference and gratitude toward their wealthy benefactors. In reality, much resentment was directed against the privileged, especially against those who lived lavishly and employed large contingents of servants and military retainers. There were, for example, over 50 peasant revolts in Russia during the 1760s alone, and while this number was unusually high, peasant grievances were many and serious across Europe.

Peasants and Serfs   It is impossible to generalize about the condition of the common people in Old Regime Europe other than to say that their numbers increased significantly during the eighteenth century. The period from 1600 to 1700 was characterized by slow demographic growth in some areas and stagnation in others, with famine, war, and disease near constants of daily life. However, populations increased after 1700, mainly because of improved agricultural techniques and more effective use of land. In 1700 an estimated 110 million people lived in Europe; by 1800 the total had reached 190 million inhabitants. The largest increases occurred in eastern Europe, especially in Russia and Hungary. The introduction of fodder crops such as clover added important nutrients to the soil, while turnips were grown to feed livestock during the winter. New crops from the Americas, especially maize (corn) and potatoes, afforded high nutritional content while yielding more food per acre than many traditional crops, such as wheat and rye. Poverty and malnutrition continued in the countryside, while urban underemployment led to much suffering in the cities. However, the steady growth in aggregate population across Europe signaled the enhanced ability of eighteenth-century society to provide for the basic necessities of life.

In England and France, most peasants enjoyed personal freedom. Further to the east, however, in the German states, Poland, and Russia, most peasants were **serfs,** legally bound to an estate and a particular landlord—often an aristocrat. Regardless of one's status, however, across the continent the class that owned the land dominated the class that worked it; social dependency in an overwhelming rural economy constituted the parameters of life for most men and women from the English Midlands to Russian Siberia. As population and food prices rose, and as farmland was consolidated in the interests of efficiency, the displacement of rural laborers and widespread urban poverty became two of Europe's most serious social problems. Charity hospitals and workhouses expanded their services in cities, but these institutions were often overwhelmed by the demand for assistance. A few hospitals resorted to lotteries to determine who would gain admission.

Conditions of work for common people varied markedly in each country, but in general more people often meant more hardship. French peasants typically owned a small piece of land, but it was seldom enough to provide for their families. Employment under the supervision of a landlord or the rental of additional land from a powerful aristocrat placed the peasant in a precarious economic position. Local fees (**banalités**) had to be paid to landowners to use their mills, ovens, and tools, and landlords had a monopoly on these items. Uncompensated work on the landlord's holdings and mandatory labor on public works projects—called the *corvée* in France—also strained the peasant's economic and physical resources. In England the emergence of commercial agriculture, initiated by a handful of improving landlords but subsequently affecting the entire kingdom, meant heavy labor demands on landless peasants and those who rented. Russian serfs, who were the virtual property of the nobility, experienced the harshest conditions. Both **Peter the Great**

Peasant Laborers in France   The *corvée* system in France required peasants to engage in public works projects like the building of roads and bridges. This mandatory labor system came to an end only after the French Revolution in 1789.

(r. 1682–1725) and **Catherine the Great** (r. 1762–1796) granted the aristocracy total control over the lives of their serfs. A Russian noble's wealth came to be measured in terms of the number of serfs (called "souls") in his possession, not the amount of land that he owned. The serf's travel, housing arrangements, and even marriages were ordered according to the wishes of the landlord.

Family Life   Western Europeans tended to work as family units, and families rarely exceeded six to ten members. Children normally resided in their parents' home and helped till the soil. Some would leave in their early teens to become servants in other families or apprentices under skilled craftsmen. Few persons lived alone, and those who did were regarded with the suspicion often associated with the rootless and the criminal. Marriages normally occurred when men and women were in their mid-twenties, and newlyweds established their own household and had children as soon as possible. In eastern Europe family units tended to be much larger, and young married couples were more apt to reside with parents. Landlords sometimes forced serfs to marry or to remarry after the death of a spouse. Arranging marriages for serfs was intended to enhance the economic position of the lord of the manor.

The role of women in the family unit was defined largely by their child-bearing capacity and their economic acumen. Young girls often left home to become paid servants in other households. However, once they accumulated a sufficient dowry and a marriage was arranged for them, brides were expected to bear children who would become assets to the family economy. Women and men worked together in the fields, plowing, planting, and producing sufficient crops to pay taxes and rent. Usually, this left only enough (in a good year) to survive until the next growing season. For the small minority of women who were married to traders or artisans and who lived in towns or cities, the death of a husband often meant that the widow would assume control of the business and even employ male apprentices. Although they were excluded from the political life of the urban center, these women could acquire economic independence after the death of a spouse.

Mortality   In this culture people were intimately familiar with the prospect of sudden death from one of a variety of causes. Even though the population of Western Europe increased sharply in the 1700s, mortality rates remained high. Perhaps the most difficult thing for us to understand about what life in the past must have been like is the experience of living and dying in a world without efficacious medicine. From the mid-eighteenth century until today, the development of narcotics and therapies capable of lessening the pain of death has altered the end-of-life experience for most people in the West. The narcotic effects of opium and its derivatives began the process that has culminated in the insensible death that millions experience in modern times. It is a death removed from public view and lacking the least element of personal oversight. By contrast, in early modern Europe most deaths occurred in the home. Immediate family and close friends assumed, in a way that could be exceptional today, a direct and continuous role in the physical and spiritual care of the person. The doctor's job, if his costly services were secured at all, was to diagnose the illness and offer a prognosis of how it would develop. He was not expected to provide a cure through aggressive intervention. Eighteenth-century Europeans, like all humans around the world at that time, lived with sickness and death as close companions.

Forging Centralized States

While life conditions might differ enormously for the poor, peasant allegiances were fiercely local throughout Europe. Everyone was aware that a rigidly stratified social structure in which appearance, diet, housing, and speech reflected one's place in the order of creation was firmly endorsed by society's religious and secular leaders. Unlike modern society, status was still largely associated with education, birth, title, legal privileges, and office, not with wealth. Loyalties to lord, priest, and community were largely taken for granted and were much stronger than any feelings toward the ruling monarch. Indeed, taxes paid to the central government provoked the greatest resentment among the peasantry, especially because these taxes rarely seemed to benefit the local community.

Political Fragmentation   Unlike the world's other major civilizations in China, Japan, India, and the Ottoman and Persian empires, the political map of late sixteenth-century Europe was characterized by hundreds of independent and semi-independent units. No European head of state enjoyed the strong centralized authority of the Ming emperors in China and the Mughal emperors in India, for example. There were hereditary kings and queens in Spain, France, England, and Scandinavia, but elective monarchs in Poland and Hungary. The Holy Roman Emperor, perhaps the most powerful European head of state in terms of lands under his nominal control, was also elected by a select group of German churchmen and princes. Important ecclesiastical cities and principalities existed in parts of Germany, and the pope ruled over a large sweep of territory in central Italy. At the regional level, hundreds of nobles and city councils dominated the political life of their respective locales. In much of Europe, the monarch was only a distant and bothersome figurehead. Most rulers found themselves leading multilingual and multicultural collections of people, all of whom were eager to protect their long-established habits of autonomy.

This localism and provincialism largely ended during the seventeenth century. The wars of religion between Catholics and Protestants that had occupied European leaders since the 1550s not only caused enormous physical destruction and human dislocation, but also contributed to the rapid enhancement of centralized state power. Royal courts expanded during this period, taxes increased, and military spending absorbed a greater percentage of national revenue. In 1500 European governments were tiny, with a small number of full-time advisors and officials. Two centuries later, the major kingdoms employed thousands of bureaucrats and professional soldiers, each one committed to enhancing the authority of the crown. Local aristocrats, clerics, regional assemblies, and urban leaders lost portions of their autonomy as monarchs moved decisively to strengthen their position as leaders of consolidated states. Sending tax collectors, military recruiters, and judicial officers into the countryside,

Europe's princes transformed their office. Abandoning the old medieval model in which they had been "first among equals," Europe's kings and queens served as divine-right agents of God on Earth.

The Church and Political Power
The most significant casualty of the sixteenth- and seventeenth-century wars of religion and the subsequent enhancement of royal power was the Catholic Church. Before the Reformation, the medieval papacy enjoyed its own international sources of revenue, its own administrative bureaucracy, its own system of courts, and a centuries-old claim to jurisdictional superiority over individual Christian princes. The Church was the only truly transnational European institution, and its clergy were encouraged to accept the authority of their ecclesiastical leaders over the wishes of their respective monarchs. The success of the Reformation in northern Europe by the mid-seventeenth century—in England, Scandinavia, parts of the Netherlands and Switzerland, and many north German states—put an end to the Roman Catholic Church's pretensions to universal religious and political authority. In Protestant territories, monarchs claimed leadership over state-supported churches, while in powerful Catholic countries like France and Spain, kings and queens played a key role in the selection of bishops and archbishops.

Political Theory and the State
Two distinct models of political authority emerged during the seventeenth century to further the goal of centralization. The theory behind each model differed, but the practical outcomes were similar. France followed the path of **absolutism** under the leadership of a powerful king. England, in contrast, curbed the monarch's discretionary authority and accorded greater political power to a Parliament dominated by aristocrats and landowners. Ironically, one of the most compelling books in support of the monarch's absolute power was written by the English King James I (r. 1603–1625), while some of the strongest arguments against absolutism were written by late sixteenth-century French authors.

Read the **Document**
On Social Order and Absolutist Monarchy
on **MyHistoryLab.com**

In *The True Law of Free Monarchies* (1598), King James insisted that hereditary monarchs enjoy their elevated status because God chose them. The book acknowledged that the monarch held a sacred trust to advance the material and spiritual well-being of his subjects. In addition, it held that kings and queens were accountable to God alone, and that subjects had a sacred duty to obey even if the monarch violated God's law. In France the period of religious wars and monarchical weakness that began in the 1560s occasioned the publication of important anti-absolutist works. Soon after a terrible attack by Catholics against French Protestants in 1572 that left 10,000 dead in the country's major cities, an event known as the **St. Bartholomew's Day Massacre,** the Protestant Françoise Hotman (1524–1590) published *Francogallia* (1573). Hotman believed that the dissolute young French King Charles IX (r. 1560–1574) had ordered the attacks. In his book Hotman claimed that history showed the French crown was not hereditary. Instead, it was conferred by the people on "those who were reputed just."

PEOPLE IN CONTEXT   King James I as Political Theorist

When he succeeded Queen Elizabeth I of England in 1603, James I was already a mature and experienced monarch. One year after his birth in 1566, James's mother, Mary, Queen of Scots (1542–1587), was forced to abdicate the throne of Scotland due to a series of scandals. Not the least of these was her reputed involvement in the suspicious death of James's father, Henry Stuart, Lord Darnley (1545–1567). Scotland was completely independent of England during the sixteenth and seventeenth centuries, as King James faced an uphill struggle to consolidate his authority against independent-minded Gaelic-speaking highland clans and lowland nobles who commanded their own fighting forces. After a long regency during which his advisors jostled for power, James began to rule Scotland directly in 1585 at the age of 21.

As King James VI of Scotland, James's intellectual pursuits reflected his desire to strengthen the power of the monarchy. In 1598 he published two books whose objective was to explain and defend divine-right monarchy. In *The True Law of Free Monarchy* and *Basilikon Doron (Royal Gift)* James insisted that only a strong executive could end the civil and religious conflict tearing Europe apart. For a monarch to be effective, however, subjects must acknowledge that royal power is a divine gift. According to James, kings represent God on Earth, and human laws could not constrain them. The sovereign must be obeyed in all things, for royal commands are the commands of God's minister. No subject had the right to resist, for only God could judge an errant king. The wise king would always try to obey human law, "yet he is not bound thereto but of his good will, and for example-giving to his subjects."

James's absolutist political theory was not well received after he became king of England. His long reign (1603–1625) was marked by repeated disagreements with Parliament. But James attempted to live by some of the more temperate advice contained in his two books. The *Basilikon Doron* was a best-selling advice book written for the king's elder son Henry. Soon after its publication, it was translated into Latin, French, Dutch, German, and Swedish. In the book, James admonished his son to "think not therefore that the highness of your dignity, diminisheth your faults (much less

TO THE MOST
HIGH AND MIGHTIE
Prince, IAMES by the grace of God
King of Great Britaine, France and Ireland,
Defender of the Faith, &c.

THE TRANSLATORS OF *THE BIBLE,*
wish Grace, Mercie, and Peace, through IESVS
CHRIST our LORD.

Reat and manifold were the blessings (most dread Soueraigne) which Almighty GOD, the Father of all Mercies, bestowed vpon vs the people of ENGLAND, when first he sent your Maiesties Royall person to rule and raigne ouer us. For whereas it was the expectation of many, who wished not well vnto our SION, that vpon the setting of that bright *Occidentall Starre* Queene ELIZABETH of most happy memory, some thicke and palpable cloudes of darkenesse would so haue ouershadowed this land, that men should haue bene in doubt which way they were to walke, and that it should hardly be knowen, who was to direct the vnsetled

The King James Bible   Title page to the 1611 English translation of the Holy Bible, commissioned by James. The Bible is dedicated to the king, and the translators make it clear that he rules "by the grace of God."

give you license to sin) but by the contrary your fault shall be aggravated, according to the height of your dignity." Absolute monarchy did not mean arbitrary monarchy. For James I of England, obedience to national law and tradition strengthened the crown and legitimized the king's right to rule. ■

QUESTION: How did the political theory of absolutism seek to enlist the support of Christianity?

Six years later another French Protestant author wrote *Defense of Liberty Against Tyrants* (1579), a book that claimed that magistrates had the right to remove a king who failed to enforce God's law. These and other resistance theorists—some of whom were Roman Catholic—had a strong impact on political theory in seventeenth- and eighteenth-century Europe. The Spanish Jesuit Juan de Molina (1536–1624) captured the essence of their position when he wrote in *The King and the Education of the King* (1598) that monarchs and magistrates were only the representatives of the people.

Absolutism in France

King **Henry IV** (r. 1589–1610) struggled mightily to bring an end to the religious divisions that had wracked France since the 1560s. With his promulgation of the Edict of Nantes in 1598, Henry granted religious toleration to the kingdom's minority Protestant population. Henry also attempted to limit the political privileges of the regional judicial courts, called *parlements,* staffed by the provincial nobility. The government introduced the labor tax, or *corvée,* and created monopolies over the production of gunpowder and salt. In the wake of his efforts to defuse religious tensions, however, the king was assassinated by a Catholic fanatic in 1610. His death left the throne to a 9-year-old male heir, **Louis XIII** (r. 1610–1643).

Cardinal Richelieu   During the minority of Louis XIII, his mother, Marie de Medici (d. 1642), appointed Armand Jean de Plessis, Duke de Richelieu (1585–1642), as principal advisor to the crown. This brilliant and shrewd Roman Catholic cardinal set about to strengthen the king's position within France and to enhance French power across Europe. **Cardinal Richelieu** assigned new government officials, called *intendants*, to each French province. These men served as the eyes and ears of the crown throughout the country, making sure that royal edicts were obeyed and taxes were collected fairly and efficiently. Richelieu also curbed the political autonomy of the Huguenots. He sent royal armies to occupy their strategic cities and abolished their separate law courts. He did not, however, interfere with the practice of their religion.

Read the Document

Richelieu on the Ancien Régime

on **MyHistoryLab.com**

On the international front, Cardinal Richelieu was convinced that the Catholic Habsburgs represented the greatest threat to France, and he assisted the Protestant states opposed to the Habsburgs during the final decade of the Thirty Years' War (1618–1648). In particular, Richelieu helped to fund the armies of King Gustavus Adolphus of Sweden (r. 1611–1642) in an effort to curb the ambitions of Habsburg Spain. Throughout his long tenure as chief minister (1624–1642), Richelieu embraced the principle of "reason of state" when formulating and implementing policy. The greater glory of France and the consolidation of royal power always superceded the interests of local officials, nobles, and even the international Catholic community.

The Personal Rule of Louis XIV

When Louis XIII died in 1643 at age 43, France was left with another child king, 5-year-old Louis XIV (d. 1715). Richelieu had died just five months before Louis XIII. The regency government set up to administer affairs during the new monarch's minority was led by another leading churchman, the Italian-born Cardinal Mazarin (1602–1661). Efforts to further Richelieu's state-building campaign involved the imposition of new taxes. In 1649 members of the Parisian nobility, led by the highest court of the land, the *Parlement* of Paris, refused to endorse a new round of taxation. Barricades were erected in the capital city, and Mazarin and the young king had to flee. The uprisings, collectively known as the **Fronde** after the slingshots used by street children, continued sporadically until 1652. Urban riots involving the poor and dispossessed so alarmed the aristocracy that they reaffirmed their support for the young king. Members of the Paris *Parlement* wanted a greater role in the formulation of royal policy, not the destruction of the existing social and political order.

□●⊢ Read the Document

Louis XIV Writes to His Son

on **MyHistoryLab.com**

Shocked by the actions of his leading subjects during the *Fronde*, Louis XIV worked throughout his long reign to transform the monarchy into the unchallenged center of political power in France. From the early 1660s until his death in 1715, he ruled without consulting a representative assembly. He made laws and appointments directly, and he built and repeatedly employed a large professional army of over 200,000 men.

Louis XIV   In this 1701 portrait of Louis XIV by Hyacinthe Rigaud, Louis XIV appears in his coronation robes projecting an image of wisdom, strength, and resolve. The portrait communicates the importance of divine-right monarchy to the stability of the kingdom. *Rigaud, Hyacinthe (1659–1743). Louis XIV, King of France (1643–1715) in royal costume. 1701. Oil on canvas, 277 × 194 cm. Louvre, Paris, France. Photo credit: Erich Lessing/Art Resource, NY*

In 1685 he transformed France into a confessional state by rescinding the limited toleration that the Edict of Nantes granted to the Huguenots in 1598. He also banned a splinter Roman Catholic movement known as Jansenism. **Gallicanism,** the idea that the French Catholic church should be a separate entity under the French crown within the Roman Catholic fold, gained increased support after 1650. The king's wish became the law of the land. Under Louis's careful guidance, France became Europe's premier political and military power during the second half of the seventeenth century.

Versailles and the Projection of Power   Constructed under the direction of King Louis XIV, the enormous Palace of Versailles was a powerful symbol of royal rule from 1682 until the start of the French Revolution in 1789. Located just 12 miles outside Paris, the property was first used by King Louis XIII as a small hunting lodge. Louis XIV committed vast resources to the construction of his new residence, employing architects, painters, decorators, and landscapers to create a palace and gardens of unrivaled scale and beauty. That Versailles was an open palace, missing the walls and battlements of medieval castles, testifies to the king's unique position in the country's political order. Construction and expansion of the palace began in 1669 and continued until Louis's death in 1715. Over 30,000 laborers were engaged in the project during the reign of the "Sun King," as Louis XIV was known. The palace could accommodate more than 5,000 people, and over 10,000 servants and soldiers were quartered in the nearby town of Versailles.

View the **Closer Look**

Versailles

on **MyHistoryLab.com**

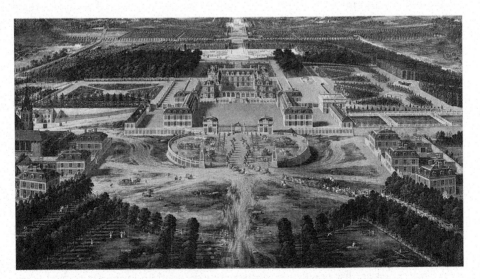

The Palace of Versailles   Built during the reign of Louis XIV, the gigantic Palace of Versailles conveys the power and opulence of French absolutism. Located a few miles west of Paris, the palace was the home of the French monarchs and the administrative center of the *ancien régime. Pierre Patel (1605–1676), "Birds Eye View of Versailles." Chateau de Versailles et de Trianon, Versailles, France. Copyright Giraudon/Art Resource, NY*

Louis XIV obliged the great nobles of the realm to spend much of the year at Versailles. This enabled the king to keep a close check on potential rivals while simultaneously denying his most powerful subjects opportunities to build independent support in the countryside. The nobility became servants of the crown at Versailles, and Louis's daily routine was carefully planned to take full advantage of this aristocratic entourage. Rising at 8:30 in the morning, Louis was bathed, dressed, and fed by those fortunate enough to be admitted into the royal bedchamber. At ten a.m. the royal party attended mass, and at 11 the king convened his various councils of state—foreign affairs, the military, finance, state, and religious affairs. A private dinner was usually served at one in the afternoon and after two the monarch would typically promenade in the palace gardens or hunt on the expansive grounds.

On these occasions even the most humble of the king's subjects could observe the court routine. Once again noble courtiers would compete with each other for the right to accompany the king, for it was in these informal settings that influence was won and lost. According to one participant, Louis de Rouvroy, Duc de Saint-Simon (1675–1755), "the frequent fetes, the private promenades at Versailles, were means on which the king seized in order to distinguish or mortify the courtiers, and thus render them more assiduous in pleasing him." More work or a social gathering would occupy the king until around ten in the evening, when a supper would be served to members of the royal family.

Royal palaces like Versailles—and monarchs built versions of the palace across Europe—were designed to showcase political power. Royal emblems and portraits of the monarchs filled the public spaces of the palace. On the ceiling of the magnificent Hall of Mirrors at Versailles, Louis commissioned paintings depicting the great events of his reign. He is portrayed as a Roman emperor, an expert administrator, and a military commander. In this imposing space the king would receive foreign ambassadors and other high dignitaries. It would have been impossible for the guest not to be impressed by the opulence and solemnity of the space. In choosing the sun as his official emblem, Louis XIV wished to evoke references to Apollo, the god of peace and the arts who was associated with the sun, while also emphasizing the sun's status as lifegiver. Royal complexes like Versailles served a variety of functions associated with a form of political control in which subjects would accept their place in a fixed social hierarchy.

Royal Bureaucrats   Louis XIV chose many of his most dedicated servants and officials from among the ranks of the middle class or bourgeoisie. These men of modest means were unlikely to build independent bases of power for themselves while serving the crown. Their success was based exclusively on loyal service to the king, and in the case of the *intendants,* they were regularly reassigned to new provinces to ensure their loyalty to the government at Versailles. The king's talented chief finance minister, **Jean-Baptiste Colbert** (1619–1683), encouraged the formation of new industries and adopted an unrelenting protectionist policy known as mercantilism. Under mercantilist practice, exports were expanded and imports curbed while the government protected French industries from foreign competition. By increasing the *taille* and better regulating its collection, Colbert gave the king the fiscal resources to pursue an ambitious military agenda (see Map 14-1).

MAP 14-1   Europe in 1714   At the end of the War of the Spanish Succession in 1714, Louis XIV was able to secure Bourbon control of the Spanish throne, but the French king failed to realize his territorial ambitions along the frontier with the Holy Roman Empire.

QUESTION: What territories did Louis XIV claim as part of France's "natural" eastern frontier?

The Wars of Louis XIV   Louis was a man of war, dedicated to securing what he defined as France's natural borders—the Pyrenees, the Alps, and the Rhine River. The king's many military campaigns led to the emergence of strategic alliances against France. Beginning in 1667 and continuing with little interruption until the end of Louis's reign, French forces attacked Spain's Belgian provinces (1667–1668), the United Provinces of Holland (1672–1679), and the free city of Strasbourg (1681). The latter assault eventually led to the exhausting 9-year War of the League of Augsburg (1688–1697) and pitted France against England, Spain, the United Provinces, and much of the Holy Roman Empire.

Finally, between 1700 and 1714, Louis pressed a claim on behalf of his grandson, Philip of Anjou (1683–1746), to the Spanish throne. The rival claimant was an Austrian Habsburg prince, and Louis feared Habsburg domination of the continent if the Austrian became king of Spain. Once again, a large coalition, including England, Holland, and the Holy Roman Empire, united against the French. During this long conflict, French resources were stretched to the limit, and English forces under the superior leadership of John Churchill, the duke of Marlborough (1650–1722), defeated a poorly organized and led French army in two decisive battles. The first took place at Blenheim in August 1704, and the second at Ramillies in 1706. Despite these setbacks, and in the face of increasing unrest at home, Louis XIV refused to concede defeat. Absent an organized political opposition in his absolutist state, his will again prevailed. At the end of the war Louis's nephew was recognized as Philip V of Spain (r. 1700–1746), although Spain had to cede its territories in Belgium and Italy to the Habsburgs and their allies.

By the time of Louis's death in 1715, France had suffered a series of agricultural disasters and a serious financial crisis. The worst years for the king's subjects were 1708 and 1709, as widespread famine and high taxes led to revolts throughout the country. Louis had lost the admiration of his people. He had failed to follow the Machiavellian and Hobbesian injunction to provide for the peace, security, and material improvement of his subjects. His successors continued to involve the country in a series of debilitating continentwide and imperial overseas conflicts against England, Austria, and Prussia during the eighteenth century. All of these conflicts led to a final reckoning for the monarchy in 1789.

Constitutionalism in England

The Early Stuarts   England followed a very different political path. The political and religious consensus that Queen Elizabeth I (r. 1558–1603) had established began to fray almost immediately after her death. The new monarch, James I, infuriated religious reformers. The reformers were convinced that the Church of England, with its reliance on bishops, elaborate rituals, and arbitrary religious courts, too closely resembled its discarded Roman Catholic predecessor. Their opponents called these would-be reformers Puritans. The Puritans attempted to use their influence in Parliament to force the king's hand. James and his successor, Charles I (r. 1625–1649), refused to make concessions, however, convinced that the Puritan demand for the abolition of the bishops would be followed by even more radical calls for the end of the monarchy.

When Charles succeeded his father in 1625, he attempted to strengthen the power of the monarchy along French lines. A protracted clash with Puritan members of Parliament led the king to dissolve the House of Commons in 1629. For 11 years Charles refused to call this representative assembly into session, leading thousands of disgruntled Puritans to strike out across the Atlantic for a new life in Massachusetts Bay colony. During the 1630s, crown revenues were raised by a variety of extraparliamentary means, and the Church of England further alienated members of the middle class and landed gentry.

Civil War   Full-scale civil war erupted in 1642 after the king unsuccessfully attempted to impose the Church of England's official prayer book on the Scottish

Presbyterian Church. The Puritan forces were led by the skilled military commander **Oliver Cromwell** (1599–1658). They repeatedly accused King Charles of taxation without the consent of Parliament, imprisonment of subjects without cause, and the illegal transformation of the Protestant Church of England into a replica of Roman Catholicism. The war continued intermittently until the Royalist supporters of the king were decisively defeated in 1649. Charles was executed, episcopacy was abolished, and the hereditary House of Lords was suspended. The country was then ruled as a semi-republican Protectorate under the heavy hand of

Read the **Document**

Cromwell Abolishes the English Monarchy

on **MyHistoryLab.com**

Cromwell as Lord Protector and the army leadership until 1660. During this period the Puritan leadership found itself unable to institute meaningful political reform, and Cromwell emerged as a de facto military dictator. Taxes escalated and general disillusionment with the Protectorate led to a restoration of the monarchy under Charles II (r. 1660–1685) in 1660.

Monarchy Restored   The civil war had resolved few of the main issues separating crown and Parliament. The period 1660 to 1688 was marked by ongoing constitutional debate over the limits of royal authority and the role of the two Houses of Parliament in the direction of national affairs. Charles II was a skilled political operative who, while envious of the power wielded by his cousin Louis XIV, was also a realist who acknowledged the historic role of Parliament in the political life of the kingdom. While sympathetic to the difficulties faced by England's small Roman Catholic minority (Charles declared himself to be a Catholic on his deathbed), the king refused to alienate his Protestant subjects by fighting for religious toleration.

His brother and successor was less adept at navigating the troubled waters of religious bigotry. King **James II** (r. 1685–1688) was a Roman Catholic in a Protestant country. His subjects were prepared to accept his inaugural pledge that he would not allow his religious preferences to influence his decisions as king of a Protestant nation. Unfortunately, their trust was almost immediately betrayed. James appointed Roman Catholics to leadership positions in the military and in the colleges at Oxford and Cambridge. He also tried to alter the process by which members of Parliament were elected from urban constituencies, and he attempted to secure religious toleration for his Roman Catholic subjects. In November 1688, just three years after James had assumed power, a group of aristocrats encouraged the king's Protestant daughter Mary and her husband Prince William of Orange to invade England on behalf of Protestantism and parliamentary government. James was accused of having attempted to abridge the rights of Parliament while forwarding a design to establish a French-style absolute monarchy.

Bloodless Revolution   In the aftermath of the successful invasion, James II fled to France, and William and Mary accepted the constitutional compromise influenced by the ideas of **John Locke** (1632–1704; see Chapter 15, "New World Views: Europe's Scientific Revolution"). A Bill of Rights, passed by Parliament and signed by William III (r. 1689–1702) and Mary II (r. 1689–1694) as joint monarchs, solidified the contractual nature of civil society. The Bill of Rights recognized the rights of the political elite to share in the kingdom's governance. Religious toleration for all Protestants who accepted the doctrine of the Trinity was secured in 1689, and king and Parliament agreed on an orderly mechanism for the peaceful succession of Protestants to the throne. While the Church of England continued to receive state support well into the nineteenth century and is still the official church of the English part of the United Kingdom, the business of government had taken a decisively secular turn in 1689.

Perhaps the clearest measure of this increasing secularization can be seen in the shifting precipitants to war. While conflicting religious outlooks had been at the heart of military confrontations in England for most of the seventeenth century, King William III engaged the enormous fiscal and military resources of England in a monumental struggle against Louis XIV's territorial ambitions. The eighteenth century would be marked by wars for empire and for trade, not for souls. In this area of human activity, religious belief was of lesser moment than the furs of North America, the sugar of the Caribbean islands, or the spices of India.

Wars of Empire and Global Markets

Beginning in the 1680s, the wars between France and the Grand Alliance in Europe involved a wider colonial dimension. In particular, the British repeatedly challenged French power in North America, the Caribbean, South Asia, the Mediterranean, and the Pacific. At the end of the War of the Spanish Succession in 1714, Britain acquired Nova Scotia, Newfoundland, and Hudson Bay territories from the French. They also received the strategic entrance to the Mediterranean at Gibraltar from the Spanish. British maritime supremacy, coupled with government support for trade and commerce, enabled this small island kingdom to become the dominant power in Europe during the second half of the eighteenth century. Whereas military conflict led to mounting debt and a weakened monarchy in France, in Britain the engagement of the aristocracy, the rising gentry, and the urban elite in the process of policymaking enhanced the power of the crown. In particular, greater access to political power strengthened the commitment of investors to fund the considerable cost of overseas warfare.

Commercial Conflict   By the start of the eighteenth century, Western Europe's colonial empires in the Americas and parts of Asia were firmly established. Non-Western peoples from Japan and the Indian subcontinent to West Africa and across the Atlantic in the Americas were forced to respond to the intrusive designs of the Europeans. Only China and Japan continued to rebuff Western efforts to secure uncontrolled trade relations. Elsewhere, the success of Western traders, settlers, and missionaries to extend their influence and to reduce the significance of cultural differences was without precedent. For good or ill, the world was becoming "Europeanized" by the eighteenth century, beginning a process that has continued with ever greater acceleration into our own day.

⊙–[Watch the **Video**
*Atlantic Connections: Sugar,
Smallpox, and Slavery*
on **MyHistoryLab.com**

In particular, overseas exploration, trade, and colonization won the enthusiastic support of Britain's political elite during the eighteenth century. This alliance of commercial capital and government military power facilitated the process of "making the world one" on European terms. Joint stock companies, the increased use of paper currency, sophisticated credit arrangements, and insurance plans all facilitated the movement of people and goods across the oceans. Beginning with the Treaty of Utrecht (1713), which ended Britain's participation in the War of the Spanish Succession, the boundaries of the respective empires were clearly established. A weakened Spanish monarchy reaffirmed its control over all of mainland South America, with the exception of Portuguese-held Brazil. Spain also held territory in Florida, Mexico, California, and the Caribbean islands of Cuba, Puerto Rico, and that part of Hispaniola that today is the Dominican Republic. Britain controlled the eastern coastline of North America together with the sugar-producing islands of Jamaica and Barbados. The French, despite their losses in the War of the Spanish Succession,

◉─⎾Watch the **Video**

Trading Empires in the New World

on **MyHistoryLab.com**

remained in possession of the lucrative sugar islands of Saint Dominique (modern Haiti), Guadeloupe, and Martinique. French traders also operated along the St. Lawrence River valley in New France, or Canada, at the mouth of the Mississippi around the city of New Orleans, and west of the Appalachian mountain range in North America. The Dutch, now pushed to the margins as a trading power in the Americas, still

The Fur Trade   A Native American hands a pelt to a European buyer. By 1700, the fur trade had decimated the beaver population in southern Canada and New England. *Fur traders and Indians: engraving, 1777.* © *The Granger Collection, NY*

ruled over Surinam (Dutch Guiana) in South America and a few Caribbean islands. The Dutch, French, and British also held lucrative trading stations along the west coast of India, and the Dutch had begun the conquest of the rich spice islands that today make up the Republic of Indonesia.

Global Clashes   Following mercantilist economic theory, colonies were valued mainly for their potential economic benefit to the home country. Each of the major powers prohibited rivals from trading with its colonies. While widespread smuggling persisted throughout the eighteenth century, colonial wars were normally fought to protect overseas markets and natural resources. The rivalry between the British and the French was especially bitter. Clashes along the lower St. Lawrence River valley, in the Ohio River valley, in the West Indies, and in India cultivated deep and lasting animosities. In addition to the War of the Spanish Succession (1702–1714), two mid-century clashes in central Europe had their counterparts in the colonies. The War of the Austrian Succession (1744–1748) and the Seven Years' War (1756–1763) drew the French and British overseas colonies into what were initially localized European conflicts. The War of the Austrian Succession began when King Frederick the Great of Prussia seized the province of Silesia from Austria's Empress Maria Teresa (r. 1740–1780). Britain, seeking to uphold the continental balance of power, supported Austria while the French, traditional enemy of the Habsburgs, sided with Frederick. During the war, French and British colonists clashed repeatedly in northern New England, New York, the Ohio River valley, the Caribbean, and India.

View the **Map**

The Seven Years' War

on **MyHistoryLab.com**

The decisive Seven Years' War actually began in the Americas in 1754, two years before the outbreak of hostilities in Europe. British colonials fought with the French and their Native American allies over lands deemed to be important in the lucrative fur trade. Confronted with about one and one-half million English colonists, the 90,000 French settlers desperately needed the assistance of their skillful Native American allies. When British Prime Minister William Pitt (1708–1778) decided that the defeat of France on the continent demanded a global strategy, he decided to send a fighting force of over 40,000 men to the colonies. It represented the largest army ever employed in colonial warfare up to that time. After initial setbacks, the British captured Quebec City in 1759 and soon won control over all French territory in Canada. The British navy also captured most of the French sugar islands in the Caribbean. In India, British Commander Robert Clive (1725–1774) won a key victory over the French in 1757 at the Battle of Plassey. In the aftermath the British secured control over the province of Bengal in northeast India. By the end of the conflict in 1763, French colonial trade had plummeted to a fraction of its prewar level, leaving Britain the undisputed leader in global commerce. In terms of mercantilist economics, Great Britain was now the predominant power in Europe.

Consequences for France   Louis XV ascended the French throne in 1715 at the age of 5, and he reigned for nearly 60 years until 1774. Like his predecessor

Louis XIV, the king claimed to rule by divine mandate, but the fiscal pressures on the government undermined royal authority. The crown wished to raise taxes to meet its mounting military obligations, but the 13 *parlements* refused to endorse any plan that would oblige the wealthy aristocracy to help reduce the national debt. All efforts to reform government finances failed, and by the early 1770s the king had become deeply unpopular. Louis's reputation for lavish spending at court and his involvement with a succession of young women further alienated his subjects. When he died in 1774, few of his subjects mourned his passing.

Central and Eastern Europe

Russian Absolutism   The dramatic overseas expansion of Europe's Atlantic kingdoms during the seventeenth and eighteenth centuries was matched by Russia's continental drive to the east. Beginning in the 1580s and continuing into the nineteenth century, Russian merchants, soldiers, adventurers, and political prisoners moved across the Ural Mountains. They gradually transformed Siberia, one of the world's key centers of mineral wealth and other natural resources. By the mid-eighteenth century, Russians had penetrated over 6,000 miles east of Moscow, first toward the fertile lands of the Ukraine and subsequently east toward the Pacific. The subjugation of Siberia alone was comparable in scale, economic impact, and strategic significance to contemporary Spanish, Portuguese, Dutch, English, and French incursions into the Americas. Siberia was a central feature of the conversion of a landlocked regime centered around Moscow into a powerful absolutist state under the leadership of the Romanov dynasty, which would rule Russia until 1917. By 1700 Russia had become the largest territorial kingdom on Earth.

Michael, the first Romanov tsar (caesar or emperor), was chosen by a group of leading nobles in 1613. They elected the 16-year-old grandnephew of Ivan the Terrible, the tsar who had ruled Russia with an iron fist from 1533 to 1584. Tsar Michael (r. 1613–1645) came to power after a period of civil unrest known as the Time of Troubles that had followed Ivan's death. Michael and his Romanov successors consolidated their power during the seventeenth century despite a number of unsuccessful revolts from the 1640s through the 1670s. Contacts with the West increased during the late seventeenth century, and when Peter I, "the Great" (r. 1689–1725), ascended the throne, the stage was set for a dynamic assertion of royal power and display.

Peter the Great   Peter I had traveled to Western Europe early in his reign, and he was deeply impressed by Western technology, military organization, and political practice. He invited numerous Western technicians and advisors to Russia and instituted government protection for new industries and commercial enterprises. The tsar insisted that his nobles become engaged in lifelong state service—either civil or military—and he created a system of bureaucratic advancement based on merit. Taxes imposed on the peasantry paid for the needs of the military, while serfs were assigned to work in state-owned factories and mines. When the leaders of the Russian Orthodox Church objected to the tsar's reforms, he attacked the church's wealth and replaced the Patriarch

Peter the Great A youthful Peter the Great appears in this portrait wearing armor. The image of determination and self-confidence enhanced his claims to absolute power.

📖 **Read the Document**

Peter the Great Correspondence

on **MyHistoryLab.com**

of Moscow, who had been the head of the church, with a new administrative office called the Holy Synod. Significantly, the leader of the Holy Synod was a lay official appointed by the tsar.

Military reform was a top priority for the energetic and ruthless tsar. Peter built a professional army of nearly 200,000 men armed with modern muskets and artillery. Engagements against the Ottoman Turks in lands adjacent to the Black Sea were unsuccessful, but after a protracted struggle (1700–1721) against Sweden, Peter secured control over the Baltic provinces of Estonia and Latvia. Confirming his gains in the Treaty of Nystad (1721), the tsar proceeded to build a new capital on the shores of the Baltic. This modern capital, called St. Petersburg, provided the Russians with an opportunity to imitate the contemporary Baroque building style of Western Europe. Peter's reforms cost money and lives. Taxes escalated fivefold during his reign, and tens of thousands died in his wars and in the building of St. Petersburg. The condition of the serfs became increasingly desperate. Serfs became the personal property of their lords, and the official distinction between a slave and a serf was ended.

Catherine the Great   Peter's male offspring predeceased him, and upon the tsar's death in 1725, Russia was subject to a period of serious political instability marked by palace coups and assassinations. In 1741 the tsar's youngest daughter, Elizabeth, ascended the throne. Elizabeth then named her nephew Peter her heir and chose an obscure German princess to be Peter's wife. Her name was Catherine, and when her weakling husband came to power in 1762, Catherine plotted his deposition and murder in collusion with a group of disgruntled military officers. With the support of aristocratic army leaders, Catherine ruled successfully until 1796. During the first decade of her reign, the empress corresponded with leading Enlightenment figures and made a range of cultural, educational, and legal reforms. But after a large revolt by

📖 **Read the Document**

Catherine the Great, Instructions for a New Law Code

on **MyHistoryLab.com**

Russian peasants in 1773 in which hundreds of influential landlords were slaughtered, Catherine's interest in reform waned. During the remainder of her reign, the condition of Russia's serfs became even more onerous even as their masters increasingly imitated the lifestyles of Western aristocrats. In 1785 Catherine extended the institution of serfdom into new areas of the empire and freed the nobility from all state taxes.

In foreign affairs Catherine was more successful than Peter the Great. The empress launched a war against the Ottoman Turks in 1768, and after six years of fighting, the Turks ceded to the Russians strategically important territories along the northern coast of the Black Sea and in the Balkans. Catherine also sought to extend Russia's frontier in the West. In a series of assaults against Poland, Russia joined with Prussia and Austria in three partitions that eventually wiped that large country off the map of Europe. When Catherine died in 1796, Russia had taken its place as one of the great powers in Europe.

Prussian Militarism   The hereditary rulers of Prussia first emerged in the German territory of Brandenburg during the early fifteenth century. The Hohenzollern family gradually added more lands to its realm. By the start of the eighteenth century, the Hohenzollern electors of Brandenburg (so called because they were one of the German ruling families who helped elect the Holy Roman Emperors) had become the kings of Prussia. They ruled over a variety of German duchies, bishoprics, counties, and provinces that constituted a total area second in size in Germany only to the Habsburg domains. During the mid-seventeenth century, Elector Frederick William (r. 1640–1688) built a strong and disciplined military establishment and a loyal administrative bureaucracy capable of uniting Prussia's disparate lands. Career officers replaced mercenary commanders, and troops were called up for specific tours of duty before returning to their agricultural pursuits. His successors, especially King Frederick William I (r. 1713–1740) and **Frederick II, "the Great"** (r. 1740–1786), were competent and dedicated rulers who built on these initial efforts. Service to the state became a central characteristic of Prussian aristocratic culture during this period.

View the **Image**

Prussian Soldiers

on **MyHistoryLab.com**

Frederick William I began the Prussian royal practice of always appearing in public in military dress, and he built the continent's third largest army (over 80,000 men). The king was reluctant to use this army, however, preferring to maintain this well-equipped fighting force as a symbol of Prussia's arrival as a great power. His son, Frederick II, demonstrated no such reservations about the employment of force. During the first two decades of his reign, he fought wars against a variety of coalition powers, including Austria, Russia, and France. During the Seven Years' War (1756–1763), Frederick's kingdom was almost destroyed. Only British financial support and Russian withdrawal from the coalition in 1762 saved Prussia. During the second half of his reign, Frederick introduced agricultural improvements, put an end to torture and capital punishment, and codified the laws of the realm. He also encouraged commerce and industry through the recruitment of enterprising refugees who were fleeing religious or political persecution in other European countries.

Europe's Declining Powers

Ottoman Decay   Russia's victory over the Turks in 1774 was symptomatic of the once mighty Ottoman Empire's long descent as a European power. At its height in the sixteenth century, the Ottoman-controlled territories stretched over an area larger than the Roman Empire. Süleyman I, "the Magnificent" (r. 1520–1566), ruled

View the Image

The Suleymaniye Mosque

on **MyHistoryLab.com**

over 14 million subjects at a time when there were only two and one-half million people living in Queen Elizabeth I's (r. 1588–1603) England. The Ottoman capital of Istanbul was much larger than any city in Western Europe, and the Ottoman bureaucracy—part of a vast military establishment—was both dedicated and competent. Ottoman military power was unrivaled in Western Europe until the late sixteenth century, when a combined Venetian, Spanish, and papal naval fleet defeated a Turkish force at the Battle of Lepanto in 1571. This military reversal was closely related to a wider set of economic, cultural, and political problems facing the Empire at a time when Western Europe was becoming innovative and aggressive (see Map 14–2).

After the death of Süleyman in 1566, Ottoman political leadership was compromised under a series of undistinguished sultans. These men failed to encourage change and risk-taking in agriculture, trade, or manufacture. In fact, manufacture declined sharply as the government curbed exports and as businessmen abandoned trade and instead purchased the right to collect taxes for the central government. The Empire's foreign trade gradually fell into the hands of Europeans resident in Istanbul. The Ottoman ruling elite lost touch with the concerns of the common people, as the bureaucracy, the military, and the sultan's courtiers preferred to exploit domestic producers. The dissemination of new ideas was hampered by conservative religious leaders who, for example, successfully destroyed an astronomical observatory on the grounds that human curiosity about divine secrets had caused a plague. Despite the

Key Developments in the Rise of the Early Modern European State

1558–1603	Reign of Elizabeth I
1598	King James I, *The True Law of Free Monarchies*
1618–1948	Thirty Years' War
1642–1949	English Civil War
1643–1715	Reign of Louis XIV
1689–1725	Reign of Peter the Great
1740–1786	Reign of Frederick the Great

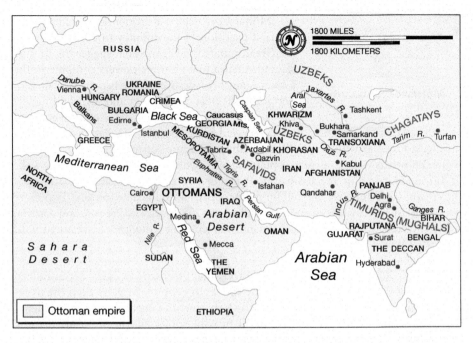

MAP 14-2   Ottoman Empire around 1600   The Ottoman Empire spanned from North Africa to the Caucasus and north to the gates of Vienna. As this map indicates, there were a number of powerful Muslim empires to the east of the Ottoman-dominated lands, but few rivaled Ottoman power, and none could match the level of often hostile contact the Ottomans had with Western Europe.

QUESTION: Why did the Habsburgs fear the Ottoman Turks?

brilliance of high culture at court and in the cities, a chasm developed between the elite ruling class and the producers of wealth. While Ottoman power remained formidable within a global context until the nineteenth century, Europe's rapid economic development after 1500 placed Ottoman accomplishments in an unfavorable light by the eighteenth century.

Poland: The Failure of Elective Monarchy   At the start of the eighteenth century, Poland was the third largest country in Europe (only France and Prussia were bigger). Situated between the expansive Russian empire to the east and the German states of the Holy Roman Empire to the west, Poland lacked any natural river or mountain frontiers. The Polish nobility clung to its privileged status, enjoying the right to elect the monarch through their control of the legislative assembly, or diet. Each new monarch found himself confirming and even expanding the legal privileges and exemptions of the aristocracy. Individual noblemen could even veto legislative initiatives in the diet. Rivalries among the nobility undermined the crown's ability to maintain state sovereignty in the face of aggressive neighbors, while waves of domestic anti-Semitism during the seventeenth century decimated the Jews who were among Poland's most enterprising communities.

View the **Image**

The Cake of Kings: First Partition of Poland

on **MyHistoryLab.com**

Military, political, and economic weakness led to the first partition of the country in 1772. Frederick the Great initiated the aggression, suggesting to Russia and Austria that all three powers combine in the assault against Polish sovereignty. Prussia took the important Baltic port city Gdansk and surrounding territory, which allowed the Prussians to unite east and west Prussia for the first time. Russia received a large portion of Poland's agricultural northeast together with one million inhabitants, while Austria seized the southern region known as Galicia, an area containing over two million inhabitants. In the wake of this initial carve-up, the aristocratic Polish diet voted to strengthen the powers of the crown. Unfortunately, the call for greater centralization came too late. Two more partitions, in 1793 by Russia and Prussia and in 1795 by Russia, Prussia, and Austria, led to the complete dissolution of Poland. The country would not be restored until the end of World War I in 1918.

Spanish Decline   The Spanish government remained largely decentralized even during the height of empire in the sixteenth century. In particular, the provinces of Catalonia and Aragon hesitated to support the expansionist ambitions of the Spanish crown that was resident in the province of Castile. Regional aristocratic assemblies called *cortes* enjoyed considerable autonomy. Despite these challenges, Philip II (r. 1556–1598) was able to employ the enormous revenues of Spain's New World empire in a monumental struggle against Protestantism in the Spanish-ruled Netherlands and in England. Both enterprises failed badly. The rebellion in the Netherlands began in the 1550s and dragged on for decades, while the massive Armada sent to destroy Queen Elizabeth I was turned away by storms and a smaller English force in 1588.

Philip's overextended government was bankrupt by the time of his death. Portugal, which had been united with Spain in 1580, reestablished its independence in 1640, and the northern Netherlands secured its freedom in 1648. During the long reign of the last Spanish Habsburg, the ineffective King Charles II (r. 1665–1700), France eclipsed Spain as Western Europe's major power. Charles, who had no children, even selected Louis XIV's grandson, Philip of Anjou (r. 1700–1746), to succeed him on the Spanish throne. At the end of the War of the Spanish Succession in 1714, Austria won control over most of Spain's Italian and Belgian possessions, while Britain secured the exclusive (and highly lucrative) right to transport African slaves to Spain's American colonies.

Although the new dynasty instituted significant military and administrative reforms, Spain never recovered its leading position in European affairs. The country's economic base remained too fragile. Relying for too long on revenues from its enormous New World colonies, the Spanish crown and the nobility failed to encourage agricultural innovations, industry, and internal commerce. The aristocracy and the church dominated Spanish society, and for these two groups manual labor and commercial enterprise were disreputable undertakings. An inventive and ambitious middle class, or bourgeoisie, never emerged as a vital force in early modern Spanish society. The French Bourbons may have replaced the Austrian Habsburgs on the Spanish throne in 1700, but the transition only temporarily arrested the process of political and economic slump that continued unabated well into the twentieth century.

The Dutch Republic   Alone among the major powers of Europe during the seventeenth century, the mainly Protestant Netherlands managed to combine a quasi-republican form of government and a small geographical base with great commercial power, political resilience, and artistic genius. All of this was achieved in the face of repeated aggression from its monarchical neighbors. The Habsburgs had controlled the Netherlands (Holland and Belgium) since the fifteenth century. In the sixteenth century it had become a vibrant manufacturing and trading center. However, during the reign of Philip of Spain, who had inherited the Netherlands from his father, the Emperor Charles V (r. 1519–1556), Holland's Calvinist minority used its naval resources to challenge the Spanish monopoly over the seaborne carrying trade. Philip responded by introducing the Inquisition accompanied by a large standing army, triggering a large-scale Dutch revolt against Habsburg rule. Once the seven northern provinces (Holland) had secured effective independence in 1609, a vibrant bourgeois republic of only one and a half million people—mostly urban dwellers—set out to dominate international shipping and manufacturing. The seventeenth century was the "golden age" of the Netherlands, as Dutch ships penetrated markets around the globe.

Under the leadership of a federal assembly, or States General, with the Princes of Orange as hereditary commanders or stadtholders, the Dutch replaced the Portuguese as Europe's main goods carrier to the Far East. Capturing the overseas spice trade propelled Dutch traders into the foreground of European commercial enterprise. Within 30 years of its founding, the **Dutch East India Company** was paying its investors healthy returns of 25 percent a year and more. In 1638 the Portuguese were expelled from Japan, and the Dutch replaced them as the only Westerners permitted to trade with the country. A small Dutch

Read the **Document**

Jan van Linschoten on Dutch Business in the Indian Ocean

on **MyHistoryLab.com**

colony was planted on the Cape of Good Hope in Southern Africa in 1652 as a supply point for ships headed to Asia. By the early eighteenth century, Dutch carriers enjoyed trading supremacy in the Indian Ocean and in the Far East. In addition to overseas trade, the Dutch also became Europe's most accomplished bankers and creditors, providing capital for many commercial and industrial ventures. Religious toleration throughout the provinces encouraged foreign investment in a wide range of business enterprises.

Despite these successes, the Dutch were unable to match their English competitors in terms of establishing permanent colonies throughout their global empire. The long and costly defensive wars against Louis XIV that began in the 1670s drained fiscal resources, and a comparatively small population base diminished the need for colonial settlements. Small Dutch colonies in North America and India could not withstand the intrusive power of the English. While they maintained their presence in Indonesia, the Dutch gradually lost their position as Europe's premier shipbuilders and traders under competitive pressure from larger neighboring kingdoms. By the 1720s, the Netherlands was no longer a major European power.

Austrian Habsburg Empire   After a century of struggle to return northern Germany to the Catholic fold, the Austrian branch of the Habsburg family accepted the autonomy of over 300 states within the Holy Roman Empire. The Treaty
of Westphalia, signed at the conclusion of the Thirty Years' War in 1648, reaffirmed
the Habsburgs as Holy Roman Emperors. But it was difficult for the emperor to coordinate policy over his multinational domains. A variety of languages, customs, and
cultures frustrated royal efforts to centralize government, even in the Habsburg hereditary lands of Austria and Bohemia. What kept the empire together was the threat
of a common enemy. The German, Czech, Magyar, Croat, Slovak, Slovene, Italian,
Romanian, and Ruthenian subjects of the Holy Roman Emperor struggled repeatedly
to roll back the Ottoman Turks who threatened the empire's southern flank. Emperor
Leopold I (r. 1657–1705) was able to strengthen his hold over his lands by defeating the Turks in a long war (1683–1689), and imperial forces subsequently extended
Habsburg authority as far south as the Balkan peninsula.

Under the terms of the Treaty of Radstadt (1714), Emperor Charles VI
(r. 1711–1740) secured additional territories in Italy and Belgium from Spain. However, Charles was obliged to spend much of his long reign winning the support of
Europe's other major powers to recognize the right of his daughter, Maria Teresa, to
succeed him. The document that was designed to guarantee a smooth succession was
known as the Pragmatic Sanction. Soon after the emperor's death, however, Frederick the Great of Prussia violated the agreement and invaded the Habsburg province
of Silesia. Maria Teresa successfully defended her title but failed to recover Silesia.
Both she and her son Joseph II (r. 1780–1790) worked diligently to bring unity and
consistency to the laws of the empire, but their scattered provinces remained divided
by a range of differences large and small. Although the dynasty survived until 1918,
the Habsburgs were never able to create a strong centralized monarchy capable of
coordinating the considerable material resources of the empire. Instead, the emperors
were constantly engaged in a series of negotiations with leaders of the constituent
kingdoms, especially Hungary. With a strong Muslim enemy to its east, the Habsburgs
never became a global colonial power.

KEY
QUESTION
REVISITED

**How do political
systems reflect the
structure of social and
economic life?**

The early modern European state-building enterprise involved,
first and foremost, a contest between landed aristocrats who
wished to preserve their local autonomy and new monarchs
committed to enhancing centralized power. For the monarchs
of the seventeenth and eighteenth centuries, royal control
over national churches, the building and equipping of standing
professional armies, the efficient collection of tax revenues,
the creation of bureaucracies whose members were dedi-
cated to the crown, and the formation of a system of rewards for loyal members of the
nobility all served to enhance the power of the national government. Most rulers aspired
to follow the model of French absolutism. In England, however, a form of limited monarchy
in which the aristocracy and the gentry participated in the political process set the stage
for unprecedented global power by the second half of the eighteenth century.

Throughout the course of this state-building enterprise, the condition of Europe's poor remained largely unchanged, with free peasants in Western Europe struggling to maintain a subsistence lifestyle. In eastern Europe, the expansion of serfdom meant that the lives of most of the population deteriorated sharply. As European monarchs successfully co-erced and co-opted the aristocracy to unite in defense of the traditional political hierarchy, new political forces were stirring in the cities, in the merchant houses, and in the overseas colonies. As we shall see in Chapter 17, "Rebellion and Revolution: American Independence and the French Revolution," the Old Regime was ill-equipped to confront these unprecedented challenges.

Europe's absolutist states were organized around the assumption that only the leader and his or her closest advisors were competent to manage the affairs of the country. Monarchy itself assumes the propriety of human inequality, privilege associated with birth, sacred status, and the purity and intelligence of the one against the sinfulness and incapacity of the many. Absolute monarchy infers that one individual alone has special access to an eternal set of rules governing society: no one has the right to challenge the ruler, even if that ruler violates his or her sacred trust. The political theory of absolutism was predicated on a very somber estimate of human nature and human potential. It also reflected the structure of much social and economic life in Europe. By the mid-eighteenth century, this centuries-old political system came under increasing scrutiny on both sides of the Atlantic, and the challenge had a good deal to do with the emergence of a more sanguine estimate of humans as rational beings. It also had much to do with the emergence of a more fluid and dynamic social and economic order, an order deeply at odds with traditional notions of hierarchy based solely upon heredity.

Key Terms

serfs, *p. 424*
absolutism, *p. 427*
St. Bartholomew's Day Massacre, *p. 427*

Fronde, p. 430
Dutch East India Company, *p. 445*

Activities

1. Compare the lives of seventeenth-century European aristocrats with the daily experiences and expectations of the peasantry.

2. Explain the rapid growth of Europe's population during the eighteenth century.

3. Describe the role of peasant women in the economic life of early modern Europe.

4. How did Europe's sixteenth-century wars of religion contribute to the formation of strong centralized states?

5. Describe the key steps taken by Louis XIV of France to build an absolutist state.

6. List the principal objectives of nations engaged in wars of empire.

7. Why was Peter I of Russia attracted by Western Europe, and how did he attempt to remold Russia along Western lines?

Further Reading

T. Blanning, *The Pursuit of Glory: Europe 1648–1815* (2007), an inclusive overview of the growth of monarchical states.

George Huppert, *After the Black Death: A Social History of Early Modern Europe* (2nd ed., 1998), a readable survey of the period.

Geoffrey Parker, *The Military Revolution: Military Innovation and the Rise of the West, 1500–1800* (1998), looks at the intersection between war, technology, and politics.

Peter Burke, *The Fabrication of Louis XIV* (1992), examines the construction of royal identity through art.

MyHistoryLab Connections

Visit **MyHistoryLab.com** *for a customized Study Plan that will help you build your knowledge of* The Early Modern State.

Questions for Analysis

1. Why did Domat advocate royal absolutism?

　　Read the **Document** On Social Order and Absolutist Monarchy, p. 427

2. Based on the letter to his son, what kind of ruler did Louis XIV seem to be?

　　Read the **Document** Louis XIV Writes to His Son, p. 430

3. Why did Cromwell abolish the monarchy?

　　Read the **Document** Cromwell Abolishes the English Monarchy, p. 435

4. How are sugar, smallpox, and slavery connected?

　　Watch the **Video** Atlantic Connections: Sugar, Smallpox, and Slavery, p. 436

5. What do Catherine the Great's *Instructions for a New Law Code* reveal about Russian society during the eighteenth century?

　　Read the **Document** Catherine the Great, *Instructions for a New Law Code*, p. 440

Other Resources from This Chapter

　　Read the **Document** Richelieu on the *Ancien Régime*, p. 429

　　View the **Closer Look** Versailles, p. 431

　　Watch the **Video** Trading Empires in the New World, p. 437

　　View the **Map** The Seven Years' War, p. 438

　　Read the **Document** Peter the Great Correspondence, p. 440

🔍 **View** the **Image** Prussian Soldiers, p. 441

🔍 **View** the **Image** The Suleymaniye Mosque, p. 442

🔍 **View** the **Image** The Cake of Kings: First Partition of Poland, p. 444

📖 **Read** the **Document** Jan van Linschoten on Dutch Business in the Indian Ocean, p. 445

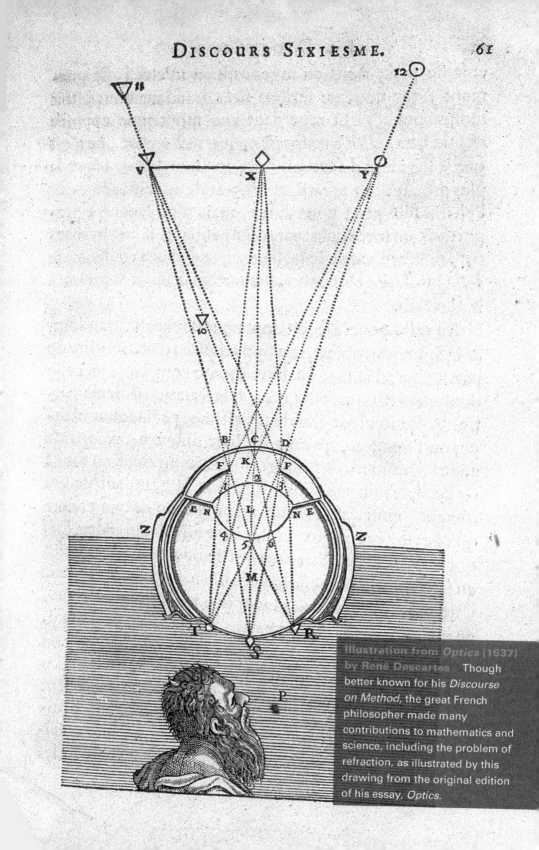

Illustration from *Optics* (1637) by René Descartes. Though better known for his *Discourse on Method*, the great French philosopher made many contributions to mathematics and science, including the problem of refraction, as illustrated by this drawing from the original edition of his essay, *Optics*.

15 New World Views: Europe's Scientific Revolution

((•—[Hear the Audio   Chapter 15 at MyHistoryLab.com

LEARNING OBJECTIVES

What were the main features of the Medieval world view? • What were the key ideas and movements that anticipated the new science? • Why did natural philosophers come into conflict with church authority? • What were the alternative modes of inquiry at the core of the scientific revolution? • How did the new science impact daily living? • How was political theory influenced by the scientific outlook? • How did church authorities respond to the implications of the new science? • How did popular superstitions test the limits of scientific rationalism?

Yet certainly there are diverse things in nature, that do much conduce to the evincing of a Deity, which naturalists either alone discern, or at least discern them better than other men.

—Robert Boyle

KEY QUESTION

How does the study of the natural world influence religious belief and the understanding of truth?

During the seventeenth century, the question just posed was much on the minds of educated Europeans. The Englishman Robert Boyle (1627–1691), for example, was easily one of the most distinguished experimental scientists of the second half of the century. Today he is remembered for his contributions to science in general and to chemistry in particular. However, Boyle's preeminent interest throughout his adult life was theology, not science, and in his will he left a considerable sum of money to endow academic lectures for the defense of Christianity against its opponents. Boyle was always troubled by what he saw as the "great and deplorable growth of irreligion, especially among those that aspired to pass for wits, and several of them too for philosophers." He was convinced that the most powerful way to counter this growing trend among educated people was to demonstrate the power and glory of God in His handiwork. The "Boyle Lectures" were designed to do just that.

It is easy to see why we find Boyle the scientist an attractive figure. The desire to know, to understand the unfamiliar, to be freed from mystery and arbitrary authority, is a commonplace of the modern human condition. We are restive with uncertainty, impatient with external authority, troubled by the unexplained. Over the past 400 years, Western culture has been interested, like Boyle, in observation, experiment, and analysis, with an approach to the natural world that we have come to call the scientific method. That approach has had a global reach. In terms of larger influences, the world's many peoples have embraced Western political forms and religious systems with varying degrees of enthusiasm, and Western economic models have had a significant impact outside of their European point of origin. Yet, virtually all cultures have eagerly embraced European science and the Western scientific outlook.

The modern world has become closely identified with science, with a belief in progress anchored in the advancement of this new way of thinking. Indeed, the foundations of our secular, materialist, and utilitarian culture are situated firmly in the Western scientific world picture. Over the past 400 years, Westerners have come to expect certain types of explanations and answers to their questions; today, the fruits of scientific investigation offer some of the most compelling responses to basic human needs. Optimism about the future, despite the horrors of two world wars and the threat of nuclear annihilation during the twentieth century, hinges largely on humanity's fascination with science and with the expectation that the fruits of scientific research will bring us closer to a mastery of the natural world. ■

The Medieval World View

Explanations, if they are to claim the assent of individuals, must provide both intellectual and emotional satisfaction. Humans respond best to interpretations of phenomena that fit closely with their dispassionate feelings about the structure or true nature of things. In the medieval West, where the influence of the church and its theological view of creation dominated local and national cultures, a picture of the cosmos where humans occupied center stage in a divinely ordered drama of salvation was accepted as simple common sense. The dignity of its subject matter made theology the foremost science on the eve of the Reformation in the early 1500s. First and last things, human purpose and destiny, the particulars of the divine mandate—all came under the heading of theological studies. Religion even shaped the contours of more mundane subjects, from diet and marriage relations to business and banking practices. Lending money at interest, for example, while common practice across late medieval Europe, was still considered a sin by church authorities.

The world of nature, in contrast, involved subjects of lesser moral significance, and religion offered little assistance in explaining how the physical world operated. Nature as experienced through the senses was, in the end, a place of trial and a temporary abode for sinful humanity. This lower world, while open to limited investigation, was also a region of perpetual change, decay, and death. In the Christian hierarchy of value that informed all things, the student of physical nature was inferior to the student of Scripture.

Church Authority and the Natural World Historians once criticized medieval church leaders for their lack of interest in the natural world, but such a position is no longer sustainable. Christian intellectuals of the High Middle Ages were genuinely interested in questions about the material environment, and the original Christian position on the nature of God's creation was central to explaining this curiosity. Unlike South Asian Hindus and Buddhists, who viewed the material world as ultimately illusory, and, unlike earlier pagans, who identified the gods with particular aspects of nature such as wind, fire, and water, Christians had a different view of the Deity and creation: God was separated from and superior to his material handiwork. Since God had created it, the material world was both good and open to human investigation.

The standard interpretation of God's command to Adam to fill, subdue, and have dominion over Earth was a powerful guide to daily Christian action. Nor did theological proscriptions hinder methodology. St. Thomas Aquinas (1225–1274) celebrated the place of reason in every compartment of human activity, and in his great poem *The Divine Comedy* Dante Alighieri (1265–1321) made the abuse of this God-given faculty subject to the severest eternal penalties. Rational inquiry was no threat to orthodoxy for most medieval thinkers, nor was the thoughtful assimilation of Arab and Greek contributions in mathematics, optics, and medicine. Aquinas built his reputation around an effort to demonstrate that Christians had nothing to fear from pagan thought.

Non-Western Contributions

Humans have always been curious about their habitat, and important intellectual breakthroughs had occurred in a variety of fields outside of the West long before a burst of activity took place in Europe beginning in the sixteenth century. Scholars in Muslim kingdoms had made essential contributions in geometry and algebra, in astronomy and in medicine, and in the overall observation of natural phenomena. Chinese advances in technology—from the simple wheelbarrow to navigational techniques, printing, and gunpowder—all were adopted by Europeans as examples of innovation based upon observation, experiment, and a desire to manipulate nature for human purposes.

Early medieval Europe had only a handful of scientific works from the ancient world, but eventually many Greek and Arab texts, copied and maintained by Byzantine and Muslim scholars, were translated into Latin. Most of the translations were made where Muslim and Christian cultures intersected in Spain and Sicily. By the thirteenth century, Christian scholars began to argue for the intrinsic value of investigations into natural phenomena. Churchmen, like Albertus Magnus (c. 1206–1280) at the University of Paris and the English monk Roger Bacon (c. 1214–1294), emphasized the propriety, if not the supreme value, of rational inquiry into God's creation. By the fourteenth century, leading European universities had established new professorships in astronomy, natural philosophy, and mathematics. Still, medieval science never disengaged itself from the theological underpinnings that informed its larger world view. These underpinnings would come under direct assault during the **Scientific Revolution** of the sixteenth and seventeenth centuries.

An Intimate Creation

Medieval thinkers saw the cosmos as limited in scale, hierarchical in structure, and monarchical in leadership. It was firmly under the providential direction of an active God, the biblical king of kings, whose knowledge and power were unlimited. The accepted picture, which most educated persons embraced because it reflected observable forces in nature, placed sinful humans and their environment at the center of a divine but ultimately mysterious creation. Building on a combination of Christian teaching, theories articulated by Aristotle (384–322 B.C.E) and further refined by the Greco-Egyptian mathematician Ptolemy (c. 90–168), the medieval cosmology comforted people whose lives were buffeted by hardships in an environment where material want was a constant close companion. Animated by angels, spirits, and the workings of unmerited divine grace, the entire physical universe was alive with energy and activity. The activity of all phenomena could be traced, in the end, to the immediate power of a God who micromanaged his handiwork. Just as the ancient Greeks believed that the god Apollo drove the sun across the sky in his chariot, so, too, medieval Christians witnessed the hand of God in events both mundane and exceptional.

The Authority of Aristotle Church authorities found much to admire in the cosmic speculations of the pagan Aristotle, not least because this Greek thinker argued that everything in nature had an individual purpose, or *telos,* that directed objects to move in certain ways. Before the investigations of the seventeenth century, educated Europeans assumed that a body remained in motion only so long as a mover was impelling it. The first or prime mover, of course, was God, but unseen hands or key intermediaries were required for the moment-by-moment action of bodies throughout the cosmos. The four elements that made up the accessible natural world—earth, water, air, fire—each had properties conducive to particular ends. For example, in the Aristotelian cosmology or world view, heavy objects made of earth naturally sought their rest at the center of the universe. Thus stones, because they are heavy, seek their repose on Earth's surface, and since the exceptionally heavy Earth did not maintain properties tending toward motion, this special planet served as the focal point of every other object.

The sun, the moon, and the other planets all revolved in perfect concentric circles around Earth, the human home. Many Christians believed that the planets, kept in motion by the labors of angels, influenced everyday lives. The planet Venus, for example, was thought to affect lovers by a special power transmitted through invisible rays. Humans might learn something about the set of physical laws that governed the region below the moon (sublunary sphere), but the larger sphere that lay above the moon (superlunary) was not subject to investigation. There, an unapproachable physical reality—a fifth element, or **quintessence**—informed the laws of motion. According to Aristotle, then, creation was dualistic at its core, with the larger portion of physical creation forever beyond human understanding. This was yet another reason, he believed, that humans should not place excessive faith in "natural philosophy," as it was known. In a cosmos informed by purpose and value, the real goal of humans was to seek the higher realm, the abode of the heavenly bodies and of the divine home itself.

Anticipating the New Science

The Aristotelian-Ptolemaic-Christian picture of the cosmos was, for almost 2,000 years, a fairly obvious and natural way of looking at observable data. After all, the sun does appear to be in motion, while no one can actually feel or experience Earth's orbit. A great conceptual and intellectual hurdle, what the modern historian of science Herbert

Butterfield once called "a transposition in the mind," was required before the modern explanation for the motion of heavenly bodies was established. Fundamental shifts in how a civilization views its place in creation do not occur suddenly, and it is fair to say that in the year 1600, despite the challenges posed by a handful of thinkers who called themselves natural philosophers, most people, even educated people, continued to accept the Aristotelian–Ptolemaic model as the most coherent explanation of observed phenomena.

This should not surprise us, especially given the deep religiosity of Europeans and the ongoing power of state authorities to coerce the unorthodox. Most countries did not enjoy genuine religious toleration until the start of the nineteenth century. Despite this serious handicap, however, by 1700 a new, less anthropomorphic or human-centered, world picture had taken hold. Social, cultural, and intellectual developments helped to set the stage for this monumental challenge to the medieval world view, fostering dissatisfaction with explanations offered solely on the grounds of tradition and ancient authority.

Renaissance Contributions   As we saw in Chapter 13, "Reformation, Religious Wars, and National Conflicts," Renaissance humanists had successfully promoted a naturalistic understanding of and appreciation for the human body, and their focus on perspective in art, where natural objects are represented on a plane surface, contributed to a more realistic rendering of the natural environment on canvas. Painters and sculptors were among the first to question established authority and to call for a more systematic observation of nature. In addition, sixteenth-century Europe's growing urban population fostered an innovative and risk-friendly approach to commercial undertakings, while transoceanic explorers exhibited a sense of curiosity about the unknown world that emboldened investigators in other areas of inquiry. Finally, the problem-solving approach of medieval artisans and craftsmen nurtured a basic interest in observation and inventiveness in the service of labor-saving devices. From windmills and plows to horseshoes and weapons, the practical labor of people who measured and mastered small corners of the natural environment promoted interest in explaining the natural world.

Voluntary Associations   Beginning in the sixteenth and seventeenth centuries, new institutions and associations began to emerge that contested the intellectual monopoly that the church and Europe's few universities had enjoyed for so long. Learned societies were founded in several capital cities; normally sponsored by wealthy patrons and attracting the educated urban middle class, their inquiries focused on the utilitarian aspects of how nature worked. England's **Royal Society** for Promoting Natural Knowledge (1662) and the *Academie des Sciences* in Paris (1666) were leaders in what had become a Europe-wide trend by the early eighteenth century. Some of the members of these organizations were also associated with an older magical and alchemical tradition. Astrologers, village "wise men," and alchemists who worked with herbs, metals, and powders all believed that nature was an organized system and that uncovering its secrets would produce practical advantages. Working out of their homes or studios on a part-time basis, natural philosophers acquired greater social prestige as the seventeenth century progressed, and more educated Europeans joined the quest for new knowledge.

Expanding Literacy   Much of the intellectual ferment after 1500 was due to the simple expansion of literacy and the growth of a reading public. Encouraging literacy was a key goal of the early Protestant reformers; if nothing else, the Reformation represented a massive dissent from religious authority. While rates of literacy were highest in Renaissance Italy during the early sixteenth century, Protestant England and the Netherlands moved ahead after 1600. English Puritans in Massachusetts and Connecticut placed a premium on education and literacy, while in eighteenth-century Prussia and Austria, the government sponsored experiments in primary education. The diffusion of new ideas in books, almanacs, journals, newspapers, and broadsheets was extensive in many urban settings, despite the continuing censorship of church and state. New knowledge could be disseminated quickly thanks to the printing press, making Western Europe arguably the most literate civilization on Earth after 1700.

Recalling Plato   One more variable, again originating in ancient Greece, profoundly influenced the unfolding of the Scientific Revolution. In their recovery and dissemination of ancient texts, Renaissance scholars in Italy, such as Marsilio Ficino (1433–1499) and Pico della Mirandola (1463–1494), had developed a strong appreciation for Plato's (c. 427–c. 347 B.C.E.) notion of a realm of ultimate reality, one located beyond everyday sensory appearances and situated in the world of forms and ideas. This invisible reality was thought to be simple, rational, and comprehensible. For scientific thinkers, the possibility that universal **laws of nature** lay within the grasp of human reason was enormously liberating. The belief that nature, once understood, might be manipulated for human good proved to be an enormous spur to the expansion of natural philosophy, alchemy, and even astrology.

New Directions in Astronomy and Physics

Ironically, the Polish mathematician and astronomer who first seriously challenged the Aristotelian–Ptolemaic model of the cosmos was also a Roman Catholic priest. After studying at the University of Krakow in Poland and in Renaissance Italy, **Nicholas Copernicus** (1473–1543), possibly influenced by neo-Platonic ideas, expressed serious concerns about the mathematical complexity of the Ptolemaic system. In particular, Ptolemy had accounted for the apparent irregular motion of some heavenly bodies by adding a series of additional mini-circles to the main path of each planet as it revolved around the sun—orbits within orbits, in effect. Copernicus insisted that these epicycles cluttered a cosmic order, which, if Plato were to be trusted, was supposed to be a work of simplicity and harmony. Copernicus was not the first to raise objections. The fifteenth-century churchman Nicholas of Cusa (1401–1464) had suggested that the world might be in motion, and the ancient Greek thinker Aristarchus of Samos (c. 310–230 B.C.E.) had proposed a **heliocentric** (sun-centered) model of the universe.

Reaffirming this bold conceptual leap, Copernicus placed the sun at the center of the universe and then attempted to assemble the mathematical proofs he needed to support a hypothesis that defied common-sense evidence.

View the **Closer Look**

The Sciences and the Arts

on **MyHistoryLab.com**

Challenging the Church   In 1543, as the first shock waves of the Protestant Reformation countermined centuries of church influence on the theological front, Copernicus published his groundbreaking *On the Revolutions of the Heavenly Orbs.*

☐●⊦ **Read** the **Document**

On the Revolutions of the Heavenly Spheres

on **MyHistoryLab.com**

Suddenly, the church was confronted with a profound dissent on matters involving the structure and operation of God's handiwork. The dissent was every bit as serious as the Lutheran and Calvinist challenge to the definition of what constitutes the true church. Just as a Catholic monk—Luther—had repudiated the apostolic and monarchical authority of the pope, now a Catholic priest who was highly respected for his mathematical skills was attempting to de-center humanity and make Earth just another planet among many, all in orbit around a fiery lantern. Biblical authority employed in the defense of the Aristotelian–Ptolemaic model of the universe now came under close and damaging scrutiny by men who wished to uncover nature's rudimentary elegance.

Tycho Brahe and Johannas Kepler   The first empirical evidence in support of the Copernican theory came, surprisingly, from a man who adhered to the

The Copernican Universe   This seventeenth-century Dutch engraving illustrates Copernicus's revolutionary "heliocentric" theories, which placed the sun—rather than the Earth—at the center of the universe.

older Aristotelian–Ptolemaic model. The Danish astronomer **Tycho Brahe** (1546–1601), working for over 20 years from an observatory on the island of Hven in the Baltic, which was paid for by the king of Denmark, collected an enormous volume of astronomical data on the movements of the heavenly bodies, including the planets. His student **Johannas Kepler** (1571–1630) used Brahe's observational data to demonstrate that the planets moved not in perfect circles, as Aristotle and even Copernicus believed, but in **ellipses,** following irregular velocities depending on the planet's distance from the sun. Kepler was a deeply mystical man and a product of the neo-Platonic tradition, which saw nature as a single explanatory system. At one point in his career he served as court astrologer and mathematician to the Holy Roman Emperor Rudolf II (1576–1612), one of Europe's leading patrons of the occult. Like so many other early scientists, Kepler was convinced that the language of nature was mathematics and that humankind had a religious duty to investigate the world machine. What eluded him in his major work, *The New Astronomy* (1609), was a plausible explanation for what kept the planets in their respective orbits. Kepler died in obscurity, reduced to telling fortunes for his income while simultaneously laboring on the frontiers of modern science.

Galileo's Breakthrough   **Galileo Galilei** (1564–1642) was a contemporary of Kepler who employed the newly invented (c. 1608) telescope and mathematics to confirm the Copernican heliocentric theory. He wrote his major statement on the subject, *Dialogue on the Two Great Systems of the World* (1632), in Italian, not Latin, and dedicated it to the pope. Like the Protestant Kepler, the Roman Catholic Galileo believed that the Platonic conception of a world of universal truth lay close at hand. He was also convinced that mathematical expression was the appropriate language for investigating the natural world. As an experimental scientist whose first interest was the motion of bodies, Galileo's major contribution to physics involved his discovery of the **law of inertia.** The established theory of dynamics claimed that the natural state of all bodies was at rest and that motion was due to an agent impelling a body. Galileo insisted that there was no natural state; if a body was in motion, it would remain in motion until another force deflected it. Working over a long career before he was silenced by the church, Galileo's contributions were varied; employing the telescope, for example, he observed the rough surfaces and mountains on the moon and spots on the sun, and discovered three moons around Jupiter. In 1610 he published *The Starry Messenger,* which provided empirical evidence for his case that the moon was not the perfect sphere that the Aristotelians posited, but instead a body whose rough surface, filled with craters and mountains, was not unlike the face of Earth.

◖ View the **Image**

Galileo's Views of the Moon

on **MyHistoryLab.com**

▢◖ Read the **Document**

Letter to the Grand Duchess Christina

on **MyHistoryLab.com**

Galileo overthrew the medieval hierarchy of the heavens and the incorruptibility of so-called superlunary matter that supposedly lay above the moon. The telescope did not lie, and according to *The Starry Messenger,* "truly demonstrated physical conclusions need not be subordinated to biblical passages." Galileo

Galileo A true "Renaissance man," Galileo Galilei excelled in many fields, but made his most lasting contributions in science and physics. This famous portrait by Giusto Sustermans captures the haunted expression that Galileo may have worn in his later years, when he was persecuted for his defense of heliocentrism. *Justus Sustermans (1597–1681), "Portrait of Galileo Galilei." Galleria Palatina, Palazzo Pitti, Florence, Italy. Nimatallah/Art Resource, NY*

was not a modest man, but in his efforts to understand the movement of bodies through the application of mathematics, especially in statics and dynamics, his labors complemented the efforts of Kepler to establish a single system of physical laws for the terrestrial and celestial realms.

Newton's Orderly Universe The capstone to the flurry of work on physics and mechanics occurred when an English professor of mathematics at Cambridge University offered a compelling physical explanation of the heliocentric theory. **Isaac Newton** (1642–1727) was a devout Christian who shared a strong interest in the study and explanation of Scripture with the philosopher John Locke (1632–1704). Both men belonged to the Royal Society for the Advancement of Knowledge, and both approached the study of nature as an exercise of Christian piety. Newton's **law of universal gravitation** demonstrated that all bodies in motion were intimately connected. His main work, *The Mathematical Principles of Natural Philosophy*, was first published in Latin in 1687. He introduced and clarified the role of gravity and motion in all aspects of physical creation, offering answers to the key issues in astronomy and physics that scholars had debated since Copernicus. His picture of the forces in play throughout the cosmos remained central to physics until the contributions of

Read the Document

Isaac Newton, from Opticks

on **MyHistoryLab.com**

View the Image

Newton's Opticks

on **MyHistoryLab.com**

Albert Einstein (1879–1955) in the early twentieth century. Newton attributed the presence of gravity to God's eternal power. His great breakthroughs were palatable to men of faith largely because in Newton's world machine, God was constantly tending to his creation. In a letter to a friend, Newton affirmed that the state of the heavenly bodies can only be explained by reference "to the counsel and contrivance of a voluntary agent." In 1705 Newton became the first scientist to be knighted by an English monarch, thus enhancing the role of the specialist academic in the broader cultural life of the nation.

Sir Isaac Newton Newton was appointed Lucasian Professor of Mathematics at Cambridge University before he was 25 years old. He made original contributions in mathematics, optics, physics, and astronomy, but like his friend John Locke, he was also deeply interested in the study of Scripture. *Sir Godfrey Kneller, Sir Isaac Newton, 1702. Oil on canvas. The Granger Collection*

New Approaches to Truth

Alternative modes of inquiry or methodology were also key components of Europe's Scientific Revolution. Whereas Aristotle had assumed that a purpose, or *telos,* was inherent in all physical and spiritual matter, the temper of Renaissance skepticism was unwilling to rest on the authority of the ancients, no matter how exemplary their contributions had been to Western thought. Talented amateurs began to investigate the practical application of natural phenomena. A more systematic approach to scientific inquiry, one devoid of respect for precedent, reputation, or grand general systems, took hold outside the walls of the medieval university, where the emphasis on tradition and hallowed authority remained firmly entrenched.

Francis Bacon   Leadership emerged from some unlikely quarters. In early seventeenth-century England, an ambitious and grasping high government official, **Francis Bacon** (1561–1626), popularized the experiential and collaborative outlook. In *The Advancement of Learning* (1605) Bacon offered a sharp critique of the old medieval scholastic method and the standard pedagogy of the universities. Urging his contemporaries to look into the nature of things themselves without respect for tradition, Bacon wished to master nature to improve the human condition. He was convinced that the sole end of scientific investigation was the enrichment of human life in concrete, even quantifiable terms. Much enamored of what later generations would label technology, Bacon held that improvements in this field could only be secured by rigorous induction, working from particular examples and experiments, and avoiding grand generalizations. He offered a method of inquiry based firmly on careful collection and observation of empirical data together with a strong commitment to collaborative work and peer criticism. His ideal society, described in *The New Atlantis* (1627), placed

[📖] **Read** the **Document**

Francis Bacon, from Novum Organum

on **MyHistoryLab.com**

Title Page from *Novum Organum* Title page from *Novum Organum* (1620) by Sir Francis Bacon. Bacon established the principles of the "scientific method," placing induction and observation ahead of traditional methods of scientific reasoning. The illustration on the title page shows a ship striking out for the unknown territories seeking, as did Bacon, for a new understanding of the natural world.

equal value on the work of manual laborers and highly educated theoreticians. Both contributed to the "relief of man's estate."

René Descartes In France the brilliant Catholic philosopher and mathematician **René Descartes** (1596–1650) sought to bypass the bitter theological controversies of the day by focusing on a method of inquiry that began with rigorous **skepticism** and strict reliance on reason. Perhaps more than any other person, Descartes helped to forge an understanding of nature as mechanism and of God as the supreme artisan who worked within the boundaries of mathematical laws and rational exposition. In his influential *Discourse on Method* (1637) Descartes called upon his contemporaries to scrutinize all past and current claims to truth. Questions sublime and mundane were equally open to the new mode of inquiry. For Descartes—whose important contributions to mathematics, optics, and analytic geometry distinguish him from gentleman amateurs like Bacon—the universe was analogous to a machine that operated according to inflexible principles. The key to genuine understanding, he felt, centered on the discovery of general laws revealed through mathematics in alliance with logical deduction. Clear and distinct ideas were the building blocks of knowledge in every compartment of life. Truth about the world and humankind's place in it could be extracted from the study of God's handiwork in addition to or in place of his written word.

View the **Image**
Descartes' View of the Universe
on **MyHistoryLab.com**

Theory and Application

Science involved much more than signal breakthroughs in astronomy and physics. More terrestrial concerns, especially those related to human health and longevity, had the greatest impact on the largest number of people during the seventeenth and eighteenth centuries. For the people of sixteenth- and seventeenth-century Europe, food and nutrition stood at the top of the basic needs list, as they had since time immemorial, and it was here that Bacon's counsel was followed to good effect.

Food Supplies and Mortality Approximately 60 million people were living in Europe in 1500, and this total grew slowly to around 110 million by 1700.

The latter figure represented about one-fifth of the world's overall population. Before 1500, indeed ever since the calamity of the Black Plague of the 1340s, Europeans rarely produced more food than they needed for survival, and in the sixteenth century Europe's economy was overwhelmingly agricultural. It was a fragile foundation; epidemic disease destroyed communities and ravaged countries well into the 1700s. Italy, Germany, Spain, and England all suffered outbreaks of plague during the 1600s, and every European state wrestled with periodic crop failures and the resulting malnutrition and even starvation.

Indeed, the expectation of severe want was a constant of human life, something that most people experienced during their normal lifetime. Lowered resistance to disease brought on by poor or inadequate diet was compounded by the depredations of opposing armies that tended to live off the land as they crisscrossed the countryside. Further, Europe's armies had more deadly military hardware thanks to innovations in cannon and rifle manufacture. Placed in the hands of larger armies, the scale of battlefield casualties increased. And finally, global climate patterns changed. From Beijing to Berlin, cooler temperatures and wetter summers prevailed. This "little ice age" of the late sixteenth and early seventeenth century may have reduced average temperatures by 1 degree centigrade. Such a shift would have abbreviated the typical growing season by three to four weeks, while also reducing the maximum altitude at which crops would ripen by some 500 feet. The result was a smaller crop yield and additional hardships for growing families.

The overall result was, from a modern perspective, a life of enormous hardship, dearth, and, comparatively speaking, brevity. Few people survived into their fifties, while poor diet meant that small stature and a generally debilitated physique were the lot of older peasants across Europe. Infant mortality rates were roughly 25 percent before the first year of life. Short life spans were a worldwide phenomenon: in 1500 the overall life span of European and non-European peoples averaged in the mid-twenties.

Agronomy and Land Management

Enhancing the quality and length of life began with improvements in the quantity and quality of food. Once agriculture began to orient itself toward production for urban and overseas markets, research and innovative experiment started to make significant headway. Improved animal husbandry, the selective breeding of domesticated animals, draining and reclamation of marginal lands, bigger farms, better seed, improved plows, and the widespread employment of wage laborers all facilitated the growth of output. This was especially the case in the Netherlands, in England, and to a lesser extent in France. The consolidation of small, inefficient farms often meant additional hardship for the peasants who lost their own farms and became employees of a market-oriented landowner. However, increased output at least reduced the frequency and severity of crop failures from weather and blight. By the eighteenth century, the introduction of turnips, clover, and legumes improved the supply of fodder, allowing farmers to maintain more food-producing animals over the long winter months. The new crops also returned precious nitrates to the soil, which increased its fertility and enabled peasants to

◉ **Watch** the **Video**

The World in 1700—Part 1

on **MyHistoryLab.com**

◉ **Watch** the **Video**

The World in 1700—Part 2

on **MyHistoryLab.com**

abandon the practice of leaving parts of their land fallow for an entire growing season. The widespread acceptance by European farmers of the American potato that began in the seventeenth century also enhanced caloric intake substantially. This allowed overall agricultural output to keep pace with Europe's expanding population.

Medical Thought and Training   Another human science that the new method of study influenced was biology. Renaissance painters were careful students of human anatomy, but strong religious injunctions against desecrating the material temple of the soul after death hampered knowledge about how the internal body operated. As in physics and astronomy, ancient Greek authority dominated medical thought and practice. Galen (c. 130–c. 201), the foremost medical authority of the ancient world, had dissected animals and studied human skeletons in an effort to explain the workings of the human body. His conclusions lay at the core of university medical training well into the seventeenth century. Key to Galen's system was the concept, based on Aristotle, that the human body consisted of four fundamental elements or humors (blood, choler, phlegm, and black bile). Sickness was rooted in an imbalance of these elements. The standard curative practice involved various purges, including bloodletting, designed to bring these elements into balance. As might be expected, recovery rates were not high. Galen also held that the human body had two kinds of blood. One ran from the liver through the veins to all parts of the body and supplied nutrients, and the other flowed through the arteries to enliven or vivify the body.

Formal medical education at the university level normally involved a professor of anatomy reading from Galen's works, or notes based on Galen, while a humble surgeon—usually trained as a barber—dissected the cadaver to confirm the Galenic principles. The professor himself would never stoop to dissect a body, and students of medicine would also often avoid it. The seventeenth-century English philosopher John Locke, who held an advanced medical degree from Oxford University, shared this disdain. Like so many of his contemporaries, he distinguished between manual labor and true intellectual work. It was an age-old attitude.

New Practitioners   Breaching the social divide separating the doctor from the barber-surgeon, however, a handful of medical practitioners across Europe eagerly embraced both physical and mental production. The maverick German physician and alchemist **Paracelsus** (1493–1541) had experimented with chemicals in lieu of purges to cure common illnesses, but the medical establishment sharply criticized his methods. Those who dared to challenge the ancient texts slowly

View the **Image**

First Printed Medical Text

on **MyHistoryLab.com**

made headway against this powerful opposition. Ironically, inhumane developments in military technology furthered their efforts. The gruesome transformation of warfare made possible by the widespread use of artillery and guns enhanced the value, if not the ability to cure, of the physician and surgeon.

In Belgium the surgeon **Andreas Vesalius** (1514–1564) called for rigorous anatomical investigation in his precedent-setting book, *The Structure of the Human Body* (1543). This work contained the first set of modern anatomical drawings available for students of medicine. Subsequently, the Englishman **William Harvey** (1578–1657), who, like Vesalius, Galileo, and Copernicus, had studied at the University of Padua

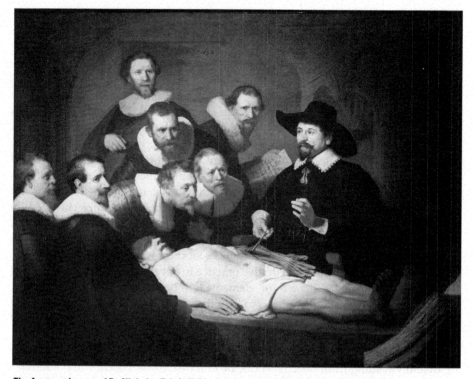

The Anatomy Lesson of Dr. Nicholas Tulp **(1632) by Rembrandt van Rijn** Anatomical training became an important feature of medical education during the seventeenth century. Physicians increasingly recognized the value of direct observation in the treatment of illness. *Rembrandt van Rijn (1606–1669). "The Anatomy Lesson of Dr. Tulip." Mauritshuis, The Hague, The Netherlands. SCALA/Art Resource, NY*

in Italy, discovered the circulation of the blood and the major function of the heart thanks to the invention of the microscope. The historian William McNeill believed that the microscope led to discoveries like microorganisms in water that were just as surprising as Galileo's identification of moons around Jupiter. Harvey approached the heart as a sophisticated mechanism, and the microscope enabled him to detect the vessels through which the blood flowed. Clinical observation and prolonged experiment, together with advances in technology, transformed the human body into a rational and comprehensible machine not unlike the cosmos in its entirety. At the close of the seventeenth century, Robert Boyle dismissed Galen's theory of the four bodily humors. Boyle argued that everything in the material world consists of tiny particles that behave in a regular, predictable fashion. Changes in the particles, not invisible spirits, spurred changes in matter. The medieval consensus, with its intelligent spirits and angelic influences, was being reduced to mere matter in motion.

Read the **Document**

William Harvey, Address to the Royal College of Physicians

on **MyHistoryLab.com**

View the **Image**

Jewish Medical Text by Tobias Cohen

on **MyHistoryLab.com**

Major Contributions to the Scientific Revolution

1543	Copernicus, *On the Revolutions of the Heavenly Orbs*
1605	Francis Bacon, *The Advancement of Learning*
1609	Johannas Kepler, *The New Astronomy*
1610	Galileo, *The Starry Messenger*
1632	Galileo, *Dialogue on the Two Great Systems of the World*
1637	Descartes, *Discourse on Method*
1687	Isaac Newton, *The Mathematical Principles of Natural Philosophy*

Politics as Science

The skepticism, empiricism, and rationalism that marked the investigation of nature after 1500 found its counterpart in the political world as Renaissance authors began to look anew at the constitutional compromises of the late medieval period. As we read in Chapter 14, "The Early Modern State," few rulers wielded effective centralized control over their respective territories during the Middle Ages. Allegiance and resentment centered on the village, the manor, and the city, as taxes and labor obligations originated with local elites. Niccolo Machiavelli's *The Prince* (see Chapter 13, "Reformation, Religious Wars, and National Conflicts") was informed by the author's deep sense of frustration over Italy's lack of political unity. Drawing conclusions from an acute observation of contemporary life, *The Prince* ignored traditional moral and religious justifications for the exercise of political power, arguing that for rulers "it is safer to be feared than loved."

Thomas Hobbes and the State of Nature   Under not entirely different political circumstances one century later, the English philosopher **Thomas Hobbes** (1588–1671), amid a bitter civil war and soon after the execution of King Charles I (r. 1625–1649) by his Puritan opponents, published his *Leviathan* (1651). Hobbes was a widely traveled intellectual who had met Descartes in France and Galileo in Italy. In his political writings he sought to discover

Read the **Document**

Hobbes' Leviathan *Excerpts*

on **MyHistoryLab.com**

natural laws of civil organization comparable with those uncovered in physics and astronomy. The experience of civil war and the chaos it unleashed propelled Hobbes's inquiries.

A dark view of human nature outside the confines of political society, where "every man is enemy to every man," obliged Hobbes to call for the creation of a social compact in which individuals surrender their right to absolute freedom in return for security and domestic peace. Humans were innately self-interested creatures who would trample the rights—and the lives—of others in pursuit of their own pleasures. In the *Leviathan,* each person surrenders the liberty that he or she enjoys in the natural state to an absolute monarch who is charged to do whatever is necessary to maintain the polity. Hobbes was no apologist for **divine-right** monarchy; instead, he felt that the ruler's success in avoiding the worst aspects of the state of nature legitimized a government's power. His daring image of a secular society where peace and personal security, not salvation and the preservation of natural social hierarchies, were the most important obligations of government anticipated many of the positions that Enlightenment thinkers advocated in the eighteenth century.

John Locke and Limited Government John Locke also experienced the mid-century breakdown of civil order in England, but he drew different conclusions from Hobbes. Locke argued that no single individual was competent to rule in an unrestrained manner, even if, as Hobbes proposed, the ruler had been raised to his position of supreme authority by an agreed social contract. Locke was troubled not only by the arbitrary tendencies of English monarchs but also at a deeper philosophical level by the question of how humans acquire knowledge.

For Locke, divine-right monarchy assumed that one individual was somehow uniquely fitted to know, interpret, and enforce God's will in the wider community. In his *Essay Concerning Human Understanding* (1690) Locke firmly rejected the argument that any one person was privileged with special innate knowledge of the divine mandate. Instead, each child was born as a blank slate, **tabula rasa,** and the sole source of human knowledge was experience of and in the world. Combined with the reflective powers of the rational mind, the raw data of sensory experience provide each person with the building blocks of knowledge, including knowledge of God and of a wider moral order. Locke was contesting the traditional Christian view that innate moral knowledge, while not fully developed in the child, was nonetheless present at birth. Absent innate knowledge, no one had the right to claim unmediated access to truth. Even kings and religious leaders were denied singular privileges in this crucial area, and it is no coincidence that the harshest critics of Locke's *Essay* were leading theologians in the Church of England.

Locke published his major political work, *Two Treatises of Government,* in the immediate aftermath of the 1688 Glorious Revolution that overthrew King James II. The same challenge to arbitrary authority that informed his theory of knowledge guided his approach to the problem of establishing a durable civil society. Locke accepted Hobbes's contract theory of government, but he imposed strict limits on the power of the sovereign. While not opposed to the institution of monarchy, Locke called for a strong legislative assembly with concrete lawmaking authority. The purpose of government, according to Locke, was to protect property, preserve political freedoms, and advance religious toleration. In one stroke, *Two Treatises* disengaged the state from the centuries-old enforcement of religious orthodoxy and secularized the civil order. Religion was a private matter, Locke stated in *A Letter Concerning Toleration* (1689). Six years later, in *The Reasonableness of Christianity* (1695), he argued that religious belief could be reduced to a few simple precepts. His title suggested that the rationalist outlook of the Scientific Revolution had now intruded itself permanently into the affairs of the spirit.

PEOPLE IN CONTEXT   Locke as Natural Philosopher

In many respects John Locke's training and interests reflect the many changes taking place in the study of nature during the seventeenth century. The son of Puritan parents of middle-class background, Locke's father fought against King Charles I in the English Civil War of the 1640s. The younger Locke attended Westminster School in London and Oxford University. Like many promising undergraduates, Locke was destined for a clerical career, but after much deliberation he declined to take holy orders, continuing on at Oxford instead for a medical degree.

Just as Bacon had done before him, Locke grew weary of what he took to be the uncritical and authority-bound nature of traditional academic life. From his journals we know that the bulk of his reading before leaving Oxford in 1667 was in medicine and chemistry.

In 1666 he supervised a dangerous operation to remove an abscess of the liver. The patient, Anthony Ashley Cooper, later Earl of Shaftesbury, credited Locke with saving his life. It was the start of a close friendship that would take Locke into the center of English political life.

Soon after relocating to London with Shaftesbury, Locke was duly elected a fellow of the Royal Society. He was on friendly terms with the chemist Robert Boyle. He later befriended Isaac Newton, and toward the end of Locke's life Newton would visit his friend not only to discuss science, but also to study and to write commentaries on the Bible. Both men believed firmly that science and religion were complementary undertakings. While Locke was often criticized by religious leaders who believed that his *Essay Concerning Human Understanding* threatened belief in an unalterable moral order, Locke insisted that his study of the mind was akin to the study of nature and that there was no inherent tension between faith and reason. ■

John Locke   Trained as a physician, Locke authored works in the fields of economics, educational and political theory, and Scripture commentary. In each area of endeavor, he emphasized the importance of empirical observation.

QUESTION: How can the study of nature claim an affiliation with religion?

Science and Religion

Replacing the concept of a universe that God governed directly and in which he regularly intervened did not mean that proponents of the new science were hostile to religion. In fact, men like Galileo, Kepler, Harvey, and Newton celebrated God's power and knowledge in the economy and exquisite order of creation. The Christian God became the great watchmaker. While humans no longer occupied the center of creation, they remained the most elevated of God's creatures by virtue of their rational nature and their ability to comprehend and utilize nature's bounty. The natural philosophers categorized their own investigations as acts of intense piety.

Medieval churchmen had been leaders in the study of the natural world for centuries, but even though the key figures in the Scientific Revolution were either devout clerics or pious laymen, Roman Catholic authorities were deeply upset with the broad theological and social implications of the new discoveries. The story of Galileo's troubles at the hands of church leaders is well known: forced to recant his acceptance of the Copernican system and placed under house arrest in Florence for the final decade of his life (1632–1642), the aged and nearly blind scientist worked in silence as the church condemned his theories and placed his publications on an index of forbidden books. When Galileo's countryman **Giordano Bruno** (1548–1600), a former Dominican monk, embraced the new learning and declared that there were innumerable planets in what amounted to an infinite universe, he was arrested, tried as a heretic, and burned at the stake. Bruno's confinement and execution, while an unusually barbaric exercise of coercive power, became a powerful rallying cry for all future advocates of freedom of thought across Western Europe.

Skepticism   Official religious opposition to the new science was not simple obscurantism, however. Scientific inquiry involved a deeper challenge to centuries-old habits of thought and belief respecting intellectual authority. The Baconian and Cartesian claims that knowledge was the end product of ardent skepticism undermined the central premise of the religious view of life. That premise was simple, and for centuries it had been compelling. It held that truths revealed to the world in canonical texts were sufficient to guide the earthly enterprise. Even Luther and Calvin, no great admirers of institutional authority and tradition, affirmed that God had communicated all that humans needed to know in the Bible. The new claim that reason was key to understanding how the world works and that it alone was sufficient in this life struck at the core of the faith traditions, Catholic and Protestant alike. The possibility that skepticism might, in the end, lead people to maintain that nothing could be known with certainty, even the existence of a creator-God, left many churchmen fearing the complete breakdown of an agreed moral order.

Blaise Pascal   Church officials were not the only ones whom the claims and implications of the new science troubled. Talented thinkers like the French mathematician **Blaise Pascal** (1623–1662) cautioned that the claims of science were exaggerated. He believed that the human condition remained one of enormous ignorance and sinfulness, that central truths were forever beyond the grasp of frail reason. For Pascal, organized religion and reliance on the operation of unmerited grace remained essential to the overall well-being of God's special creation. Science and reason were valuable components of Christian living, but by themselves they could not offer humans a satisfactory picture of creaturely purpose and destiny. "The God of the Christians is not simply the author of geometrical truth," pleaded Pascal in response to the ambitions of Descartes. Scientism would destroy all spiritual values if left unchecked, fostering a misplaced sense of confidence in human power and autonomy. Pascal's admonitions retain their power even today, in a world where material ambitions and values often outpace otherworldly perspectives on life.

Superstition and Its Victims

The rationalist outlook of the Scientific Revolution may have upset church authorities and thoughtful laymen like Pascal, but for Europeans outside of the intellectual elite, the reality of a realm of power and influence beyond the purview of reason was compelling and frightful. Most Europeans continued to believe in the power of demonic forces, while occult practices and magic maintained their hold on the educated and uneducated alike. While the privileged paid astrologers to identify propitious days for marriages, common people turned to sorcerers when a crop was endangered. In periods of social and political dislocation, blame was often ascribed to the practitioner of magic. Parallel with the growth of natural science during the sixteenth and seventeenth centuries was the intensification of witchcraft persecution.

Charging one's neighbors with the practice of harmful magic and witchcraft seemed to provide the accusers with an explanation for a wide variety of natural misfortunes and harmful occurrences. Preliterate village cultures in every global setting have accepted the claims of certain individuals to special powers over nature. "Cunning folk" were expected to protect communities from the worst effects of natural disasters and to serve as healers for the sick and infirm. The practices associated with the magician often had ancient, pre-Christian roots. In some cases the peasant who engaged in such practices and claims to special powers was seeking to establish a modicum of social respectability in a sharply hierarchical society. However, their claims came into direct conflict with the institutional church. The sacramental power of the Roman Catholic clergy was a form of magic, and while church authorities had always stressed the reality of demonic power in the world, it did not allow the laity a special role in combating that power. "Cunning folk" were unwelcome rivals.

Women and Witchcraft   Thousands of people were accused of witchcraft during the age of great scientific discoveries, and the majority of the accused were women. Most of the victims of witch hunts were single or older widowed women. They were vulnerable targets in a society dominated by men and where the accused were often seen as burdens on the community. Such women served as convenient scapegoats during periods of religious upheaval and conflict, where the older certainties of

View the **Map**

Witchcraft Persecutions

on **MyHistoryLab.com**

Combating Witchcraft Three women are burned to death as witches in Baden, Germany. Their alleged crimes are depicted on the right, where they are seen feasting with demons. Three witches burned alive from a German Broaside, *circa 1555. Courtesy of Stock Montage, Inc.*

👁️‍🗨️ **Watch** the **Video**

Hunting Witches

on **MyHistoryLab.com**

religious orthodoxy were under attack. By the mid-sixteenth century, Catholic and Protestant religious leaders were equally strident in their condemnation of witchcraft and magic for evil. Witches were accused of using their special access to the devil to undermine the fabric of Christian society. The accusation, prosecution, torture, and execution of women who were associated with destructive forces beyond the reach of rational understanding allowed communities under strain to demonstrate that they could take to the offensive in an inhospitable world.

KEY
QUESTION
REVISITED

How does the study of the natural world influence religious belief and the understanding of truth?

The controlling feature of the cosmic structure as formulated by the ancients and endorsed by the medieval church was its hierarchical structure. Multiple layers of value, dignity, nobility, and purity were associated with various types of matter and motion. The analogy between the human body and the cosmos was a popular one for the medieval mind. Microcosm and macrocosm were integrated; from thunderstorms and the appearance of comets to the death of a child or defeat in war, all physical phenomena were interrelated in a complex web of meaning. Of deeper significance was that this value-laden hierarchy of the heavens was thought to be the natural counterpart of hierarchies in the social and political domains, in the realm of personal relations (especially the family), and in the institutional church. Equality was a distant concept for most medieval thought, while rank and accompanying privilege based on sex, birth, and office defined access to social, economic, and political power.

The anti-authoritarianism of the scientific outlook had little immediate social impact. Women, for example, continued to be excluded from university life and from the new scientific societies. Most men considered women their intellectual inferiors, and the developing physical and biological sciences were all but closed to them. In fact, the period of the Scientific Revolution, with its appeal to reason and truth, was also an age of heightened witch hunts, with upwards of 100,000 people (mostly women) sentenced to death for their alleged involvement in black magic and witchcraft. Similarly, little political or religious freedoms were extended to the peasants. Most Europeans remained illiterate, devoid of access to political power, and firmly committed to their traditional religion.

But even after taking account of these significant limitations, by 1700 the hierarchical world view—a cosmic and terrestrial "great chain of being" linking all creation—was under sustained and probing attack. Attempts to understand the component parts of the physical world in terms of purpose or ends had been confidently discarded, and the aesthetic or even emotional assurances provided by the older world picture were forever abandoned. The Scientific Revolution introduced a mechanical picture of creation and described an inert physical order that humans could understand, especially in mathematical language. The closed and finite universe of medieval consciousness was replaced by an expansive and perhaps infinite clockwork. A secular and rational approach to life began to shape the thought and habits of the educated elite, and science as a realm of inquiry separate from theology gained significant new ground.

Newton had demonstrated that everything in the known universe influenced everything else; that one set of physical laws kept the constituent parts of creation neatly in their proper places. God as workman had erected a knowable mechanism. The study of nature prompted a significant challenge to traditional authority during the sixteenth and seventeenth centuries. If Francis Bacon was correct and the artisan was as essential as the aristocrat to the advancement of the human condition, if God could be known through his works alone, and if the ancient biblical injunction calling for dominion over Earth was still valid, then the next century, the century of Enlightenment, offered tremendous potential for human transformation.

Key Terms

Scientific Revolution, *p. 453*
laws of nature, *p. 456*
skepticism, *p. 461*

divine right, *p. 466*
tabula rasa, p. 466

Activities

1. Why was the medieval cosmos intellectually and emotionally satisfying for over 1,500 years?

2. In what respects did the medieval church encourage the investigation of nature?

3. Why were many leading figures in the Scientific Revolution strongly influenced by the occult, magic, and alchemy?

4. Describe the genuinely international character of scientific discovery.

5. Outline the role of skepticism in seventeenth-century political thought and practice.

6. Explain why women were singled out for the practice of witchcraft.

Further Reading

S. Shapin, *The Scientific Revolution* (1996), a survey that focuses on social factors.

J. Repcheck, *Copernicus' Secret: How the Scientific Revolution Began* (2007), an engaging biography.

L. Jardine and A. Stewart, *Hostage to Fortune: The Troubled Life of Francis Bacon* (1999), a fresh look at one of the first propagandists for science.

D. Sobel, *Galileo's Daughter: A Historical Memoir of Science, Faith and Love* (1999), explores the life of the great scientist through the letters of his eldest daughter.

MyHistoryLab Connections

Visit **MyHistoryLab.com** for a customized Study Plan that will help you build your knowledge of New World Views: Europe's Scientific Revolution.

Questions for Analysis

1. What are some of the innovations celebrated in the Sciences and the Arts?

   View the **Closer Look** The Sciences and the Arts, p. 456

2. How did Copernicus frame his argument in hopes of convincing Pope Paul III of its validity?

   Read the **Document** *On the Revolutions of the Heavenly Spheres*, p. 457

3. What are some of the global changes that occurred when Europeans began to cross the oceans?

   Watch the **Video** The World in 1700—Part 1, p. 462

4. How did China influence European thought in the seventeenth and eighteenth centuries?

   Watch the **Video** The World in 1700—Part 2, p. 462

5. How were witch hunts used to persecute marginalized members of society?

   Watch the **Video** Hunting Witches, p. 470

Other Resources from This Chapter

View the **Image** Galileo's Views of the Moon, p. 458

Read the **Document** Letter to the Grand Duchess Christina, p. 458

Read the **Document** Isaac Newton, from *Opticks*, p. 459

View the **Image** Newton's *Opticks*, p. 459

Read the **Document** Francis Bacon, from *Novum Organum*, p. 460

View the **Image** Descartes' View of the Universe, p. 461

View the **Image** First Printed Medical Text, p. 463

Read the **Document** William Harvey, Address to the Royal College of Physicians, p. 464

View the **Image** Jewish Medical Text by Tobias Cohen, p. 464

Read the **Document** Hobbes' *Leviathan* Excerpts, p. 465

View the **Map** Witchcraft Persecutions, p. 469

Monticello Thomas Jefferson's estate in Virginia is one of the most striking examples of the Enlightenment in North America. Pictured here is Jefferson's bedroom, which was modeled on classical sources and featured several innovative design elements. A few hundred yards away, Jefferson's African-American slaves slept in much more modest quarters. *Monticello/Thomas Jefferson Foundation, Inc.*

16

The Age of Enlightenment: Rationalism and Its Uses

((•—[Hear the Audio   Chapter 16 at MyHistoryLab.com

LEARNING OBJECTIVES

Who were the principal critics of the Old Regime in Europe?   •   What were some of the key plans for the reform of economic and social life?   •   Why were some European monarchs in favor of limited reform?   •   Who was excluded from the Enlightenment?   •   How did the arts reflect the rationalism of the eighteenth century?

I have sometimes been ready to think that the passion for liberty cannot be equally strong in the breasts of those who have been accustomed to deprive their fellow creatures of theirs.

—Abigail Adams to John Adams, March 31, 1776

KEY QUESTION

Can the principle and practice of human equality ever be truly inclusive?

As the spouse of one of the leading revolutionaries in the struggle for American independence against Great Britain, Abigail Adams (1744–1818) knew a great deal about the ideas that inspired the resistance to Old World monarchy. There was much talk about human equality and the right to national self-determination within Britain's 13 colonies in the years before 1776. But Adams was perceptive enough to realize that the rhetoric of men like her husband was directed solely toward their educated male peers. Women, landless laborers, African-American slaves—all were excluded from the debate over what Thomas Jefferson termed "inalienable rights."

When eighteenth-century men used the word **Enlightenment** to describe their own age, they were eager to separate themselves from what had gone before and to emphasize a firm commitment to the improvement of the human condition without reference to religious systems. Plans for the improvement of political institutions, reform of the criminal code, enhancement and expansion of education, economic development, and religious toleration all assumed a more optimistic view of human nature, or at least human potential. The possibility that institutions might be organized in harmony with what were believed to be universal principles of human reason led many thinkers to call for reform irrespective of tradition and authority. While the Enlightenment focused on practical change in the interest of efficiency and material improvement, it also promoted the idea that progress was a law of nature. Enlightened thinkers believed that the enhancement of the human condition was possible through the discovery and application of scientific principles in every sphere of human activity. This was a new outlook on life, one that was not shared by the overwhelming majority of Western Europeans who for centuries had lived in conditions where change and improvement were unfamiliar. ■

Critiquing the Traditional Way of Life

Life in the Old Regime   The eighteenth century in Europe did not signal a basic transformation in the way most people lived. They continued to cultivate the land, worship in a traditional Christian church, and pay land and labor taxes without any expectation that they would either choose their leaders or influence political decisions. Most would remain illiterate, working in harmony with the seasons and preparing their simple meals in a one-room cottage of timber, thatch, wattles, and dirt. More often than not, these Europeans spent their lives in an isolated village or hamlet where news of great events was neither offered nor expected. Most people were more concerned about the impact of influenza, typhoid, smallpox, intestinal worms, infantile diarrhea, and dysentery than they were about the decisions of administrators in Berlin or members of Parliament in London. It is difficult for those of us used to the insatiable drives of a consumer culture, where university-trained advertisers sell products to an eager public, to understand a world where it was the demands of the natural environment that dictated abstinence and restraint, self-sufficiency, and artisanal competence. Villages of a hundred or so inhabitants, often coinciding with a parish, might be located miles from the next area of population, and roads, if they existed at all, were in the best of times rutted, muddy, and frequented by bandits.

These isolated farming archipelagos lacked even the idea of personal privacy. The individual and the community were one in terms of labor on the land, use and maintenance of tools and livestock, dress, diet, language, and, perhaps most importantly, the struggle for collective security. Community feeling, unlike anything our intensely individualistic modern culture knows, was, in the words of historian Michael Kamen, "perhaps the most powerful social force in early modern Europe." Eating, sleeping, entertaining, praying, quarreling, loving, and dying in their anonymous cottages, regulating their lives around the seasons, the weather, and the church's ritual year, the eighteenth-century peasantry knew nothing about concepts of change and innovation.

The general impoverishment of the peasant majority had never been a deep concern of Europe's political elite. In fact, some believed that the deprivation of the majority actually enhanced social order. Cardinal Richelieu, chief minister to King Louis XIII of France from 1624 to 1643, wrote that "all students of politics agree that when the common people are too well off it is impossible to keep them peaceable." If they are not constantly engaged in securing the bare necessities of life, the poor "find it difficult to remain within the limits imposed by both common sense and the law." Here was a harsh estimate of the human potential for peaceable improvement. It was this very perspective that would be overturned, at least in the minds of a distinct minority, during the eighteenth century. The two great political upheavals of the century, the successful American colonial revolt against Britain and the more radical French Revolution of 1789, together pointed toward the potential for change through education and a new outlook about what formal human associations like government were supposed to do.

Key Figures and Texts of the Enlightenment

1690	Locke, *Two Treatises of Government* and *An Essay Concerning Human Understanding*
1721	Montesquieu, *Persian Letters*
1733	Voltaire, *Letters on the English*
1739	John Wesley begins open-field preaching
1751	Diderot, first volume of *Encyclopedia*
1759	Voltaire, *Candide*
1764	Beccaria, *On Crimes and Punishments*
1764	Rousseau, *Discourse on Inequality*
1776	Smith, *Wealth of Nations*
1790	Paine, *Rights of Man*

The Community of *Philosophes*   It is difficult to associate the eighteenth-century Enlightenment with a set of firm, easily delineated ideas. What united a wide range of thinkers (most of whom, interestingly, were not associated with Europe's intellectually conservative universities) was a more general attitude toward the human condition. This attitude reflected confidence in the possibility of progress through the application of human reason to a variety of fields. Most seventeenth-century Europeans did not believe that the future could be better than the past. Western culture had always looked backwards for models of the good society: The Greeks recalled a mythical world of gods and heroes, and Romans of the later Empire remembered the vanished Republic. Christianity had its Garden of Eden, the Middle Ages turned to the rugged simplicity of the early faith, and the Renaissance looked to Greece and Rome for inspiration and imitation. The achievements of natural philosophy—the belief that the environment could be understood, measured, and mastered—helped to transform this retrospective outlook. In a protracted literary debate around the turn of the eighteenth century, what has come to be known as the quarrel between the ancients and the moderns, the latter group, led by the Frenchman **Bernard de Fontenelle** (1657–1757), asserted that contemporaries could build on the collective wisdom of the past. They could utilize an established core of knowledge to exceed the accomplishments of all previous ages.

Emerging in part out of the Scientific Revolution, the most recognizable figures of the Enlightenment were less original thinkers than their predecessors. But they were enormously effective popularizers of new ideas, new methods of intellectual inquiry, and new views on educational theory. Like the Scientific Revolution, however, the Enlightenment was an international undertaking. It was centered in France but included figures as diverse as the Scottish professor of political economy **Adam Smith** (1732–1796),

View the **Map**

Science and the Enlightenment

on **MyHistoryLab.com**

the German philosopher **Immanuel Kant** (1724–1804), the French satirist and advisor to kings Voltaire, and the American president Thomas Jefferson. Most were from either aristocratic or middle-class backgrounds and had received the benefit of a traditional university education. Collectively referred to by the French word ***philosophes*** (philo-sophers), these men—and a few, mainly aristocratic women—took all fields of knowledge under their charge. In an essay titled "What Is Enlightenment?" Kant described the movement as a call to think for oneself, to question and reflect, to understand the world according to one's own rational lights. If fol-

[□●┤ Read the **Document**

Immanuel Kant Defines the Enlightenment, 1784

on **MyHistoryLab.com**

lowed closely, the injunction would subject a wide range of institutions to scrutiny: the church, the state, the universities, the legal system, and, more generally, the whole design of authority.

The Power of Environment   When John Locke died in 1704, the major breakthroughs in physics and astronomy had been consolidated by his compatriot and fellow Christian Isaac Newton. In a short work titled *Some Thoughts Concern-ing Education* (1693), Locke had argued that "all the men we meet with, nine parts of ten, ninety-nine of one hundred, are what they are, good or evil, useful or not, by their education." Here was an emphatic affirmation of the argument for nurture over nature that lay at the heart of the better-known *Essay Concerning Human Understanding*. Locke's claim that education was key to shaping the student's character as well as informing the content of his mind called into question a long-

[□●┤ Read the **Document**

John Locke, Essay Concerning Human Understanding

on **MyHistoryLab.com**

standing consensus about humanity's inherent depravity and sinfulness. Locke even included sections on the education of women, insisting that no one was exempt from the influences of family, community, and formal instruction. Environment determined human character.

This radical empiricism or environmentalism spurred a reexamination of many established precedents and practices in religion, ethics, politics, econom-ics, and social life. Extending the belief in natural laws that lay at the core of the Scientific Revolution to the realm of human affairs, the *philosophes* claimed that progress was itself a general law. They believed that the application of reason to all human activities could accelerate the march of progress. In the late 1690s, the French Protestant **Pierre Bayle** (1647–1706) condemned the religious intolerance of Louis XIV's government on the grounds that alleged "truths" beyond the test of reason were inherently unstable. In his *Historical and Critical Dictionary* (1697), Bayle maintained that the only legitimate test of truth is conformity with ratio-nal understanding. Dogmas that transcended the embrace of human reason could never be obligatory. More controversially, Bayle asserted that morality and religion were separate spheres. He held that one could reject divine revelation and still conduct oneself in harmony with a rational standard of morality. Bayle was fond of saying that "errors are none the better for being old," and he articulated the interna-tionalism of the Enlightenment when he stated that the true scholar "should forget that he belongs to any country.... I am neither French nor German, nor English nor Spanish, etc., I am a resident of the world."

The argument that individuals might be good without the oversight of religious authorities and nationally based institutions encouraged eighteenth-century reformers to leave no organization, system, or custom outside the purview of independent reason. In an effort to reach the widest possible audience, many of the *philosophes* deliberately adopted a popular and accessible form of exposition. They wrote philosophy to fit the tastes and the comprehension of a growing urban middle-class. Journals, fiction, histories, satires, plays, letters—all avenues were exploited in a broad effort to subject hallowed conventions to the test of reason. One of the more influential strategies for expanding readership in this growing republic of letters was the exotic traveler's tale, stories written from the perspective of the non-Western visitor to Europe.

The Literature of Reform   Two Frenchmen excelled in the use of this genre, even deriving significant income from the sale of their works. **Baron de Montesquieu**'s (1689–1755) widely popular *Persian Letters,* published in the Netherlands in 1721 (French censorship was still strong), critiqued European customs from the perspective of two Persian travelers. Anticlerical in tone and sympathetic to non-Christian traditions, the book capitalized on Europe's growing awareness of divergent world cultures. On a more regional level, Francois Marie Arouet, better known to the world under his pen name **Voltaire** (1694–1778), contrasted English freedoms with French autocracy in his influential *Letters on the English* first published in 1733. The book popularized the work of Locke and Newton for a French reading public. It also championed the English constitutional system in which Parliament limited the monarch's powers. Voltaire's immensely popular novel *Candide* (1759) focused on the adventures and troubles of a single young character in order to chastise more radical thinkers who thought that progress in this world was somehow predestined. In Ireland the Protestant churchman **Jonathan Swift** (1667–1745) wrote satirical essays decrying England's treatment of its Irish colony. His *Gulliver's Travels* (1726), another work of fantasy literature with a strongly moralizing tone, reached a broad audience.

Efforts to classify, systematize, demonstrate, and disseminate new knowledge became a central goal of the Enlightenment. Pierre Bayle's *Dictionary* was in fact the first encyclopedia, organized alphabetically by topic and

Read the **Document**

Voltaire, Letters on the English

on **MyHistoryLab.com**

Voltaire   Voltaire was the most influential critic of Europe's religious institutions during the eighteenth century. He was a historian, dramatist, and poet whose works reached a wide readership. *Nicolas de Largilliere. Portrait of Voltaire at age 23, bust length, 1728. Private Collection, Paris. Bridgeman-Giraudon/Art Resource, NY*

MAP 16-1 The Influence of Diderot's *Encyclopedia* This map indicates where subscriptions were taken out for Denis Diderot's *Encyclopedia*. This huge endeavor at compiling scientific, technological, and mathematical knowledge expressed the Enlightenment beliefs in reason and progress.

QUESTION: Why were the largest numbers of subscribers found in France?

View the Image

Diderot's Encyclopedia— *Illustration of Agricultural Techniques*

on **MyHistoryLab.com**

Read the Document

Denis Diderot, Preliminary Discourse from The Encyclopedia *(France), 1751*

on **MyHistoryLab.com**

offering synopses of the most up-to-date scholarship on a wide range of topics. It was followed in the 1720s by an English-language production, stressing the arts and sciences, under the authorship of the Scotsman Ephraim Chambers (1680–1740). But no one person could write a truly comprehensive encyclopedia. Beginning in the 1740s, a new effort was undertaken by a group of Parisian publishers. They appointed **Denis Diderot** (1713–1774) as general editor for what would become a multivolume collaborative effort to distill recent learning, especially in science, technology, and mathematics. In a preface co-authored by Jean le Rond d'Alembert (1717–1783), Diderot announced that the project was designed to "contribute to the certitude and progress of human reason." Thanks in no small measure to the indulgent attitude of the French government's chief censor, the first volume of the great *Encyclopedia* appeared in print in 1751. Six more volumes were issued annually until 1759, when a royal decree quashed the release of volume eight. France was at war with England by this date, and the government suspected that many of the contributors to the *Encyclopedia* were Anglophiles with little loyalty to the French state. Yet Diderot persisted, recruiting a wide range of *philosophes* as contributing authors. Eventually, in 1766 the 17 volumes were finished. Another 11 volumes of plates and additional volumes containing supplementary material and an index reached the bookshops in the 1770s. By the start of the French Revolution in 1789, over 20,000 full sets of the *Encyclopedia* had been sold (see Map 16–1).

Masonic Lodges and Salons

In addition to the popular *Encyclopedia*, new ideas were discussed in Masonic lodges that were located in every major European city by the mid-1700s. The first Grand Lodge had been established in London in 1717, bringing together a number of smaller discussion circles. The movement known as **Freemasonry** offered alternatives to traditional religious houses of worship. Complete with their own rituals, fostering a sense of intellectual community, and even engaging in charitable activities, the Masons attracted members who were eager to share their engagement in the world of new ideas with like-minded men. Also key to the dissemination of knowledge during the Enlightenment were the aristocratic *salons,* or discussion circles, held in private homes and provincial literary academies. In Paris the *salons* were the center of activity. Normally hosted by influential women and serving as places where writers and their aristocratic patrons could interact, these meetings helped to make the French capital the center of Enlightenment thought.

Jesuit Education

The Roman Catholic Society of Jesus, or Jesuit Order, was established in 1540 during the Reformation era Council of Trent. Dedicated initially to reconverting Protestants to the Catholic faith, by the 1700s the Jesuits had become the premier educators in most Catholic countries, and in particular within France. The Jesuits were men of the world, counselors to kings and missionaries to distant lands such as India, China, and the Americas.

> **Read** the **Document**
>
> *Jesuits in India (1530s–1550s), St. Francis Xavier*
>
> on **MyHistoryLab.com**

In seventeenth- and eighteenth-century China, Jesuit missionaries even served as astronomers and cartographers at the Ming and Qing courts.

Many of the intellectual leaders of the Enlightenment were educated at Jesuit schools. Francis Bacon, although a Protestant, had spoken highly of Jesuit education in the early seventeenth century. The Jesuits were clearly the most influential teachers in the Age of Enlightenment. Students received rigorous training in the classics, rhetoric, and the latest sciences. The virtues stressed by Jesuits—discipline, self-control, intellectual exactitude—were endorsed by the *philosophes.* However, some former students turned their skills against their teachers. René Descartes

> **Watch** the **Video**
>
> *The Global Mission of the Jesuits*
>
> on **MyHistoryLab.com**

was trained in mathematics by Jesuits, but he later rejected their steadfast position on authority and obedience. Voltaire, another Jesuit student, had been expelled as a ne'er-do-well.

The Church as Enemy

One of the most bitterly contested issues during the eighteenth century was the status of revealed religion and the power of the church to

Salon of Marie-Therese Geoffrin   Salons provided a forum for Enlightenment thinkers to bring their ideas to the attention of a larger audience. Wealthy women often provided the patronage needed to sustain writers and reformers.

regulate people's lives. Outside of England and the Netherlands, official state churches afforded little toleration to religious minorities. Orthodoxy was enforced through censorship and the courts, and civil authorities employed the coercive power of the state to support the official faith. The Inquisition, for example, remained active in Spain, and non-Catholics were prohibited from traveling to Spain's colonies in the Americas. The same proscription applied against French dissenters; Protestants were banned from New France (Canada). National churches controlled vast tracts of land, and church leaders, especially within the Roman Catholic tradition, were often drawn from the aristocracy. In many ways, state churches were the chief buttresses of the Old Regimes across Europe, utilizing the power of the pulpit to inculcate obedience to civil authority and deference to superiors. The *philosophes* equated such power and control with bigotry and decried intolerance as the root cause of human divisions.

Deism   For Voltaire, established religious institutions stood squarely in the path of human freedom and progress. Some of his most vitriolic attacks were reserved for the Roman Catholic establishment in France. Censorship authority and control over education were the two areas where the malevolent influence of the hierarchical church was most pronounced. Opposing the creeds, dogmas, legal systems, and rituals of Europe's Protestant and Catholic churches, Voltaire spoke for an increasing number of educated believers who sought to simplify Christianity while bringing it in line with the mandate of universal reason. In his *Philosophical Dictionary* (1764), he articulated the essential position of those who referred to themselves as Deists (Voltaire preferred the word "theist"). God exists, and in the end

Baruch Spinoza   The great Jewish philosopher Spinoza (1632–1677) was a major influence on the Deists and other Enlightenment thinkers of the next century. Spinoza sought to reconcile faith with reason and challenged many deeply held theological beliefs of Judaism and Christianity.

He rewards and punishes His creatures on the basis of their conduct in this life. But He is a remote Creator who does not intervene in the daily affairs of individual believers, and He has certainly not saddled humanity with the incapacitating burden of original sin; each person enjoys the freedom to choose or reject salvation. There exists one universal and primitive religion, embracing Muslims, Buddhists, Hindus, Jews, Christians—indeed people of all faith traditions. Differences between these eclectic paths are only unfortunate human contrivances.

Deism rejected the incarnation and the doctrine of the Trinity, accepting Jesus as a great moral teacher but not God. Worship the one transcendent God and deal justly with others: this was the simple creed of most Deists from the plains of central Europe to the plantations of Virginia. A handful of thinkers took the critique of religion one step further. The Scottish philosopher **David Hume** (1711–1776) concluded that miracles, which by definition eluded the confines of rationality, lay at the core of Christianity. Hume's claim that even reason could not demonstrate the existence of God led to charges of atheism and, among other hardships, cost him a coveted professorship at Edinburgh University. The Jewish philosopher **Baruch Spinoza** (1632–1677) believed that all sacred texts should be scrutinized at the bar of reason. In his best-known book, titled *Ethics,* he seemed to approach a pantheistic faith in his identification of God with all of nature. This, at least, is how his many critics interpreted his arguments, and he was excommunicated from his synagogue. Other influential figures, including Denis Diderot, Julian Offray de la Mettrie (1709–1751), and the German Baron d'Holbach (1723–1789), concluded that the idea of God was the great superstition of the ages.

Formulas for Improving Material Conditions

The social sciences as a distinct area of study were born during the Enlightenment, and the issue of wealth creation received special attention as Europe's colonial holdings matured and the Industrial Revolution began in Britain. Mercantilism, the belief that the total amount of wealth in the world was finite and that a country's share of this wealth depended on its ability to protect its own agricultural and manufacturing sectors from foreign competition, was the leading economic theory. Its impact reached across Europe and the Americas from the 1500s to the late eighteenth century. Dissenters from the orthodox model included merchants in Britain's North American colonies who were eager to trade with every European state, whether friend or foe of Britain, and a group of French reformers known as **physiocrats.** Arguing that the only genuine measure of wealth lay in the agricultural sector, these theorists, led by **Francois Quesnay** (1694–1774), physician to King Louis XV (r. 1715–1774), called for the state to promote human happiness and its correlate individual liberty. The state could do this by refraining from interference with the operation of natural economic forces except to protect agricultural property. This meant that for the first time in Western history, getting and consuming—an ethic of private appropriation—was being championed as one of the principal objectives of civil society, and governments were now to be judged according to how well they advanced this hedonistic ethos.

Adam Smith   The case for government noninterference on economic activities was taken into the industrial age by a professor of moral philosophy at the University of Edinburgh, Adam Smith (1723–1790). In 1776 he published a groundbreaking work that would have enormous influence into the twentieth century. In *The Wealth of Nations* Smith argued that society as a whole is best served when individuals are permitted to seek, secure, and hold their private material gains under conditions of minimal state interference. Only when government abandoned mercantilist protectionism, which in Smith's mind amounted to a discriminatory subsidy for one group of businessmen and a handicap against all other subjects, would broad-based material progress occur. In concrete terms, Smith's pioneering work called for an end to all tariffs, protective duties, subsidies to particular industries and enterprises, and the privileging of domestic over foreign manufactures.

▣◉ **Read** the **Document**

Introduction to the
Wealth of Nations

on **MyHistoryLab.com**

A hands-off, or *laissez-faire,* approach to economic development would also lead to true social harmony. Smith posited the operation of an "**invisible hand**" or universal law of economics. According to Smith, freeing individuals to pursue their own rational, selfish interests would in fact further the material well-being of the entire community, both at the local and national levels. He rejected the mercantilist idea that total global wealth was limited, arguing instead that opportunities for wealth creation were as varied as the talents of the world's many peoples. Freeing those many talents, celebrating self-reliance, allowing the pressures of the marketplace to determine product, quantity, and price, were the inflexible laws that, if adhered to, would best serve every people irrespective of cultural differences. In this respect Smith was a proponent of the essential equality of economic man. Although after his death he became the darling of liberal capitalism and big business, Smith was no apologist for the uninhibited business tycoon. Indeed, he believed that employers who conspired to hold down wages often oppressed workers. Removing the heavy hand of government from economic affairs, he was convinced, would improve workers' ability to negotiate with their wealthy employers.

Crime, Punishment, and Reform   The problem of crime and the treatment of criminal offenders were also priorities of Enlightenment discourse. The conventional wisdom held that crime was to be equated with sinfulness, the fruit of human depravity. Once tried and convicted, the prisoner should be exposed to a regime of corporal punishment, torture, and, for many offenses, the death penalty. Europe's legal systems drew few distinctions between what today would be called misdemeanors and serious felonies, while in prisons murderers were held alongside debtors and petty thieves. The Italian reformer **Cesare Beccaria** (1738–1794) led the field in questioning the accepted wisdom. He called for a reform of irrational legal systems and focused on the need to rehabilitate the offender. In his popular *Crimes and Punishments* (1764), Beccaria condemned the use of torture and capital punishment as counterproductive vengeance, not deterrence. He called for new law codes that would enhance human happiness, what he termed "the greatest happiness of the greatest number," and not just reflect someone's personal understanding of divine law. More controversially, Beccaria alleged that criminality was not unrelated to wide disparities in wealth, leading the poor to operate outside of a legal system that they could not change.

Read the **Document**
Crimes and Punishments
on **MyHistoryLab.com**

Enlightened Despots

Just as there were many targets of the overall Enlightenment critique, so, too, there were differences of approach to the common problems that reformed thinkers identified. This was especially true of the political arena. On one hand, a few of Europe's monarchs encouraged and supported those *philosophes* who endorsed absolute rule. On the other hand, a thinker like **Jean-Jacques Rousseau** (1712–1778) put the good of the community before that of the individual and attacked society itself for corrupting human nature.

Catherine the Great   None of the *philosophes* endorsed democratic rule. Despite broad agreement over the importance of education to rational living, few envisioned an age when most people would be fit to exercise political rights. This was no

Catherine the Great of Russia   After securing the throne in 1762, Catherine worked to create an efficient government informed by Enlightenment ideas. During the early years of her reign, the empress supported legal and educational reform, but she was reluctant to surrender any of her powers as an absolute monarch.

small comfort to Europe's crowned heads. As we read in Chapter 14, "The Early Modern State," Catherine the Great (r. 1762–1796) sought to transform a state that had lacked strong leadership since the reign of Peter the Great (r. 1689–1725) into a model of monarchical efficiency and innovation. During the first 15 years of her reign, the empress subsidized the publication of the French *Encyclopedia,* supported the foundation of schools, encouraged the fledgling Russian publishing industry, and created a legal reform commission that included commoners as well as noblemen. Catherine's program for legal reform was influenced by her reading of Beccaria's work, and the final document or "instruction" she gave her commission was translated into a number of European languages. Voltaire even received a personal copy from the empress (thanks to Catherine's interest, most of Voltaire's manuscripts today reside in Russia). Sadly, aristocrats and commoners on the special commission quarreled endlessly over serfdom, and in the end few reforms were implemented.

Frederick the Great   The most celebrated "**enlightened despot**" was the Prussian king Frederick the Great (r. 1740–1786). Fond of describing himself as the "first servant of the state," he was never directly accountable to his subjects, but he acknowledged a moral obligation to work for the good of the broader national community. Frederick was one of only a handful of rulers who, from an early age, developed an appreciation for and interest in music, literature, and philosophy. As king, he continued to perform in private concerts as a flutist and exchanged letters with Europe's leading thinkers. His first correspondence with Voltaire dates from 1736, and the stormy friendship that developed between the two men culminated in Voltaire's residence at Frederick's court in Berlin from 1750–1753. Frederick's official actions early in his reign reflect the essential Enlightenment belief that problems and errors are manmade, not cosmic constants of the human condition. The king reformed the criminal code and abolished torture. He embraced religious toleration at a time when few rulers were willing to accept dissenters, and he promoted agricultural reform in the tradition of the physiocrats.

However, Frederick the Great, like Catherine the Great, was not solely interested in lessening misery and increasing happiness. Neither ruler hesitated to go to war when the opportunity arose to expand his or her territory and power. A series of partitions from 1772 to 1795 dismembered Poland, as Russia, Austria, and Prussia divided up the spoils. Neither Frederick nor Catherine was committed to reform at the cost of alienating the nobility. Frederick had little faith in the abilities of his nonnoble subjects. When the French Revolution broke out in 1789, Catherine firmly rejected the position that the masses were equipped to carry out reforms similar to the ones she had enacted. Soon after Frederick died in 1786, almost all of his unique alterations, including the unprecedented edict against serfdom, were swiftly overturned.

Joseph II   The only "enlightened" eighteenth-century ruler who dared to take on fundamental questions of social rights and economic reform was Emperor Joseph II of Austria (r. 1780–1790). Joseph had become Holy Roman Emperor in 1765 after the death of his father. However, he had to wait for the passing of his strong-willed mother, Maria Teresa (r. 1740–1780), before he could begin to reform his far-flung, diverse, and economically backward empire. The emperor's Italian, Flemish, Magyar,

Frederick the Great   Frederick II valued his exchanges with Enlightenment thinkers, but he was committed to reform only within the context of enhancing state power. In this painting, the king performs on the flute during a private concert.

Polish, Czech, Croatian, and German subjects had little in common, but Joseph was undaunted by the scale of the task before him. During his ten-year reign, he issued thousands of royal edicts in an effort to realize some of the key goals of Enlightenment thinkers. Censorship was relaxed, religious toleration was declared, and Jews were given more freedom to worship and greater civil rights. The legal system was transformed as torture was abolished and capital punishment restricted. Most importantly, equality before the law was enforced. In the most dramatic decision of his brief reign, Joseph abolished serfdom within the empire, ending with the stroke of a pen centuries of social and material oppression. The opposition of the privileged classes and the church was both unanimous and loud, and after a decade of frenetic activity, the emperor had earned for himself the disdain of his nobles, priests, and the provincial legislatures that these social groups dominated. Absent this support, most of his innovations could not be sustained.

Critiquing the Enlightenment

Jean-Jacques Rousseau   The troubled loner Jean-Jacques Rousseau would have little to do with the top-down reforms of enlightened despots. Born in the Republic of Geneva in French-speaking Geneva, Rousseau's mother died soon after his birth, and his father abandoned him ten years later. The poor and ill-educated young man served several apprenticeships before leaving his natal land for France. Involved in a number

Read the Document

Jean-Jacques Rousseau, Emile

on **MyHistoryLab.com**

Jean-Jacques Rousseau "Man is born free, and everywhere is in chains," wrote the great Enlightenment thinker. Rousseau diverged from many of his fellow *philosophes* in his advocacy of a "social contract." Rousseau's writings and example would serve as an important inspiration for the French Revolution.

of romantic affairs, Rousseau, like his father, abandoned his own children. In the midst of this erratic personal life, he began to critique the very foundations upon which his society rested. In his *Discourse on the Origin of Inequality* (1755), *Emile* (1762), and *The Social Contract* (1762), Rousseau denied that humans were inherently evil or corrupt at birth. He insisted instead that society itself was to blame for the poor state of human relations. Rousseau overturned the Hobbesian description of the hypothetical state of nature, claiming that before the imposition of rules of property and formal institutions of government, self-interest and materialism were not central features of human comportment, that a genuine communism prevailed on Earth.

But since the fateful step had been taken to create civil society, Rousseau was prepared to offer his own model of the best possible polity. He disavowed the widespread assumption, shared by most of the *philosophes,* that society was simply an aggregate of individuals seeking personal goals and protected in their quest by a government of laws. Locke was wrong: property was no natural right but a curse. Instead, Rousseau demanded that people enter into a social contract whereby they surrender their individual wills for the greater "freedom" of the common good. A **general will,** the embodiment of what each person would will for himself if he were thinking in a truly rational manner, must be the guiding principle around which the just society is constructed and maintained. Many of Rousseau's erstwhile friends saw in the concept of the general will not the liberation of the individual but the seeds of despotism and stultifying conformism. Rousseau's pursuit of the just society, his critics alleged, came at too high a price. Minorities and dissenters would find little solace in the unlimited power of the general will.

Montesquieu and Law   A more modest approach to the "science" of politics, but one equally troubling to the Enlightenment faith in universal natural laws, was provided by Montesquieu. Like his compatriot Voltaire, Montesquieu had traveled to England and was an admirer of Locke. He titled his study *The Spirit of the Laws* (1748), and in true Baconian fashion the author advanced his novel thesis only after assembling broad comparative data on governments around the world. In this respect it could be considered an early work in sociology as well as political science. For Montesquieu, no one formulaic model of government was applicable everywhere. Rather, a country's size, climate, population, religious and social customs, together with its economic structure, provided keys to the form of government that was best for current conditions. France, for example, was ideally situated to be organized under a limited monarchy, where the regional aristocratic courts or *parlements* (of which Montesquieu was a member) checked the ruler's powers. The guiding spirit or informing principle of limited monarchy was honor. The city-states of Geneva and Venice, in contrast, where virtue and moderation were the animating ideals, could function effectively under a republican system due to their modest size and cultural homogeneity. Montesquieu sharply disparaged despotisms, where fear prevailed, although they had once served well in large, heterogeneous empires like Rome.

Montesquieu's typologies for government even helped to inform thinking in Britain's former North American colonies. The framers of the Constitution of the United States, a document first drafted in 1787, embraced the idea of separation of powers (dividing executive, legislative, and judicial functions) contained in *The Spirit of the Laws*. While Montesquieu made many naive assumptions on the basis of climate and geography—northern peoples, he concluded, were more courageous than their southern neighbors, and Asians were less vigorous than their Western counterparts—his efforts to uncover a set of invariable laws (as opposed to a single law) of political evolution boosted interest in the study of society as a fledgling science.

Read the **Document**

Baron de Montesquieu, Excerpt from The Spirit of the Laws

on **MyHistoryLab.com**

Women and the Age of Reason   Wealthy patronesses frequently provided essential financial support for writers like Rousseau, and politically connected aristocratic women also facilitated contacts and helped controversial works get published. King Louis XV's mistress **Madame de Pompadour** (1721–1764), for instance, helped to temper official criticism of the multivolume *Encyclopedia*. She even wrote an article on cosmetics for one of the volumes. Émilie du Châtelet (1706–1749) was wealthy and highly educated, and her marriage to another man did not prevent her from forming a close bond with Voltaire. She was interested in physics and translated Newton's *Principia*; her early death was a crushing blow to Voltaire.

Overall, however, the major Enlightenment thinkers were not champions of sexual equality or what would later be termed women's rights. Married women had few property rights, and the conduct of husbands within the household was virtually unassailable, no matter what abuses took place. Locke had questioned the biblical grounds for the ascendancy of the father in his *Two Treatises of Government,* but the *philosophes* did not share his judgment. The great *Encyclopedia* did not bother to address the contributions of women. Immanuel Kant felt that too much education overtaxed the female intellect. Rousseau believed that women were the natural inferiors to men and should be confined to the home. He unapologetically stressed that the education of women ought to center on domestic and child-rearing responsibilities. Rousseau was a man of his word in this respect, regularly mistreating and then abandoning the many women with whom he fathered his offspring. A few, like Locke and Montesquieu, were sympathetic to greater educational opportunities for women and disputed the notion that unbridgeable intellectual differences existed between the sexes. However, none envisioned women playing an equal role with men in the political realm. The double standard in sexual conduct remained firmly in place, and child-rearing duties continued to be associated exclusively with the mother.

The Scotsman David Hume, with characteristic bluntness, alleged that men were led to repress women to preserve their own power. However, he was not troubled enough by this analysis to call for any change. The American Abigail Adams felt no such inhibitions. Upon hearing from her husband John that the 13 colonies were set to declare their independence from Britain, she reminded him that "in the new code

of laws which I suppose it will be necessary for you to make, I desire you would re-
member the ladies and be more generous to them than your ancestors."

Three years after the start of the French Revolution, one extraordinary woman
indicted the wholesale hypocrisy of the Enlightenment project with respect to the place
accorded one-half of the population. **Olympe de
Gouges** (1748–1793), the daughter of a butcher, boldly
extended the revolutionary *Declaration of the Rights of
Man and Citizen* (1789) to females with her 1791 *Declaration of the Rights of Women and Citizen.* Calling for
equal rights before the law and in property relations,
she spoke for many working-class women who were
active in the early years of the French Revolution.

[●] Read the Document

Olympe de Gouges,
Declaration of the Rights
of Woman and the Female
Citizen

on **MyHistoryLab.com**

The English author **Mary Wollstonecraft** (1759–1797) followed the work of
de Gouges with her widely read *A Vindication of the Rights of Woman* (1792). The
London-born daughter of a weaver, Wollstonecraft traveled to Paris in 1792, just before King Louis XVI was executed by his republican opponents. Her book set out
to demonstrate that the progress of humanity could not occur so long as women
remained the virtual slaves of men. Wollstonecraft
called for equal educational opportunity for boys and
girls, and she insisted that existing social norms were
the exclusive cause of women's alleged incapacities.
Not content with mere assertions of equality absent
empirical evidence, Wollstonecraft forwarded the
Baconian call for rigorous experiment and data col-
lection. "Let [women's] faculties have room to unfold, and their views to gain strength,
and then determine where the whole sex must stand in the intellectual scale." Men
constantly complain about the frivolity and intellectual weakness of women while
simultaneously keeping women "in a state of childhood."

[●] Read the Document

*Mary Wollstonecraft,
Introduction to* A Vindication
of the Rights of Women

on **MyHistoryLab.com**

Slavery and Inequality   Europeans were latecomers to the African slave
trade, but their involvement, while comparatively brief to that of native African
rulers and Arab slave traders, was unrivaled with respect to the demographic,
physical, and psychological impact slavery caused. The movement of black slaves
northward across the Sahara Desert began more than 500 years before the first Portuguese traders arrived on the west coast of the continent in the mid-fifteenth century. These early centuries were dominated by Muslim middlemen who sold their
captives as concubines, eunuchs, and domestic servants in Muslim lands across
North Africa, the Near East, and as far east as India. Over the centuries, millions
of African men and women were forced to trek thousands of miles in harsh desert
conditions to reach their ultimate destination. Islam forbade the enslavement of
other Muslims, but infidels could be denied their freedom with impunity. While
slaves in the Muslim world could occasionally rise to positions of considerable authority, disparaging assessments of Africans based on race were not the monopoly
of later Europeans. The fourteenth-century Arab historian Ibn Khaldun expressed
a commonplace view when he wrote that "the only people who accept slavery are
the Negroes owing to their low degree of humanity and their proximity to the
animal stage."

PEOPLE IN CONTEXT   Olympe de Gouges

Olympe de Gouges (1748–1793) was born in humble circumstance and managed to educate herself before relocating to Paris after the death of her husband in the late 1760s. Once in the capital, she set out to become a playwright and political pamphleteer. By all accounts, she was a quarrelsome personality, and other writers tired of her efforts to dominate literary gatherings. She wrote on many subjects, including the abolition of slavery, but she is best remembered as an early champion of women's rights. Her *Declaration of the Rights of Woman* was composed in a climate of enormous social and political upheaval, when women were enjoying newfound influence.

Women's Patriotic Club   Women's clubs, such as the one depicted here, flourished during the revolutionary period in France and focused mainly on philanthropic work.

Despite her strident call for women's rights, de Gouges was a royalist who even dedicated the *Declaration* to the embattled Queen Marie Antionette. She called upon the Queen "to give weight to the progress of the rights of women, and to hasten its success." In 1792 she came to the defense of King Louis XVI, attacking the radical leader Maximillien Robspierre, and referring to him as an "egotistical abomination." In 1793 de Gouge called for a national plebiscite to determine the government of France. Arrested, tried, and convicted of sedition by the new republican government, she attempted to delay her execution by feigning pregnancy. In one hostile obituary, Olympe de Gouges was not only labeled a traitor, but condemned "for having forgotten the virtues which befit her sex." ■

QUESTION: Can human equality be secured under traditional political institutions?

Ironically, it was just as human bondage was disappearing in Europe that the horrific black African slave trade began in earnest. Africans were first brought to Portugal for sale in 1444. Thereafter, the sale of captive Africans expanded dramatically in the wake of Europe's colonization of sugar-producing islands off the west coast of Africa and subsequently in the Americas. The extremely high mortality rates from disease that Amerindians suffered soon after the arrival of whites from across the ocean opened up an acute need for labor in cash-crop, plantation-based economies.

The Spanish crown began licensing slave traders to the Americas in the 1550s. Before slavery was brought to a close in the late nineteenth century, upwards of 22 million Africans had been forcibly removed from their homes and transported to the Americas. Historian Philip Curtin estimated that 42 percent of all African slaves lived and worked in the small sugar-producing islands of the Caribbean. Another 38 percent engaged in plantation agriculture in Brazil, and five percent resided in North America. Plantation labor was so harsh that the slave population died faster than it could reproduce itself. In 1800 there were about eight and one-half million Africans born in the Americas, which was less than the total number of Africans that had been brought across the Atlantic since the year 1600. Despite European willingness to pay for slave labor, the sale of slaves by African rulers to European traders contributed nothing to the economic or social advancement of nascent West African states. Indeed, the scale of the trade undermined the ability of African governments to begin the process of agricultural reform or manufacture. Handicrafts never evolved into viable manufacture for export, and not a single West African kingdom transformed itself into a cash-crop exporting area comparable with the West Indies. Africa's main export product became the essential labor force for Europe's transformation of the New World.

View the **Closer Look**

A Sugar Plantation in the West Indies

on **MyHistoryLab.com**

Most of the *philosophes*, while perhaps opposed to the institution of slavery, declined to take a strong stand against slavery. Nor did they reflect seriously on the impact that the removal of so many able-bodied young men and women had on the indigenous peoples of Africa. Voltaire attributed the institution to humanity's penchant for power and domination. A strongly worded essay in the *Encyclopedia* condemned the institution, and the volume's wide readership may have contributed to the growth of a movement in favor of emancipation. By the third quarter of the eighteenth century, more voices were being raised in opposition. In Britain's American colonies, the pamphleteer **Thomas Paine** (1737–1809) rebuked his countrymen for tolerating the nefarious system at the very time that they were calling for their own freedom from royal authority. However, it was not the *philosophes* who led the antislavery drive, but dissenting Protestant religious groups.

Challenging the Enlightenment Faith   In many respects, the enthusiasm of the Age of Reason, the intoxicating effects of progress, and the conviction that social phenomena were amenable to scientific analysis and manipulation prompted a sharp reaction from a variety of thinkers. In particular, those who found the arid rationalism of the *philosophes* both emotionally unsatisfying and intellectually arrogant voiced the strongest objections. Rousseau suggested that feeling was of greater value than raw intellect in his novels *The New Heloise* (1761) and *Emile* (1762). Samuel

Richardson's popular novel *Pamela* (1749) elevated sentiment and habits of the heart above rational understanding. However, it was in religious circles that the biggest response to the ascent of reason took place, and especially among dissenting voices within the established Protestant churches.

Efforts by select churchmen to harmonize reason and revelation left many believers with little sense of the beauty and mystery, the emotive and transformative side of essential faith. By the mid-eighteenth century, a number of restorative movements were underway. In Germany it was Pietism, in England Methodism, and in North America the **Great Awakening.** Each of these corrective endeavors took aim at the rigidity and complacency of the state-sponsored religious establishments, calling for a return to revelation absent rationalist interpretations. The Moravians in Germany were a Pietist group who found refuge in North America, and one of their number had a powerful influence on the Church of England cleric **John Wesley** (1703–1791). Wesley, along with his brother Charles (1707–1788), founded a dissenting branch of the official Anglican church that became known as Methodism. In America the evangelist **George Whitefield** (1714–1770) transformed the message of unmerited free grace and the need for personal transformation into a mass movement called the Great Awakening during the 1740s. While most popular in rural areas, even growing cities like Boston embraced the spirit of revival Whitefield fostered. For the religious leaders of these grassroots journeys, the power of human reason was as nothing compared to the glory and majesty of the personal God of Christianity.

The Arts in the Age of Reason

In terms of original thought and creation, one area of artistic endeavor reached new levels during the eighteenth century. European music entered an exceptionally vibrant and diverse period after 1700. The major royal courts and *salons* commissioned a stream of works while patronizing various composers, and a growing number of public concert halls offered a wide range of religious and secular music to urban audiences. While opera remained popular, new forms of instrumental and orchestral music appeared. Perhaps most significantly, eighteenth-century Western music began to reflect the rationalism of the age in its emphasis upon formality, harmony, control, and studious adherence to the original composition at each performance. Spontaneity, emotion, and improvisation in performance, central to musical traditions in the non-Western world, were discouraged in favor of balance and order. While compositions dedicated to religious themes and ritual observances remained at the forefront of artistic endeavor in music, composers also began to write secular works for entertainment.

Classical Music   A new musical style, described as "classical" both for its enduring as opposed to ephemeral impact and for its efforts to imitate the symmetry, clarity, and measured restraint of Greek and Roman art, emerged around mid-century. It continued to dominate the compositional arena until the early 1800s. As in so many Enlightenment endeavors, the movement was international in scope, although the leading composers came from Germany and Austria. The central performance innovation was the birth of the orchestra, complete with groups of related instruments (strings, brass, woodwinds, and percussion). Musical instruments evolved rapidly, with the piano enjoying primacy of place. The Austrian **Franz Joseph Haydn** (1732–1809) rose from humble circumstances to music director for a wealthy and powerful Hungarian noble family, the Esterhazy. Over a long career, Haydn composed operas, string quartets, music for religious services or liturgies, and symphonies. During a stay in London in the early 1790s, he composed additional symphonies for large orchestra (some 60 players) and won the acclaim of a large urban public.

Mozart   The preeminent artist of the century was doubtless the Austrian-born **Wolfgang Amadeus Mozart** (1756–1791). He began to compose at the age of 6, and his overall output when he died at age 35 included more than 600 works, among them 41 symphonies and 22 operas. In 1788 alone, Mozart composed three symphonies in six weeks. Like so many of his contemporaries, the young Mozart supported himself by seeking private appointments to play and compose in the courts of Europe's noble families. However, despite the quality and quantity of his artistic output, Mozart never amassed great wealth and was buried without circumstance in an unmarked grave.

Architecture, Painting, and Sculpture   In architecture, the fascination with ancient Greece and Rome that had informed the spirit of the Renaissance grew, especially after fresh archeological studies gave scholars more artifacts from early sites. Excavations at two buried Roman towns near Naples, Herculaneum, and Pompeii, fascinated the reading and traveling public and became "must see" for aristocratic gentlemen making the "grand tour" of Europe's cultural sites. For those who could not travel to original sites, sketches and engravings offered architects a wealth of ideas. A "**neoclassical**" style began to inform design and construction across Europe and even reached the United States by the early nineteenth century. Eighteenth-century designers believed that buildings should reflect the reason, order, and clarity that purportedly lay at the heart of the Enlightenment project. Gone was the riotous detail and elaborate ornamentation of an earlier Baroque style. No longer projections of mystery and absolute power, the neoclassical buildings—public and private—of the eighteenth century emphasized mathematical proportion and refined taste.

Even painting, portraiture, and sculpture began to respond to the Enlightenment call for directness, realism, balance, and harmony. In **Jacques-Louis David**'s (1748–1825) famous *Oath of the Horatii,* three brothers swear to fight a rival family in a struggle to determine the fate of Rome. The enormous canvas, completed in 1782, was 14 by 10 feet, and the viewing public embraced it with enthusiasm.

Life lived in earnest, the virtues of self-sacrifice and patriotism, the ascendancy of principled intellect over the varied and unreliable emotions—these were the themes extracted from David's work. The artist's equally well-known and popular *The Death of Socrates* appeared in 1785. Here the great philosopher is unflinching in his acceptance of an unjust sentence, resolute and composed as he consumes the deadly hemlock. Working in a different genre, the English engraver **William Hogarth**'s (1697–1764) many explorations into the lives of common people offered unadorned, if sometimes highly satirical and moralistic, portrayals of eighteenth-century urban existence at every social level.

View the **Closer Look**

An Eighteenth-Century Artist Appeals to the Ancient World

on **MyHistoryLab.com**

Oath of the Horatii   Jacques-Louis David rendered several of the most famous paintings of his era. This 1782 painting—which covered a huge canvas, measuring 14 by 10 feet—invokes an ancient Roman ritual in order to promote self-sacrifice and patriotism. David would later turn his attentions to contemporary affairs, while retaining his flair for the dramatic. *Jacques-Louis David,* The Oath of the Horatii. *1784. Oil on Canvas. 10'10" × 13'11" (3.3 × 4.25 m). Musée du Louvre, Paris. RMN Reunion des Musées Nationaux/Art Resource, NY*

KEY
QUESTION
REVISITED

Can the principle and practice of human equality ever be truly inclusive?

During the Enlightenment era, ideas of human flourishing were built on the foundations of a new view of human potential. Some seven decades ago, the historian Carl Becker alleged that the *philosophes* had dismantled St. Augustine's otherworldly City of God, the city of Christian believers, as part of a larger effort to rebuild that city on Earth with more up-to-date materials. What Becker meant by this analogy was that the Enlightenment thinkers were just as clearly men of faith as those whom they so publicly disparaged. Faith in progress, in reason, in secular versions of human flourishing, and in humankind's ability to fashion a self-referential heaven on Earth placed the *philosophes* on the same level of intellectual rigor as the churchmen and "mystery-mongers" whom they so disparaged in their writings.

Becker's views were challenged and amended by scholars like Peter Gay in the 1960s, and today our estimate of the Enlightenment is much more complex—confusing even. The movement consisted of varied streams of thought, and the family of enlightened thinkers, like all large families, was replete with problem children and stubborn debate. Yet there were important areas of consensus, and these included a suspicion of emotion and intuition, a desire for efficient and orderly institutions of governance, a willingness to place all traditions under the critical lens of rational inquiry, and, perhaps most eventfully, a willingness to broaden the circle of discussion beyond the confines of the university and the courts of princes. Abigail Adams was part of Enlightenment discourse even though she was denied political rights. While no democrats, the *philosophes* had made an enormous intellectual concession to the idea of human equality, if only in principle. For them, progress and human flourishing were the product of the application of reason to the affairs of daily life. Before the century concluded, serious revolutionaries on both sides of the Atlantic would attempt to translate this belief into action.

Key Terms

Enlightenment, *p. 475*
philosophes, p. 478

Deism, *p. 483*
enlightened despots, *p. 486*

Activities

1. Why did the *philosophes* object to the influence that traditional religions exercised?

2. How did the Enlightenment affect the lives of common people?

3. Outline the main principles of Deism.

4. Is it fair to argue that modern social science began in the eighteenth century?

5. Was enlightened absolutism a serious institutional mechanism for reform?

6. Draw up a detailed list of the failures and limits of the Enlightenment.

7. Describe the main features of the "Enlightenment style" in the arts.

Further Reading

Jeremy Black, *Eighteenth-Century Europe* (1990), a solid overview of political developments.

Roger Pearson, *Voltaire Almighty: A Life in Pursuit of Freedom* (2005) is a good introduction to the life of one of the most influential figures of the Enlightenment.

Perez Zagorin, *How the Idea of Religious Toleration Came to the West* (2003) details an important modern movement.

C. A. Kors, *Encyclopedia of the Enlightenment* (2002) offers clear introductions to many of the major intellectual themes of the period.

MyHistoryLab Connections

Visit **MyHistoryLab.com** *for a customized Study Plan that will help you build your knowledge of* The Age of Enlightenment: Rationalism and Its Uses.

Questions for Analysis

1. How did Kant characterize the Enlightenment?

Read the **Document** Immanuel Kant Defines the Enlightenment, p. 478

2. How does Voltaire compare and contrast the ideas of Descartes and Newton?

Read the **Document** Voltaire, *Letters on the English,* p. 479

3. What is the global mission of the Jesuits?

Watch the **Video** The Global Mission of the Jesuits, p. 481

4. What does *Declaration on the Rights of Woman and the Female Citizen* reveal about where women stood in the social order in eighteenth-century France?

Read the **Document** Olympe de Gouges, *Declaration of the Rights of Woman and the Female Citizen,* p. 490

5. What are some of the social values reflected in *The Oath of the Horatii?*

View the **Closer Look** An Eighteenth-Century Artist Appeals to the Ancient World, p. 494

Other Resources from This Chapter

View the **Map**   Science and the Enlightenment, p. 477

Read the **Document** John Locke, *Essay Concerning Human Understanding,* p. 478

View the **Image**   Diderot's *Encyclopedia*—Illustration of Agricultural Techniques, p. 480

Read the **Document** Denis Diderot, Preliminary Discourse from *The Encyclopedia* (France), 1751, p. 480

Read the **Document** Jesuits in India (1530s–1550s), St. Francis Xavier, p. 481

Read the **Document** Introduction to the *Wealth of Nations,* p. 484

Read the **Document** *Crimes and Punishments,* p. 485

Read the **Document** Jean-Jacques Rousseau, *Emile,* p. 487

Read the **Document** Baron de Montesquieu, Excerpt from *The Spirit of the Laws,* p. 489

Read the **Document** Mary Wollstonecraft, Introduction to *A Vindication of the Rights of Woman,* p. 490

View the **Closer Look** A Sugar Plantation in the West Indies, p. 492

17 | Rebellion and Revolution: American Independence and the French Revolution

((•—[Hear the Audio   Chapter 17 at MyHistoryLab.com

LEARNING OBJECTIVES

Why did the American colonies reject British crown authority?   •   How did the French Revolution transform European political thought and practice?   •   Did Napoleon Bonaparte champion or repudiate the French Revolution?   •   What impact did the French Revolution have on developments in Latin America?

Having it at last in my power to visit my American friends, I hastened to the well known, and heartily beloved shores of this continent, and now feel happy to think, I once more am within the limits of the United States.

—Marquis de Lafayette, 1783

KEY QUESTION

Can political change occur without social and economic upheaval?

In 1776, the Marquis de Lafayette (1757–1834) signed an agreement to serve as a major general in the Continental army of the newly established United States of America. Lafayette was a wealthy French aristocrat who had begun his military career as a cavalry officer at age 16. In America he fought and distinguished himself under the command of General George Washington (1732–1799). In letters home to family, friends, and government officials, Lafayette faithfully promoted the America cause, and he was a key figure in forging a military alliance between the monarchy of King Louis XVI and the American republic. After returning to France in 1781, Lafayette served as a liaison between the French government and two American ambassadors to France, Benjamin Franklin (1706–1790) and Thomas Jefferson (1743–1826).

Why did this member of the European nobility risk his life in defense of a republic that repudiated both monarchy and titled aristocracy? When he first agreed to fight in America, the 20-year-old Lafayette saw only an opportunity to enhance his professional skills and to win renown on the battlefield. Writing in 1779, he admitted that he could recall "no time in my life when I did not love stories of glorious deeds, or have dreams of traveling the world in search of fame." But upon his arrival in the rebellious colonies, Lafayette was almost immediately inspired by the principles that had rallied the American patriots. "Never before had such a glorious cause attracted the attention of mankind; it was the final struggle of liberty, and its defeat would have left it neither asylum nor hope." In the years leading up to the French Revolution of 1789, Lafayette worked on behalf of a range of liberal causes: the liberation of African slaves, religious freedom for French Protestants and Jews, and the creation of a constitutional monarchy for France. When the Revolution broke out, this aristocratic friend of the United States drafted a statement of rights modeled after the Declaration of Independence. The revolutionary French National Assembly incorporated many of Lafayette's ideas into the *Declaration of the Rights of Man and Citizen* (1789), the central text of the French Revolution. That same year, now serving as commander of the Paris National Guard, a newly formed citizen militia, Lafayette sent the symbolic key of the old royal fortress-prison of the Bastille to his "adoptive father," President Washington. Today that symbol of what Lafayette called the "fortress of despotism" hangs in Washington's home in Mount Vernon, Virginia. ■

America Rejects Europe

Rebellion or Revolution?   In certain respects, the American colonial revolt against Britain that began in 1776 was fundamentally different from the French Revolution. Strong social and economic grievances (except among African-Americans) were absent from the American conflict, religious issues were insignificant, and the post-independence political system remained unchanged except for the withdrawal of American allegiance to the British crown. In short, the American break with Britain was not a genuine revolution, if one associates revolution with profound social, economic, religious, and political upheaval. All of these factors were present in the uprising that began in France in May 1789.

Conversely, ideas and events in America from the end of the French and Indian War in 1763 to the successful conclusion of the American war of independence in 1783 had a profound impact on developments in France. Political leaders in America were familiar with French Enlightenment thought, while America's successful experiment in republican government inspired antimonarchical elements in France during the 1790s. Eager for an opportunity to avenge its loss in 1763, the French government of Louis XVI exploited the differences between Britain and its North American colonies; when the American war effort began to falter, French financial and military assistance enabled the rebellious colonists to prevail in their struggle against the world's greatest power. However much the French government disliked American **republicanism,** it decided that the opportunity to strike a blow against British power was worth the risk involved in assisting the rebels.

Britain's Fiscal Crisis   The British national debt had doubled during the French and Indian War. At the start of the eighteenth century, that debt stood at 14 million pounds; in 1763 it totaled nearly 130 million pounds. With the successful conclusion of the war in 1763, King **George III** (r. 1760–1820) and the leaders of Parliament decided to raise crown revenues and service the debt. They planned to do this by enforcing mercantilist trade regulations on the colonies and by imposing new tax measures designed to relieve the burden on English taxpayers. The British expected the Americans to cooperate with these measures because the war had largely

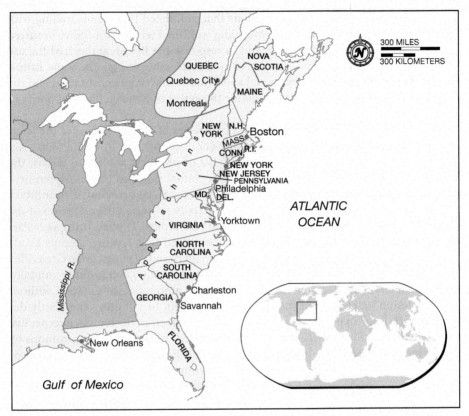

MAP 17-1   North America in 1763   Britain's victory over France in 1763 presented authorities in London with two difficult challenges: how to pay for the cost of the empire and how to administer newly acquired North American territories.

QUESTION: Why did British authorities seek to restrict settlement to lands east of the Appalachians?

been fought to increase the security and prosperity of Britain's American colonies. The costs associated with administering the empire stood at about 70,000 pounds in 1756. After the war, those costs increased five times, largely because the imperial government stationed troops along the Appalachian frontier (see Map 17–1). British attempts to redefine the relationship between the colonies and the home country precipitated a crisis of trust less than a decade after the defeat of the French.

A New Tax Regime   Beginning with the establishment of the Virginia House of Burgesses in 1619, most of the original 13 British colonies in North America had created legislative assemblies that were modeled after the Parliament in London. By the mid-eighteenth century, colonial governors, all appointed by the king, led **bicameral assemblies.** The governor appointed the members of the upper house, and property-owning white males elected the lower house. Despite their extensive executive powers, most governors worked closely with their legislatures. The British government had allowed the colonial governments to administer their own affairs as long as the colonies obeyed the laws of trade. However, ambitious colonial merchants grew increasingly restive with restrictions that prohibited them from trading with other European powers. Extensive smuggling with the French West Indies occurred during the French and Indian War, and in response the British authorized the use of general search warrants in an effort to confiscate smuggled goods. Some British colonists insisted that such actions violated Britain's unwritten constitution and the "rights of Englishmen." The move to define the extent of Parliamentary authority in the colonies had begun.

In 1764 the British enacted the first of a series of tax plans. Under the leadership of Prime Minister George Grenville (1712–1770), the so-called Sugar Act became law. In addition to expanding the list of products subject to tariffs, the legislation called for customs agents in all colonial ports to rigorously enforce procedures for collecting revenue. Smugglers were to be prosecuted in military courts. Assemblies in nearly every colony officially protested the adoption of the Sugar Act, sending petitions to London asking for repeal. The following year Parliament approved the **Stamp Act.** This law required that revenue stamps be affixed to all legal documents and even to newspapers and playing cards. Grenville's government hoped that the excise would raise around 60,000 pounds annually. Outspoken colonists declared that the Stamp Act amounted to "taxation without representation," a claim that members of Parliament in London vehemently denied. In fact, English politicians claimed that all subjects of the crown, irrespective of where they resided, were "virtually" represented in the House of Commons by members who placed the interests of the British Empire before provincial concerns. The government of George III believed that American objections to the Stamp duties represented simple tax evasion, a selfish unwillingness to assume some of the costs of administering the British Empire to which the colonists belonged and from which they benefited.

View the Image

Stamp Act Protest

on **MyHistoryLab.com**

The Americans countered by insisting that from the period of the earliest colonial settlements, representatives lived in the districts that they served. The idea that a member of Parliament who had never been to America could adequately represent local interests was incomprehensible to the colonial mind. Colonial assemblies passed resolutions condemning the Stamp Act, angry mobs threatened and intimidated Stamp tax collectors, and most businesses and legal transactions took place absent the hated tax. American merchants then began boycotting British goods. Under extreme pressure from irate British merchants, moderates in Parliament decided to withdraw the tax in March 1766. Colonial politicians and merchants were jubilant, but when British lawmakers coupled the withdrawal of the tax with a **Declaratory Act,** stating that Parliament could enact any law it wished to bind the colonies, the issue of sovereignty was again placed in dispute.

Constitutional Conflicts   By the 1760s, the colonial understanding of *representation* and *constitution* diverged significantly from the interpretations put forward in London. The same words were used, but the opposing sides attached different meanings to them. While representation in colonial assemblies meant advocacy on behalf of one's local constituency, in Britain it meant a more comprehensive view of imperial interests. In the colonies constitutions were written documents that delineated the specific powers granted to the government. The British constitution, however, was not a single charter or document but the totality of laws, customs, and institutions basic to the life and culture of a people. In effect, the constitution was fluid, always changing and responding to the needs of the kingdom.

As Parliament attempted to assert its sovereignty over the North American colonies, this semantic divide compounded the differences between a provincial outlook and its imperial counterpart. Leaders in the colonies were increasingly convinced that the liberties and "rights of Englishmen" that had been secured in the Glorious Revolution of 1688 were under attack by corrupt politicians who were determined to erect a tyrannical state. This, at least, was the view of a group of republican writers called the **Commonwealthmen** who saw England as the only state in Europe not governed by an absolutist monarch. Especially active at midcentury, their arguments resonated in the colonies, and all plans to tax the colonies were viewed through this ideological prism. When the English radical **John Wilkes** (1727–1797) was expelled from the House of Commons in the 1760s for his criticism of the king and his ministers in the newspaper *The North Briton,* colonists who followed these developments saw a sinister pattern developing. England was slipping into tyranny, with the royal executive attempting to emulate his peers on the continent. The Commonwealth perspective was represented throughout the colonies in newspaper articles, in public demonstrations, and in mob actions against "corrupt" representatives of the crown.

In 1767 the new British finance minister, Charles Townshend (1725–1767), imposed fresh tariffs on glass, lead, tea, and paper imported into the colonies. Again, the Americans organized boycotts of British goods. Troops were sent to Boston to protect the customs agents who were charged with collecting the levies, and in March 1770 clashes between townspeople and soldiers led to an exchange in which five civilians were killed. This so-called **Boston Massacre** temporarily galvanized colonial public opinion against the crown, and Townshend's tariffs were withdrawn (with the sole exception of the tariff on imported tea). For the next two years, there were no major incidents, and British imports returned to

Boston "Massacre"   Just as the Declaration of Independence would unfairly portray King George III as a tyrant, this view of the Boston Massacre by Paul Revere was an effective piece of propaganda to generate support for the colonial resistance effort. The innocent civilians who were being fired upon were actually members of a violent mob who had provoked the British troops.

their preboycott levels. Not until a group of Bostonians destroyed a shipment of imported East India Company tea in May 1773 did the government of King George III take robust and determined action against the colonies.

This Boston "Tea Party" outraged the British government. The king resolved that "we must master them or totally leave them to themselves." The port of Boston was ordered closed, and the Massachusetts colonial assembly was suppressed until reparations were paid to the East India Company. For the first time in almost two centuries, the Bay Colony had lost its right to self-government. In 1774 Parliament also passed the **Quebec Act,** extending the boundaries of that mostly French-speaking Catholic territory into the Ohio River valley. The Quebec Act also put the province under a royal governor with no assembly (which was how Quebec had been ruled by France). Together the actions in Massachusetts and Quebec seemed to confirm the worst fears of colonial radicals that Britain wished to destroy self-government in America.

View the **Image**

Boston Tea Party

on **MyHistoryLab.com**

Continental Congress and Independence   Representatives from each of the 13 British colonies maintained close lines of communication throughout 1763–1774. In September 1774 these political figures organized the First **Continental Congress** in Philadelphia to plan a joint strategy. The following summer pitched battles between British troops and colonial militia took place at Lexington and Concord in Massachusetts.

A Second Continental Congress met in May 1775 in an attempt to work out a compromise with the British. Failing in this effort, the Congress moved to organize a unified government for the colonies. King George III declared the colonies in open rebellion in August 1775, and over the winter a short pamphlet called *Common Sense* helped to build broad public support for an American repudiation of British rule. The author was **Thomas Paine** (1737–1809), an English-born artisan who had been in America for less than one year and who would later relocate to France during the French Revolution. In July 1776 the Continental Congress adopted a **Declaration of Independence** written by Thomas Jefferson, a 33-year-old delegate from Virginia.

Read the **Document**

Thomas Paine, Common Sense

on **MyHistoryLab.com**

Read the **Document**

Rough Draft of the Declaration of Independence

on **MyHistoryLab.com**

Watch the **Video**

The American Revolution as Different Americans Saw It

on **MyHistoryLab.com**

The spirit of the European Enlightenment informed the American Declaration of Independence. With the Declaration, monarchy was nullified, aristocracy renounced, and the equality of white male citizens established as the basis of national sovereignty. Consisting of two parts, the general statement of the right to revolution, a right that Jefferson based on natural law, "self-evident" reason, and the defense of "certain inalienable rights," has inspired people around the world for over 200 years. The second part, a personal indictment of King George III, served as a brilliant polemic during the course of the war for independence. Together they provided an unprecedented public justification for political rebellion, a statement designed as much for a Europe-wide audience as it was for the 10 to 15 percent of colonists in America who opposed independence.

War and Republican Rule   During the first year of fighting, Britain employed a seasoned and well-trained army, together with German mercenaries, against an inexperienced colonial militia led by George Washington. In addition to large numbers of Tories (colonists who supported the British), thousands of colonists were indifferent to the outcome of the struggle, making Washington's task extremely difficult. After a series of setbacks on the battlefield, the American Continental army finally won a crucial victory at Saratoga, New York, in October 1777. Almost 6,000 British troops surrendered to American forces. King **Louis XVI,** whose government had been sending arms and supplies to the American patriots, now quickly recognized the independence of the United States. Within six months, France signed a formal treaty of alliance with the fledgling republic. The French loaned the U.S. government over eight million dollars and sent a large fleet and army to North America. In October 1781 Washington and his French allies won a decisive victory over British forces at Yorktown in Virginia. In 1783, the British signed a formal treaty in Paris acknowledging American independence and ceding some colonial possessions to France and its ally Spain.

Read the **Document**

Letter from a Revolutionary War Soldier

on **MyHistoryLab.com**

Constitution Building   The Continental Congress had served as America's national government during the war with Britain, and in 1781 its legal basis was established with the ratification by each state of the **Articles of Confederation.**

Read the **Document**

Articles of Confederation

on **MyHistoryLab.com**

Under its provisions, states retained their sovereignty and independence, with the federal government denied the power to tax or print money. No executive office was created under this instrument of government, and judicial power remained at the state level. Each state enjoyed one vote in the unicameral Congress, and unanimity was required before important legislation could become law. The Articles of Confederation reflected American fear of coercive central government under the leadership of a single British executive. But decentralized power was not a complete success; by the mid-1780s, many political leaders were calling for the formation of a stronger national government. Foreign affairs, military preparedness, and internal development all required a government with the power to raise revenue and print money. The loose alliance of 13 states, while preserving sovereignty at the local level, hindered the formation of mutually beneficial trade policies and weakened the ability of the United States to negotiate successfully with foreign powers.

In 1787 the Congress approved a meeting in the city of Philadelphia, where delegates were to work on revisions to the Articles of Confederation. Broadly interpreting their mandate, the assembled delegates jettisoned the Articles and drew up a new instrument of government. The final product was sent to the states for ratification, and it was approved by late 1788. The **Constitution of the United States** established a presidential system, with a separate judiciary and a strong legislative branch.

Read the **Document**

Bill of Rights

on **MyHistoryLab.com**

Watch the **Video**

Slavery and the Constitution

on **MyHistoryLab.com**

A **Bill of Rights** was added to the document in order to protect individual citizens from possible government abuse of power. The new Constitution permitted the national government to tax citizens, regulate interstate and foreign commerce, and raise and maintain an army and navy. States lost their right to issue money or to make treaties with foreign governments. The framers of this second Constitution believed that the new instrument of government provided an adequate set of checks and balances to prevent any single branch from abridging the "natural rights" of the citizenry.

Impact in Europe and Latin America   Leading figures in America's successful bid for independence, men like Thomas Jefferson, **Benjamin Franklin,** and **John Adams** (1735–1826), embraced the Enlightenment's call for the critical evaluation of all institutions and ideas. The American adoption of religious toleration, the insistence upon trial by jury, freedom of speech and religion, an expansive franchise, and government by the consent of the governed all served to animate European and Latin American reformers and revolutionaries during the next century. The success of the American republic encouraged opponents of the Old Regime across the European continent and in Spain's American empire; for European royalty and the titled aristocracy, however, the United States stood as a dangerous challenge to the inviolability of the hierarchical social order, to the belief that only a chosen few were born to rule. The government of Louis XVI had taken a huge gamble by backing the American cause. Britain may have been humbled by America's successful colonial revolt, but over the next 20 years, its government would weather the upsurge in European republicanism while the Old Regime in France would be overturned.

Key Developments in the American and French Revolutions

	AMERICA		FRANCE
1763	Britain victorious in Seven Years' War	1789	Meeting of Estates General
1765	Stamp Act	1789	Fall of the Bastille
1770	Boston "Massacre"	1792	Outbreak of war with Austria
1774	First Continental Congress	1793	Execution of Louis XVI
1775	Second Continental Congress	1793–1794	Reign of Terror
1776	Declaration of Independence	1799–1804	Napoleon's Consulate
1778	France joins American war effort against Britain	1802	Napoleonic Code
		1804	Napoleon declared Emperor of the French
1781	British defeated at Yorktown		
1783	Treaty of Paris recognizes American independence	1814	Collapse of French Empire

Revolution in France

Crisis of the Old Regime   When Louis XVI (r. 1774–1793) assumed the French throne upon the death of his grandfather, the country was facing a pronounced fiscal emergency. The unsuccessful French and Indian War (1754–1763) had been largely funded by loans secured against a government guarantee of military victory. New sources of taxes were desperately needed, but those individuals and institutions most able to pay—the aristocracy and the church—consistently refused to register royal decrees thanks to their control over the 13 regional *parlements*. French peasants, who were better off than peasants elsewhere in Europe, shouldered the bulk of the tax burden in the country. Louis XVI compounded the financial crisis by supporting the American war of independence. By the time that the Americans had secured their freedom from Britain, more than half of the French national budget was dedicated to interest payments on loans taken to support earlier military ventures.

Louis XVI appointed a series of reform-minded finance ministers, but each man was forced to resign in the face of strident aristocratic opposition. When one of these ministers, Charles Alexandre de Calonne (1734–1802), proposed a tax on land and the sale of church property, the wall of privileged opposition reached new heights. Nobles

REVEIL DU TIERS ETAT.

Ma foute, il étoit tems que je me réveillasse, car l'opression de mes fers me donnoient le cochemar un peu trop fort.

"The Third Estate Awakens"   An illustration from the early days of the French Revolution shows the "third estate" awakening—and arming itself—while the First and Second Estates (the clergy and the nobility) recoil in horror. The violence of the Revolution is further suggested by the destruction of the Bastille in the background.

spoke of the "rights of man" and the government's attack on individual freedom. Clearly, the first two orders or estates of the realm, the clergy and the nobility, were attempting to use the rhetoric of Enlightenment in a base effort to maintain their varied financial exemptions. In frustration, the king agreed to call a meeting of the **Estates General,** a medieval advisory body that had not convened since 1614. The king's advisors hoped that this assemblage, which included representatives from all three estates—nobility, clergy, and commoners—could muster the required moral authority to break the deadlock.

○─【**View** the **Closer Look**

Challenging the French Political Order

on **MyHistoryLab.com**

A troubling set of demographic and economic indicators compounded the fiscal crisis. Population grew at a brisk pace during the eighteenth century, and while food production managed to keep up with the increases, long-term inflation made food more expensive and undermined the ability of poor peasants to maintain themselves. As the population expanded, landlords attempted to protect themselves against inflation by holding down wages while simultaneously raising rents and dues. A series of bad harvests during the 1780s aggravated conditions; thus, when elections to the Estates General were held in 1789 a mixture of anger, resentment, and high expectations influenced the outlook of millions of French men and women.

From Estates General to National Assembly   The meeting of the Estates General provided the **Third Estate,** which included urban laborers, peasants, artisans, businesspeople, lawyers, bankers, and financiers, an unprecedented opportunity to influence national politics. Delegates arrived at Versailles with a list of grievances *(cahiers de doleances)* drawn up by their local constituencies. A more perceptive monarch than Louis XVI would have realized that decades of pent-up frustration over the high cost of food, inequitable tax and service burdens, urban underemployment, and chronic government inefficiencies would result in a contentious meeting. The impact of books, political pamphlets, and broadsides published during the Age of Enlightenment was bound to be significant, at least in shaping the outlook of the reading public. During the 1790s, France's political, social, and religious institutions would be shaken to their foundations. Millions of French men and women would become involved in some form of political action, and their status as subjects would be transformed into the role of citizen.

☐●─【**Read** the **Document**

Emmanuel Joseph Sieyès, What Is the Third Estate?

on **MyHistoryLab.com**

When the Estates General first assembled at Versailles in early May 1789, the Third Estate had already received royal permission to double its delegation. According to the protocol of the last meeting in 1614, each estate was allowed to elect 300 delegates. Because it represented most of the French population, the Third Estate sent 600 delegates to Versailles. How each estate was to vote was a more difficult issue. Traditionally, each estate cast one vote, a procedure guaranteed to enable the clergy and nobility to defeat all reforms originating with the commoners. For weeks, the first two Estates refused to amend the voting process. Finally, on June 17, 1789, the Third Estate, together with a handful of sympathetic clergy and nobility, declared itself the **National Assembly** of France and pledged not to disband until the country had a new constitution. As newspaper accounts and eyewitness reports of the events at Versailles spread throughout the country, peasants and urban workers were suffering after an especially harsh winter and faced escalating food prices. They looked upon the actions of the Third Estate with a sense of renewed hope for change.

Fall of the Bastille   Initially, King Louis XVI was unwilling to accept the legitimacy of the National Assembly. When he began to increase the number of troops at Versailles and in Paris, fears of a violent crackdown grew. Some 800 Parisians responded on July 14 by storming the **Bastille,** a royal armory that doubled as a debtor's prison. After overwhelming the handful of troops stationed at the Bastille, the enraged mob killed the governor of the fortress and some of his soldiers. Subsequently forming a citizen militia called the National Guard and led by Lafayette, the radicalized Parisians—most of whom were members of the middle class—instantly became the military wing of the Third Estate. Lafayette suggested an insignia for the Guards, a tricolor of blue, white, and red stripes, which became the new flag of revolutionary France.

Declaration of the Rights of Man and Citizen   Similar urban revolts took place in cities throughout France. The formation of regional militia groups modeled after the National Guard led to the resignation of many royal government officials who feared for life and limb. In the countryside, landless, hungry, and desperate peasants began to attack the homes of local nobles, pillaging and destroying any legal papers related to dues and services owed by local peasants to their superiors. Their actions led liberal nobles and churchmen in the National Assembly to renounce their feudal privileges. Equality before the law had been conceded in the face of direct

The Storming of the Bastille   The attack on the Bastille on July 14, 1789, marked the first time that ordinary Parisians shaped the course of the French Revolution.

📖●▐ Read the Document

Declaration of the Rights of
Man and Citizen

on **MyHistoryLab.com**

action by the peasantry. On August 27, 1789, the National Assembly approved the **Declaration of the Rights of Man and Citizen,** a statement of political principles modeled after America's Declaration of Independence. All men were declared free and equal citizens, religious toleration was adopted, and taxation based on the ability to pay was accepted as a basic constitutional principle. Women were not mentioned in this watershed document, but women were coming to play an important role in the Revolution. In Paris the high price of bread—the staple food of the urban poor—led some 7,000 women (armed with knives, swords, and pikes) to march on Versailles in early October. After skirmishes in which a few royal guards were killed, the women compelled Louis and his queen, Marie Antoinette (1755–1793), to accompany them back to the capital. The king was now forced to recognize the de facto power of the National Assembly, whose bourgeois delegates were committed to the formation of a constitutional monarchy.

A Written Constitution for France   In 1791 the Assembly created a constitutional monarchy whereby the king now exercised a delaying, but not a permanent, veto over legislation passed by a unicameral Legislative Assembly. The members of the new legislature had to meet high property qualifications in order to serve, although all males who paid local taxes equal to three days' labor wages could vote for electors who then picked the legislators. In effect, only about 50,000 of France's 25 million people could hold public office under the new constitution. However, the criterion for officeholding had shifted from birth to wealth, opening new opportunities for nonnoble citizens to shape public policy at the national level. In fact, all titles of nobility were abolished. A uniform court system staffed by professional judges replaced the feudal *parlements,* and 83 administrative regions called *departements* of roughly equal size replaced the medieval provinces. In an effort to rationalize economic policy, free trade policies were adopted and restrictive guilds were suppressed. French women were denied political rights under the new constitution, and some, like the self-educated commoner **Olympe de Gouges** (d. 1793),

📖●▐ Read the Document

Olympe de Gouges,
Declaration of the Rights
of Woman and the Female
Citizen

on **MyHistoryLab.com**

called for an extension of civil rights. In her *Declaration of the Rights of Woman and the Female Citizen,* de Gouges rephrased the *Declaration of the Rights of Man* by inserting the word *woman* wherever the initial document used the word *man.* Her efforts to make natural rights language more inclusive failed, but the active role played by women in the Revolution kept the issue of human equality alive.

Attacking the Church   Unlike most revolutionary regimes in recent centuries, the French National Assembly reluctantly assumed all of the debts of the previous royal government. To address the acute financial crisis, the new government ordered the confiscation of the property of the Roman Catholic Church. In addition, all clergy were required to take loyalty oaths to the new government, in effect transferring their allegiance from the pope in Rome to the national state. The Assembly also reduced the number of bishops to conform to the new administrative *departements.* Church property was offered to investors, and *assignats,* or government bonds, were sold to the public on the expectation that revenue generated from sales of church land would service the bonds. However, the income derived from this one source failed to make a significant impact on the gigantic debt. In addition, the actions taken against the church enabled opponents of the Revolution to rally common people to their cause; the revolutionaries were increasingly portrayed as destroyers of traditional religious values, and the Roman Catholic Church set out on a course of opposition to liberalism and revolution that would continue for most of the nineteenth century.

The Radical Revolution and End of the Monarchy, 1792–1794

During the first two years of revolutionary change, King Louis XVI had reluctantly assented to the measures taken by the National Assembly, even approving the shift to constitutional monarchy. Equality before the law, careers open to talent, a written constitution—liberals were pleased with the accomplishments of the Revolution and wished to build upon these moderate reforms. However, many French aristocrats, including the king's younger brothers, the counts of Provence (1755–1824) and Artois (1757–1836), fled to neighboring countries and worked to build a counterrevolutionary movement. In June 1791, Louis XVI, feeling increasingly insecure in Paris and opposed to the measures taken against the church, was persuaded to join them. Disguised as commoners, the king and his immediate family attempted to flee the country but were discovered at Varennes in eastern France. They returned to Paris as virtual prisoners. Sympathizing with Louis's predicament, Queen Marie Antoinette's brother, Emperor Leopold II of Austria (r. 1790–1792), together with Prussia's King Frederick William II (r. 1786–1797), threatened intervention if the French royal family was harmed. Within a year the French government declared war on both countries (ostensibly for harboring French aristocrats who were plotting against the government), confident that military conflict in defense of the homeland would rally the French people to the revolutionary cause.

However, poor laborers, shopkeepers, and artisans had less to show for their efforts. Beginning in 1792, these **sansculottes** (referring to the long trousers that workingmen wore instead of aristocratic knee breeches) called on the government to address the problem of economic inequality by increasing wages, controlling food prices, and raising taxes on the wealthy. The *sansculottes* also called for a more democratic political order in which the voice of the common citizen would be heard. In their view the middle-class leaders of the Revolution were content to slow reform down now that they enjoyed political privileges once held by the aristocracy of the Old Regime.

The outbreak of war with Austria and Prussia in April 1792 worsened the economic situation and led to dissension within the ranks of the Legislative Assembly. Lacking strong military leaders in the wake of numerous defections by aristocratic officers (among them Lafayette, who was afraid of the increasing radicalization of the Revolution), the French army fared poorly on the battlefield. As enemy troops penetrated deeper into France, panic spread in Paris. Acting on wild rumors that disaffected priests and nobles who had been arrested were about to break out of custody, mobs attacked prisons and murdered over 1,000 inmates. Earlier, the people of Paris had also assaulted the royal residence, killed hundreds of the royal guards and servants, and demanded **universal manhood suffrage,** decentralized government, and economic justice. Radicals succeeded in forcing the Legislative Assembly to "suspend" the king

PEOPLE IN CONTEXT   Edmund Burke on Revolution

Edmund Burke (1729–1797) was born in British-controlled Ireland and attended Trinity College, Dublin, before moving to London in 1750. During Britain's conflict with its American colonies, Burke was a member of Parliament who took the unpopular position that the king and Parliament should work to conciliate the colonists by trying to understand their constitutional grievances. In speeches before Parliament, Burke appealed for the abandonment of colonial taxation and the promotion of colonial freedoms as consistent with the history of British involvement in North America. In a "Speech on Conciliation with the Colonies" (1775) Burke stated that English settlers "have turned a savage wilderness into a glorious empire, and have made the most extensive and the only honorable conquests, not by destroying, but by promoting the wealth, the number, the happiness of the human race. Let us get an American revenue as we have got an American empire. English privileges have made it all that it is; English privileges alone will make it all it can be." For Burke, the essence of political wisdom lay in a respect for precedent, the accumulated wisdom and traditions of centuries. He believed that government efforts to enforce new tax schemes on the colonists after 1765 smacked of innovation and constituted a violation of English liberties.

This same conservatism, the defense of tradition and custom, led Burke to come to the defense of Irish Catholics (Burke's mother was Catholic) who sought to practice their religion in freedom and Irish merchants who sought to trade on equal terms with their English counterparts. Once again, Burke took an unpopular stand in pleading for colonials, whom most English politicians considered troublesome. When the French Revolution began in 1789, many liberals in England and America applauded the efforts of the National Assembly to curb the power of the crown and to establish a new constitution. But at this juncture Burke broke with many in his own political party, the Whigs. In *Reflections on the Revolution in France* (1790) Burke denounced the revolutionaries even before the radical stage had begun. He doubted whether the newly elected French assembly could control the forces of change in a manner consistent with order and tranquility. "The objects of society are of the greatest possible complexity," he maintained, and hastily drawn up blueprints for the good society, implemented without regard for a particular nation's heritage, were a formula for disaster.

Edmund Burke Burke was a defender of the American colonists in their quarrel with Britain and later wrote a powerful indictment of the moderate stage of the French Revolution. In both instances, Burke insisted that he had remained faithful to his conservative principles.

Thomas Paine responded to Burke's *Reflections* with *The Rights of Man* (1794). Burke was opposed to the Enlightenment language of "natural rights" and claimed that "Government is not made in virtue of natural rights, which may and do exist in total independence of it." Instead, "Government is a contrivance of human wisdom to provide for human wants," and only men who worked within the framework of existing national institutions and practices could successfully guide the state. He believed that the French Revolution would go violently wrong because its leaders sought to do away with a centuries-old political system. Effective political systems were for Burke akin to organic systems, complicated and delicate, and while these systems should evolve over time, forcing change through revolution was self-defeating. During the nineteenth century, Burke's ideas were influential in conservative circles across Western Europe and in America. ■

QUESTION: Is conservatism always opposed to change?

and call for elections to a new national government. This "Convention" government, named after the American Constitutional Convention of 1787, was elected on the basis of universal male suffrage and charged with drawing up a more radical constitution. Almost immediately, the newly elected delegates proclaimed France a republic and moved to prosecute the monarch for conspiring against the liberty of the French people.

Louis XVI, derisively referred to by his accusers as "Citizen Capet" after the Capetians who had founded the dynasty in 987, was tried and convicted in December 1792. On January 21, 1793, he was beheaded by the newly invented guillotine. Marie Antoinette, the frivolous queen who had become the supreme symbol of royal indifference to the suffering of the French people, followed her husband to the guillotine in October (Olympe de Gouges, who had spoken out for the queen, was executed in November). The war with Austria and Prussia intensified, and the Convention government's difficulties were compounded when the anti-French coalition expanded to include Britain, Holland, Portugal, Spain, Sardinia, and Naples. For the leaders of the Revolution, the European conflict was now about the defense of new political principles and fundamental social transformation. Europe's monarchs and titled aristocrats, they believed, were committed to the destruction of their enlightened republic, and extreme measures were justified in the heroic struggle ahead.

〇─[View the Image

French Revolution, Execution of Louis XVI

on **MyHistoryLab.com**

Marat Jean Paul Marat was one of the most radical of the revolutionary leaders. He published a newspaper called *The Friend of the People* and was popular among Paris's *sansculottes.* This painting by the great French artist Jacques-Louis David depicts Marat's 1793 assassination, in his bathtub, by a royalist named Charlotte Corday.

Jacobin Rule and the Reign of Terror   In June 1793 a group of radical leaders in the Convention, known as **Jacobins** (after the name of a former Dominican monastery in Paris where they met informally), began to dominate the proceedings. The Jacobins favored strong central control over the *departements* and emergency powers to address the economic and military crisis. The urban *sansculottes* supported the Jacobin leaders, and in early June 1793 a mob surrounded the Convention and demanded the expulsion and arrest of the more moderate members, known as **Girondins** (from the *departement* of Gironde), who were seized and executed. The Jacobins were now emboldened to pursue their revolutionary plans. In the face of emerging peasant counterrevolution in the countryside, foreign invasion from the east, and economic breakdown everywhere, the Jacobins persuaded the Convention to delegate executive power to the 12-member **Committee of Public Safety,** which they dominated.

These fervent republicans instituted an unprecedented draft of unmarried men between the ages of 18 and 25 and built a citizen army of over 800,000 men. Women and children were called upon as well, stitching clothing and manufacturing bandages for the troops. These citizen-soldiers were inspired by French nationalism to fight for the revolutionary ideals of liberty, equality, and fraternity—not for a divine-right monarch who cared little for their plight. Fired by patriotism and led by battle-hardened officers who had risen through the ranks, the rejuvenated army managed to roll back the enemy and even take the offensive in Belgium and the Rhineland by the summer of 1794.

The Committee of Public Safety fought an even more bloody war on the domestic front. Led by **Maximilien Robespierre** (1758–1794), the radical leaders were intent on creating a "republic of virtue" in which ignorance and superstition would be expelled and there would be no extremes of wealth and poverty. A Law of the Maximum, designed to control the price of bread and flour, was instituted in order to appease the *sansculottes,* and a new draft constitution (never implemented) promised rights to education and basic subsistence. Influenced by the thought of Rousseau and convinced that they alone understood the general will of the French people, Robespierre and his colleagues on the

Committee of Public Safety attacked Girondin critics of the regime, peasant opponents of centralized rule, royalist priests, nobles, and their supporters—anyone who disagreed with Jacobin leadership. A brutal terror campaign was inaugurated against the varied "enemies of the people." It began with royalists in

Maximilien Robespierre   Known as "The Incorruptible" for his austere lifestyle and revolutionary ethics, Robespierre emerged as leader of the Committee for Public Safety during the "Reign of Terror." Robespierre was eventually claimed by the Terror; he was beheaded in July 1794.

the capital and eventually consumed members of every social class and most political perspectives. Upwards of 30,000 people, most of them peasants and workers, were put to death before Robespierre turned against his own allies. In self-defense, members of the Convention arrested Robespierre and his key lieutenants and executed them—by guillotine—in July 1794.

□|●|⌐ **Read** the **Document**

Maximilien Robespierre "Speech to National Convention: The Terror Justified"

on **MyHistoryLab.com**

The End of the Terror   With the invading enemy armies defeated and internal rebellion contained, few French citizens saw any justification to continue the type of idealistic political extremism sponsored by the Robespierrists. The **Reign of Terror** began in an effort to forge a rationalistic republic of virtue and ended by repudiating the humane ideals of the Enlightenment. The property-owning bourgeoisie quickly regained control of the government, imprisoned and executed Jacobins, purged the army leadership, and removed many of the restrictive measures imposed by the previous regime. A new constitution, adopted in 1795, limited the right to vote to wealthy property owners. All executive functions were reserved for five individuals—named the **Directory.** Over the next four years (1795–1799) the government continued to face challenges from disgruntled royalists on the right and Jacobins on the left, the war dragged on, and finances remained precarious. The role of the army in maintaining the authority of the increasingly corrupt Directory became greater each year, creating an opportunity for ambitious military commanders to influence state policy.

An Assessment in 1795   The Directory government wished to refocus the revolutionary impulse back to the reform agenda of the early years. The accomplishments had been significant: the formal abolition of feudalism, an end to legal privileges based on status and title, the repudiation of divine-right monarchy, government accountability to property-owning males, the dramatic fall of church influence in affairs of state, the emergence of citizen armies, and anticipations of modern patriotic nationalism. For the first time in European history, a significant number of common people—wage earners, shopkeepers, peasants— had become political actors capable of influencing the national agenda in a significant manner. The ideas generated by the *philosophes* during the eighteenth century, especially their discussion of natural rights and liberties, religious freedom, and the accountability of magistrates, were now implemented. These ideas animated a kingdom where economic hardship was acute and where society's traditional leaders seemed out of touch with conditions experienced by the majority of the population.

In some respects the Americans had paved the way for the French Revolution. Many French soldiers—like Lafayette, who had fought in the American war for independence—returned home with a new sense of possibilities for their own country. However, Americans before 1776 did not have to contend with a titled aristocracy, an entrenched state church, grinding poverty in the countryside, and high urban unemployment. The French Revolution undermined the corporate and hierarchical nature of society. In its place a society emerged where talent, not title, mattered, where the mandate of the people, not the mandate of God, legitimized civil authority. There is perhaps no better illustration of the new principles in action than the meteoric career of **Napoleon Bonaparte** (1769–1821).

Napoleon Bonaparte and the Export of Revolution, 1799–1815

Born on the Mediterranean island of Corsica just after it became French territory, Napoleon Bonaparte attended a French military school and received a commission as a second lieutenant at age 16. As a commoner, he was resentful of the aristocratic officers who secured their positions on the basis of status. When the French Revolution began, Napoleon quickly sided with the Revolutionaries. His successes on the battlefield brought him to the attention of the National Convention, and in 1795 he was charged with suppressing a crowd of royalist insurgents in Paris. He was then assigned to lead a French army fighting in Italy, where he won a series of important victories over the opposing Austrians and Sardinians. Napoleon established a number of Italian republics in the wake of his military successes. He then accepted command of an expeditionary force of 35,000 troops whose task was to attack British interests in Egypt. Although Napoleon was victorious on land, the British prevailed at sea, with Admiral Horatio Nelson (1758–1805) crushing the French fleet at the Battle of the Nile on August 1, 1798. Stymied, Napoleon was able to slip back into France, and he carefully controlled the reports coming out of Egypt.

[◉⊦Read the Document

Rise of Napoleon

on **MyHistoryLab.com**

When he arrived in France, conservative factions were planning to overthrow the government of the Directory. The conspirators needed a popular general to serve as a figurehead leader, and Napoleon was recruited to lead the coup d'état. The French population, wearied by a decade of political instability, economic hardship, and foreign war, accepted the appointment of the popular military commander as "first consul" under a constitution created in 1799. Two additional consuls initially served as executives with him. However, Napoleon quickly consolidated support, and by 1802, he was made first consul for life with the exclusive right to name his successor. Two years later, in an elaborate ceremony at Notre Dame Cathedral in Paris, Napoleon crowned himself Emperor of the French, restoring the hereditary monarchy. Shrewdly, Napoleon called for **plebiscites** (popular votes) to ratify his many changes, thus allowing him to claim that he ruled by popular will. Thanks to the opportunities presented by the Revolution, the obscure commoner had risen to the heights of political power in less than a decade.

◉⊦View the **Closer Look**

The Coronation of Napoleon

on **MyHistoryLab.com**

Domestic Reform   Napoleon recognized that his past military accomplishments would soon be forgotten if he failed to address pressing needs at home. He won the support of the conservative peasantry by his reconciliation with the Roman

Coronation of Napoleon   On December 2, 1804, Napoleon crowned himself Emperor of the French in Notre Dame Cathedral. In this painting by Jacques-Louis David, Pope Paul VII raises his hand in blessing as Napoleon places a crown on the head of his wife, Josephine. *Jacques Louis David (1748–1825) Consecration of the Emperor Napoleon I and Coronation of Empress Josephine, 1806–1807. Louvre, Paris. Bridgeman-Giraudon/Art Resource, NY*

Catholic Church in 1801. By the terms of the Concordat, or agreement, concluded with the papacy, Napoleon recognized Catholicism as the faith of the majority of the French and allowed the pope to consecrate all new bishops. The Emperor was not a devout man, but he recognized the value of religion for its potential extrinsic function: it served to keep the people quiet and obedient. In return for official recognition, the French clergy were to be paid by the state, and land confiscated from the church during the 1790s would remain in the hands of its new owners. Napoleon also permitted freedom of worship for Protestants and Jews.

On the economic front, the Emperor supported businessmen with protective tariffs and government loans, while large public road, canal, and bridge-building projects enabled goods to move more freely around the country. The Bank of France was established to handle government funds and to regulate the currency. Hard-pressed peasants and workers were provided with subsidized bread, and the old feudal obligations were not restored. The principle of careers open to talent meant that enterprising common people could rise through the ranks in Napoleon's army, in the bureaucracy, or in private enterprise. These and other policies won Napolean wide support, even though political liberties and freedom of the press had been eliminated by a ruler whose power was now more absolute than that enjoyed by any Old Regime king of France.

Legal Reform   The legal systems in prerevolutionary Europe were both many and arbitrary. In most countries, traditional practice and the preference of the ruling monarch normally set the parameters of civil and criminal law. In France what passed as law varied from province to province, with over 350 different codes in place when the Revolution began in 1789. In the north of the country, customary Germanic law tended to dominate, while in the south Roman law was more widespread. Voltaire once quipped that in France travelers change legal codes as often as they changes horses. The early reforms of the French Revolutionaries added thousands of additional decrees to the existing laws, making some sort of overhaul necessary.

In an effort to streamline and rationalize French law, the National Convention attempted to frame a new system of law in 1793. It was rejected, however, and the governments of the 1790s never succeeded in revamping the existing patchwork. In 1800 Napoleon undertook to complete the project. He appointed a commission of influential jurors to examine all French civil (not criminal) laws and to synthesize these into one code that the average citizen could understand. Bonaparte presided at many of the meetings, and the Code received its legitimacy through his dictate. The final version of the Civil Code (popularly known as the **Code Napoleon**) consisted of over 2,000 articles with sections covering persons and property. It became the law of the land in 1804.

The Code recognized the inherent equality of males, freedom of religion and separation of church and state, the inviolability of property, and freedom for the individual to choose a career. It represented a great victory for the property-owning middle class, and it boosted Napoleon's popularity at home and abroad. The export of the Code's provisions throughout Napoleon's European empire effectively destroyed the feudal system of privilege and private jurisdictions that had dominated life for centuries. Napoleon later sponsored reform of the Code of Civil Procedure (1806), Commercial Code (1807), and the Penal Code (1808), bringing greater system and order to these three areas.

The Code also reflected Napoleon's deep distrust of women in public life. Not only were women denied the vote, but husbands enjoyed complete control over family property, and divorce, while allowed in limited cases, was difficult for women to secure. Napoleon believed that civil marriage "should contain a promise of obedience and fidelity by the wife. She must understand that in leaving the guardianship of her family, she is passing under that of her husband." Unmarried women had few rights, with the Code emphasizing the importance of the traditional male-dominated household. The children of divorced parents remained in the custody of the father, while illegitimate children were denied rights of inheritance.

Despite these weaknesses, the Code Napoleon emphasized the modern conception of a free and equal citizenry, sanctity of contract and property rights, the secularization of civil society, and unified standards of conduct irrespective of location or circumstances of birth. The Code also contributed to the enhancement of nationalism within each country where it was adopted. Its influence spread far beyond France, shaping the civil codes in the Low Countries, Northern Italy and Germany, parts of South America, the state of Louisiana in the United States, and Quebec Province, Canada. The Enlightenment ideal of a society guided by reasonable law and not by arbitrary individuals was first adopted, ironically, under a ruler who would tolerate no opposition to his vision of reform. Napoleon considered law reform to be his most important contribution to society; it was certainly his most lasting.

War and Expansion   As a political leader, Napoleon had taken important steps to restore public order, but the military side of his personality yearned for new challenges and triumphs. He had concluded hostilities with Russia in 1801 and with Britain with the **Peace of Amiens** in 1802, but Napoleon's ambitions inevitably clashed with Great Britain's desire to maintain the balance of power on the continent. War erupted again in 1803, and within two years Napoleon massed an enormous army for a planned invasion of Britain. He had a large, though poorly trained and commanded fleet at his disposal, but the logistics involved in an amphibious assault were too complicated. On October 21, 1805, British naval forces under the command of Admiral Nelson smashed the combined fleets of France and its Spanish ally, and Napoleon's dream of occupying Britain faded. Instead, Napoleon turned to the east and won a string of remarkable victories over Austrian, Russian, and Prussian forces between 1805 and 1807. When the Austrians renewed the struggle in 1809, Napoleon's forces crushed them again.

By 1810, Napoleon and his disciplined, patriotic troops had upset the balance of power and redrawn the political map of Western Europe. The Holy Roman Empire was dismantled in 1806, while Holland and Italy came under French control. Spain was reduced to a client state, and Austria, Russia, and Prussia were forced into the status of French allies. Only Great Britain remained as a viable opponent. In the areas where French forces were triumphant, Napoleon appointed his brothers as monarchs; Joseph held the throne of Naples and then of Spain, Jerome became King of Westphalia in Western Germany, and Louis took the royal office in Holland (see Map 17–2). The reforms previously introduced in France were exported to all occupied lands. Serfdom was abolished, equality before the law and careers open to talents introduced, religious toleration observed, and the Code Napoleon adopted. European liberals and the long-suffering serfs welcomed the reforms, but the spirit of nationalism that French soldiers carried with them was contagious. Before long many Europeans, especially in Spain and parts of Germany, were calling for an end to French control.

Decline and Fall   In 1812 Tsar Alexander I of Russia (r. 1801–1825) broke with Napoleon and joined the British side. In Spain, native guerilla fighters assisted by a British expeditionary force proved to be a constant irritant to Napoleon for six years (1808–1814). Napoleon elected to focus his military might on Russia, and in June 1812 an army of half a million men invaded the Russian Empire. Russian imperial troops withdrew into the interior vastness. When Napoleon reached Moscow in September, he found a city set aflame by its residents to deny the French winter quarters. In the countryside the Russians destroyed grain and shelter, leaving the enormous French army without adequate clothing, food, or shelter for the harsh Russian winter. Forced to retreat, Napoleon's army numbered fewer than 100,000 when it finally returned to France. The defeat signaled the broad expansion of Britain's war effort. Prussia,

MAP 17-2 Napoleon's Empire in 1812 By 1812, Napoleon had reached the height of his power. Spain, parts of Italy, and a number of German states had been incorporated into the French Grand Empire, while Austria and Prussia were forced into alliances with Napoleon. The invasion of Russia signaled the decline of the French Empire.

QUESTION: How did Napoleon attempt to govern his far-flung European territories?

Austria, and Sweden now joined the anti-French alliance. By April 1814, Napoleon's army had been defeated and France occupied. Napoleon abdicated and was exiled to the small Mediterranean island of Elba. He escaped confinement and returned briefly in March 1815 to lead French forces in one last campaign that ended with the famous **Battle of Waterloo** in Belgium in June. Surrendering again, he was sent to another island exile, but this time far away in the South Atlantic on St. Helena. Having dominated the continent for more than a decade, Napoleon's lasting achievements were only marginally related to his considerable military skills and battlefield victories. Rather, the influence of French—and Napoleonic—ideas, particularly legal, educational, and political ideas built on the twin principles of liberty and equality, would continue to inform the culture of Western Europe into the Industrial Age of the nineteenth century.

The French Revolution and the Americas

The success enjoyed by the independent United States inspired Spanish, French, and Portuguese colonials to seek greater political and economic freedoms for themselves. Many in the United States initially applauded the French Revolution; liberals were encouraged by what appeared to be another effort to implement the principles of the Enlightenment. Inspired by the rhetoric of human equality, a rebellion by black slaves in St. Dominique (Haiti), France's largest sugar-producing colony in the Caribbean, began in 1791. Led by **Toussaint L'Ouverture** (1743–1803), the rebels claimed equality with whites and independence from France. An independent state was established on the island in 1804, but not before Napoleon attempted (unsuccessfully) to return the former colony to French control. Haiti quickly became a beacon to black slaves and poor people of color throughout Latin America because the independence struggle there represented a genuine social revolution.

In Spanish Latin America the independence movements were led by the property-owning Creole elite (American-born whites of Spanish descent) who deeply resented the monopoly over political power enjoyed by *peninsulares* (whites from Spain). Like their counterparts in the United States, these landowners, merchants, and traders also wished to put an end to the restrictive mercantilist controls placed on the colonies by Spain. When Napoleon deposed the Spanish Bourbons and placed his brother Joseph on the Spanish throne in 1807, the Spanish colonists in America refused to accept the new king and pledged their allegiance to their legitimate rulers.

The Bourbons were restored to power under Ferdinand VII (r. 1813–1833) after the defeat of Napoleon in 1814. The colonial rebellions ceased at this point, but the Spanish king's reactionary policies soon led to renewed calls for independence. By 1825, all of Spain's mainland colonies in South America had achieved their goals. **José de San Martin** (1778–1850) led armies of liberation from his base in the Rio de la Plata (modern Argentina) across the Andes Mountains into Chile (1817) and Peru (1820). In the north, armies under the direction of **Simon Bolivar** (1783–1830) defeated forces loyal to Spain in Columbia, Bolivia, Ecuador, and Venezuela. Due to the large sweeps of territory involved in the independence struggles, separate nations emerged across South America during the nineteenth century. Most of these states were led by Creoles who had little

Toussaint L'Ouverture   One of the leaders of the Haitian revolution, which freed the Caribbean island from French rule, abolished slavery, and established an independent republic. Toussaint (right) became a hero to many blacks and slaves throughout the Americas.

interest in popular democracy. In New Spain (modern Mexico, Texas, and California), what began in 1811 as a popular revolt led by Roman Catholic priests, who stressed land reform and social equality, ended in 1821 as an independence movement firmly under the control of conservative landowners. These men strongly opposed any alteration in economic or social life (see Map 17–3).

When Napoleon invaded Portugal in 1807, the royal family fled to Brazil. Their arrival transformed the city of Rio de Janeiro into a bustling commercial center and imperial capital. King John VI (r. 1816–1824) reluctantly returned to Portugal in 1820, and Brazil achieved formal independence in 1822 after the Portuguese parliament tried to reassert mercantilist controls. Unlike the former Spanish colonies, all of which initially adopted a republican form of government, Brazil remained a monarchy under John VI's son, Pedro I (r. 1822–1831), who had stayed in Brazil, and Pedro's son Pedro II (r. 1831–1888). For several decades Brazil remained the most prosperous and unified state in Latin America. In the United States, fear that other European powers might attempt to take advantage of the new countries, all of which maintained trade relations with Europe, led to the issuance of the **Monroe Doctrine** in 1823, a warning against the establishment of any new European colonies in the Americas. In practical terms the U.S. government was incapable of backing up its warning with significant military force. However, Britain's commercial interests coincided with the American position. The British wished to trade with each of the newly independent Latin American states, and the reestablishment of Spanish and Portuguese authority would have meant the return of mercantilist restrictions. During the nineteenth century, the British navy, not the Monroe Doctrine, served as the major deterrent to the return of European colonialism in the Americas.

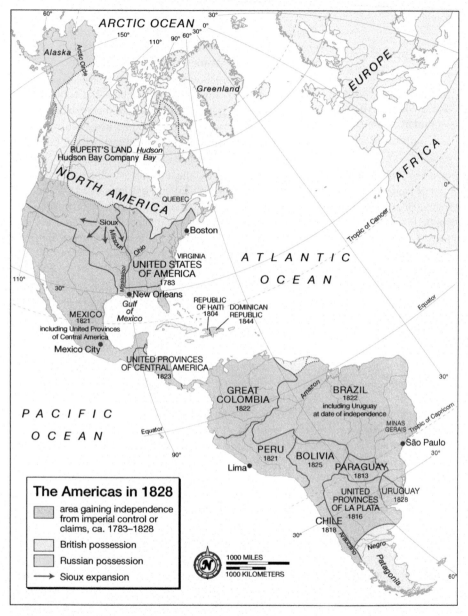

MAP 17-3   The Americas in 1828   Between 1811 and 1830, most of South America won its independence from European rule. José de San Martin and Simón Bolivar emerged as the two most powerful leaders of the independence movements.

QUESTION: Why did the newly independent Latin American republics fail to establish stable democracies?

QUESTION
REVISITED

Can political change occur without social and economic upheaval?

The Estates General opened its first session (May 5, 1789) only five days after George Washington was inaugurated as the first president of the United States of America. The Estates General represented the great medieval divisions of society—nobles, clergy, and commoners—but soon after its convocation, the Third Estate claimed that it alone represented all Frenchmen. Washington had assumed the presidency of a nation that rejected legal distinctions based on status. Now the leaders of the French National Assembly would seek the same reforms in a country, and on a continent, with a centuries-old tradition of social hierarchy based on privilege. The American experiment forwarded political and constitutional patterns inherited from the colonial experience; the French, however, were involved in a revolution whose outcome would have a lasting imprint on modern European history. Political change occurred in North America without social and economic upheaval. In France political change could not be realized without dramatic change in the social and economic order.

Britain's American colonists did not face the combination of hardships that made the situation of Frenchmen so desperate in 1789. The British Empire was at its height after the defeat of the French in 1763, and as late as 1775, most Americans (with the obvious exception of black slaves) were proud to be members of this great empire. A tax system that exempted those most able to pay, widespread social injustices, legal privileges for the clergy and nobility, food shortages and high inflation, government fiscal crisis—Americans suffered under none of these conditions when they repudiated their allegiance to Britain. Instead, Thomas Jefferson claimed in the Declaration of Independence that King George III and Parliament were attempting to undermine traditional English rights with their unprecedented tax schemes. According to Jefferson, "the laws of nature and nature's God" legitimized the American call for independence. Informed by Enlightenment values, the dissolution of Britain's empire in America did not threaten the social or political status quo in the 13 states.

The same cannot be said for developments in France, where the upheaval that began in 1789 altered the basic fabric of political, social, and religious life. The French Revolution was important not only for one country, but for all of Europe. France was the greatest military power on the continent, and in many ways it was the cultural and intellectual leader as well. Fundamental change in Old Regime France was bound to influence conditions elsewhere in Europe. Over the space of two years, the great and lasting changes had been achieved. Between 1789 and 1792 the feudal order was dismantled, and upon its ruins the signposts of modernity were erected. Legal equality, freedom of expression, the sanctity of property, the abolition of serfdom and the right to choose one's career path, popular sovereignty and the separation of executive and legislative powers, a written constitution, religious toleration—these groundbreaking changes ushered in the modern age in Western politics.

Even the language of modern politics finds its roots in the Revolution: The terms *Left* and *Right* emerged from where delegates sat in the Convention. The terms *Conservative* and *Liberal* were not used until the early nineteenth century, but they served to identify where one stood politically on the changes instituted by the French Revolution. Napoleon's megalomania guaranteed that many of the reforms would reach a Europe-wide audience. Between 1801 and 1814 the Old Regimes across Europe were introduced to French-style legal and administrative reform, to the principle of meritocracy, and, most importantly, to the power of nationalism. The nineteenth century would be a century of nation building and of liberal revolution across Europe. The American and French examples of popular self-government served as the beacon for all who would fight to translate revolutionary ideas into practice.

Key Terms

republicanism, *p. 500*

Commonwealthmen, *p. 503*

Continental Congress, *p. 504*

Articles of Confederation, *p. 505*

Bill of Rights, *p. 506*

sansculottes, p. 511

Jacobins, *p. 514*

Reign of Terror, *p. 515*

Activities

1. How was "representation" defined by members of Parliament in London and by colonial legislators in America?

2. Describe the essential "rights of Englishmen" as understood by English colonists in America.

3. Why did the French monarchy support the American republic, and what problems did this support present for France?

4. What were the causes of France's fiscal difficulties in the 1780s, and what was the major impediment to reform?

5. Explain how Edmund Burke could sympathize with the Americans in 1776 and condemn the French in 1789.

6. Outline the permanent social and economic changes that took place in France in the midst of the French Revolution.

7. Was Napoleon a child of the Enlightenment and a champion of the French Revolution, or was he the restorer of absolute monarchy in France?

Further Reading

Gordon Wood, *The Radicalism of the American Revolution* (1990), a compelling account that sets the American experience into a broader context.

David Armitage, *The Declaration of Independence: A Global History* (2007), sets the revolutionary experience in a broader context.

Simon Shama, *Citizens* (1991), a lively and insightful narrative of the French Revolution.

Ruth Scurr, *Fatal Purity: Robespierre and the French Revolution* (2007), an analysis of one of the key radical leaders.

David Bell, *The First Total War: Napoleon's Europe and the Birth of Warfare as We Know It* (2007), an account of the modern culture of war.

MyHistoryLab Connections

Visit **MyHistoryLab.com** *for a customized Study Plan that will help you build your knowledge of* Rebellion and Revolution: American Independence and the French Revolution.

Questions for Analysis

1. What were some of Thomas Paine's criticisms of English government and the English constitution?

⬚●─Read the Document Thomas Paine, *Common Sense,* p. 504

2. What were some of the different perspectives and goals of those who took part in the American Revolution?

👁─Watch the Video The American Revolution as Different Americans Saw It, p. 504

3. What were some of the different arguments surrounding the question of whether or not slavery was constitutional?

👁─Watch the Video Slavery and the Constitution, p. 506

4. How was French society structured prior to the French Revolution?

🔍─View the Closer Look Challenging the French Political Order, p. 508

5. What kind of society did Robespierre envision for post-revolutionary France?

⬚●─Read the Document Maximilien Robespierre "Speech to National Convention: The Terror Justified," p. 515

Other Resources from This Chapter

🔍─View the Image Stamp Act Protest, p. 502

🔍─View the Image Boston Tea Party, p. 504

⬚●─Read the Document Rough Draft of the Declaration of Independence, p. 504

⬚●─Read the Document Letter from a Revolutionary War Soldier, p. 505

⬚●─Read the Document Articles of Confederation, p. 505

⬚●─Read the Document Bill of Rights, p. 506

Read the **Document** Emmanuel Joseph Sieyés, *What Is the Third Estate?*, p. 508

Read the **Document** *Declaration of the Rights of Man and Citizen*, p. 510

Read the **Document** Olympe de Gouges, *Declaration of the Rights of Woman and the Female Citizen*, p. 510

View the **Image** French Revolution, Execution of Louis XVI, p. 513

Read the **Document** Rise of Napoleon, p. 516

View the **Closer Look** The Coronation of Napoleon, p. 516

PART SIX

Europe Triumphant:
1815–1914

Gustave Caillebotte, *Paris Street; Rainy Day*, 1877. *Gustave Caillebotte (French 1848–1894), Paris Street; Rainy Day. 1877. Oil on Canvas. 83½" × 108¾" (212.2 × 276.2 cm). Charles H. and Mary F. S. Worcester Collection, 1964. 336. Photograph © 2006, The Art Institute of Chicago. All Rights Reserved.*

The century between the final defeat and exile of Napoleon Bonaparte and the start of World War I (1815–1914) represented the apogee of European power in the world. After a series of failed revolutions in 1848, middle-class liberals embraced nationalism and began to win new political powers under the leadership of conservative leaders like Otto von Bismarck in Germany and Emperor Louis Napoleon in France. By the start of the twentieth century, universal manhood suffrage had been achieved across most of Western Europe, while women began to organize and press for their political rights.

The birth and rapid growth of industry transformed the material and intellectual landscape of Western Europe during the 1800s. Wherever the factory system emerged, a large migration from rural to urban settings followed. Problems associated with an urban lifestyle served to focus the attention of political leaders and to prompt new responses to pressing public needs. On the global stage, Europe's industrial might enabled a number of countries to extend their political, military, and economic influence. By the last third of the nineteenth century, rival states in Europe began to build extensive overseas empires, each one dedicated to the economic well-being of the imperial heartland.

T I M E L I N E

	ENVIRONMENT AND TECHNOLOGY	SOCIETY AND CULTURE	POLITICS
1815	Manchester-Liverpool railway line (1830)	Romantic era (c.1815–1848)	Congress of Vienna (1814–1815)
1830	Cholera epidemic strikes Europe (1831)	Death of Beethoven (1827)	Revolutions in France, Italy, Belgium, and Poland (1830)
	First trans-Atlantic steamship crossing (1833)	Majority of Britons live in cities and towns (1830)	Reform Bill in England (1832)
	Telegraph (1837)	First factory acts passed in England to regulate labor (1830s)	First Opium War (1839)
	Cunard Lines begins regular trans-Atlantic service (1840)	Neo-Gothic Houses of Parliament (1836)	Marx, *Communist Manifesto* (1848)
	Famine in Ireland (1846–1848)		Revolutions across Europe (1848)
1850	Suez canal opens (1869)	Crystal Palace exhibition (1851)	Civil War in United States (1861–1865)
	Telephone (1876)	U.S. forces opening of Japan (1853)	Austro-Prussian War (1866)
	Electric light (1879)	Darwin, *Origin of Species* (1859)	Franco-Prussian War (1870)
			Unification of Germany (1871)
1900	Theory of Relativity (1905)	Emancipation of Serfs in Russia (1861)	France becomes a republic (1871)
	Ford's mass-produced autos (1909)	Dreyfus Affair (1897–1899)	Triple Alliance (1882)
		European population reaches 285 million (1870)	Berlin Conference coordinates the carve-up of Africa (1884–1885)
		Radicalization of British suffragettes (1910)	Russo-Japanese War (1904–1905)
			Norway becomes first nation to grant women the vote (1907)
			First Balkan War (1912)
1914			Start of World War I (1914)

Women's Work Women workers, with barely enough room to maneuver, stoop over piles of cloth in a vast hat factory in Manchester, England, around 1900.

18 Industry, Society, and Environment

((●─Hear the Audio   Chapter 18 at MyHistoryLab.com

LEARNING OBJECTIVES

Why did industrialization begin first in the West?   ●   How did agricultural production change with the advance of industry?   ●   What were the key technological breakthroughs of the industrial age?   ●   What were the social consequences of industrialization?

It is not the consciousness of men that determines their being, but, on the contrary, their social being that determines their consciousness.

—Karl Marx (1818–1883)

KEY QUESTION

How do technology and urbanization influence the relationship between humans and nature?

Karl Marx's friend and collaborator, Friedrich Engels (1820–1895), lived and worked in Britain's first industrial city, Manchester, during the 1840s. Engels was the son of a German manufacturer who owned a textile factory in Manchester, and in 1844 Friedrich published a moving indictment of living conditions in that booming city. Along the Irk River in the heart of the mill district, Engels described how

... the left bank grows more flat and the right bank steeper, but the condition of the dwellings on both banks grows worse rather than better. He who turns to the left here from the main street, Long Millgate, is lost; he wanders from one court to another, turns countless corners, passes nothing but narrow, filthy nooks and alleys, until after a few minutes he has lost all clue, and knows not whither to turn. Everywhere heaps of debris, refuse, and offal; standing pools for gutters, and a stench which alone would make it impossible for a human being in any degree civilized to live in such a district.

Yet thousands of people did live in these conditions, and the overcrowding and filth continued throughout the nineteenth century as masses of displaced rural workers moved to factory towns like Manchester, hoping that the fruits of industrial technology would improve their lives.

The description of working-class conditions in Manchester offered by Engels might be criticized on the basis of the author's radical political ideology. He did, after all, reject capitalism and, together with Karl Marx, forecast its ultimate destruction in 1848 in *The*

Communist Manifesto. However, abundant and compelling evidence of the hardships working people suffered during the industrial era confirms his indictment. Like Manchester, the town of Little Bolton is located in Lancashire, and much of the coal that powered the mills in Manchester came from this nearby source. In 1842 Parliament established a committee of inquiry to investigate conditions of labor in the mines. Betty Harris, aged 37, testified that she first entered the mines at Little Bolton at age 23, having worked as a weaver since she was 12. "I am a drawer" (carrying coal to the surface), she reported. "I have two children, but they are too young to work. I worked at drawing when I was in the family way [pregnant]. I have drawn till I have the skin off me; the belt and chain is worse when we are in the family way."

This testimony, like the stories of many other workers in the mines and factories, suggests that just under two centuries ago a small fraction of the world's population entered into a new relationship with the natural environment. Separation from and dominion over nature became hallmarks of what we call industrial capitalism. At once enormously dynamic and cruelly debilitating, the combination of capitalist market forces and machine technology redefined life and culture in ways that have strained the planet's capacity to sustain life and our ability to solve acute environmental problems. Industrialization has also raised important questions about human nature—about how people ought to live and whether labor that is divorced from basic human needs and is carried out in a large impersonal setting undermines both the dignity of the individual and the integrity of culture and community. ▪

From Rural to Urban Lifestyles in Europe

The widespread shift in labor patterns from farm and household to factory and mine, from human and animal power to machine power, is what French observers in the 1820s first termed the **Industrial Revolution.** Historians still use the term today, and for good reason. We tend to associate the term *revolution* with rapid and sometimes violent political change, but it can also describe a broad economic and social upheaval. Measured by its effect on human life over the past two centuries, this ongoing Industrial Revolution is far more significant than the American, French, or Russian revolutions. It began in Britain around the third quarter of the eighteenth century, spread to Belgium by the early nineteenth century, and gradually affected most of Western Europe and North America by 1900 (see Map 18–1). In a short span of time, the revolution led to the most fundamental alteration in European, and then global, society since early humans replaced their hunter-gather lifestyles with agriculture.

For countless generations, human life had been based on physical toil in nature. Abundant human capital, not precious metals or currency, was the crucial resource that successful landowners and employers coveted. Most people were peasant farmers who worked generation after generation in family and village units on lands owned by a local member of the gentry or aristocracy. The coming of industrial production shattered this age-old pattern. In 1900 relatively few persons in Western Europe were employed in settings that their grandparents would have found familiar, and many workers had no economic interests in common with their employers. Peasant farmers and skilled craftsmen who had worked in or adjacent to their homes had become

MAP 18-1 The Industrial Revolution in Europe   Industrial growth was dependent on abundant supplies of coal and iron ore. Railroads facilitated the movement of raw materials, finished goods, and people. New manufacturing centers emerged across Western Europe during the nineteenth century.

QUESTION: Was political stability essential to industrial growth in nineteenth-century Europe?

machine operators and clerks within the confines of impersonal factories and offices, and most Europeans had lost their close connection to the natural environment. They had become instead residents of large cities and grim factory towns where food was consumed far away from the farmer that produced it. In 1800 Europe had just 20 cities with populations over 100,000, but by 1900 almost 150 such cities existed in Europe. Industrialization transformed Western Europe economically, socially, and culturally. It altered the social structure and highlighted the importance of class. It fostered new political movements based on the interests of semiskilled and unskilled workers. It emphasized the distinctions between rural and urban lifestyles, between home and workplace, and even between the economic functions of individual family members.

Why the West?   Historians often debate why Europe enjoyed a head start in industry. After all, imperial China seemed poised to become the first great workshop of the world as early as the sixteenth century. European trade with China during this period was driven largely by the popularity of Chinese luxury products in the West. In fact, much of the silver that Europeans extracted from mines in Central and South America eventually found its way to Beijing as payment for Chinese porcelains, silks, and tea. However, China's Confucian culture had elevated the scholar and the rural gentry over the merchant and the artisan. Except for a brief period in the early fifteenth century, the Chinese imperial government did not support the development of manufacture for export or a large merchant fleet to carry products to distant markets. A similar situation existed in the expansive Muslim world, and especially in Mughal India, where trade links with the West beginning in the sixteenth century failed to lead to the development of a Mughal overseas commercial empire.

European heads of state, however, had ample reasons to support commerce, not the least of which involved intra-European political, religious, and military rivalries. War and the threat of war in Europe, and the absence of any Europe-wide centralized authority competent to dictate economic policy, meant that the innovative, entrepreneurial spirit was given free reign. The creation of private wealth enhanced national power, and many European monarchs encouraged and protected overseas trade in the interests of national defense. East India companies, Africa companies, Near East companies, and other "regional" companies were sanctioned by European heads of state and even given monopolies over trade with specific parts of the world.

Why Britain?   The Industrial Revolution began first in Britain thanks to the convergence of a number of key economic, political, and social factors. Abundant capital was available due to profits from two centuries of global trade, including the nefarious trade in slaves. Britain had the world's largest merchant fleet by the 1700s, and its military triumph over France in 1763 enabled it to dominate overseas commerce. Despite the loss of its American colonies in 1783, Britain's colonial empire remained enormous. British investors and traders eagerly brought their risk-taking mentality to the factory floor, while the government encouraged the formation of large investment partnerships. These partnerships were designed to generate profits from domestic production instead of overseas commerce.

Internally, Britain's stable political order, together with a comparatively fluid social structure, an abundant supply of coal and iron ore, a unified and tariff-free internal market, a broad network of navigable rivers and canals for the movement of bulky commodities like coal, a mature financial system, a small military establishment, and comparatively low taxes, all hastened the development of new methods of finance, manufacture, transportation, and distribution. Compared with other European nations, British merchants, manufacturers, bankers, and entrepreneurs were accorded great respect in society. Even the younger sons of the landed aristocracy could take up careers in the business world. Many inventors were religious dissenters, barred from careers in government because of their refusal to accept the official Church of England but allowed to pursue opportunities in business. In France, by contrast, nobles who invested in commercial pursuits normally did so with the short-term goal of purchasing offices, new titles, or land; the business activities themselves remained suspect. Those French entrepreneurs who did invest in manufacturing tended to focus on the luxury goods market, avoiding mass production of cheap goods for the majority of consumers. A tangle of internal tariffs also inhibited investment in industry in France and in most countries on the continent.

Developments in Germany illustrated the close connection between political stability and industrial expansion. Before 1870 Germany was divided into a number of small states, none of which was a major economic power. Only after political unification in 1871 did the German economy begin to compete with its British neighbor, and by 1900 German industrial output in iron, steel, and machinery had overtaken its rival.

Watch the **Video**

19th Century Industrialization

on **MyHistoryLab.com**

Similarly in the United States, the North's victory in the bloody and protracted Civil War in 1865 greatly strengthened the American economy. By 1900 it, too, had surpassed Britain. National unification during the 1860s enhanced opportunities for industrial growth even in Italy, which for centuries had been divided and under the political control of Spain, France, and Austria. In all these countries the creation of uniform laws, currency, tariff policy, and administration created conditions under which investors were more willing to accept long-term risk.

Agriculture, Demographics, and Labor

The domestication of plants and animals that had first taken place some 10,000 years before the Common Era ushered in a new and revolutionary phase in human existence. Nomadic hunter-gatherers became sedentary laborers; kinship social organization gave way to formal institutions of government; tribute was exacted and paid to military, religious, and political elites; and permanent villages, towns, and cities were built and defended against raiders. In the new environment survival increasingly depended upon the production of crops cultivated under labor-intensive conditions. For approximately the next 12,000 years, agricultural productivity set the limits to demographic growth, while attitudes toward land hampered agricultural output.

A Modern Revolution in Agriculture   In the late 1700s most Europeans were still subsistence farmers. They cultivated the land in ways that had not changed much since the Middle Ages. Most farmers grew the same crops each year, left between one-third and one-half of their land fallow to avoid soil exhaustion, and kept only enough fodder to preserve a few draft and breeding animals over the long winter months. Large areas of forest and field were left uncultivated as common land where locals could cut wood for fuel and graze their animals. In close contact with the rhythm of nature, Europeans worked the land in a manner that was both physically demanding and technologically unsophisticated. Few peasants believed they had a choice about how they would feed and shelter themselves and their families. A dramatic enhancement in the soil's ability to produce was neither expected nor encouraged.

A modest but sustained increase in population during the eighteenth century obliged farmers to intensify traditional methods. Marginal land was cleared and put under the plow, swamps were drained, and the owners of large estates in Holland and Britain began to experiment with new crops. The biggest breakthrough came when "improving" landowners began to alternate grain crops like wheat and barley, both of which consumed the soil's nitrogen, with crops like turnips, clover, and alfalfa. These latter crops restored nitrogen to the soil and could be used as fodder. This system basically doubled the amount of land that could be cultivated in a given year and enabled farmers to feed more livestock during the lean winter months. Increased numbers of

Lincolnshire Ox England's "agricultural revolution" of the 1700s enabled it to take the lead in the Industrial Revolution later in the century. The "Lincolnshire Ox" was an enormous, 3,000-pound animal that represented British advances in breeding and other agricultural techniques.

cattle and swine meant more protein-rich foods for humans, while additional horses and oxen meant more productive capacity to work the land and more manure to enrich the soil. The potato, first introduced from America as fodder for animals in the early sixteenth century, began to appear more frequently in the peasant diet during the eighteenth century. Since this highly nutritious root vegetable produced a high yield per acre, it appealed to families with additional mouths to feed.

Technology and science also contributed to agricultural output. Better iron plows and harrows (used for breaking up clods of earth) enabled farmers to dig deeper into richer soils. During the second half of the eighteenth century, inexpensive artificial fertilizers made their appearance thanks to the application of chemistry to agriculture. Surpluses were sold in urban markets at handsome profits, while fewer hands were needed to work the land. The prospect of famine, a constant since the dawn of agriculture, began to fade in lands west of Russia after 1850. Small, independent farmers who did not or would not adopt these new approaches to working the land were unable to compete. Many of them left for the cities, where they became part of a growing pool of urban labor.

Finally, the practice of enclosing common land with fences and hedges to create larger farms dedicated to a single crop accelerated after 1750. Some innovative landowners practiced **convertible husbandry.** This involved plowing the soil and growing crops when grain prices were high and shifting to pasture, sheep, or cattle when the market price of wool or meat increased. Under this pattern of land use, workers could be hired and dismissed as needed. Enclosure and specialization obviously meant hardship or unemployment for the small landholder, as wage labor in the agricultural sector replaced the more familiar pattern of traditional family links to the manor and village. Land was increasingly treated as a commodity to be exploited for profit in a wider market. Supporters of the changes, mostly wealthy landowners, argued that improved management helped to end the age-old cycle of sufficiency and dearth, which had previously acted as a brake on the rapid and sustained expansion of population. More mouths were fed at lower cost, and increased population created added demand for basic consumer goods. Displaced farmers obviously disagreed with this analysis, but one fact is indisputable: the Industrial Revolution would not have been possible without the efficiencies introduced by new practices in agriculture.

Food and Population   The nineteenth century ushered in the modern age of statistical data. For the first time, governments across Western Europe collected reliable numbers on population trends and other vital information. The collection of birth and death records by civil authorities began in France in 1792, while Britain compiled its first census in 1801. The advent of this age of demographic measurement, so familiar to us today, meant that governments could better assess potential fiscal and human resources when formulating domestic policies. Accurate information about population was key to political decision making. In 1800 approximately 190 million persons lived west of the Ural Mountains in Russia. This figure was up from roughly 100 million a century earlier. By 1914, at the start of World War I, Europe's population had expanded to an amazing 463 million persons.

This extraordinary increase occurred despite massive overseas migration to the Americas, Australasia, and parts of Africa. During the eighteenth century, for example, approximately two million Europeans had settled in the Americas. Over the next century, however, the number escalated in dramatic fashion. By 1914, close to 60 million Europeans had departed for opportunities on other continents. Britain alone sent 17 million emigrants to points around the globe. Looking at this demographic data in a global context is helpful. In 1800 roughly one-quarter of all humans lived in Europe; by 1920 the percentage had increased to one-third. Population growth and overseas migration greatly facilitated the emergence of industry in Europe. Europeans abroad often built their regional economies to supply raw materials and foodstuffs to Europe and to import manufactured goods from it.

Increased agricultural output was essential to population growth, but Europe was well positioned for rapid demographic expansion after 1815 for other reasons as well. The general peace that prevailed from 1815 (the defeat of Napoleon) until 1914 meant that most of Europe avoided the civilian hardships associated with military occupation and conflict. The destruction of crops and the breakdown of supply networks were the greatest hardships. Improved transportation systems, beginning with sophisticated canal networks, helped to mitigate food shortages. Beginning in the 1860s, steam-propelled railroads and ships brought down long-distance transport costs. By the end of the century, the United States, Canada, Argentina, Uruguay, Australia, and New Zealand provided grain and livestock to European consumers at competitive rates. Similarly, after 1870 the railroad and steamships on the Black Sea allowed Russian growers to sell their products in eastern and Western Europe, linking the Russian economy to the wider European market. As food supplies became more

Chicago Packinghouse at the Turn of the Century   The meatpacking industry epitomized some of the social ills that accompanied the Industrial Revolution. Social reformers like the American socialist Upton Sinclair brought attention to the dangerous and squalid working conditions in packinghouses.

secure and predictable, the cost of feeding one's family declined and discretionary spending increased.

In addition to improved nutrition and sanitation, important contributions in medicine led to higher birth rates and lower death rates. Before midcentury, relatively few people survived into their forties. The employment of **antiseptics** beginning in the 1860s made childbirth safer, while real progress against two fearful killers—tuberculosis and cholera—was made in the 1880s. Other epidemic diseases, such as typhus, typhoid, smallpox, and diphtheria, were effectively treated by medical professionals by the start of the twentieth century. Vaccination and the isolation of infected persons became standard approaches to combating the spread of illnesses. For the first time, hospitalization became an accepted method of addressing serious medical problems. The development of **anesthetics,** especially ether and chloroform during the 1840s, made surgical procedures less painful. Once viewed as places where poor persons went to die, urban hospitals now became centers of effective treatment and rehabilitation.

Better personal hygiene, cleaner water, and improved nutrition were especially important in reducing child mortality. Before the mid-nineteenth century, one out of every five children died before reaching his or her first birthday. This was true even in advanced countries like Britain and France. In Germany the figure was one in four, while in eastern Europe one in three perished. This began to change after 1850, as more vegetables, dairy products, and meat became a part of the common person's diet. A rapidly growing population meant that abundant and youthful human resources were available for prospective employers. Increased population also meant new demand for basic infrastructure projects—more housing stock, better transport systems, ready-made clothing, provision for primary education. Each variable—more people, calls for infrastructure, overseas migration, demands for new sources of productive power, capital available from global trade—converged to inspire inventors and entrepreneurs to look for ways to increase productive capacity.

Innovations in Production

Many rural families in early modern Western Europe supplemented their income from the land by taking in wool or linen for spinning and weaving. However, with the enclosure of common lands reducing many farmers to the status of poorly paid wage laborers, the supply of potential workers for basic manufacturing tasks grew rapidly. Responding to greater demand for clothing by a growing population, merchants turned to the countryside to increase textile production. They stimulated "cottage industries," or what was also called the "putting out" system of commercial manufacture. Previously, urban clothing guilds had regulated most textile production. Rural laborers now offered merchants a low-cost alternative. In addition to the raw materials, urban entrepreneurs would often supply rural workers with a spinning wheel and a simple handloom. Because spinning and weaving were relatively unskilled jobs, women and children did much of it, anticipating their crucial role in later factory labor. In the cottage system, merchants paid their employees on the basis of how much finished cloth they produced during a set interval. The work was not dangerous, but it was monotonous and poorly paid. Together with commercial farming, the cottage industries introduced a money economy to the rural sector and integrated the peasant into a broader national and international economy.

Early Advances in Technology   The period and place that historians traditionally identify with the origins of the Industrial Revolution, between 1760 and 1820 in Britain, hardly struck most contemporaries as a significant social or economic age. Their attention was occupied by the conflict with the American colonies and the wars of the French Revolution, not by the emergence of machine-driven manufacture in cities like Glasgow, Manchester, and Leeds. Still, the breakthroughs in machine building that took place during this period had a broad and lasting impact on society. Some of the breakthroughs did not involve a change in power source, but rather tinkering with and constant improvement upon existing technology. During the early stages of the Industrial Revolution, mechanics and solitary inventors who often lacked formal education were the key figures. Cotton production serves as a good illustration. Britain's American colonies provided an abundant source of raw cotton throughout the first three-quarters of the eighteenth century. Female spinners operated wooden wheels to spin the thread, while male weavers ran simple handlooms. The demand for cotton cloth was rising, but output remained flat.

The invention of John Kay's (1704–1764) **flying shuttle** in 1733 assisted weavers, but the paucity of spun thread created a serious production bottleneck. James Hargreaves (1720–1778) introduced the **spinning jenny** in 1768, which solved the problem. The jenny consisted of a wooden frame that contained a number of spindles

Unskilled Labor Operating Power Looms   By 1830, the cotton industry had become completely mechanized. Women and children were employed at low wages, and hand weavers were supplanted by unskilled workers.

around which the thread was drawn by a hand-operated wheel. Richard Arkwright's (1732–1792) water-powered spinning machine made its debut in 1769, and its stronger rollers produced more durable threads for cotton cloth. All of these machines required space, and it was judged more economical to centralize the production in one place rather than divide it among hundreds of separate cottages. The problem was that water provided the main source of power, and useful rivers and hillside streams were often far away from where most people lived. It was also expensive to move goods overland from these water-powered mills.

Steam Technology   The answer to the location and transportation problems was found by applying steam power to the process of spinning and weaving. Thomas Newcomen (1663–1729) had built a primitive machine in 1705, but the first efficient **steam engine** was pioneered by **James Watt** (1736–1819) in the 1760s. The earliest "Watt" machines were used to help pump water out of coal mines. Coal had become an important fuel during the eighteenth century, since the traditional practice of burning charcoal to smelt iron ore (a process designed to remove other compounds from iron) had deforested much of Britain. Smelting with coal led to improvements in basic metallurgy, which in turn led to the construction of better steam engines.

The success of steam engines in draining water from mines led to a number of creative adaptations to power heavier machinery. In particular, the effective employment of coal and steam in place of water power to drive textile machines or operate iron-smelting furnaces meant that centers of production no longer needed to be situated near running water on rural hillsides. Factories were now portable and could be constructed near or within population centers. Overall, the substitution of inanimate

fossil fuels (coal and subsequently petroleum products) for water power and human forms of energy greatly increased the ability of Europeans to manipulate and transform their natural environment.

By 1820 the steam-driven power loom had largely overtaken hand weavers in the British cotton industry. Power machinery made spinning jennies that wound fiber into thread and the flying shuttle for weaving enormously efficient. A handful of factory workers could operate many **power looms** simultaneously, increasing production while simultaneously reducing labor costs and the price of consumer goods. Production of cheap cotton cloth soared during the first half of the nineteenth century. Thanks to the growth of its colonial empire, Britain sold these goods across the globe. By 1850, almost 40 percent of all British exports consisted of finished cotton products. To keep pace with the insatiable demands of machines that never rested, raw cotton for British factories was imported from India, Egypt, Brazil, and the United States. New industrial cities emerged near abundant sources of coal, dictating new lifestyles and working conditions for thousands of domestic migrants.

The Railway and Steamship Age   Steam power lifted the limits that human, animal, and water power had imposed on productive capacity. While the technology was adapted to different forms of rotary power, none was more ingenious than steam locomotion. Moving bulky coal to factories and moving finished industrial products to markets near and far presented a logistical challenge to ambitious industrialists. All of these manufacturers struggled to satisfy an almost insatiable demand for the products of industry. A canal-building frenzy during the late eighteenth century alleviated some of the difficulties. In England over 2,500 miles of canals were in operation by 1830, and private companies built dozens of hard-surfaced roads.

However, the real breakthrough came in 1830, when a mining engineer named **George Stephenson** (1781–1848) developed a locomotive, called "the Rocket," that could haul a load three times its own weight on iron rails at the extraordinary speed of almost 30 miles per hour. That same year the industrial city of Manchester was linked to the port city of Liverpool by iron rail. Originally designed to move coal and other heavy goods, the Manchester-Liverpool line became an instant hit with passengers, thousands of whom took passage on the "iron horse" during its first years of operation. One early passenger marveled at "how strange it seemed to be journeying on thus, without any visible cause of progress other than the magical machine, with its flying white breath and rhythmical, unvarying pace…" Subsequent railroad lines were built with both freight and passenger service in mind.

By mid-century, Britain, France, Belgium, and the German states all had extensive rail networks. Speculators eagerly bought shares in railway stocks. The British Parliament authorized thousands of miles of rail construction, while the governments of Germany and France built rail systems as a part of national economic development policy. In the United States the national government offered free right of way to railroad developers. The train quickly became essential to the movement of coal from its point of extraction to the factory furnace, while rail lines boosted demand for iron and steel, created new employment opportunities for skilled civil and mechanical engi-

◉–[Watch the Video

Railroads and Expansion

on **MyHistoryLab.com**

The Third Class Carriage   By the mid-nineteenth century, railway travel featured a variety of accommodations. In this 1862 painting, the artist foregrounds the simple dignity of working-class people crowded into cars equipped with hard, wooden benches. *Honore Daumier, French, (1808–1879). The Third Class Carriage, Oil on Canvas, H 25.75 × 35.5" (65.4 × 90.2 cm). The Metropolitan Museum of Art, Bequest of Mrs. H. O. Havemeyer Collection 1929, (29.100.129). Photograph © 1992 The Metropolitan Museum of Art, Art Resource, NY*

neers, and helped to solidify the interdependence of each nation's regional economy. More than any other aspect of industrial technology, the railway linked the rural countryside with the expanding urban centers and port cities. Migrants to the cities and people seeking to emigrate abroad increasingly began their journeys by rail. Rail companies even offered day excursions and short holiday packages to maximize revenues. Travelers could select various levels of service, but as costs declined, even the working-class family could enjoy this revolutionary high-speed transport.

Steam was also applied to water transportation. Here the Americans took the early lead in 1807 when **Robert Fulton** (1765–1815) experimented with a steamboat on the Hudson River in New York state. The first trans-Atlantic steamship crossing took place in 1833 when the *Royal William* traveled from Nova Scotia to England. By 1840, steam-propelled ships had reduced the time of an Atlantic crossing by half, to an average of two weeks. In 1840 Samuel Cunard's (1787–1865) steamship line announced the beginning of regular trans-Atlantic steamship service and even published dates of departure and arrival beforehand. This information could be communicated across the Atlantic instantly after 1866 thanks to the installation of the first trans-Atlantic electric **telegraph** cable. By the close of the century, steamships were carrying thousands of migrants at

View the **Image**

Laying the Transatlantic Telegraph Cable

on **MyHistoryLab.com**

low cost to new homes in the Americas. The same ships that moved people also featured refrigeration compartments that enabled producers to move perishable goods across the oceans for surprisingly low costs.

Second-Generation Power and Industry   The first phase of the Industrial Revolution was based on coal and steam. During the final three decades of the nineteenth century, a second phase, anchored in the chemical, electrical, and petroleum industries, accelerated the process. Instead of solitary inventors, new discoveries and advances tended to emerge from universities, where teams of highly trained specialists worked in formal laboratory settings. The results have become familiar "requirements" of the modern Western lifestyle. During the 1860s, for example, natural gas was used to power an **internal combustion engine.** These engines were lighter and more portable than the earlier generation steam engines, but since natural gas was difficult to store and transport, the new power plant had to wait until the 1880s, when liquid petroleum was substituted for natural gas as a fuel. After this date the popularity of the portable internal combustion engine in Europe increased demand for oil. Sources as far away as Pennsylvania in the United States and southern Russia met the initial demand for petroleum products. In 1877 the first European pipeline to transport oil was built in Russia; two years later the first oil tanker was put into service.

Another second-generation power source was electricity, with the first electric generator developed in 1870. Countries such as Italy and Switzerland, which lacked large coal reserves, especially favored electric power, since electric current could be produced with the aid of water or wind power. Improved turbines in the 1880s made hydroelectric power production feasible. In America, **Thomas Edison**'s (1847–1931) invention of the incandescent electric light marked the start of a new age of artificial light. Among other uses, the incandescent light

Watch the Video
Edison's Punching the Clock
on **MyHistoryLab.com**

helped to inaugurate the round-the-clock shift work in some factories, again reshaping the lives of the **working class.** German scientists took the lead in the electrical and chemical industries, and worldwide sales helped to fund further research into "cutting edge" technologies. The first public electric power station was built in England in 1881, but it was constructed by a German firm, Siemens Brothers.

Key Inventions of the Industrial Revolution

1733	John Kay's "flying shuttle"
1760s	James Watt modernizes the steam engine
1764	James Hargreaves's "spinning jenny"
1769	Richard Arkwright's "spinning frame"
1807	Robert Fulton's steamboat
1830	George Stephenson's "The Rocket" locomotive

The Social Consequences of Industrialization

Before the Industrial Revolution, most urban centers were located in fertile valleys and flood plains or near rivers and natural ports. The size of cities depended on the ability of the adjacent countryside to provide surplus foodstuffs and on the incidence of disease in crowded, unsanitary surroundings. In general, high mortality rates meant that cities needed a constant influx of migrants from the countryside to maintain their population levels. When plague struck—as it often did in the early 1700s—the well-to-do fled the cities for country retreats, leaving the poor to suffer alone. This pattern changed dramatically during the nineteenth century thanks to advances in agriculture, transportation, medicine, and public health. Clean water supplies, centralized and efficient sewage systems, and improved food preservation techniques, such as canning and refrigeration, were crucial to the demographic shift from countryside to city. After World War I, most Germans, Britons, Belgians, Dutch, and Americans lived in towns and cities; worldwide almost one-fifth of humanity lived in urban settings, a social transformation that was unparalleled in human experience (see Map 18–2).

From Workers to Proletariat   In 1800 the wealthiest members of the middle class were merchants and traders. One century later the middle class was led by captains of industry, the owners of machines and factories, and the employers of propertyless wage workers. Bankers and businessmen involved in commerce continued to make modest gains, but in comparison to the industrialist, the old middle

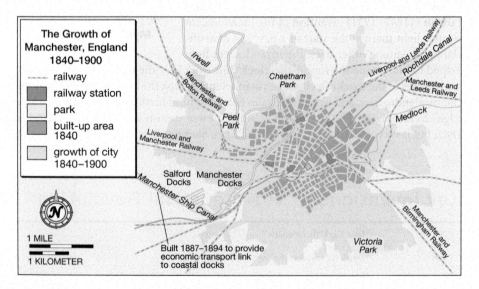

MAP 18-2   Manchester, England   A major textile-producing city, Manchester was at the forefront of the Industrial Revolution. In 1800, 75,000 people lived in the city. Fifty years later the population had increased to over 300,000.

QUESTION: Why did Manchester require so many rail lines going in and out of the city?

class was under assault. The same relative disadvantage faced the working class. The word ***proletariat*** refers to a new type of worker who was entirely dependent upon wage labor for his or her survival. In general, the urban proletariat could not afford private homes, did not own land or small businesses, and had nothing to offer for compensation but physical labor. The raw materials that the laborers extracted, the tools that they used, and the power equipment that they operated were owned by the person or persons who had provided the capital to build the factory and purchase the machinery. Skilled and semiskilled artisans, such as weavers, blacksmiths, and glass blowers, found themselves reduced to operatives in huge factories that did not require specialized abilities.

The relationship between the owner of the means of production and the employees became impersonal and limited to the workplace. In these factories hundreds of workers tended machines that never got tired. Factory owners were well aware that business failures and bankruptcies were widespread and that constant competition threatened their substantial investments. Advanced technology and machinery involved considerable capital investment, and as industry grew, the role of banks and corporations expanded, with shareholders demanding even greater efficiencies in the workplace. Managing the workplace became a high priority. Harsh rules regarding tardiness, drunkenness, theft, and failure to keep pace with the machinery placed the employee—often a recent arrival from the countryside, where the seasons and the weather had regulated the workday—in an unfamiliar and demoralizing situation. This harsh physical environment was what Karl Marx had in mind in the opening quote to this chapter when he stated that mens' social being determined their consciousness.

In the factory, the whistle, the time clock, and the automated machine imposed a new discipline that was oppressive and monotonous. Large work crews in factories were subject to regimentation and to limited, repetitive tasks. Overpopulated cities meant that employers could recruit unskilled machine operatives, even children, from a large pool of potential laborers. Hired to work long (sometimes 16-hour) shifts when demand was high and as easily dismissed when the economy faltered, workers were unlikely to receive a sympathetic hearing from government officials before midcentury, since they did not enjoy the right to vote. Industrialization therefore tended to accentuate economic or class differences in nations where machine production involved a significant percentage of the overall population. In the early nineteenth century skilled English handloom weavers attempted to smash power machinery in a desperate

Read the **Document**

The Sadler Report: Child Labor in the United Kingdom, 1832

on **MyHistoryLab.com**

effort to save their traditional form of employment. It was a futile protest. The British Parliament quickly made industrial sabotage a capital offense. Neither Europe's traditional political leaders nor the industrial bourgeoisie were particularly sensitive to the needs of the emerging working class or to those skilled artisans whose livelihoods were destroyed by the coming of the factory. This is not to say that agricultural laborers lived under more gentle superiors in the form of landowners; working conditions in the commercial agricultural sector were also driven by the demands of the market, and rural poverty and child labor remained endemic problems. However, the novel setting for industrial labor, the city environment, and the rules, fines, and lockouts associated with the factory created a special set of challenges for workers.

Consumer Culture   Despite the many hardships associated with industrialization, during the 1800s Europeans and North Americans became wealthier and
more comfortable than their counterparts in other societies. Not only more wealth
but a greater concentration of the world's wealth in the West marked the age of the
machine. Thanks to industry and science broadly defined, Europe was able to feed and
employ—or transport overseas—its expanding population. Office employment increased as industries and corporations hired clerks, accountants, and sales and secre-
tarial staff. Highly specialized tasks became the rule in this "white collar" employment
sector just as they had on the factory floor, and close supervision of staff by managers ensured maximum productivity. A strong and ever-expanding consumer sector
developed, especially within the ranks of the middle class, and advertising in mass-
circulation newspapers and magazines became an important part of the sales strategy.
Buying on credit, market research, enticing window displays, money-back guarantees,
and many other modern sales techniques originated in the mid-nineteenth century.

While still largely beyond the reach of the working class, whose disposable income was limited by the high cost of housing, the culture of consumption gained
increasing support across Europe and in North America. Large department stores
began to encroach on the small specialty shop. In Paris the innovative *Bon Marché*
department store opened its doors in 1852 (and is still in business). By the 1890s, the
store had over 40 different departments plus a mail-order division. The ideal life was
defined in terms of the constant acquisition of material goods and services. Personal
identity was increasingly linked to personal possession, the ability to purchase the
many fashionable products now available in shops and stores. The English potter **Jo-
siah Wedgwood** (1730–1795) earned a fortune selling "Queen's ware" table settings to
middle-class consumers who wished to associate themselves with the trappings (albeit
invented) of royalty. According to Wedgwood, "fashion is superior to merit," and his
fabulous commercial success appeared to confirm the maxim.

In the United States pioneering efforts in manufacturing led to the development
of interchangeable parts, allowing the production process to become ever more efficient. By the early twentieth century, for example, the automobile manufacturer
Henry Ford (1863–1947) instituted the assembly-
line technique and the use of interchangeable parts.
Ford's factories produced vehicles that were within
the financial reach of the workers who built them.
Producers like Ford made enormous profits by extending the products of consumer culture to average
working families.

⊙ View the Image

*Automobile Assembly Line,
1925*

on **MyHistoryLab.com**

Dominion over Nature   Factory life and the use of tireless machines to produce
goods changed the relationship between individuals and the natural world. In Britain,
1850 was a watershed year: For the first time in history, more than one-half of a nation's population did not work in agriculture or live in the countryside. As more workers
ceased to depend upon the soil for their livelihood, and as technology replaced human
power, a sense of human superiority over nature displaced the traditional understanding
of the role of humans as dependent on nature. Science and technology offered multiple
examples of how nature might be controlled and dominated in the interests of material

Interior of Crystal Palace The exhibit hall of the Crystal Palace (1851) showcased the latest technology and labor-saving devices of the industrial era.

advancement. Economic "progress" became a principal responsibility of governments during the nineteenth century. Official circles downplayed the potential negative consequences of unimpeded development and industrial expansion. Preservation of the natural environment was not a public priority, and few inventors or entrepreneurs considered the harmful side effects of industry. Cities might be unpleasant, dirty, and dangerous, but in comparison to a life without ready-made clothing, electric lights, and rapid steam transport, the environmental costs seemed relatively minor.

View the **Closer Look**
The Great Exhibition in London
on **MyHistoryLab.com**

Voices of Dissent   Despite official lack of interest, however, influential writers and poets of the mid-nineteenth century did discuss many of the social and environmental problems associated with rapid industrialization and consumerism. In Britain **Charles Dickens** (1812–1870) often focused on the shattered lives of industrial workers as they sought to find meaningful work in ugly and unhealthy cities. The fictional "Coketown" of Dickens's *Hard Times* (1854) is inhabited by unscrupulous and callous capitalists and educators who have reduced beauty to production quotas and efficiency goals. In the novel, even union leaders fall into the trap of equating wage levels with human happiness. Dickens was writing only three years after Britain hosted a large-scale international celebration of technology—the Crystal Palace exhibition—in London. The spectacular glass and iron exhibit hall attracted millions of visitors from across Europe and America, who were invited to marvel at the latest labor-saving machinery.

PEOPLE IN CONTEXT   Alfred Krupp

Alfred Krupp (1812–1887) was a pioneer metallurgist and industrialist who transformed a small steel firm established by his father Friedrich (1787–1826) into a major producer of sophisticated military hardware. Krupp was born and raised in the city of Essen in the German Rhineland. He assumed control of his father's firm at the age of 14, at a time when sales of steel were modest and when there were only five company employees. By the time of his death in 1887, Alfred Krupp had expanded his labor force to over 20,000, and his firm was a key supplier of military hardware to over 40 nations. Until World War II, the Krupp family company was one of the world's largest steel and weapons manufacturers.

Krupp's early efforts in steel production focused on small domestic products. He manufactured and sold scissors, dies, machine tools, and rolling mills for use in minting coins. In the late 1840s he developed a popular muzzle-loading gun of cast steel for the military while simultaneously working on improved railway components. The firm acquired Europe-wide recognition in 1851 when Krupp displayed heavy cannons and a two-ton steel ingot (mold) at the Crystal Palace exhibition in London. The ingot was nearly twice as heavy as the one produced by its nearest competitor. New orders began to flow to the Essen plant, and in 1852 Krupp designed a seamless steel railway wheel, which became an instant commercial success. Profits from these early enterprises enabled Krupp, who was a consummate salesman, to concentrate on securing large military contracts from European governments. He sold guns and cannons to Egypt, Belgium, Russia, and Prussia. Once the German states achieved political union in 1871, sales of Krupp ordnance to the new German Empire began to soar. The "cannon king," as he was called, even purchased iron and coalmines across Germany to control the extraction and transport of these essential raw materials.

Industrial Empire   Aerial view of the Krupp armaments factories in Essen, Germany. *Marc Charmet/Picture Desk, Inc./Kobal Collection*

Some historians have cast an unfavorable light on the Krupp family, seeing them as merchants of death who had no higher interest beyond their firm's profit margin. Krupp armaments were used in many conflicts. Another, more charitable perspective focuses on the firm's special relationship with its workforce. As one of Europe's first self-made industrialists, Alfred Krupp was one of only a handful of large employers to offer his workers a package of comprehensive welfare benefits. In 1836 he started a sickness and burial fund, and in 1855 introduced a pension plan for workers who had become disabled on the job. Krupp then began to construct company houses, and as neighborhoods developed adjacent to the sprawling factory complex, schools, parks, libraries, and churches emerged—all with financial support from the Krupp family. He resisted the "hire and fire" mentality based on swings in the business cycle, working to maintain jobs even during periodic downturns in business. While these innovations were obviously paternalistic and designed to avoid labor disputes that might interrupt production, Krupp did create a dedicated and fiercely loyal workforce. ■

QUESTION: In light of his success, how did Krupp and men like him contribute to the process of redefining the relationship between humans and their natural environment?

Women, Children, and Immigrants The Industrial Revolution had a profound impact on the role that women played in the larger economy. In the family economy of rural Europe, women worked in and near the home, often alongside their husband and children. In addition to long hours working the land, women were also responsible for housekeeping duties and child care. They might also do piecework, spinning fibers into thread for male handloom weavers under the cottage industry system. The labor was hard and often repetitious, but it allowed family and neighbors to work together.

⬚●⬚ Read the Document

Industrial Society and Factory Conditions (Early 1800s)

on **MyHistoryLab.com**

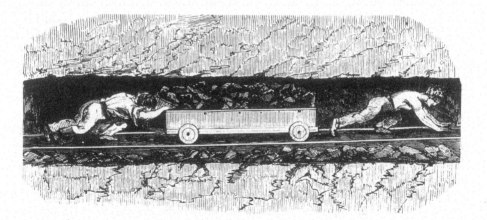

Trolley Boys Until child labor laws were enacted and enforced, youngsters were employed in factories and mines. Orphans and pauper children were especially vulnerable to this type of exploitation. In this illustration, young children remove coal from a mine shaft on a trolley. The mine shaft is illuminated by candlelight.

In the industrial city many working-class women became wage laborers in mills and factories separate from the rest of their household. The work discipline of the factory severely limited a woman's ability to care for family members, particularly children. Single women often toiled as domestics in the homes of the middle class. Neither work environment offered much prospect of advancement or of earning a living wage. Income differences between the sexes were significant. In 1900, for example, women in industry earned on average less than half of what their male counterparts earned. As the population of urban centers grew, the cost of housing mounted, making the income secured by women essential to a family's survival. Children and recent U.S. immigrants also played significant roles in the urban workforce. Like women, these two groups were thought to be more compliant than native-born adult males. All could be paid significantly less, and, it was argued, they would also be less likely to unionize.

Middle-class women also experienced the separation of the workplace from the home, but in an entirely different manner. The wives of the bourgeoisie were expected to stay at home, raise the children, and supervise the servants. In the home they would provide hospitality and refuge from the stresses of the new economy in a manner befitting their husbands' professional status. These women lived in homes that no longer contributed to the traditional family economy but were centers of the moral economy, promoting values that were at odds with the competitive spirit of the business world. A unique "domestic sphere" was constructed in which the middle-class home became the focus of the emerging consumer economy. There was no expectation that middle-class women might enter institutions of higher education or train for the professions.

Working-Class Organizations   The factory system destroyed the medieval guild practice of protecting skilled labor while ensuring product quality. A few employers adopted a paternalistic model of management, constructing worker housing and company stores, providing minimal medical care, and occasionally offering basic educational training. In Lowell, Massachusetts, for example, mill owners provided their mostly female (and single) workers with room and board. However, paternalism could quickly deteriorate into coercion, with threats of eviction used against workers who sought to organize for better wages. Even after the advent of factory production, traditional labor organizations, such as mutual aid societies and fraternal organizations, continued to assist workers in their transition to the unfamiliar industrial setting. Formal labor unions were illegal in Britain between 1799 and 1824, when the government finally allowed workers to organize but denied them the right to strike. Normally limited to skilled labor, the first industrial unions focused their attention on incremental change within the framework of the capitalist system.

Early unions for skilled workers offered their members accident insurance, modest retirement benefits, and accidental death and burial payments. After midcentury, however, union organizers shifted their attention to the growing ranks of unskilled workers. In most industrialized countries, wages were creeping up for the average laborer, but working conditions remained poor. The right to strike was finally recognized in Britain in 1875, an important milestone in a nation where factory workers made up more than one-half of the total workforce. Nine years later the French government sanctioned union activity, and by 1900, the French syndicates or labor unions included half a million members. Industrial unions for unskilled workers began to clash openly with employers in the final decades of the century, using strikes as their major weapon.

In 1889 a strike at the London docks briefly crippled the movement of goods destined for overseas ports. Despite the sporadic victories of organized workers, however, most of Europe's labor force remained outside of unions at the start of World War I.

Education in the Industrial Age   During the early stages of industrialization, factories did not require educated workers. As late as 1860 most Europeans remained illiterate. The wealthy had always secured their education through tutors or in expensive private institutions. The few primary schools that existed in cities were operated by churches, but they reached only a small fraction of the working class. Most poor families were reluctant to support plans for mandatory education because they needed the income their children earned in the factories. After midcentury, however, industry's growing need for literate clerks, accountants, and men with some technical training led to calls for state-supported and directed schools.

Supporters of compulsory elementary schooling advanced three basic arguments. For those who worried about the potentially disruptive power of large numbers of poorly paid urban dwellers, a carefully managed system of literacy and indoctrination offered the best guarantee of popular loyalty to the state and respect for private property. The virtues of discipline, obedience, and self-help could be communicated by trained professionals. The French statesman (and historian) **François Guizot** (1787–1874) believed that "the opening of every school house closes a jail."

Pupils and Teachers   The Reverend Thomas Guthrie (1803–1873) was an ardent social reformer in Scotland in the middle of the nineteenth century. Among his many causes, he championed the creation of nonsectarian schools. Guthrie can be seen here standing at a blackboard, accompanied by a female aid, instructing young pupils at the Ragged School in Edinburgh, Scotland. One of Guthrie's former pupils said that "he was all the father I ever knew."

More idealistic supporters focused on the remedial and transforming power of basic education. These proponents were heirs of the Enlightenment tradition, eager to advance equality of opportunity and a new "aristocracy" of talent. Economic progress required state-sponsored schools. Finally, champions of an extended franchise insisted that as more and more men secured the right to vote, it was essential to have an educated citizenry to avoid the rise of demagogues and would-be tyrants.

In 1833 Guizot introduced legislation that called for an elementary school in every French parish. It was an ambitious agenda, and the goal was not fully realized until 1882. The French initiative was also repeated elsewhere in Western Europe. Great Britain began subsidizing its existing religious schools in 1870 while simultaneously supporting the formation of secular institutions at the elementary level. School attendance was first made compulsory for British youth in 1880 and for French children in 1882. Germany, Holland, Belgium, Italy, Switzerland, and Scandinavia all embraced the trend, and by the end of the century, most remaining tuition fees were abolished across Western Europe.

The movement for universal primary education (for children under the age of 14) was strongest in those parts of Europe and America where the process of industrialization was well underway. By World War I, most men and women in these nations could read and write, and many had received specialized technical training. A large corps of professional teachers emerged, and pupils from working-class backgrounds were provided with the basic intellectual tools necessary for entry-level white collar employment. Bank clerks, secretaries, machine operators, postal service employees—all needed basic education to carry out their tasks. The schools did promote responsible self-government, but more problematically, they also became training camps for strong and unreflective nationalism in an age of European expansion and imperial rivalry.

The Changing Role of the State   Optimists on both sides of the Atlantic hoped they could reduce poverty and illness and expand material comforts by alleviating the physical burdens of work through the application of technology. The promises of industry—efficiency, increased productivity, and lower costs for mass-produced goods—all seemed within reach under the appropriate political conditions. Those conditions, at least from the point of view of liberal economists and politicians, involved minimum interference from the state. According to Edward Baines (1800–1890), author of *The History of the Cotton Manufacture in Great Britain* (1835) and an enthusiastic supporter of modernization, "under the reign of just laws [in England], personal liberty and property have been secure; mercantile enterprise has been allowed to reap its reward; capital has accumulated in safety." More controversially, Baines claimed that the working class also benefited from a laissez-faire economic order.

National incomes did increase tremendously in Europe in the century before World War I, and free labor replaced onerous slave systems in the United States and in the British Empire. Yet the income gap between employer and employee appeared to grow wider each decade. Religious organizations like the **Salvation Army** in Britain, founded in 1878, attempted to assist men and women who faced poverty and despair, but

View the **Image**

Salvation Army Workers

on **MyHistoryLab.com**

their resources were limited. The fabulous wealth enjoyed by successful businessmen, investors, and owners of large factories, when juxtaposed with the difficult circumstances of workers during the early stages of industrialization, prompted European governments to intervene in a small way in the private sector. Precedents for state action abounded, ironically in the area of government assistance for capitalist ventures. Adam Smith's doctrine of laissez-faire (see Chapter 16, "The Age of Enlightenment: Rationalism and Its Uses") was faithfully championed by industrial capitalists when it came to employer/employee relations, but businessmen were aggressive supporters of government investment in infrastructure. Land grants and tax incentives for transport companies (road and bridge building, railroads, harbor projects), together with tariff protection for infant industries facing stiff foreign competition, were all time-honored exceptions to the free market confession of faith.

By 1900, all of the major European states except Russia had adopted less restrictive electoral systems. This process of democratization helped to intensify efforts to improve the lives of the working class. France had universal manhood suffrage in 1848, while Britain extended the franchise to working men in voting reform acts of 1867 and 1884. Germany, Britain's biggest rival in the race for industrial supremacy, instituted universal manhood suffrage in 1871. Amendments to the U.S. Constitution after the Civil War in 1865 called for the enfranchisement of free black males, but that struggle continued well into the 1960s. By the start of World War I, Spain, Belgium, France, Norway, Italy, Switzerland, Austria, and the Netherlands each broadened their franchise to include every adult male, and strenuous efforts were underway to enfranchise women. Norway, in 1907, became the first European state to give the vote to women.

☐●〉Read the **Document**

National Woman Suffrage Association, Mother's Day Letter

on **MyHistoryLab.com**

🔍〉View the **Image**

Suffragist Speaking

on **MyHistoryLab.com**

🔍〉View the **Map**

Woman Suffrage before the Nineteenth Amendment

on **MyHistoryLab.com**

Extending the Enlightenment principle that legitimate governments derive their powers from the consent of the governed, and not from an assumed divine mandate, had the unanticipated effect of enhancing the power of national governments across Western Europe. Patriotic and nationalist rhetoric allowed Europe's democratizing states to cultivate popular support in pursuit of expansionist domestic programs and imperial adventures. Thanks to universal manhood suffrage, serious reform could now take place within the political and economic arenas. Socialist political parties were committed to improving living and working standards for the working class, and conservative and liberal politicians responded by introducing their own programs for social reform. In an economic and cultural environment of rising expectations, where centuries-old assumptions about the inevitability of poverty for the many were no longer accepted, Europe's leaders became increasingly alarmed by the prospect of social conflict. To defuse this potential, governments began to invest heavily in education, housing provision, sanitation, pure water and food supplies, adequate policing, and street lighting.

KEY
QUESTION
REVISITED

How do technology
and urbanization
influence the
relationship between
humans and nature?

Technology and **urbanization** had a profound impact on the relationship between humans and nature during the Industrial Revolution. At the time of the French Revolution, Europeans still depended upon wind, water, and animal and human muscle to supply the energy they needed for their daily work. For the most part, that work took place in close connection with the natural environment. The work routine was regulated in large measure by available sunlight, the condition of the soil, and climatic variables. In the nineteenth century this traditional pattern of life and work was gradually replaced by a capital-intensive economy based on manufacturing. Although most people in southern, eastern, and central Europe remained in rural economies at the start of the twentieth century, industrialization had transformed life in Belgium, Britain, France, Germany, the Netherlands, Scandinavia, northern Italy, and in pockets of Austria-Hungary. Across the Atlantic, the United States experienced the full force of the Industrial Revolution after 1865.

In addition to new patterns of organizing human labor, the substitution of factories for small shops and home workrooms, and the emergence of large industrial centers, the Industrial Revolution redefined the relationship between humans and the natural environment. Nonrenewable natural resources such as coal and oil were depleted at a fast pace, while renewable resources such as water and timber were consumed at an unsustainable rate. Trees were felled at an alarming rate to construct houses and factories, create railway lines, and build roads. Factories spewed smoke into the atmosphere and discharged waste products in rivers. Cotton workers were exposed to brown-lung disease, while miners suffered and died from black-lung disease. Poisoning from mercury, lead, and the ingestion of metal shavings became distressing features of industrial life. Traditional sources of drinking water now became convenient dumping points for human and industrial waste, while smoke from coal-fired engines was often the first signal that the traveler was approaching an urban center. Shabby housing in unplanned, overcrowded, and disease-ridden neighborhoods contributed to the overall pattern of environmental degradation.

Still, before 1900, few reformers paid much attention to the environmental consequences of rapid industrialization. Women and men continued to flock to the cities in search of jobs in factories, construction, domestic service, stores, and offices. Despite the pressures of factory discipline, families adjusted to their new environments. The city offered anonymity and freedom of action; traditional values and practices were replaced by new options in personal relations. One's choice of marriage partner, for instance, now transcended the confines of the village. Rates of divorce increased, as did illegitimate births. Even the choice to remain single, always suspect in the rural village, became easier to realize in the city. An increasing emphasis on rights over obligations, especially to social superiors, was perhaps one of the most significant aspects of the new freedoms the large urban setting provided.

By 1914, the condition of the working class in Western Europe was much improved, and some of the conveniences of the expanding consumer economy were within reach of laborers. Adult males had won the right to vote in most countries; children were now afforded primary education at public expense; the disgruntled and the ambitious had the option of cheap passage to the Americas or Australasia. State intervention in the workplace addressed the worst elements of early industrial life. In particular, government-mandated health and safety regulations, better wages, and accident and retirement provisions allowed common people to reach levels of material security never before available. The Western industrial lifestyle was even embraced by colonial peoples who sought both to emulate the West's economic transformation and to free themselves from European control. Unfortunately for people in countries where industry had not taken root and where opportunities for migration were negligible (India and China, for example), acute economic crises, political unrest, and recurrent food shortages became the norm.

Technology and urbanization had redefined the relationship between humans and nature, but in the early nineteenth century, the separation of large numbers of people from the rhythm of life on the land and in small communities seemed, on balance, to have resulted in a better quality of material life for everyone. Industrialization had weakened the influence of both the traditional aristocracy and the official state churches. The middle class rose to political and social power thanks to the economic rewards associated with industrial production. The working class had not been pressed to the limits of physical endurance as the Marxists had predicted at midcentury. Increasing secularization and confidence about the future replaced older, less optimistic assumptions about the possibility and value of change. On the eve of World War I, industrial prowess enabled Europeans to dominate the globe, and few people worried about the capacity of industrialized nations for widespread human and ecological destruction. All of this would change after war began in 1914.

Key Terms

Industrial Revolution, *p. 532*
steam engine, *p. 540*
internal combustion engine, *p. 543*

working class, *p. 543*
proletariat, *p. 545*
urbanization, *p. 554*

Activities

1. Explain how changes in agriculture expedited the process of early industrialization.

2. Why did governments intervene in the private sector on behalf of industrial workers?

3. List the factors that enabled Britain to become the world's first industrial nation.

4. Why was steam power so central to the early stages of the Industrial Revolution?

5. List the main objectives of the first industrial unions.

6. What role did manufacturers play in the development of a middle-class consumer culture?

7. Describe the changing roles of working-class and middle-class women during the Industrial Revolution.

Further Reading

Kenneth Morgan, *The Birth of Industrial Britain: Social Change, 1750–1850* (2004), a fresh look at the first industrial nation.

Peter Stearns, *The Industrial Revolution in World History* (2007), places the Western experience in global context.

Deborah Cadbury, *Dreams of Iron and Steel: Seven Wonders of the Nineteenth Century, from the Building of the London Sewers to the Panama Canal* (2004), provides a snapshot of transformative projects.

Deborah Valenze, *The First Industrial Woman* (1995), explores the impact of industrialization on the work of women.

MyHistoryLab **Connections**

Visit **MyHistoryLab.com** *for a customized Study Plan that will help you build your knowledge of* Industry, Society, and Environment.

Questions for Analysis

1. How did industrialization affect cities and rural communities in the nineteenth century?

    ◉─[Watch the **Video** 19th Century Industrialization, p. 535

2. What is the relationship between railroads and settlement patterns in the United States during the nineteenth century?

    ◉─[Watch the **Video** Railroads and Expansion, p. 541

3. What was life like for children working in factories in the early nineteenth century?

    ▢◉─[Read the **Document** The Sadler Report: Child Labor in the United Kingdom, 1832, p. 545

4. How did the organizers of the Great Exhibition in London characterize "progress"?

    ◉─[View the **Closer Look** The Great Exhibition in London, p. 547

5. Based on the interactive map, what observations can be made about women's voting rights prior to passage of the Nineteenth Amendment to the U.S. Constitution?

    ◉─[View the **Map** Woman Suffrage before the Nineteenth Amendment, p. 553

Other Resources from This Chapter

    ◉─[View the **Image** Laying the Transatlantic Telegraph Cable, p. 542

    ◉─[Watch the **Video** Edison's Punching the Clock, p. 543

🔍 **View** the **Image** Automobile Assembly Line, 1925, p. 546

📖 **Read** the **Document** Industrial Society and Factory Conditions (Early 1800s), p. 549

🔍 **View** the **Image** Salvation Army Workers, p. 552

📖 **Read** the **Document** National Woman Suffrage Association, Mother's Day Letter, p. 553

🔍 **View** the **Image** Suffragist Speaking, p. 553

Soldiers Firing on Civilians Revolution spread across Europe during the spring and summer of 1848, but in most cases the established authorities used force successfully to defeat their opponents. The revolutions were led by fragile coalitions between the middle and working classes. Ideological differences weakened the opposition in every country.

19 The Age of Ideology

LEARNING OBJECTIVES

What was the European "Congress System"?   •   What were the main differences between liberals and conservatives after 1815?   •   Why did revolution spread across Europe in 1848?   •   How did Britain achieve political reform before 1848?   •   What were the main values of the Romantic movement?   •   What were the principle characteristics of utilitarianism and socialism?   •   How did Marxism challenge political and economic orthodoxy?

Fight on, embattled Russia mine, Recall the rights of ancient days! The sun of Austerlitz, decline! And Moscow, mighty city, blaze! Brief be the time of our dishonor The auspices are turning now; Hail Moscow—Russia's blessings on her! War to extinction, thus our vow!

—Alexander Pushkin, "Napoleon" (1821)

KEY QUESTION

What leads people to repudiate traditional ideas, beliefs, and practices?

In recalling Napoleon's invasion of his homeland in 1812, the Russian poet and dramatist Alexander Pushkin (1799–1837) focused not on the destruction and loss of life caused by the Grand Army led by Bonaparte, but instead on the emergence of Russian national feeling. Pushkin's pride in his country was matched by a strong commitment to political freedom and the advancement of individual rights. Neither goal was realized in Russia during Pushkin's brief lifetime, but the ideals of national autonomy, freedom, and the dignity of the individual became key features of European culture in the three decades following the defeat of Napoleon Bonaparte at Waterloo in 1815.

A wide range of ideological "isms" emerged on the European political scene during these years. Most of these terms and movements are recognizable today—liberalism, conservatism, romanticism, utopianism, industrialism, nationalism, socialism, and Marxism. But most found their definitive modern expression during or in the aftermath of the great French Revolution that began in 1789. Most of them would play decisive roles in shaping the lives of Europeans as they responded to the disruptions caused by two decades of military conflict and the beginnings of an unprecedented change in patterns of labor and production associated with the rise of industry.

Napoleon's imperial dreams may have been shattered decisively at Waterloo, but there was little hope that the intellectual assumptions and beliefs of Old Regime Europe could be restored fully in the nineteenth century. As monarchies were reconstituted and efforts undertaken to affirm the legitimacy of Europe's hereditary rulers, the forces in support of responsible self-government, individual rights, religious pluralism, and civil and legal reform continued to attract additional followers from within the ranks of the expanding middle class. By 1848, a series of liberal and nationalist revolutions across Europe demonstrated the power of ideas first put to the test during the French Revolution. Napoleonic dictatorship and reform by fiat had been rejected in 1815, but no one knew for sure what model of social and political order would take its place. On a continent where the unprecedented forces of industrialization were contributing to a fundamental reordering of established cultural values, ideological commitments repeatedly fueled political action in the streets of Europe's capitals. ■

The Congress System and the Conservative Agenda

After Napoleon's abdication and banishment to Elba in 1814, Russia, Prussia, Austria, and Britain concluded a lenient "First Peace of Paris" with the defeated French. Louis XVI's young son had been recognized by the other European rulers as Louis XVII after the execution of his father in 1793, but the boy died while being held captive by the revolutionaries and never exercised power. As a result, after the fall of Napoleon, the younger brother of the executed monarch was installed as King Louis XVIII (r. 1814–1824). The restored Bourbon ruler always carried the taint of having been imposed on the French people by the powers who had vanquished Napoleon, but despite this awkward start, the king was welcomed by most of his subjects. The boundaries of the restored monarchy were cut back only to their 1792 dimensions, giving the French territory they had not held when the French Revolution began in 1789.

After settling affairs in France, the victorious powers agreed to meet again in the Austrian capital of Vienna in September 1814 in order to make additional adjustments to the political map of the continent. As the delegates assembled, the most pressing problems before them involved the reestablishment of political stability and the creation of a balance of power in Europe. The leading figures at the meeting were Austria's chancellor, Prince **Clemens von Metternich** (1773–1859), British foreign secretary Robert Stewart Viscount Castlereagh (1769–1822), Russian Tsar Alexander I (r. 1801–1825), the aged Baron Hardenberg of Prussia (1750–1822), and France's minister for foreign affairs, Charles Maurice Prince de Talleyrand (1754–1838). They were joined by dozens of rulers who had been summarily dispossessed of their lands by Napoleon and by a host of lesser figures who sought to avenge some slight received during the revolutionary era. Most of the leading figures at Vienna were members of Europe's old aristocracy. They were men who were suspicious of liberal political ideas and who viewed the middle class as

[◼▶️[Read the Document

Metternich on the Revolutions of 1848

on **MyHistoryLab.com**

Prince Clemens von Metternich   The leading figure at the Congress of Vienna, Metternich would remain an important spokesperson for nineteenth-century conservatism until he fled from Vienna during the revolution of 1848.

troublesome upstarts. The war and chaos of the preceding 20 years, they believed, had been occasioned by the dangerous belief in human equality. The delegates were intent upon destroying the revolutionary impulse and reasserting their traditional leadership prerogatives.

Containing the French

One of the main principles at the **Congress of Vienna** was monarchical "legitimacy." Many of the rulers abridged or revoked the civil and legal reforms Napoleon had introduced. As a result, the prerevolutionary dynasties returned to their respective capitals. The Vienna meeting was interrupted by Napoleon's 100-day return to power in March 1815 and defeat at Waterloo in June. In the aftermath of this crisis, France was forced to pay a 700 million franc indemnity, accept the imposition of foreign troops until the indemnity was paid, and retract its eastern frontier to the boundaries of 1789. The creation of strong states along France's eastern border was thought to be in the interest of Europe-wide peace and order; thus, the delegates granted Prussia new lands along the Rhine River while the Protestant Netherlands and Catholic Belgium were joined to make the kingdom of the Netherlands under the rule of William I (r. 1815–1840).

In Italy, where the Napoleonic reforms had taken deep root, the return of the House of Savoy to an expanded kingdom of Piedmont-Sardinia in the northeast, coupled with direct Austrian rule in Venice and Lombardy, led to simmering local discontent. Napoleon, who as a native Corsican was in certain respects more Italian than French, had dismantled the old feudal order and succeeded in winning broad support for the Napoleonic Code. The entire peninsula reverted to rule by more or less reactionary monarchs, including the pope, who returned as ruler of the Papal States.

New Boundaries

The leading powers also took the opportunity to expand their own territories. Poland was restored as a state, but under the rule of the Russian tsar and subject to Russian military occupation. Tsar Alexander also won control over Finland, previously ruled by Sweden. The Swedes, in return, acquired Norway, which had been governed by Napoleon's ally Denmark. Prussia acquired part of Saxony and all of the central German province of Westphalia. It emerged from the Congress as the second most powerful state in the former Holy Roman Empire. Not to be outdone, Britain received strategically important naval bases at Helgoland in the North Sea, Malta in the Mediterranean, Cape Colony in South Africa, and the island of Ceylon off the southern coast of India. The Papal States were restored to the Roman Catholic Church under the leadership of Pope Pius VII (r. 1800–1823), and in Spain the Bourbons returned to their capital at Madrid. The defunct Holy Roman Empire was replaced by a loose confederation of 39 German states featuring a federal diet based in Frankfurt. While the "Congress System" was subject to serious strain in the nineteenth century, the Vienna settlement did inaugurate a century in which there was no general European war. The leading states of Western Europe would expand their influence around the globe between the defeat of Napoleon in 1815 and the start of World War I in 1914, but during this period, no one power would come to dominate the continent and threaten its neighbors (see Map 19-1).

Challenging the Peace of Europe   In France the government of Louis XVIII quickly paid its indemnity and was admitted into an alliance of five great states (known as the Quintuple Alliance) that included Russia, Austria, Prussia, and Great Britain. Committed to upholding the territorial and political settlements reached at

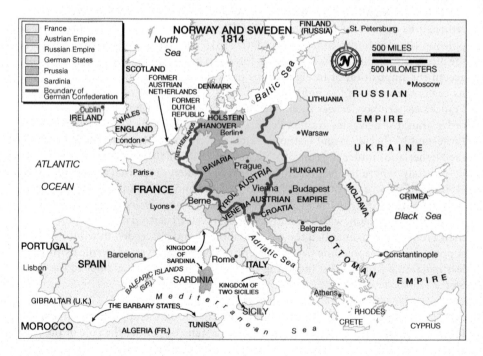

MAP 19-1   Europe in 1815   The delegates at the Congress of Vienna dismantled Napoleon's empire and made a wide array of territorial adjustments. The Holy Roman Empire was not restored; instead it was replaced by a new German confederation.

QUESTION: Did the Congress of Vienna acknowledge nationalist sentiments?

Vienna, the governments of the restored monarchies cracked down on liberal activists, censored the press, and used their armies to crush revolutionary movements whenever and wherever they emerged. A second and overlapping alliance, the so-called Holy Alliance, involved Russia, Austria, and Prussia. It committed the signatories to upholding the Christian faith throughout the continent.

As early as 1821, Austrian forces overturned a liberal revolution in the southern Italian Kingdom of the Two Sicilies and another in Piedmont. Two years later, 100,000 French troops were sent across the Pyrenees to assist Spanish King Ferdinand VII (r. 1813–1833) against a liberal revolution. The revolutionaries were led by disgruntled soldiers and had forced the king to restore the liberal constitution of 1812, established during the Napoleonic occupation of the country. In Russia, the death of Alexander I in December 1825 led to a revolt by army officers who had been exposed to liberal political ideas and who had founded a number of secret societies dedicated to undermining autocracy in Russia. Lacking broad support, the revolutionaries were easily defeated by troops loyal to the new tsar, Nicholas I (r. 1825–1855). In the aftermath of this "Decembrist" uprising, the tsar inaugurated a rigorous program of censorship and control over foreign travel. The secret police were granted wide powers of surveillance over the Russian population.

There were exceptions to the Vienna consensus. The British were unenthusiastic about Metternich's brand of repression, and they refused to participate in the Holy Alliance. Tsar Alexander's plan to organize a Russian fleet to crush the rebellions that had broken out in Spain's American colonies won little support among the Congress powers. When Greek rebels took up arms against their Turkish overlords in 1821, Britain, France, and Russia supported the revolutionaries despite the protests of the arch conservative Metternich. In 1827 the three powers signed a formal treaty pledging support for the Greek insurgents. European leaders who were educated in the Greek classics, and who associated the Greek fighters with the ancient Spartans and Athenians, felt compelled to assist in the struggle against the Muslim Turks. By 1830, the Greeks had secured their independence. While few Europeans remained alive who had lived through the age of the French Revolution, the memory of reform continued to inspire a new generation.

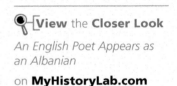

View the **Closer Look**

An English Poet Appears as an Albanian

on **MyHistoryLab.com**

Ideological Ferment

Conservatism   The Greek struggle for independence during the 1820s was but one of a number of events that highlighted a protracted debate between advocates for change and defenders of tradition and the status quo. Following in the footsteps of Edmund Burke, European conservatives argued that social order and political stability could best be realized in a climate where tradition, hierarchy, and corporate relationships were preserved and respected. For nineteenth-century conservatives, society was made up not just of individuals who had rights—it was a complex organism that had developed slowly over centuries. This organism was best directed by men who had inherited their positions of leadership. Conservatives like the Frenchman

Joseph de Maistre (1753–1821) wrote that the state must play an active and directive role in the life of the nation, supporting religious institutions, encouraging educational initiatives, and inculcating a sense of moral authority through example.

According to conservatives, monarchy, aristocracy, and church were the essential anchors of long-term social harmony. Unlike modern conservatives, early conservatism valued the heavy hand of the state because conservatives rejected the Enlightenment faith in universal truths that were applicable to all people in every circumstance. Instead, each state must follow social, religious, and political paths unique to its cultural traditions. The state must be the arbiter of rights that were not universal but were peculiar to one people. Conservatives valued community and duty, by which they meant the obligations that bound individuals to each other and to the state. The experience of the French Revolution and the tyranny of Napoleon were, for conservatives, nearly fatal to the whole concept of civilization. They rejected the Enlightenment's faith in human perfectability and the idea that "all men are created equal." Instead, their picture of human nature and human potential emphasized human frailty and sinfulness.

Liberalism Nineteenth-century European liberals represented a different point of view. For increasing numbers of bankers, businessmen, traders, manufacturers, lawyers, and other professionals, the defeat of Napoleon did not mean that the values of the American republic or the French Revolution were invalid. Where conservatives stressed duty, tradition, and hierarchy, liberals believed that human beings were individuals who possessed inherent rights. They called for political reform, equality before the law, and economic freedom. They also espoused the sanctity of private property and supported written constitutions that restrained the power of the state.

During the nineteenth century, liberalism appealed most directly to the aspiring middle class. These were men who had acquired significant economic power but who lacked political rights and social status. They believed that talent, ambition, and material success qualified one for high social status and a role in the political decision-making process. They also held that through education and personal freedom, everyone could live as a rational, self-directed citizen. Maximizing personal autonomy and limiting the power of the state to the basic needs of national defense and law enforcement were, for liberals, key ingredients to personal and corporate happiness. Most liberals were not democrats; they pushed for a moderate extension of the franchise to include men (never women) of property, but did not believe that workers, peasants, the poor, and the uneducated should be given a voice in government.

Political Economy The personal freedom advocated by liberals after 1815 also included the freedom to fail. With a state limited to protecting the person and property of the individual, and with all monopolies and restrictions on trade lifted, the autonomous citizen would be free to pursue economic advancement without hindrance from the state. However, autonomy and personal responsibility also meant that the state in particular and society as a whole were under no obligation to provide for the destitute or unemployed. Nor was the government charged with overseeing the conditions of labor, regulating wages in the marketplace, or setting minimum standards in housing. Adam Smith had claimed that natural laws existed in the marketplace just as surely as they existed in the heavens, and the first law stated that the economy would remain in balance only if the meddling hand of the state were restricted. The rational self-interest of employers and employees would ensure material well-being for all. Under such an understanding of basic economic forces, those who experienced poverty had no one but themselves to blame.

Some economists, while supportive of Smith's laissez-faire (noninterference) formula, were less optimistic about its impact on the poor. The English clergyman **Thomas Malthus** (1766–1834) believed that population would always outstrip food supply in a free-market economy. Malthus's *Essay on the Principle of Population* (1798) did not advocate state action in the face of this impending crisis, however. Any effort on the part of the government to raise wages would simply lead Europe's masses to have more children, thus plunging them back to the margins of survival. In the *Principles of Political Economy* (1817), **David Ricardo** (1772–1823) endorsed the gloomy "Malthusian" prediction, concluding that the wage worker must engage in a constant struggle with his employer for salary increases. Unfortunately, as the population grew, wages would be pushed down due to the inevitable oversupply of labor. According to Ricardo's "iron law of wages," salary deflation was the only force capable of curbing population growth. In the opinion of Europe's expanding working class, the theories of Malthus and Ricardo offered a troubling justification for the ongoing callousness and apathy of the wealthy, the owners of the means of production.

Read the **Document**

Laws of Population Growth *(1798), Malthus*

on **MyHistoryLab.com**

Read the **Document**

David Ricardo, Excerpt from Principles of Political Economy and Taxation

on **MyHistoryLab.com**

The "dismal science" of political economy may have pleased middle-class liberals who fought for the right to utilize their property as they saw fit, but for employees, the need for state intervention in the workings of the private sector seemed obvious.

The Revolutions of 1830–1832   By the third decade of the nineteenth century, the Vienna settlement, also known as the Concert of Europe, had been put to the test repeatedly. In most instances it had succeeded in preventing serious upheaval in the major states. In France the restored Bourbon king reluctantly accepted limits on his powers. A constitutional charter established a two-chamber legislative assembly, rights to free expression, and legal equality among all Frenchmen. About 90,000 Frenchmen, or one in 300, enjoyed the right to vote for members of the Chamber of Deputies.

Unfortunately, Louis XVIII's younger brother and successor, Charles X (r. 1824–1830), was less pragmatic and forcefully asserted his right to rule without legislative hindrance. Backed by conservative nobles known as "ultras," Charles curbed press freedoms and worked to extend the authority of the Catholic Church. For example, sacrilege against the church was made a crime punishable by imprisonment and even death. Charles also sought to compensate aristocratic families who had lost lands during the revolutionary era. When the king's party failed miserably in the legislative elections of 1830, the monarch dissolved the Chamber of Deputies and instituted a new franchise by decree that was designed to give conservative landowners more electoral power than the wealthy members of the French middle class. The press was also censored. These actions outraged the king's opponents and denied them their only outlet for peaceful political expression at the national level.

These royal decrees coincided with an escalation of food prices throughout the country during the spring of 1830, which created discontent among the urban masses. In a spontaneous uprising in July, barricades were erected in Paris, and clashes between citizens and soldiers ensued. However, the army lost control of the streets, and the urban bourgeoisie abandoned the king. The defiance soon spread to the countryside, and calls for a republic were heard within working-class circles. After Charles X abdicated and left for a life of exile in Britain, the wealthy middle class, fearful of republican rhetoric, threw their support behind Charles's cousin, the duke of Orleans. Proclaimed King **Louis Philippe** (r. 1830–1848), the new monarch recognized that he owed his position to the support of the wealthy bourgeoisie. His government consistently supported the interests of this liberal element until another popular revolution overthrew the monarchy in 1848.

In the neighboring Low Countries the Catholic Belgians were disgruntled by the 1815 union of their state with the mostly Protestant Netherlands. They reacted to the events of 1830 in France by declaring their own independence. A food crisis similar to the one in France triggered the Belgian revolt and call for autonomy. The Belgians stressed the importance of their Catholic traditions, their native language, and their desire for a written constitution. After the Dutch failed to defeat the Belgians, the

Delacroix, *Liberty Leading the People* Eugene Delacroix's famed painting dramatized the French uprising of 1830. This painting helped to popularize the image of Marianne, who symbolizes the French nation and the republican values of liberty, fraternity, and equality. *Eugene Delacroix (1798–1863),* Liberty Leading the People. *July 28, 1830. Painted 1830. Oil on canvas, 260 325 cm. Photo: Hervé Lewandowski. Musée du Louvre/ RMN Reunion des Musées Nationaux, France. SCALA/Art Resource, NY*

great powers recognized Belgian independence on the condition that the new state adopt a posture of neutrality. The 1831 constitution that created the Kingdom of Belgium instantly became a beacon of hope for liberals across Europe. Although only 1% of the male population was afforded the right to vote (the franchise was expanded in the 1840s), both houses of the new bicameral legislature were elected (in most countries the upper house was appointed by the crown). Members of the judiciary were granted autonomy from the government, and the Catholic clergy were denied political influence.

Further to the east, revolution in Poland threatened Russia's hold over its western neighbor. The Polish diet had been restored after 1815, but real political power rested with the Russian governor (and the tsar's brother), Grand Duke Constantine (1779–1831). After news of events in Paris reached Warsaw, disgruntled Polish army officers and university students—and even some members of the aristocracy—joined in what became a call for national independence and constitutional government. The uprising began in November 1830, and it took almost one year for the Russian army to crush the insurgency. The Austrians faced similar threats to their control over portions of Italy. Early in 1831 the northwestern Italian states of Parma and Modena attempted to free themselves from Austrian control, and in central Italy's Papal States, nationalists fought to strip the Roman Catholic Church of its political monopoly. In both instances the rebels failed, but Italian nationalists maintained their goals through a number of underground movements that would return to action in 1848.

Read the **Document**

Adam Mickiewicz: Excerpts from The Books of the Polish Nation 1830–1831

on **MyHistoryLab.com**

View the **Map**

Map Discovery: Unrest of the 1820s and 1830s: Centers of Revolutionary Action

on **MyHistoryLab.com**

The Revolutions of 1848

In the spring of 1848 a series of revolutions swept across the continent in dramatic fashion. They threatened the restored regimes of Western Europe and featured a radical dimension that questioned the legitimacy of the monarchical principle. The revolutions also introduced the prospect of a society reordered along more equalitarian lines. Beginning in France, spreading east and south into the small German-speaking states and Italy, and finally engulfing Central Europe, the revolutionary agenda demonstrated that the core ideals of the French Revolution could not be excised by government repression; and in Poland, Italy, Ireland, Hungary, the Czech lands, and Germany, the push for broader political rights and constitutional reform was combined with parallel demands for national autonomy and national unity (see Map 19–2).

The Spread of Ideas   The persistent calls for parliamentary government under a constitutional monarch during the 1830s and 1840s were strengthened by two changes in the intellectual culture of Western Europe. The first force for change involved the universities, where faculty and students for the first time in Western history had a distinct impact on political thought and action. The second involved

MAP 19-2   The Revolutions of 1848   Revolution was widespread in 1848. As this map indicates, the call for political reform and the recourse to violence in order to secure reforms was concentrated in Italy, France, and Germany.

QUESTION: Why did Britain escape revolution in 1848?

the expansion of literacy and the resulting growth of the popular press. Newspapers and periodicals became important vehicles for shaping public opinion in the West, especially middle-class opinion. Censorship continued to be applied by governments across the continent, and the further east one traveled, the harsher the controlling arm of the state became. While mass circulation newspapers did not appear until the last decades of the century, the influence of the print media far exceeded its subscription lists. The dissemination of information reached new levels, and papers critical of government policies enjoyed strong popular support. For the first time in Europe, common people, especially urban dwellers, came to understand the importance of politics in their daily lives and began to take direct action to advance their agendas.

The revolutions took place during a period of acute economic hardship. Food shortages across Europe began with the decimation of the potato crop in 1845, affecting peasants from Ireland to Prussia. Famine conditions (the last time that Europe was faced with a severe food crisis) threatened wide areas of the population. Persistent drought also weakened grain production on the continent. For peasants and urban workers, high food prices and the prospect of malnutrition undermined their innate conservatism and weakened their support for existing regimes. The physical hardship that the unemployed, the malnourished, the bankrupt businessman, and the middle-class investor experienced sharpened the intensity of calls for political reform.

Beginnings in France   For British-controlled Ireland, famine conditions provided ample cause for a popular uprising, but instead of widespread violent revolution against hated British rule, millions of desperate peasants emigrated to England, Canada, and the United States. In France no such outlets for the wretched and the discontented existed. The government of King Louis Philippe had consistently opposed the extension of the franchise to members of the lower middle class, and the police kept a close watch on republican organizations. Restrictions on the press intensified during the 1840s, just as poor harvests and financial reverses pushed the country into an economic crisis. French workers were not allowed to go on strike. Their inability to vent their anger at the ballot box created a situation in which the regime was linked with the narrow economic interests of the urban bourgeoisie.

When protestors began to circumvent the ban on public demonstrations by holding reform banquets, the government tried to proscribe all large meetings. In February 1848 workers in Paris took to the streets, setting up barricades and defying the government's orders. Clashes between soldiers and citizens took place in the capital. In what would become a familiar pattern across Western and central Europe over the succeeding months, the governing elite panicked and lost confidence in its ability to control the situation. Despite having 40,000 soldiers at his disposal in Paris, King Louis Philippe refused to entertain the prospect of large scale violence. He abdicated on February 24, and a republic was quickly declared by the provisional government that took power after he fled.

Working-Class Demands   Immediately after the king departed, a coalition of moderates who wished to see an extension of the suffrage and radicals who wanted the government to provide extensive social benefits to the workers took control in an uneasy alliance. The government gave the vote to all adult male Frenchmen. The "right to work" radicals succeeded in having a socialist named **Louis Blanc** (1811–1882) appointed to establish a series of "national workshops" to address the problem of massive unemployment in Paris. The planned workshops drew thousands of unemployed workers from the surrounding countryside into the capital, all desperate to secure a state-sponsored job. Taxes were raised to finance the various work projects, creating peasant discontent in the rural areas. In May 1848 an increasingly conservative government closed the workshops, and this triggered a worker's revolt in Paris the following month.

Barricades reappeared, calls for the redistribution of property were made, and the desperately poor of the capital city demanded a new social order. The republican government, with the overwhelming support of rural France, crushed the rising in three days, but not before some 1,500 people had been killed in fierce street-by-street fighting. The workers' vision of a society where economic equality complemented political equality had been eradicated, but deep class divisions emerged in every major city in France. The radical revolution suppressed, in December 1848 the new mass French electorate chose Louis Napoleon

View the **Image**

Louis Napoleon v. General Cavaignac—British Cartoon, 1848

on **MyHistoryLab.com**

(1806–1873), a nephew of Napoleon Bonaparte, to lead the nation as president of the Second French Republic. Within three years, Louis Napoleon overthrew the republic and declared himself emperor of the French as **Napoleon III.** His actions were subsequently approved by a majority of Frenchmen in a national plebiscite.

Expanding the Revolution in Germany   Popular demonstrations in favor of constitutional reform, political rights, and civil liberties soon spread to numerous other countries. Between March and April 1848, the rulers of the small German states of Wurttemberg, Bavaria, Saxony, Hanover, and Baden all instituted reforms. These occurred in the wake of vocal protests and uprisings led by middle-class liberals, skilled artisans whose careers were threatened by factory mass production, and university students. Hard-line government ministers were quickly dismissed, press freedoms introduced, and legislative assemblies promised. In Prussia King **Frederick Wilhelm IV** (r. 1840–1861) ordered his troops out of Berlin after clashes with protesters led to the erection of barricades in the city. Overestimating the extent of popular support for the uprising, the king hastened to allow the formation of a Prussian parliament and declared freedom of the press.

Across Germany, liberal politicians worked to forge a pan-German national parliament under the leadership of a single constitutional monarch. An inaugural meeting of the parliament was called for May in Frankfurt with the goal of drafting a unified constitution for all of Germany. Delegates to the assembly were elected on the basis of universal manhood suffrage, but virtually all of those elected came from the professional middle class. In 1849 a majority of delegates offered a new German crown to the Prussian king, who led the largest and most powerful German state, but he refused to accept the title "from the gutter." One year after the initial protests had forced the king's hand in Berlin, Frederick Wilhelm IV gained new determination not to let middle-class reformers dictate the terms of German unification. While he desired a greater role for Prussia within the German Confederation, he wished to lead this effort according to his own timetable and in consort with Prussia's traditional leadership elite of landowning aristocrats and army officers.

The Habsburg Lands   In the Austrian Empire, the revolutionary movement enjoyed a series of initial successes, as liberals and nationalists appeared to win major concessions from the emperor. The Habsburg Empire was especially vulnerable to the rising tide of nationalism in Europe. This multiethnic, multilingual empire stretched from German-speaking Austria in the west to Magyar-dominated Hungary in the east. Poles, Czechs, Serbs, Ruthenians, Croats, Slovaks, Slovenes, Italians, and Romanians all owed allegiance to the weak-minded Emperor Ferdinand I (r. 1835–1848) in Vienna. Metternich, the Austrian chancellor, recognized that the forces of liberalism and nationalism threatened the integrity of the empire. As a result, Austria had some of the most repressive laws in Europe.

Despite the controls, the revolution in France triggered calls for constitutional change across the empire. In the imperial capital of Vienna, large crowds of students and workers demonstrated in the streets. Unwilling to use overwhelming force to end the activities, the emperor and his principal advisors followed the pattern set elsewhere in Europe and made important concessions. By March, Metternich had resigned and fled, a constitutional assembly was established, and serfdom was outlawed in Austria. Disturbances in Hungary and Bohemia placed additional strain on the government. In Hungary ethnic Magyars began the process of creating an autonomous state under the leadership of **Louis Kossuth** (1802–1894). Kossuth and his allies declared independence for Hungary in the spring of 1848, but the minority Serb, Croatian, and Romanian populations that would be placed under Magyar rule did not support the break and instead backed Austrian efforts to reconquer the territory. The Magyars were defeated by Austrian forces under the command of Count Joseph Jellachich (1801–1859) in the fall of 1848. A second attempt at securing national independence in March 1849 was suppressed with Russian help. Imperial troops also quashed a pan-Slavic insurrection in Prague during June 1848.

Italian Nationalism   In Italy, where the Habsburgs had exercised significant political control since 1815, a strong nationalist movement led by **Giuseppe Mazzini** (1805–1872) and **Giuseppe Garibaldi** (1807–1882) inspired liberal revolutions in Naples, the Papal States, Piedmont-Sardinia, Lombardy, and Venetia. However, like the revolutions in France and Prussia, the initial successes could not be sustained. In mid-March rebels in the city of Milan succeeded in forcing Austrian troops to withdraw, and King Charles Albert of Piedmont (r. 1831–1849) declared war against the Habsburgs. It took the Austrians less than two months to defeat the Piedmontese, but revolutionary activity now shifted south to the Papal States. The revolutionaries had high hopes for the reformist impulses of the new pope, **Pius IX** (r. 1846–1878), who had relaxed some restrictions on the press after assuming office in 1846. Radical calls for a Roman Republic, and the assassination of one of the pope's chief ministers, destroyed whatever sympathy the pontiff may have had for political reform. In November 1848 he took refuge in a Neapolitan fortress. The following year, French president Louis Napoleon Bonaparte, eager to court favor with French Catholics, intervened militarily and restored papal authority. Further south, the reactionary King Ferdinand II of Naples (r. 1830–1859) was finally able to crush an uprising that had started in January 1848.

Assessing the Revolution
The initial successes enjoyed by revolutionaries in 1848 were reversed by Europe's dynastic rulers once they recognized that their liberal

Giuseppe Garibaldi (1807–1882)   Seen here toward the end of his life serenely dressed in his trademark poncho (a mode of dress he adopted in the 1830s and 1840s as a freedom fighter in South America), Garibaldi was a forceful and spiritual leader of the movement for Italian unification, which was achieved, after many conflicts, in 1861.

PEOPLE IN CONTEXT Giuseppe Mazzini

Giuseppe Mazzini (1805–1872) was one of the principal leaders of the Italian nationalist movement of the mid-nineteenth century. He was born in Genoa and attended the university there, beginning his studies at age 14. Mazzini received a law degree in 1827 and began his association with outlawed reform groups called Carbonari. An informant betrayed Mazzini to the police, and after his arrest and brief imprisonment, Mazzini left for his first period of exile in France. He was impressed by the ideas of Henri de Saint-Simon (1760–1825), the founder of French socialism, especially Saint-Simon's faith in progress under enlightened leadership.

In 1831 Mazzini (now living in the French city of Marsailles) founded Young Italy, an association of liberal intellectuals who dedicated themselves to the unification of Italy under a strong central government. The government of King Louis Philippe allowed considerable press freedoms at this time, and Young Italy sought to win support through the dissemination of ideas. The goal was daunting, especially in light of the repressive rulers who controlled most of Italy. However, by 1833, an estimated 50,000 to 60,000 Italians had joined the association. From abroad Mazzini called for the removal of all Austrian influence, an end to the pope's temporal power over the Papal States, and the creation of a republican national government. Rome would serve as the capital of this revolutionary republic, and the Italian people would become the standard bearers of enlightened self-government across Europe, a model society for oppressed peoples everywhere.

When the revolutions of 1848 began in France, Mazzini was living in exile in England (the nation where he spent most of his adult life). During the long years of exile, he had supported a variety of conspirators who attempted to organize popular uprisings in Italy, but all had failed miserably. In March 1848 he reluctantly supported King Charles Albert of Piedmont-Sardinia in the monarch's declaration of war against Austria. Mazzini returned to Italy in April, residing in Milan until the Austrian army retook the city in July. In March 1849 Mazzini relocated to Rome, where a popular revolution had forced Pope Pius IX to abandon his capital.

A portrait of Giuseppe Mazzini, from about 1865.

The revolutionaries declared the formation of a republic, and Mazzini moved into the pope's former residence at the Quirinal Palace. The United States was the only country to extend diplomatic recognition to the Roman republic. After five months, Louis Napoleon of France dispatched troops to restore the pope. After two months of fighting, the republic was defeated.

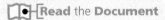

Read the **Document**

Life and Writings of Giuseppe Mazzini, 1805–1872

on **MyHistoryLab.com**

Despite the failed revolutions of 1848, Mazzini's reputation actually grew in international circles. The Roman republic had introduced universal manhood suffrage, instituted government control over clerical salaries, and founded popular political clubs designed to attract the support of the common man. During years of reimposed exile, Mazzini continued to champion republicanism over monarchy, universal manhood suffrage, the end of serfdom, tax credits for the working poor, a progressive income tax, and free education for all citizens. When he died in March 1872, Italy had achieved national unification under a constitutional monarch. Mazzini had dedicated his life to the cause of national unity, but his vision of a democratic republic would not be achieved before the mid-twentieth century. ∎

QUESTION: Why do revolutionaries attract international attention?

opponents did not enjoy broad-based popular support. The fragile alliance of middle-class liberals, students, and urban workers was fraught with ideological disagreements. While liberals sought to obtain limited constitutional change and political power for the educated and property-owning middle class, the radicals who enjoyed the support of urban laborers pushed for more basic alterations in the social and economic fabric. The latter wished for a new world, not simply a more responsible government. Once Europe's monarchs recognized that they could count on the support of their armies and that the use of force would be supported by the majority peasant population who distrusted the urban working class, the revolutions in the cities were doomed to failure.

Yet the core of the revolutionary agenda—written constitutions, freedom of speech and press, representative political institutions based on an extended franchise, military forces subordinate to civilian authority—was not extinguished by the failure of middle- and working-class insurgency in 1848. The tillers of the soil, still the overwhelming majority of Europe's population in 1848, may not have supported the revolutionaries at midcentury, but over the next 50 years wider political rights were realized and greater government involvement in the economic welfare of the general population was achieved.

Britain and Reform

The only major European power fortunate enough to avoid revolution throughout the period 1815 to 1848 was Great Britain. Given that the country was in the midst of unprecedented social and economic change brought about by rapid industrialization (see Chapter 20, "The Consolidation of Nation-States"), Britain's ability to undertake constitutional reform without recourse to violence was exceptional. While Britons may have enjoyed the broadest political and religious freedoms in Europe, the country was far from tolerant and democratic in 1815, and civil liberties had been sharply curtailed during the Napoleonic wars. The titled aristocracy controlled the House of Lords, while the vast majority of the House of Commons were men of substantial property. Less than five percent of the male population had the right to vote in 1815. In addition, the growth of industrial towns during the early nineteenth century had not led to a reapportionment of seats in Parliament. As a result, densely populated industrial centers in the Midlands and in the north of the country had no members of Parliament, while underpopulated rural areas, dominated by a handful of powerful elites, did. Liberal reformers wished to put an end to these "**rotten boroughs**" (seats in the House of Commons that had few electors or were owned outright by a single wealthy individual) while simultaneously extending the franchise to members of the commercial and industrial middle class.

Repression at Peterloo   Initial efforts at reform were met with official repression. The end of the Napoleonic wars found returning veterans struggling to find work in a depressed civilian economy. In 1819 workers assembled in St. Peter's fields near the city of Manchester to protest their worsening economic plight and to demand the right to vote. Government forces panicked and attacked the 50,000 unarmed protestors. Hundreds of civilians were injured and 11 killed in what became known as the "**Peterloo Massacre**" in mock comparison with the great victory over Napoleon at Waterloo. In the aftermath of the attack, the conservative government passed legislation that placed restrictions on public meetings and called for the rigorous prosecution of political radicals.

The Great Reform Bill   The repression did not last for long, however. During the 1820s, the government made a series of important concessions to liberal demands. In 1828 Roman Catholics and Protestant Nonconformists were granted political rights. In British-controlled Ireland, the Catholic Emancipation Act meant that property-owning members of Ireland's Catholic majority could now hold public office. The government also began to back away from some of the more reactionary international policies advocated by Metternich. However, it was not until 1830, when the conservative Tory government was replaced by a more moderate Whig party, that serious discussion over the franchise took place. Sponsored by the Whigs and reluctantly supported by King William IV (r. 1830–1837), the **Great Reform Bill** of 1832 acknowledged the changing structure of economic power in the country. Britain's ruling elite recognized that the nation's prosperity and international power were made possible by the successes of the middle class.

View the Image

Reform Bill of 1832—Cartoon

on **MyHistoryLab.com**

Under the terms of the Reform Bill, the right to vote in parliamentary elections was extended to the property-owning middle class (especially the wealthy industrial manufacturers) for the first time. This meant the enfranchisement of about 650,000 males, by no means a majority in a nation of some 10 million. Still, the inclusion of Britain's industrial leaders in the political process helped to ensure a large measure of social order in a period of great change resulting from the industrialization of the country. With the precedent established, future Parliaments, in 1867 and again in 1872, would extend the right to vote even further, although Britain would not enjoy universal manhood suffrage until 1918.

Additional Peaceful Reforms   Other important changes followed the passage of the Reform Bill. Slavery was outlawed in all British colonies in 1833. This change was the result of decades of activism on the part of middle-class humanitarians, many

House of Commons   With the passage of the Great Reform Bill of 1832, the membership of Britain's House of Commons began to include representatives drawn from new urban centers.

of whom were associated with the country's evangelical churches. The government compensated slaveowners for the loss of their "property," thereby easing the process of abolition. Towns and cities gained new powers of self-government under the Municipal Corporations Act of 1835, and elected officials were now empowered to address growing social problems associated with the rise of industry. Parliament also turned to the problems faced by industrial laborers. In a series of reform measures taken during the 1830s and 1840s, the conditions of work were ameliorated and the commitment to laissez-faire principles gradually abandoned. The first **Factory Act** was passed in 1833, limiting the number of hours children under age 13 could work (a nine-hour maximum!) and restricting those under age 18 to 69 hours of labor per week.

Successive laws regulated labor in mines and addressed the conditions of work for women. A parliamentary inquiry into the conditions of labor in the country's numerous coalmines led to swift remedial action. After sometimes harrowing testimony by children before parliamentary committees, the government banned the employment of children under age 10 in the mines while limiting the number of hours to 10 that women and boys under age 18 could work underground. Adult male workers continued to work long hours for another quarter century.

The Chartist Movement   The drive for comprehensive political rights after 1830 was led by a coalition of middle-class political radicals and working-class leaders. They called for a new political charter that would guarantee universal manhood suffrage, the secret ballot, annual parliaments, and salaries for members of Parliament. Led by **William Lovett** (1800–1877) and a group of London-based artisans, most of these "Chartists" embraced peaceful reform, sponsoring rallies and sending

Key Political Developments in Europe, 1815–1848

1814–1815	Congress of Vienna
1825	"Decembrist" uprising (Russia)
1830	Greek independence
1830	Belgian independence
1830	Revolution in France
1832	Great Reform Bill (Britain)
1830s–1840s	Chartist Movement (Britain)
1848	Revolutions across Europe

petitions with millions of signatures to Parliament. The Charter was presented to Parliament on three separate occasions, and its supporters published a newspaper, *The Northern Star*. Although the movement failed to achieve its main objectives by 1848, it did provide an important outlet for disenfranchised workers to express their many grievances. Chartism represented the first mass political movement in Britain and contributed to a faith in peaceful change through legislative means that enabled the country to avoid revolution at midcentury.

☐☐●☐Read the **Document**

Chartist Movement: The People's Petition of 1838

on **MyHistoryLab.com**

The Chartist Movement   A Chartist demonstration in 1842. The Chartists were the first large working-class organization in Britain. Their efforts to extend the right to vote and other political rights contributed to the birth of modern trade unionism and socialism in Europe.

The Romantic Movement

The attention given to reason and natural law during the Enlightenment had informed many of the political transformations in America and France at the end of the eighteenth century. However, it also generated a reaction and the emergence of an alternate perspective on truth, beauty, and the individual during the first half of the nineteenth century. Although it is always difficult to periodize movements in literature and the arts, certain features distinguish what has come to be known as **Romanticism** from the neoclassical style of the mid-eighteenth century. A concern with individual creativity anchored in the emotions, a stress on the unique and even spiritual nature of the creative process, and a celebration of spontaneity informed by imagination as an avenue to truth distinguished aspects of European cultural life in the first half of the nineteenth century. It is appropriate to place these features under the general heading of Romanticism.

Romantic authors, painters, and musicians represented a wide variety of political and religious perspectives, but all of them questioned the value of rational inquiry as the sole avenue to the discovery of universal truths. In France the novelist Victor Hugo (1802–1885); in England the poets William Blake (1757–1827), Samuel Taylor Coleridge (1772–1834), William Wordsworth (1770–1850), and John Keats (1795–1821); in Russia the poet Alexander Pushkin (1799-1837); and in the German-speaking states the composers Ludwig van Beethoven (1770–1827) and Franz Schubert (1797–1828) all emphasized the importance of the subjective imagination in human expression. The generic concerns of the *philosophes,* especially their unwavering dedication to the principle that progress issued solely from the exercise of reason, struck the Romantics as too simplistic. Such an approach overlooked the multidimensional nature of humans as creative agents. Against the Enlightenment's focus on general rules and features of human nature shared by all, the Romantics dedicated themselves to the celebration of exception, to personal differences, to the unusual and the aberrant. Beethoven, for example, was reluctant to immerse himself in the music of other composers out of fear that it would inhibit or contaminate his own musical ideas.

View the **Image**
Blake's Image of Creation
on **MyHistoryLab.com**

View the **Image**
Beethoven Sonata
on **MyHistoryLab.com**

Jean-Jacques Rousseau (1712–1778), who in some respects anticipated the Romantic impulse, believed that in nature humans were pure and good; society—even rationally ordered society—corrupted an otherwise healthy human nature. For Romantics, reason was an insufficient guide to authentic living.

Romantic poets and writers claimed that as a way of knowing truth and penetrating life's deepest mysteries, their method was more productive than formal philosophical inquiry. Indeed, Romantic artists argued that for reason to function at all, it had to be informed by the nonanalytical imagination. The imagination could not be cultivated through the study of rules and manuals, but instead through the experience of nature, the pain of personal loss, the joy of fresh encounters. The poet and artist **William Blake** believed it was a focus on the particular, not the general, that enabled great minds to view the sublime. Instinct and feeling were rooted in what would later be labeled the unconscious; for the Romantics, the inner recesses of the soul would find productive expression only if each person's emotional side were allowed free play in the world as experienced.

William Blake's *Jerusalem*   The visionary poet and artist William Blake was a key figure in the Romantic movement. The Romantics did not share the Enlightenment's faith in reason, instead extolling emotion, spontaneity, and human instinct. Blake spent many years on his prophetic book, *Jerusalem*, in which he created his own mythological world through etchings and symbolic prose.

In some respects this feature of Romanticism was anti-egalitarian; the unique genius, the seer, was valued over the ordinary mortal whose only guide was the mundane faculty of reason.

Inspired by the work of Kepler, Galileo, Descartes, and Newton, the Enlightenment had treated the natural environment as a giant clockwork, orderly and predictable. The laws of nature were open to human investigation through the application of the scientific method, and since rationality and predictability governed the cosmos, the same principles ought to guide our terrestrial affairs. Romantics strongly disagreed with this picture of nature. Instead of viewing the environment as a machine whose component parts can be measured and mastered, nature was valued as a spiritual touchstone, a moral teacher, a guide to the emotions, and the principal source of artistic inspiration. It was often the particular in nature, the single example, and not nature as a large system that provided valuable guidance in life's journey. In "The Tables Turned," poet **William Wordsworth** wrote

> One impulse from a vernal wood
> May teach you more of man,
> Of moral evil and of good,
> Than all the sages can.

While not all Romantics were devout Christians, the symbolic, aesthetic, and otherworldly side of Christian religious expression had great appeal to many poets, artists, writers, and composers. God as nurturer and spiritual force, immanent in nature and receptive to emotional forms of worship and expression, stood in stark opposition to the Enlightenment's picture of the deity as an orderly and disinterested workman. The medieval period, with its great gothic cathedrals, its pilgrimages, and its unified faith tradition, appealed to a generation wearied by decades of war and political upheaval. History, particularly the history of the Middle Ages, fascinated the Romantics. The *philosophes* had dismissed the Middle Ages as a protracted period of superstition, intolerance, and economic stagnation. Romantics, in contrast, were apt to idealize the simple life of the peasantry, the bond of community in medieval agricultural society, the richness of local cultures and languages, and the inherent dignity and originality of folk traditions. The popularity of the novels of **Sir Walter Scott** (1721–1832), stories of adventure and heroism performed by ordinary people in the Middle Ages, testified to the growing appeal of history for the literate middle class.

The Impact of Romanticism   The aesthetic contributions of Romanticism included a renewed and enhanced respect for human creative impulses rooted in the emotions. While not disparaging the place of reason in the quest for a more humane and just society, the Romantic movement reclaimed the importance of passion, intuition, and will in the creative process. Overall, Romantics did not fall captive to the claim that truth was singular and personal. Most accepted that truth was independent of the seeker, but they wanted the seeker to employ a variety of tools in the search for truth. In addition, Romanticism had an unmistakable impact on political and social developments during the first half of the nineteenth century. Criticism of living and working conditions in the rising industrial towns often found eloquent voice in Romantic novels. Many of the most memorable characters in the novels of **Charles Dickens** (1812–1870), for example, were those whose lives had been crushed by the factory routine and the logic of laissez-faire economic theory. The strong and deliberate leadership of Napoleon Bonaparte was held up by Romantics as an example of how one man from modest circumstances could transform the continent through force of personality and broad vision. Many of the leaders of nationalist movements in Italy, Poland, France, Prussia, and Austria launched the revolutions of 1848 against enormous odds. Outmanned and outgunned, the insurgents found much of their inspiration in myths created around cultural identity and national destiny. Rational calculation and a balanced assessment of the strength of the opposition would have dictated caution and even inaction in 1848.

Utilitarianism and Utopian Socialism

Early nineteenth-century liberals were not democrats. They were horrified by the excesses of the French Revolution and feared that if political rights were extended to the uneducated masses, the result would be a return to tyranny under the leadership of a despot like Napoleon. To liberals, the uneducated lower classes were incapable of making rational political decisions; given the opportunity, they would advocate policies inimical to the interests of property owners. Poor people, liberals believed, always preferred equality to liberty. The revolutions of the period 1815–1848 may have enjoyed the support of the working classes, but the leaders of these revolutions were deeply suspicious of their allies. As a rule, liberals sought to end revolutionary action as soon as they achieved their limited goals. Only toward the end of the nineteenth century did the twin goals of political democracy and economic justice attract the majority of those who identified themselves as liberals.

Utilitarian Reform   Prior to 1848 a modest number of political radicals moved beyond the liberal camp and supported genuine popular sovereignty. They were convinced that the common man deserved political rights by virtue of his status as citizen. In Britain, **Jeremy Bentham** (1748–1832) rejected the natural rights philosophy of the Enlightenment and instead maintained that the purpose of all formal institutions, including institutions of government, was to promote the greatest happiness for the greatest number of people. This principle of utility assumed that all humans seek happiness and prefer pleasure to pain. Bentham and his followers argued that the fundamental measure of good laws, good economic systems, good judicial decisions, and good educational endeavors was the extent to which they afforded the greatest happiness to the inhabitants of a particular state. Utilitarianism called for reform based on the immediate needs of the majority—a creed of self-interest—not the abstract principles formulated by an "enlightened" intellectual elite.

Socialist Options   Concern over growing economic disparities and the failure of middle-class reformers to support popular democracy resulted in the emergence of socialist alternatives to the individualistic, competitive, and property-rights orientation of liberal and utilitarian reformers. Early socialism interpreted the Enlightenment's call for a rational society as a mandate for economic equality. In some respects early socialist theory also incorporated elements of the Romantic movement. The socialists believed that a new social and economic order would free individuals to pursue their expressive talents in a setting where everyone's basic needs were met in a community of sharing. In France **Henri Count de Saint-Simon** (1760–1825) and **Charles Fourier** (1772–1837) were two of the leading socialist thinkers. Saint-Simon was a member of the aristocracy, but he renounced his title and privileges and called for a new social order led by scientists, industrialists, and other professionals. These specialists would be charged with leading society into a new age of collective abundance through science and technology. Fourier was uncomfortable with the type of large collectives supported by disciples of Saint-Simon. Instead, he believed that human happiness could best be promoted in small communities of about 1,500 citizens. Organized into these small "phalansteries," residents would live a simple lifestyle where agriculture and artisanal enterprises would form the core of economic activity.

Saint-Simon and Fourier were theorists of socialist society; British industrialist **Robert Owen** (1771–1858) became a practitioner. Born into poverty, Owen went to work at age 9 and rose to become a great textile manufacturer in the city of Manchester. Deeply troubled by the hardships of the factory environment, Owen experimented with socialist alternatives at his cotton mills in New Lanark, Scotland. He became convinced that healthy profits for owners of the means of production could be combined with economic justice for employees in the mills. At New Lanark he improved wages, provided housing for his workers, established

[ ]●[ ]**Read** the **Document**

Robert Owen, Excerpt from Address to the Workers of New Lanark

on **MyHistoryLab.com**

pension and sick funds, and built schools for the children of his employees. Owen believed that by providing a healthier lifestyle for working families, his factories would produce more and better quality products.

His philanthropic activities attracted the attention of a wide audience. In 1825, for example, Owen was invited to address a special session of the U.S. Congress.

In Britain, Owen urged Parliament to embrace factory reform, but the scale of his proposals frightened fellow industrialists who believed that free-market principles and the sanctity of property offered the best model of industrial organization. Frustrated by his lack of progress at home, Owen spent his entire fortune establishing socialist communities. In New Harmony, Indiana, Owen's cooperative community attracted thousands of sympathizers. Like many other similar ventures in the United States during the 1830s, however, the experiment in cooperative living did not endure. The utilitarian claim that people are motivated solely by self-interest seemed to receive validation in the collapse of the Owenite communities.

The Marxist Challenge

The revolutions of 1848 were led by middle-class professionals eager to secure constitutional change and political enfranchisement for themselves, but many of their allies within the ranks of the working class demanded more basic social and economic rights. At the midpoint of the nineteenth century, the Industrial Revolution had not touched the lives of most Europeans. However, for the inhabitants of the growing cities of Britain, France, and the German states, the harsh conditions of labor within the factory environment would continue so long as working people were denied direct access to political power. The enfranchisement of the bourgeois factory owner, accountant, or lawyer promised little benefit for the uneducated and unskilled city dweller.

Utopian socialists believed that a society based on cooperation instead of competition could be secured in a peaceful manner with the assistance and goodwill of scientists, skilled administrators, and economic managers. Utopian thought minimized the prospect of inevitable violent conflict between economic classes while placing great faith in the willingness of the owners of property to address problems of inequality after a rational assessment of its causes. The German philosopher **Karl Marx** (1818–1883) was less confident in the ability of self-interested producers to ameliorate the plight of their less fortunate neighbors. The son of a middle-class lawyer, Karl Marx was raised in the city of Trier close to the French border. He attended university to train for the legal profession, but his interest in philosophy led him in new directions.

Marx received a Ph.D. in philosophy from the University of Jena and turned his talents to journalism instead of the academic life. He traveled to Paris in the 1840s and familiarized himself with the socialist ideas of Fourier and Saint-Simon. While in Paris he first met his future collaborator and financial supporter, **Friedrich Engels** (1820–1895). Like Marx, Engels was of German birth, but his father was a successful textile manufacturer who owned factories in Manchester, England. In February 1848 Marx and Engels published a short tract that coincided with the outbreak of revolution across Europe but was destined to have a far greater impact on European—and global—thought than the violent upheavals of that spring. *The Communist Manifesto* called upon the working class to overthrow the capitalist economic system by force. Happiness was to be secured in this life, not in some hoped-for heavenly abode. For Marx and Engels, the religious world view was the creation of self-interested elites who sought to legitimize their privileged status by creating otherworldly consolation stories for the poor and oppressed.

> **Read the Document**
>
> *Capitalism Challenged:* The Communist Manifesto *(1848),* Karl Marx and Friedrich Engel
> on **MyHistoryLab.com**

Like his Enlightenment forebears, Marx believed in the existence of scientific laws of historical development operating in nature. Once these laws were understood, working people could take charge of their destiny. The primary law held that the means of production, the way that goods are produced and wealth is distributed within society, determines the shape of culture, ideas, politics, and even morals. Those who hold material power determine the shape of a culture's dominant ideas and institutions. For example, industrial capitalists and the values of free-market individualism replaced lords of the manor and feudal obligations as soon as machine production deposed cottage manufacture and guild regulations. Throughout the course of the human experience, class conflict stood at the center of material life. It was a conflict between the owners of the means

Karl Marx Marx was deeply affected by the human costs associated with the rise of industry, and his socialist philosophy provided comfort to those who looked forward to the end of capitalist economies.

of production and the laborers who, according to Marx, were exploited by their social and economic superiors. From master/slave relationships in the ancient world, to lord and serf in the medieval context, to factory owner and the proletariat, the group that controlled economic power controlled the state. That same group controlled the legal system and the bureaucracy and forwarded the material and ideological interests of the ruling class.

Despite **Marxism**'s emphasis on class conflict throughout history, Marx was an optimist about the future. He believed that in his own day the rise of the industrial middle class or urban bourgeoisie signaled imminent changes in the political system. The urban bourgeoisie were about to break the monopoly over political power enjoyed by the landholding elite for centuries. However, the economic interests of the bourgeoisie—their faith in free markets, free labor, competition, and the sanctity of private property—were deeply at odds with the concerns of the working class. Once the forces of industrial capitalism and the misery of factory conditions had touched the lives of enough people, the final stage in the historical process—the overthrow of the capitalist system—would take place. It would occur under the leadership of men committed to a genuinely equalitarian social and economic system. The start of the revolution would be in Britain, the most advanced industrial nation. Marx even predicted that national differences would fall away once the proletariat understood that **nationalism** and state rivalries were simply productions of the ruling elite.

After the failure of the 1848 revolutions, Marx returned to Germany and briefly edited a newspaper in Cologne. His radical ideas made him an unwelcome figure in the eyes of the authorities, and in 1849 he and his family moved to London, where he would spend the rest of his life writing and preparing for the great revolution that never came. Engels provided much-needed financial support during these years. British authorities were content to let Marx carry out his research and writing in peace at the library of the British Museum. According to Marx, the capitalist stage in history would not endure for long due to the rapid pace of commercial and industrial expansion. As small businessmen were plunged into the ranks of the proletariat due to intensive competition, as wages fell in direct response to the needs of the producer to lower costs, and as members of the burgeoning proletariat recognized their common plight thanks to the aid of communist intellectuals, the few capitalists who remained after eliminating their smaller rivals would be destroyed in a massive popular revolution.

In its wake private property would be abolished, and workers would control the material means of production. Only then would new ideas and plans for a society where cooperation replaced competition find their way to the center of human thought.

Marx's belief that material culture determines human consciousness meant that a new consciousness, a new human nature, in fact, would be the final result of the communist revolution. Combining elements of both the Enlightenment and the Romantic traditions, Marx was the author of a secular religion replete with a judgment day in the revolution and an earthly Eden where all would be free to fulfill their potential, "from each according to his abilities, to each according to his needs." In the second half of the nineteenth century, Marx's theory of history was embraced by intellectuals and workers alike as possessing the ring of scientific certainty. By the 1880s, the trend in industry toward greater concentration of economic power, where small competitors were gobbled up by their massive rivals, appeared to legitimize the communist forecast. By this date, a number of European governments began to respond to the horrors of child labor, low wages, and long hours by legislating rules of work and providing minimum employee benefits. These actions belied Marx's prediction that capitalism would collapse under the weight of its own competitive dynamic. Whatever one thought of his theory, however, Marx's basic message provided hope and comfort for large numbers of men and women whose lives were being forever changed by modern capitalism.

KEY QUESTION REVISITED

What leads people to repudiate traditional ideas, beliefs, and practices?

In the aftermath of the 1848 revolutions, three overriding trends in the intellectual and political life of Europe came into sharper focus. First and foremost, the liberal political agenda, born in the heat of the French Revolution and centered on the establishment of responsible constitutional governments with voting rights for the property-owning middle class, continued to win peaceful incremental victories across the continent. The revolutionaries were defeated by superior force in 1848 to 1849, but Europe's traditional leaders then moved to adopt key elements of the liberal agenda. The liberal economic program evolved from the simple protection of property rights to an acknowledgment that the state had some role to play in protecting the health and well-being of the working public.

Romanticism, with its emphasis on the strengths of unique languages, histories, and cultures, gave an enormous boost to the forces of nationalism, which became one of the most dynamic and destructive forces of the twentieth century. Finally, the social dislocation and sharpening of differences between middle-class liberals and workers, intensified by the advent of large-scale industrial production, set the stage for new political and economic debate during the second half of the century. Calls for universal manhood suffrage and greater economic justice would repeatedly engage the attention of European leaders just as the formation of modern nation-states reached its culmination.

In a global context, Europe's "Age of Ideology" would have a dynamic and formative impact on the world's peoples. The ideas associated with liberalism, embraced by colonial elites studying in European universities, would be turned against authoritarian rulers the world over during the late nineteenth century and against European imperialists themselves during the first half of the twentieth century. Nationalism and the Romantic stress on the integrity of specific cultural identities helped non-European peoples to first resist European expansion and to later win their freedom from European control. Finally, and ironically, the impact of Marxist thought in agrarian Russia, China, and Southeast Asia would change those societies in an integral manner, destroying centuries-old imperial structures and creating new forms of authoritarian rule under leaders who became locked in ideological combat with the West's liberal democracies. Europe's economic and military preeminence around the world by 1900 was prefigured by the ideological struggles of the period 1815 to 1848; the ferment of ideas and the force of revolutionary activity during these decades paved the way for the emergence of strong centralized states. In Western Europe these states would gradually extend political rights to the entire male population while simultaneously intervening in the workplace to prevent the very revolution that Marx had predicted was inevitable.

Key Terms

Congress of Vienna, *p. 561*

Peterloo Massacre, *p. 574*

Great Reform Bill, *p. 574*

Romanticism, *p. 577*

Marxism, *p. 582*

nationalism, *p. 582*

Activities

1. How did the goals of middle-class and working-class revolutionaries differ in 1848?

2. How did Britain manage to avoid revolution in 1848?

3. Describe the main features of Romanticism and explain the movement's relationship to the Enlightenment.

4. Describe Karl Marx's view of the industrial middle class.

5. List the main features of nineteenth-century conservatism.

6. Describe the role the state played in the development of liberal economic theory.

7. What features distinguished the Austrian Empire from its neighbors in 1848?

Further Reading

Paul Schroeder, *The Transformation of European Politics, 1763–1848* (1994), a study of European diplomacy.

Tristram Hunt, *Marx's General: The Revolutionary Life of Friedrich Engels* (2009), provides a forceful account of an important figure in revolutionary thought.

Benedict Anderson, *Imagined Communities: Reflections on the Origin and Spread of Nationalism* (1991), offers a good introduction to the changing nature of nationalist thought.

Karl Marx and Friedrich Engels, *The Communist Manifesto* (2011), a modern edition of one of the key texts of the nineteenth century.

MyHistoryLab **Connections**

Visit **MyHistoryLab.com** *for a customized Study Plan that will help you build your knowledge of* The Age of Ideology.

Questions for Analysis

1. What is the significance of Lord Byron's attire in the painting and how does it relate to his position on Greek independence?

   View the **Closer Look** An English Poet Appears as an Albanian, p. 563

2. What were Malthus's concerns about population growth and the ability to produce sufficient supplies to meet increasing demand?

   Read the **Document** *Laws of Population Growth* (1798), Malthus, p. 565

3. Why did Mazzini believe so strongly in the nationalist cause in Italy?

   Read the **Document** Life and Writings of Giuseppe Mazzini, 1805–1872, p. 572

4. What were some of the basic principles around which Owen's ideal society would be organized?

   Read the **Document** Robert Owen, Excerpt from *Address to the Workers of New Lanark,* p. 580

5. Why did Marx consider private property to be the number one target of the proletarian revolution?

   Read the **Document** Capitalism Challenged: *The Communist Manifesto* (1848), Karl Marx and Friedrich Engels, p. 581

Other Resources from This Chapter

Read the **Document** Metternich on the Revolutions of 1848, p. 560

Read the **Document** David Ricardo, Excerpt from *Principles of Political Economy and Taxation,* p. 565

Read the **Document** Adam Mickiewicz: Excerpts from *The Books of the Polish Nation* 1830–1831, p. 567

View the **Image** Unrest of the 1820s and 1830s: Centers of Revolutionary Action, p. 567

View the **Image** Louis Napoleon v. General Cavaignac —British Cartoon, 1848, p. 569

View the **Image** Reform Bill of 1832—Cartoon, p. 574

Read the **Document** Chartist Movement: The People's Petition of 1838, p. 576

View the **Image** Blake's Image of the Creation, p. 577

 View the **Image** Beethoven Sonata, p. 577

Proclamation of the Third Republic Crowds in Paris celebrate the proclamation of the Third Republic in 1870 during the Franco-Prussian War.

20 The Consolidation of Nation-States

LEARNING OBJECTIVES

How did Italy achieve political unification? • How did the German states achieve political unification? • What were the main constitutional changes in France and Britain? • Why did the eastern empires lose power and influence? • What factors enabled the United States to become a major power after 1865? • How did nationalism change in the late nineteenth century?

The Great Decisions of the time will not be resolved by speeches and majority decisions—that was the mistake of 1848 and 1849—but by iron and blood.

—Otto von Bismarck

KEY QUESTION

Is nationalism a constructive force in the modern age?

The statement previously quoted was from a speech by Otto von Bismarck (1815–1898), Prussian prime minister, to the Prussian Parliament in September 1862. In his speech Bismarck argued that within the German Confederation of States, Prussia was admired as a leader not because of its attachment to liberal political principles but because of its military power. He believed that Prussia must maintain its military readiness in preparation "for the favorable moment" when it could create a larger German state. For Bismarck and for those who supported his policies, the creation of a unified German Empire under one monarch was the prerequisite to future economic progress and social order. Only large unified states, led by men who understood and practiced power politics, could command the respect of the international community.

Modern **nationalism,** defined by loyalty to the state and its abstract ideals, began during the wars of the French Revolution. For the first time in European history, large conscript armies fought bravely on behalf of a set of political ideas, not for a dynasty or a particular ruler. During the second half of the nineteenth century, Europeans and Americans would fight and die to secure the privilege of living in autonomous nation-states. Membership in these states was determined on the basis of a shared language, traditions, and cultural patterns. Early nationalism during the era of the French Revolution tended to promote the values of participatory government, personal freedom, the promotion of universal rights, and the separation of church and state. After 1850, the rhetoric of national self-determination changed. In a disturbing manner, it began to descend into the realms of power politics, militarism, jingoism, racism, and cultural imperialism. Some of this new spirit can be detected in Bismarck's speech.

The formation of the modern nation-state as the highest expression of political power shattered the universalist ideals that had stood at the core of medieval Christian thought. The conviction that humans owed primary allegiance to a power located outside of the territorial borders of the state in which they lived had first been challenged by the Protestant revolt against the authority of the Roman Catholic Church. The momentum of modern nationalism completely undermined what was left of these universalist ideals. Unsentimental and hostile to the revolutionary impulse, the principal architects of the new nation-states were political realists who sought to win the support of their respective citizenry through measures designed to enhance collective self-esteem. Few of these leaders had much respect for the masses, yet they skillfully adapted themselves to the onset of democratic politics in Western Europe by appealing to the common bond of national identity.   ◼

Italian Unification

A Pragmatic Approach   The 1848 revolution in Italy had failed to create a unified state. Giuseppe Mazzini's (1805–1872) dream of a liberal Italian republic designed by idealistic and romantic student revolutionaries was swiftly and decisively rejected by superior military force. The Austrians remained in control of the provinces of Lombardy and Venetia in northern Italy, while a French army guaranteed the integrity of the pope's territories (the Papal States) in the middle of the peninsula. The north-central duchies of Parma, Modena, and Tuscany were under the control of princes allied to the Austrians, and in the south, a reactionary Bourbon monarch ruled the Kingdom of the Two Sicilies. Within 23 years of the failed 1848 revolution, however, full Italian unification had been achieved under the leadership of the northeast Kingdom of Piedmont (officially called the Kingdom of Sardinia).

The path to political union and constitutional government was forged by Count Camillo Cavour (1810–1861), chief minister to King Victor Emmanuel II (r. 1849–1878) of Piedmont-Sardinia. Cavour was a strong monarchist and a political realist who recognized that professional armies would always defeat a mass uprising by untrained revolutionaries. His strategy to achieve Italian unification involved building the power of Piedmont by modernizing its economy. Creating a modern state, he believed, was an essential precondition to removing the Austrians from northern Italy. In 1855 Piedmont joined Britain and France in a war against Russia (the Crimean War) even though the Italians had no strategic interest at stake in the conflict. Cavour believed that Piedmont's participation on the side of the two major Western powers would win their support for Italian unification. The British held back, but Emperor Napoleon III (r. 1852–1870) of France soon became a sympathetic ally. In 1858 Napolean III and Cavour reached a secret agreement whereby France would come to the aid of Piedmont if Austria attacked the small Italian state. In return for French aid, Cavour was prepared to transfer the Piedmontese territories of Nice and Savoy, which were predominantly French speaking, to France (see Map 20–1).

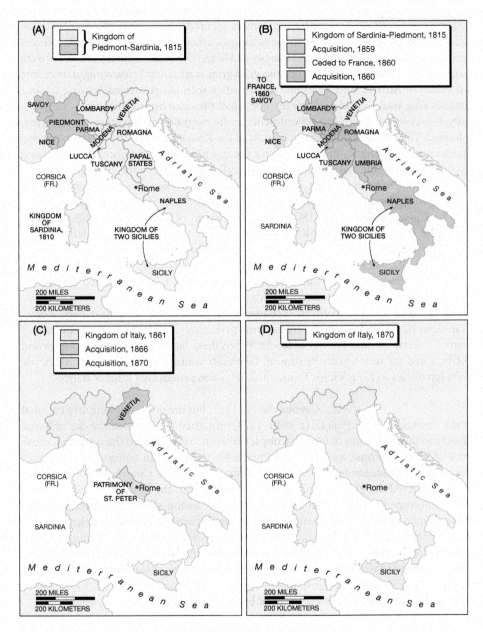

MAP 20-1   The Unification of Italy   The struggle for political unity began soon after the defeat of Napoleon in 1815 and continued until 1870. The northern Kingdom of Piedmont took the lead in the process, aided by a wide range of nationalists from throughout the peninsula.

QUESTION: How was Italian unification complicated by the influence of the Roman Catholic Church?

War with Austria   With an agreement secured, Cavour provoked the Austrians into declaring war in April 1859. In the ensuing conflict, French and Piedmontese forces quickly conquered Lombardy and the city of Milan. The initial military successes were not exploited, however. By June, Napoleon III grew fearful that Prussia might intervene on behalf of Austria, and he signed an armistice with the Austrians, leaving Cavour and his king with a good deal less territory than they had hoped to secure. Unexpectedly, however, revolutionary governments in the neighboring Italian states of Parma, Modena, Tuscany, and the papal provinces of the Romagna voted to join the expanded Italian state, making Piedmont-Sardinia the dominant power in northern Italy and giving Cavour additional support for the overall goal of uniting the entire peninsula.

Piedmont's success against Austria inspired rebels in the southern Italian Kingdom of the Two Sicilies to take action against their Bourbon king, Francis II (r. 1859–1861). Led by Giuseppe Garibaldi (1807–1882), the island of Sicily was quickly liberated. Garibaldi then crossed to the Italian mainland and, welcomed by a jubilant population, captured the capital city of Naples in September 1860 without a fight. With all of southern Italy under his control, Garibaldi decided to attack Rome and its French garrison. This decision provoked Cavour to intervene. Cavour disliked Garibaldi's republicanism, his commitment to gender and racial equality, and his defense of the right of workers to organize. In exchange for a commitment not to occupy Rome, Napoleon III allowed the Piedmontese army to occupy all of the Papal States outside of a small enclave around the city of Rome. When these lands, together with Naples and Sicily, voted for union with Piedmont, Garibaldi voluntarily surrendered his newly won territories to King Victor Emmanuel, who was proclaimed king of Italy.

Venetia and Rome   Cavour died in 1861, but the quest for complete national unity continued. Pope Pius IX (r. 1846–1878) remained in control of the city of Rome thanks to the protection of French troops, while Austria still ruled the northeast province of Venetia. Rome was the most intractable issue. Italian nationalists could not conceive of an independent Italy without Rome as its capital. Church authorities vehemently rejected the idea that the administrative heart of the Roman Catholic Church should become the capital of a Western European nation-state. After 1848, compromise seemed unlikely. A war between Prussia and Austria in 1866 solved the Venetian problem: Italy sided with the victorious Prussians and was rewarded with the contested province. Four years later Italian troops wrested Rome from the pope after Napoleon III was obliged to withdraw his garrison with the outbreak of war between France and Prussia. France's defeat at the hands of the superior Prussian army led to the fall of Napoleon III and the end of centuries of French involvement in Italian affairs.

Unfulfilled Promises   The long struggle for Italian unification had been undertaken with the implicit understanding that a future nation-state would afford its citizens all of the benefits of economic modernization. Hopes were raised that the new government would provide education, jobs, and an improved standard of living. Unfortunately for Italians, the high expectations were never met. Illiteracy rates remained high, especially in the rural south, and only about two million males had the right to vote in a country with a total population of almost 28 million. The king appointed the prime minister and the members of the upper house of parliament, who served for life. A lower house was elected, but its members tended to ignore the concerns of the rural peasants, who formed the majority of the population but lacked the right to vote. A great deal of localism remained, with northern industrial workers and illiterate peasants feeling little patriotic allegiance to the state. In addition, the Roman Catholic Church refused to recognize the legitimacy of the new state and warned Catholics not to participate in national politics.

Politicians claimed that Italy had become one of the great powers after the country joined with Germany and Austria in a defensive alliance in 1882. However, an 1896 military disaster in Abyssinia (modern Ethiopia) marked Italy as the only European power to have lost a war to an African opponent. By 1914, Italy had failed to achieve even one-quarter of the industrial strength that Britain enjoyed. Much of the population did not see the benefits of industrialization in their daily lives. On the eve of World War I their sovereign nation was a place where nationalism had yet to transplant centuries of provincialism, conservatism, and poverty.

The Creation of Modern Germany

Otto von Bismarck   Just as the Italian quest for national unity was guided by the pragmatic Cavour after the failed revolutions of 1848, in Prussia an aristocratic practitioner of ***Realpolitik*** (power politics) took the lead in the broader German struggle to achieve national unity. Otto von Bismarck (1815–1898) was a conservative aristocrat who believed that the king of Prussia, William I (r. 1861–1888), ruled by divine right and that society's natural leaders (landed aristocrats called Junker in Prussia) should determine the shape of any future national German state. Bismarck's

appointment as chancellor (prime minister) of Prussia took place at the height of a constitutional struggle between King William I, who wished to reorganize the Prussian army as a counter to Austrian power, and the liberals in the Prussian assembly, who refused to approve the funds to pay for the king's proposal. Bismarck secured the backing of the army and his fellow Junkers, brusquely

Otto von Bismarck   Bismarck was the most influential European statesman during the period 1850 to 1890. He employed military force in order to unify Germany under Prussian leadership, but worked to maintain peace in Europe after 1871. *Franz von Lenbach (1836–1904). Prince Otto von Bismark in uniform with Prussian helmet. Canvas. Kunsthistorisches Museum, Gemaeldegalerie, Vienna, Austria.* Photograph © Erich Lessing/Art Resource, NY

violated the constitution, and ordered that taxes be raised despite parliament's opposition to fund the reforms. Bismarck was gambling that the liberal members of the Prussian parliament would forgive his extra-constitutional actions if he could create a larger, more prosperous German state under the leadership of Prussia.

Not willing to wait on events, the Prussian chancellor, like Cavour in Piedmont-Sardinia, moved quickly to demonstrate Prussia's new claims to leadership. In 1864 Prussia declared war on Denmark when the Danish government tried to incorporate two formerly autonomous German-speaking territories, Schleswig and Holstein, which had long been ruled by the Danish crown, into the Danish national state. Austria was reluctantly drawn into the quarrel on the side of Prussia when Bismarck skillfully portrayed the conflict as an issue of broader German nationalism. After Denmark was defeated, the two provinces were placed under the joint rule of Prussia and Austria. This proved to be an unworkable situation that was bound to lead to friction between the two powers.

War with Austria   Austria, with its large population and varied territories, viewed itself as the leader of the German Confederation. During the 1830s many member states of the Confederation had entered into a customs union (**Zollverein**) that abolished all tariff barriers. By 1853, Austria was the only German state that did not accept the union, and when the economic benefits of the **Zollverein** began to become apparent, the movement for greater political unity under Prussian leadership intensified. Bismarck began to quarrel with the Austrian leadership over the disposition of Schleswig and Holstein while simultaneously winning support from the Italians by supporting their claim to the province of Venetia and from the Russians by supporting the tsar's suppression of a Polish rebellion.

In 1866 Austria declared war on its ambitious Prussian neighbor, convinced that now was the time to reassert the Habsburgs' role as the leader of the German-speaking peoples. It was a gigantic miscalculation. Superior Prussian military technology, greater troop mobility due to more efficient rail transport, and better generalship led to a humiliating defeat for the Austrians after just seven weeks of fighting. Under the terms of the Treaty of Prague, Prussia expelled Austria from the German Confederation and annexed a number of smaller German states that had supported Austria in the conflict. However, unwilling to humiliate the vanquished and thus foster a desire for revenge mentality, Bismarck resisted the call of his king and generals to annex Austrian territories.

Read the Document

Letter from Otto von Bismarck, 1866

on **MyHistoryLab.com**

In the aftermath of this stunning military triumph, most Prussian legislators forgave Bismarck's earlier anticonstitutional sins. The cause of national unification, once the cornerstone of liberal ideology, had been co-opted by the conservative Bismarck. The government moved to found a new North German Confederation that featured a legislative assembly (the **Reichstag**) whose members were elected by universal manhood suffrage. This concession to democratic forms, however, did little to hide the fact that the Confederation was really an autocratic state in which the chancellor (Bismarck) served at the discretion of the king. The legislature was denied control over the military and, more importantly, over the budget. An important transformation took place in Prussian political culture in the aftermath of the war. Most liberals abandoned their decades-long struggle for responsible constitutional government and joined the call for greater political and cultural unity. While Bismarck's accomplishments were exceptional, his agenda was not yet complete. A number of south German (and Catholic) states remained outside of the Confederation, and Bismarck now focused on strategies that were likely to persuade them to accept Prussian leadership by stirring up a greater sense of German nationalism (see Map 20-2).

War with France   Germany's "Iron Chancellor" did not have to wait long for a new opportunity to further his nation-building goals. Napoleon III and French public opinion were alarmed by the rapid rise of Prussian power. In 1870, when the Spanish crown was offered to a cousin of Prussian King William I, the French, who feared encirclement by German rulers, insisted that the German candidate decline the offer. A diplomatic crisis ensued. Bismarck edited a crucial telegram that made it appear that the Prussian king had insulted the French ambassador (something that had not actually occurred). The telegram was then made public, infuriating French public opinion and provoking France into declaring war on July 19.

As in the case of Bismarck's quarrel with Austria, on paper it looked as though the opposition (in this case France) possessed far greater resources and military might.

MAP 20-2 The Unification of Germany   Under the leadership of Prussia and guided by Bismarck, the German nation was created in 1871. The new state quickly rose to a preeminent position in Europe, becoming a leader in industry and empire.

QUESTION: Given its location, why did Germany seek to maintain close relations with the Habsburg Empire?

However, Bismarck's gamble again paid off. The south German states came to the aid of their northern neighbors, putting aside their historic differences with the Protestant north. Rapid German military victories followed, and the French emperor himself was captured after the Prussians encircled a French army at Sedan on September 1. Upon hearing news of the emperor's dilemma, liberals in Paris declared the establishment of a republic and unwisely refused to end the war. Paris was besieged and forced to surrender in January 1871. Meeting at Versailles in the wake of this conquest, the assembled German princes declared that William I was now kaiser (emperor) of a unified German empire.

War and the Nation-State   Given the importance of nationalism as an ideological force during the second half of the nineteenth century, it is surprising that European wars were not more frequent and protracted. Most governments were prepared to go to war to protect or expand their alleged national interests, and new military hardware was readily available to states whose buoyant economies allowed for a more robust international posture. The wars that did occur on the continent in the century after Napoleon's fall in 1815 were comparatively brief affairs (months, not years, in duration) thanks in large measure to the overwhelming military superiority of one of the combatants. Even casualties were relatively light. In 1866, for example, the year when Prussia handily defeated Austria, more people died from cholera than from battlefield injuries. The total number of dead and wounded at the 1870 battle of Sedan (where Emperor Napoleon of France was captured) was 26,000, and only 9,000 of these were German. The only exception to this pattern occurred in America, where more than 600,000 died in a four-year civil war.

The impact of nineteenth-century European wars on civilian populations and on national economies was also generally light. The normal "campaigning" season began in May and ran through September. Despite the use of modern rail transport to move men and material, fighting was normally concentrated in a small geographical area. Most of the population in a country at war was unlikely to experience any immediate disruption of daily life unless the population happened to exist near the battle zones. Unlike previous centuries, civilians did not suffer at the hands of undisciplined armies bent upon pillaging food and destroying the enemy's transportation and supply network.

Perspectives on the desirability of war tended to reflect class interests and values. Middle-class businessmen were prone to disparage military adventures. They believed that military conflict disrupted normal business channels, manufacture, and opportunities for international trade. With the obvious exception of large arms manufacturers, producers of industrial goods and agricultural products looked upon war as the betrayer of capitalism, ushering in periods of political and economic uncertainty. In particular, international businesses stood to lose money in the event of war between European neighbors. Across the continent, politicians who favored a "peace policy" commanded broad support from the middle class.

Aristocrats and traditional landed elites were less troubled by the prospect of international conflict. These were men who staffed the embassies, served as high-ranking military officers, and held seats in the appointive or hereditary upper chamber of the national legislature. War and training for war had been the special preserve of the aristocracy for centuries, and even with the rise of political democracy in most

Western European states by 1900, the politics of deference continued to play an important role in the life of each nation-state. Foreign policy, issues of war and peace, remained the preserve of the monarch and his closest advisors.

These traditional leaders were often joined in their bellicose sentiments by a wide array of intellectuals. According to Walter Bagehot (1826–1877), an influential journalist and interpreter of the British constitution during Queen Victoria's reign, the strongest nations were also the best nations. Samuel Smiles (1812–1904), the author of an immensely popular book called *Self-Help* (1859), sang the virtues of military drill and discipline. Preparation for war transformed complacent citizens into vigilant patriots. Smiles believed that if the entire population were exposed to the rigors of military training, "the country would be stronger, the people would be soberer, and thrift would become much more habitual." The influential Swiss historian Jacob Burckhardt (1818–1897) was convinced that long periods of peace weakened the national spirit. War provided opportunities for heroism, collective moral rejuvenation, and commitment to something higher than bourgeois individualism. Even the novelist George Eliot (born Mary Ann Evans, 1819–1880) remarked that the German victory over France in 1870 represented the triumph of progressive forces over decadent ones.

[□|●|─Read the Document

Excerpt from Self-Help

on **MyHistoryLab.com**

The widely shared belief that warfare was a legitimate and relatively low-cost means of national advancement continued to inform European consciousness during the high tide of global imperialism. As the great powers extended their territorial and economic sway across Africa and Asia, the willingness to use sophisticated military forces to achieve strategic objectives prepared the way for an increasingly truculent international climate during the first two decades of the twentieth century. The myths of the cleansing value of military conflict and of the tendency of new technology to make wars short would only be dispelled after the outbreak of World War I in 1914.

Bismarck Ascendant, 1870–1890

As the emerging national power in central Europe, Germany combined autocratic government with industrial prowess and cultural self-assurance. While the German empire was federal in structure, with certain powers reserved for its member states, the two-chamber legislature did not enjoy significant political power. The franchise was extended to all adult males, but universal manhood suffrage did not translate into democratic rule. Bismarck remained chancellor of the German Empire until 1890. Like the rest of the cabinet, he served at the discretion of the kaiser or emperor. Foreign affairs remained the prerogative of the kaiser, while most important legislative initiatives began with the chancellor. A large conscript army was maintained in peacetime, led by Junker aristocrats. The higher ranks of the civil service also remained the preserve of the aristocracy, which in turn helped to shape a government culture committed to the glorification of the state, not the extension of individual rights and liberties.

The Social Question

With unification secured, Bismarck turned his attention to pressing domestic challenges in a country undergoing rapid industrialization. The chancellor remained disdainful of political democracy, and he viewed political parties as little more than selfish interest groups that were to be manipulated for the benefit of larger state interests. Bismarck's campaign against the Catholic Church during the 1870s, called the ***Kulturkampf*** (struggle for civilization), was an energetic example of his approach to political alliances. The chancellor was convinced that German Catholics, who constituted almost 40 percent of the nation's population, owed their first allegiance to the pope. He was joined in this controversial position by German liberals, most of whom objected to the role of the Catholic Church in German political and cultural life. Indeed, for liberals the Church was the enemy of the modern secular state. Bismarck supported liberal legislation that expelled the Jesuits from Germany, instituted civil marriage and state oversight of the Catholic and Protestant churches, and favored secular state education over religious schools. In response, German Catholics fought back by organizing the Center Party, which became one of the largest parties in the *Reichstag,* the elected branch of the German federal parliament.

⊶—[View the **Closer Look**

Conflict between Church and State in Germany

on **MyHistoryLab.com**

Bismarck also attacked German socialists, arguing that members of the German **Social Democratic Party,** or SPD, were, like German Catholics, untrustworthy nationalists, since socialists believed in the international brotherhood of the working class. Three years after its founding in 1875, the chancellor outlawed the party,

Church-State Conflict   The struggle between the imperial German government and the Catholic Church was one of the most intense cultural conflicts of the late nineteenth century. In this cartoon from the 1870s, Pope Pius IX and Otto von Bismarck, the German chancellor, play a game of political chess. Each piece on the chessboard represents a German church leader whom Bismarck sought to remove from public life. Bismarck is clearly winning the game, while the Pope considers his next move.

declaring that its internationalist and anti-capitalist views represented a fundamental threat to the security and prosperity of the German Empire. He used the excuse of two assassination attempts against Emperor William I in 1878 to make his case that socialist internationalism had to be destroyed. In a calculated effort to weaken the appeal of socialism among the German working class, Bismarck supported legislation designed to address a number of problems caused by industrialization. During the 1880s, the government approved legislation instituting accident, sickness, and old age insurance. Contributions to the old age and disability plans came from individual workers and employers, but the state organized the plans. Bismarck's brand of paternalistic "**state socialism**" improved the quality of life for German workers, but it did not succeed in marginalizing the SPD. Despite the chancellor's repressive measures, individual socialist candidates continued to run for and win seats in the *Reichstag*. In 1891 the party adopted an official statement, called the Erfurt Program, which reaffirmed its Marxist faith in the ultimate destruction of capitalism. The party simultaneously pledged to pursue this goal through the existing political process. Similarly, the Catholic Center Party continued to win electoral victories in the wake of the *Kulturkampf*. In 1878 Bismarck quietly entered into negotiations with Pope Leo XIII (r. 1878–1903) and accepted an agreement that put an end to official religious bigotry.

Read the **Document**

The Gotha Program

on **MyHistoryLab.com**

Kaiser William II and German Power

In 1888 William II (r. 1888–1918) succeeded to the throne. The new emperor clashed with Bismarck over foreign policy and over the chancellor's antisocialist campaign. William II believed that the best way to win the allegiance of the German worker was to provide him with tangible evidence of German greatness through an aggressive policy overseas. Within two years of ascending the throne, the kaiser dismissed Bismarck and replaced him with a more pliable chancellor. Antisocialist legislation was allowed to expire, and the SPD became the biggest Marxist political party in Europe. Over the next quarter century, German industrial growth rivaled and in some areas exceeded rates in Britain and the United States, while Germany pursued the kaiser's imperial ambitions in Africa and Asia (see Chapter 21, "Global Empire and European Culture"). The lives of German workers continued to improve during these decades, which strengthened the regime's legitimacy. However, German economic growth and military power were built upon a political foundation that was less responsive to the give and take of the parliamentary process than either its British or American counterparts. The government allied itself firmly with powerful industrial and landowning interests, while the kaiser's desire to build a fleet comparable to Britain's was predicated on the assumption that the German Empire must extend beyond the confines of the German-speaking lands of Europe.

Constitutional Change in France and Britain

The Second French Empire

Louis Napoleon Bonaparte (1808–1873), the nephew of Napoleon I, came to power in France in the aftermath of the failed 1848 revolution. Elected president of the Second French Republic in 1848, he promised to restore order and prosperity to a country torn between urban political radicals and the more conservative peasantry. Within three years of his election, however, Bonaparte dismantled the republic in a coup d'état rather than accept a constitutional require-ment that prohibited the president from running for a second term. Resistance to his usurpation of power was light, although the government subsequently deported thousands of opponents. Once firmly in control, Louis Napoleon held two plebiscites in which over 90 percent of the electorate affirmed his assumption of hereditary power as Emperor Napoleon III (Napoleon I's son had died in 1832) in December 1852.

During the first decade of imperial rule, Napoleon cracked down on opposi-tion groups, censored the press, and denied the national legislature any substantive political power. Controls were relaxed after 1860, however, as the emperor sought to encourage industrialization and economic expansion. Press restrictions were removed, individual liberties guaranteed, unions permitted, and political prisoners pardoned. Paris, once an unsanitary and dangerous city, was rebuilt into a modern urban showpiece, with broad boulevards, parks, and impressive public buildings testi-fying to the power and prestige of the regime. Napoleon III's advisors were convinced that economic prosperity could eliminate France's social problems and political divi-sions. Charity hospitals, facilities for the elderly, new housing stock, schools, and a network of railroads and canals all seemed to suggest that quality of life issues were uppermost in the mind of the emperor and his closest advisors.

However, while his domestic improvements won the emperor broad popular support, his ambition extended beyond the boundaries of the nation-state. For the first time since the defeat of Napoleon I, France became a significant military force beyond its own borders. Napoleon joined Britain in the costly Crimean War against Russia in 1853, intervened in Italy on the side of Piedmont and against Austria in 1859, and even attempted to establish the archduke Maximilian, a Habsburg prince, as Emperor of Mexico in 1862. This last venture ended in disaster in 1867 when the French army withdrew and Emperor Maximilian (1832–1867) was executed by Mexi-can nationalists led by Benito Juarez (1806–1872). The rise of Prussia further eroded Napoleon's prestige. In an effort to bolster his regime, the emperor instituted new reforms and asked the French people to vote on a more liberal constitution. This was overwhelmingly approved in May 1870. Two months later, however, the ailing emperor blundered into a disastrous military conflict with Prussia.

The Third French Republic   French national pride was deeply wounded by the humiliation suffered at the hands of the Prussian army in September 1870. The capture of Napoleon at Sedan sealed the fate of the Second Empire. In Paris, what began as a refusal to accept an armistice with the Prussians escalated into a rejec-tion of the new French provisional government. The "**Paris Commune**" included republicans and socialists who fought a bitter defensive campaign against both the Germans, who cut off supplies to the city and then bombarded it, and their own coun-trymen. Elections in early 1871 led to the formation of a provisional government that was committed to ending the war and to pacifying the defiant Parisians. To end the

View the **Map**

Paris Commune, 1871

on **MyHistoryLab.com**

war, France ceded Alsace and most of Lorraine to the new German Empire. To regain control of Paris, gov-ernment forces attacked the city and executed over 20,000 resistance fighters who were hastily buried in mass graves. Humbled by Germany and torn apart by bloody civil war in the capital, France in 1871 was a nation-state divided between monarchists and republicans. Quarrels among the monarchists over who should be king allowed the republicans to set up the Third Republic, but it was an unstable regime with a multitude of parties and shifting political alliances.

Despite the appearance of chronic instability and the reality of a number of embarrassing government scandals, the liberals and conservatives who vied for power nonetheless managed to introduce a number of significant reforms during the 1870s and 1880s. Compulsory public education at the primary level spread a common set of patriotic values, while the historic role of the Catholic Church in education was curbed. A new professional military force was established under a compulsory service law. This helped to bolster national identity and loyalty to the state.

Domestic Crises   The durability of the Third Republic was severely tested by two political crises of the late nineteenth century. The first involved a direct challenge to the integrity of the Republic. When General George Boulanger (1837–1891), backed by disgruntled right-wing supporters, undertook a national campaign to restore authoritarian, one-man rule to France, the defenders of parliamentary government were placed on the defensive. Despite his appeal to monarchists and elements in the military, Boulanger failed to win sufficient popular support, and he fled the country in 1889. The second challenge involved the integrity of the French justice system. In 1894 a Jewish army officer was accused—falsely, as it turned out—of selling military secrets to the Germans. Captain Alfred Dreyfus (1859–1935) was tried for treason in a military court, convicted, and sentenced to a life of solitary confinement at Devil's Island, an overseas penal colony. (This was known as the **Dreyfus Affair.**) In the midst of the trial, a wave of xenophobia and **anti-Semitism** swept across the country. Most of the country seemed satisfied with the conviction, but a number of prominent republicans, including the novelist Emile Zola (1840–1902) and a future prime minister, Georges Clemenceau (1841–1929), argued that the evidence against Dreyfus was fabricated. The political right, however, vociferously defended the conviction. The conviction was overturned in 1906, but not before deep fissures emerged in the political culture of the nation. The anti-Semitism associated with the case continued to play a poisonous role in French politics, especially in German-occupied France (1940–1944) during World War II.

Key Developments in the Rise of European Nationalism

1848	Revolutions in most of Western and central Europe
1866	Austro-Prussian War
1870–1871	Franco-Prussian War
1870	Third Republic is proclaimed in France
1871	Unified German Empire proclaimed
1871	Italy is unified

Trial of Alfred Dreyfus   Anti-Semitism was widespread in late nineteenth-century Europe. Captain Alfred Dreyfus, standing on the right at his military trial, was convicted in 1894 and exonerated in 1906.

In the three decades prior to the outbreak of World War I, France's economy did not match that of Britain and Germany. Although some regions of the country were heavily industrialized, France remained a nation of artisans and peasant farmers. Labor unions, especially those focusing on the unskilled, remained relatively small and decentralized. Despite the efforts of trade unionists and socialists, the country lagged behind in welfare provision and the regulation of workplace conditions. French socialists and anarchists engaged in a number of strikes in the early twentieth century, but in general their deep suspicion of politics limited their ability to influence the formulation of national policy. The church, the army, the unions, and the political parties all appeared to lack appeal much beyond their own particular constituencies. Ironically, the onset of a horrific war in 1914 would finally galvanize the nation under one patriotic banner.

[■] Read the **Document**

Emile Zola, Nana

on **MyHistoryLab.com**

The Advent of Democracy in Britain   Great Britain's midcentury status as the world's leading industrial power was achieved within the context of peaceful political change. While the monarchy under **Queen Victoria** (r. 1837–1901) remained the symbolic heart of the political system, real power had shifted to the House of Commons, where two major parties, the Liberals and Conservatives, vied for leadership. In 1867 the Conservative Prime Minister Benjamin Disraeli (1804–1881) co-opted a liberal plan and introduced legislation to expand the electorate by approximately 1 million voters, from 1.5 to 2.5 million. Both parties recognized that further democratization was key to economic progress, and Disraeli hoped to win the support of the working and lower middle class with his proposal. His efforts were to bear fruit in the long run for the Conservative Party, but in 1868 the Liberal Party, under William Gladstone (1809–1898), won control of the House of Commons in national elections.

Gladstone's first ministry (1868–1874) marked the high tide of liberal reform in Victorian Britain. The monopoly that members of the state church, the Church of England, had long enjoyed over access to university education, civil service posts, and military appointments was broken. Competitive examinations now determined appointment to government service, Oxford and Cambridge Universities admitted students without reference to religion, and a secret ballot was introduced. Gladstone's reform program sought to create a society in which skill and merit, not patronage or family lineage, determined the bounds of economic, educational, and professional opportunity. While Disraeli and Gladstone were intense rivals, they both sponsored important social legislation. When Disraeli returned to power in 1874 to 1880, for example, public health, housing, and trade union legislation all

View the **Image**

Gladstone and Disraeli

on **MyHistoryLab.com**

improved conditions for the working class. As leader of the Conservatives, Disraeli was more sympathetic to the idea of using state power to solve social problems, while the Liberals under Gladstone focused more on individual initiative.

In 1884 Gladstone sponsored another reform bill. Now almost two-thirds of all males, irrespective of whether they owned property, had the right to vote. The extension of democracy transformed the political process. To appeal to the new mass electorate, party leaders now took to the rails and visited cities and towns throughout the country during political campaigns. A new form of political journalism arose, as reporters for serious broadsheet, and less serious tabloid, newspapers began to accompany candidates at mass rallies that drew thousands of supporters. Gladstone also attempted to address the long-standing demands of Irish nationalists who called for the end of British rule in Ireland. The prime minister attempted to pass home rule bills for Ireland in the House of Commons in 1886 and again in 1893, but the legislation was defeated on both occasions. In Northern Ireland, Protestant politicians who opposed home rule feared that the Catholic majority in Ireland would be hostile to the Protestant population, and many of these politicians threatened forceful resistance if Irish home rule became law.

In 1901 Britain's Trades Union Congress founded the **Labour Party** to advance the political interests of the working class. In the general election of 1906, Labour won 29 seats in the House of Commons. Further to the left of the Labour Party was the Fabian Society, a socialist organization founded in 1884 and led by a number of important non-Marxist intellectuals. Sidney (1859–1947) and Beatrice (1858–1943) Webb, George Bernard Shaw (1856–1950), and H. G. Wells (1866–1946) were among those who sought to convince their countrymen that they could achieve collective ownership of the means of production in a gradualist, peaceful manner. This was the thesis of an influential book called *Evolutionary Socialism* (1899) written by the German author Eduard Bernstein (1850–1932). Bernstein was familiar with the British Fabians, and his book called into question the need for the sort of revolutionary activity required by orthodox Marxists.

The socialists remained a tiny minority in Britain before World War I, in no small part because the major political parties had taken steps to respond to working class demands. When the aristocratic House of Lords objected to the growing cost of government-sponsored welfare plans, the House of Commons, in alliance with the king, passed the Parliament Act of 1911. This was a groundbreaking piece of legislation that limited the legislative veto of the Lords. When large strikes occurred involving the railways, docks, factories, or mines, the government intervened to mediate the dispute. By 1914, most Britons enjoyed free elementary education; minimum wage laws; accident, health, and unemployment insurance; and the enormous psychological advantage of belonging to the world's greatest imperial power. For most British voters and trade union members, political democracy and industrial capitalism appeared to be the key to global power and material prosperity at the start of the twentieth century.

The Waning of the Habsburg, Russian, and Ottoman Empires

Nationalism and Dual Monarchy   Prussia's resounding victory over Austria in 1866 signaled the permanent eclipse of Habsburg leadership within the German Confederation. The military debacle, coming so quickly after defeat at the hands of France and Piedmont-Sardinia in 1859, reflected the corrosive power of modern nationalism in a multilingual, multicultural, and multiethnic empire. Unlike any of the other great powers, the Austrian Empire represented the negation of the modern nation-state with its German, Magyar, Czech, Slovak, Polish, Croat, Italian, Slovene, Serb, and Romanian populations. All owed allegiance to the Habsburg emperor, Francis Joseph (r. 1848–1916). However, during the second half of the nineteenth century, a heightened sense of history and culture led most of the non-German subject groups to challenge the legitimacy of the imperial structure (see Map 20–3).

The usual instruments of repression—a secret police and the military—were utilized in an attempt to quash liberal dissent after the revolutions of 1848, but these blunt instruments swiftly devolved into a rearguard action. Some modest reforms, such as the establishment of a bicameral parliament with an elective lower house, had been agreed to by the conservative Francis Joseph, but no significant steps were taken to integrate non-Germans into the highest levels of administration. Many Austrian Germans were disdainful of the various minorities within the empire. The Roman Catholic Church continued to wield considerable control over education, while the landed aristocracy remained the dominant force in local affairs. Francis Joseph appointed government ministers and the members of the upper chamber of parliament; when the imperial parliament (the *Reichsrat*) was not in session, the emperor could rule by royal decree.

In the immediate aftermath of the Prussian victory in 1866, Emperor Francis Joseph was forced to make significant political concessions to the Magyars of Hungary, the most

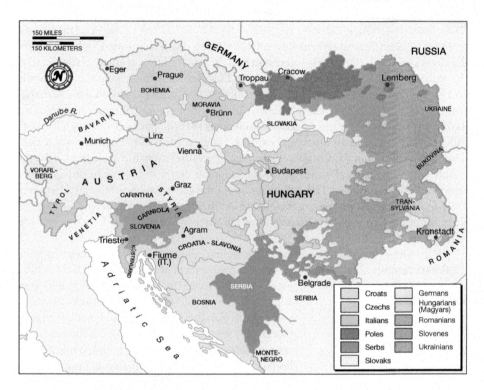

MAP 20-3   The Habsburg Multiethnic Empire   Nationalism posed a serious problem for the Habsburg rulers of the Austro-Hungarian Empire. While the Magyars of Hungary achieved significant autonomy in 1867, the aspirations of other ethnic groups remained unfulfilled.

QUESTION: How does the Habsburg Empire illustrate the problems of nationalism in the late nineteenth century?

powerful non-German national group. In 1867 a compromise (*Ausgleich*) was reached whereby Austria and Hungary were split into two territories, a dual monarchy, under Francis Joseph, who was named king of Hungary and emperor of Austria. Joint ministers appointed by the monarch handled foreign affairs, defense, and finance. Beyond this, however, the Magyars won complete control over their internal affairs. Henceforth, Austria and Hungary had separate parliaments and prime ministers. The Magyars' success inspired other minorities, especially the Czechs, Romanians, Ruthenians, and Croatians, to press their claims for greater autonomy. By the close of the nineteenth century, the Austrian parliament became a political flashpoint where members disrupted meetings over the question of nationalist self-determination within the empire. The dual monarchy of Austria-Hungary failed to find a satisfactory solution to the dilemma. As a result, the authorities were unable to use the nationalist banner to solidify popular support for the government or promote industrial development. In a Europe of nation-states, Austria-Hungary remained a multiethnic state based on loyalty to a supranational dynasty—the Habsburgs. Ethnic tension and nationalist aspirations within the Habsburg lands would play a crucial role in the outbreak of World War I in 1914.

The Traditional Power: Russia, 1861–1914

Tsar Peter the Great's (r. 1682–1725) efforts to reform Russia from the top down, combined with Catherine the Great's (r. 1762–1796) early interest in Enlightenment ideas, seemed to suggest that the Russian Empire qualified as a genuinely European power. During the eighteenth and nineteenth centuries, most Russian efforts at territorial expansion were focused, with great success, on the East, whereas Russian thought and Russian high culture looked to the West. After the defeat of Napoleon in 1815, it appeared as though Russian influence in European affairs would expand. Harsh control over Poland, regular bullying of the Ottoman Turks, and claims to a special relationship with the Christian peoples of the Balkans all signaled Russia's ongoing desire to be recognized as a preeminent European power. The hollow nature of the claim was demonstrated between 1854 and 1856, when poorly organized and led British and French forces defeated the Russians in the Crimean War (named after the Black Sea peninsula where the war was largely fought).

The military mismatch revealed the economic and technological backwardness of the Russian empire. At mid-century, more than 90 percent of the population lived at subsistence level. Despite the abolition of serfdom by Tsar Alexander II (r. 1855–1881) in 1861 (just two years before American President Abraham Lincoln declared that slavery was at an end), the plight of Russia's peasant population continued to deteriorate. While 22 million serfs secured legal freedom, they did not get land. Instead, portions of the land that the peasants had worked as serfs became the property of village communes, and the peasants who made up the communes had to compensate their former lords for whatever they were given. Most poor farmers fell into serious debt. It was not until 1906, in the aftermath of a serious revolution, that the government canceled the remaining debt and allowed the peasants to hold title to their own land.

View the Map

The Crimean War

on **MyHistoryLab.com**

View the Closer Look

The Crimean War Recalled

on **MyHistoryLab.com**

Assassination and Repression

Tsar Alexander II attempted to appease Russia's small middle class and provincial aristocracy by establishing local political councils called *zemst'va*. He also encouraged the establishment of primary schools and instituted reforms in the military, reducing terms of enlistment to six years (down from 25) and enlisting the support of Western technical advisors. However, the tsar refused to allow the formation of a national legislative assembly. The Russian intellectual elite who were familiar with political developments in Western Europe insisted that genuine modernization required broader political participation. The tsar's intransigence led to the formation of terrorist cells. One of these, known as the People's Will, assassinated Alexander II in March 1881. The murder was the most infamous in a wave of assassinations and terrorist acts that had taken place. The new ruler, Tsar Alexander III (r. 1881–1894), responded to the terror by expanding the powers of the secret police, censoring the press, and rolling back many of his father's modest reforms. The regime sought to strengthen itself by identifying closely with Russian nationalism and by persecuting minority groups within the Russian Empire, especially Jews.

In one area alone did Alexander III demonstrate appreciation for the forces that were shaping the modern world. During the 1890s, the tsar committed his government to a program of rapid industrialization. Under the direction of an innovative finance minister, Sergei Witte (1849–1915), the government sponsored railroads and industrial plants. It also encouraged foreign investment. The French, eager to forge a defensive alliance with Russia, emerged as the key financiers. By 1900, foreigners owned much of the industrial plant in Russia. Yet, while productive capacity grew, the social inequalities and political repression characteristic of absolutist regimes remained. Moscow, St. Petersburg, and a few other cities witnessed the emergence of a small industrial working class. Workers were denied political expression, however, and when a Marxist Social Democratic Party emerged in 1898, the regime drove its leaders into exile. One of the leaders of the Marxist exiles was Lenin (1870–1924), the future leader of the Communist Revolution in Russia. After being exiled to Siberia in 1895 (his brother had been executed by the government in 1887 for participating in a plot to murder the tsar), Lenin spent the years 1900 to 1917 in Switzerland, writing and organizing for revolution. In 1902 he wrote *What Is to Be Done?*, a call to establish a small, elite party of leaders who could guide an overwhelmingly peasant Russia to a proletarian revolution. In 1902 such a revolution seemed unlikely. Since Russia had only 3 million industrial workers out of a total population of 150 million in 1914, the Marxist program had little resonance beyond a few cities. At the start of the twentieth century, it remained to be seen whether Russia's reactionary monarchy could both modernize its economy and assuage worker discontent.

View the **Closer Look**

*Bloody Sunday,
St. Petersburg 1905*

on **MyHistoryLab.com**

The early signals were not propitious. The new tsar, Nicholas II (r. 1894–1917), was not sympathetic to political reform. His government pursued an expansionist

Russian Peasants after Emancipation   Although serfdom was abolished by Tsar Alexander II in 1861, the condition of the peasantry continued to deteriorate. In this painting peasants wait outside a government building while officials inside finish their lunch.

policy in east Asia at the expense of Japan, another rapidly industrializing power. In 1904 the two countries clashed in the Russo-Japanese War, and Russia was defeated on land and at sea. In the midst of these military setbacks, worker discontent, middle-class and student anger over the absence of constitutional government, and mutinies in the navy forced the tsar to set up a national parliament, called the **Duma.** Elections to the Duma took place, but the tsar retained control of foreign and military affairs, finance, and the appointment of government ministers. The gesture toward constitutional government had been made under duress. Once the embarrassment of defeat at the hands of the Japanese was over, the imperial government muddled along without any vision or long-term program to face the challenges of the modern world.

The Ottoman Failure

Throughout the nineteenth century, the absolutist Ottoman state struggled to maintain its considerable holdings in the Balkans, the Near East, and North Africa. Not unlike its Habsburg neighbor to the north, the sultans ruled over a multiethnic and religiously diverse population numbering some 40 million at the start of the nineteenth century. However, the spread of nationalist ideas, together with the ambitions of the great powers, threatened the territorial integrity of this once-powerful Muslim empire. Centuries of autocratic rule had bred corruption and inefficiency at the highest levels of government in Istanbul. Younger, Western-educated reformers attempted to introduce political and economic reforms in the 1870s, but Sultan Abdul Hamid II (r. 1876–1909) refused to embrace these efforts. His oppressive reign featured a complete rejection of the legal and constitutional changes being adopted in the industrializing states of Western Europe.

Nationalism had its most disruptive impact in the Ottoman Empire's Balkan territories, which were mostly Christian. Beginning with Greece in the 1820s and continuing into the 1870s, a series of Balkan rebellions and wars against Turkish rule placed enormous strain on the fiscal and military resources of the empire. A war between Russia and Turkey (1877–1878) resulted in complete Turkish defeat. Brokered by Bismarck, the European powers then met in Berlin and recognized the full independence of Serbia, Montenegro, and Romania. They also awarded Cyprus to Britain and placed the Turkish provinces of Bosnia and Herzegovina under Austrian administrative protection. In 1885 an autonomous principality of Bulgaria was created, which achieved full independence as a kingdom in 1908 (see Map 20–4).

⊙ [Watch the **Video**

The Ottoman Tanzimat Period (1839–1876): The Middle East Confronts Modernity

on **MyHistoryLab.com**

In the nineteenth century Europe's great powers were a constant threat to the integrity of the Ottoman Empire. There had never been any love lost between Christian Europe and the Muslim Turks. The Muslim intellectual elite were staunchly anti-Western, while the sultans, as leaders of the largest Muslim empire, viewed themselves as caliphs, spiritual heirs of the Prophet Muhammad. Claims to absolute power aside, Ottoman military strength was predicated on the constant acquisition of new territories; once the process of expansion stopped as it did in the seventeenth century, the resources of the empire began to atrophy. The empire lacked a vibrant middle class, and the sultans failed to promote commercial enterprise. To finance its activities, the government contracted loans from Western governments and private financiers. By 1881, however, the empire

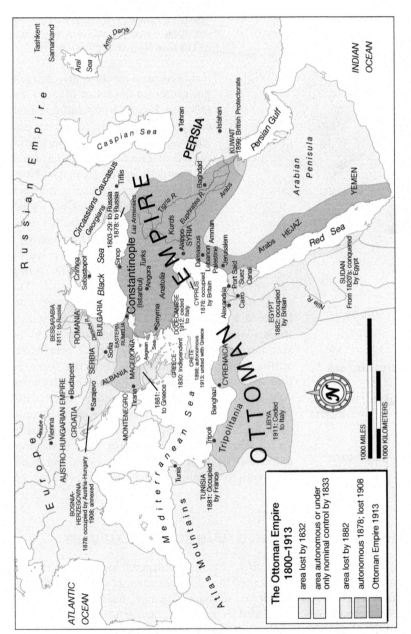

MAP 20-4 The Decline of the Ottoman Empire, 1800–1913   Through the seventeenth and eighteenth centuries, the Ottoman Empire was one of the world's largest and most powerful. But by the nineteenth century, competition from Europe, nationalism in the Balkan regions, and autocratic and corrupt rule led to the empire's steady decline.

QUESTION: Approximately what percentage of the Ottoman Empire was lost between 1800 and 1913?

Abdul Hamid II, Turkish Sultan   The leader of the Ottoman Empire from 1876–1909, Abdul Hamid II presided over the massacre of tens of thousands of Armenians in the mid-1890s. The massacre earned the sultan the nickname, "The Great Assassin." Slow to embrace reform, Abdul Hamid II was overthrown by the military coup of the "Young Turks" in 1909.

had become so indebted that the great powers forced the sultan to create the Ottoman Public Debt Administration, an agency staffed by foreigners and empowered to collect revenues from various state monopolies. At the turn of the twentieth century, foreign investors controlled Ottoman banking, railways, mining, and public utilities. For a small core of Turkish nationalists, this situation was intolerable and humiliating.

In 1909 a military coup led by reformist army officers, "the **Young Turks**," ousted Abdul Hamid II. The rebels installed a compliant successor named Muhammed V (r. 1909–1918), but their efforts to cultivate a sense of Turkish nationalism failed. As in the Habsburg Empire, a variety of subject peoples resented the centuries-old hegemony of the Turks, be they divine-right caliphs or reformist military men. Albanians, Arabs, Greeks, Armenians, Kurds, and others demanded independence. From 1910 until they decided to cast their lot with the Germans in World War I in 1914, the "Young Turk" leadership found itself in constant crisis and regional war, especially with its remaining Balkan subjects.

View the **Image**

Young Turks Overthrow Abdul Hamid II, 1908

on **MyHistoryLab.com**

Read the **Document**

The Young Turk Revolution

on **MyHistoryLab.com**

The United States and Western Europe

Two Economies   During their first 75 years of independence, the former British colonies in North America had adapted their federal system of government to accommodate the economic priorities of two separate economic zones. In the northern states, independent small farmers produced for an internal market, while the inhabitants of coastal cities like Boston, New York, and Philadelphia provided capital and free labor for a vibrant commercial economy. Starting in the 1820s with canal building and shifting by mid-century to railroad development, the northern United States was poised for industrial development. By 1861, the northern states were home to almost 90 percent of the country's manufacturing establishments. In the southern states, the economy remained predominantly agricultural, with large planters producing cash crops like tobacco and cotton for an overseas market. Labor in the South was divided between poor whites (many of whom were illiterate) and unfree black slaves. Southern leaders, acutely sensitive to antislavery arguments in the North and wary of Britain's efforts after 1815 to interdict the trans-Atlantic slave trade, emphasized the rights of states to control their own affairs. Northern states that wanted federal aid for transportation and infrastructure projects tended to support a more interventionist role for the national government.

Civil War   The continuation of chattel slavery in the South was the catalyst for a secession movement that gained force during the 1850s. Southern slaveholders viewed abolitionism as an assault on their economic and political power. They argued that the United States was the states united, a voluntary alliance of sovereign states. When Abraham Lincoln (1809–1865) was elected president in 1860, his opposition to the spread of slavery led to a breakup of the union and to a bloody civil war. Unlike the lightning victories of Prussia over Austria and France in 1866 and 1870, the American conflict turned into a five-year war of attrition in which some 600,000 lives were lost. In the end, the superior numbers and industrial might of the North prevailed. The union was preserved, and the slave system abolished, although free blacks remained subject to appalling discrimination for the next century.

Watch the **Video**
The Plantation System
on **MyHistoryLab.com**

Watch the **Video**
The Slave Trade
on **MyHistoryLab.com**

Watch the **Video**
The Civil War
on **MyHistoryLab.com**

Watch the **Video**
The Meaning of the Civil War for Americans
on **MyHistoryLab.com**

The half century following the Civil War was marked by three significant developments in the United States, all of which affected Western Europe. First and foremost, America's growing industrial power transformed the material and social landscape. Railroad developers enjoyed lavish government subsidies, free right of way over public land, and plentiful European investment capital. By 1914, British, French, and German venture capitalists had invested some $12 billion in American industry. The telegraph, and after 1870 the telephone, began to shrink distances between American cities. Steel, coal, oil, and textile production increased dramatically, employing thousands in ever-expanding production facilities in the North. By the start of the twentieth century, one man or a small group of men dominated most major industries. The Scottish immigrant Andrew Carnegie (1835–1919) controlled the steel industry, John D. Rockefeller (1839–1937) consolidated his hold over oil production and distribution, and J. P. Morgan (1837–1911) was the leading railroad magnate and banker. Income disparities between America's industrial elite and its working class were glaring in 1900. In response, "Progressive" reformers fought to raise wages, limit work hours, and enact health and safety requirements in the workplace. Both major political parties responded to the demand for change.

Read the **Document**
Herbert Croly, The Promise of American Life *(1914)*
on **MyHistoryLab.com**

Republican President Theodore Roosevelt (1858–1919) and Democratic President Woodrow Wilson (1856–1924) both incorporated elements of the Progressive agenda in their policies and legislative programs.

The second major development involved the changing demographic profile of the American republic after 1865. Immigration, in terms both of the numbers of new arrivals and the diversity of European countries from which they came, helped to create a truly multicultural society. In 1860 over 80 percent of all foreigners living in the United States were British, Irish, or German. Thirty years later this majority had shrunk to 64 percent of the total, and by 1920 that majority had become a minority of only 25 percent. New arrivals from Italy, Scandinavia, Eastern Europe, the Balkans, and Russia had altered the balance. Most of the new immigrants crowded into America's major coastal and industrial cities, there to become essential, albeit unappreciated, contributors to the nation's unprecedented industrial expansion. Opportunities for public education at the primary and secondary levels expanded after 1900, and the process of assimilating and "Americanizing" these new arrivals proceeded rapidly. As the United States prepared to take its place as one of the world's preeminent economic and military powers, it would make the transition within a democratic political framework where the state protected individual rights. The significance of this connection between great power status and responsible, constitutional government would not be lost on opponents of totalitarian political systems during the twentieth century.

The third development, westward expansion, was closely related to the first two. Westward expansion had been a focus of settlers in British North America since the mid-seventeenth century. Clashes with Native Americans, wars of empire against France and Spain during the eighteenth century, and the expropriation of Mexican lands in the Southwest during the 1840s had all fit the larger pattern of Western territorial aggrandizement. However, during the second half of the nineteenth century, Western railroad-building enabled thousands of Americans and recent immigrants to relocate to regions where they could find new economic opportunities. The mining and cattle industries benefited enormously from the new railroads. As population increased along the eastern seaboard, enterprising Midwestern farmers and cattle ranchers could move their products efficiently and profitably to market.

The obvious losers in the process of Western development were the Native Americans, who despite centuries of abuse still inhabited roughly one-half of the continental United States just before the start of the Civil War. Pressured to cede territory to white settlers and prospectors, the Plains Indians rose up against the government during the Civil War. After 1865, they were dealt with harshly. Forced to settle on reservations and to abandon their hunter-gatherer lives for settled agriculture, the Native American population dwindled. Those who remained were granted citizenship provided, according to the Dawes Severalty Act of 1877, that Indians "adopted the habits of civilized life." White American attitudes toward native peoples assumed that traditional cultures were stagnant, uncreative, and even uncivilized. Lacking individualistic notions of property, failing to embrace a sedentary lifestyle, and following a spiritual order that did not accord with Western monotheism, the invasion and appropriation of Native American lands was seen as a

[●]┤Read the Document

The Dawes Act

on **MyHistoryLab.com**

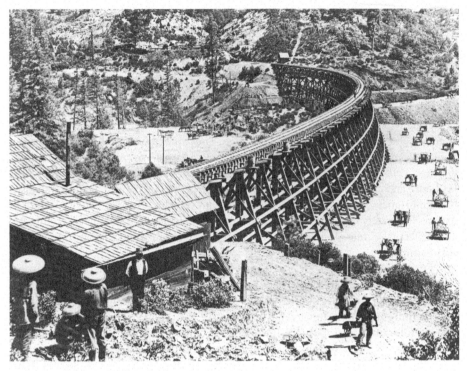

Immigrant Labor in the Building of the American Railroads   The extension of railroads was integral to the United States' westward expansion in the 1800s. Immigrant workers, such as the Chinese "coolies" in this photograph, performed much of the labor for railroad construction, usually enduring harsh working conditions.

progressive and enlightened undertaking. The Dawes Act assumed that a federal law could immediately transform an entire culture.

Nationalism and Race

The decline of Native American culture in the late nineteenth century is an important illustration of the diverging nature of nationalism. During the first half of the century, proponents of national identity and autonomy associated the movement with the Enlightenment emphasis on natural rights. Early nationalists such as Giuseppe Mazzini saw no contradiction in their call for human equality within a civil framework of sovereign territorial states.

The rhetoric of nationalism changed sharply in the late nineteenth century, however. An increasing emphasis on the nation as the repository of culture and values began to replace talk about individual rights and freedoms. The glorification of the state as the embodiment of particular racial values, a form of modern tribalism, also found a receptive audience. Extreme nationalists highlighted differences between peoples, not similarities, and it became popular to talk of superior and inferior races. Minority peoples were accused of defiling national culture, while neighboring states were viewed exclusively as rivals. Even democratic political institutions were attacked, especially by nationalists who feared that minority voters would hamper the state's exercise of its powers. Ethnicity became the barometer of good citizenship, and worship of the state and its core values emerged as a new secular religion.

Extremes in Germany   The rapid industrialization and rise to political power of Germany led some extremists to argue that the energy and dynamism of the new state was due to its unique cultural heritage. They maintained that since the days of the late Roman Empire, when the first Germanic peoples had migrated westward, the German *Volk* or people had demonstrated their superior genius for survival and the resilience and creativity of German culture. Many of the *Volkish* propagandists stressed the importance of race in history, claiming that everything from creativity to morality was intimately connected to racial characteristics. Racist thought contributed to an intellectual climate in Germany that fostered imperialism and, more immediately, anti-Semitism.

Disdain for and oppression of Jews had a long and tragic history in Europe. Portrayed as murderers of Christ and as disloyal subjects, Jewish communities throughout Europe were subject to periodic persecution and mob violence. During the Enlightenment, however, a lessening of the bigotry seemed to suggest that a more tolerant, cosmopolitan outlook might emerge. Most European countries eliminated legal restrictions on Jews, although informal discrimination continued. The great German Jewish scholar Moses Mendelssohn (1729–1786) urged his

Anti-Jewish Pogrom   A violent rampage against Jews in Russia in the 1880s. Jews suffered discrimination and persecution in Europe for many centuries and in parts of Russia and Poland were still victimized by pogroms well into the twentieth century.

PEOPLE IN CONTEXT   Theodor Herzl and Jewish Nationalism

Theodor Herzl (1860–1904) was born in Budapest, Hungary, to a family of merchants who had sought to assimilate into the majority culture. He secured a law degree from the prestigious University of Vienna, but his passion for journalism led him into a career as a foreign correspondent. At age 31, Herzl was assigned to Paris, where he witnessed the tide of anti-Semitism surrounding the trial of Captain Alfred Dreyfus. From this point until his death, Herzl focused his energies on the plight of European Jews and on the need for the establishment of a Jewish homeland in Palestine.

In 1895 Herzl published a short pamphlet called *The Jewish State.* Considering the intensification of anti-Semitism during the late nineteenth century, he wrote, "In vain are we loyal patriots, our loyalty in some places running to extremes; in vain do we make the same sacrifices of life and property as our fellow-citizens; in vain do we strive to increase the fame of our native land in science and art, or her wealth by trade and commerce." The so-called Jewish question, he asserted, is neither a social nor religious one, but a national one, and it was now time for Jews all over the world to work in unison for a national homeland in Palestine. "'Next year in Jerusalem' is our old phrase," he recalled. "It is now a question of showing that the dream can be converted into a living reality."

In 1899 Herzl organized and presided over the First Zionist Congress

Theodor Herzl, champion of Zionism

in the Swiss city of Basel. The chief goals of the Congress were to heighten Jewish self-awareness and to coordinate efforts aimed at achieving statehood. Local Zionist organizations emerged wherever Jews had emigrated. Herzl secured meetings with the German kaiser and the Ottoman sultan. In *The Jewish State,* Herzl had recommended that in return for Palestine, the Jews might assist the Turks in the regulation of their badly mismanaged fiscal affairs. It was not until the end of World War I, however, when the British ruled Palestine that European Jews were allowed to settle there in considerable numbers.

Herzl's rejection of assimilation was controversial within the European Jewish community. Some of his liberal critics claimed that his skepticism regarding the possibility of assimilation undermined the position of Jews in modern industrial society. On the other hand, his plans for a future state alienated some cultural Zionists who disliked Herzl's secular and Western-oriented focus. They also disliked Herzl's willingness to consider alternative locations for the future state. Between 1901 and his death in 1904, for example,

Herzl discussed with British authorities the possibility of claiming the island of Cyprus or the Sinai Peninsula for European Jews. He clearly underestimated the potential for conflict between Arabs and Jewish settlers in Palestine, hoping that both peoples could work together to improve the quality of life for all inhabitants. Unlike the American conquest of the West, he argued, where the "settlers assemble on the frontier, and at the appointed time make a simultaneous and violent rush for their portions," Jewish settlement in Palestine would be orderly and humane. While Herzl's dream of a nation-state for Jews would be realized by the middle of the twentieth century, the process was both difficult and bloody. ■

QUESTION: How did Zionism complement nationalism?

fellow Jews to accept the nation-states in which they lived and to become more active participants in European cultural life. Mendelssohn emphasized the connections between Christian and Jewish culture, and he sought to promote a sense of unity between the two traditions. By the 1880s, Jews had become prominent members of most professions and served in a variety of political offices in Western and Central Europe.

The social disruption and insecurity caused by industrialization, urbanization, and class tension, however, provided fertile ground for those who sought to reduce complex problems to simple, all-encompassing myths—and the myth of the evil and disloyal Jew was always close at hand. The worst treatment occurred in eastern Europe, where over 70 percent of the world's Jewish population lived. Russian authorities—not for the first time—indulged in pogroms (organized attacks or persecutions against Jews) in the wake of the assassination of Alexander II in 1881. Jews were beaten up and killed, their shops destroyed, and their property confiscated. Millions of Russian Jews, finding no future in the land of their birth, relocated to the United States between 1881 and 1914. In Germany and in German-speaking Austria, late nineteenth-century racial nationalists focused much of their irrational animus on the Jewish community. An anti-Semitic congress held in the German city of Dresden in 1882 called for an end to Jewish influence in political life throughout Europe.

The Birth of Jewish Nationalism   As part of the larger reaction to the wave of persecution Jews experienced in much of Europe, a Jewish nationalist movement called Zionism arose. It held that the Jewish people would never be accorded equal status in Europe and that they could achieve permanent security only through the creation of a Jewish state in the ancient biblical homeland of Zion (Palestine). The movement was inspired by the success of state-building efforts in Italy and Germany, together with nationalist movements in Ireland, Poland, and the Balkans. Many Jews, led by an Austrian journalist named Theodor Herzl (1860–1904), worked tirelessly to encourage Jewish immigration to Palestine. Despite Ottoman opposition to migration schemes (Palestine was part of the Ottoman Empire until 1918), some 1,000 Jews had settled in Palestine by 1900, with another 3,000 arriving annually until the start of World War I in 1914.

KEY
QUESTION
REVISITED

**Is nationalism a
constructive force in
the modern age?**

The formation of independent nation-states in Western Europe during the second half of the nineteenth century represented the culmination of efforts begun during the era of the French Revolution and Napoleon. However, the proponents of nationalism after 1850 were often conservative elites who adopted the nationalist agenda to solidify their social and economic privileges. Cavour in Italy, Bismarck in Germany, and Louis Napoleon III in France all promoted the goal of national unity along linguistic and cultural lines from the standpoint of *Realpolitik*. Dismissing the nationalist idealism of an earlier liberal and Romantic tradition, the new architects of the sovereign state were interested in the military, economic, and political advantages that the unified state gave them. They also abandoned the older conservative assumption that governments were distinct from their populations, and instead skillfully portrayed their nation-building crusade as the collective embodiment of and capstone to each citizen's individual genius.

By the closing decades of the nineteenth century, nationalism had become the tool of leaders who cared little for the historic keystones of liberal ideology: individual rights, international cooperation based on the equality of peoples, and the freedom to dissent. National honor and the respect of rival states in a highly competitive state system made the international order increasingly fragile. Although there had been no general European war since the fall of Napoleon Bonaparte in 1815, nationalist politicians dedicated enormous fiscal resources to their military establishments. As we shall see in the next chapter, those military forces were employed repeatedly overseas as Europe's leading powers established huge colonial empires.

In France after 1848, in Italy after 1860, in the United States after 1865, in Britain after 1867, and in Germany after 1871, strong nationalist sentiments developed in concert with an extended franchise and with a more active role for government in labor relations, public health and safety, and education. The great fear of the ruling class that political democracy would mean the end of their ascendancy and perhaps even the overthrow of the existing social order was shown to be misplaced. Instead, universal manhood suffrage, when combined with better material conditions for Europe's working class, became the great bulwarks of the existing order. The bond of national unity proved to be stronger than either the Enlightenment appeal to internationalism or the socialist creed of worker cooperation and class consciousness. The territorial nation-state, sovereign and sacred, the chief object of each citizen's allegiance even to the death, had by 1914 become the new political orthodoxy. The fate of nations and the defense of their honor were about to replace loyalty to a ruling dynasty (even in states with monarchs) as the central concern of the twentieth century.

So powerful was the appeal of nationalism after 1900 that those governments, irrespective of their apparent military prowess, that failed to frame their claims to legitimacy in nationalist terms did not survive. From the collapse of the Austrian Habsburg Empire after World War I to the disintegration of the Soviet Empire in the late 1980s, states that did not self-consciously foster nationalism have faltered. The appeal of nationalism, its ability to rally public support around a set of symbols and myths respecting an alleged common culture, has been essential to the formation of the modern state system. However, nationalism also contributed to a disturbing trend after 1870 in which foreigners became "the other," and where the formation, preservation, and expansion of the territorial state bred both distrust and disdain in a global community in which Europe was coming to dominate peoples on every continent.

Key Terms

nationalism, *p. 587*

Realpolitik, p. 591

Kulturkampf, p. 596

state socialism, *p. 597*

Dreyfus Affair, *p. 599*

anti-Semitism, *p. 599*

Activities

1. How did approaches to national unification change in Western Europe after the failed revolutions of 1848?

2. Explain how traditional elites and conservative political leaders used nationalism to strengthen their hold on power after 1850.

3. What role did industry play in the creation of centralized nation-states in Europe and America?

4. How did the rhetoric of nationalism shift during the second half of the nineteenth century?

5. Analyze the reasons for the failure of the Austrian Habsburg Empire to maintain its leadership within the German Confederation.

6. What internal and external factors undermined the Ottoman Empire during the nineteenth century?

7. Describe how British nationalism differed from nationalism on the European continent.

Further Reading

Geoffrey Wawro, *Warfare and Society in Europe, 1792–1914* (2000), a treatment of military factors in the emergence of modern nation states.

David Blackbourn, *The Long Nineteenth Century: A History of Germany, 1780–1918* (1998), a readable and balanced survey.

Michael Bentley, *Politics without Democracy, 1815–1914* (1984), a treatment of major trends in Britain.

John Stuart Mill, *On Liberty* and *The Subjection of Women* (2007), a modern edition of two key works in nineteenth-century political thought.

MyHistoryLab Connections

Visit **MyHistoryLab.com** *for a customized Study Plan that will help you build your knowledge of* The Consolidation of Nation-States.

Questions for Analysis

1. What does the excerpt from *Nana* reveal about Parisian society during the Second Republic?

Read the **Document** Emile Zola, *Nana,* p. 600

2. What were some of the ways in which modernization took place during the Ottoman Tanzimat period?

👁─Watch the Video The Ottoman Tanzimat Period (1839–1876): The Middle East Confronts Modernity, p. 606

3. What were some of the principles that the Young Turks embraced?

📖─Read the Document The Young Turk Revolution, p. 608

4. Beyond the atrocity of slavery itself, what other atrocities resulted from the domestic slave trade in the United States?

👁─Watch the Video The Slave Trade, p. 609

5. What are some of the differences between how white Americans have viewed the Civil War and how African-Americans have viewed the war?

👁─Watch the Video The Meaning of the Civil War for Americans, p. 609

Other Resources from This Chapter

📖─Read the Document Letter from Otto von Bismarck, 1866, p. 592

📖─Read the Document Excerpt from *Self-Help,* p. 595

🔍─View the Closer Look Conflict between Church and State in Germany, p. 596

📖─Read the Document The Gotha Program, p. 597

🔍─View the Map Paris Commune, 1871, p. 598

🔍─View the Image Gladstone and Disraeli, p. 601

🔍─View the Map The Crimean War, p. 604

🔍─View the Closer Look The Crimean War Recalled, p. 604

🔍─View the Closer Look Bloody Sunday, St. Petersburg 1905, p. 605

🔍─View the Image Young Turks Overthrow Abdul Hamid II, 1908, p. 608

👁─Watch the Video The Plantation System, p. 609

👁─Watch the Video The Civil War, p. 609

📖─Read the Document Herbert Croly, *The Promise of American Life* (1914), p. 609

📖─Read the Document The Dawes Act, p. 610

Imperial Dress Members of the Freemason's Lodge in Freetown, capital of the British colony of Sierra Leone, address the Duke of Connaught, a son of Queen Victoria, in 1910. Dressed in evening suits, the African dignitaries look every bit as formal as their British counterparts.

21 Global Empire and European Culture

((•⎯ Hear the Audio   Chapter 21 at MyHistoryLab.com

LEARNING OBJECTIVES

What were the main motives for the new imperialism? • Why did the European imperialists target Africa? • How did south and east Asia come under Europe's influence? • What was the European view of colonial peoples? • How did artists gain influence as cultural leaders in the late nineteenth century?

Dreamers and visionaries have made civilizations. It is trying to do things that cannot be done that makes life worth while.

—Cecil Rhodes

KEY QUESTION

How does the projection of power reflect wider cultural values?

In 1877 London-born Cecil Rhodes (1853–1902) published a "Confession of Faith" in which he reflected on the chief good in life. Rhodes had migrated to British-controlled southern Africa in 1870 where he quickly amassed a large fortune in the diamond industry. His company, De Beers Consolidated Mines, Ltd., became the dominant producer and marketer of fine diamonds worldwide. One might expect a self-made man like Rhodes to focus on wealth creation as the greatest good in life, but instead he said that the overseas migration of Britons, "the finest race in the world," provided his greatest personal satisfaction. He asked his readers to consider those parts of the world "that are at present inhabited by the most despicable specimens of human beings" and how much better things would be if these lands "were brought under Anglo-Saxon influence."

In the late nineteenth century, Rhodes was not alone in his estimate of Europe's beneficent impact on the rest of the world, even if it meant the subjection of indigenous peoples by violent means. Europe's industrial and military prowess, its sophisticated transportation and communications networks, its advances in public health and education, and its representative political institutions all seemed to demonstrate that the West deserved to dominate less advanced continents. Coupled with the rise of a body of social thought that carelessly extended Charles Darwin's new theory of

▢•⎯ **Read** the **Document**

Cecil Rhodes, "Confession of Faith"

on **MyHistoryLab.com**

biological evolution to social, moral, cultural, intellectual, and political development, Europeans in the late nineteenth century confidently and aggressively imposed their rule, their institutions, and their values on non-Western peoples around the globe. By 1914, most of Africa and large parts of south and east Asia had come under the direct or indirect control of Western Europe's most powerful nation-states. Indeed, only one-fifth of the world's land mass was not under a European flag when World War I began. The process was so rapid and wide-reaching, and the potential for overseas conflict between rival European states so great, that scholars have described the phenomenon as the "**new imperialism**" to distinguish it from the colonization efforts of the seventeenth and eighteenth centuries.

Most Europeans were supremely confident that global dominance was not at odds with the Enlightenment tradition of inalienable human rights, natural law, the equality of peoples, individual liberty, and rational conduct. Yet, however hard they labored to justify imperialism in terms of spreading Enlightenment ideals, a basic shift in European consciousness occurred during the final decades of the nineteenth century. It emphasized the aggressive and irrational side of human nature, the subconscious impulses and drives that often extolled violence and struggle. Suddenly it seemed to many thinkers that reason was a fragile instrument and that powerful, and little understood, nonrational forces defined human nature. In the late nineteenth century these forces often found their outlet in the cruel quest for empire. During the twentieth century, they would be manipulated by fascist political demagogues who repudiated the liberal tradition of enlightened rationalism. ▪

The New Imperialism: Motives and Methods

Imperialism was not a new feature of European life. Beginning in the late fifteenth century, the kingdoms of Spain and Portugal began a process of global expansion that was to involve every major European power and continue until the end of World War II in 1945. It began with the conquest of the Americas, Siberia, and central Asia, followed by the peopling of these lands with European migrants and, in America, African slaves. During the late eighteenth and early nineteenth centuries, successful revolutions in the Americas transformed most settler colonies into independent nation-states, but Europe's global predominance continued in new directions. By the third quarter of the nineteenth century, European states expanded former slave stations along the coast of Africa, together with trading posts in India, China, and Southeast Asia, into territorial empires. With political control came cultural and economic domination. Even in those areas where the Western powers did not exercise direct political ascendancy—in the Ottoman, Persian, and Chinese empires, for example—Europe's economic superiority dictated the formation of a semicolonial relationship.

Economic Factors   Three features distinguish late nineteenth-century imperialism from all previous forms. The first involves the role of economics. As European states experienced the early stages of industrialization, many politicians and industrialists believed they needed to secure reliable international markets for their country's manufactured products. It was thought that in a highly competitive capitalist society, the ability of producers to cultivate a transnational consuming public would largely determine success. Earlier proponents of free trade and followers of Adam Smith (see Chapter 16) argued that colonies were unnecessary so long as all producers had equal access to markets. However, national competition within Europe made the free-trade argument vulnerable after 1850, especially when countries began to raise tariffs to protect their own industry. Colonies, the argument ran, could absorb Europe's surplus products and investment capital. Proponents of overseas empire also maintained that colonies would serve as potential sources of strategic (and inexpensive) raw materials, such as rubber and petroleum, and as a demographic safety valve for Europe's surplus population. The Russian communist Lenin (1870–1924), a harsh critic of empire, believed that imperialism was inherent in the dynamic of capitalism and that, in order to survive, capitalist economies had to find new markets for their surplus products.

Few colonies proved profitable. Most of them turned out to be far more costly to secure, protect, and maintain than anyone anticipated. The healthiest markets for Europe's manufactured products were in other advanced and affluent states, not in underdeveloped and impoverished colonies in Africa or south Asia. Similarly, European investors put little of their capital in overseas possessions that were not populated by European settlers and their descendants. While overseas migration peaked in the late nineteenth century, few white Europeans elected to settle in the many African or East Asian colonies established by the imperial powers.

National Rivalry   The second important feature of the new imperialism involved a self-imposed competition for international prestige engendered by the rise of nationalism. Europe's political leaders, eager to enhance popular support for the state while defusing potential social unrest at home, skillfully directed state resources into the establishment of overseas empires. World powers needed secure ports, coaling stations for their navies, and the ability to raise colonial armies in any potential conflict. The acquisition of new lands overseas would provide these assets and win accolades for politicians who set the ambitious agenda. Governments boasted about the achievements of their armed forces in colonial wars. French acquisitions in North and sub-Saharan Africa and Indochina partly compensated for defeat at the hands of the Germans in 1870; Italy's military adventures in Libya and Somalia provided evidence of that nation's great power status despite the country's relative underdevelopment when compared with its northern neighbors; and Germany's role in southwest Africa (Namibia) and Tanganyika, and its influence in China, all confirmed Emperor William II's (r. 1888–1918) assertion that his empire was gaining its rightful "place in the sun."

Culture and Race   The final and most pernicious factor undergirding the intensive pace of late nineteenth-century imperialism involved European attitudes toward non-Western, non-Christian cultures. Some apologists for imperialism insisted that territorial expansion was a moral enterprise designed to bring the blessings of a superior civilization to benighted millions. French politician Jules Ferry (1832–1893) argued that "the superior races have a right vis-à-vis the inferior races . . . they have a right to civilize them." British poet Rudyard Kipling's (1865–1936) famed 1898 poem **"White Man's Burden"** captured this combination of paternalism and racial disdain, referring to the colonized

Read the **Document**

Imperialism and the White Man's Burden *(1899)*, *Rudyard Kipling*

on **MyHistoryLab.com**

peoples as "half-devil and half-child." However offensive it may seem today, the appeal of what Kipling called the "White Man's Burden" involved an implicit conviction that non-Western peoples had the potential to be like their imperial mentors and that the entire imperialist project was at its core a gigantic educational enterprise, a global extension of the European Enlightenment.

Many advocates of imperialism insisted that evolutionary theory confirmed lingering suspicions about race and cultural development. They argued that just as the animal kingdom was organized hierarchically, so, too, were human cultures and "races." Depending on their level of cultural and intellectual development, some cultures were deemed superior to others, which made up the essence of **racism.** Race was the defining characteristic in this pseudoscience, which was given an intellectual façade through the efforts of French aristocrat Arthur de Gobineau (1816–1882), Houston Stewart Chamberlain (1855–1927), and others. White European, especially northern European, culture was superior to all others, they argued, and these views were widely accepted throughout the continent by the end of the century. The European conquest and subjection of other races was only the natural working out of the laws of competition and survival where only the fittest would—and should—prevail. Here was a sharp repudiation of the Enlightenment tradition, particularly in the areas of universal human rights and the equality of peoples. This "law of nature" privileged struggle and conflict between peoples and celebrated irrational vitality and a subconscious will to power. The good and the just were reduced to whatever values the victor chose to impose.

Read the Document

Karl Pearson, "Social Darwinism and Imperialism"

on **MyHistoryLab.com**

Scientific Racism This chart purports to show the superiority of white Europeans over other "races." Europeans became obsessed with racial categories in the late nineteenth century and often camouflaged racist ideas with scientific language.

Methods of Control   Once they had established their claim to control overseas territories, the European powers adopted a number of strategies to preserve and exploit their acquisitions. Annexation and direct colonial rule using European administrators were the most costly options. This was the approach most European powers took in sub-Saharan Africa beginning in the 1880s. An alternative approach was a protectorate arrangement. In a protectorate, the local ruler and his government continued to function, but the Europeans controlled the country's military, foreign affairs, and economy and intervened whenever imperial interests were threatened. This was how the British ran Egypt from 1882 to the 1920s and how the French imposed their authority over Tunisia in 1881. Another approach was referred to as a "sphere of influence." This meant that a non-European country granted a European state certain exclusive economic privileges in part or all of its territory. Europeans living or working in that territory were also exempted from the jurisdiction of the local legal system and resided in their own autonomous sections of foreign cities and towns. Here they attempted to recreate many of the amenities of their home country. These privileges became the norm in Europe's relations with the once powerful Chinese Empire during the nineteenth century.

> ◉─[**Watch** the **Video**
> *Imperialism*
> on **MyHistoryLab.com**

Educating the Colonial Elite   European colonizers also asserted and maintained their control through the cultivation of an indigenous elite. Recognizing the need for this base of support—and convinced that European culture was vastly superior to anything that was embraced by indigenous peoples—the imperialists undertook to provide a Western-style education for native leaders. Often, the initiative was led by Christian missionaries who viewed the transmission of Western culture as part of a larger civilizing mandate. These initiatives were in general limited to males. A select number of colonial subjects received their university training in Western Europe and upon their return were immediately selected for significant posts in the colonial bureaucracy. It was hoped that these Western-educated intellectuals would begin the process of translating and communicating the "blessings" of Western scientific and philosophical thought to a wider native audience. This would solidify colonial allegiance to the imperial state. Irrespective of their educational accomplishments or their demonstrated loyalty to the empire, however, the members of the new elite were never accepted as genuine equals by white Europeans, for whom the highest appointments in the colonial service were reserved. It was therefore not surprising that many of the Western-educated native elites became the most forceful critics of Western imperialism during the late nineteenth and early twentieth centuries. Their study of European political institutions and Western philosophical ideas spurred the growing call for civil equality and the right to national self-determination. While few of the Western-educated elite actually identified with the illiterate and impoverished majority in their homelands, they began to claim the mantle of leadership in the drive to end colonialism. Their efforts would finally bear fruit in the aftermath of World War II.

The Scramble for Empire: Africa

The most dramatic manifestation of the new imperialism was the division of Africa among the European powers between the 1880s and 1914. Prior to the 1870s, most of the vast African interior was unknown to Europeans (see Map 21–1). Whites had seldom penetrated far beyond the coasts. There were scattered forts and former slave stations along the west coast of Africa, and the French had conquered most of Algeria in North Africa during the 1830s. Morocco was independent. Tunisia, Libya, and Egypt were autonomous provinces of the Ottoman Empire. However, the peoples of sub-Saharan Africa continued to follow traditional kinship patterns of social and political organization without interference from the West. European missionaries and explorers like David Livingstone (1813–1873) and Henry Stanley (1841–1904) had visited part of the interior of the continent after midcentury, but their presence had only a nominal impact on local culture.

◉-⎡View the **Closer Look**

The French in Morocco
on **MyHistoryLab.com**

◉-⎡Watch the **Video**

The Origins of Modern Imperialism and Colonialism
on **MyHistoryLab.com**

This situation changed swiftly and dramatically in the mid-1870s as Belgian, French, German, and British interests in sub-Saharan Africa led to a series of territorial disputes. King Leopold II of Belgium (r. 1865–1909) took the lead by securing almost one million square miles of territory in the Congo as his private domain. Leopold's expansive appropriation was based on the work of his personal agent, the formidable Henry Stanley, who secured highly questionable "grants" of land from indigenous leaders. To rule this vast area, Leopold set up the International Association of the Congo, which inaugurated a brutal regime dedicated solely to extracting raw materials, especially rubber and ivory. Germany, Portugal, Britain, and France quickly followed Leopold's lead in the race for prime real estate in central and southern Africa. Each country was eager to reap profits and prestige no matter what the cost to native peoples.

⎡◉-⎡Read the **Document**

Imperialism in Africa (1880s)
on **MyHistoryLab.com**

Berlin Conference   In the fall of 1884 German Chancellor Otto von Bismarck (1815–1898) and French Premier Jules Ferry (1832–1893) arranged for a special conference on African affairs to be held in Berlin. Fourteen nations, including the United States, sent delegates, but not a single African leader was invited to attend. The meeting was designed to establish rules for the campaign of empire building. It became the unofficial starting point for a territorial "**scramble for Africa**" that continued until the entire continent, except for Liberia and Ethiopia, was under European political control. The imperial powers established borders with little regard for the concerns of indigenous peoples. Traditional political and cultural rivals found themselves joined politically within a single European colony, while other tribes were divided among several colonies. Exploitative labor regimes, arbitrary land taxes, and the proselytizing activities of Christian missionaries disrupted centuries-old patterns of social organization.

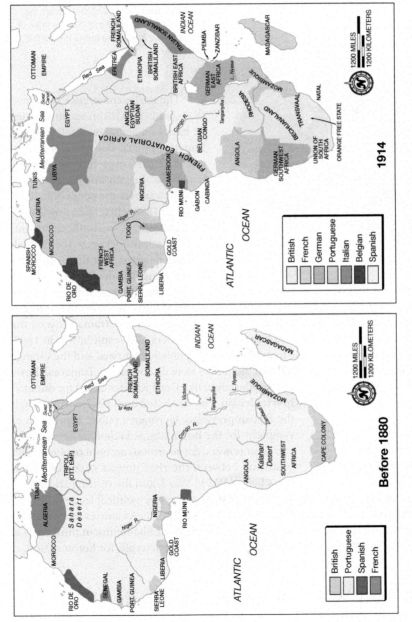

MAP 21-1 European Colonies in Africa in 1914 Prior to the 1880s, Europe's presence in Africa was limited to the coastline. Between 1880 and 1914 the continent was divided by the Western powers. Liberia and Ethiopia were the only countries to retain their independence.

QUESTION: How did Europeans determine colonial boundaries in Africa?

THE RHODES COLOSSUS
STRIDING FROM CAPE TOWN TO CAIRO

Cecil Rhodes and the New Imperialism "The Rhodes Colossus," a cartoon depicting English-born Cecil Rhodes striding over the African continent. The views of Rhodes, and many other imperialists, were summed up in his declaration, "I contend that we are the finest race in the world and that the more of the world we inhabit the better it is for the human race."

The Berlin conference stipulated that claims to African territory must be based on actual occupation by an imperial power, but there were frequent clashes over territorial proclamations. Britain and France came close to war over the upper Nile River valley in 1898 when opposing armies met at Fashoda in southeastern Sudan. Tensions between the French and the Belgians over the Congo and between the British and the Germans respecting claims to territory in southeast Africa each threatened to escalate into armed conflict. In South Africa, where the British had captured Cape Town on the southern tip of the continent from the Dutch during the Napoleonic wars, strains between the British and the descendants of Dutch settlers (called Boers) did result in war in 1898. Many Boers had fled British rule to establish two republics, Transvaal and the Orange Free State, in the 1850s. When gold and diamonds were discovered in Transvaal, however, imperialists like Cecil Rhodes called for annexation to Britain. The war lasted until 1902, and although the British prevailed, Germany's public expression of sympathy for the Boers strained relations between the two great powers. An enormous amount of bluster and posturing between the rival powers occurred in the years before World War I, and the reading and voting public appeared to support the stridency of their respective political leaders. Talk of war over the defense of colonial possessions became stock news stories for the cheap tabloid press. The spirit of internationalism promoted by Enlightenment thinkers was being replaced by a dangerous bellicosity and emotion-laden calls for heroic action.

○⌐View the **Image**

Belgian King Crushing the Congo Free State—Cartoon

on **MyHistoryLab.com**

The Scramble for Empire: South and East Asia

The Indian Raj British involvement in India began in the early seventeenth century, when commercial agents representing the British East India Company established trade relations with the powerful Mughal Empire. As Mughal power declined during the eighteenth century, the company began to form commercial and military alliances with rival Indian princes while simultaneously building a large private army of native troops known as *sepoys.* A rebellion against the East India Company took place in 1857, but it was brutally suppressed. In the aftermath Parliament put an end to East India Company rule and declared the entire subcontinent to be a part of the British Empire. Queen Victoria was proclaimed Empress of India in 1877, and the Indian Raj, or rule, quickly became the centerpiece of Britain's global empire.

Under the Raj, a small elite British civil service consisting of roughly 1,000 men was stationed in India to supervise a much larger Indian staff. These bureaucrats governed a population of nearly 300 million. Britain also stationed more than 100,000 British troops in India and raised an Indian army of about 300,000 men under British officers. British rule brought some benefits: Western medical practices and improved agricultural techniques contributed to a rapid rise in overall population. The subcontinent was unified for the first time in its history, and an extensive system of railroads, bridges, and roads was built. However, it is doubtful that the quality of life for average Indians improved much during this period. Moreover, a policy of racial discrimination whereby Indians were denied access to the highest levels of administration and were excluded from British clubs, hotels, and other private venues fanned the resentment of the Indian elite. In the 1880s a group of educated Indians founded the Indian National Congress, a political organization whose members were animated by a strong sense of nationalism. On the eve of World War I, Indian leaders were calling for some degree of autonomy. In a country with hundreds of language groups and a wide variety of religious traditions, the Indian National Congress struggled to forge a common identity using the tools of empire—English language, Western technology, and Western political values, including nationalism, to challenge the Raj.

China and Europe   European demand for China's luxury products—silks, porcelains, teas, spices—had been strong since the early sixteenth century. While eager to trade with China, Western merchants decried the fact that access to China's markets was limited by the authoritarian Ming (1368–1644) and Qing (1644–1912) dynasties. China's rulers had traditionally considered their country to be the most advanced civilization in the world. Since China had no need for Western products (although it did benefit immensely from the introduction of American maize [corn], peanuts, and sweet potatoes), an "unfavorable balance of trade" developed: The West had to pay for Chinese goods with gold and silver. The Chinese considered trade to be a privilege, not a right. The privilege was bestowed on barbarian Westerners according to terms set by the Chinese emperor, the "Son of Heaven." Those terms restricted all foreign trade to the single port of Canton, where a group of Chinese commercial firms, known as *cohongs,* held the exclusive right to interact with Western merchants.

View the **Image**

Chinese Destroying Opium

on **MyHistoryLab.com**

Read the **Document**

Letter to Queen Victoria 1839, Lin Zexu

on **MyHistoryLab.com**

Opium Wars   The West's subordinate association with China changed dramatically with the Industrial Revolution. Beginning in the early 1840s,

Opium Wars in China Superior naval power enabled the British to defeat the Chinese in two wars fought between 1839 and 1860. In this illustration, Chinese rioters attempt to destroy British warehouses during a conflict in the 1850s.

Britain employed its superior naval might to force the Chinese government to open its markets to foreign products, including opium produced in British India by the East India Company. Opium was illegal in China, but British and American smuggling had produced an enormous addiction problem among the Chinese. The Qing government acted decisively to end the opium trade by destroying stocks of opium it discovered in Canton, but this bold action precipitated a lopsided war with Britain. After China's defeat in the first Opium War (1839–1842), the Chinese government was obliged to cede the island of Hong Kong to the British (it would not be returned until 1997) and to open up five additional ports to foreign traders.

Another Opium War was fought between 1856 and 1860. This time Britain was joined by France, and the two powers occupied Beijing and forced the Chinese government to grant concessions that further undermined China's sovereignty. Foreign missionaries were now allowed to travel freely throughout the empire, opium was legalized, and Western gunboats were permitted access to many of China's most important rivers. In the late nineteenth century China also fought two more unsuccessful wars against France (1884–1885) and Japan (1894–1895) in which it had to surrender control over Vietnam and Taiwan, respectively. By the 1890s, France, Russia, Germany, Japan, and the United States had all laid claim to spheres of influence on the Chinese mainland. A final Chinese effort to expel foreigners in 1900, called the **Boxer Rebellion** by Europeans, was crushed by an international force of European, American, and Japanese troops. The Chinese government had become simply another inferior power in a world increasingly dominated by the industrialized West, and in 1912 the ancient dynastic system was abolished (see Map 21–2).

Japan Imitates the West   The first European merchants and missionaries to Japan had arrived in the sixteenth century. However, all except the Dutch had been forced to leave in the seventeenth century. Japan remained an isolated country for the next 200 years, until the American naval commander Matthew Perry (1794–1858) arrived in Tokyo Bay with a fleet in 1853 and demanded the right to trade. Unlike the Chinese, Japan's elite responded to these demands by transforming their country

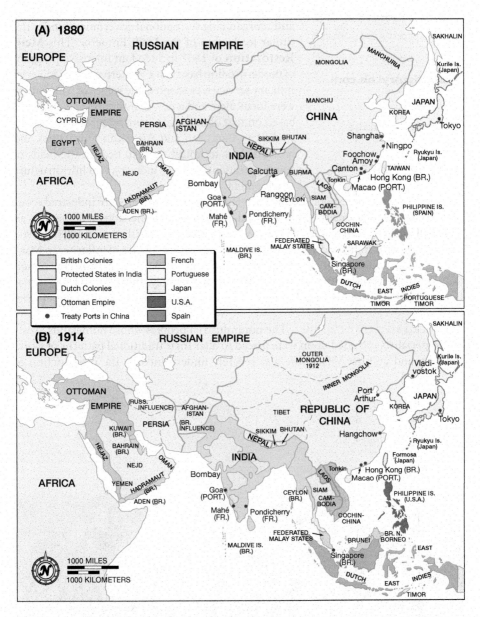

MAP 21-2   European Colonies in Asia by 1914   The extension of European power into Asia occurred simultaneously with the carve-up of Africa. Japan and the United States joined the list of imperial powers in Asia prior to World War I.

QUESTION: What role did superior technology play in Europe's Asian empires?

⬚●⊦ **Read** the **Document**

Meiji Constitution (1889)

on **MyHistoryLab.com**

🔍⊦ **View** the **Image**

Emperor Meiji

on **MyHistoryLab.com**

and reorganizing the national government under the titular leadership of the Meiji Emperor. This **Meiji Restoration** of 1867 included an intensive program of modernization based on a Western model. Universal military service was adopted, the values of nationalism were inculcated, and a new constitution was approved based on that of imperial Germany. Japanese students studied in European and American universities and brought their technical skills to bear in the fields of communications, mining, industry, and infrastructure development.

By 1900, a resource-poor state had been transformed into a modern industrial economy. So rapid was Japan's rise to power under its reformist leadership that it became an imperialist aggressor in east Asia. Taiwan was wrested from the Chinese in 1895. In 1905 Japan's surprising military defeat of Russia over the issue of spheres of influence in Manchuria and Korea (which became a Japanese colony in 1910) helped to dispel the notion that the Western powers were invincible. The victory not only strengthened Japanese nationalism but also inspired anti-Western and anti-imperial sentiments throughout Asia.

The Legacy of Empire   The nonindustrial peoples whose homelands Western imperialists intruded upon were forced to alter their traditional patterns of work, thought, and culture. Village life was severely undermined by the introduction of

The Scramble for Africa   Diamond mining in South Africa in 1872. Africa's rich deposits of such natural resources as diamonds, gold, and rubber made the continent the object of European competition.

European labor requirements. Large mining operations in Southern Africa, for example, obliged African men to leave their villages for distant work sites to earn enough income to pay newly imposed imperial land taxes. Once colonial peoples began producing cash crops and raw materials for a Western and global market, rural economies became dependent on fluctuating global economic conditions. In terms of material culture, late nineteenth-century imperialism represented the consummation of a process of worldwide economic integration that had begun in the early sixteenth century. The production and consumption of goods within a transnational context were made possible by Europe's control over non-Western peoples. By 1900, the age of independent civilizations was at a close.

Imperialism, Intellectual Controversy, and European Culture

As Europe's power spread around the globe, so too did Western ideas, institutions, and values. English and French became international languages, just as Spanish and Portuguese had in the sixteenth century. Christian missionaries and entrepreneurs worked under the protection of superior military forces, while Western science, medicine, educational theories, and legal forms all found expression in cities where Western-style architecture increasingly replaced indigenous styles. Even Western fashions became commonplace, with educated African and Asian people dressing like Europeans. Not every imposition was exploitative, however. Imperialists played a significant role in the suppression of the Muslim slave trade in Africa, in the abolition of *sati* (the immolation of widows on the funeral pyres of their deceased husbands) in India, and in the elimination of foot binding in China. Most importantly, Western democratic values, especially Enlightenment ideas about responsible self-government, the rule of law, and individual freedom, galvanized educated non-Europeans to work for greater autonomy and, ultimately, national independence.

Ironically, the Enlightenment tradition of natural rights and fixed, natural laws began to take hold in Europe's many colonies just at the moment when that tradition was being undermined by new intellectual trends in the West. The scientific quest for certainty and useful truths was anchored in the Enlightenment assumption that space, time, matter, and energy were independent realities within a fixed and knowable universe. Humans were reasonable creatures capable of investigating the natural laws that governed God's clockwork universe in a dispassionate, objective manner. The continuous improvement of the human condition through the application of the scientific method stood at the core of middle-class ideas of progress. However, during the period of Europe's imperial expansion, these rationalist assumptions were called into question by biologists, physicists, and by professionals (especially psychologists) in the emerging social sciences.

Darwin, Biology, and Deity   The English naturalist **Charles Darwin**'s (1809–1882) monumental contributions to biology were the product of years of study, field-based data collection, and rigorous analysis. Untroubled by theological ideas about the status of humans, Darwin's evolutionary theory was as significant to biology as Newton's work had been to physics. The biblical account of humankind's creation remained a compelling and emotionally satisfying story for most Europeans well into the nineteenth century. In less than a week, God had created each species of plant and animal life in its fixed and finished form. Each species was endowed with features designed for a specific purpose, and the entire creative act had taken place a mere 6,000 years ago.

Darwin's *Origin of Species by Means of Natural Selection* (1859) raised fundamental questions about both the timeframe and the process of creation. Instead of a single divine creative act six millennia ago, he introduced a more fluid model in which some creatures came into being and others became extinct and in which the creative process unfolded, and continued to unfold, over millions of years. Darwin's theory, while shocking to traditional religious believers, was in fact the culmination of work carried out by a variety of biologists and geologists for over a century. Darwin's grandfather, Erasmus Darwin (1731–1802), argued in his *Zoonomia, or the Laws of Organic Life* (1794) that Earth existed long before the appearance of humans. In the 1830s Sir Charles Lyell (1797–1875) published his *Principles of Geology*, in which he argued that Earth had evolved over millennia. The discovery of the skeletal remains of extinct species and the extraction of dissimilar fossils at different geological strata indicated a strong connection between the environment and animal forms. Even contemporary experiments in crossbreeding plants and animals suggested that the creative process was much more varied and dynamic than the biblical account allowed for.

Read the **Document**

Origin of Species, *Charles Darwin 1859*

on **MyHistoryLab.com**

Read the **Document**

On Darwin 1860s

on **MyHistoryLab.com**

Origin of Species was significant because it offered an explanation—the principle of **natural selection**—for the process of evolution. It even argued for links between extinct and living species. Darwin's path-breaking theory of natural selection maintained that in the ongoing struggle for food and for security against predators, some species are more successful than others at adapting to changes in the environment. Offspring are not exact duplicates of their parents; small and sometimes random variations in speed, strength, color, dexterity, size, and many other features can determine which plants and animals are most likely to reach maturity and have offspring of their own. Those that do survive are apt to pass on their superior attributes to the next generation.

The process was imperceptible, covering millions of years and involving all living organisms, including humans. While Darwin received full credit for the theory of natural selection, his contemporary Alfred Russell Wallace (1823–1913) had reached similar conclusions while working independently. However, neither man could explain the origin of chance variations that gave some organisms an advantage over others in a given species. Not until the work on heredity pioneered by the Austrian monk Gregor Mendel (1822–1884) and expanded by the Dutch botanist Hugo De Vries (1848–1935) became available did scientists solve this puzzle. De Vries asserted that instead of evolution resulting from small variations, as Darwin had claimed, radical change or mutations were key. Genetic mutations that were appropriate for a particular environment enabled the individuals who possessed them to dominate and to pass these qualities along to their descendants.

Charles Darwin and Evolution Darwin's theory of natural selection represented a significant scientific advance but provoked opposition among many Europeans, as seen by this cartoon. Although Darwin was not an atheist, his scientific method was rejected by those who believed in a literal interpretation of the Bible. *Private collection/The Bridgeman Art Library*

At one level, the theory of biological evolution conformed nicely with the nineteenth century's ascendant culture of progress. Creation was not an act but a process, and the law governing the process assured that only the best adapted species would survive. Only favorable characteristics emerge and thrive in the race to adapt to an ever-changing natural environment. In 1871 Darwin published his *Descent of Man* in which he explicitly included human beings in the evolutionary paradigm. Darwin insisted that a creator God still had a pivotal role in the process of evolution. However, instead of a solitary act, Darwin's deity provided the physical matter and the form (natural selection) whereby all life emerged. The ability to adapt was the prerequisite for a species' survival over thousands of years.

Such an unconventional perspective on God was cold comfort to many Christians. Darwin's work sparked an intense controversy between traditionalists who accepted Scripture as infallible and members of the scientific community who insisted that the empirical data in favor of evolution were irrefutable. Critics of Darwin understood that the impersonal process of natural selection stood in bleak opposition to the biblical story of a loving God and to the belief that humankind was a special creation endowed with an immortal soul. Darwinism banished the supernatural and the mysterious from the creation narrative and in the process reconfirmed an argument, first introduced by Galileo in the early seventeenth century, that the Bible had no place in the arena of science. The drama of salvation now stood in stark opposition to uncaring natural processes and chance variations. If nature had no enduring order or design, then could one assume that there were universal rules in the social or political spheres? Could one continue to insist on the existence of a moral order that was applicable to all humans? "Best adapted" seemed to be a morally neutral term. Was there such a thing as fixed truth?

Herbert Spencer   One troubling response to these questions came from the British philosopher Herbert Spencer (1820–1903), who applied evolutionary theory to ethics. According to Spencer, competition and struggle were essential to progress, and those who rose to economic, political, and cultural predominance were justified in imposing their rule over the weak. Spencer coined the term ***survival of the fittest.***

Policymakers used it to limit state assistance to the poor at home and to oppress colonial peoples abroad. Helping those who had so clearly failed in a competitive environment, these "Social Darwinists" alleged, would undermine the best qualities of the species. Religious scruples about the plight of the poor had no place in a world where compassion became a synonym for cultural decay.

Friedrich Nietzsche and the Will to Power   Influenced by the new trends in biological thought, increasing numbers of European intellectuals began to question the primacy of rationality in human culture, focusing instead on the instinctive, emotional, and unreflective side of human conduct. Imperialist adventures certainly generated a large measure of unreflective and highly emotional jingoism. While some thinkers celebrated the creative potential of the irrational in the arts, religion, and mythology, others cautioned that these forces could easily overwhelm political life. In an increasingly democratic age, the potential for demagogues and unscrupulous politicians to play upon the fears, hopes, and ambitions of the electorate was immense.

The German philosopher Friedrich Nietzsche (1844–1900) was one of the most vehement critics of liberal culture, Christian morality, the ideology of progress, and the belief in reason. Nietzsche viewed mass democratic politics and parliamentary government with contempt. He claimed that the dominant middle-class values were decadent and sterile, committed to materialism and mediocrity. The popular assumption that rational thought was what distinguished human beings from animals, an assumption that could be traced back to the ancient Greeks, was to Nietzsche the grand lie. In fact, he was convinced that the excessive development of reason had led to the enfeeblement of the human species. In a hostile world lacking either divine order or creative purpose, Nietzsche discovered meaning in the simple struggle to create new values through the heroic cultivation of long-submerged instincts and unconscious striving. Since God was a fiction and Christianity was a "slave morality," eternal truths did not exist. Nietzsche was a destroyer of all conventional orthodoxies at the very moment of Europe's material primacy. Three decades after his death, Nazi ideologues distorted his theory of the heroic *Übermensch* (super-man) to advance their myth of the superior race in Aryan Germany.

☐●⊏ **Read** the **Document**

Friedrich Nietzsche, Beyond Good and Evil

on **MyHistoryLab.com**

Freud and the Unconscious   The Viennese physician Sigmund Freud (1856–1939) was an ardent supporter of the Enlightenment tradition. Like the *philosophes* of the eighteenth century, and unlike Nietzsche, he associated reason and science with the highest achievements of civilization. As a doctor who specialized in treating mental disorders, however, Freud's research led him to highlight the role of nonrational and destructive forces in people's lives. Nietzsche celebrated these primal qualities; Freud feared them and worked both to explain their origins and to offer a systematic clinical approach to controlling them. Since he was convinced that nonrational drives threatened civilization, Freud undertook his studies as part of a defense of reason in modern life.

The task before him was daunting because Freud conceded that reason did not regulate most of human behavior. Instead, powerful but little-understood instincts and subconscious drives motivated most decisions and actions. In 1900 he published a controversial book, *The Interpretation of Dreams,* in which he argued that dreams were specific expressions of unconscious desires that the rational, waking self struggles to suppress. By studying irrational phenomena like dreams, the scientist could better explain conscious behavior and help to treat neurotic illnesses. Freud's later work sought to describe the connections between the rational and irrational sides of the mind. He paid particular (and controversial) attention to the role of sexual drives as the strongest human impulse. He used the now famous terms *id* (for the primitive and irrational drives), *superego* (for the faculty that internalizes the moral rules of society), and *ego* (the mediating force) to explain commonplace behavior. According to Freud, within the mind the *ego* was engaged in a constant struggle to repress the destructive features of the *id* while helping the individual to internalize the moral code set by the dominant culture and embodied in the *superego.*

While he believed that the *id* was at odds with the requirements of civilized living, Freud also expressed deep concern that repressing the irrational side of the human personality contributed to mental disorders. Paradoxically, he also believed that human progress could only occur so long as self-denial and repression were effective. In the aftermath of World War I, Freud published *Civilization and Its Discontents* (1927), a brief but wide-ranging book that placed that horrific experience within the context of his broader psychological theory. Freud interpreted the unprecedented bloodletting of the war as a civilization-wide discharge of aggressive impulses that modern culture had sought to repress. Freud found no solution to humankind's dilemma in religious experience. Like Marx and Nietzsche before him, he dismissed religion as a neurotic manifestation of the immature mind, and he placed his trust in a naturalistic explanation of the universe.

Ironically, Freud's secularized picture of human nature, in which humanity's base instincts and desires must be controlled if civilization is to be preserved, had something in common with the early Christian perspective, where fallen men and women were incapable of obeying God's law and where sacrifice and struggle were essential to the human experience. Freud's most promising student, Carl

Sigmund Freud Freud's exploration of nonrational forces undermined the strength of the Enlightenment tradition in Western thought. Although he championed rationality, Freud alerted his readers to the existence and power of instinctive, aggressive, and amoral drives that could be controlled only through deliberate effort.

Jung (1875–1961), did not share his mentor's disdain for religious experience. Jung took issue with Freud's emphasis on the primacy of sexual drives in the formation of the personality and instead emphasized the role that collective memories, which he called archetypes, played in the development of the subconscious. Much to the chagrin of the rationalist Freud, Jung introduced a mystical element into psychoanalysis, legitimizing the role of religion in personality development.

Einstein and the New Physics

The Newtonian picture of the physical universe, where solid objects moved in absolute time and space irrespective of the observer and where humans could discover unchanging, mechanistic, physical laws, suggested the possibility that all of the secrets of nature might one day be discovered. Newton's contribution had inspired eighteenth-century thinkers to draw comparisons between the apparent order and rationality of the physical universe and the disorder and irrationality of Europe's social, religious, and political landscape. The Enlightenment hope for a society ordered by reason was in large measure impelled by the discovery of new truths about God's physical creation.

During the late nineteenth and early twentieth centuries, many of the Newtonian assumptions about physical matter were superceded by a second great revolution in physics; this one associated with the German-born Swiss theoretical physicist Albert Einstein (1879–1955). At the age of 26, while working as a clerk in the Swiss patent office, Einstein published his **"Special Theory of Relativity,"** which included the radical theory that absolute space and time were not fixed realities independent of human experience, as Newtonian physics had long assumed. Einstein demonstrated that there existed no absolute frame of reference in the universe, and that instead space, time, and motion were relative to one another and to the human observer. Probing beneath the surface of experienced reality, Einstein's work appeared to reinforce the antirationalist arguments current in other fields of research.

Einstein's subsequent research revealed the tremendous energy contained in simple matter. By showing that very small amounts of matter could be converted into enormous energy, Einstein broke with the conventional Newtonian treatment of matter and energy as independent quantities. Suddenly, the universe seemed unfamiliar and disorienting. The practical end product of Einstein's path-breaking theoretical work was just as unsettling. The development of the atomic bomb in the 1940s transformed international relations by virtue of the massive destructive power made available to humankind.

The Birth of the Social Sciences

The many tangible benefits of late nineteenth-century science and technology, especially their ability to improve the material quality of life, raised the prestige of those who engaged in scientific activities and encouraged other specialists to claim that their disciplines were also sciences. New and existing fields of study, including sociology, anthropology, economics, history, and archaeology, each proudly declared that it followed the same rigorous empirical and experimental standards as the biological and physical sciences.

In Germany the historical profession was given its specialist credentials early. Leopold von Ranke (1795–1886) argued that each period in the human past was "equidistant from eternity" and must be studied on its own terms; scholars had to reject popular legend and rely on archival source material whenever possible.

Dispassionate investigation of social processes also became popular. The word *sociology* was coined by August Comte (1798–1857), and by the end of the century, sociologists concerned themselves with the problem of creating and maintaining social order in a period of rapid urbanization and industrialization. The French scholar Emile Durkheim (1858–1917) was the most influential successor to Comte. Although a defender of modern civilization and an admirer of science, Durkheim warned that some of the main features of modern society, particularly competitive individualism and secularism, could trigger social disintegration. With the loss of communal identity and the weakening of collective spiritual beliefs, modern men and women faced a hostile world without the benefits of companionship. Because people lacked common values and social conventions and were encouraged by popular culture to raise their material expectations, Durkheim believed that a situation of anxiety, or *anomie,* had emerged at the core of advanced Western culture.

The leading social theorist at the turn of the century was the German Max Weber (1864–1920). He, too, applauded the achievements of rationalism in science, economic and political organization, law, and administration. However, the rationalization of life had unfortunately contributed to the erosion of life-sustaining customs and beliefs. The modern outlook dismissed religion as superstition, emotion as dangerous, and tradition as reactionary. Awash in material abundance, the modern citizen, immersed in the institutions and bureaucracies of his own creation, struggled to find meaning in life. Many sought to find that meaning in the supposed glories of overseas empire. Anticipating some of the darker developments of twentieth-century politics, Weber cautioned that in time of economic crisis, citizens in a society where happiness was equated with possessions would be quick to support charismatic leaders who promised wide-ranging and easy solutions to their plight.

Feminism and Inequality   The calls for equality between the sexes issued by Mary Wollstonecraft and Olympe de Gouges in the 1790s (see Chapter 16, "The Age of Enlightenment: Rationalism and Its Uses") had not been heeded during the first half of the nineteenth century. In the United States, a national women's suffrage movement met at Seneca Falls, New York, in 1848 and issued a *Declaration and Statement of Principles* echoing Thomas Jefferson's Declaration of Independence, but little came out of it. Some intellectual leaders did support the cause of civil equality for women, but these voices were out of the mainstream. In England, John Stuart Mill (1806–1873) published *The Subjection of Women* in 1867 and spoke on behalf of women's suffrage in Parliament, but the proposal was decisively rejected by his colleagues. Even Queen Victoria (r. 1837–1901) rebuked women who agitated for political rights.

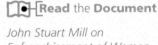
Read the Document

John Stuart Mill on Enfranchisement of Women

on **MyHistoryLab.com**

The old argument that women were not capable of responsible, rational conduct in the public sphere was strengthened by some of the conclusions of social science and especially by the proponents of Social Darwinism. Women's "nature," it was alleged, was emotional, irrational, unstable, and frivolous. Lacking self-control, women were more likely to make decisions on the basis of those dark irrational forces that adversely affected human life. Since rationality was the one fragile power keeping civilization on its current progressive path, any extension of civil and political rights to women was bound to end badly. Toward the end of the century, as feminists like Emmeline Pankhurst (1858–1928) in England began to engage in acts of civil disobedience, the evidence of women's essential irrationality seemed clear to opponents of equal rights. Reports of arrested feminist militants being force-fed by authorities after going on hunger strikes to protest their status not only shocked the public but in many cases confirmed antifemale prejudice.

Transformation in the Arts

As European states projected their power around the world in the form of territorial and commercial empires, important developments in the arts reflected the broader tension between the Enlightenment heritage and a more subjective and nonrational view of human nature. A general climate of restlessness, directness, and anxiety informed literature as well as the visual and performing arts. Authors and artists emerged as cultural leaders and respected critics; their ability to highlight the pressing issues of the day—poverty, urbanization, women's rights, empire—led Sigmund Freud to describe them as the first psychoanalysts.

Realism and Naturalism   Beginning in the second half of the nineteenth century, many artists and writers rejected the romantic style of expression and adopted a realistic idiom that reflected science and technology's fact-driven, experiential approach to truth. Authors investigated the gritty contours of city life, the personal and the private, the ordinary and the exceptional, in a manner that captured the complexity of living in a society where the forces of industrialization were invalidating traditional norms and values. Mary Ann Evans (1819–1880), who wrote under the name George Eliot in England; Emile Zola (1840–1902) in France; Leo Tolstoy (1828–1910) in Russia; and Henrik Ibsen (1828–1906) in Norway each created characters whose psychological development was detailed within the context of new social forces. In her novel *Middlemarch,* for example, Evans introduced a wide range of fascinating characters, from the idealistic and progressive medical doctor and his ambitious but insecure wife, to the hypocritical banker whose false piety and condescension are betrayed by the revelation of a youthful affair and his abandonment of his mistress and their child. Ibsen's best-known play, *A Doll's House,* detailed the psychological burdens imposed on a woman whose conventional middle-class husband refuses to acknowledge his wife's longing for an independent identity, which shockingly, she chooses anyway.

Modernism   Not surprisingly, the literary and artistic response to the uncertainties introduced by modern biology, physics, and psychology involved a sharp rejection of realism and a vigorous engagement with the subjective, the introspective, the irrational, and the abstract. Conventional literary and artistic forms were deemed inadequate to the task of exploring beneath the surface of rational appearances. Authors such as James Joyce (1882–1941), Thomas Mann (1875–1955), D. H. Lawrence (1885–1930), Virginia Woolf (1882–1941), and Franz Kafka (1883–1924) wrote about the inner psychological conflicts and antisocial penchants of men and women who rejected the conventions of bourgeois existence.

PEOPLE IN CONTEXT   Marie Curie and Modern Physics

Marie Sklodowska Curie (1867–1934) was born in Warsaw, Poland, to parents who were both employed as teachers. Her mother was a devout Catholic, but her father, a mathematics and physics instructor, was an agnostic freethinker. Marie, who shared her father's religious outlook, excelled in school as a child and embraced the dream of becoming a scientist at a time when few women had professional careers. This was especially true in Russian-dominated Poland. After working as a tutor and governess, Marie moved to Paris in 1891. At age 24, she began attending lectures at the Sorbonne, met a number of leading physicists there, and secured a post as laboratory assistant. In 1894, one year after taking her degree in physics, she met Pierre Curie (1859–1906), a shy and introverted man who shared Marie's passion for pure research in the natural sciences. They were married the following year.

Working together in a poorly equipped laboratory, the husband and wife team made a series of important discoveries in physics. In 1896 they discovered the highly radioactive elements polonium and radium, and in 1903 they shared a Nobel Prize in physics with Henri Becquerel (1852–1908) for their joint discovery of natural radioactivity. Although the money from the Nobel Prize freed them from financial worries, the resulting public attention disrupted their personal and professional lives. When World War I began in 1914, Marie Curie was busy establishing the Radium Institute of the University of Paris. She served as the Institute's first director, and during the war she worked on using X-rays to locate shrapnel and bullets so that soldiers might be operated on more effectively. She also pioneered the use of portable X-ray machines in vans to treat the wounded closer to the front.

Family life, including the birth of two daughters in 1897 and 1904, and the tragic death of her husband in an accident in 1906, did not inhibit Curie's professional career. Offered a pension, she refused to accept it, commenting that she was 38 and fully capable of earning a living. After Pierre's death, she was selected to fill his professorship at the Sorbonne. Curie was the first female to hold a faculty position at this leading research institution. In 1911 Curie was awarded a second

Marie and Pierre Curie   Despite the widespread sexism and anti-Semitism of her day, Marie Curie rose to prominence in physics and chemistry and is still the only person to win Nobel prizes in two separate scientific fields. She is pictured here with her husband, Pierre, who was also an outstanding scientist—the two were jointly awarded the Nobel Prize in 1903—but who died in a carriage accident in Paris three years later.

Nobel Prize, this time in chemistry, for her work on the isolation of pure radium. Just after receiving this unprecedented second prize, Curie was denied admission to France's prestigious Academy of Science. Sexism, anti-Semitism, and disdain for foreigners outweighed the importance of her remarkable scientific work in the eyes of many of her male colleagues. The right-wing press suggested that although Curie was from a Catholic household, her father's name (Sklodowska) suggested that she might be of Jewish origin. The rejection by the Academy deeply wounded Curie.

Exposed to high degrees of radiation during her career, Marie Curie died of leukemia at age 67. She had spent her professional life committed to the belief that science must help lessen human suffering. In 1995 the French government moved the remains of Marie and Pierre Curie to the famous Pantheon mausoleum in Paris. ∎

QUESTION: What conventions did Curie break during her career?

Major Works of the Nineteenth and Early Twentieth Centuries

1859	Charles Darwin, *On the Origin of Species by Means of Natural Selection*
1867	John Stuart Mill, *The Subjection of Women*
1871	Charles Darwin, *Descent of Man*
1878	Leo Tolstoy, *Anna Karenina*
1879	Henrik Ibsen, *A Doll's House*
1886	Friedrich Nietzsche, *Beyond Good and Evil*
1900	Sigmund Freud, *The Interpretation of Dreams*
1905	Albert Einstein, "On the Electrodynamics of Moving Bodies"
1925	Franz Kafka, *The Trial*
1928	D. H. Lawrence, *Lady Chatterley's Lover*

A new frankness about the role of sex, a willingness to highlight the power of the instinctive and the primitive, and a penchant for detailing the everyday and often sordid aspects of human life in a world of disorder all distinguished the modern mood in literature.

Modern Art and Music   Since the Renaissance, leading artists endorsed the view that art should imitate the world as the senses perceive it. Rules of perspective and proportion set the parameters of what was judged worthy of serious consideration. The finest art would follow a certain structure and attempt to mirror nature, and those who strayed from convention were generally dismissed as insubordinate hacks. Around the middle of the nineteenth century, the French artist Gustave Courbet (1819–1877) inaugurated the Realist movement in landscape and genre painting. Joined by the

American Thomas Eakins (1844–1916) and the Englishman Ford Madox Brown (1821–1893), the realists painted what they saw, no matter how appealing or distasteful. Painting the laboring classes instead of the elite, urban slums and factories instead of country estates, the actual conditions of industrial life became the focus of what deserved the attention of the artist.

Some mid-century artists believed that reality was more complex than merely representational. In particular, a group of painters known as **Impressionists** began to turn away from the deliberate representational form and experiment with personal interpretations, especially the first glance, or "impression," of external reality. Parallel with the development of modern photography, many artists cast off their previous interest in recreating mere surface images. Edouard Manet (1832–1883), Edgar Degas (1834–1917), Claude Monet (1840–1926), and Pierre Auguste Renoir (1841–1919) produced works that mediated between a fascination with nature and a desire to record. Particularly in their treatment of light and form, the Impressionists conveyed a sense of the elusiveness of sensory reality. By the 1890s, post-Impressionist artists like Paul Cézanne (1839–1906) and Vincent van Gogh (1853–1890) worked to portray inner feelings and personal perspectives of reality, largely without regard to the tastes of the public or private patrons.

Vincent Van Gogh   *The Night Café* is characteristic of Van Gogh's work in its brilliant and turbulent use of colors. Like many of his late paintings, *The Night Café* leaves the viewer unsettled because of its expressionistic and vaguely nightmarish qualities. *Vincent van Gogh (1853–1890), Night Cafe (Le Café de nuit). 1888. Oil on canvas, 28 1/2 36 1/4 in. 1961. 18.34. Yale University Art Gallery, New Haven, Connecticut/Art Resource, NY*

Modernist artists of the early twentieth century reconstructed their discipline by legitimizing the unconventional and the introspective. Reality was no longer confined within the boundaries of sense experience and rational understanding. **Modernism** heralded the advent of multiple realities, each of which had to be approached in a highly individualistic and personal fashion. The Modernist artist was concerned primarily with the process of expression, the aesthetic experience, and only marginally with the final outcome or outside reality. Similarly, since the finished product no longer depicted a fixed reality, the viewer was invited to share in the highly personal process of interpretation. Reason, order, and clarity were replaced by ambiguity, tension, lack of form, and an appeal to the subconscious. For the modernist, the wellspring of creativity, be it in the artist or the viewer, no longer resided in the rational and conscious mind. With the birth of Cubism just before World War I, artists led by Pablo Picasso (1881–1973) struggled to represent the multiple realities of modern existence on a single canvas.

The same desire to communicate multiple realities inspired the French composer Claude Debussy (1862–1918), who was influenced by the exotic music of Bali in Indonesia when he heard it performed at the Paris Exposition of 1889. His *Prelude to "The Afternoon of a Faun"* (1894) combined a dreamlike melody with innovative chords. The Austrian composer Arnold Schoenberg (1874–1951) and his Russian counterpart Igor Stravinsky (1882–1971) were even bolder. Schoenberg's music employed dissonant chords, abandoning the traditional technique of organizing tones around a musical key and instead treating all 12 notes equally. Stravinsky's ballet *The Rite of Spring* (1913) incorporated a variety of musical styles, including jazz rhythms, to produce a highly dissonant composition that deals with the disturbing theme of primitive Slavonic peoples engaged in human sacrifice. Just as many painters and sculptors of the early twentieth century turned for fresh artistic ideas to the customs and practices of peoples who had avoided modernization, composers sought a new direction in what was termed **primitivism.** Audiences were sometimes outraged. When *The Rite of Spring* was first performed in Paris, the highly discordant and jarring music elicited catcalls, shouts, and boos from members of the audience. The police were called in to restore order, and the composer was obliged to depart through a backstage window. The public was ill-prepared for such a radical challenge to the culture of order, reason, progress, and power that Europeans had projected around the world during the previous quarter century.

KEY
QUESTION
REVISITED

How does the projection of power reflect wider cultural values?

By 1914, Europe's rapidly expanding population could confidently claim that the West was the dominant global civilization. There was a widespread popular conviction, held most strongly by the middle class, that the great problems of life could and would be successfully addressed. Famine, sickness, ignorance, underemployment, poverty, war—the many ills that had been constants of the human experience for centuries—would be removed with the help of highly educated specialists in education, medicine, sociology, psychology, administration, and politics. More troublesome developments in theoretical science, philosophy, and the arts did not alter the generally confident outlook of most Europeans. Equating science with the benefits of technology, they went about the business of educating themselves, seeking better careers, and consuming new industrial products without giving much thought to the implications of evolutionary theory in biology, Freudian psychology, relativity theory in physics, or modernist art. Even traditional religious forms, while under assault, continued to appeal to millions of Europeans.

Most people maintained their belief in the values and goals of the Enlightenment, including responsible, representative government, the rule of law, protection of individual liberties, religious freedom, the sanctity of property, and a social and economic order responsive to merit and talent.

Overseas empire was commonly justified as the extension of these "universal" values to the peoples who inhabited less-developed areas of the world. At the height of empire, few Europeans questioned the propriety of their nation's overseas conquests; the link between progress and control over non-Western peoples was considered self-evident. Most of the approximately 60 million Europeans who migrated overseas during the nineteenth and early twentieth centuries would have endorsed the claim by Cecil Rhodes respecting the backwardness of indigenous peoples. In the period between 1870 and 1914, the Europeanization of the global community was intimately connected with the gospel of unlimited progress, with a faith in the universality of Western ideas, even when those ideas legitimized the subjection of non-Western peoples.

Key Terms

new imperialism, *p. 620*   Boxer Rebellion, *p. 628*   survival of the fittest, *p. 633*
racism, *p. 622*   Meiji Restoration, *p. 630*   Modernism, *p. 642*

Activities

1. Why did a new European race for imperial possessions begin during the last quarter of the nineteenth century?

2. Explain how traditional elites and conservative political leaders used nationalism to strengthen their hold on power after 1850.

3. How did the new physics undermine the Newtonian picture of the universe?

4. What was the nature of Nietzsche's relationship with the Enlightenment tradition?

5. Does Freud's assessment of human rationality have any bearing on Europe's treatment of non-Western peoples?

6. Describe how views on the role of women in society reflected changing cultural norms.

7. What were the principal goals of Modernist art and how did they differ from earlier aesthetic standards?

Further Reading

David Abernethy, *The Dynamics of Global Dominance: European Overseas Empires, 1415–1980* (2000), a comprehensive survey.

J. Burrow, *The Crisis of Reason: European Thought, 1848–1914* (2002), a study of major intellectual trends.

Peter Bowler, *Evolution: The History of an Idea* (2003), a solid introduction.

Peter Gay, *Freud: A Life for Our Time* (1998), a standard biography by a leading scholar of the period.

Joseph Conrad, *Heart of Darkness* (1999), a modern edition of a classic fictional exploration of the effects of imperialism on Europeans.

MyHistoryLab Connections

Visit **MyHistoryLab.com** *for a customized Study Plan that will help you build your knowledge of* Global Empire and European Culture.

Questions for Analysis

1. How does Cecil Rhodes justify British imperialism?

▢●⌐Read the Document Cecil Rhodes, "Confession of Faith," p. 619

2. How did the notion of imperialism evolve during the time span between the Roman Empire and the early twentieth century?

◉⌐Watch the Video Imperialism, p. 623

3. How did the French justify the colonization of Morocco?

◉⌐View the Closer Look The French in Morocco, p. 624

4. What are the origins of what is known as the new imperialism of the late nineteenth century?

◉⌐Watch the Video The Origins of Modern Imperialism and Colonialism, p. 624

5. What did Mill find compelling about the "Women's Rights Convention" and what concerned him about the proceedings?

▢●⌐Read the Document John Stuart Mill on Enfranchisement of Women, p. 637

Other Resources from This Chapter

▢●⌐Read the Document *Imperialism and the White Man's Burden* (1899), Rudyard Kipling, p. 621

▢●⌐Read the Document Karl Pearson, "Social Darwinism and Imperialism," p. 622

PART SEVEN

Europe in Crisis:
1914–1945

Pablo Picasso, *Guernica* (1937). Oil on canvas, 350 × 782 cm. Museo Nacional Centro de Arte Reina Sofia, Madrid, Spain. © *2004 Estate of Pablo Picasso/Artists Rights Society (ARS), New York. John Bigelow Taylor/Art Resource, NY*

No one alive in Europe in the summer of 1914 had ever experienced a general war involving multiple states with well-equipped and well-trained armies. The last time the continent had been engulfed by conflict on multiple fronts was during the Napoleonic era. There had been a number of regional wars, but the evidence seemed to suggest that modern military conflict involved rapid troop movements, limited casualties, and quick resolution. World War I shattered each of these misconceptions. Plunging from the pinnacle of global power to the depths of financial insolvency and psychological self-doubt, Western Europe failed to find a durable solution to the problem of international rivalry.

A troubled interregnum of 20 years followed the conclusion of World War I and the start of another, more deadly, global conflagration. The Western democracies, especially Britain and France, appeared incapable of responding to the challenge of fascism in Italy and Germany or to the rise of communism in the Soviet Union. The United States retreated into isolationism during the 1920s and 1930s. Those states that repudiated the Enlightenment tradition of responsible, constitutional government, individual rights, and free expression boldly proclaimed the dawn of a new age where race and class were the benchmarks of power.

Between 1939 and 1945, another world war claimed the lives of over 50 million people, combatants and noncombatants alike, around the globe. The unrivaled barbarism of the Jewish Holocaust, together with the inhumanity exhibited by Japanese occupying forces in the Pacific theater, suggested to many in the West that the Enlightenment faith in human rationality had been misplaced. At the end of the war, two great ideological power blocs emerged, one led by the United States and the other dominated by the brutal Stalin regime in the Soviet Union. Western Europe, with its economic base in tatters and its populations wearied by a half-century of distrust and war, surrendered its global primacy in political affairs.

T I M E L I N E

	ENVIRONMENT AND TECHNOLOGY	SOCIETY AND CULTURE	POLITICS
1914	Poison gas, airplanes, and tanks employed in war (1914–1918)	European population reaches 450 million (1914) Spengler, *Decline of the West* (1918)	Start of trench warfare (1914)
	Bauhaus school founded (1919)	Jazz age in America (1920s)	United States enters World War I; Bolshevik Revolution in Russia (1917)
	First radio broadcast station opens in France (1920)	Rampant inflation in Germany (1923)	Russian civil war (1918–1921)
	Electronic television broadcast begins; penicillin discovered (1928)	General strike in Britain (1926) Women secure franchise in Britain (1928) Collectivization of Soviet agriculture begins (1928) Great Depression begins (1929)	Treaty of Versailles (1919) Mussolini's "march on Rome" (1922) Stalin consolidates power (1927) Japan invades Manchuria (1931)
1930	Radar technology developed (1935)	Stalin's purges begin (1934) Picasso, *Guernica* (1937)	Hitler becomes chancellor (1933) Civil war in Spain (1936–1939) World War II begins (1939)
1940	Jet engine invented (1941)	Holocaust (1941–1945)	Battle of Britain (1940) Germans invade Soviet Union; Pearl Harbor attacked (1941) Atomic bombs dropped on Hiroshima and Nagasaki (1945)

WOMEN OF BRITAIN SAY – "GO!"

Recruitment Poster When orders for mobilization went up on walls and were broadcast in newspapers across Europe in the summer of 1914, a generation of young men lined up for battle. They went in high spirits, cheered on by their mothers, unaware of the horrors they were about to face.

22

World War I: The End of Enlightenment

 **Hear the Audio** Chapter 22 at MyHistoryLab.com

LEARNING OBJECTIVES

How did Europe's system of alliances increase the possibility of major military conflict? • How did trench warfare differ from anything soldiers faced in earlier conflicts? • What role did colonial empires play in the World War I? • What was the significance of America's entry into World War I? • How did World War I affect the lives of civilians on the home front? • What were the principal factors behind the triumph of Bolshevism in Russia in 1917? • What were the main challenges facing the victorious powers after World War I?

If in some smothering dreams, you too could pace
Behind the wagon that we flung him in,
And watch the white eyes writhing in his face,
His hanging face, like a devil sick of sin . . .
My friend, you would not tell with such high zest
To children ardent for some desperate glory,
The old Lie: Dulce et decorum est
Pro patria mori (it is sweet and proper to die for one's country)

—Wilfred Owen

KEY QUESTION

Are nation-states inherently adversarial?

The British poet and officer Wilfred Owen (1893–1918) died on the battlefield just a few hours before the armistice ending World War I was signed. Like many young men, Owen had volunteered for military service out of a deep sense of patriotism and commitment to the ideals of the British Empire. When the war began in August 1914, few of the combatants on either side expected it to last more than a few months. Most planned to be home by Christmas, having defeated the enemy in rapid order thanks to the employment of the latest military technology. Their predictions were based on solid empirical evidence. No general European war had been fought for over a century, and those conflicts that had taken place were brief and involved few casualties. There had not been a military clash in Europe between two major powers since 1870, when a better-trained and better-equipped German force triumphed over France in less than six months.

Many strident European nationalists, encouraged by the easy successes of colonial wars, celebrated military conflict as a heroic, purifying, and liberating experience. They believed that the excitement, emotional intensity, and drama of the battlefield would strengthen the national community and provide a sense of purpose to factory workers, office clerks, and students who found little pleasure or meaning in their dull, repetitive civilian tasks. In the days immediately after the outbreak of World War I, men eagerly lined up at recruiting stations, young soldiers were applauded as they paraded on the way to the front, and serious newspapers praised the renewed sense of national unity and vigor that appeared to affect entire populations. Most socialist politicians abandoned the rhetoric of international working-class solidarity and joined the outpouring of support for the sacred nation-state.

There was an eagerness for war in 1914. The same martial spirit and thirst for glory that gripped the common people of Britain, France, Germany, Austria-Hungary, and Russia also captured the imaginations of Europe's intellectuals, including such well-known scholars as Sigmund Freud. Here was an opportunity to put an end to the complacency of bourgeois life with its focus on getting and spending. The triumph of the nation-state would restore meaning and a sense of collective purpose to modern civilization. Those few voices opposed to the war were treated harshly by their countrymen. In Britain, for example, Ramsey MacDonald (1866–1937) resigned his leadership of the Labour Party in opposition to the war, the plays of pacifist George Bernard Shaw (1856–1950) were boycotted, and the philosopher Bertrand Russell (1872–1970) was jailed. The summer and fall of 1914 were cruel seasons for those who cautioned restraint.

The high expectations were dispelled within a few months. Hopes of rapid victory proved illusory as the anticipated war of movement degenerated into a stalemated and gruesome campaign of attrition. New military technology—machine guns, poison gas, high explosives—magnified the carnage. Military leadership proved to be uninventive and undistinguished, while the bellicose and punitive rhetoric of popularly elected politicians mitigated against diplomatic initiatives and compromise. As the conflict dragged on, disillusionment and despair replaced enthusiasm. Casualty rates were so high that by 1916, the British government was obliged to institute military conscription for the first time in British history to maintain force levels on the continent. The following year French troops mutinied, refusing to follow senseless orders to advance to their deaths across "no-man's land" on the Western Front.

The war quickly engaged Europe's colonies in Africa and Asia, involved combat on land and sea, terrorized civilian populations, and led to massive physical destruction in wide stretches of Western and eastern Europe. By the end of 1917, tsarist Russia had been destroyed, and the American republic had been drawn into the conflagration. European civilization, at the moment of its apogee, decisively forfeited its global primacy in what was akin to a fratricidal civil war. The nation-states of Europe had failed the test of mutual accommodation. ▪

The Alliance System

When a young Serbian terrorist named Gavrilo Princip (1895–1918) assassinated the heir to the throne of Austria-Hungary on June 28, 1914, he also set off a diplomatic crisis in each of Europe's major capitals. Archduke Francis Ferdinand (1863–1914) and his wife were on an official state visit to Sarajevo when they were murdered, and in response the imperial authorities in Vienna decided that now was the moment to crush the Serbian-inspired, pan-Slav separatist movement in Bosnia. The provinces of

Bosnia and Herzegovina, nominally part of the Ottoman Empire, had been administered by the Austrians since 1878, and in 1908 they were officially annexed by the multinational Austrian Empire. Since much of the population in these areas were Eastern Orthodox in religion and were ethnically related to the Serbs, the annexation caused consternation in Belgrade, the capital of independent Serbia. A strong nationalist movement had emerged in Serbia during a long and ultimately successful struggle for independence from the Ottoman Empire. Once independence was achieved, Serbia turned its nationalist energies against the Austrians. The Serbs dreamed of a greater union of all south Slavs, including the over seven million who lived under Austrian rule.

Read the **Document**

The Murder of Archduke Franz Ferdinand at Sarajevo (1914), Borijove Jevtic

on **MyHistoryLab.com**

View the **Map**

Linguistic Groups in Austria-Hungary

on **MyHistoryLab.com**

Still, the assassination of Francis Ferdinand need not have led to a general European war. Austrian authorities had been faced with violent secession movements in the past, but they had always been able to address the problem through a combination of military force, political compromise, and the co-option of nationalist leaders. Unfortunately, the Serbian threat had wider international implications. In particular, the Russians had long portrayed themselves as the protectors of their Serb co-religionists. In 1908 Tsar Nicholas II's (r. 1894–1917) government had concluded an informal arrangement with Austria whereby Russia would acquiesce in the Austrian plan to annex Bosnia and Herzegovina in return for Austrian support for Russia's bid to secure naval

Assassination of Archduke Franz Ferdinand, June 28, 1914 Shortly before this photograph was taken the Austrian archduke and his wife were assassinated by members of a secretive Serbian nationalist group, indirectly sparking the World War I. Here, one of the assailants is captured by police.

access from the Black Sea to the Mediterranean through the Ottoman-controlled Dardanelles (adjacent to Istanbul). Austria did annex the provinces, but Britain and France strenuously objected to a Russian fleet in the Mediterranean, and Tsar Nicholas was forced to back down. It was the latest in a string of diplomatic and military humiliations that the Russians had suffered since their defeat by Japan in 1905, and as a result the Russian government was in no mood in 1914 to allow Austria to bully Serbia.

The Triple Alliance and Triple Entente   Otto von Bismarck (1815–1898) had pursued a nonaggressive foreign policy in Europe after Germany was unified in 1871. To solidify his country's position in Europe and prevent an attack by France, Bismarck forged a defensive **Triple Alliance** in the 1880s with Austria-Hungary and Italy. He also concluded a nonaggression pact with Russia, but this was allowed to expire in 1890 after Bismarck left office. Kaiser William II (r. 1888–1918) disagreed with Bismarck's cautious policy on the continent. The Triple Alliance remained in force, but, with strong encouragement from German nationalists, the kaiser began an ambitious naval-building program that was designed to rival the British fleet. William also expanded the size of the German army and inaugurated an expansionist colonial policy. When combined with its industrial, technical, and educational accomplishments, Germany's newly assertive posture on the international front deeply troubled policymakers in Britain, France, and Russia.

In 1893, five years after William assumed the throne and three years after he dismissed Bismarck, Russia and France entered into their own defensive alliance. In 1904, Britain resolved its outstanding differences with France over colonial issues and concluded a defensive understanding, the *Entente Cordiale.* The pact was tested by the German emperor at an international conference held in Algeciras, Spain, in 1906 to decide the fate of Morocco, over which the French were gradually establishing a protectorate. Kaiser William announced that Germany favored independence for Morocco, but only Austria supported its German ally. Britain, Russia, Spain, the United States, and even Italy, which was also still formally a German ally, sided with France. In the aftermath of the conference, the British and French military staffs began to discuss how their forces would cooperate if Germany attacked.

In 1907 the French acted as intermediaries to get Britain and Russia to settle their competing imperial claims in Afghanistan, Tibet, and Persia. The system of alliances that was now in place seemed to represent an important step toward ensuring peace in Europe. No single power would be reckless enough to provoke another state, it was assumed, because any attack could mean war against an entire military partnership. Each country's professional diplomatic corps was charged with settling international disputes. Failing this, the direct intervention of Europe's monarchs, some of whom were relations, would prevent the inconceivable from happening. Rival nation-states appeared capable of establishing formal and adequate mechanisms for avoiding war.

The Balkan Tinderbox   A second Moroccan Crisis occurred in 1911 when a German gunboat arrived in the Moroccan port of Agadir, just as the French were quashing a rebellion. The British feared that the kaiser was seeking to secure a Mediterranean port for Germany's growing navy. The Germans eventually recognized French claims to Morocco, but the dispute bolstered the view in Britain that its security was best served by forging even closer military ties with France. For its part,

Germany, recognizing that it could no longer count on Italian support, became even more committed to the support of its one sure ally, Austria-Hungary. Austria's annexation of Bosnia and Herzegovina in 1908 had infuriated Serbian nationalists, while in Vienna key Austrian officials, supported by their German allies, debated strategies for ending Serbian agitation once and for all. In 1912 Serbia joined with Greece, Bulgaria, and Montenegro in a war against the Ottoman Turks that all but expelled the Turks from the Balkans. For a brief moment, the victorious Serbs gained coveted access to the Adriatic coastline, but Austria (with German backing) forced them to surrender this territory and to permit the formation of the independent state of Albania in 1913. After this last Serbian indignity, the Russians concluded that they could not afford to lose any more credibility in the eyes of their Orthodox "little brothers" in Serbia.

Final Breakdown   In the aftermath of this tense situation, the heir presumptive to the Austrian throne made his fateful trip to Sarajevo. Francis Ferdinand, whose wife was a Czech countess, was genuinely interested in seeking political compromise with the empire's Slavic subjects, and his assassination guaranteed that the voice of moderation would no longer prevail in Vienna. The Serbian newspapers reported the murder with satisfaction, and there is evidence that the Serbian government was complicit in the act. With full backing from its German ally, Austria presented Serbia with an ultimatum that included a demand that Austrian authorities conduct an investigation, on Serbian soil, into the murder. The Serbians, afraid of what the Austrians might discover, accepted the other parts of the ultimatum but rejected this last demand as a violation of the rights of a sovereign nation, and Russia supported this interpretation. The Austrian army was then mobilized for action, and on July 28, 1914, the multinational Habsburg Empire declared war on Serbia.

Two days later, Russia began mobilizing its forces. Since most statesmen interpreted full mobilization to be an act of war, Germany sent Russia a 12-hour ultimatum demanding immediate demobilization. When this was ignored, Germany mobilized and formally declared war on Russia on August 1. It was an enormous gamble, but the German army's general staff believed it was best to fight now rather than to wait for the forces of Slavic nationalism to undermine the integrity of the Austrian Empire, Germany's one reliable ally in Europe. Within 48 hours, the Germans also declared war on France, convinced that the French would honor their pact with Russia and anxious to implement a detailed plan for a two-front war that the German army had drawn up years earlier. The defensive alliance systems, rather than preventing war, actually ensured that a regional conflict would escalate into a continent-wide catastrophe. The job of coordinating the movement of men and massive amounts of material via railway networks required strict adherence to preestablished timetables. Any last minute alterations or changes of plan could spell disaster. In the five weeks between the assassination of Francis Ferdinand and the start of war on August 4, military planners on both sides resisted appeals for delay or contingency planning.

The Experience of Modern War

Into the Abyss   Germany's war plan, developed by Count Alfred von Schlieffen (1833–1913) while he was chief of the German general staff, was a desperate gamble to deal with the problems of having to fight a two-front war against France in the west

View the **Map**

Map Discovery: The
Schlieffen Plan and France's
Plan XVII

on **MyHistoryLab.com**

Watch the **Video**

The Outbreak of World War I

on **MyHistoryLab.com**

and Russia in the east. The plan envisioned a quick knock-out of France by an invasion through neutral Belgium and Luxembourg, followed by a rapid transfer of troops via railway to the eastern front to rebuff the enormous but slow-moving Russian army. Britain had pledged to guarantee Belgian neutrality in a treaty of 1839, and as German troops rolled through Belgium en route to France during the first three days of August 1914, the British were quick to respond. They entered the war against Germany on August 4, confident of victory and believing that Kaiser William II and his closest military advisors were solely to blame for the conflict. Only the British Foreign Secretary, Sir Edward Grey (1862–1933), appeared to recognize the gravity of what was about to occur. "The lights are going out all over Europe," he commented, "and we shall not see them lit again in our lifetime."

Stalemate in the West   The first few weeks of combat in the Western theater seemed to confirm the predictions of those who had anticipated a short war of movement. The Germans were able to outflank most French defenses by invading from the northeast through Belgium. Their highly mobile troops moved rapidly into French territory, reaching the Marne River, within 40 miles of Paris, during the first month of fighting. The **Schlieffen Plan** called for German troops to envelop the French defensive forces by sweeping around Paris and attacking the French armies from the rear. At the bloody week-long Battle of the Marne, however, the French, with the assistance of a small British expeditionary force, stopped the German advance and forced the Germans to retreat. In the following weeks, each side desperately tried to outflank the other to secure the ports along the English Channel in what scholars refer to as "the race to the sea." The war now entered an unanticipated phase on the Western Front. Each side began constructing a vast network of defensive trenches stretching from Belgium's North Sea coastline across northern France to the Swiss border in the south. For 400 miles the trench lines snaked their way across devastated countryside. Between the opposing trenches stood nests of barbed wire, shattered trees, and churned up farms. Heavy artillery, poison gas, land mines, and machine guns guaranteed that any assault across this **"no man's land"** would result in heavy casualties. During the first four months of fighting, 700,000 German, 850,000 French, and 90,000 British troops were either killed or wounded. Again and again over the next four years, however, unimaginative military leaders on both sides disregarded the deadly fact of defensive superiority and sent tens of thousands of men "over the top" of the trenches in repeated efforts to break through the enemy's lines and reignite the war of movement. Most of the troops never returned to the filth and squalor of their defensive positions, having been mowed down by the efficient weaponry of the modern age. The average life expectancy for junior officers who had to lead these attacks was just two months (see Map 22–1).

View the **Closer Look**

The Development of the
Armored Tank

on **MyHistoryLab.com**

Read the **Document**

François Carlotti, from
"World War I: A Frenchman's
Recollections"

on **MyHistoryLab.com**

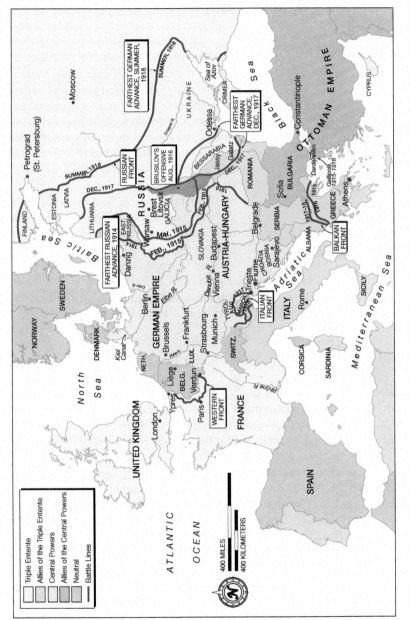

MAP 22-1 World War I in Europe The Central Powers were obligated to fight on two fronts after the failure of the Schlieffen Plan in August 1914. Important battles took place across the globe, but the major theater remained in Europe throughout four years of conflict.

QUESTION: Which nation suffered the greatest physical destruction on the Western Front?

The Experience of the Trenches   The stalemate on the Western Front led to four years of trench warfare. Conditions in the trenches were extremely difficult. During long stretches of inactivity, soldiers battled cold, wet, the smell of decaying bodies, and the fear of imminent death from enemy shelling.

The psychological strain imposed by life in the trenches was enormous. Months of inactivity amid wounded and dying men, the smell of human and animal excrement and decaying flesh, the cold damp climate, the always expanding rat and lice population, and the sound of heavy bombardments and the cries of the wounded stranded in no man's land all combined to undermine morale. Within one year of the start of the war, the dreams of heroic combat and national glory were dead. The unexpected war of attrition in the heart of Western Europe, where lines of advance were measured in feet and where casualties were counted in hundreds of thousands, contributed to an atmosphere in which cynicism and despair replaced idealism and courage. "War is hell," wrote Siegfried Sassoon (1886–1967) from the trenches, "and those who institute it are criminals."

Verdun and the Somme   After almost two years of fruitless combat, German commanders decided in February 1916 to concentrate their destructive might against the defenses around the historic French city of Verdun. The plan was simple in its brutality. The Germans expected the French to defend this fortress city to the end. By inflicting massive casualties on the defenders of Verdun, the Germans hoped to break France's will to fight. The French commander, Henri Petain (1856–1951), became a national hero for his success in resisting repeated assaults, but the human cost was astronomical. Before the Germans abandoned the assault in December 1916, over one million German and French combatants were either killed or wounded at Verdun. To help the French, the British opened their own offensive against the Germans at the Somme River in northeastern France in July 1916. The assault from the trenches was preceded by a week-long bombardment of the German lines by heavy artillery. This preparatory "softening up" was a complete failure. On the first day of the attack, 60,000 British soldiers were either killed or wounded as they crossed "no man's land" into a hail of German machine gun fire. The battle and the butchery continued at the Somme until November, but neither side capitulated. The

▶ Read the Document

British Soldiers on the Battle of the Somme

on **MyHistoryLab.com**

British assault at Passchendaele in Flanders during the summer and fall of 1917 followed a similar frontal approach, with disturbingly similar results—this time

300,000 casualties. That same year the French commander General Robert Nivelle (1856–1924) ordered yet another massive assault into the heavily defended German lines. On this occasion the Germans inflicted almost 200,000 casualties on the French over a 10-day period. Mutinies ensued in almost one-half of the French divisions on the front. Thousands of soldiers were eventually court-martialed for refusing to obey orders, but subsequent commanders agreed to forego any future frontal assaults from the trenches.

The Eastern Front and Europe's Empire

One reason the Schlieffen Plan faltered in August 1914 was that the German High Command had redeployed 100,000 troops (four divisions) to the east at a critical moment in the Western campaign. The redeployment was in response to Russia's invasion of East Prussia and Austrian Galicia. The Germans were able to defeat the enemy at the Battles of Tannenberg and Masurian Lakes, destroying the Russian Second Army and capturing 100,000 Russian soldiers. During the next year the kaiser's forces pushed some 200 miles into Russia's Baltic and Polish territories, inflicting almost two million casualties before the end of 1915 and gaining control over 30 percent of Russia's key industries and 20 percent of its population.

In the Balkans, the Austrian assault against Serbia was unsuccessful. A battle-hardened Serbian army of 350,000 men forced the Austrians onto the defensive within the first two weeks of fighting. The Germans were obliged to come to the assistance of their ill-prepared allies. After intense fighting, a combined Austrian, Bulgarian, and German force finally eliminated Serbia from the war in October 1915. Ottoman Turkey joined Austria and Germany (now called the Central Powers) in 1914 and repulsed an Anglo-French expeditionary force that attempted an ill-prepared landing at **Gallipoli** near the Dardanelles. This ill-fated amphibious campaign, planned by Britain's naval chief, Winston Churchill (1874–1965), was designed to break the deadlock on the Western Front by knocking the Turks out of the war and opening up the supply lines to Russia.

Secret Treaties and Broken Promises   After the humiliation of Gallipoli, the British led an effort to arouse Arabs in the Middle East against the Ottoman sultan in return for British assistance in creating an Arab state under the prince of Mecca, Emir Hussein (1853–1931). British forces based in Egypt with Arab troops under the leadership of T. E. Lawrence (1888–1935), "Lawrence of Arabia," gradually pushed back the Turks. Jerusalem fell in 1917 and Damascus in 1918. At the same time that British authorities were making promises to the Arabs, they were also offering assurances to the World Zionist Organization and to the approximately 60,000 Jewish settlers in Palestine. The 1917 **Balfour Declaration** supported Zionist aspirations for the creation of an independent Jewish homeland in Palestine—so long as it did not interfere with existing Palestinian civil and religious claims. These contradictory commitments resulted in serious problems for British authorities during the 1920s and 1930s.

Read the **Document**

The Balfour Declaration, 1917

on **MyHistoryLab.com**

Italy joined the Allied effort in 1915 after receiving secret promises of Austrian territory. While Italian troops fared poorly against their outnumbered Austrian and German opponents, combat in northern Italy did draw precious German resources away from the Western front. For their part, the Germans attempted to distract British forces by appealing to nationalist sentiments in British-controlled Ireland, to Poles in Russian-dominated Poland, and to Muslims in Egypt and India. A rebellion against British rule in Ireland during Easter week 1916 was put down with dispatch, but it increased London's anxiety about the security of its colonial holdings elsewhere. In the Far East, the Japanese, who had been Britain's ally since 1902, captured German colonies in China and the South Pacific.

The Allies relied heavily on support from their colonial (and former colonial) subjects. More than one million Indians, 640,000 Canadians, 330,000 Australians, and 100,000 New Zealand troops fought alongside the British, while hundreds of thousands of Algerians, Indochinese, and black African soldiers from France's colonies served on the Western front. In the aftermath of the war, many of these colonial peoples demanded independence. The war shook European claims to superiority, and colonial leaders based their demands for freedom on the principle of national self-determination first articulated by American President Woodrow Wilson.

India and Britain's Need   India's experience in World War I provided a good illustration of the Wilsonian principle in action. When the British declared war against Germany on August 4, 1914, the vast Indian subcontinent, home to over 300 million people and source of enormous material wealth, immediately became embroiled in the struggle. Four years earlier, the King-Emperor George V (r. 1910–1936) presided over an imperial *durbar* (reception) in the new capital at Delhi. Every ruling prince of India was obliged to pay his respects to the newly crowned imperial master. Now, without their consent, the Indians were being asked to contribute their blood and treasure to a war effort that seemed both distant and irrelevant to India itself. Remarkably, most Indian nationalist politicians eagerly supported the British cause, while leaders of the Congress movement firmly believed that cooperation in Britain's hour of need would translate into more freedom for India once the war was concluded. Mohandas Gandhi (1870–1948) organized a field ambulance training corps for use in the war effort. The Indian Viceroy, Lord Hardinge (1858–1944), portrayed the conflict as a global struggle between freedom and slavery. Indians naturally hoped for an extension of the former in the subcontinent once the war was over.

The first Indian expeditionary force left the port city of Karachi (now in Pakistan) for the Western Front on August 24, 1914, reaching Marseilles in southern France on September 26. The troops immediately joined their British and French counterparts in the struggle to rebuff the initial German assault. Within two months over 7,000 Indians had lost their lives in Europe.

The decision of the Ottoman Empire to join the Central Powers in November 1914 caused considerable unrest in India. There were over 60 million Muslims in India, and most considered the Ottoman caliph the leader of the international Islamic community. From the British point of view, however, preventing Germany from accessing Persian Gulf oil justified the use of Indian troops against Ottoman forces in

The "Camel Corps"   An Indian military unit that fought on behalf of the British empire during World War I. The British army enlisted more than one million Indian troops during the war. Britain promised that the Indian contribution to the war effort would enhance the colony's prospects for independence, but this would not be achieved for another 30 years.

Mesopotamia. By October 1915, over 12,000 British-led Indian troops were within reach of Baghdad before they were pushed back and defeated by Turkish forces in April 1916. Poor leadership and inadequate supplies spelled disaster on this front. In Egypt, almost 30,000 Indian troops stood ready to defend the Suez Canal from Ottoman attack.

Overall, approximately 1.2 million Indian troops and support staff were sent overseas to fight, and just over 100,000 were killed during the war. India also contributed 30 million pounds annually to the British war effort. In return, the British government stated its support for "the gradual development of self-governing institutions, with a view to the progressive realization of responsible government in India as an integral part of the Empire." This was in August 1917, and the proposal appeared to mirror the arrangements already in place in Canada, Australia, South Africa, and New Zealand.

Unfortunately, immediately after the war, the imperial authorities in India decided to continue wartime measures on press censorship, trial without jury, and internment without trial. India's nationalist leaders raised a storm of protest, and riots ensued in which several British civilians were killed. On April 13, 1919, in the city of **Amritsar,**

📖 **Read** the **Document**

Summary of Orders (for Martial Law in the Districts of Lahore and Amritsar, India), 1919

on **MyHistoryLab.com**

as several hundred men, women, and children assembled (in violation of an official ban on public gatherings) for a protest meeting, British-led troops opened fire without warning for 10 minutes—379 unarmed people were killed, and another 1,200 were wounded. This brutal action transformed millions of Indians into strident nationalists; it marked the beginning of the end of Britain's Indian Empire.

Naval War and American Entry

Although the British and German navies were formidable in terms of size, number, and firepower, there was only one large-scale naval battle during World War I. Britain had imposed a tight blockade of all German ports using its large surface fleet, while the Germans employed deadly submarines called U-boats in an effort to prevent food and strategic supplies from reaching Britain. When the German surface fleet finally emerged from its bases in 1916, a large battle ensued off Jutland in the North Sea on May 31, and although Britain lost more battleships than Germany did, the German fleet was obliged to return to port, where it remained for the rest of the war. Ironically, the massive prewar German naval buildup that had so worried British policymakers turned out to be a negligible factor in determining the outcome of World War I.

Early in the war, Germany had declared the waters around Britain off-limits to commercial shipping, and its U-boats attacked neutral vessels with impunity throughout the Atlantic. When the British luxury liner *Lusitania* was torpedoed off the southern

🔍 **View** the **Image**

Sinking of the Lusitania— New York Tribune

on **MyHistoryLab.com**

coast of Ireland in 1915, resulting in the loss of 1,200 lives (including 128 Americans), pressure from the United States led the German navy to refrain from such attacks without first warning the target vessel. This gave the allies (Britain and France) a temporary advantage in the war of attrition, since the expensive German surface fleet was confined to port. Most trade from the neutral United States now made its way to British and French ports, but no further. Germany and Austria-Hungary began to suffer serious shortages of food and material.

Woodrow Wilson   President Woodrow Wilson (1856–1924) wished to maintain America's neutrality, especially in light of the ethnic diversity of the nation's voters. More than one-third of America's 92 million residents were foreign born. Citizens of English descent tended to support the allied cause, but 4.5 million Irish-Americans and eight million German or Austrian-Americans sympathized with the Central Powers. In 1914 when the war began, Wilson insisted that Americans must remain neutral in thought and deed, and he naively claimed that neutral nations must be allowed to trade with all belligerents. By 1916, heavy British and French borrowing from American banks, coupled with the fact that America's industries were now producing military and civilian goods primarily for the Allied market, tilted U.S. foreign policy away from neutrality. While commerce with the Central Powers all but disappeared, that with Britain and France rose from $825 million in 1914 to over $3.2 billion in 1916. If Germany won the war, Allied debts would be repudiated and American creditors would be ruined. Germany's cessation of submarine warfare against merchant ships on the Atlantic was clearly undermining the German war effort.

⬚⬛⬚ Read the Document

Eugene V. Debs, Critique of World War I *(1918)*

on **MyHistoryLab.com**

In January 1916 Wilson asked both sides for their peace terms and worked to reach a negotiated settlement. Neither bloc was willing to forego its hopes for victory at this point, however, and the American offer was rejected. By 1917, the situation had changed significantly. The British naval blockade was creating enormous civilian and military hardship in the Central Powers. Acute food shortages were now commonplace, food riots had occurred, and infant mortality rates were rising rapidly. German strategists had concluded that the Allied powers would prevail unless Germany could sever Allied supply lines from America. In early February the Germans announced they would resume unrestricted submarine warfare, even at the risk of bringing the Americans into the war on the side of the Allies. At the end of February an intercepted secret telegram from the German government offering to help Mexico recover its "lost territories" in the American Southwest inflamed U.S. public opinion. One month later, the autocratic tsarist government collapsed. Russia was now led by Western-leaning members of the Duma, or national legislature. These three events convinced President Wilson, who viewed the European conflict in moral terms as a war to make the world safe for democracy, that the full military might of the United States must be brought to bear on the side of the Allies. In April 1917 Congress declared war on Germany.

The entry of the United States into the war, with its vast industrial, financial, and human resources, assured that the Allies would eventually prevail. American naval ships now protected trans-Atlantic merchant convoys. U.S. troops were trained and transported across the Atlantic in time to assist weary British and French forces as the German High Command planned and executed a final great offensive in the spring of 1918. In late March, following a plan devised by General Erich Ludendorff (1865–1937), the Germans broke through Allied lines and pushed to within 60 miles of Paris. American soldiers played a key role in what now became the Second Battle of

"Doughboys" Though inexperienced, American soldiers—called "doughboys," perhaps in reference to the large buttons on their uniforms, though the exact reasons are unclear—played a critical role in the eventual Allied victory. The photo here shows American machine gunners in action at the second Battle of the Marne in July 1917.

View the **Image**

American World War I Poster

on **MyHistoryLab.com**

the Marne in mid-July. By this date over 300,000 U.S. troops under the command of General John Pershing (1860–1948) were deployed on the front lines. It had now been four years since the Germans had been first rebuffed at the Marne, upsetting the Schlieffen Plan and inaugurating the long stalemate of **trench warfare.**

Final German Advance   By August, when a final German drive began, a total of one million German soldiers had become casualties in the Ludendorff offensive. The Allies, under the overall command of French General Ferdinand Foch (1851–1929), began a dogged counterattack. Lacking adequate reserves and afraid that the war would be carried onto German soil, the German army under Ludendorff advised William II to set up a civilian government along democratic lines. This government asked for peace on the basis of principles put forward by President Wilson in 1917. Ludendorff cynically hoped to pin the blame for defeat on the new civilian government, and during the 1920s and early 1930s this myth that Germany was "stabbed in the back" by civilian defeatists would be a powerful weapon the Nazis used in their quest for total power. Disorder did break out in Germany, the navy mutinied, and on November 9 Kaiser William II abdicated. Two days later, on November 11, 1918, the civilian, socialist-led government signed the armistice that ended the four years of carnage. The poet Wilfred Owen was one of the last victims.

Assigning Blame   By the terms of the **Treaty of Versailles,** which was signed in 1919, Germany and her partners were forced to accept complete responsibility for the war. While this clause in the final treaty was a source of great resentment in Germany, most modern historians believe that Kaiser William II and his advisors did act in a provocative and irresponsible manner in giving Austria a "blank check" to deal with the Serbian problem. According to this interpretation, the Germans realized in 1914 that Austrian military action against Serbia would almost certainly lead to Russian intervention and thus to a wider conflagration. Other scholars see a more complicated picture. Searching for the more systemic and long-term causes, they point to imperial rivalries, angry nationalism, the bombast of elected leaders and hereditary monarchs, and the tendency in Europe to celebrate power and the "cleansing" role of conflict. European civilization, this view concludes, was in serious moral disarray in the early twentieth century, unable to avoid destroying the fabric of material abundance created during the Industrial Age. All of the great European powers, not just Germany, bore some responsibility for the carnage.

The Impact of Total War at Home

World War I was really the first military conflict in history in which almost every member of society and every aspect of the economy became engaged in the struggle for victory. During the first Battle of the Marne in September 1914, the sight of Paris taxicabs rushing troops to the front lines gave an early indication that this war would involve large numbers of civilians. As German airships later flew over London, dropping largely ineffective bombs, the place of innovative technology in combat confirmed that everyone had become a target in this total war. As taxes rose and supplies of food and consumer goods diminished, entire populations were obliged to change their lifestyles. Armies required enormous quantities of machines, armaments, and ammunition, and these were produced by a civilian sector that came under the close scrutiny and control of the state. National governments repeatedly intervened in the private sector to assure that every aspect of business, agriculture, manufacture, and transportation was focused on the war effort. State agencies set aside free-market principles and established production targets, regulated wages and prices, and even imposed rationing. A special Ministry of Munitions was established in Britain under the direction of David Lloyd George (1863–1945) in 1915. In the United States a War Industries Board was established in 1917 and given almost total power to regulate materials, production standards, and prices. Similar state-run agencies appeared in all of the belligerent states. Governments also worked to secure strategic raw materials from neutral nations on favorable terms. This was especially true of Britain's relationship with the United States during the first two years of the war.

Women and Work   As casualties mounted, governments recruited new sources of domestic labor, businesses entered into partnership with labor unions, and working hours grew longer to meet the needs of the armed forces. Women entered the industrial workforce in huge numbers, taking positions that previously were reserved for men. By 1918, women constituted approximately one-third of the labor force in most countries. They drove taxis and operated trams; worked as safety officers, firefighters, and nurses; and became key operatives in the steel and munitions industries. Some women even took white collar jobs and supervised office staffs in a wide variety of businesses. In Russia women served in the armed forces. While some female workers experienced new freedoms as full-time employees in crucial sectors of the wartime economy, others struggled to balance work outside the home with their traditional family responsibilities. At the conclusion of the war, the long-standing demands of European suffragists would finally be met as women secured the right to vote at the national level in Britain, Germany, and other countries.

Maintaining Morale   Another wartime first involved the official use of mass communications to vilify the enemy and to ensure support for the government's war effort. Press censorship and state-sponsored propaganda became normal aspects of domestic life. As the death tolls mounted, democratically elected politicians assured the voters that the enemy would be punished severely after victory was achieved. Dissent was not tolerated. Police powers were extended, civil liberties abridged, and strikers arrested. In the United States, Congress passed a Sedition Act in 1918 that made it a crime to speak or publish material critical of the government. The law also criminalized opposition to the sale of war bonds. On a more positive note, class distinctions in most European countries began to break down as the priorities of the wartime economy demanded contributions from all citizens, irrespective of their background or training. Aristocrats worked alongside urban laborers in service and volunteer agencies. Under rationing, food allocations were based on need, not social status or income. Nutrition

Women Munitions Workers The labor shortage on the home front led to important social changes during World War I. Factories across Europe and in the United States relied heavily on women to build the weapons of war. At the end of the conflict, returning soldiers displaced their female counterparts on the factory floor, but many women retained their jobs outside the home.

actually improved for the poorest sectors of British and French society, while in Germany the combination of a potato crop failure in 1916 and the strict British blockade reduced the entire population to a "turnip winter" in which caloric intake was halved. Some German soldiers organized attacks simply to raid the enemy's food stores.

The Russian Revolution

Military Failure   The Russians had entered World War I with enormous human resources, but with limited industrial and military capacity. Tsar Nicholas II and his closest advisors hoped that a short conflict in the Balkans on behalf of Serbia would restore Russia's diminished international prestige while simultaneously uniting the tsar's subjects under the banner of nationalism. This was a disastrous miscalculation. Lacking adequate transportation, armaments, and supplies, Russia was not prepared for modern mechanized warfare. Once the Ottomans joined the conflict on the side of the Central Powers, a crucial supply line from the West through the Dardanelles was cut off. In 1915 Tsar Nicholas made a fateful decision to take personal command of the armed forces (the only head of state to do so) while affairs in the capital fell under the baneful influence of his German-born wife Alexandra (1872–1918) and her corrupt advisor, the Orthodox faith healer Grigori Rasputin (1871–1916). Even though the tsar's generals actually ran military affairs, further reverses on the battlefield were bound to be blamed directly on him.

In June 1916 Russian General Aleksei Brusilov (1853–1926) launched a massive offensive against Austria-Hungary. The attack came close to crippling the enemy, but lack of supplies and military hardware, together with a high rate of desertion, hampered the Russian effort. Soldiers were even sent into battle unarmed, advised to scavenge a rifle from a fallen colleague or dead enemy. A German counteroffensive led to over one million Russian casualties. By the spring of 1917, Russian troop morale was awful, and the rate of desertion had skyrocketed. Food shortages in Russia's cities and towns led to strikes and protests, many led by women. By March, the tsarist administration was breaking down. With his leadership discredited and soldiers in the capital mutinying and unwilling to fire on unarmed demonstrators, Nicholas abdicated on March 15, and the Duma organized a provisional government.

While promising civil liberties, universal manhood suffrage, equality before the law, a written constitution, and social reforms, the leaders of the provisional Russian government did not do what the Russian people wanted most—withdraw from the war. Liberal members of the Duma felt that Russia remained obligated to its French and British allies. The collapse of the tsarist autocracy also meant the collapse of traditional authority. As domestic conditions deteriorated during the summer and fall of 1917, calls for peace, bread, and land reform were heard throughout the country. Angry peasants began to seize land and hoard food, exacerbating hardship in the cities. Morale at the front collapsed, and disillusioned soldiers began to return home to make land claims of their own. Radical exiles who had been forced out of the country by the tsar's secret police began reappearing in Russia's major cities, where they formed political organizations of workers and soldiers called soviets. The most influential returnee was Vladimir Ilich Ulyanov (1870–1924), better known by his revolutionary name, Lenin.

The Germans had actually transported Lenin in a sealed train from his exile in Switzerland to the city of Petrograd (St. Petersburg), hoping he would undermine the ability of the provisional government to maintain its war effort. Their hopes were almost immediately realized. After one failed attempt to overthrow the government (in the aftermath of yet another disastrous military campaign), Lenin and his leading collaborator, Leon Trotsky (1879–1940), led a coalition of workers and soldiers to seize power in Petrograd on November 6, 1917. Trotsky's forces captured the strategic communications and rail hubs as well as key government offices in the city. The leader of the provisional government, Alexander Kerensky (1881–1970), fled the city. The Bolsheviks had come to power in an almost bloodless fashion.

Read the Document

Bolshevik Seizure of Power, 1917

on **MyHistoryLab.com**

Early Bolshevik Policy   The Bolshevik revolutionaries still had to win the support of Russia's peasants, who made up the vast majority of the population. Lenin had argued that a genuine Marxist revolution could take place in rural Russia even though the country lacked a large proletariat, or industrial working class. Marx had written that a communist revolution could only succeed in a fully industrialized state,

V. I. Lenin and Leon Trotsky The two principal leaders of the Bolshevik revolution of 1917. Trotsky is wearing the uniform of the Red Army, which he led to victory in Russia's brutal civil war.

where workers had been reduced to the level of landless industrial laborers and where working-class consciousness was strong. Lenin and the Bolsheviks, in contrast, believed that an intellectual vanguard of professional revolutionaries could lead peasants and workers to create a stateless socialist society. Immediately after seizing power in Petrograd, Lenin nationalized land ownership and turned production over to the peasants, repudiated the debts incurred by the tsarist government, and entered into negotiations with the Germans to end the war.

Sensing Bolshevik weakness, the Germans drove a hard bargain. An armistice was signed in December 1917, and under terms of the **Treaty of Brest-Litovsk** in March 1918, the Bolshevik government surrendered claims to Poland; Finland; the Baltic states of Latvia, Lithuania, and Estonia; and Ukraine. The Russians also agreed to pay Germany a large indemnity and to provide enormous supplies of grain and other foodstuffs. Fierce resistance to the newly established communist regime began almost immediately and continued until 1921. Internal opponents of the regime, called the White Army and representing a wide spectrum of political views, were joined by over 100,000 foreign troops from 14 different countries. The foreign forces were led by the United States, Britain, France, and Japan, former Russian allies now intent on destroying the fledgling communist state. During this protracted civil war (1918–1921), Bolshevik armies under Trotsky's leadership repulsed the invading forces. In the midst of the struggle the Bolsheviks murdered the tsar and his family, instituted a reign of terror using the secret police to execute opponents of the new regime, and began the monumental process of transforming an overwhelmingly agrarian and war-torn country of 150 million people into a socialist society.

The Threat of Communism   The overthrow of the tsarist regime in Russia led to widespread fear in European capitals that war-weary citizens might support similar movements in the West. Lenin's Russia may have been excluded from the Versailles peace conference and gripped by civil war, but the ideology of revolutionary Marxism easily transcended geography. Lenin had written that the war was nothing more than a predictable clash of capitalist economies and that true peace would never be achieved until the entire capitalist system was destroyed. In a speech before the Petrograd Soviet, Lenin stated that "it is necessary to overthrow capitalism itself. In this work we shall have the aid of the world labor movement, which has already begun to develop in Italy, England, and Germany."

> **View** the **Image**
> *Bolshevik Revolution Poster*
> on **MyHistoryLab.com**

In the war's aftermath, the communist appeal for a new social order resonated with members of Europe's socialist parties, many of whom had enthusiastically supported their country's war effort in 1914. Each major European postwar democracy soon had a revolutionary communist party and fledgling soviets. In Germany the counterpart of Lenin's Bolsheviks was the **Spartacist League,** led by Karl Liebknecht (1871–1919) and Rosa Luxemburg (1871–1919). The interim German government was led by moderate socialists, and they used the armed forces to destroy the Spartacists. In December 1919 Liebknecht and Luxemburg were killed,

> **View** the **Image**
> *Spartacist Demonstration*
> on **MyHistoryLab.com**

along with a thousand of their supporters. In Hungary, a short-lived Soviet republic was established in March 1919 under the leadership of Bela Kun (1886–1939). That same year Lenin organized an international umbrella organization called the Comintern to provide leadership for the various communist parties in Western Europe. It was a rigidly top-down organization, following Lenin's conviction that the revolutionary vanguard must direct the less enlightened, but it nevertheless attracted support among European communist parties.

As the German and Hungarian examples illustrated, the threat of a communist revolution outside Russia seemed a distinct possibility in the years immediately after the war,

Russian "May Day" Poster   Paraphrasing Karl Marx, this poster declares, "You have nothing to lose but your chains, but the world will soon be yours." The zeal and enthusiasm of the early days of the **Russian Revolution** is evident in this image, one of many such posters produced at the time. *Museum of the Revolution, Moscow, Russia/Bridgeman Art Library, London*

PEOPLE IN CONTEXT   John Reed and Bolshevism

The American journalist John Reed was born in Portland, Oregon, in 1887. He graduated from Harvard University in 1910 and worked as a writer for a variety of leftist and radical magazines, including *The Masses,* for which Reed was reporting in Petrograd when the Bolsheviks seized power in November 1917.

Reed published an eyewitness description of the November Revolution, titled *Ten Days that Shook the World,* in 1919. The book was translated into many languages, with an introduction by Lenin that appeared after Reed's death in 1920. Reed was a partisan journalist, and his sympathies lay with the Bolshevik insurgents. *Ten Days* provided a rare firsthand account of events from the perspective of an American intellectual who found much to admire in Lenin's repudiation of the capitalist West.

Reed returned to the United States at the end of the war. In 1919 he founded the Communist Labor Party during a fractious meeting of the Socialist Party of America in Chicago. To secure recognition for his new party from Lenin's Comintern, he set off again for Russia in the fall of 1919. He left just as the United States attorney general established a new General Intelligence Division in the Department of Justice headed by a young J. Edgar Hoover (1895–1972). The division was charged with collecting information on radical organizations, including communist political groups. In January 1920 police arrested over 6,000 persons in 33 cities across the nation. Many detainees were held without charge for weeks. A handful were deported in this Red Scare. Reed was already back in Russia when the mass arrests took place, but he had been indicted for treason during the panic.

John Reed

In Russia Reed met with Lenin, and he was elected to the Executive Committee of the Comintern. But soon he was struck with typhus. He died in Moscow on October 19, 1920, and was buried with other Bolshevik heroes in the Kremlin. Reed's activities helped arouse deep public suspicion in the West that a handful of dedicated communists were working to overthrow the Western capitalist democracies. Given the success of the small Bolshevik minority in Russia, it was felt that a ruthless cadre could endanger the stability of the postwar West at a moment's notice. ■

QUESTION: What would an educated young American find appealing about the Russian Revolution of 1917?

and Russian agents fanned across the globe to advance the cause of world revolution. The United States experienced a "**Red Scare**" in 1919 as government agencies trampled civil liberties in search of radicals, while in Europe fear of communist insurgency led many political moderates to turn toward far-right political parties. In particular, emerging Fascist parties were adept at promoting their anticommunist credentials. Less than one year after assuming power in Hungary, Bela Kun's Soviet state was toppled by invading Romanian troops. In its place a right-wing authoritarian government was established with the full support of the anxious Allied powers.

The Peace Settlement and European Consciousness

What has come to be known as the Great War ended with the armistice signed by Germany on November 11, 1918. The Ottoman, Russian, German, and Austrian empires were dismantled, and the Habsburg, Hohenzollern, Romanov, and Ottoman dynasties abolished. Almost 10 million people had been killed in battle during four years of fighting, and another 15 to 16 million had been wounded. Virtually every family in France, Britain, Russia, Germany, and Austria-Hungary had lost a loved one. In France alone the total population was reduced by one-twentieth, and most of the dead were young men in their most productive years. Millions of civilians also lost their lives during the conflict. As if war-related deaths were not enough, in 1919 a worldwide **influenza epidemic** killed another 27 million people.

The war severely damaged the national economies of each of the European combatants, with the total direct cost of the conflict estimated at $180 billion. Most governments, unwilling to raise taxes at a time when their populations were making so many other sacrifices, borrowed heavily.

The United States was the biggest lender, and in the process it transformed itself from a debtor to a creditor nation. In 1919 the Europeans owed American creditors $3.7 billion. Europe had suddenly and decisively lost its status as the center of global politics, culture, and economics. Social Darwinist arguments now rang hollow across a continent where once imperial states were reduced to poverty and political instability. The war's savagery had destroyed faith in the inevitability of progress and the primacy of reason in human affairs. Widows, fatherless children, amputees, and the maimed found it difficult to resume their broken lives. The poet T. S. Eliot (1888–1965) expressed the sense of alienation brought forward by the conflict in his poem "The Hollow Men," with its haunting depiction of the war's survivors, while the Irishman William Butler Yeats (1865–1939) wrote about the decay of Western civilization. In "The Second Coming" Yeats reflected how

> Things fall apart; the center cannot hold;
> Mere anarchy is loosed upon the world,
> The blood-dimmed tide is loosed, and everywhere
> The ceremony of innocence is drowned;
> The best lack all conviction, while the worst
> Are full of passionate intensity.

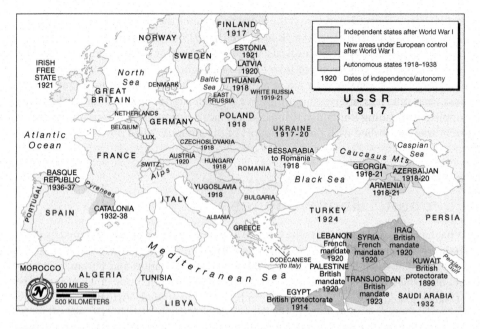

MAP 22-2 Postwar Europe While new nations were created at the end of the war, the principle of national self-determination was not applied in a uniform manner. New areas of European control were established in the Middle East, while Africa and South Asia remained under European rule.

QUESTION: How was the principle of national self-determination applied in eastern Europe after World War I?

In postwar Europe, and especially in Fascist Italy and Nazi Germany during the 1920s and 1930s, the final two lines of this stanza were to be borne out in full measure. After a respite of two decades, "the worst" would lead Europe's nation-states into another, even more costly global struggle (see Map 22–2).

The Versailles Conference   The representatives from 32 victorious states who assembled in the great palace of Versailles outside Paris in January 1919 faced enormous challenges. The leaders of the Big Four—France, Britain, the United States, and Italy—would make the major decisions, and they had promised their peoples compensation for the enormous sacrifices on the battlefield. Germany and Austria-Hungary were excluded from the deliberations, as was Russia, which was now under communist control. Delegates from some of Europe's many colonies also attended in the expectation that their pleas for independence would be acknowledged, especially in light of the fact that millions of colonial troops had fought with distinction to save European civilization.

Two of the leading figures, American President Woodrow Wilson and French Premier Georges Clemenceau (1841–1929), had irreconcilable agendas. The idealistic Wilson, representing a nation that had entered the war late and incurred comparatively few casualties, wished to secure "peace without victors" and to rebuild the continent according to the principle of national self-determination (although no one, including

Wilson himself, was sure what self-determination meant). He had first outlined his views one year earlier in his famous "**Fourteen Points**" speech justifying America's involvement in the war. According to Wilson, secret diplomacy must end, colonial claims for self-governance must be heard, freedom of the seas must be protected and free trade promoted, and armaments must be reduced. Both sides to the conflict had accepted Wilson's outline for an equitable peace before the armistice. Wilson also called on the delegates to establish a permanent **League of Nations** where future international disputes could be settled without recourse to violence. Clemenceau, in contrast, wished to punish the vanquished states (Germany, Austria, Hungary, Bulgaria, and Turkey). In particular, Clemenceau sought to cripple Germany's war-making capacity. France had been invaded twice by Germany during Clemenceau's lifetime (in 1870 and 1914), and the most brutal fighting in the Western theater during World War I had taken place on French soil. The French had good reason to fear another German invasion. Germany's larger population and greater industrial capacity made the French delegation extremely wary of the principle of peace without victors.

Retribution and Resentment   In the end the delegates settled for a compromise that included a number of punitive elements. The principle of national self-determination, while laudable in theory, was difficult to apply in practice. At what point, for example, was it legitimate to include disgruntled minorities within the boundaries of a new state? One-third of the population of Poland did not speak Polish; Romania contained one million Magyars; Czechoslovakia had almost one million Germans; Catholic Ireland remained under British rule. Since many areas in Europe contained a mixture of nationalities, redrawing the map on nationalist lines was particularly difficult. No solution was likely to please every interested party.

However, the victors enjoyed distinct advantages. Alsace and Lorraine, lost to Germany in 1871, were restored to France. The Rhineland territories, Germany's industrial heartland, were demilitarized and were to be occupied by Allied troops for 15 years. Germany also forfeited all of its overseas colonies, ceded Polish-speaking areas of eastern Germany to a resurrected Polish state, and accepted the creation of a "Polish corridor," which cut through German territory to provide Poland with an outlet to the sea at the international—but German inhabited—city of Danzig. The German army was limited to 100,000 troops, the powerful navy was scrapped, and a large but undetermined war indemnity imposed. In 1923 the heavy indemnity was set at $33 billion, creating an enormous fiscal burden for the newly established German republic.

Four separate treaties with Germany's wartime allies were concluded during the six months of negotiations at Versailles. The Austrian Empire, home to 50 million subjects of the Habsburgs, had imploded during the final months of the war, and a series of breakaway states were recognized at Versailles. Smaller, independent Austrian and Hungarian states were created, and an independent Czechoslovakia, uniting Czech and Slovak lands, emerged in the heart of Europe. The break-up led to serious economic dislocations as the new states established trade and tariff policies that hindered the movement of raw materials to factories that were once located in the same country. Some Austrians wished to merge with Germany to the north, claiming the primacy of language bonds, but the victors forbade this move. The Serbs realized their goal of a South-Slavic nation with the establishment of Yugoslavia in the Balkans, while the Turks created a republic based on the Turkish-speaking lands of Anatolia. To the north, Finland, Latvia, Estonia, and Lithuania became independent states, while Poland was restored to nation-state status after almost 150 years. The British and French divided the Ottoman Empire's Middle Eastern territories between themselves, with the French claiming Lebanon and Syria while the British took administrative control over Palestine and Mesopotamia (Iraq).

The League of Nations   For the first time in history, the Americans wielded direct and decisive influence over European affairs. Woodrow Wilson, discouraged by the punitive features of the Versailles settlement, pushed hard for the establishment of a permanent international body dedicated to the peaceful resolution of international disputes and to the promotion of global health and economic issues. The League of Nations was incorporated into the final peace treaty, but opposition to the League by isolationists in the United States Senate doomed the president's desire that the United States play a larger role in international affairs. In 1920 the Senate refused to ratify the treaty. The absence of the United States, together with the exclusion of Germany and Russia from membership in the League, undermined the League's influence and effectiveness. Lacking a military force of its own, the League council

Arab Delegates to the Paris Peace Conference, 1919   T. E. Lawrence (middle row, second from the right)—the fabled "Lawrence of Arabia"—with Arab leaders. The British undermined Ottoman control of the Middle East by promising to support local rulers who sought to break free from the Ottoman Empire.

could only apply economic sanctions against future aggressors. France and Britain joined the organization along with 40 other states (26 members of the League were non-European), but there was little enthusiasm in either Britain or France for the League's broadly internationalist agenda. In one area only did the victors support the League, and that was due to the problems of empire. Germany's former colonies, together with former Ottoman lands in the Middle East, were assigned to Britain and France by the League under a "mandate" system. Ostensibly, the imperial powers were charged with preparing their mandated territories for eventual independence under League supervision. In practice, however, these lands were administered as colonial possessions.

A Legacy of Distrust   The war to "make the world safe for democracy"— to use Woodrow Wilson's words—ended in a climate of mutual dissatisfaction and distrust. The French felt betrayed by the failure of their allies to impose a harsher peace on Germany or to ratify a promised alliance to come to the aid of France if Germany attacked again. The Italians resented the Allies' refusal to satisfy their claims to more former Austrian- and Turkish-controlled territories. The German military constructed the myth of civilian betrayal, while the German public resented the "war guilt" clause and the demand that Germany pay reparations. The Americans withdrew into comfortable isolationism while refusing to forgive or even to renegotiate Allied loans taken out during the war. Bolshevik Russia was ostracized by the Western democracies. Colonial peoples in Africa and Asia felt duped by imperial masters who had no intention of extending the right of self-determination beyond the confines of Europe. The Japanese resented the delegates' refusal (at the behest of the United States) to declare formally the equality of all races. In the Middle East, Arabs and Jews quarreled over which duplicitous promise made by the British during the war ought to be honored. Nothing in the treaties addressed the crucial matters of reconciliation

Major Events of World War I

June 28, 1914	Assassination of the Archduke Francis Ferdinand
August 1–3, 1914	Germany declares war on Russia and France
August 4, 1914	Britain declares war on Germany; war begins
September 1914	Battle of the Marne; German retreat signals long stalemate
February 1916	Battle of Verdun begins
July 1, 1916	Battle of the Somme begins
April 1917	United States declares war on Germany
November 1917	Bolshevik revolution in Russia
November 11, 1918	Armistice is signed, ending the war
June 28, 1919	Treaty of Versailles is signed

and rebuilding. Having barely survived the deluge, the victors could not see their way clear to a better Europe.

In *The Economic Consequences of the Peace*, published in 1919, the young British economist John Maynard Keynes (1883–1946) argued that the new German government was incapable of meeting the reparations demands of Britain and France and that the resulting hardships would make future conflict more likely. Recalling the Roman destruction of Carthage after the Third Punic War (149–146 B.C.E.), Keynes described the Treaty of Versailles as the equivalent of a "Carthaginian peace." At the time of the book's publication, few would have anticipated his forecast that the treaty would lead to future conflict would come to pass in less than 20 years. Like Woodrow Wilson, Keynes recognized that Germany—now a democracy—must be reintegrated into the European state system if the future of the continent was to be peaceful and prosperous. Few Europeans were prepared to be generous and forgiving in 1918. The intensity, longevity, and brutality of the encounter with modern warfare precluded a rational assessment of Europe's predicament.

◉—⟨Watch the **Video**

The Continuing Legacy of World War I in the Middle East

on **MyHistoryLab.com**

KEY QUESTION REVISITED

Are nation-states inherently adversarial?

Are nation-states doomed to quarrel with each other? The experience of 1914 to 1918 would suggest that they are. Looking at a map of the world in 1920, it appeared that Europe was still the most powerful region in the world. European national flags still flew in scores of colonies around the globe. In the French and British cases their colonial possessions actually increased thanks to their mandates in Africa and the Middle East. The map was misleading, however. World War I had diminished Europe's states economically, militarily, politically, and intellectually. The sense of confidence and superiority that most Europeans felt about their own civilization was consumed by the four long years of carnage, official lies, and punitive settlements. A war that began with widespread public support ended in widespread popular disillusionment and despair. "An old bitch, gone in the teeth," was the American poet Ezra Pound's (1885–1972) diagnosis of Western civilization. The German historian Oswald Spengler (1880–1936) perhaps best captured the mood of the postwar generation with his influential *Decline of the West*, first published in 1920 and premised on the idea that the West had entered an age of "gigantic conflicts." All civilizations, Spengler argued, have natural life cycles, and anyone familiar with the trenches on the Western Front would have been compelled to admit that Europe had reached the end of its primacy.

While Europe's traditional elite, what historian Barbara Tuchman (1912–1989) called "the Proud Tower," were key players in the decision to go to war, the voting public overwhelmingly supported their elected and hereditary leaders. In light of this fact, the biggest casualty of the war may have been Europeans' faith in the value of traditional political systems, whether parliamentary or monarchical, and in the primacy of rational decision making. Nationalist ideology, the conviction that the sovereign state was master of its own destiny, accountable to no higher authority, had successfully preempted another Enlightenment value: belief in the equality of persons across artificial international boundaries. Late nineteenth-century colonial disputes, intense economic rivalries, and an inflexible system of military alliances all contributed to the breakdown of the European order during four years of total war. For the next two decades, the core values of liberal democracy were called into question in much of Europe. During the interwar years, the subject of the next chapter, parliamentary government, individual rights, and the rule of law would all be challenged by new leaders who publicly repudiated the Enlightenment tradition.

Key Terms

Triple Alliance, *p. 652*
Entente Cordial, p. 652
Balfour Declaration, *p. 657*

trench warfare, *p. 662*
Treaty of Versailles, *p. 662*
Treaty of Brest-Litovsk, *p. 666*

Russian Revolution, *p. 667*
League of Nations, *p. 671*

Activities

1. Assemble the evidence and assess responsibility for World War I.

2. Why was there enthusiasm for war in 1914?

3. What role did military strategy play in prolonging trench warfare?

4. Why did the United States wish to remain neutral, and why did America eventually side with the Allies?

5. What role did propaganda play on the home fronts? How did the war involve Europe's civilian population?

6. Analyze the main flaws in the Treaty of Versailles.

7. Explain the reasons for the Bolshevik rise to power in 1917.

Further Readings

Jeremy Black, *The Great War and the Making of the Modern World* (2011), a recent treatment by a leading scholar.

Neil Ferguson, *The Pity of War* (1998), an engaging but controversial study of the origins and prosecution of the war.

Paul Fussell, *The Great War and Modern Memory* (2000), examines the cultural responses to the war through the lens of poetry, prose and letters.

Vera Brittain, *Testament of Youth* (2005), a new edition of one of the most powerful accounts of the war.

MyHistoryLab Connections

Visit **MyHistoryLab.com** for a customized Study Plan that will help you build your knowledge of World War I: The End of Enlightenment.

Questions for Analysis

1. What was the significance of Archduke Franz Ferdinand's trip to Sarajevo in June 1914?

👁️ Watch the Video The Outbreak of World War I, p. 654

2. Based on the account by François Carlotti, how was the war experienced on the home front?

📖 Read the Document François Carlotti, from "World War I: A Frenchman's Recollections," p. 654

3. Based on the excerpts from the soldiers' diaries, what are some of the ways in which the soldiers' depiction of the Battle of Somme might differ from accounts of the battle by contemporary journalists and government officials?

📖 Read the Document British Soldiers on the Battle of the Somme, p. 656

4. Why does Lenin advocate censorship of the press and how might his position be related to the kind of coverage reflected in the excerpt from the newspaper *Izvestia*?

📖 Read the Document Bolshevik Seizure of Power, 1917, p. 665

5. How has World War I influenced the modern Middle East?

👁️ Watch the Video The Continuing Legacy of World War I in the Middle East, p. 674

Other Resources from This Chapter

📖 Read the Document The Murder of Archduke Franz Ferdinand at Sarajevo (1914), Borijove Jevtic, p. 651

🔍 View the Map Map Discovery: Linguistic Groups in Austria-Hungary, p. 651

🔍 View the Map Map Discovery: The Schlieffen Plan and France's Plan XVII, p. 654

🔍 View the Closer Look The Development of the Armored Tank, p. 654

📖 Read the Document The Balfour Declaration, 1917, p. 657

📖 Read the Document Summary of Orders (for Martial Law in the Districts of Lahore and Amritsar, India), 1919, p. 660

🔍┤**View** the **Image** Sinking of the *Lusitania—New York Tribune*, p. 660

📖┤**Read** the **Document** Eugene V. Debs, *Critique of World War I* (1918), p. 661

🔍┤**View** the **Image** American World War I Poster, p. 662

🔍┤**View** the **Image** Bolshevik Revolution Poster, p. 667

🔍┤**View** the **Image** Spartacist Demonstration, p. 667

18
ULIO

1936
1939

The Spanish Civil War This poster, created in support of the Nationalist side of the war, provides witness to the intense ideological struggles of the interwar period. The conflict began in July 1936. When it ended in 1939, half a million Spaniards had lost their lives.

The Troubled Interwar Years

LEARNING OBJECTIVES

What were the main challenges facing postwar governments across Europe? • How did the Great Depression undermine confidence in democratic governments? • What were the main features of Italian fascism? • How do we explain the rise of authoritarianism in Spain and eastern Europe? • How did Hitler undermine the Weimar Republic? • What was the root cause of Japanese imperialism? • How did Stalin repudiate the vision of Marxian communism?

The völkisch *(racial) state must free all leadership and especially the highest—that is, the political leadership—entirely from the parliamentary principle of majority rule.*

—Hitler

KEY QUESTION

Does personal liberty matter to people who suffer under conditions of acute material hardship?

Writing from prison in 1923, the leader of Germany's National Socialist (Nazi) Party discussed how to win popular support in a democratic age. Adolf Hitler (1889–1945) placed special emphasis on the role of propaganda in democratic culture. "All propaganda," he insisted, "must be popular and its intellectual level must be addressed to the most limited intelligence among those it is addressed to … we must avoid excessive intellectual demands on our public, and too much caution cannot be exerted in this direction." For Hitler and for many others ambitious for political power in postwar Europe, the advent of mass democracy presented a unique opportunity for charismatic leaders to channel popular discontent into political action. By showing contempt for the reasoning power of the average citizen, and by blaming Europe's complex postwar problems on the machinations of traitors, foreign enemies, and inferior races, unprincipled men hoped to destroy liberal democracy and create their own distorted versions of the perfect society.

During the two decades after World War I, Europe's liberal democracies came under increasing pressure from authoritarian, anti-individualistic ideologies on the right and left of the political spectrum. Fascist regimes rose to power by constitutional means in Italy and Germany, while in the Soviet Union the Communist Party wielded absolute and arbitrary authority under the brutal direction of Joseph Stalin (1879–1953). These antidemocratic regimes used propaganda, technology, and large, impersonal bureaucracies to suppress individual liberties, rival political parties, the autonomy of the artist, and the security of private property. Their leaders sought to establish complete control over individuals while elevating party ideology and the cult of their own personality to the level of unquestioned truth. In the case of **Fascism,** the leadership appealed directly to base emotions and the prejudices of the masses to win approval for a variety of inhumane policies. Fascist leaders skillfully exploited democracy in order to secure power, then used that power to destroy democracy once they took office. In the Soviet Union, the Enlightenment inheritance of individual rights and the sanctity of property perished before the forces of state-imposed collectivization, the rejection of the rule of law, and Stalin's megalomania.

By the 1930s, as worldwide economic depression smashed the hopes and dreams of millions in the West, many Europeans lost faith in the ability of liberal democracy to solve life's most pressing daily problems. Two centuries of struggle to achieve political freedoms and civil rights now appeared hollow in the face of hunger and massive unemployment. As the decade wore on, the shrill appeal of leaders who promised jobs, the restoration of national greatness, or the triumph of the international working class began to make headway. Demagogues who appealed to pent-up hatreds and to the darker side of human nature came to power in several European countries and triggered a crisis of confidence in those states that struggled to preserve their democratic institutions.

Postwar Problems in Western Europe

The perceived inadequacies of the Versailles settlement afforded governments across Europe the opportunity to rally popular support for revising the treaties. In democratic states elected politicians were expected to restore prewar prosperity. However, the widespread destruction caused by the Great War and the fact that millions of men in their most productive working years had been killed or maimed on the battlefield undermined efforts to rebuild the continent's economic fabric. Rail systems and industrial plants had been severely damaged or destroyed, especially in areas such as northern France and Belgium, where the most prolonged fighting had taken place. In addition, the creation of new nation-states in central and eastern Europe complicated trade policies and fragmented transportation and production networks. Demand for European manufactures declined as the United States raised tariffs and extended its global market presence. Europe was no longer the financial hub of the global community. That distinction had passed to the Americans, and the enormous debts owed by victor and vanquished alike weakened the ability of postwar European governments to control their own economies.

For those who had fought in the war and survived, a sense of incompleteness and a belief that their sacrifices on behalf of the homeland were not being recognized or properly compensated often accompanied a return to civilian life. High rates of unemployment, continuing food shortages, and the absence of friends and loved ones who had died in the conflagration all contributed to the mood of despondency. The Wilsonian rhetoric of a "world made safe for democracy" meant little to many Europeans in the postwar environment. If anything, they resented the United States' unwillingness to forgive debts that had been incurred during the war. To meet their obligations to repay the United States, the British and the French sought to extract reparations from Germany. Germans in turn resented the terms of what they called the dictated peace of Versailles.

The Price of Victory

Irresolute Britain   The end of the war brought about further democratization in Britain. In 1918 the franchise was extended to all men over the age of 21 and to women who were at least 30 years of age. In 1928 this age discrimination was abolished, and universal suffrage at age 21 became the rule. The Labour Party replaced the Liberals as the main opposition to the Conservatives. Under the leadership of Ramsay Mac-Donald (1866–1937), Labour successfully fought for reforms to improve the lives of the working class. A

View the **Image**

London Stock Exchange, 1920s

on **MyHistoryLab.com**

general strike came close to provoking social unrest in 1926, but in general, unemployment benefits, housing subsidies, and old-age pensions defused class tensions in a period of economic uncertainty.

Unemployment rates in Britain remained high throughout the 1920s. The economic hard times were in large measure the result of fresh competition from the United States and Japan, which lessened the worldwide demand for British goods. Many of Britain's manufacturing plants had been built in the nineteenth century, and many factories had become outdated by the 1920s, while the destruction of a large portion of the merchant fleet during the war slowed the movement of British goods overseas. Since prewar Germany had been Britain's second best market (the United States was first), political leaders in London were eager to see Germany return to its prewar prosperity so that Germans could afford to buy British goods. Since Germany was now a democratic republic, British policymakers were increasingly sympathetic to the German argument that the Versailles Peace Treaty undermined the very form of political order that the Allies said they had been fighting for.

The Defense of France   French political leaders remained focused on national security. They were troubled by the failure of Britain and the United States to guarantee they would come to France's aid if Germany attacked again. Lacking these guarantees, the French formed defensive alliances with several small Eastern European powers. Poland, Yugoslavia, Czechoslovakia, and Romania joined with France in an effort to further isolate Germany and the Soviet Union. Even in defeat, Germany's growing population of 60 million threatened France's comparatively stagnant 40 million. While the fighting during World War I had devastated France's most industrialized region, Germany's large industrial and transportation infrastructures remained intact, since no fighting had occurred on German soil. In the years immediately after the war, the French government worked continuously to keep Germany weak. Insisting on heavy reparations and the demilitarization of the industrial Rhineland, French politicians remained suspicious of a resurgent German state, even a democratic one.

Hyperinflation in Germany, 1923   A woman in Berlin uses worthless marks (the German currency) to start a fire in her stove. Germany experienced one of the most severe inflations in modern European history in 1923. Germany's severe economic crisis contributed to the political instability that aided Adolf Hitler's rise to power.

Weimar Republic   With the Hohenzollern monarchy abolished in November 1918, German liberals and Social Democrats established the Weimar Republic (after the city where it was founded) in August 1919. The new constitution claimed that all political authority "derives from the people." A president, elected by secret ballot on the basis of universal suffrage (women were given the vote in 1919), a Reichstag whose powers included the right to initiate all legislation, a cabinet system that made ministers responsible to the popularly elected legislature, and the protection of civil liberties all reflected enlightened liberal ideals. Unfortunately, the new constitution was adopted just as the government, headed by the Social Democrats, was forced to sign the humiliating Versailles Treaty. The Weimar Republic thus began its brief life under the cloud of national defeat and the burden of heavy war reparations. Throughout the 1920s, angry nationalists and their military supporters blamed the republic for everything that went wrong.

Economic problems were the key to popular discontent. Weimar authorities were saddled with the debts that the former government had incurred during the war. The new government elected to honor these commitments and satisfy its reparations obligations by printing additional paper money. The result was hyperinflation and the precipitous collapse of the German mark. During the years 1919 to 1923, pensioners, veterans on disability, government bond holders, mortgage and insurance policyholders, and the owners of personal savings accounts all saw their benefits, finances, and savings evaporate. Many lower- and middle-class Germans were reduced to a barter economy as national wealth was transferred to Britain and France in the form of war reparations.

American Intervention   The economic situation in Germany had become unsustainable by November 1923. New ideas were desperately needed if the German economy was not to collapse entirely. In 1924 British and American authorities, led by American banker Charles Dawes (1865–1951), proposed a plan that reduced and rescheduled Germany's payments while also guaranteeing American loans to the Weimar government. The French were persuaded to agree to the arrangement and pledged not to use military force in the event that Weimar failed to meet its deadlines. Despite the emergency situation, the United States remained unwilling to cancel the wartime debts owed by Britain and France. The imposition of a high tariff by the U.S. Congress made it difficult for any of the European nations to sell their products in America. Since the potential market for European-manufactured products in the United States was strong, the inability of producers to sell in the United States hampered the overall recovery that was in the best interest of every Western capitalist nation.

A Moment of Promise   With the Dawes plan and American loans, the German currency was at last placed on a firm basis. Germany would use the funds to pay reparations and jump-start its economy. A circular flow of capital began: Germany borrowed from the United States to pay reparations to France and Britain, who used those payments to repay their debts to the United States. This arrangement worked as long as America's economy remained healthy—and it did, at least until the fall of 1929. Germany's economy also seemed to recover. Industrial output grew, foreign investment returned, unemployment fell, and trade grew with other European states. The economic turnaround was matched by a reduction in international tensions. At a meeting in Locarno, Switzerland, in 1925, France, Belgium, and Germany formally agreed to accept their common borders, while Britain and Italy promised to oppose any state that violated the pact. The next year, guided by foreign minister Gustav Stresemann (1878–1929), Germany was admitted to the League of Nations.

Popular Culture and Consumerism   The momentary return of economic stability across most of Western Europe prompted manufacturers to focus on new technologies for a consumer market. Radios, washing machines, refrigerators, vacuum cleaners, and irons all began to appear in middle-class homes. The passion for private transportation spurred the automobile industry and road-building projects. Airplane design improved, and commercial airlines began to appeal to the affluent and adventuresome. The service sector expanded, especially in large towns and cities. Sales jobs in large retail firms, repair services for the myriad new products, travel agencies, gardening centers, telephone operators, home builders, plumbers, electricians, hair stylists, hospital workers, counselors, and therapists all provided new services to a population that for the first time since the war began in 1914 actually could hope for a better future based on material progress. Despite political uncertainties and the financial strain of rebuilding the war-torn north of the country, France remained the acknowledged center of European cultural life during the 1920s. Artists and writers from around the world made their home in Paris. The American expatriate community was especially influential. African-American artists and the new jazz style in music found receptive audiences in the French capital.

For those Europeans with adequate disposable incomes in the 1920s, leisure activities became more diverse and innovative. The motion picture industry blossomed, and movie stars became cultural icons. While most moviegoers sought pure entertainment in the new "movie palaces," some film producers and directors tackled compelling social and intellectual issues. Trends in fashion, often prompted by films, took on added urgency for the middle class. Personal hygiene and beauty products,

Bauhaus School, Dessau, Germany   Designed by Walter Gropius, this building—the headquarters of the Bauhaus School in the late 1920s—was typical of Bauhaus architecture and graphic design. The Bauhaus style was sleek and modernistic, emphasizing function and simplicity.

especially women's cosmetics, were marketed and sold as keys to professional success, psychological well-being, and sexual appeal. Family holidays and shopping excursions became part of middle-class culture. The city became the focal point for new ideas. As skyscrapers began to transform the skyline of major cities in the United States, in Europe the **Bauhaus school,** established by German architect Walter Gropius (1883–1969), introduced a style that reflected the streamlined efficiencies of the modern factory. Emphasizing function in design and employing the latest synthetic materials, Bauhaus buildings, furniture, and fixtures all shared a stark simplicity. Affordability and utility were hallmarks of what became known as the "international style."

The Great Depression, 1929–1939

The optimism of the late 1920s was short-lived, however, and did not survive the **Great Depression** that began with the stock market crash in New York in October 1929. The prosperity of the 1920s rested on shaky foundations. Throughout the decade wages lagged behind rising levels of productivity. This meant that by the late 1920s manufacturers were producing more goods than consumers could afford to purchase, so factories began to slow production and lay off workers. Improvements in farming methods and expanded tillage increased output but had the unintended effect of lowering grain prices.

The combination of rural poverty and flat wage levels for urban workers meant that income disparities were pronounced. In the United States, for example, a mere

Unemployed Miner The collapse of the American stock market and the onset of the Great Depression led to widespread unemployment. As workers like this British coal miner lost their jobs, confidence in Western liberal democracy began to decline. Fascists and communists insisted that liberalism was doomed.

five percent of the population controlled one-third of total personal wealth. Capital investment and industrial expansion continued, while the potential global market for goods shrank. Non-Western developing countries were unable to buy European manufactures, since high protective tariffs in the West made it nearly impossible for these countries to earn capital through the sale of their agricultural products and raw materials. The reckoning came quickly in October 1929. Within one month of the initial stock market crash, overall stock values dropped by 40 percent, and the decline continued for the next three years. Suddenly, credit was no longer available for businesses or for foreign governments. Panic spread across borders, and massive layoffs began throughout the industrialized West. American banks, unable to recover loans made before October 1929, failed in record numbers. One-third of them had closed by 1932. Even prestigious European banks declared insolvency, and by 1933, the international reparations system had broken down completely. Leading Marxist theoreticians predicted the imminent collapse of world capitalism under the weight of its own contradictions.

The Social Impact The most crushing feature of the Great Depression was the loss of millions of jobs. One-fourth of the labor force in Britain and in the United States were out of work by 1933. Unemployment rates in Germany were even higher. Productivity plummeted as factories closed. Most governments were ill-prepared to deal with this crisis. Orthodox economic theory called for cuts in government spending and patience while the market corrected itself. However, as each nation erected even higher tariffs in a desperate attempt to protect its own producers, the resulting decline in international trade aggravated the overall crisis. The British economist John Maynard Keynes called for massive **deficit spending** by leading countries to stimulate their economies, but most policymakers dismissed this option (now commonplace in

Read the **Document**

The Great Depression: An Oral Account (1932)

on **MyHistoryLab.com**

View the **Image**

Migrant Mother, Great Depression

on **MyHistoryLab.com**

the West) with contempt. In the meantime, homelessness and malnutrition mounted, savings accounts were depleted, family farms were foreclosed, and peoples' confidence in themselves and in their political leaders tumbled.

The Democratic View   The second half of the 1920s had provided a brief respite for what was an otherwise gloomy economic situation during the interwar period. In retrospect, the victors had never recovered their momentum after so many millions had died in the period 1914 to 1918. In particular, the multiparty democracies seemed unable to provide their citizens with a compelling sense of purpose or collective identity. Rifts between right-wing and left-wing parties seemed unbridgeable. When the French socialist premier, Léon Blum (1872–1959), took office in 1936 and began a reform program that included a 40-hour work week, right-wing politicians denounced him as a Jew who was trying to recast France into a communist state. In Britain, the economic situation was so grim that King George V (r. 1910–1936) called upon the Labour, Conservative, and Liberal parties to form a joint "national" government in 1930 to deal with the economic crisis. However, neither the national government nor the Conservative ministry of Stanley Baldwin (1867–1947) that succeeded it was able to devise a creative solution to Britain's problems. American President Franklin Delano Roosevelt (1882–1945) took a number of modest, although controversial, steps to stimulate the U.S. economy. Centralized planning and a host of new government make-work agencies constituted Roosevelt's "**New Deal.**" Nevertheless, it was not until Britain and the United States began to re-arm in the late 1930s that the worst effects of the depression began to abate (see Map 23–1). Historian William Keylor has noted that one of the tragic ironies of modern history is that "organized violence on a large scale, or the preparation for it, has proved to be the most effective remedy for the economic problems of underconsumption and unemployment."

◉—Watch the **Video**

Responding to the Great Depression: Whose New Deal?

on **MyHistoryLab.com**

▢◉—Read the **Document**

An Attack on New Deal Farm Policies (1936)

on **MyHistoryLab.com**

◉—Watch the **Video**

Prosperity of the 1920s and the Great Depression

on **MyHistoryLab.com**

The Totalitarian View   The only governments that appeared to act decisively in the face of the global economic crisis were totalitarian ones under the leadership of a charismatic and intolerant leader. A central tenet of Enlightenment political theory involved the primacy of law over the will of the individual leader. In totalitarian systems, the leader was above the law, and his directives, no matter how irrational and irresponsible they appeared, became the embodiment of the national will. Unquestioning obedience to the leader was required at all times. Any opposition was considered treason and punished accordingly. This leadership principle was combined with an ideology that proclaimed human history could be reduced to one great myth or higher truth. Often that myth privileged one group of people over others on the basis of culture, race, or class; and the state was dedicated to realizing the triumph of that group.

MAP 23-1   The Great Depression in Europe   Europe was wracked by instability throughout the 1930s. This map indicates the extent of unemployment and political unrest, as well as the rise of right-wing and left-wing governments.

QUESTION: Which countries were hardest hit by the Depression?

During the 1920s and 1930s, both Fascism and Soviet communism cast them-selves as heroes in a herculean struggle against great evil. For Italian Fascists, that evil was synonymous with the liberal parliamentary state, and for German Nazis, it was with worldwide Jewry. The Soviets under Lenin—and especially under Stalin—associ-ated evil with capitalists, with their parliamentary political systems and meaningless nationalism, both of which prevented the world's working class from recognizing its common interests. Totalitarian regimes need enemies to justify their existence. The totalitarian state can never achieve complete victory, because a world without en-emies would remove the justification for pervasive state control. Totalitarian regimes politicized all aspects of life; they recognized no distinctions between the public and the private spheres. Schools, literature, art, scientific inquiry, voluntary associations, religious institutions, and popular culture all were controlled and supervised by the state. Since they viewed themselves as idealists pursuing the goal of social order and harmony, supporters of the totalitarian state felt justified in taking extreme actions against perceived enemies. With the party and its leader defining truth and goodness, individual conscience was nullified, and unspeakable actions in the name of the perfect society were legitimized.

Italy: The First Fascist State

Italy had joined the Allied side in World War I, but Prime Minister Vittorio Emanuele Orlando (1860–1952) walked out of the Paris Peace Conference after it became apparent that Italian demands for former Austrian territories along the Adriatic coast would not be met. Postwar Italian governments were weak and indecisive. Italy continued to wrestle with a deteriorating economy, rural poverty, inflation, and social unrest. Returning veterans could not find work, food shortages were commonplace, industrial strikes disabled production, and peasants began to occupy large estates. Southern Italy became a hotbed of banditry and disorder. Many Italians who had suffered hardships during the war, including relatives of the half-million war dead, began to long for a strong regime.

Benito Mussolini   Into this gathering disorder stepped Benito Mussolini (1883–1945). A veteran of the Great War and an ex-socialist, in 1919 he organized the Fascist Party (from *Fascio di Combattimento,* or League of Combat) in the city of Milan. Recruitment was especially strong among the unemployed ex-soldiers, while industrialists and other businessmen who feared a communist revolution provided financial support. For those seeking adventure, Mussolini evoked the history of the

Roman Empire; for factory owners and merchants, he promised to fight communist insurgency; and for the middle class, he promised to restore economic security and national purpose. Mussolini's black-shirted street fighters beat up socialists and strikers, often with the connivance of the police and military.

[◘] Read the **Document**

Mussolini, Political and Social Doctrine of Fascism

on **MyHistoryLab.com**

In 1922 Mussolini ordered a "march on Rome" to secure national power. When King Victor Emmanuel III (r. 1900–1946) refused to use the military to stop the march, the liberal cabinet resigned. On October 29, 1922, the king named Mussolini prime minister.

Eliminating the Opposition   Once in power, Mussolini consolidated his authority. In 1924 a new election law gave the political party with the largest popular vote two-thirds of the seats in parliament. The Fascists then called new elections and used their majority to pass legislation giving Mussolini the right to rule by decree. Opposition political parties were outlawed, the press was controlled, and Fascist gangs intimidated and in a few cases killed opponents of the regime. By the end of 1926, Mussolini was the unchallenged ruler of Italy with the title *Il Duce* (the leader).

One potential opponent of the regime was the Roman Catholic Church. The Vatican had been at odds with the Italian government since Italy seized the papal city of Rome in 1870. Mussolini shrewdly settled this dispute in 1929. Italy agreed to

Benito Mussolini   Italy's *"Il Duce"* in a characteristic pose atop an armored tank. This image conveys the militaristic, aggressive style of Fascist politics. Mussolini's government attacked Ethiopia in 1935, but the Italian army later found itself outmatched in World War II.

compensate the Catholic Church for the property it had seized and exempted remaining Church lands from taxation. Mussolini also recognized Vatican City as an independent state, made religious instruction mandatory in schools, and declared Roman Catholicism to be the religion of the nation. In return, Pope Pius XI (r. 1922–1939), who saw Mussolini as a bulwark against communism, recognized the legitimacy of the Italian state and encouraged Roman Catholics to cooperate with the Fascist regime. The Church later took issue with Mussolini's anti-Semitic laws and with his alliance with Germany, but it never broke ties with Italian Fascism.

Domestic Policy   Italian Fascism condemned liberalism, socialism, communism, and the equality of peoples. According to Mussolini, "Fascism conceives of the state as an absolute, in comparison with which all individuals and groups are relative, only to be conceived of in their relation to the state." However, when compared with Nazi Germany or Stalin's Russia, the Italian Fascist Party's efforts to control every aspect of life were far from successful. Fascist youth groups were organized to indoctrinate students, but many young Italians did not bother to attend their meetings. Women were encouraged to leave the workplace and remain at home, but this caused great resentment. Italy's military forces remained more loyal to the king than to the Fascist Party. Similarly, the large landowners and industrialists who funded the Fascist Party never fell completely under its control. Independent labor unions and the right to strike were outlawed, but worker unrest persisted, and strikes occurred anyway, even during World War II. Mussolini's attempts to make Italy economically self-sufficient through high import tariffs merely increased the price of domestically produced goods and food.

Fascist Italy remained a relatively poor and backward country where the image of strength and action was more important than reality. The poor remained poor, and corruption grew in the Fascist Party. In the 1930s Mussolini used foreign policy to distract the Italian people. He proclaimed that "war alone … puts the stamp of nobility upon the peoples who have the courage to meet it." In October 1935 he defied the League of Nations and invaded Ethiopia, one of only two independent states left in Africa. The stage was set for his fateful alliance with Nazi Germany and the so-called Rome-Berlin Axis.

Authoritarian Regimes in Spain and Eastern Europe

Spanish Civil War   In 1931 the Spanish monarchy collapsed and Spain became a republic. The domestic policies of the republican government alienated powerful conservative groups across the country, while socialist and anarchist groups grew stronger. Catholics, landowners, business groups, and the army grew increasingly restive, especially after a left-wing "Popular Front" alliance won national elections in February 1936. In July of that year, General Francisco Franco (1892–1975) launched a military revolt that soon led to civil war. The Spanish Civil War became a test case in the ideological struggle between European authoritarianism and democracy. Franco, a conservative Catholic, entered into a tactical alliance with Spain's Fascists, known as the *Falange*. Hitler and Mussolini supported him with troops and weapons. Stalin backed the republic, and by 1937 Soviet agents took over its security forces. Britain, France, and the United States stayed aloof, although tens of thousands of left-wing volunteers from the West joined the beleaguered republican loyalists. The war was bitterly fought, and both sides committed atrocities. After three years of fighting, however, Franco's superior military power, aided by German air power, prevailed. The German bombing of the town of Guernica in northern Spain became emblematic of the horrors of the war and prompted Pablo Picasso to paint his famous work (*Guernica*, 1937), expressionistically depicting the carnage. By the time the republic fell in 1939, almost half a million Spaniards had lost their lives; in the wake of his victory, Franco imprisoned an additional one million republican loyalists, many of whom were sent to concentration or labor camps. Pitting the forces of right-wing nationalism and fascism against those of democracy as well as socialism, the Spanish Civil War can now be seen as a dress rehearsal for the world war that would soon begin.

Eastern Europe   In the 1920s and 1930s democratic institutions faltered in the restored state of Poland, in the successor states to the Austro-Hungarian Empire, and in the Balkans. Poland had been divided into Russian, German, and Austrian spheres since the late eighteenth century. When a Polish state was resurrected after World

War I, its multiparty system did not produce stable or effective government. In 1926 a military takeover by Marshal Josef Pilsudski (1857–1935) established an authoritarian regime. Similar right-wing governments emerged in Romania, Bulgaria, and Greece.

In Hungary, Admiral Miklos Horthy (1868–1957) took power in 1920. Horthy's conservative royalist government was backed by an alliance of military and church leaders and large landowners. To the south in the new kingdom of Yugoslavia, Orthodox Serbs clashed repeatedly with Roman Catholic Croats and Slovenes, and with Bosnians and Albanians. In 1929, King Alexander I (r. 1921–1934) tried to suppress the disputes by banning political parties. He was assassinated by Croatian fanatics in 1934, but authoritarian rule continued under a regency government for his young son Peter II (r. 1934–1945). The breakup of Yugoslavia in the 1990s was in large measure the product of ethnic and religious divisions that flared up in the 1920s and 1930s. In all of eastern Europe only Czechoslovakia remained a parliamentary democracy during these years, and even there ethnic tensions among Czechs, Slovenes, Germans, and other groups threatened to break up the state.

The Emergence of Nazi Germany

The Great Depression shattered the stability of the Weimar Republic. As the unemployment lines swelled and the price of basic commodities increased, political parties quarreled over how to address the crisis. To break the stalemate, in 1930 Chancellor Heinrich Bruning (1885–1970) invoked a clause in the Weimar Constitution (Article 48) that allowed the president to issue emergency decrees. The president of Germany was the aged World War I military leader Paul von Hindenberg (1847–1934). When he dissolved the Reichstag in September 1930 and called for new elections, he set the stage for the meteoric rise of the ultraright National Socialist or Nazi Party.

Hitler's Rise to Power Adolf Hitler, the leader of the Nazis, had served in World War I and returned from the war a deeply embittered man. In 1919 Hitler joined the National Socialist German Workers' Party (Nazis) and rose to the position of its leader, or Fuehrer. In 1923 he tried to overthrow the state government of Bavaria. Imprisoned for nine months, Hitler spent his time behind bars composing his hate-filled autobiography, *Mein Kampf* (My Struggle). Mixing crude Social Darwinism, anticommunism, and anti-Semitism, the book endorsed the myth of the superior German race descended from the ancient Aryans. Hitler called for national renewal through the demolition of the liberal Enlightenment tradition and the expansion of the master race to the east, eliminating inferior Jews and Slavs in the process.

Read the **Document**

Excerpt from Mein Kampf

on **MyHistoryLab.com**

During the 1920s the Nazi Party did poorly at the polls. In 1928 the Nazis had only 12 seats in the Reichstag and little middle-class support. The party's fortunes changed decisively, however, once the Great Depression hit Germany. In the September 1930 elections, Hitler's party won 107 seats in the Reichstag and received 18 percent of the vote. The Nazis were now attracting the support of more affluent Germans who were worried about the economic crisis. Hitler promised to reestablish confidence in

PEOPLE IN CONTEXT José Ortega y Gasset

The Spanish philosopher José Ortega y Gasset (1883–1955) was a critic of mass democracy who believed that only the leadership of an intellectual elite could preserve modern civilization. He was educated in Jesuit schools and at the University of Madrid, where he was appointed professor of philosophy in 1910. A liberal in politics, he went into exile during the Spanish Civil War, returning to Spain only after the end of World War II in 1945.

In his most influential work, *The Revolt of the Masses* (1929), Ortega warned that the rise of irrationalism and violence in mass culture was plunging European civilization into a dark period. Ortega believed that mass culture led to conformism and support for mediocre politicians who appealed to base instincts. It would crush "everything that is different, everything that is excellent, individual, qualified and select. Anybody who is not like everybody, who does not think like everybody, runs the risk of being eliminated...." His critique was confirmed during the 1930s, as the Nazis in Germany and Stalin in the Soviet Union used modern communications, surveillance, and terror tactics to eliminate all personal freedoms.

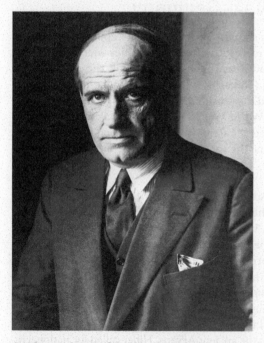

José Ortega y Gasset Spanish writer, playwright, and philosopher, in a photograph from the 1940s.

Ortega felt what he called "mass man" was both mentally unassertive and quick to hand over leadership to the undeserving. The ideas of the masses did not represent the best of culture, yet their numbers transformed vulgar ideas into a new orthodoxy. Ortega was convinced that modern mass culture and the primacy of the commonplace undermined the liberal adherence to fixed truths. Under Fascism, "there appears for the first time in Europe a type of man who does not want to give reasons or to be right, but simply shows himself resolved to impose his opinions. This is the new thing: the right not to be reasonable, the 'reason of unreason.'" The rise of communism and Fascism were for Ortega symptoms of unreflective mass society, where immediate and easy solutions to problems replaced any commitment to higher ideals or serious debate in a climate of mutual respect. ∎

QUESTION: Why is democratic culture susceptible to the lures of antidemocratic politicians?

the economy and destroy German communism. He also pledged to undo the hated Versailles Treaty and restore German military greatness.

Hitler was assisted by ever-increasing unemployment. By March 1932, some six million Germans were out of work, three times the number in 1930. Some of the unemployed found a sense of purpose and fellowship in the Nazi SA or storm troopers, paramilitary forces who, like their Italian Fascist counterparts, specialized in intimidation and terror tactics. There were 100,000 members of the SA in 1930 and one million in 1932. The SA attacked communists and socialists and staged mass rallies that appealed to German national pride. Still, many

Germans who voted for the Nazis did so with little enthusiasm, seeing the Hitler movement as merely the lesser of two evils when compared with the apparent paralysis of Weimar multiparty democracy.

In the presidential election of March 1932, Hitler narrowly lost to Hindenburg. However, in July elections to the Reichstag, the Nazis took 230 seats out of a total of 549, winning almost 40 percent of the popular vote and becoming the largest party in the legislature. Hoping to control Hitler, the 83-year-old Hindenburg and his conservative advisors offered Hitler the Chancellorship in January 1933. The government was supposed to be a coalition in which most of the ministers were non-Nazis. For years Hitler had been railing against the failings of the Weimar government; now he would be obliged to demonstrate that his policies could pull Germany out of economic depression. To remain in power, it was assumed, the Nazis would be forced to tone down their anti-Semitic, racist, and antidemocratic rhetoric. It was a fatal miscalculation on the part of Hitler's conservative political opponents.

The Nazi State   Chancellor Hitler immediately called for new elections to the Reichstag. Nazi propaganda and bullying frightened many voters who supported anti-Nazi candidates. A few days before the elections, a mysterious fire destroyed the Reichstag building in Berlin. Hitler blamed the communists, suspended civil liberties, and insisted that Germany was under attack from left-wing terrorists. The Nazis and their conservative allies won a majority of the seats in the elections, and in March 1933 the Reichstag gave Hitler dictatorial power for four years. Without hesitation the Nazi leader outlawed all other political parties, and when Hindenburg died in 1934, Hitler took over complete executive authority. Seeking to secure the support of the German military, whose generals disliked the rival paramilitary SA, Hitler ordered an elite force within the Nazi Party, the SS, to kill the SA leadership. Under Heinrich Himmler (1900–1945), the SS would become a ruthless and murderous organization dedicated to Hitler's world view. The elimination of the SA leaders achieved two goals for Hitler. The German army took a personal oath of allegiance to him as Fuehrer (not to the German state), and Hitler's principal rival within the Party, SA leader Ernst Roehm (1887–1934), was executed.

The Nazis took direct aim at the constitutional liberties guaranteed by Weimar democracy. Freedom of speech, assembly, and press were eliminated, and a secret police force, the Gestapo, rooted out any effective opposition. Nazi officials monopolized key government posts. Schools, professional associations, and even leisure orga-

Key Developments in Hitler's Rise to Power

1920	Hitler becomes leader of the Nazi Party
1923	Nazis stage "Beer Hall Putsch" in Munich
1924	Hitler writes *Mein Kampf*
1930	Nazis win 107 seats in parliamentary elections
1933	Hitler appointed chancellor
1934	Hitler eliminates SA leaders
1935	Nuremburg Laws
1938	"Kristallnacht"

View the **Closer Look**

The Nazi Party Rally

on **MyHistoryLab.com**

View the **Image**

German Painting Idolizing Hitler

on **MyHistoryLab.com**

nizations were forced to conform to Nazi directives. The Hitler Youth indoctrinated boys with Nazi ideology while the League of German Girls inculcated young women with the virtues of motherhood and of women's subordination to men. Campaigns were conducted to eliminate birth control, homosexuality, and abortion and to "improve" the German racial stock. Large families received special encouragement from the Nazi state with pensions and medals for women who gave birth to more than four children. Hitler's regime also controlled artistic expression, condemning American jazz and modernist art. University professors and their students publicly burned books thought to be subversive. Faculty who objected lost their posts.

Under the direction of propaganda minister Joseph Goebbels (1897–1945), the print and electronic media (radio and films) emphasized the infallibility of the Fuehrer and the submission of the individual to the totalitarian state and to the greater good of the master race. Goebbels embraced film as a powerful tool in shaping Fascist identity and in highlighting the differences between the harsh realities of Depression-era Germany and the renewal of national life under the Nazis. In 1933 he established the Reich Film Chamber, which became responsible for approving scripts, screening productions, and approving personnel. A state-controlled credit bank provided financing for filmmakers, and in 1934 the Reich Cinema Law outlawed Jewish participation in the industry. Many talented Weimar-era filmmakers fled the Nazi regime for America during the 1930s.

View the **Image**

Nazi Party Congress, Nuremburg

on **MyHistoryLab.com**

The young actress and filmmaker Leni Riefenstahl (1902–2003) put her talents at the disposal of the Hitler regime, producing masterful propaganda films that recorded the enormous rallies the Nazis held during the 1930s. *The Triumph of the Will* (1934) employed a production crew of 120, more than 30 cameras, and

Hitler and Propaganda   The Nazis staged large political rallies designed to highlight the dynamism and resolve of state authorities. In this photo from 1938 Hitler salutes from an open vehicle while troops and Nazi banners provide the backdrop.

a wide range of techniques, including shots of the Fuehrer in an airplane en route to the Nazi Party rally at Nuremberg. Masses of soldiers formed geometric lines and frames for the long distance shots at the rally, where Hitler strode up the stairs to deliver an emotional speech. Riefenstahl portrayed Hitler as decisive, all-knowing, eternally energetic, and the object of worshipful reverence and respect. Two years later, Riefenstahl produced *Olympia,* an evocative account of the 1936 Berlin Olympics. She emphasized the Nazi concern with physical superiority, using slow motion segments, underwater shots of swimmers, and panoramic scenes. Riefenstahl could not escape her association with Nazi propaganda, and she was briefly imprisoned after World War II. Al-

View the **Image**

1936 Berlin Olympics

on **MyHistoryLab.com**

though most of the approximately 1,100 feature films produced during the 12 years of the Third Reich were entertainment/escapist movies, the 10 percent that were overt propaganda films centered on the themes of preparation for war, Nazi Party ideology, and anti-Semitism.

Rebuilding the Economy   Unlike most other leaders in Europe during the 1930s, Hitler was willing to engage in deficit spending to jump-start the national economy. His confidence was based on the assumption that Germany would recoup its investments through future military and territorial aggression in Eastern Europe. Large public works, especially the creation of a modern transportation infrastructure, put thousands of Germans back to work. In 1933 Hitler repudiated the military provisions of the Versailles Treaty, withdrew from the League of Nations, and began a massive rearmament program under Hermann Goering (1893–1946). The military buildup led to full employment by the late 1930s. The six million Germans who were unemployed when Hitler took office in 1933 now had jobs, and to many the loss of personal freedom and the increasing intolerance of the Nazi regime were a small price to pay for economic security. Hitler had forged a strong sense of national purpose within a few years. Some observers in the Western democracies, still mired in the Great Depression, envied Germany's economic rebound and began to wonder whether a dictatorship was the only viable path to material abundance. Small Fascist movements emerged in France and Britain, while in the United States right-wing demagogues accused the Roosevelt administration of sympathizing with communism.

Anti-Semitism   German Fascism thrived on excluding and demonizing groups it deemed enemies of the German people. Hitler and the Nazi leadership despised leftists, homosexuals, gypsies, and Jehovah's Witnesses; members of these groups were persecuted and imprisoned without trial. In 1939 the regime even approved "euthanasia" programs for the mentally ill and infirm, leading to the murder of tens of thousands of Germans. However, drawing upon 2,000 years of European anti-Jewish prejudice, Nazism reserved its deepest animosity for Germany's Jews. For Hitler, Jews were disloyal internationalists who were committed to poisoning the superior "Aryan" racial stock. In 1935 the **Nuremberg Laws** stripped Jews of their citizenship. They were subsequently denied entry into the medical, legal, educational, and music professions and were forced to wear a Star of David on their garments. Non-Jews were forbidden to marry or have sexual relations with Jews.

On the night of November 9, 1938, Nazi gangs destroyed thousands of Jewish shops, synagogues, and homes in towns and cities across Germany. Thousands of Jews were imprisoned without trial in concentration camps, and the state seized their property. After this program—which came to be known as *Kristallnacht* (Night of Broken Glass)—those Jews who could do so emigrated, leaving behind most of their possessions. By the start of World War II in September 1939, over one-half of Germany's Jewish population had fled. While a small number of individual Christian

Kristallnacht   A synagogue burns during the "Night of Broken Glass" (*Kristallnacht*), November 9–10, 1938. This anti-Jewish rampage was an ominous milestone in the Nazis' persecution of German Jews, heralding a more openly violent policy.

clergy spoke out in protest, neither Protestant nor Catholic church leaders publicly opposed Nazi persecution of the Jews. Together with most German intellectual leaders,
influential Christians remained loyal to the Nazi regime even after the war began, and
they remained silent during the Holocaust. The Nazi goal of stripping individuals of
the capacity for independent thought had made enormous headway by the end of the
1930s. Rational thought and humane instincts had crumbled before the forces of intimidation and state-sponsored domestic terror. Few Germans at the time either recognized the full extent of the transformation that had occurred in less than one decade
or understood the implications of Nazi policy for the future of European civilization.

Imperial Japan

The rise of authoritarian, antidemocratic government in Western Europe was mirrored by developments in Asia's single industrialized state. Like the United States,
Japan had emerged from World War I in a relatively strong position. In the 1920s a
vibrant two-party political system developed, with all males over the age of 25 eli-
gible to vote in national elections. A series of social reforms were undertaken, labor
unions grew, and military expenditures fell. Japan was the best-educated and most
modernized country in Asia. However, since most Japanese were peasants and urban
workers who earned low wages, the domestic market for consumer goods was small,
and Japanese industry relied heavily on foreign markets to sell its products. When the
global depression struck and nations began to raise import tariff barriers to protect
domestic industry, Japan's overseas trade, particularly with the United States, plummeted. One-half of all Japanese factories were closed in 1931. As exports dropped by
50 percent between 1929 and 1931, crop failures in the north of the country led to
famine conditions in 1931 and 1932.

Invasion of Manchuria   Ultranationalists and army officers began to argue
that economic security required secure Asian markets, preferably in territories that
Japan controlled directly or indirectly. It was time to create an Asian Empire under the
direction of the military and the emperor. First on the
list of potential additions was Manchuria, a fertile and
resource-rich region in China's northeast. The attack
on Manchuria began in September 1931, and within
six months the Japanese had defeated the Chinese Nationalists and installed the former Chinese emperor,
Henry P'u Yi (1906–1967), as ruler of a new puppet
state named Manchukuo. When the League of Nations condemned the invasion, Japan
withdrew from the League. The ease with which Japan flouted the League's authority
was not lost on Fascist leaders in Italy and Germany.

View the **Image**

*Japanese in Tsingtao, China,
1920s*

on **MyHistoryLab.com**

Extreme Nationalism   In the spring of 1936 a group of right-wing army
officers attempted to overthrow Japan's parliamentary government. They sought to
put an end to Western-style democracy and looked with envy on Nazi Germany's
accomplishments. They promoted the values of emperor worship and the samurai
code of honor. Although the coup failed, the ultranationalists' rhetoric of "Asia for the

Asians" and their belief in Japan's racial superiority resonated with a large segment of the public. Japan continued its aggression against Nationalist China, and by 1938, Japan was selling almost half of its exports to Manchuria, Taiwan, and Korea—all lands under Japanese control. Because Japan still lacked the essential raw materials and fuels that modern industrial economies needed, Japanese military and political leaders now began to consider further expansion in Asia. Of particular interest were the rubber plantations of British Malaya and the oil produced in the Dutch East Indies (Indonesia). Japan's aggression against its Pacific neighbors alarmed Washington. Fear of American opposition proved to be crucial in the military's decision to attack United States naval forces at Pearl Harbor in December 1941.

The Soviet Union under Stalin

The repressive single-party state that emerged in Russia after the triumph of the Bolsheviks in the civil war against the White Russian forces and their foreign allies (1918–1921) was similar to Europe's Fascist regimes in several important respects. Once in power, the Bolsheviks ruthlessly eliminated their political rivals. They rejected the liberal concept of human rights and the rule of law, created a powerful secret police to root out dissent, and glorified the cult of the all-knowing and all-powerful leader. The good of the state as defined by the Communist Party leadership always took precedence over the economic, political, religious, cultural, and intellectual claims of the individual.

However, the Bolshevik government also rejected some of the key components of the Fascist world view. First and foremost, the leaders of the Soviet Union's Communist Party fervently believed that the revolution in Russia was but the first stage in what would become a global struggle to overthrow the capitalist political and economic order. Their appeal to international worker solidarity and their belief that the Russian Revolution was the dawn of a new age assumed that all human beings were equal. Social Darwinist pseudoscience, racism, and imperialist nationalism, all key components of Fascist thought, never played a significant role in Bolshevik ideology. The Soviet experiment also lasted much longer. The murderous German Third Reich lasted only 12 years, Japanese militarism endured barely a decade, and Mussolini's tenure was less than 25 years. The Soviet Union, by contrast, survived for three-quarters of a century before its demise in 1991.

The Early Soviet Economy   Although the Red Army prevailed during the civil war, conditions in Russia during the early 1920s were desperate. Famine and disease killed between five and seven million people, the economy was in tatters, strikes were commonplace, sailors from the Baltic naval fleet mutinied, and peasants refused to meet government grain requisitions. The promised fruits of a socialist society under the "dictatorship of the proletariat" were nowhere in sight. The Bolsheviks faced an overwhelming economic challenge at home and widespread international hostility. A small group of Communist Party leaders reserved all power to themselves and struggled to turn a backwards economy into a modern, industrialized socialist system. As the head of a seven-man Politburo (political bureau) that set policy for the larger Central Committee of the Communist Party, Lenin decided that he had to postpone his outline for a top-down planned economy. In a strategic retreat in March 1921, he announced the **New Economic Policy** (NEP). Peasant farmers were now allowed to manage their own plots of land and sell their surplus grain on the open market in return for the payment of a tax in kind. Similarly, small businesses and retail stores were allowed to operate along market lines. The change in policy had an immediate and positive impact; by 1927, industrial production had returned to pre-World War I levels.

Read the Document

Lenin Calls for Electrification of All of Russia (1920)

on **MyHistoryLab.com**

Succession Struggle, 1924–1928 When Lenin died in January 1924 after a series of strokes, a power struggle broke out to succeed him. Leon Trotsky, who advocated worldwide revolution, seemed to be the most likely successor, but the youthful Nikolai Bukharin (1888–1938), a man with wide-ranging interests and a strong supporter of Lenin's NEP, also enjoyed a great deal of influence. One other contender, Joseph Stalin, was not a native Russian but a Georgian from the Caucasus Mountain frontier zone. Raised in poverty, Stalin briefly attended an Orthodox seminary before becoming a Marxist revolutionary and follower of Lenin at the turn of the twentieth century.

Although Lenin had deep reservations about him, Stalin rose quickly to prominence in the Communist Party after the 1917 Revolution. Appointed general secretary of the Central Committee of the Communist Party in 1922, Stalin was no match for either Trotsky or Bukharin as a thinker, nor did he possess much knowledge of the West, having never lived in exile. But Stalin was a masterful propagandist and manager of the Communist Party apparatus. With control over the bureaucracy, which included admission to and promotion within the Communist Party, Stalin built his support within the lower ranks of the administration. He also led a movement to elevate the deceased Lenin to cult hero status and claimed to be Lenin's closest associate. In 1924 Stalin denounced Trotsky's appeal for world revolution and instead called for the creation of "socialism in one country." He also remained unenthusiastic about the NEP, preferring to push for total collectivization of agriculture and rapid industrialization. By 1927, Stalin had effectively marginalized both of his rivals. Trotsky was driven into exile in 1929, eventually finding his way to Mexico, where Stalin's assassins killed him in 1940. Bukharin was ousted from the Politburo and murdered in 1938.

The Stalin Terror State Between 1928 and the start of World War II in June 1941, Stalin transformed the Soviet Union into one of the world's premier industrial and military powers, but at a cost in human life that is hard to imagine. At least 20 million Soviet citizens died during this frenetic race to modernize an overwhelmingly agrarian empire. Many died from overwork and exhaustion; others were the victims of collectivization of agriculture and the resulting mass starvation. Millions more were shot or died in prison camps, having been arbitrarily defined as opponents of the all-knowing Soviet leader.

Read the Document

Stalin Demands Rapid Industrialization

on **MyHistoryLab.com**

View the Image

Stalinist Poster, 1931

on **MyHistoryLab.com**

Five-Year Plans Under Joseph Stalin, the Soviet Union embarked upon an accelerated program of industrialization. During the first Five-Year Plan (1933), posters like this encouraged an all-out effort to raise production. The words at the bottom read, "Industrialization is the road to socialism."

Stalin believed that the Soviet Union could not survive in a world of hostile capitalist nation-states unless it could match the West's industrial prowess. Setting aside the gradualist NEP, he established a state planning commission, or *Gosplan,* to oversee a series of **Five-Year Plans** built around the idea of state ownership in every sphere of economic life. The first target was the collectivization of agriculture. Soviet bureaucrats used the armed forces to put an end to private farming and forced the peasantry to work on large state-owned and managed collective farms. The government set production targets and used surpluses from the sale of farm products to finance industrialization.

There was enormous resistance to collectivization, especially among prosperous peasants. Many farmers even destroyed their own crops and livestock rather than surrender them to the state. However, Stalin was undeterred. Between 1929 and 1933, millions of landowners, called *kulaks* by Soviet authorities, were either killed or exiled to Siberia where they later perished in state-run labor camps. Agricultural output plunged during these years, and famine returned. Millions of people died of starvation, even as Soviet authorities exported grain produced on collectivized farms to raise capital for industrial projects. The greatest brutalities took place in Ukraine, the traditional breadbasket of the Russian Empire. Approximately seven million people died in Ukraine during the years of forced collectivization, most from starvation, but many at the hands of Soviet officials who killed resisters with impunity.

Forced labor on collectivized state farms eventually ended the famine and raised production levels. Thousands of excess workers were shifted to urban centers where they worked in newly established factories. The picture of Soviet life communicated to the outside world during the first Five-Year Plan (1928–1933) was one of agricultural surpluses, the building of new heavy industries and power plants at astonishing speed, and happy workers exceeding production targets. Carefully crafted media images of inspired workers and well-fed peasants, all committed to the dream of a cooperative socialist society, contrasted sharply with unemployment lines and business failures in the capitalist democracies. Some in the West believed that the Soviet system had avoided the ravages of the global depression. Few observers in the United States and Europe realized the enormous cost in human life resulting from forced collectivization. Nor did they appreciate the scale of Stalin's murderous repression.

Repression and Political Purges   Every sector of Soviet society was mobilized to support the modernization programs. Soviet schools inculcated the virtues of worker discipline, while newspapers, radio, and film applauded Stalin's vision and selflessness. Party officials and the secret police, the *Cheka* (later known as the KGB), ensured that political dissent was swiftly suppressed. Women were recruited into the workforce in large numbers, while mothers were taught to raise their children to serve the state. Soviet authorities imposed an official style in the arts, called "socialist realism," which was dedicated to eliminating decadent bourgeois themes. Artists, musicians, writers, and dramatists were all obliged to have their productions approved by communist bureaucrats. A cult of Stalin developed, and his image appeared on enormous posters, in paintings, in newsreels, and as statues in public places.

Stalin's growing paranoia and crude hunger for absolute power led him to equate debate with betrayal and treason. Beginning in 1934, he began to eliminate most of the old Bolsheviks, the founders and top leaders of the Communist Party, charging them with conspiracy to destroy the Soviet State. In a series of publicized show trials, high-profile defendants confessed (usually after torture and threats of retribution against their families) to a variety of treasonable offenses. All were executed. In parallel secret purges, members of the military high command were condemned and then killed by Stalin's agents. Once the Party and military leadership had been eliminated, Stalin turned against large numbers of middle-class professionals, including scientists, scholars, artists, and engineers. Millions of Soviet citizens, the well-known and the obscure, were killed without the least hesitation. Total conformity and unflinching obedience were required; family members were encouraged to inform on loved ones, and even children were drawn into the net of accusation and denunciation. No one was safe, as this period of the "Great Terror" concluded, and the only truth was that which issued from the diseased mind of the Party leader. By 1938, the Stalinist dictatorship had become a cruel caricature of Karl Marx's stateless communist society. The Russian people, less than two decades removed from tsarist absolutism, were now subject to levels of control and servility of which the tsars had never dreamed.

KEY QUESTION REVISITED

Does personal liberty matter to people who suffer under conditions of acute material hardship?

The interwar period failed to achieve either political reconciliation between former adversaries or lasting economic security for the peoples of Europe and the United States. The Versailles Treaty set the stage for future conflict by imposing harsh terms on the vanquished. Europe's fiscal indebtedness to the United States hampered efforts at economic reconstruction across the continent. The Soviet Union repudiated the debts of the tsarist regime, thereby guaranteeing that the West would offer no economic assistance. After a brief period of modest prosperity during the second half of the 1920s, the Great Depression plunged the Western democracies into an unprecedented crisis. As millions of citizens were reduced to the ranks of the unemployed, confidence in the ability of liberal democratic governments to respond effectively to the emergency tumbled. Across Europe the constitutional ideals of the Enlightenment, including responsible elective government, civil rights, equality under the law, and the guarantee of personal liberty, all seemed of minor importance in the face of acute material hardship.

Into this crisis of liberal democracy stepped radical politicians on the right and the left who declared that the Enlightenment tradition was bankrupt and that true greatness and material abundance could be secured only under the direction of charismatic and decisive leaders. Fascist leaders appealed to irrational impulses, ethnic and religious prejudice, hyperbolic nationalism, and aggressive militarism in pursuit of absolute political power. Rejecting parliamentary democracy as a government of weaklings and divisive special interests, authoritarian and Fascist leaders claimed that the future belonged to their movement. Writing at the end of World War II, the exiled German philosopher Ernst Cassirer (1874–1945) described the Fascist phenomenon as the victory of the grand myth over hard reality. The myth was multifaceted, but it was anchored in the rhetoric and action of inhumanity.

Soviet totalitarianism took a different form. The same malignity and repression of the individual was central to the power of both Fascist and communist regimes, but Stalin's call for worker solidarity and the creation of the classless society served as the basis of opposition to Western liberal democracy. Stalin sought supreme power for himself and to make the Soviet Union a modern economic and military power at any cost. By 1939, he had achieved these goals, but Soviet modernization emphasized industrialization for the sole purpose of national defense, while the consumer sector was largely ignored. Soviet citizens lived under a government that put people to work and, by the mid-1930s, offered food and shelter where too often in the past there had been poverty and starvation. However, tens of millions of lives had been lost in the process of building the Soviet economy. A man for whom truth was simply the successful application of power in society, Stalin did not recognize Western liberal definitions of freedom and dignity.

While Western Europe's democratic states maintained personal liberty, defenders of the rationalist-humanist tradition were hard-pressed during the interwar period. The appeal of totalitarianism, its simple solutions to complex problems, its call to instinct and action, and its focus on larger collective goals appealed to many Europeans seeking renewal in a deeply troubled postwar culture. In those countries where democracy had taken deep root—Britain, France, Switzerland, Ireland, and in the United States—personal liberties were protected despite acute material hardship. Where democratic practices had not taken root, the promise of material security under authoritarian political systems, while destroying individual autonomy and the right to dissent peacefully through the political process, was too seductive to be ignored. Once seduced, however, the citizen became a subject, the leader became a secular god, and the dignity of the individual evaporated before the shrine of state power.

Key Terms

fascism, *p. 680*
Great Depression, *p. 684*

New Economic Policy, *p. 699*
Five-Year Plans, *p. 700*

Stalin's Purges, *p. 701*

Activities

1. How did the West's liberal democracies respond to the Great Depression? How did Fascist and communist regimes respond?

2. Explain how the Great Depression advanced Hitler's rise to power.

3. Outline the main features of the totalitarian state in the 1930s.

4. How did Stalin modernize the Soviet Union in less than a decade? Why did the Soviet economy appear to be moving forward while Western economies stagnated?

5. How did Mussolini's Fascists manage to secure power in 1922?

6. Analyze the factors contributing to Japan's descent into militarism and imperialism in the 1930s.

7. How did Nazism repudiate the central tenets of the Enlightenment tradition?

Further Reading

Richard Evans, *The Coming of the Third Reich* (2004), a treatment of the years leading up to the Hitler regime.

John Stevenson and Chris Cook, *The Slump: Britain in the Great Depression* (2010), a moving account of public policy and daily life in the 1930s.

Anne Applebaum, *Gulag: A History* (2003), looks at one feature of Stalin's brutality.

Arthur Koestler, *Darkness at Noon* (1984), a modern edition of one of the twentieth-century's most important political novels, set in the Soviet Union in 1938.

MyHistoryLab Connections

Visit **MyHistoryLab.com** *for a customized Study Plan that will help you build your knowledge of* The Troubled Interwar Years.

Questions for Analysis

1. What was the Bonus March and how did the U.S. government respond to the demands of the World War I veterans that took part in the march?

Read the **Document** The Great Depression: An Oral Account (1932), p. 685

2. What are some of the outside forces that contributed to and shaped the New Deal?

Watch the **Video** Responding to the Great Depression: Whose New Deal?, p. 686

3. What are some of the parallels between Hitler's early years in power and Roosevelt's early years in power as both confronted severe economic crises?

Watch the **Video** Hitler and Roosevelt, p. 693

4. How were symbolism and mythology used by the Nazis to win public support for their policies?

View the **Closer Look** The Nazi Party Rally, p. 694

5. Why did Stalin make rapid industrialization such an important policy goal?

Read the **Document** Stalin Demands Rapid Industrialization, p. 699

Other Resources from This Chapter

View the **Image** London Stock Exchange, 1920s, p. 681

View the **Image** Migrant Mother, Great Depression, p. 685

Read the **Document** An Attack on New Deal Farm Policies (1936), p. 686

Watch the **Video** Prosperity of the 1920s and the Great Depression, p. 686

Read the **Document** Mussolini, *Political and Social Doctrine of Fascism*, p. 688

Read the **Document** Excerpt from *Mein Kampf*, p. 691

View the **Image** German Painting Idolizing Hitler, p. 694

View the **Image** Nazi Party Congress, Nuremberg, p. 694

View the **Image** 1936 Berlin Olympics, p. 695

View the **Image** Japanese in Tsingtao, China, 1920s, p. 697

Read the **Document** Lenin Calls for Electrification of All Russia (1920), p. 699

View the **Image** Stalinist Poster, 1931, p. 699

Liberation The citizens of Palermo, Sicily, welcome American forces into their city after it surrendered to Allied forces on July 22, 1943.

24 World War II: Europe in Eclipse

((•[Hear the Audio   Chapter 24 at MyHistoryLab.com

LEARNING OBJECTIVES

Why was appeasement so popular in the 1930s? • How was Nazi Germany able to dominate its enemies before 1942? • How did the Nazis govern their occupied territories? • What was the role of women on the home front? • How did the tide of war turn after 1942? • How did members of the Grand Alliance plan for the postwar world?

We shall never surrender; and even if, which I do not for a moment believe, this island or a larger part of it were subjected and starving, then our Empire beyond the seas, armed and guarded by the British Fleet, would carry on the struggle, until, in God's good time, the New World, with all its power and might, steps forth to the rescue and liberation of the Old.

—Winston Churchill

KEY QUESTION

Can deeply held ideas and values sustain a civilization under violent attack?

In early June 1940, after the conquest of Poland, Denmark, Norway, Belgium, Luxembourg, and Holland by Germany, and as the last troops of the British Expeditionary Force were being hastily evacuated by sea from the beaches at Dunkirk in France, Prime Minister Winston Churchill (1874–1965) addressed the House of Commons and spoke the words just quoted. The defeat of France was now imminent, but Churchill remained defiant. He assured his parliamentary colleagues and the nation that the war against Nazi aggression, what he had earlier termed "a monstrous tyranny, never surpassed in the dark lamentable catalogue of human crime," would continue until victory was achieved.

Churchill seemed to be confident that if Germany invaded the British Isles, the colonial subjects of King George VI (r. 1936–1952) would come to the defense of the Empire. After all, they had done so once before. Churchill took it for granted that Britain's subject peoples would assist Britain in its new moment of peril. Remarkably, most colonials responded positively, again sacrificing their sons for the preservation of a state and a system committed to the principles of liberal democracy, even though those principles had not been extended to the colonies themselves. Churchill also spoke of the New World, with its power and might, coming to the aid of the Old. This, too, was a bold prediction, especially in light of America's strongly isolationist political culture during the 1930s. But it also came true. The United States entered the war in December 1941 and afforded Britain the material resources to sustain its commitment to democratic culture. With the military support of the United States, Western Europe would reject Nazi absolutism and return to the path of democracy. However, it could no longer follow that path unassisted or unprotected. Europe had been eclipsed. ■

The Process of Appeasement, 1933–1939

Hitler had stated clearly in *Mein Kampf* that Germany's future greatness was contingent upon war and expansion into eastern Europe. The Slavic peoples, including the Russians, were from inferior racial stock and needed to be subordinated to the master Aryan inhabitants of Germany. The persecution of German Jews and the destruction of Weimar democracy during the 1930s should have signaled the danger of the Fascist threat to Western civilization. Nazi domestic policy was always formulated in the expectation of future territorial expansion and the inevitability of war. Throughout the 1930s Germany's neighbors, particularly France and Great Britain, failed to recognize the depth of the Nazi commitment to war. They chose instead to believe that if only Hitler's latest territorial demand was met in the best spirit of international cooperation, conflict could be avoided and the Nazi state integrated into the European political system. Appeasing Hitler seemed to be the best way to avoid repeating the horrors of World War I. The memory of that conflict was still fresh in the 1930s, and for many British and French policymakers, **appeasement** was a reasonable, positive approach to international relations on the continent.

◉⌐View the Image

Nazi Book Bonfire, 1933
on **MyHistoryLab.com**

Germany's Neighbors Hesitate   Hitler's decisions to withdraw from the League of Nations in 1933 and to begin rearming Germany were the first of many calculated gambles that the Nazi leader took, but given the League's failure to act against Japan after that country invaded Manchuria in 1931, it was unlikely that the international organization would intervene. Hitler's assumption was correct. In 1934 the Nazi regime signed a nonaggression pact with Poland, an agreement that increased nervousness in France, which considered Poland a potential ally. It was followed by the restoration of the German air force and the creation of a 500,000-man German army—both violations of the Versailles Treaty.

Instead of a collective response, Germany's neighbors hastened to cut individual deals. Britain, for example, sought to maintain its historic naval superiority by entering into a separate agreement with Hitler. The British approved the construction of a German fleet that would be one-third the size of Britain's Royal Navy. France signed a five-year defensive alliance with the newest member of the League of Nations, the Soviet Union, in May 1935. The French military also constructed a series of defensive installations, called the Maginot Line, to repel any future German attack. The French and British also negotiated regional pacts involving Turkey, Greece, Romania, and

Yugoslavia to preserve the status quo in the Balkans. However, none of these agreements or alliances curbed the remilitarization of the German state. Neither did they inhibit Hitler's demands that all German-speaking people be united to Germany or his strident calls for more living space (*Lebensraum*) at the expense of "inferior" Slavic peoples.

The Rhineland Wager

When Mussolini attacked Ethiopia in 1935, the League of Nations imposed weak economic sanctions on Italy but took no military steps to preserve the independence of the African state. In a further blow to League credibility, oil companies in the United States, against the wishes of President Roosevelt, continued to supply the Italian armed forces with fuel. Always the opportunist, Hitler now prepared another strike against the hated Versailles Treaty. He entered into a defense pact with Italy, and both countries were joined by Japan in what was ostensibly an anticommunist alliance. In March 1936 Hitler ordered German troops into the demilitarized Rhineland, the industrial heart of Germany. It was another high-stakes gamble, opposed even by the leaders of his own military who feared that the French would attack and occupy the Rhineland. Hitler's estimate of British and French resolve proved to be on target. British leaders were willing to look the other way, since the Germans were not annexing new territory but simply asserting full sovereignty over a part of Germany itself—and France was unwilling to act without British support.

Austria, Czechoslovakia, and "German" Unity

Hitler was a native Austrian, and he passionately believed that all Germans, especially Austrians, should be united in one state. The idea of unification, or *Anschluss,* between Germany and Austria had been discussed in 1919, but the Versailles Treaty forbade it. By the late 1930s, Austria was weak and divided with a large Nazi Party. In March 1938 Hitler used the pretext of possible civil disturbances in Austria to order the German army to occupy the country. France and Britain took no action. Austria's 6.5 million people became part of the German Reich (empire). Hitler used the rhetoric of national self-determination to legitimize an annexation that was in any case highly popular with the Austrian people.

Almost immediately after his successful Austrian gambit, Hitler took up the question of the 3.5 million Germans living in a region of western Czechoslovakia known as the Sudetenland. Again he used the rhetoric of national self-determination to make a power grab. Although many of the Sudeten Germans disliked Czech rule, Czechoslovakia was the only genuine democracy in central Europe. Czech authorities stood firm even though Hitler's propaganda machine decried the "persecution" of Czechoslovakia's German minority. By September 1938, war seemed imminent, especially since Czechoslovakia had treaties of alliance with France and the Soviet Union. To avert a European war, British Prime Minister Neville Chamberlain (1869–1940) entered into direct negotiations with Hitler, and Britain and France put pressure on Czechoslovakia to yield to Hitler's demands.

After a series of complicated negotiations, Mussolini called for a four-power conference at Munich. Chamberlain and French Premier Edouard Daladier (1884–1970) met with Hitler and Mussolini at the conference, which ran from September 22 to September 29, 1938. Czechoslovakia and the Soviet Union were not invited to attend. The meeting ended with France and Britain awarding Hitler the Sudetenland. France refused to honor its military commitments to Czechoslovakia, while the Soviets were infuriated by their exclusion from the meeting. Chamberlain represented a nation that was neither prepared for war nor completely unsympathetic to the German claim that the Versailles Treaty had arbitrarily assigned Germans against their will to the new Czech republic. In addition, many British policymakers, while disdainful of the Nazi regime, viewed Hitler as a potential ally against international communism. Chamberlain returned home to announce that with the **Munich agreement,** Hitler's territorial demands had been satiated. The settlement had achieved "peace in our time." Churchill was less certain. In the House of Commons he stated that Chamberlain had been defeated in Munich and that the German dictator, "instead of snatching the victuals from the table, has been content to have them served to him course by course."

[●] **Read** the **Document**

Neville Chamberlain, In Search of Peace

on **MyHistoryLab.com**

[○] **View** the **Image**

Hitler and Chamberlain, 1938

on **MyHistoryLab.com**

The Destruction of Czechoslovakia   Hitler interpreted the Munich agreement as a further sign of Western weakness. The truncated Czechoslovak state was doomed. Poland and Hungary received parts of it, and in March 1939, on the pretense of protecting the Slovaks who were in revolt against Czech rule, German troops occupied Prague and ended Czech independence (see Map 24–1). This invasion destroyed the pretense that Hitler was simply interested in national self-determination for Germans. It now became apparent that the policy of appeasement, based on the assumption that Hitler was a reasonable statesman who would not recklessly plunge Europe into another world war, was a failure. Britain and France at last began to take steps to resist further Nazi aggression. They did not have long to wait.

Poland and the Resumption of War   For the first time since the Bolshevik Revolution of 1917, the Western democracies and the Soviet Union faced a common threat. Hitler's opposition to communism and his stated desire for "living space" in the east posed a long-term challenge to Stalin's totalitarian regime, while the assault on democracy in Central Europe dispelled any lingering Western illusions about the Nazi agenda. Immediately after the carve-up of Czechoslovakia, the Soviets called for a six-nation conference (Britain, France, Russia, Poland, Rumania, and Turkey) to discuss the possibility of joint measures against further Nazi attacks. Most of these states were fearful of Soviet intentions, and the conference was never held. However, when Hitler began to bully Poland in early 1939, Britain and France pledged to come to its aid in the event of a German attack. The Versailles peace settlement had awarded parts of eastern Germany to the Polish state. Hitler now called for a revision of this settlement. His ultimate objective was either to reduce Poland to the status of a puppet state or to destroy it entirely. Poland would not be bullied, and by June 1939, the German army completed plans for an invasion.

Hitler-Stalin Pact   At this critical juncture, the Germans reached a surprise nonaggression pact with the Soviet Union. Stalin was suspicious of the West, and in an attempt to buy Hitler off, he agreed (in secret provisions) to remain neutral while

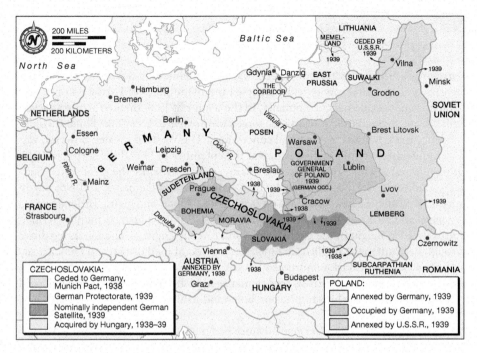

MAP 24-1   The Partitions of Czechoslovakia and Poland 1938–1939   Adolf Hitler's obsession with greater "living space" (*Lebensraum*) for the German people led him to steadily encroach upon countries to the east and south of Germany in the late 1930s.

QUESTION: Why were the other European powers unable to stop German expansion?

Hitler's forces dismantled Poland. Stalin had never accepted Russia's loss of territory in 1918 and 1919. The pact with Hitler gave the Soviet leader a free hand to reoccupy these lands, including a large part of eastern Poland. The Nazi-Soviet nonaggression pact was signed on August 23, 1939. Less than two weeks later, on September 1, 1939, Germany invaded Poland using tanks and air power. Within one month, this ***Blitzkrieg*** (lightning war) overwhelmed the Poles. The Soviets invaded eastern Poland, and again the country was wiped off the map of Europe.

War Resumes   The British and the French declared war two days after the German invasion. However, they did nothing to assist the beleaguered Poles and remained passively on the defensive on the Western front. After two decades of uneasy peace, Europeans were once again at war. When it ended six years later, the Western world would be changed forever. Unlike they had in 1914, no one in Britain, France, or Germany rejoiced at the outbreak of the conflict; none of Europe's leading intellectuals mused about the cleansing effects of battle; no parades were organized for the departing troops. After years of hesitation and hope against hope that Hitler would act responsibly once the harsher provisions of the Versailles Treaty were withdrawn, Europe's major constitutional democracies went to war as a last resort against a regime that contemptuously equated truth with power.

Nazism Triumphant, 1939–1941: Europe and North Africa

Germany's swift destruction of Poland was accompanied by Soviet advances from the east. Stalin's Red Army quickly occupied the Baltic states of Latvia, Estonia, and Lithuania, and seized part of Romania. In the winter of 1939 the Red Army attacked Finland, but strong Finnish resistance forced the Soviets to recognize Finland's independence in exchange for territorial concessions. The Western theater, however, was largely quiet between the outbreak of war in September 1939 and the spring of 1940. Often referred to as the "phony war," it was an eerie calm before the great storm. Suddenly, and with overwhelming force, the Nazis occupied Denmark and Norway in April 1940, inflicting heavy damage on British naval forces and giving Hitler access to key naval and air bases for a future assault against Britain. The next month German troops invaded Belgium, the Netherlands, and tiny Luxemburg. The Blitzkrieg drove through Belgium to the English Channel, forcing a combined British and French army to the beaches at Dunkirk in northern France. Despite German aerial bombardment, over 300,000 French and British troops managed to flee across the Channel aboard everything from small ships to pleasure boats and fishing craft.

Fall of France   The German advance had outflanked the well-defended Maginot Line through the Ardennes Forest and into northern France. Well-armed but poorly led French troops quickly lost heart after the Dunkirk disaster. Mussolini, eager to share in the spoils now that a German victory seemed certain, invaded southern France on June 10. The French easily repulsed the Italians, but Paris fell to the Germans on June 13, and French political leaders, after only five weeks of combat, decided to sue for an armistice. It was solemnly signed on June 22, 1940, in the same railway car where Germany had capitulated to the Allies in 1918. Germany occupied northern France and the strategically important coastline. The new French government, led by the aged hero of Verdun, Marshall Henri Philippe Petain (1856–1951), was located in the southern city of Vichy. It agreed to collaborate with the Nazis in areas of France under German occupation. Not all French leaders, however, accepted defeat. General Charles de Gaulle (1890–1970), from exile in London, organized a Free French government and vowed to continue the struggle. For French citizens who remained behind, however, the hard reality of military occupation called for sullen adjustment and resignation. The German juggernaut appeared unstoppable in the summer of 1940, a fact that led Hitler to assume that the British would swiftly accept the new political order on the continent.

View the Closer Look

The Vichy Regime in France on **MyHistoryLab.com**

Battle of Britain   Winston Churchill became prime minister in May 1940 at the head of a coalition government dedicated to continuing the war. Churchill had been a consistent opponent of appeasement, and he used his oratorical skills to rally the British public for the fight ahead despite seemingly impossible odds. In August the German air force, the *Luftwaffe,* began attacking British naval and military installations in preparation for a cross-Channel invasion. When the British responded by

German Troops Occupy Paris   French defenses proved to be woefully inadequate against German assault in 1940. In this photo, Hitler's troops march down the Champs-Élysées in the capital city of Paris.

bombing German cities, Hitler began a nightly bombardment of London. For two months, the battle for mastery of the skies over Britain raged between the Royal Air Force (RAF) and the *Luftwaffe*. German losses were twice as high as those incurred by the RAF, and for the first time in the war, Hitler was forced to abandon his offensive plans.

The Battle of Britain united the British public as never before. Although Britain stood alone against the previously unstoppable tyrant, Churchill's leadership and the bravery of a handful of combat pilots had scored an important victory. Referring to those pilots on August 20, Churchill told Parliament that "never in the field of human conflict was so much owed by so many to so few." Even the royal family became a symbol of popular resistance. When large portions of central London were destroyed by Nazi bombs and while other European monarchs were forced to flee their homelands, King George VI (r. 1936–1952) and Queen Elizabeth (1900–2002) remained at their home, Buckingham Palace. The monarchs visited bomb sites across the city on a regular basis, especially the poor districts of the heavily damaged East End. After Buckingham Palace was hit by bombs and rockets, Elizabeth said, "It makes me feel I can look the East End in the Face." The Queen made a point of wearing bright pastel colors and exhibited great warmth on these walkabouts. Her radio addresses, along with those of Churchill, brought comfort and resolve to the nation at its darkest hour. Hitler referred to Elizabeth as the most dangerous woman in Europe.

▶ **Read the Document**

Churchill, Their Finest Hour

on **MyHistoryLab.com**

In the spring of 1941, President Roosevelt, despite strong isolationist sentiment in Congress, established the **Lend-Lease Program** in which American goods and services, including military hardware, could be transferred to any country whose defense the president deemed vital to the security of the United States. Congress approved the expenditure of $7 billion for war materials under Lend-Lease, and the American navy began patrolling the North Atlantic and assisted the British in tracking down German submarines. From Hitler's perspective, the United States had become an undeclared enemy. Its overwhelming material resources would enable Britain to defy Germany throughout 1941.

North Africa and the Balkans   Eager to match Germany's military feats, in September 1940 Mussolini ordered his forces in the Italian colony of Libya to attack British-controlled Egypt. The Italians also began operations against Greece from bases in occupied Albania. In both assaults the Italians were humiliated. Hitler felt obliged to assist his hapless ally, assigning General Erwin Rommel (1891–1944) to the North African theater. Rommel was a skillful tank commander, and his Afrika Korps armored divisions drove the British back from Libya into Egypt. His goal was to gain control over the Suez Canal, Britain's lifeline to its South Asian Empire. Nazi forces also conquered Greece and Yugoslavia and forced Hungary and Romania to join the **Axis** (as the German-Italian alliance was called). Romania's oil fields were crucial to the German war effort, and Hitler needed to secure the Balkans before attacking the Soviet Union. By the spring of 1941, Germany dominated the continent and was poised for an assault against Stalin's totalitarian empire (see Map 24–2).

War in Russia   Hitler had always planned to destroy the Soviet Union despite the nonaggression pact he had signed with Stalin in 1939. He hoped to knock Britain out of the war before turning east, but in June 1941, with Britain still unsubdued, Hitler ordered a massive land and air assault, code named **Operation Barbarossa** (after the medieval German crusader emperor Frederick Barbarossa), against the communist regime. The invading army consisted of over three million men plus thousands of tanks and aircraft. Hoping to repeat Germany's other rapid military successes on the continent, optimistic German generals anticipated the destruction of Soviet forces within six weeks. Hitler apparently believed that by swiftly defeating the Soviet Union, he would convince the British of the futility of continuing the war. In fact, it was imperative that the German campaign reach a successful conclusion before the start of the long Russian winter.

The early stages of the German advance seemed to confirm the original timetable. Despite Stalin's buildup of the Soviet military during the 1930s, Russian forces were caught off-guard. The German *Luftwaffe* destroyed thousands of Russian aircraft while they were still on the ground, and over two million Russian soldiers were killed, wounded, or captured during the first six months as German tanks repeatedly smashed through Russian lines. Resistance was fierce, however, and when the autumn rains became the snow and sleet of the harsh Russian winter, the invaders found themselves straining to maintain communication and supply lines. The Germans nearly reached Moscow by December 1941, but a bold Russian counterattack saved the city. To the north, the inhabitants of Leningrad found themselves surrounded by German troops but refused to surrender. The Blitzkrieg was over as the war bogged down in conditions that placed the invaders at a severe disadvantage.

MAP 24-2 Axis Powers in Europe   In the spring of 1941, Nazi Germany and its allies dominated the European continent. The United States had not yet entered the war, and Hitler's forces were poised to invade the Soviet Union.

QUESTION: What were the advantages of Germany's position in 1941? What were the disadvantages?

The German Empire

By the winter of 1941, Hitler's armed forces had conquered most of Europe, making Hitler master of an empire larger than that of either Charlemagne or Napoleon. The Nazi ruler spoke vaguely of a New Order for Europe and of a thousand-year German Reich. However, the Nazis had no clear blueprint for the future. Instead, Hitler constantly improvised, guided more by racist prejudice than by geopolitical calculation. Where the Nazis did not annex lands and rule directly, they set up puppet regimes and used collaborators to assist their war effort. Foodstuffs, manufactured goods, armaments, oil, and coal flowed into Germany from the defeated and demoralized states of Hitler's continental empire. Millions of forced laborers were brought to Germany

PEOPLE IN CONTEXT   Charles de Gaulle and Free France

With much of France under German occupation and collaborationist Vichy France in control of the rest of the country, General Charles de Gaulle (1890–1970) refused to accept France's defeat. Throughout the war de Gaulle lobbied hard with both the British and Americans to provide additional aid to his Free French movement, often infuriating the Americans but always impressing Churchill with his tenacity and patriotism.

De Gaulle was born in Lille, France, the son of a philosophy and literature professor at a Jesuit college. He graduated from a military school in 1912, served in World War I, and was wounded and captured by the Germans in 1916 at Verdun. During the 1930s, he wrote a number of books and articles that criticized the Maginot Line defensive strategy

Return to Paris   Charles de Gaulle enters the capital after it was liberated by Allied forces in March 1944.

and called for the creation of mechanized armored forces and a modern air force. His advice was not heeded by France's military and political establishment.

When the German assault began in May 1940, de Gaulle was commander of the Fourth Armored Division. In June he was appointed undersecretary of state for war and argued vigorously against surrender. He advised the government to withdraw to Algeria if the Germans overran France. His superiors overruled him, and de Gaulle fled to London. Here, in a radio broadcast to occupied France, he called upon his fellow citizens to continue the struggle against Hitler. On June 28 the British government recognized him as the leader of the Free French. The following month a Vichy court-martial convicted de Gaulle of treason *in absentia*.

A number of the French colonies in sub-Saharan Africa rallied to the Free French. Small Free French units fought alongside the British in North Africa and against Vichy forces in Syria and Lebanon. On Bastille Day in 1941 de Gaulle made a strong plea for American entry into the war on behalf of Western democracy and against the Fascist menace. Once the United States was in the war, however, de Gaulle felt betrayed by President Roosevelt's willingness to negotiate with Vichy governments. By 1944, however, de Gaulle's French Committee of National Liberation had become the provisional government of the French Republic, and de Gaulle was its unquestioned leader. Hundreds of thousands of Free French soldiers fought alongside the Allies in the Italian campaign and in the Normandy invasion of June 1944. The Free French Second Armored Division led the Allied advance toward Paris, and on August 26, 1944, de Gaulle entered the city of Paris in triumph.

De Gaulle was elected president of the provisional postwar government in October 1945, but he resigned in January 1946 after failing to secure a constitution that included a strong presidency. However, he returned to power in 1958 and was elected president of the Fifth French Republic under such a constitution. He served as president, pursuing a largely independent course in foreign relations, until his resignation in 1969. ◼

QUESTION: How does de Gaulle's experience in exile relate to the larger issue in this chapter?

to work in factories and mines, on farms, and in other war-related enterprises. The Nazis also looted art treasures and gold from defeated countries and forced them to pay for the troops who were occupying them.

Nazi Brutality   In the occupied lands, hundreds of thousands of innocent people were summarily jailed, tortured, and executed. Some of the worst abuses took place in occupied Poland, where schools and churches were shut down; local political, religious, and community leaders killed; and farmers forced off their land. German soldiers and SS guards reserved their harshest treatment for Russians. As the German army pushed toward Leningrad and Moscow in 1941, captured Soviet leaders were murdered while the civilian population was starved. Hitler believed that the Russian people who survived the war should be either enslaved or forced into central Asia, leaving their fertile lands for German soldier-settlers. The head of the SS, Heinrich Himmler (1900–1945), preferred to

View the Image

Nazis Executing Russian Civilians

on **MyHistoryLab.com**

Russian Women Digging Anti-Tank Trenches   The Soviet government enlisted civilian help to prepare for the German assault on Moscow, October 1941. After initial defeats, the Soviet Union rallied to halt and eventually reverse the Nazi advance during the winter of 1941–1942.

eliminate at least 30 million Slavs in order to provide Germany with living space in eastern Europe.

Resistance to the Nazi regime in Europe was strongest among the various European communist parties after the invasion of the Soviet Union. Other resistance fighters were nationalists who took enormous risks in an effort to free their countries from the Hitler regime. In Vichy France, Norway, Czechoslovakia, and other countries where authorities collaborated with the Nazis, the resistance passed intelligence information to the Allies, engaged in sabotage and assassination, assisted escaped prisoners, and distributed resistance literature. The Croatian communist Josip Broz (1892–1980), who went by the alias Tito, fought a protracted guerilla war against the German and Italian occupiers of Yugoslavia. At the end of the war Tito became the leader of an independent communist Yugoslavia. Many resisters were betrayed and captured by the Nazis, who also tortured and killed the family members of those who dared oppose them.

The Destruction of the Jews   Hitler wished to rid Germany and Europe of its Jews as part of his policy of racial purification, and the war gave him the opportunity to annihilate them. In *Mein Kampf* Hitler decried "the black-haired Jewish youth" who with "satanic joy in his face . . . lurks in wait for the unsuspecting girl whom he defiles with his blood, thus stealing her from her people. With every means he tries to destroy the racial foundations of the people he has set out to subjugate. . . ." Operating on the perverse assumption that an entire people had colluded in a malicious grand design to destroy the German "race," Hitler employed all of the resources of modern technology, bureaucracy, and propaganda to murder an entire people. Himmler was placed in charge of this fiendish business, and he took to his assignment with enthusiasm. In addition to the half million Jews living in German-occupied Western Europe, defeated Poland was home to between two and three million Jews, while another three million lived in the German-controlled areas of the Soviet Union. All were targets of the barbaric Himmler and his faithful subordinates in the SS. Beginning in 1941 with the use of firing squads in Poland and Russia, and then mobile gas vans, the SS-directed **genocide** (race or nation killing) against the Jews reached new levels of brutal efficiency with the opening of massive extermination camps in eastern Europe in 1942 (see Map 24–3).

☐☐●⊢Read the **Document**

The Wannsee Protocol: Planning the Holocaust

on **MyHistoryLab.com**

Approximately six million Jews perished in the Nazis' "final solution to the Jewish question" before the war ended in 1945. Rounded up and herded into cattle cars for what the Jews were told was "resettlement," many died of dehydration, disease, and starvation en route to the camps. Those who survived the nightmare journey were separated upon arrival into two groups: those fit for slave labor and those to be killed immediately (young children, pregnant women, the old, the debilitated, and the sick). The laborers were then simply worked to death or sent to the gas chambers when they could no longer work. A few became the victims of cruel medical experiments carried out by Nazi physicians. Most died soon after their arrival. In the camp at Auschwitz, one of six major killing factories located in occupied Poland, an estimated one million were murdered by gassing, while another half million succumbed to disease and starvation. The entire operation was a model of depraved indifference: Gold was extracted from the teeth of corpses, hair was used to stuff mattresses, bones were crushed for phosphates, and fat was used to make soap. After the corpses were incinerated, the ashes were carried away as fertilizer. The horrors of the camps, the screams, the beatings, the systematic torture, and the starvation were in part pure racism and in part designed to convince the inmates that they were indeed less than human. As the German war effort faltered in 1943 and 1944, the genocide intensified, continuing until the Reich collapsed in 1945.

The Jewish **Holocaust** was the absolute repudiation of the Enlightenment faith in progress and human rationality. Hitler's executioners and the massive bureaucracy that supported them annihilated two-thirds of Europe's Jewish population, and they completed their work with fanatical dedication and moral indifference to human suffering and to the status of civilians during wartime. The Allies could have alleviated some of the horror by bombing rail lines and even the camps themselves, and

◉⊢Watch the **Video**

Nazi Murder Mills

on **MyHistoryLab.com**

some Jewish leaders in the West called for such attacks. However, the military claimed that other targets took priority in the struggle to defeat Nazism.

Some commentators have interpreted the genocide as further evidence of the irrationality and penchant for violence at the core of human personality. Others attribute this callous evil to modern totalitarianism. When combined with the millions of Russians and Ukranians who died to satiate Stalin's megalomania in the

MAP 24-3 The Holocaust After years of increasingly harsh persecution of Jews within its borders, Germany embarked upon the Holocaust—the systematic physical elimination of all Jews, as well as other "undesirables"—during World War II.

QUESTION: Which countries had the largest number of Jewish victims? Which had the fewest?

1930s, and with the additional millions who lost their lives under Mao Zedong's (1883–1976) communist dictatorship in China in the 1950s and 1960s, Hitler's depravity appears symptomatic of totalitarian regimes' indifference to human life. Still others see something unique in Western anti-Semitism, a centuries-old sickness that repeatedly spread its hatred across Christian culture. What sets the murders of Nazi Germany apart is the way it applied modern industrial technology to premeditated mass murder.

Buchenwald Concentration Camp, April 1945   When American troops arrived at Buchenwald, one of the Nazis' most notorious camps, they found thousands of emaciated, starved inmates. These were among the survivors of the Holocaust, which claimed six million Jews and millions of non-Jews.

The Home Front and the Role of Women

Expanding Government   As in World War I, national governments assumed both a directive role over their economies and an intrusive power over the individual citizen. Ironically, Germany was the last major belligerent to interfere directly with civilian life. For the first two years of the war, German food supplies were adequate and the production of consumer goods continued. Elsewhere, and especially in Britain, the Soviet Union, and the United States, government agencies directed all aspects of industrial production. The type and quantity of goods and conditions of employment—including wage levels and prices—were regulated to further the war effort. Soviet authorities ordered the dismantling and removal to the east of entire manufacturing plants in the fall of 1941 lest the advancing Germans capture them. In the West governments employed scientists from the private sector and universities in weapons production.

View the **Map**

World War II on the Home Front: War Industry and Relocation

on **MyHistoryLab.com**

View the **Image**

Ration Stamps

on **MyHistoryLab.com**

Rationing became commonplace, and the military was given priority access to raw materials. In Britain the use of private automobiles was sharply curbed to conserve fuel, and marginal lands were put under the plow to raise more food. In the United States the federal government spent more money between 1941 and 1945 than it had in the entire history of the country.

Civil liberties were obviously nonexistent in totalitarian countries, but even in the Western democracies the constitutional rights of individuals and groups were violated with impunity during the conflict. The American government, for example, ordered the detention and relocation of about 100,000 Japanese-Americans in 1942 after Japan's attack on Pearl Harbor. Official government-sponsored propaganda portrayed the enemy in the harshest light, engendering racist sentiments in both Axis and Allied countries. The need for a united front against the Nazi menace even led to the propagandistic reinvention of the bloody dictator Stalin into the benevolent "Uncle Joe," the ally of Britain and the United States from late 1941 until 1945. Stalin's communist credentials were replaced by nationalist ones as he met Roosevelt and Churchill in a series of strategic meetings.

◉—Watch the **Video**

Conformity and Opposition in Nazi Germany

on **MyHistoryLab.com**

Women and War   As the war continued and military conscription depleted the ranks of the civilian workforce, women once again stepped in to meet the military's production needs. Around six million women entered the workforce in the United States after 1941, and almost half of them were in the manufacturing sector. In Britain many women served in the armed forces, carrying out essential military duties on the beleaguered home front. Russian women, as they had in the previous war under the tsar, took up arms in defense of their country and accounted for many of the 16 million Russian war dead. Women held one-half of all manufacturing jobs in Russia and constituted three-quarters of all agricultural workers. Only the Nazis continued to insist that women stay at home and bear children. Instead of women, the Nazis used forced laborers and war prisoners to fill vacant industrial and agricultural posts.

During World War II it was difficult to draw a clear distinction between the war front and the home front; air power brought the war home to Europe's civilian

U.S. Army Poster "Join the WAAC"—the Women's Army Auxiliary Corps—implores this World War II poster. To a greater degree than ever before, women and civilians were encouraged to contribute, in various ways, to the war effort in the United States and Europe.

Speed them back Join the WAAC

WOMEN'S ARMY AUXILIARY CORPS ★ U.S. ARMY
APPLY AT ANY U. S. ARMY RECRUITING AND INDUCTION STATION

population in a way that would have been unimaginable 20 years earlier. Close to 600,000 German civilians were killed during Allied bombing raids on German cities; more than half of the victims were women and children. Comparable mortality rates applied wherever heavy bombing occurred. The involvement of women in the war effort and their sacrifices as cities and towns were destroyed enhanced their status as citizens and patriots. At the end of the war in 1945, women in the Western democracies who had played a crucial role in defeating Nazism were not prepared to return to their domestic duties. They had been encouraged, and sometimes forced, to do so after World War I. The post-1945 Western world, with its strong women's movement, would begin the difficult struggle to afford women equality of opportunity in education, the workplace, and especially the professions.

War in Asia and the Pacific

China's Ordeal   For the inhabitants of Nationalist China, World War II—or at least the myriad horrors associated with total war—began in 1937, two years before Nazi Blitzkrieg in Poland plunged Western Europe into the abyss. During the late 1920s and early 1930s, Chinese Nationalist leader Chiang Kai-shek (1887–1975) used his Soviet-trained and (after 1927) German-trained army of over 300,000 men to

The "Rape of Nanjing"   Japanese attacks on China culminated in the 1937 takeover of several of China's major cities. Japanese soldiers massacred hundreds of thousands of civilians in Nanjing, an episode that is remembered as one of the great atrocities of the twentieth century. In this photo, Japanese soldiers bayonet helpless civilians.

fight various warlords and a small communist movement. After ruthlessly purging the communists in the city of Shanghai in 1927, these troops drove the communists out of their mountain strongholds in the southwest in 1931. Some 90,000 communist troops fled north over 6,000 miles in what has come to be called the "**Long March.**" Only 20,000 survived the ordeal; one of them was Mao Zedong, who managed to win leadership of the Party with a call for revolution based on peasant support and resistance to Japanese aggression in China.

By the mid-1930s, the Nationalists controlled most of China, but Japanese incursions posed a growing threat. In 1936 Chiang reluctantly agreed to form a united front against Japan with Mao's small communist force. A clash between Japanese and Chinese troops outside Beijing in July 1937 precipitated a full-scale Japanese attack. By December, Beijing, Shanghai, and Nanjing (the Nationalists' capital) had all fallen to the Japanese. The attack on Nanjing was particularly barbaric; hundreds of thousands of Chinese civilians were massacred after the city fell. Chiang retreated to the west and established a new capital at Chungking, but with Japan in control of the most populous regions of the country, the credibility of the Nationalist government declined rapidly. Despite receiving military aid and advice from the United States after 1941, Chiang refused to commit his troops to fighting the Japanese. Instead, he chose to preserve his assets for a battle against the communists once the war was over. Mao's communist fighters, however, conducted guerilla operations against the Japanese and won the support of the peasantry due to their efforts to promote literacy and agricultural reform. Their grassroots efforts to assist the peasantry while fighting the Japanese led many Chinese to conclude that Mao's communists were the true Chinese nationalists.

Japan Attacks America   The Japanese became allies of Germany and Italy after the outbreak of war in Western Europe. They also signed a treaty of neutrality with Russia in April 1941. Taking advantage of France's surrender and Britain's weakness, the Japanese military moved into French Indochina and threatened the Dutch East Indies (Indonesia) and British Malaya. In response the United States froze all Japanese assets and imposed a complete economic embargo against Japan in the summer of 1941. Britain and the Netherlands followed with embargos of their own. The cutoff of American and Dutch oil supplies represented a serious threat to Japan's industrial economy. The prowar faction in Japan, led by General Hideki Tojo (1885–1948), decided that a quick but devastating strike against the Pacific naval forces of the United States would allow the Japanese sufficient time to invade and secure the Dutch East Indian oil reserves and the rubber and tin of British Malaya.

On the morning of December 7, 1941, the Japanese launched a surprise attack against Pearl Harbor, America's principal naval base in the Pacific. A large portion of the U.S. fleet and hundreds of airplanes were destroyed. Almost 2,500 military personnel were killed. Fortunately for the Americans, their strategically important aircraft carriers were at sea and missed the attack. Japanese planners knew they could not win a protracted war against the United States. They hoped the shock of Pearl Harbor would at least lead the isolationist Americans to acquiesce in Japan's creation of a Southeast Asian sphere of influence. Instead, the attack put an end to American isolationism. On December 11, three days after Congress declared war on Japan, Hitler

View the **Image**

Japanese Bombing of Pearl Harbor

on **MyHistoryLab.com**

and Mussolini gratuitously announced that the Axis was at war with the United States. A number of Latin American countries then joined the Allies, and the war assumed truly global proportions.

((•—Hear the Audio

Pearl Harbor Performed by New York, Georgia Singers on **MyHistoryLab.com**

The Japanese swiftly "liberated" much of southeast Asia from the forces of Western imperialism, expelling Allied troops and creating what it called the Greater East Asia Co-Prosperity Sphere, a euphemism for a Pacific Empire based in Tokyo. The Americans were forced out of the Philippines, Guam, and Wake Island. Early in 1942, the Japanese overran Hong Kong, Thailand, Burma, Malaya, and the Dutch East Indies. The Japanese forces appeared to be unstoppable, but in May 1942 the Americans slowed the advance and at least temporarily freed Australia from the threat of invasion by defeating the Japanese at the Battle of the Coral Sea. In June, as a large Japanese fleet approached Midway Island, over 1,000 miles northwest of Hawaii, the momentum shifted. In a decisive air battle between planes launched from the decks of aircraft carriers, the Americans sank four of Japan's big carriers. Henceforth, Japan was on the defensive (see Map 24–4).

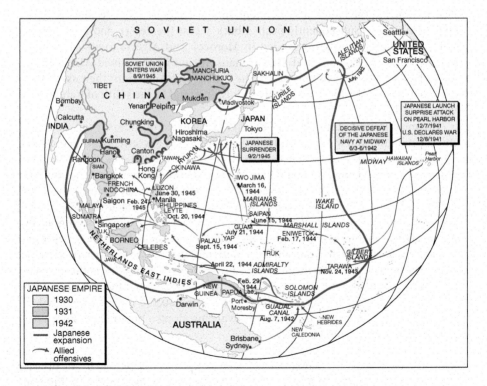

MAP 24-4   The Pacific War   The Japanese followed their attack against the United States at Pearl Harbor with a rapid takeover of key areas in Southeast Asia and the Pacific. Allied war efforts in this theater involved protracted and bloody assaults on these positions from 1942 through 1945.

QUESTION: What role did naval power play in the Pacific theater?

The Tide Turns, 1942–1945

While the fighting would continue for another three years, America's superior industrial and military capacity would prove to be too much for the aggressors. The Japanese attack on Pearl Harbor solidified public opinion behind President Roosevelt's war policy, and the American economy shifted quickly to a war footing. The coalition, or **Grand Alliance,** now opposing the Axis powers (Germany, Italy, Japan) included Britain, the Soviet Union, Nationalist China, and the United States. The Americans began sending huge quantities of military aid in the form of trucks, tanks, planes, and weapons to its beleaguered allies. German submarines sank a great many ships, but a large naval convoy system, together with new sonar and depth-charge capabilities, enabled the Americans to prevail in the protracted Battle of the Atlantic by early 1943. For the duration of the war, the fight for the unconditional surrender of a common enemy overcame most ideological divisions among the Allies.

El Alamein and Stalingrad   The American victory at Midway was one of three decisive battles in the second half of 1942 that changed the tide of the war. The second occurred in North Africa, where in October 1942 the British, under the command of General Bernard Montgomery (1887–1976), were at last able to defeat Rommel at the battle of El Alamein, just 70 miles west of Alexandria, Egypt. The Germans were subsequently pushed back across the desert, and in November a joint Anglo-American army landed in Morocco and Algeria to attack Rommel from the west. The Italians and the Germans, including the famed Afrika Korps, were forced to surrender in May 1943. The British and Americans then used North Africa as a springboard to attack Sicily in July and land in the south of Italy the following month.

The most important battle of 1942 to 1943 occurred on Russian soil. Failing to capture Leningrad and Moscow, Hitler ordered his forces to concentrate on the south in an attempt to deny the Red Army continued access to the oil fields of the Caucasus. The assault began in June 1942, and like the previous summer, the first months were successful as German tanks advanced rapidly across the Russian plains. When German forces reached the Volga River to the north of the city of Stalingrad in August, Soviet troops dug in for a long battle. Hitler's generals wished to bypass Stalingrad, but Hitler overruled them and ordered an attack on the city. The fighting was intense and often at the level of hand-to-hand amid the ruins of the city. In November, two Russian armies counterattacked from the north and the south of Stalingrad, and the Germans suddenly found themselves surrounded in the city. By February, the remnants of the frozen and malnourished German Sixth Army, some 80,000 men, surrendered. By the end of the winter, Soviet troops were advancing along a broad front. Like Japan, Germany, too, was now on the defensive.

Campaign in Italy   Mussolini had been completely discredited by the disaster in Africa and the subsequent Anglo-American invasion of Sicily. King Victor Emmanuel III (r. 1900–1946), on the advice of dissident Fascists, dismissed *Il Duce,* and a new government coalition under the leadership of Marshal Pietro Badoglio (1871–1956) signed an armistice with the Allies in September 1943. Hitler was unwilling to permit the Allies to secure a base to Germany's immediate south, however, and German troops seized Rome and the northern half of Italy. The Germans set up Mussolini as the puppet ruler of a Fascist republic. For the next year and a half, American and British troops fought a bloody campaign up the Italian peninsula, capturing Rome in June 1944.

The Second Front   Almost as soon as the Americans entered the war, Stalin called for the establishment of a second front in Western Europe to take pressure off Soviet forces in the east. Soviet military and civilian casualties were dramatically higher than those suffered by either Britain or the United States, and despite the infusion of massive American aid beginning in 1942, Stalin resented the Allies' decision to invade North Africa instead of Western Europe in 1942. Nor did he consider the invasion of Italy an adequate substitute. Under the command of General Dwight D. Eisenhower (1890–1969), the Allies finally invaded France in Normandy on June 6, 1944 (D-Day), against heavily defended German positions. That an American commander led this operation from British soil showed how dependent Britain had become on American aid. After establishing a beachhead, the Allies were able to land more than two million men over the course of the next few months. In August a second landing in southern France contributed to the rollback of German forces. Paris was liberated on August 25–26, 1944, with the Free French led by General Charles de Gaulle playing a prominent role.

The expulsion of the Nazis from France, after more than four years of occupation, had been preceded by a long and intensive aerial bombing campaign that targeted German military installations and entire German cities. Most of Germany's cities were leveled, with the loss of almost 600,000 civilian lives, many of them women and children. The morality of these attacks on nonmilitary urban targets was debated at the time within the Allied command and continues to be controversial at the start of the twenty-first century. During 1943 the bombing took place around the clock, with the British flying at night and the Americans attacking during daylight hours. Hundreds of planes and their crews were lost over the skies of Germany, but by early 1945 the German air force had been all but destroyed.

Soviet Advances   While the Allies pushed from the west toward the Rhine River and onto German soil, Russian troops continued their heroic efforts in the east. The Red Army liberated Crimea and Ukraine by spring 1944 and then opened a wide offensive that summer. Poland was taken, and Romania and Bulgaria joined the Soviet side. Fearing that they would be trapped by the advancing Soviet army and its allies, German troops quickly withdrew from the Balkans, leaving resistance fighters like Tito of Yugoslavia in control. The Germans were able to mount one final winter offensive in December 1944 through Belgium's Ardennes Forest (where the Nazis had begun their invasion of France in 1940), but Allied forces prevailed in this Battle of the Bulge and crossed the Rhine River in March 1945.

By April 1945, the Soviets had captured Vienna and were attacking Berlin. Unlike the conclusion to World War I, this time there was no doubt that Germany had been defeated on the battlefield. On the last day of April, Hitler took his life in a Berlin bunker. Two days earlier, Italian partisans had captured and shot Mussolini. On May 7 the last German forces surrendered throughout Europe. The thousand-year Reich had lasted only 12 years, but it had scourged a continent.

Partisans in Yugoslavia   The German occupiers were faced with irregular, "guerilla" or partisan warfare in much of Europe. Led by the Communist leader Josip Broz Tito, the Yugoslav partisans—who included a large proportion of women—liberated much of their country from the Nazis.

The Defeat of Japan

The campaign against Japan in the Pacific theater was difficult and costly. In late 1942 the Americans began a slow and tenacious island-hopping campaign, which drew ever closer to the Japanese mainland. Once they took possession of the Mariana Islands, the Americans could use long-range bombers to attack Japanese positions in the Philippines, on the Chinese mainland, and in Japan itself. Many Japanese soldiers and pilots preferred death to surrender; thus, each American assault on a Japanese-held island involved colossal loss of life on both sides. During the battle for the island of Okinawa, Japanese pilots dive-bombed their planes into Allied ships, killing thousands of sailors on board. Once Iwo Jima and Okinawa fell to the Americans in the spring of 1945, additional bases became available for heavy bombers that now concentrated their destructive payloads against Japan's industrial centers and major cities. The bombing caused huge firestorms that killed hundreds of thousands of civilians.

Despite destruction at home and the steady advance of America's superior military power, the Japanese military refused to surrender. It seemed likely that the United States would have to invade the Japanese home islands with horrific casualties. President Roosevelt had died on April 12, 1945, and the new American president, Harry S Truman (1884–1972), concluded that the projected loss of American life in an invasion of Japan was too great. Instead, he authorized the use of a powerful new weapon. During the war, the government had funded a $2 billion secret research program (the

Manhattan Project) to investigate the military uses of atomic energy. Some of the key researchers were refugees from the Hitler regime.

On August 6, 1945, after successful tests in the New Mexico desert, an American aircraft dropped an atomic bomb on the Japanese city of Hiroshima. The initial blast killed approximately 80,000 people, while thousands more perished later from the effects of radiation. On August 9 a second bomb killed 50,000 people in Nagasaki. On August 8 the Soviets declared war on Japan and invaded Manchuria and Korea. The decision to use nuclear weapons has been debated since their first (and thus far only) use. More people died in conventional bombing raids on Dresden, Germany, and Tokyo earlier in 1945 than at Hiroshima

Read the Document

An Eyewitness to Hiroshima

on **MyHistoryLab.com**

Read the Document

The Effects of Atomic Bombs on Hiroshima and Nagasaki

on **MyHistoryLab.com**

and Nagasaki. In July 1943 British and American bombers killed 50,000 people in Hamburg, Germany, most of them women and children. Still, the debate has centered around the necessity of using atomic weapons in 1945. Critics of Truman's decision have argued that a demonstration test on a deserted Pacific island with Japanese observers present would have served the same purpose in speeding a surrender. Others

Atomic War   On August 6, 1945, an American bomber dropped an atom bomb on the Japanese city of Hiroshima. Over four square miles of the city were destroyed by the blast. Three days later the United States dropped a second bomb on the city of Nagasaki.

◉—⌐Watch the **Video**

*Truman on the End of World
War II*

on **MyHistoryLab.com**

have claimed that a total blockade of Japan, coupled
with the precision bombing of its transport infrastructure, would have starved the Japanese into submission
within a few months. Whatever the hypothetical arguments, the Japanese people looked for leadership
from their emperor. On August 15, 1945, the people of
Japan heard the voice of Emperor Hirohito (r. 1926–1989) for the first time. Without
once using the word *surrender,* the divine emperor took to the radio to tell his subjects that the war must end. "Should we continue to fight," he warned, "it would not
only result in an ultimate collapse and obliteration of the Japanese nation, but also it
would lead to the total extinction of human civilization." The emperor's request was
heeded immediately. After the deaths of 2.3 million soldiers and 800,000 civilians, the
Japanese people accepted a humiliating directive from the man whom they revered as
a god. The surrender was made official aboard the U.S. battleship *Missouri* anchored
in Tokyo Bay on September 2.

Planning for the Postwar World

In August 1941, four months before the United States entered the war, Roosevelt
and Churchill met on a ship off the coast of Newfoundland to agree on a set of
principles to guide the future rebuilding of Europe. The principles resembled those
put forward by President Wilson at the end of World War I: self-determination of
peoples, democratically elected governments, and the creation of an international
peacekeeping organization. Once the Grand Alliance was formed, the Soviets were
willing to pay lip service to these neo-Wilsonian principles in the interests of wartime solidarity.

The Tehran Conference   The British and the Soviets jointly occupied Iran
during the war, and in November 1943 Churchill, Roosevelt, and Stalin met in Tehran,
the Iranian capital, to plan for the projected—or in Stalin's view, long delayed—invasion of Western Europe. In return Stalin pledged to join the fight against Japan once
the Nazi menace was eliminated. There was little concern raised at the time about the
future status of Eastern Europe should Soviet forces roll back the Germans in that
area. The next year, however, as Soviet forces entered Poland and then turned south
to occupy Romania and Hungary, the British and Americans began to contemplate the
possibility of a postwar Soviet Empire in Eastern Europe. The Western allies conceded
that innocent Russians had suffered the most at the hands of the invading Germans,
but since Britain and France had declared war in 1939 to preserve the territorial and
political integrity of Poland, the desire to see democratically elected governments in
Eastern Europe was strong.

Meeting in Yalta   The leaders of the Grand Alliance met again in the Russian resort city of **Yalta** on the Crimean peninsula in February 1945. With Soviet
and Western forces closing in on Berlin, Stalin was eager to impose a harsh peace on
Germany, reminiscent of Versailles. Churchill and Roosevelt, however, feared that the

breakup of Germany would lead to a power vacuum in Central Europe—one that the Red Army would quickly fill—and economic instability for the Western democracies. The Yalta Conference did not resolve the question of Germany's future, but the participants did agree to a temporary partition of the country into four military zones under American, British, French, and Soviet administration.

View the **Image**

The Big Three at Yalta
on **MyHistoryLab.com**

Watch the **Video**

The Big Three Yalta Conference
on **MyHistoryLab.com**

The future of Poland became the major point of dispute at Yalta. In 1943 the Soviets had withdrawn their recognition of the London-based Polish government in exile after its leaders accused the Soviets, justly, of atrocities in eastern Poland. In its place Stalin organized a Russian-based, pro-communist Polish leadership. When the pro-London Polish underground rose up in revolt in Warsaw against the Germans on August 1, 1944, the Red Army, located just a few miles outside the city, refused to help them. The Russians allowed the Germans to crush the rebellion at the cost of thousands of Polish lives. Stalin then recognized the pro-Soviet group as the official government of "liberated" Poland. At Yalta, Stalin agreed to include a few noncommunists in this government and to free elections after the war. Roosevelt returned home from the meeting hopeful that a free and independent Poland could be established. He died soon after reaching the United States. For his part, Stalin returned to Moscow determined to maintain Soviet influence over Poland, the state whose independence had been the occasion for the outbreak of war six years earlier.

The Cost of War   Atomic weapons ended the most destructive war in human history. Almost 50 million people had been killed. One-half of the dead were civilians; more than one-third of the total were Russians (20 million). Stalin's postwar policy toward Eastern and central Europe would be shaped by the overriding desire to protect the Soviet Union from another assault from the West. The physical destruction was in harrowing proportion to the human wreckage: major cities lay in rubble, transportation infrastructures—bridges, waterways, rail lines, roads—were inoperative, and agricultural production was reduced to subsistence levels. Homelessness and forced migration were commonplace, hunger the companion of millions. In China more than 90 million people had abandoned their homes during the Japanese occupation; in Europe millions had fled the Nazis; and in Eastern Europe millions more flooded west to escape the Red Army's advance.

As the historian Roland Stromberg reminds us, many who were alive in 1945 could recall the Bolshevik terror in Russia, the rise of black- and brown-shirted thugs in Germany and Italy, the destruction of republican Spain, the loss of hope in the depths of the Great Depression, death from the air during saturation bombings, the barbarity of the concentration camps, invading armies, and "a European atmosphere heavy with the smell of death." At the end of it all, Europe had been eclipsed, occupied and awaiting its fate at the hands of outsiders. American soldiers were stationed in Western Europe, Japan, and Australia. Soviet troops took up positions in all of Eastern Europe and in northern China, and the two most powerful partners in the Grand Alliance were beginning to quarrel about the contours of the postwar world.

Key Dates for World War II

March 1935	Germany begins remilitarization
1936–1939	Spanish Civil War
March 1938	Germany annexes Austria
September 1938	Munich conference
August 1939	German-Soviet "nonaggression pact"
September 1939	Germany invades Poland
May 1940	Germany invades Belgium, Holland, and France
July 1940–June 1941	Battle of Britain
June 1941	Germany invades Soviet Union
December 1941	United States enters the war
September 1942–January 1943	Battle of Stalingrad
July 1943	Battle of Kursk
June 1944	D-Day: Allies land in Normandy
May 1945	Germany surrenders
August 6–9, 1945	United States bombs Hiroshima, Nagasaki
August 14, 1945	Japan surrenders

KEY QUESTION REVISITED

Can deeply held ideas and values sustain a civilization under violent attack?

World War II in Europe erupted after just 20 years of uneasy peace. Some scholars have referred to the entire period from 1914 to 1945 as the Second Thirty Years' War. It certainly matched and then exceeded its seventeenth-century counterpart in terms of ideological fervor, indiscriminate violence, and physical devastation. In such a climate it was perhaps understandable how the British author H. G. Wells (1866–1946) concluded in *Mind at the End of Its Tether* (1946) that civilization was fast approaching its end. As Churchill indicated in a speech before Parliament, Nazism was "a monstrous tyranny, never surpassed in the dark lamentable catalogue of human crime." For Churchill, the triumph of Hitlerism would have marked the beginning of a new European Dark Age made more malevolent through the power of science and technology.

From the fall of 1939 (1937 in the case of Japanese aggression in China) until the middle of 1942, the Axis powers triumphed over their opponents with remarkable speed and appalling cruelty. Hitler was master of Western Europe, while the Japanese replaced the Western powers as the imperial authority in East and Southeast Asia. The entry of the

United States into the war transformed two separate fields of conflict into a truly global war, and once the Americans were fully mobilized, the economic and military might arrayed against the Axis powers would prove to be overwhelming. At some point during the conflict, perhaps as news of the concentration camps began to emerge, World War II became for the Allies a moral conflict, a battle to defend the much-maligned principles of liberal civilization. In the Soviet Union, the ideas of communism and nationalism sustained the Red Army and millions of civilians. The residual power of liberal democracy in the West, and of communism and impassioned nationalism in the Soviet Union, prevailed over the forces of racism and inhumanity.

Key Terms

appeasement, *p. 708*
Munich agreement, *p. 710*

Lend-Lease Program, *p. 714*
Holocaust, *p. 719*

Grand Alliance, *p. 726*
Yalta, *p. 730*

Activities

1. Why did Britain and France appease Hitler during the 1930s?

2. Explain how science and technology erased the distinction between the war front and the home front during World War II.

3. Why did Stalin agree to a nonaggression pact with the anticommunist Hitler?

4. Explain how the Allies were able to turn the tide of the war.

5. How did the Holocaust change the course of Western civilization?

6. List the factors that led the Japanese to attack the United States in 1941.

7. In what respects was European civilization eclipsed during World War II?

Further Reading

Gerhard Weinberg, *A World at Arms: A Global History of World War II* (1994), remains one of the most highly readable surveys.

John Keegan, *The Second World War* (1990), a lively narrative with a focus on the military dimension.

Richard Overy, *Why the Allies Won* (1997), a study of technological factors in World War II.

Omer Bartov, *Murder in Our Midst* (1996), looks at the Holocaust within the wider context of twentieth-century history.

Elie Wiesel, *Night* (2010), a new edition of a key text in Holocaust literature.

MyHistoryLab Connections

Visit **MyHistoryLab.com** *for a customized Study Plan that will help you build your knowledge of* World War II: Europe in Eclipse.

Questions for Analysis

1. In light of the actions that Hitler ultimately took, how would you characterize Chamberlain's position on whether Britain should go to war with Germany?

▐●▌Read the Document Neville Chamberlain, *In Search of Peace*, p. 710

2. How did Churchill frame his argument that Great Britain had no choice but to defeat Germany at all costs?

▐●▌Read the Document Churchill, Their Finest Hour, p. 713

3. How was the Volkswagen car a symbol of the betrayal of the German people by the Nazis?

◉Watch the Video Conformity and Opposition in Nazi Germany, p. 722

4. How does John Siemes describe the aftermath of the atomic bomb attack on Hiroshima?

▐●▌Read the Document An Eyewitness to Hiroshima, p. 729

5. How does the U.S. government report describe the devastation that followed the atomic bomb attacks on Hiroshima and Nagasaki and how does this description compare with Siemes' account?

▐●▌Read the Document The Effects of Atomic Bombs on Hiroshima and Nagasaki, p. 729

Other Resources from This Chapter

View the Image Nazi Book Bonfire, 1933, p. 708

View the Image Hitler and Chamberlain, 1938, p. 710

View the Closer Look The Vichy Regime in France, p. 712

View the Image Nazis Executing Russian Civilians, p. 717

▐●▌Read the Document The Wannsee Protocol: Planning the Holocaust, p. 719

◉Watch the Video Nazi Murder Mills, p. 719

View the Map World War II on the Home Front: War Industry and Relocation, p. 721

View the Image Ration Stamps, p. 721

View the Image Japanese Bombing of Pearl Harbor, p. 724

PART EIGHT

The Postwar Western
Community: 1945–2012

Multiculturalism. **Turkish women perform a traditional dance in Berlin in 2006.**
Muslims make up five percent of Germany's population.

The second half of the twentieth century was a period of retreat, retrenchment, and renewal in Western Europe. The United States assisted many countries in their efforts to
rebuild after the war, and by the 1950s the idea of greater European integration and cooperation had found powerful supporters. In Soviet-dominated Eastern Europe, authoritarian
governments and socialist economies were imposed. The 40-year Cold War (c. 1946–1989)
served as a costly focal point around which the world's two nuclear superpowers set their
international priorities. A divided Europe was one consequence of the ideological split between the United States and the Soviet Union. Europe played a much-diminished role in
international affairs during these decades, withdrawing—largely in a peaceful manner—
from colonial commitments and focusing on domestic priorities.

Paradoxically, just as the political might of Western Europe waned, Western civilization's
enduring values spread rapidly around the world. The collapse of communism in the late
1980s in Eastern Europe and by 1991 in the Soviet Union strengthened the appeal of Western democracy and free-market economics in the non-Western world.

Economic and political cooperation were key features of the European Union at the
start of the new century, but serious challenges to greater unity remained, especially in

southeastern Europe where the collapse of communism led to violent ethnic and religious conflict in the 1990s. Sixty-five years after the end of World War II, and more than two decades after the end of communism, the Western community has again become an important source of power and influence in what is now a multipolar world.

	ENVIRONMENT AND TECHNOLOGY	SOCIETY AND CULTURE	POLITICS
1945	U.S. and Soviet possess hydrogen bombs (1953)	Beauvoir, *Second Sex* (1949)	United Nations founded (1945)
	Structure of DNA mapped (1954)	Orwell, *1984* (1949)	India secures independence (1947)
			Israel established (1948)
		Beckett, *Waiting for Godot* (1953)	Communist Revolution in China (1949)
			Korean War (1950–53)
1956	Launch of first artificial satellite, Sputnik (1957)	Formation of European Common Market (1957)	Suez Canal Crisis (1956)
	First manned space flight (1961)	Grass, *The Tin Drum* (1959)	Cuban missile crisis (1962)
	First successful heart transplant (1967)	Heller, *Catch-22* (1961)	
	First moon landing (1969)	The Beatles record their first album (1963)	
	OPEC oil embargo (1973)	Cultural Revolution begins in China (1966)	
1975	Smallpox eliminated (1977)	Conflict and ethnic cleansing in the former Yugoslavia (1991–1999)	Americans withdraw from Vietnam (1975)
	Personal computers available (1980)	Birth of world's first mammalian clone, Dolly the sheep (1997)	Islamic revolution in Iran (1979)
	AIDS virus identified (1983)	Euro currency introduced (1999)	Margaret Thatcher becomes first female Prime Minister of Britain (1979)
	Chernobyl accident (1986)	World's population exceeds 6 billion (2000)	Gorbachev comes to power (1985)
	Exxon Valdez oil spill (1989)	190 people killed in terrorist bombing in Madrid (2004)	Fall of communism in Eastern Europe (1989–1990)
	Internet becomes key communications tool (1993)	Riots in France by young Muslims against discrimination (2006, 2007)	Collapse of Soviet Union (1991)
	Kyoto Protocol on climate change (1997)	Over 100 million iPods sold since its introduction in 2001 (2008)	Democratic elections in South Africa (1994)
			Genocide in Rwanda (1994)
			Wars in Chechnya (1994, 1999)
			U.S.-led "War on Terror" begins (2001)
			U.S. and Britain invade Iraq (2003)

The End of Empire, 1970   A statue of Queen Victoria is removed in Georgetown, Guyana, in preparation for the former British colony's transition to independence.

25 Decolonization and the Cold War

((•─[Hear the Audio   Chapter 25 at MyHistoryLab.com

LEARNING OBJECTIVES

Why did postwar optimism evaporate by 1947?   •   What were the leading factors in the collapse of European empire?   •   How did the Cold War spread to nations around the globe?   •   How did the nuclear threat shape superpower foreign relations?

At the present moment in world history nearly every nation must choose between alternative ways of life. The choice too often is not a free one.

—Harry S Truman, March 12, 1947

KEY QUESTION

How does ideology shape public policy?

When Harry S Truman (1884–1972) became vice president of the United States in 1945, he knew little about international affairs. He had been abroad only once, as a soldier in France during World War I. He had served in the Senate for 10 years, but he had focused his legislative energies on domestic issues. He knew few of the world's political leaders. During Truman's 83 days as vice president, President Franklin Delano Roosevelt excluded him from all discussions about negotiations with the Soviets and the development of the atomic bomb. When Roosevelt died on April 12, 1945, and Truman succeeded him as president, most of what he knew about Roosevelt's face-to-face meetings with Soviet leader Josef Stalin and of America's wartime weapons program came from what he had read in the newspapers.

Within six months of assuming office, however, Truman had authorized the use of atomic weapons against Japan, confronted the Soviet Union over postwar reconstruction in Eastern Europe, and warned against the dangers of isolationism in foreign affairs in a radio address to the United Nations. The president, who one day after assuming the presidential office confided to a friend that "I'm not big enough for this job," had within months taken the lead in shaping the political contours of postwar Western Europe. Truman's understanding of the Soviet system in general—and of Stalin in particular—would deeply inform American actions around the globe in the decades after 1945. ▨

The Eclipse of Postwar Optimism

New Directions in Western Thought   In 1945, Europeans were faced with a troubling set of questions regarding the centrality and universality of their Enlightenment heritage. In Africa, south and east Asia, and throughout the Muslim world, the rhetoric of Western cultural superiority had been tested and found wanting during the nightmare of two fratricidal wars. On the material front the continent was a shattered hulk, stripped of prestige and influence and emphatically eclipsed by the upstart Soviet Union and the United States. The "truths" and values that had guided Europeans in their boastful expansion around the planet after 1500 were now thrown into doubt, and a deep sense of the fragility of all civilizations took hold in a variety of intellectual circles.

Perhaps the most unsettling trend was the suspicion that fixed truths—so much a part of historic Western Christian culture—were in fact no more than points of view relative to time and place. For growing numbers of Europeans after World War II, values appeared to be more the product of culture, constructed by humans in response to pressing contingency, than the inflexible result of rational inquiry and discovery. The certainties that had informed Western culture at the turn of the twentieth century had broken down in the aftermath of total war and genocide. Faith in human rationality, or at least the potential for humans to live in a rational manner, was severely tested by the horrors of totalitarianism and the physical destruction wrought by Europeans against their neighbors. For some intellectuals, the years after 1945 represented "the end of ideology," the abandonment of faith in progress. Even scientific specialization and the fruits of technology now appeared under a darker guise, fostering a bland consumer mentality in the West and opening an unbridgeable chasm between the "expert" and the average citizen.

Existentialism   A new and more exacting view of reality known as **existentialism** emerged in the West out of this predicament. Led by the French philosopher Jean-Paul Sartre (1905–1980) and novelist Albert Camus (1913–1960), existentialist writers rejected belief in moral absolutes that existed independent of human agents. Some existentialists went so far as to deny any larger meaning to the human journey outside of birth,

Albert Camus   A leader of the existentialist school of literature and philosophy, which came to prominence after World War II. Camus wrote some of the most important novels of the 1940s and 1950s, including *The Plague* and *The Stranger*.

existence, and death. If there are to be values worth defending, then these must be constructed by individuals and groups who take full responsibility for their creations. In popular novels such as *The Plague* (1947), Camus portrayed individuals who were attempting to come to grips with a world without purpose or meaning. The playwright Samuel Beckett (1906–1989) captured the spirit of the existentialist school in plays like *Waiting for Godot* in which the main characters are homeless tramps waiting for someone who never arrives—the essential forlorn condition. Sartre's most famous play, *No Exit*, was first performed after the liberation of Paris in 1944. The play depicted hell as a place where people are simply stuck in meaningless isolation.

In a very key respect, existentialism called into question the enormous expansion of state power (and its accompanying ideologies) over the individual that had taken place during the first half of the century. This expansion was captured in disturbing fashion by George Orwell in his widely read novel *1984*. Enormous disenchantment with the intrusion of the state into almost every compartment of life fostered a misplaced assumption that the parameters of life ought to be defined, regulated, and protected by civil authority. Existentialism insisted on individual responsibility and emphasized personal choice as a moral obligation confronting every person; "following orders" was simply no longer an adequate defense for acts of inhumanity.

Hopeful Beginnings   The call to choose came quickly. The official end of World War II in Europe on May 7, 1945, inaugurated a brief period of euphoria and solidarity among the victorious Allies. In particular, the convergence of Soviet and American troops at the Elbe River in Germany, troops that had endured a bloody and protracted struggle against Nazi forces, showed that two hostile political systems could come together to confront a great evil. Soon a peaceful world would be restored, civilian pursuits resumed, and a new international order established on the solid foundations of shared experience in battle. In the summer of 1945 delegates from 51 nations met in San Francisco to establish the **United Nations Organization.** Its multilateral charter pointed toward a new era of international cooperation that would avoid the mistakes made after World War I. Committed internationalists like Franklin Roosevelt believed that cooperation and reconciliation would replace traditional balance-of-power politics.

Read the **Document**

Charter of the United Nations

on **MyHistoryLab.com**

The ideological and territorial divisions that hardened into the Cold War were not fixed in 1945. Germany's military and political institutions were, in the estimate of its enemies on all sides, disqualified from playing any role in the reconstruction of central Europe. New structures of authority were needed straightaway. The de facto force for order became the Soviet and Western armies, each occupying territory it had taken during the fighting. Surprisingly, anticommunist political parties were allowed to operate without hindrance for some time in the Soviet-controlled zone, and noncommunists and communists joined in coalition governments across postwar Eastern Europe. In France, Italy, Belgium, and Greece, communist parties enjoyed considerable strength, with party members even holding cabinet rank. Across the Channel in Britain, a new Labour government committed to the establishment of a wide-ranging socialist economic program replaced a respected wartime coalition headed by Conservative Prime Minister Winston Churchill. The ideological divide separating East and West, the historic barriers between communist and capitalist systems, appeared permeable in the immediate aftermath of the terrible conflict.

Early Tensions and Western Suspicions   Still, there was no denying that underlying disagreements existed among the Allies. First and foremost was Stalin's deep suspicion that the British and Americans had delayed the opening of a western front against Germany until June 1944 in order to undermine Soviet resources. From the moment that Britain and the Soviet Union had signed a pact of mutual assistance in July 1941, Stalin had called for an assault by British forces into occupied France to relieve the strain on the Red Army in the east. Only at a meeting in Tehran, Iran, in November 1943 did Stalin receive assurances from Roosevelt and Churchill that the planned offensive would be centered on northern France. By this date, the Red Army had already begun to expel the Germans from Soviet territory. Historians continue to debate the rationale for the joint Churchill-Roosevelt position on a cross-Channel invasion; what mattered in 1945, of course, was how the paranoid Soviet dictator chose to understand events.

The second area of disagreement involved Stalin's insistence that future Soviet security demanded friendly governments in Eastern Europe. The Soviets had incurred staggering human losses during the war: The Nazis had killed more than 15 million Soviet soldiers and civilians. When we add to this figure deaths related to malnutrition, forced labor, and physical dislocation, a total of 20 to 25 million Soviet citizens perished during the four-year confrontation. Together with the widespread destruction of farms, livestock, agricultural machinery, factories, and homes during the German occupation, it is hardly surprising that the Russians demanded secure frontiers. The Nazi invasion, while certainly the most destructive experience in Russian history, merely reinforced the popular perception that from Napoleon to Kaiser Wilhelm to Hitler, Russia's sorrows originated in the West.

For Stalin, friendly states meant client-states, especially in terms of their political, economic, and military organization. During a summit meeting with Roosevelt and Churchill in the Crimean city of Yalta in February 1945, the Soviet dictator called for the imposition of a harsh peace against Germany, one that would require the country to pay heavy reparations and undergo extreme political reconstruction. While he promised that free elections would take place in Soviet-occupied Poland after the war, Stalin had no intention of allowing Western-style liberal democracies in Soviet-occupied countries. At a July 1945 summit in Potsdam, Germany, he confronted two new and untested leaders: Clement Atlee (1883–1967) of Britain and Harry S Truman of the United States. At this summit, the Soviet leader refused to follow through on his promise to permit elections.

View the **Image**

Truman, Atlee, and Stalin at the Potsdam (Berlin) Conference

on **MyHistoryLab.com**

The United States had emerged from the war as the dominant global power, with a monopoly (albeit only until 1949) on atomic weapons, the strongest economy, and the most advanced manufacturing base. Russia may have been a major military power in May 1945, but economically it was poor and backwards. However, the rapid postwar demobilization of American troops in Western Europe, made necessary by political opinion in the United States, meant that a Soviet military force of close to 4 million men was in a strong position to enforce Moscow's dictates on its zone of influence. Thousands of Soviet prisoners of war returned home only to be exiled to forced labor camps or executed for fear that they had been contaminated by anti-Soviet ideas during their imprisonment. Under directions from the Kremlin, the Red Army began to install pro-Soviet puppet regimes across Eastern Europe. Over the next three years, from 1946 to 1948, the countries of Eastern Europe were compelled to adopt Soviet-style political systems and state-dominated command economies, and to support Russian foreign policy. The communists overthrew a coalition government in Czechoslovakia in 1948. In 1956, when the Hungarian communist government of Imre Nagy (1895–1958) attempted to introduce a multiparty political system and withdraw from the Warsaw Pact (the Soviet military alliance), Russian forces invaded Hungary and killed thousands.

View the **Image**

Hungarian Uprising, 1956

on **MyHistoryLab.com**

The German Dilemma   To policymakers in the West, including those within the new Truman administration, an effective countervailing force was necessary to prevent the extension of Soviet power—indeed, possible Soviet hegemony—throughout the continent. Balance-of-power politics was about to replace internationalism and the hope for greater postwar cooperation. In a famous speech delivered at Fulton, Missouri, in March 1946, Churchill warned his American audience that "there is nothing they [the Russians] admire so much as strength, and there is nothing for which they have less respect than for military weakness." Declaring that an "Iron Curtain" had been established across the continent, Churchill counseled that security depended on an alliance among the Western democracies.

Read the **Document**

Churchill's "Iron Curtain" Speech (March 5, 1946)

on **MyHistoryLab.com**

Churchill's speech encapsulated the broader ideological division, or opposing world views, guiding policymakers on both sides. For the Western democracies, Soviet expansion into the European heartland meant the repudiation of the 200-year-old Enlightenment project, with its emphasis on individual rights, the sanctity of property, freedom of thought and expression, self-government, and religious pluralism. From the Russian, and later Chinese, communist perspective, the West had established a long record of global imperialism. Now the United States had become the unrivaled imperialist power in the Pacific basin, establishing a string of military bases with distinctly offensive capabilities. The hostility of the capitalist West toward all communist states demonstrated that those states needed to adopt a strong defensive posture if the Marxist alternative to capitalism were to survive. One month before Churchill's "Iron Curtain" speech, Stalin and Soviet Foreign Minister Vyacheslav Molotov (1890–1986) stated publicly that the Western democracies had become the enemies of the Soviets.

Read the **Document**

Joseph Stalin, Excerpts from the "Soviet Victory" Speech, 1946

on **MyHistoryLab.com**

The physical cost of the total war was difficult to calculate, but its punishing nature was apparent to occupying troops. Hitler had exhausted the natural and human resources of occupied countries in his racist bid for mastery, while massive German and Allied bombing of major cities, factories, and communications and transportation networks had crippled Europe's productive capacity. In addition to the millions of war dead, over 50 million refugees wandered across shattered lands, and millions more were homeless and malnourished. The Soviets, along with their Polish, Romanian, and Czechoslovakian clients, expelled more than 13 million ethnic Germans, and most of these people ended their involuntary flight in the western portion of the crippled and divided former Third Reich. Economic collapse was the norm everywhere. Churchill referred to the continent as "A rubble heap, a charnel house, a breeding ground for pestilence and hate." George C. Marshall (1880–1959), the U.S. secretary of state, warned that this situation created "the kind of crisis that communism thrived on." Despite the momentary euphoria of victory in the spring of 1945, Europe's postwar governments faced a monumental task.

At the center of the early Cold War conflict lay the fate of Germany. The victors had established four temporary occupation zones—British, American, French, and Soviet—immediately after the Nazis were defeated. They imposed a similar model on Berlin, located deep in the heart of the Soviet zone. The financial cost of administering each respective zone was high. The Americans, for example, spent $700 million in 1946 alone to provide basic food, clothing, and housing for the desperate population of their zone. The following year, France, Britain, and the United States elected to unify their zones to increase fiscal efficiency. Rather than continue a punitive peace similar to the one adopted at Versailles in 1919, the Western powers, led by the United States, sought to rebuild the continent in general and Germany in particular. Rebuilding meant a democratic political order and free market economics.

The Soviet decision to move natural resources—and even entire factories—from the zone it controlled in Germany to Russia also helped trigger the West's decision. The United States, whose economy had grown during the war and whose land mass no enemy had touched, condemned what it saw as a cynical property grab on Stalin's part. The Soviet leader justified these actions as part of an overall reparations program, but the Western allies interpreted it as a deliberate attempt to permanently impoverish Germany.

The opposing visions reached a crisis point when the United States, Britain, and France introduced a new currency in the western zones of Germany as part of a larger set of incentives to improve the economy. Stalin responded by blocking land access to the Western-controlled sectors of Berlin. For 11 months beginning in June 1948, the United States organized 277,000 airlifts into the city, bringing essential supplies and foodstuffs and circumventing the Soviet land blockade. The Soviets finally reversed their policy, but not before the Western powers decided to unify their three zones in West Germany into a new state: the German Federal Republic. The Soviets responded in October 1949 by forming the German Democratic Republic in their zone, inaugurating what would become a nearly 40-year division of Germany into capitalist and communist spheres.

The Marshall Plan   Crucial to the overall strategy of rebuilding Europe's war-torn economies was the implementation of the **Marshall Plan** for Europe, named after American Secretary of State George C. Marshall. Beginning in 1947, the United States offered massive economic aid to all war-torn countries in Europe, including the Soviet Union and its satellites, but the Soviets rejected the offer and prohibited their client-states from participating. Ostensibly, the Soviets objected to the

Berlin Airlift of 1948   After World War II Berlin was divided into four zones, controlled by the United States, Britain, France, and the Soviet Union. As diplomatic tensions developed between the Western powers and the Soviet Union, the U.S.S.R. cut off land access to western Berlin, prompting the United States to organize airlifts of food and other supplies.

Plan's requirement that the United States have some supervisory privileges over and access to the budgetary records of the receiving countries. Stalin chose to interpret these conditions as a violation of national sovereignty. The additional requirement that Marshall Plan money be used to purchase American products

Read the Document

George C. Marshall, The Marshall Plan, 1947

on **MyHistoryLab.com**

struck the Soviets as yet another attempt to extend the influence of the capitalist system. The Cominform, the international propaganda wing of the Soviet state, denounced the Marshall Plan as a sinister ploy to "establish the world supremacy of American imperialism." In response, Moscow established in January 1949 the Council for Mutual Economic Assistance to coordinate the rebuilding of those states under Soviet control.

Sixteen European nations, all outside of the Soviet sphere of influence, welcomed the American offer. Each received a substantial aid package, supervised by the recently formed Organization for European Economic Cooperation. By 1952, the United States had extended over $13 billion in grants and credits (worth perhaps $650 billion in today's money) to participants. The enormous infusion of resources helped to restart Europe's industrial base and modernize its agricultural sector. In West Germany the funds facilitated a remarkable resurrection of its industrial economy; by 1952, German production had climbed more than 50 percent over

Rebuilding Western Europe President Harry S Truman awards a Distinguished Service medal to General George C. Marshall in a ceremony at the Pentagon. Both men were instrumental in the establishment of an economic recovery package for Western Europe, and both were leaders in the creation of postwar foreign policy.

prewar levels. The contrast between civilian life in East and West Berlin (especially in the availability of consumer goods and services) became obvious to all visitors and reflected poorly on the Soviet alternative. Overall, the economies of Western European states were growing by five percent annually by 1952. The United States also reaped significant long-term benefits. Almost two-thirds of postwar European imports originated in America, and the reemployment of Europe's laboring population translated into the rapid stabilization of Europe's democratic political systems. The effort to undermine the appeal of the communist alternative through economic revival had passed a crucial test.

The Truman Doctrine   While the Soviet presence in Eastern Europe seemed irreversible short of a major military clash that few in the West welcomed, President Truman and his advisors were eager to foil potential Soviet influence elsewhere. Formal and highly secretive security intelligence gathering and espionage organizations, led by the **Central Intelligence Agency** (CIA) and the National Security Council (both established in 1948), faced off against their Soviet counterparts in an ever-expanding theater of operations around the world, but most immediately along the southern rim of Asia. The first crisis occurred in Iran, where the Soviet Union encouraged a secessionist movement in the northern province of Azerbaijan. Strong British and American opposition led to the grudging withdrawal of Soviet troops that had been in Iran alongside British forces during the war. In Turkey fear of the growth of communist influence, and in particular Western resentment over Stalin's call for Russian access to the Mediterranean via Turkish waters, led to a swift and dramatic American response. United States naval forces were dispatched to the eastern Mediterranean by President Truman, who announced they would remain there permanently.

Further to the west, a communist guerilla insurgency against a pro-Western monarchist government in Greece led the American president to announce a new foreign policy priority. During 1946 the Greek government appealed to the United States for

Read the **Document**

Truman Doctrine

on **MyHistoryLab.com**

financial and material assistance against the rebels. In early 1947 Britain (which had already intervened in the Greek conflict) told the United States that it could no longer afford to give Greece economic or military assistance. It was a watershed diplomatic acknowledgment of the coming end of the British Empire. Henceforth the Americans would have to assume the burden of repulsing communist insurgency. Truman responded in March 1947 in an address before a special joint session of Congress. In what came to be known as the Truman Doctrine, the president stated that "it must be the policy of the United States to support free people who are resisting attempted subjugation by armed minorities or by outside pressures."

In the two years that followed, the United States spent nearly $700 million to shore up the Greek army and provide economic assistance. By 1949, the communists had been defeated, but not before American military trainers had begun to work closely with Greek forces in the field. The Truman Doctrine helped refocus American public opinion about the West's former wartime ally, putting the Soviet Union on notice that the United States would not withdraw from Europe as it had after World War I. A program of "**containment**," which meant opposing further Soviet expansion, was first articulated by George Kennan (1904–2005), a seasoned foreign service officer stationed at the American embassy in Moscow. After 1949, the idea of containment became central to American foreign policy around the globe.

Read the Document

George Kennan,
Containment (1947)

on **MyHistoryLab.com**

The Creation of Israel   In 1945 and 1946 many European Jews who survived the Holocaust pressed the international community to recognize their claim to relocate in Palestine. During World War I, the British had promised to establish a Jewish homeland in Arab-inhabited Palestine, and in the interwar years, thousands of European Jews migrated there, buying land and clashing with Muslim inhabitants. In 1947 the British, unable to control fighting, referred the problem to the United Nations, which recommended dividing Palestine between Jews and Arabs. In the process many Palestinians were driven from lands where they had lived for generations.

In May 1948, Jewish settlers declared the establishment of an independent state called Israel, and the United States quickly recognized the new nation under its first prime minister, David Ben-Gurion (1886–1973). War erupted almost immediately between Israel and its Arab neighbors, and the Israelis were able not only to defeat their opponents but in the process extend the borders of the country beyond the limits established by the U.N. The United States became Israel's staunchest backer during the Cold War, while the Soviet Union increasingly gravitated toward some of the Arab states, such as Egypt, Syria, and Iraq.

Read the Document

Press Release Announcing
U.S. Recognition of Israel

on **MyHistoryLab.com**

Nuclear Arms Race   Soon after the United States deployed atomic weapons against Japan, Stalin accelerated the Soviet wartime program of nuclear research and development. The Russian scientific community, assisted by captured German researchers, became part of the Soviet defense establishment. Their work put an end to America's atomic monopoly in 1949; three years later both countries had developed hydrogen bombs, devices with a destructive capacity far exceeding the bombs that had destroyed Hiroshima and Nagasaki in August 1945. Both sides then introduced inter-continental ballistic missile delivery systems (**ICBMs**) and satellite technology, round-ing out the early advances in weapons of mass destruction. Over the next 30 years, the United States and the Soviet Union spent billions of dollars "enhancing" their stockpiles of weapons and "improving" delivery systems. Inevitably, the technology proliferated, with France, Britain, China, India, Pakistan, and Israel eventually joining the nuclear club. The cycle of weapons development, deployment, and proliferation continued as the superpowers confronted each other around the world.

The End of European Empire

At the conclusion of the war in 1945, almost 750 million people, or nearly one-third of the world's population, lived under the control of a foreign government. Most of-ten these governments were European, and despite their relative weakness after the defeat of **Nazism,** none of the imperial states was keen to shed itself of its colonial holdings. The United States and the Soviet Union, despite their own efforts to influ-ence domestic politics in developing nations, encouraged European states to grant independence to their colonies (see Map 25–1). It was apparent by the early 1950s that victorious European powers could neither afford the cost of maintaining global empires nor deny the aspirations of colonial peoples without repudiating the very commitment to democracy that stood at the core of the war against Fascism. Pushed by the United States to withdraw from their colonial possessions around the world and stung by Soviet denunciations of old-style imperialism, Western Europe pre-pared to disengage from its many overseas colonies. By 1985, almost 100 countries had secured their independence—new states that included one-third of the world's total population.

Britain Departs from South Asia   India was by far the largest European colony to gain its independence after the war, raising its national flag for the first time on August 15, 1947. The new country instantly became the world's most populous de-mocracy, adopting a parliamentary system of government that the country's Western-trained elites had learned to admire, despite the fact that British authorities had denied educated Indians access to the highest levels of power in the colonial government. The **Indian National Congress** had supported Britain during World War I, and Indian troops fought bravely in a number of the-aters in the hope that independence would be granted after the conflict. That hope was quickly dashed. A postwar government crackdown against opponents of empire prompted indigenous leaders like Mohandas Gandhi to organize a sophisticated campaign of nonviolent resistance to British rule that won broad-based support during the 1930s. When the British unilaterally announced at the start of World War II that India was also at war with Nazi Germany, the Hindu-dominated Congress Party passed a "Quit India" reso-lution that led to the banning of the party and the incarceration of leaders like Gandhi and Jawaharlal Nehru.

◉—⎡**Watch** the **Video**

Gandhi in India

on **MyHistoryLab.com**

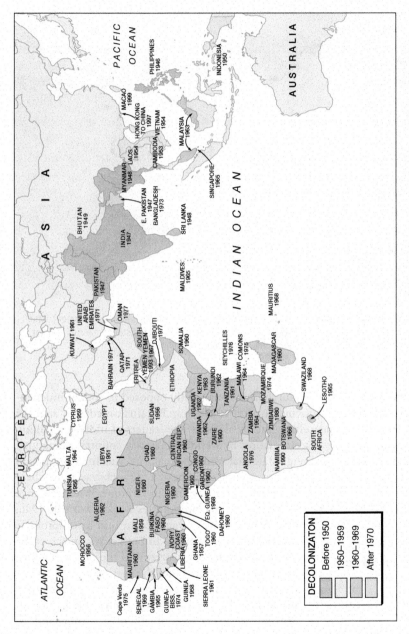

MAP 25-1 Postwar Decolonization The enormous cost of World War II combined with an upsurge in calls for political independence after the defeat of Germany and Japan signaled the end of the European empires. In Africa and Asia new nations emerged, each one struggling to achieve economic security and material progress.

QUESTION: Did decolonization mean the end of Western influence in newly independent states?

Jawaharlal Nehru and Mohandas Gandhi Nehru and Gandhi led India's independence movement, which freed India from British colonial rule in 1947. Gandhi's tactics of nonviolent resistance exerted a major influence throughout the world in the second half of the twentieth century.

Prime Minister Winston Churchill was adamantly opposed to Indian independence, but the Labour government that came to power in Britain immediately after the war was committed to a peaceful withdrawal. Sadly, the leaders of India's 95 million Muslims, fearing possible discrimination in a Hindu majority country, demanded the creation of a separate sovereign state that would be majority Muslim. Gandhi and the Congress Party opposed partition, arguing in favor of a nonsectarian state where all faith traditions would find a home. When violence between the two communities escalated during 1946, British negotiators scrambled to find a compromise that would be acceptable to both sides. In the end a two-state solution was agreed in the face of terrible sectarian bloodshed. Once the partition took place in August 1947, millions of Hindus fled from northwest India (now Pakistan) while a comparable exodus of Muslims departed India for their new homeland. In the midst of the chaos approximately a quarter of a million people were killed fleeing their homes and crossing the border. Another 17 million became long-

☐●☐Read the **Document**

Gandhi Speaks against the Partition of India (pre-1947)

on **MyHistoryLab.com**

☐●☐Read the **Document**

The Tandon Family at Partition (1947), Prakash Tandon

on **MyHistoryLab.com**

term refugees. Under the leadership of Nehru, India emerged as a stable parliamentary democracy, pursued a non-aligned foreign policy, and maintained cordial relations with its former imperial overlord. Pakistan was less fortunate, entering into a long period of troubled democracy and intermittent military rule. Both countries faced enormous economic challenges in the immediate postwar years, and a legacy of distrust soured bilateral relations and led to a series of military conflicts over the disputed territory of Kashmir that further undermined efforts to address pressing domestic needs.

France Withdraws from North Africa

In an effort to retain its considerable holdings in Africa, France's postwar government conferred metropolitan citizenship on its colonial subjects and attempted to create a wider French Union. The North African colonies of Morocco and Tunisia were committed to full independence, however, and in 1956 the goal was achieved peacefully. The outcome was very different in French Algeria, a colony since the 1830s and home to over one million politically powerful French settlers. The Muslim population of nine million was determined to dislodge the settlers, and a bloody war of national liberation began soon after the French withdrew in defeat from their Southeast Asian colony of Vietnam in 1954. The brutal conflict in Algeria raged for eight years, leading to the collapse of the Fourth Republic and to the return of General Charles de Gaulle as president of a new Fifth Republic. Under de Gaulle's lead, French forces finally withdrew from Algeria in 1962, followed by approximately 1.5 million deeply embittered white settlers. They left behind a war-ravaged country where over one million Algerians had died, and where the fledgling government faced an enormous task of reconstruction.

Democratic Promise in Sub-Saharan Africa

India's successful independence struggle set a powerful example for nationalist movements in dozens of sub-Saharan African colonies. There were only three independent African states in 1945 (South Africa, Liberia, and Ethiopia), but as world opinion turned sharply against colonialism in the years immediately after the war, Africa's Western-educated leaders pressed for a complete end to decades of exploitative outside control. During the late 1950s and continuing through the 1960s, more than 30

African Decolonization This 1960 cartoon depicts the sweeping out of the former colonial powers from the African continent. Most of Africa gained its independence in the 1950s and early 1960s.

new nation-states were created on the African continent, with most of the fledgling states maintaining the old colonial boundaries that had been set by Europeans in the late nineteenth century.

The British and the French were the first European countries to accept **decolonization** in sub-Saharan Africa. For the most part, the process of liberation took place in an orderly and peaceful manner. In the West African British colony of Gold Coast, for example, a charismatic and American-educated leader named Kwame Nkrumah led his Convention People's Party to independence in 1957. Under Nkrumah's guidance, the renamed state of Ghana set out to become a model of African democracy in the postcolonial era. With abundant mineral-ore, hardwood, and cocoa reserves that were in strong demand overseas, and with Nkrumah's vision for stronger pan-African unity and cooperation, initial hopes were high for the rapid social and economic development of West Africa's first independent state.

Unfortunately, the high expectations were never realized. Nkrumah's consuming interest in pan-African unity distracted his attention away from pressing domestic issues, and when he began to rule in an increasingly undemocratic manner, restricting press freedoms and detaining critics, popular support eroded. As the mismanaged economy began to falter in the 1960s, the goal of rapid industrialization failed to move forward. Nkrumah was removed from office by the

[●] Read the Document

Kwame Nkrumah on African Unity (1960s)

on **MyHistoryLab.com**

military while the president was on a state visit to China and Vietnam in 1966. It was a pattern of civilian to military rule that became all too familiar on the African continent as the grandiose promises of democratically elected politicians remained unfulfilled in the years immediately after independence. In reality, few of Africa's postwar leaders embraced nationalism as a vehicle for needed social change. In too many cases they had opposed European imperialism because it prevented them from assuming positions of authority at the highest levels.

Independence from the direct control of Western Europe, however exhilarating during the first months and years of freedom, did not set in motion a course of unimpeded progress for new states in South Asia, the Middle East, Africa, and Southeast Asia. Most of these nations found themselves drawn into the Cold War conflict between the superpowers after 1945, often becoming Soviet or American clients in exchange for needed financial and military support. In addition, the economic foundations of nascent postcolonial states frequently rested on the production of single cash crops for a global market. Increasing global economic interdependence often meant that for newly sovereign states in the developing world, the search for autonomy was elusive, with economies disadvantaged in the competition with more mature, industrialized (and usually Western) countries. Finally, the early leaders of former European colonies faced a host of formidable obstacles in their quest to create stable political institutions. Over the last 60 years, nationalist leaders of newly independent states had repeatedly promised significant improvements in the quality of life for their citizens. When these promises were not kept and economies faltered, the recourse to authoritarian and military government followed, inaugurating an unhappy cycle of official corruption, ever-expanding poverty, and civil unrest.

Migration to Europe from the Colonial Periphery   Europe had been the world's principal sending zone since the late sixteenth century. As migrants settled and appropriated lands in the Americas and Australasia, native populations were decimated by a series of infectious diseases introduced inadvertently by Europeans. After 1945 the process of relocation was reversed, with Western Europe becoming a net immigration zone for the first time in over 400 years. As part of the rebuilding of Western Europe's war-torn infrastructure, and in the context of Europe's stagnant or declining birth rate, former colonial subjects and others from less-developed regions around the world were invited to become a part of the workforce on what was envisioned as a temporary basis. Immigration authorities were eager to maintain maximum flexibility with respect to residency. Thus, a series of guest-worker schemes were devised to control the flow of new arrivals.

West Germany, France, Belgium, Switzerland, the Netherlands, and Britain all recruited temporary laborers after the war, with West Germany facing the most acute shortages in its mines, factories, and construction trades. Between 1945 and 1961, much of the demand for workers was met by migrants fleeing communist-controlled Eastern Europe. Over eight million ethnic Germans were forced out of their homes in the east immediately after the war, and a voluntary exodus followed once living conditions in the Soviet Bloc deteriorated. With the erection of the Berlin Wall in 1961, however, the flow westward was arrested and West German authorities were obliged to turn to residents of southern Europe and Turkey for assistance. By the early 1970s many of West Germany's 2.6 million foreign workers were from Turkey, and generous family reunification policies led to the arrival of additional nonworkers. Ethnic

Evicting Immigrants   Police in Paris, France, in August 2006 evict immigrants from the Ivory Coast and Mali who refused to move into government housing. France has one of the highest immigrant populations in Europe.

enclaves emerged in a number of cities, and anti-immigrant sentiment rose during periods of economic downturn. This was especially true after the oil shocks of the early 1970s, when economies throughout the industrialized West faced inflation and higher levels of unemployment.

In Britain, colonists and citizens of recently independent **Commonwealth states** were allowed to enter the country and could apply for British citizenship. By the early 1960s over 3.2 million persons had taken advantage of this generous policy. Most settled in the industrial cities of the English midlands where they worked in factories and established small service-oriented businesses. But as racial tensions rose in the early 1960s between native Britons and recent arrivals from India, Pakistan, and sub-Saharan Africa, the government began to place restrictions on immigration. By the early 1980s, only those applicants who possessed specialized skills in targeted sectors found an official welcome. France faced comparable challenges in its efforts to assimilate settlers from its former colonial empire. A National Office of Immigration, created in 1945, regulated the flow of immigrants. In addition to two million Europeans who entered the country between the end of the war and 1974, almost one million Tunisians, Moroccans, and Algerians gained admittance. Here, too, tensions between the majority population and migrants from Muslim North Africa, especially during the recession of the 1970s, fueled nativist sentiment and **xenophobia.** Demographically stagnant Western Europe needed foreign labor resources to rebuild after the war, but seemed reluctant to embrace the multicultural implications of the new immigration (see Map 25–2).

Expanding the Cold War

NATO and the Warsaw Pact   The Western European democracies became central players in the emerging Cold War conflict. Heavily dependent on American economic assistance, France and Britain accepted American forces and weapons systems while also increasing their own military budgets. Given the much larger Soviet ground forces stationed in Europe throughout the Cold War, America's nuclear "umbrella" appeared to be the only guarantee against a potential Soviet incursion. Switzerland, Sweden, Ireland, and Finland managed to follow a neutral course; Austria embraced neutrality after securing independence in 1956; and Marshall Tito's (1892–1980) communist Yugoslavia avoided Soviet domination. Elsewhere, however, Europe's many states felt the pull of American and Soviet power (see Map 25–3).

In 1949 the United States took the unprecedented step of formalizing the military cooperation that already existed among the Western allies. The **North Atlantic Treaty Organization,** or **NATO,** was presented as a defensive alliance in which all the members would regard an attack against one member state as an attack against the entire alliance. In direct response to the formation of NATO, the Soviet Union created its own alliance system, the **Warsaw Pact.** During the 1950s, as the two sides stockpiled weapons and consolidated their positions in Europe, superpower Cold War conflict broadened to embrace peoples around the globe.

East Asia   The first phase of the Cold War ended with the promulgation of the Truman Doctrine and the adoption of containment theory as the basis of America's

MAP 25-2   Muslim Population of Western Europe, c. 2005   Much of Western Europe saw its Muslim population increase in the 1990s and in the first years of the new century. This growth has generated new social issues related to immigration and anti-Muslim prejudice.

QUESTION: Which European countries have the highest percentage of Muslims? Are there historical factors that account for these trends?

posture toward the Soviet Union. Abandoning any thought of rolling back the existing Soviet sphere of influence, Western foreign policy and military strategy, led by the United States, would now focus on resisting communist expansion around the globe. Securing reliable allies who embraced the anticommunist position began to take precedence over concerns about the human rights record of these potential allies. During the

MAP 25-3 **The Cold War in Europe** The member states of the NATO alliance faced the Soviet-dominated Warsaw Pact from the late 1940s until the late 1980s. Ideological differences between the two superpowers had broad implications for the peace and security of Europe.

QUESTION: To what extent was the Cold War about the future of Europe?

next 40 years, diplomatic backing of and military assistance to anticommunist regimes often meant American support for repressive regimes whose policies ran counter to the U.S.-professed stand for individual freedom, political democracy, and civilian rule.

The defeat of Japan in August 1945 meant the collapse of an enormous East Asian Empire and created a power vacuum in a number of strategic areas. American forces occupied Japan's main islands, the Soviets took charge in Manchuria, and the two powers organized a temporary partition of Korea between them along the thirty-eighth parallel. However, elsewhere in the former Japanese Empire, the struggles among rival claimants to postwar political power inevitably became part of the Cold War. East Asia, which before the rise of Japanese imperialism had been part of the larger European-dominated world system, was now drawn into the Washington-Moscow rivalry.

View the **Image**

Tokyo Shanty Town

on **MyHistoryLab.com**

The Struggle for China The principal setting for this ideological struggle was China, an enormous nation that had suffered greatly from Japanese invasion and

civil conflict between the Nationalist government and rural-based communist insurgents since the late 1920s. In this nation of over 300 million people, the anticommunist Nationalists under the leadership of Chiang Kai-shek (1887–1975) enjoyed
the backing of the United States. Chiang's forces were often incompetent and poorly
led. Despite an infusion of American military aid, the Nationalists had failed to win a
single significant battle against the Japanese.

In the rural areas and along the coast of China, however, an alternative movement under Mao Zedong (1893–1976) had won the support of increasing numbers of
resistance fighters. As early as the 1920s, Mao had insisted (in opposition to classical
Marxist-Leninist theory) that the revolutionary potential and leadership capacity of
the peasantry were enormous. The communists culti-
vated the support of the oppressed peasantry by lowering rents and attacking exploitative landlords. By
1945 Mao stood at the head of a communist (mostly
peasant) army of over one million men. The communist **People's Liberation Army** (PLA) controlled large
sweeps of territory across China, and Mao's call for fundamental land reform, something that the Nationalists had never taken seriously, gave his movement enormous
political advantage.

Read the Document

*Mao Zedong, "From the
Countryside to the City," 1949*

on **MyHistoryLab.com**

对伟大导师毛主席心怀一个"忠"字
对伟大毛泽东思想狠抓一个"用"字

Mao Zedong   This poster from the 1960s stresses the leader principle in Chinese communism. Mao
Zedong towers over his peasant supporters, all of whom hold a copy of Mao's teachings, the "Little Red
Book." The words at the bottom read, "Be loyal to the great leader, Chairman Mao. Put his ideas into
practice."

While the Americans continued to send military and financial aid to Chiang Kai-shek, by 1947 it had become obvious that the Nationalists' corruption and complacency could not be reversed. Frustrated by the lack of progress, U.S. forces were withdrawn from China, and American-sponsored mediation efforts between the two sides, led by General George C. Marshall, the future secretary of state, were abandoned. By the spring of 1948, the Nationalists' military situation on the mainland had become untenable, and in 1949 Chiang withdrew to the island of Taiwan. After this stunning military victory, achieved without the support of the Soviet Union and against the American-armed Nationalists, Mao officially announced the formation of the Communist **People's Republic of China** on October 1, 1949. This momentous victory occurred barely one year after a Soviet takeover in Czechoslovakia and the Berlin blockade, and in the same year that the Soviets successfully tested an atomic bomb. Many Western observers incorrectly linked the rise of Communist China with a Soviet-led worldwide conspiracy.

Conflict in Korea   Superpower differences in the evolving bipolar conflict reached their first flashpoint on the occupied Korean peninsula in 1950, less than a year after the creation of the People's Republic of China. The Soviets and Americans had failed to reach agreement on plans for Korean reunification. After each side installed separate governments in the north and the south (both of which claimed sovereignty over the whole of Korea), the Soviet and American armies had withdrawn in 1948. They left behind a highly volatile stalemate in which neither North nor South was prepared to make tangible concessions to the other. The leader of the U.S.-backed state, the authoritarian Syngman Rhee (1875–1965), vowed to unify Korea by force if necessary. Military and financial assistance flowed into both Koreas over the next two years, and on June 25, 1950, a North Korean army of some 100,000 men, with the endorsement of the Soviet Union, crossed the thirty-eighth parallel to "liberate" the people of the South from their "reactionary" Nationalist government. Stalin and North Korean leader Kim Il Sung (1912–1994) were gambling that the Truman administration would not intervene to save the dictatorial Rhee regime.

The American response, however, conditioned by recent developments in China and by memories of the appeasement of Fascist aggression in 1930s Europe, was immediate. Advocates of containment within the Truman administration insisted that a credible reaction must include military intervention on behalf of the South. President Truman told reporters that the Korean situation represented "the Greece of the Far East," and his advisors were convinced that the invasion was a Soviet-led test of American resolve in the Pacific. Truman dispatched American forces from nearby Japan under the command of General Douglas MacArthur (1880–1964), and the Security Council of the United Nations (in the absence of the Soviets who were protesting the exclusion of Communist China from the United Nations) voted to legitimize the U.S. intervention.

What began as a limited defensive action in Korea quickly developed into a full-scale war. After a series of attacks and counterattacks, a military stalemate ensued along the thirty-eighth parallel. The fighting continued for three years, with the United States incurring over 100,000 casualties as leader of the U.N. army. Chinese and North Korean dead and wounded reached an estimated one million soldiers; the same ghastly count applied to South Korean combatants. North Korean cities suffered heavy damage from American bombers, and before an armistice was signed in 1953, the posture of the United States toward both China and Stalin's Soviet Union had hardened into deep disdain.

Read the **Document**

Korean War Armistice

on **MyHistoryLab.com**

Southeast Asia   The Philippines, liberated from Japanese occupation in 1944, secured its full independence from the United States in 1946. However, in the wake of the Korean conflict, the Philippine government extended long-term leases on military bases and airfields to the Americans, and a defense treaty pledged U.S. assistance in the event of communist aggression. The United States also entered into a mutual defense pact with Australia and New Zealand in 1951 (ANZUS), signaling the replacement of a century of British protection for these European settler countries and former British colonies in the South Pacific. The shadow of one great empire was replaced by the protective military and financial umbrella of a country that for most of its history as an independent nation had eschewed the temptations and burdens of global power.

While the Americans played the predominant role in postwar Japan and South Korea, the British, Dutch, and French returned to their former colonial holdings in Southeast Asia. For Britain and the Netherlands, the reversion was in some cases a temporary measure designed to facilitate the creation of independent, pro-Western, and anticommunist governments. The French were less realistic. In 1946 French soldiers and administrators returned to Indochina, hoping to resume their rule over the region's diverse population. In Vietnam, however, they confronted an indigenous guerrilla movement led by the communist leader Ho Chi Minh (1892–1969).

Vietnam   The United States had originally viewed French operations in Indochina as a misguided attempt to restore an old-style empire. In 1950, however, in the wake of the Chinese Revolution and Soviet sponsorship of North Korean aggression, the Truman administration changed its posture. Having "lost" China, the hard-line American policymakers resolved not to repeat the debacle in Southeast Asia. U.S. military hardware and economic aid now began to flow freely to the French.

Despite the infusion of American material assistance, early in 1954 French forces suffered a humiliating defeat at the hands of the communists, with 10,000 French troops surrendering a strategic redoubt at **Dien Bien Phu.** The French now conceded that they could not win the war; they had already suffered 100,000 casualties, and French public opinion turned decisively against the undertaking. Although of little economic value in terms of its global influence, Vietnam attracted the attention of the superpowers when peace negotiations were opened between communist and noncommunist representatives from Vietnam. The United States, Britain, the Soviet Union, and China all sent delegates to the conference, and once

Read the **Document**

*Ho Chi Minh,
Self-Determination*

on **MyHistoryLab.com**

again a disputed land was partitioned pending promised national elections set for 1956. Ho Chi Minh accepted the terms of the accord, confident that the communists would win an overwhelming majority in nationwide balloting.

The elections never took place. The United States recruited a Nationalist leadership for the South, provided military training and funding for a new South Vietnamese army, and spent almost $1 billion to forge a pliable client-state. A communist

MAP 25-4   War in Vietnam   Southeast Asia became a flashpoint in the Cold War as French and subsequently American forces tried (unsuccessfully) to defeat communist insurgents in Vietnam. For American strategists in the 1950s and 1960s, the fall of Vietnam would have strengthened the global reach of communism.

QUESTION: How did Vietnam's proximity to China affect the way the United States viewed it?

revolution in Cuba in 1959 influenced the American commitment to remain engaged in Vietnam. The United States interpreted Fidel Castro's victory as a major breach of the containment policy. President John F. Kennedy (1917–1963) was unwilling to allow a similar reversal in Southeast Asia. As early as 1956, while he was still a U.S.

senator, Kennedy had stated that "Vietnam represents the cornerstone of the Free World in Southeast Asia." By the time of Kennedy's assassination in 1963, over 15,000 American military advisors were stationed in South Vietnam. The new president, Lyndon Johnson (1908–1973), inherited a rapidly deteriorating and chaotic situation in Saigon. Over the next two years, South Vietnamese generals struggled for mastery as more of the countryside fell to communist forces. The social and economic disorder visited upon the civilian population, both North and South, was without precedent in the history of the region (see Map 25–4).

PEOPLE IN CONTEXT Ho Chi Minh

Like his Chinese counterpart Mao Zedong, Ho Chi Minh believed strongly in the revolutionary potential of the peasantry, and his insistence upon the need for fundamental land reform attracted many impoverished Vietnamese to his guerilla insurgency against the French.

Ho was born in 1890, the youngest of three children. He spent his youth in central Vietnam and participated in local tax revolts against the French. In 1911 he traveled to Paris and worked as a photo restorer. In 1919, still living in France, Ho joined the Communist Party. He hoped that French rule would end after World War I, but the peace conference at Versailles declined to address the issue of French colonialism in Vietnam.

In the 1920s Ho served as a covert Soviet agent in Asia. In 1929 he established the Indochinese Communist Party. When the Japanese invaded Vietnam in 1940, Ho began to organize the Vietnam Independence League, or Vietminh. He brought to the movement a sense of dedication and purpose unrivaled by other anticolonial groups. When the French refused to recognize Vietnamese independence after World War II, Ho's resistance organization withdrew to the countryside and formed a guerilla movement similar to the one previously established by Mao Zedong in the north of China.

In the late 1950s Ho had warned that the insurgency against colonial rule might last for another 30 years. Unconventional guerilla tactics shortened the struggle, but not before millions had lost their lives. When Ho died in 1969, his armies still faced years of conflict before the country was reunified. However, his refusal to compromise with the French and Americans, and his disagreements with Chinese communists, marked his movement as a nationalist struggle first and a communist revolution second. ∎

Ho Chi Minh Meeting with advisors in 1954, Ho Chi Minh (center) directs the insurgency against French colonial forces. The North Vietnamese fought an unconventional guerilla war against both the French and Americans.

QUESTION: What role did traditional forms of nationalism play in Ho Chi Minh's struggle against France and America?

The Cold War and Nuclear Threat

Cuban Missile Crisis   During the early 1950s, Cuban dictator Fulgencio Batista (1901–1973) banned the Communist Party and established close relations with the United States in return for military aid and business investment. In a small island nation of seven million people, a tiny Cuban middle class benefited greatly from its economic ties to the American colossus to the north. Sugar exports and the tourist trade stood at the heart of the relationship, but improved economic conditions for some could not compensate for the absence of political freedoms under a regime that did little to improve the lives of most Cubans. A youthful reform-oriented opponent of U.S. influence in Cuba, Fidel Castro (b. 1926), staged a successful revolt against the Batista regime in 1958. In his subsequent assumption of political power, Castro was able to unite disparate ideological forces: communists, socialists, and anti-Batista liberals who advocated social justice and land reform for the rural poor. U.S. officials, pleased to see the end of the corrupt and ineffective Batista dictatorship, held out modest hope that the coalition would hold, especially since Castro himself seemed to have no clear agenda beyond a call for national renewal.

Within three years of his initial victory, however, Castro had broken with most of his allies over the issue of free elections, erected a one-party state, began to create a Soviet-style command economy, and turned to the Soviet Union for essential foreign aid. Political dissent, press freedoms, foreign ownership of established business enterprises, and landed estates were all forbidden. By the end of the Eisenhower presidency in 1960, Castro had seized the property of all U.S.-owned businesses in Cuba, worth several billion dollars, and the United States had adopted a full embargo on trade with the island. As Castro turned to the Soviets for technical advice, economic assistance, and trade agreements, the new Kennedy administration prepared to fight the Cold War in its own hemisphere.

In April 1961 a U.S.-organized and funded group of 1,400 Cuban exiles disembarked from American naval vessels at the **Bay of Pigs** on the Cuban coast. Their assault was short-lived, with Cuban authorities arresting sympathizers and Cuban troops quickly defeating the rebel contingent on the landing beaches. In the aftermath of this debacle, Castro proclaimed his adherence to the Marxist-Leninist community of anti-imperialist nations. While he did not secure the formal military alliance with the Soviet Union that he desired, Russian leader Nikita Khrushchev (1894–1971) did offer Castro medium- and intermediate-range ballistic missiles on the condition that the Soviets install and control the weapons in Cuba. Castro consented, and in the fall of 1962 the lethal hardware, together with thousands of Russian technicians and military personnel, began to arrive at its destination less than 100 miles off the southern coast of Florida (see Map 25–5).

Speculation continues to this day over the Soviet decision to confront the Americans in their own hemisphere. Khrushchev may have hoped to use the missiles as a bargaining chip to eliminate the Western enclave in Berlin or to remove American ballistic missiles stationed near the Soviet border in Turkey, but no single motive is clear. What is clear is that the subsequent Cuban Missile Crisis brought the world's two superpowers to the edge of nuclear war just 17 years after they had been allies in

MAP 25-5 The Cuban Missile Crisis The Soviet Union and the United States avoided armed conflict with each other throughout the Cold War, but in 1962 the two superpowers came close to nuclear warfare.

QUESTION: Why did the United States feel threatened by the events in Cuba of the early 1960s?

defeating Nazism in Europe. With missiles in Cuba, America's major cities were vulnerable to a direct Soviet nuclear strike. In October the United States began an air and naval blockade of Cuba and insisted that the Soviets withdraw the missiles. Kennedy received

◉─[Watch the Video

The Cuban Missile Crisis

on **MyHistoryLab.com**

NATO backing for his position and declared that any missile launched from Cuba against any nation in the Western hemisphere would result in American nuclear retaliation against the Soviet Union.

A tense week of threats and counterthreats ensued as 19 American warships prepared to stop and board Russian cargo ships bound for Havana. Without consulting Castro, Khrushchev finally agreed to remove the weapons in return for a U.S. pledge not to

◉─[Watch the Video

Cold War Connections: Russia, America, Berlin, and Cuba

on **MyHistoryLab.com**

attempt the overthrow of the Castro government. The Soviet leader also requested the removal of the U.S. missiles in Turkey; while Kennedy officially refused, the weapons were quietly removed from their forward positions in 1963. The world had narrowly avoided a violent conclusion to the Cold War that no one would have survived.

Divisions and Détente   The political and ideological divisions that emerged within the larger family of Marxist states belied Western fear that communism represented a monolithic force committed to the overthrow of capitalist democracies. Mao's relations with Stalin were always icy, and in the 1960s the Soviets began withholding economic and technological aid that they had promised to the Chinese. Nor did communism diminish the historic and deeply rooted animosity between the Vietnamese and their Chinese neighbors to the north. In the 1970s, while the United States was still deeply engaged in the Vietnam conflict, China and the United States began to normalize diplomatic and commercial relations. In February 1972 Richard Nixon (1913–1994) became the first American president to visit China. In Cuba, while Castro's regime continued to receive substantial economic assistance from the Soviets until the late 1980s, the resolution of the missile crisis demonstrated how unequal the relationship between Castro and his Soviet patrons was throughout the years.

Despite the many tensions Cold War rivalries generated, the United States and the Soviet Union were able on occasion to use their diplomatic power to diffuse potentially dangerous military situations. In 1956, for example, Egyptian President Gamal Abdel Nasser (1918–1970) nationalized the Suez Canal, precipitating a British and French invasion designed to protect their interests and influence in North Africa and the Near East. The United States forced its European allies into a humiliating withdrawal, while the Soviets loudly supported Egypt, one of its Arab allies. Israel, which had invaded Egypt's Sinai and Gaza Strip in conjunction with the British and French, was also forced to withdraw. The incident demonstrated that the two superpowers could restrain their respective allies from military adventures that might easily escalate into wider conflicts.

Suez Canal Votes   In an attempt to prevent Egyptian leader Gamal Abdel Nasser from nationalizing the Suez Canal in 1956, Britain, France, and Israel intervened militarily. This provoked a furious response from the United States, which led to a worldwide condemnation of the assault and a debate on the issue at the U.N. Security Council. In the photograph here, the contrasting votes of the U.S. and British ambassadors are starkly contrasted.

During the height of the Cold War, the threat of nuclear annihilation led both superpowers to seek ways to regulate the production and deployment of weapons of mass destruction. Under the 1963 Nuclear Test Ban Treaty, over 100 nations agreed to stop testing nuclear devices in the atmosphere, under the oceans, and in space. In 1968 the **Nuclear Non-Proliferation Treaty** obliged more than 100 signatories to refrain from developing these weapons. Although China, Israel, France, and India refused to sign the U.N.-sponsored treaty and proceeded to develop their own nuclear capabilities, the two superpowers continued to work toward greater regulation of their respective weapons arsenals. President Nixon visited Moscow in May 1972, just three months after his visit to China. He met with Soviet leader Leonid Brezhnev (1906–1982) and signed an interim arms control agreement. It placed limits on the number of intercontinental ballistic missiles (ICBMs), antiballistic missiles (ABMs), and submarine-launched missiles each side could deploy. At the end of the meeting, a confident Brezhnev told his aids, "You can do business with Nixon." This period of U.S.-Soviet relations, often referred to as *détente* continued until 1979. A series of agreements reached at Helsinki, Finland, in 1975 committed Europe, the United States, and the Soviet Union to recognize the existing borders in central Europe, thus bringing to a close debates that had been ongoing since the end of World War II. The signatories also agreed to share technical and scientific information in an effort to reduce Cold War tensions.

Read the **Document**

Test Ban Treaty

on **MyHistoryLab.com**

Power and Principle   Committed first and foremost to stopping the expansionism thought to be inherent in capitalism and communism respectively, both sides in the Cold War too often pursued strategic goals with a disregard for their own ideals. The Soviet, Chinese, North Korean, North Vietnamese, and Cubans sacrificed the quest for a just social and economic order in the name of party discipline, military preparedness, and the cult of leadership. The Marxist ideal of the classless society in which human potential would at last be realized under conditions of genuine majority rule was repeatedly subordinated to the territorial and nationalist ambitions of the leadership elite. The very concept of the nation-state, so anathema to the Marxist ideal of international proletarian solidarity, emerged as the central focus of the communist bloc. The strained relations that emerged within the family of communist states after 1945 testified to this ideologically awkward reality.

On the other side of the ideological divide, the United States advertised itself as the defender of the Enlightenment tradition of liberalism, including the defense of individual liberty, national self-determination, and the right to overthrow repressive regimes. Along with its West European allies, the Americans claimed the moral high ground over the Soviets by virtue of their respect for the will of the majority and the right of minorities to freely dissent. Unfortunately, as Cold War suspicions intensified, policymakers in the United States interpreted postcolonial nationalist revolts through the lens of containment theory. Alliances predicated solely on a state's anticommunist credentials undermined America's reputation throughout the developing world. From Korea and Southeast Asia in the Pacific theater to Cuba, Guatemala, and Nicaragua in Central America, the United States repeatedly propped up undemocratic and brutal regimes in the interest of anticommunist solidarity.

Key Dates in the Cold War and Decolonization

1946	Churchill gives "Iron Curtain" speech
1947	India gains independence
1947	Truman Doctrine
1948	Marshall Plan
1949	Formation of NATO
1954	Battle of Dien Bien Phu
1954–1962	Algerian war of independence
1955	Formation of Warsaw Pact
1956	Suez Canal crisis
1961	Berlin Wall is built
1962	Cuban Missile Crisis

QUESTION REVISITED

How does ideology shape public policy?

It has been argued that disagreement between the Soviet Union and the United States after the defeat of Fascism was the predictable outcome of great power relations. Throughout history, major states have distrusted each other; while occasionally avoiding outright war, they have taken rivalry and rhetorical sparring for granted. What one side may consider essential to its defense often strikes the other as insidious expansionism, while the formation of extensive alliance systems and friendship pacts merely makes the other side uneasy.

Another interpretation sees the postwar U.S.-Soviet antagonism in starkly ideological terms. Two opposing systems of political, social, and economic organization, both "revolutionary" in terms of the long sweep of global history, each viewed the collapse of Nazi totalitarianism and the end of colonial empires as an opportunity to rebuild the world in their own image. For the United States, the heir of a liberal democratic revolution that was 200 years old, humanity's best hope centered on the primacy of the individual. Freedom to pursue one's material goals in a market economy, to seek social change within a democratic polity, and to differ without fear from one's neighbor under conditions of free expression were the benchmarks of civilized living. They were also the inalienable rights for which so many millions had already sacrificed their lives during the first half of the twentieth century, the bloodiest half-century in history.

For the Soviet Union, heir to a more recent Marxist revolution, the promises of liberal capitalism, of markets, and of selfish individualism rang hollow in light of the class conflict and economic inequality that characterized societies that the Enlightenment project had spawned. According to this world view, liberal capitalism would never lead to true human dignity and material sufficiency. Lenin had identified the natural tendency of capitalist states to foster a competitive culture that in the end would consume them; communists believed that it was time to escape from the grip of a system whose inherent dynamic was to guarantee the misery of the majority. That the Soviet system had not evolved into the noncoercive classless social order Marx envisioned was due solely, its defenders argued, to the ongoing hostility of the Western capitalist states to the socialist experiment.

The dangerous dynamic of great power rivalry, of ideological confrontation, not only informed political and military decisions but also shaped economic priorities on both sides, fostering what President Dwight D. Eisenhower (1890–1969) lamented as the "military-industrial complex" in the West. This same complex denied Soviet citizens a genuine consumer sector as Stalin and his successors doggedly pursued military parity with the United States. The struggle, and particularly the failure to honor the aspirations embodied in the founding ideas of their respective systems, diminished both sides.

Key Terms

existentialism, *p. 740*
Nazism, *p. 748*

decolonization, *p. 752*
Marshall Plan, *p. 754*

NATO, *p. 754*
Warsaw Pact, *p. 754*

Activities

1. How justified were Stalin's suspicions of the Western democracies after World War II?

2. Outline the Soviet case for refusing to accept Marshall Plan funding.

3. Describe how the Truman Doctrine helped to redefine America's role in the global community.

4. Why did China's Nationalist government fail to defeat communism?

5. Describe containment policy and provide some examples of its implementation during the 1950s.

6. What was the purpose of NATO and the Warsaw Pact?

7. How did both sides in the Cold War violate their founding principles?

Further Reading

John Gaddis, *The Cold War: A New History* (2005), offers a balanced and up-to-date account.

John Hargreaves, *Decolonization in Africa* (1988), provides an overview of Europe's withdrawal from this important continent.

David Halberstam, *The Coldest Winter: America and the Korean War* (2007), a highly readable study by a noted journalist.

Nelson Mandela, *Long Walk to Freedom* (1995), an autobiographical account by South Africa's first post-apartheid President.

MyHistoryLab Connections

Visit **MyHistoryLab.com** *for a customized Study Plan that will help you build your knowledge of* Decolonization and the Cold War.

Questions for Analysis

1. Why did Gandhi believe nonviolence to be a more effective form of resistance than violence when confronting colonial power?

👁—Watch the Video Gandhi in India, p. 748

2. According to Kwame Nkrumah, what were the advantages of a united Africa and how did Nkrumah respond to those who feared that unification would encroach on the sovereignty of the member states?

📖—Read the Document Kwame Nkrumah on African Unity (1960s), p. 752

3. What was Mao's strategy for victory and what were some of the key components of this strategy?

📖—Read the Document Mao Zedong, "From the Countryside to the City," 1949, p. 757

4. What were some of Ho Chi Minh's short-term and long-term goals for Vietnam?

📖—Read the Document Ho Chi Minh, *Self-Determination*, p. 759

5. What had Nikita Khrushchev hoped to accomplish by placing missiles in Cuba in 1962 and what was the outcome of this plan?

👁—Watch the Video Cold War Connections: Russia, America, Berlin, and Cuba, p. 763

Other Resources from This Chapter

📖—Read the Document Charter of the United Nations, p. 741

📍—View the Image Truman, Atlee, and Stalin at the Potsdam (Berlin) Conference, p. 742

📍—View the Image Hungarian Uprising, 1956, p. 743

📖—Read the Document Churchill's "Iron Curtain" Speech (March 5, 1946), p. 743

📖—Read the Document Joseph Stalin, Excerpts from the "Soviet Victory" Speech, 1946, p. 743

[📖] **Read** the **Document** George C. Marshall, The Marshall Plan, 1947, p. 745

[📖] **Read** the **Document** The Truman Doctrine, p. 746

[📖] **Read** the **Document** George Kennan, *Containment,* (1947), p. 747

[📖] **Read** the **Document** Press Release Announcing U.S. Recognition of Israel, p. 747

[📖] **Read** the **Document** Gandhi Speaks against the Partition of India (pre-1947), p. 750

[📖] **Read** the **Document** The Tandon Family at Partition (1947), Prakash Tandon, p. 750

[🔍] **View** the **Image** Tokyo Shanty Town, p. 756

[📖] **Read** the **Document** Korean War Armistice, p. 759

[👁] **Watch** the **Video** The Cuban Missile Crisis, p. 763

[📖] **Read** the **Document** Test Ban Treaty, p. 765

Smokestacks at Drax Power Station, England Industrial chimneys belch smoke at the Drax power station in northern England. Its coal-fired plants emit over 20 million tons of carbon dioxide a year—an amount that exceeds the yearly CO_2 emissions of over 100 countries.

26 Western Civilization and the Global Community

((•─Hear the Audio   Chapter 26 at MyHistoryLab.com

LEARNING OBJECTIVES

What were the key factors leading to the end of Communism? • What were the main political and economic components of the European Union? • How did science and technology transform the postwar environment? • How did the postwar feminist movement advance the struggle for equality? • What role did religion and ethnicity play in post–Cold War politics? • What are the main features of the postindustrial West?

Politicians are rightly worried by the problem of finding the key to ensure the survival of a civilization that is global and at the same time clearly multicultural. How can generally respected mechanisms of peaceful coexistence be set up, and on what set of principles are they to be established?

—Vaclav Havel

KEY QUESTION

Has the West defined the process of globalization?

Former president of the Czech Republic Vaclav Havel (b. 1936) spent five years in prison during the period when Czechoslovakia was under communist control. The dissident and playwright was first elected president of Czechoslovakia in December 1989, and during the 1990s he became a leading voice in discussions about the West's role in a new global community. The speech just quoted was delivered at Independence Hall in Philadelphia on July 4, 1994. Havel called for all humans to transcend their individual national identities and "start from what is at the root of all cultures." By this he meant that all peoples must recognize "that we are not here alone nor for ourselves alone" but instead are part of a larger "miracle of Being." Survival depends on our ability to engage in a constructive manner with "what we ourselves are not" and on our ability to value coexistence with people from different cultures and traditions.

[❚●─Read the Document

Vaclav Havel, "The Need for Transcendence in the Postmodern World"

on **MyHistoryLab.com**

With the end of the Cold War and the collapse of the Soviet empire, Western political, economic, and cultural values have begun to exercise enormous influence around the globe. European economic integration has made the continent an economic force as powerful as the United States. Both the Americans and the Europeans have had an inordinate influence on non-Western civilizations. This influence is especially felt in the developing world, where Western values are reflected in everything from popular music, dress, and architecture to political and economic priorities.

Instantaneous communication through emails, mobile phones, and Internet-based social media has lessened the importance of state borders and highlighted global interdependence. However, **globalization** has also threatened traditional societies and challenged cultural pluralism. Resistance to globalization has manifested itself in many forms. In particular, the Western model of development, a model that emphasizes material comfort and consumerism, is being questioned both in the West and in non-Western civilizations. Some opponents of Western culture have even resorted to violence in protest against what they see as a Western, and particularly American, drive for world domination. ■

The End of Communism

The ideological conflict between the communist and capitalist worlds, led by the Soviet Union and the United States, respectively, came to an abrupt halt in the late 1980s and early 1990s. The conflict had been responsible for an unprecedented arms buildup between the two superpowers; it had ignited and fueled proxy wars in Korea, Southeast Asia, Latin America, and Africa, and it contributed to an enormous waste of human and material resources. The policy of **mutually assured destruction** (MAD), for example, where a nuclear first strike by one side would be met by massive retaliation, cost the Americans and the Soviets billions of dollars over a 40-year period. That money might have been invested in any number of more productive and certainly more humane public enterprises from improved health care to literacy programs. Rarely before in history had two wartime allies descended so quickly into so costly a confrontation. By 1980, this confrontation seemed to be a permanent fixture of international life. Suddenly, however, during the second half of the 1980s, new leadership in the Kremlin began a process of reform that was initially designed to strengthen and update the Soviet system but ended up destroying it.

Soviet Economic Troubles   The heavily bureaucratized and centralized Soviet system did not respond well to technical innovations in industry. By the late 1970s, factories were failing to keep pace with the changing needs of the consumer. Few starved, but consumer goods were often shoddy and monotonous, and long waits in line outside understocked shops had become a way of life for the average Soviet citizen. Moreover, the Soviet state, which put a premium on controlling access to information, was highly suspicious of the emerging information technology sector. The controlled Soviet economy neither allowed nor rewarded flexibility or risk taking.

Soviet workers had little incentive to work harder, since the state guaranteed their positions for life, while managers were reluctant to challenge the decisions of Party leaders regarding economic priorities. The same inefficiencies plagued the agricultural sector. Private ownership of land was forbidden, and farmers had to labor on collective farms. As a result, Soviet economic growth rates declined; by the late 1970s, the government had to import grain from the capitalist West to feed an increasingly disgruntled population. Only the Communist Party elite was exempt from the growing economic problems, living lavishly and enjoying access to the latest in Western goods and services. A few Soviet citizens became active in dissident movements, but most sank into apathy and resignation, convinced that the Marxist ideal had been a cruel hoax.

When Ronald Reagan (1911–2004) became president of the United States in 1981, he accelerated the pace and cost of the Cold War arms race. The Soviet invasion of Afghanistan in 1979, together with earlier Soviet efforts to aid Marxist regimes in Ethiopia and Angola, confirmed American fears of Soviet global expansionism. Reagan publicly described the Soviet state as an "evil empire," and the United States pumped billions of additional dollars into its defense budget. In an effort to keep pace, Soviet leaders diverted precious fiscal resources away from the struggling civilian economy. Leonid Brezhnev (1906–1982) failed to recruit younger Party members for leadership posts, and his death was followed by a period of drift under two

Read the Document

Ronald Reagan, Speech at the Brandenburg Gate (1987)

on **MyHistoryLab.com**

sickly and uninspiring elderly leaders, Yuri Andropov (1914–1984), and Constantin Chernenko (1914–1985). Corruption and mismanagement became commonplace, while political dissidents were hounded and exiled. The Soviet Union appeared to be losing its way under a bureaucracy that seemed dedicated to propping up a failing ideological status quo.

Rise of Gorbachev   To the surprise of many, after the death of Chernenko in 1985, Mikhail Gorbachev (b. 1931) emerged as the new Soviet leader. Committed to reform in the interests of saving the Soviet system, Gorbachev implemented an economic program called *perestroika* (restructuring) that reduced the size and power of central bureaucracies and introduced limited free-market principles. Not unlike Lenin's New Economic Policy of the 1920s, *perestroika* aimed to increase production levels while rewarding those workers and factory managers who were able to meet pent-up consumer demand for goods and services. Shortages continued during the transition, however, and Gorbachev took a further step to bolster confidence in the system by allowing public discussion and criticism of the Communist Party. This policy of *glasnost* (openness) introduced unprecedented freedoms. National minorities began to express their dissatisfaction with the Soviet federal system, and dissidents won political office.

Read the Document

Mikhail Gorbachev on the Need for Economic Reform (1987)

on **MyHistoryLab.com**

In 1989 Gorbachev was able to extract Soviet troops from Afghanistan, a costly and demoralizing imperial misadventure begun under Brezhnev. The Soviet leader also took steps to end the ruinous arms race with the United States. The growth of nuclear stockpiles, coupled with the advent of new technologies that allowed the superpowers to achieve even more lethal advantages without violating existing treaties, seemed to make the world less secure during the early 1980s. Of particular concern was the development of multiple independently targeted reentry vehicles (MIRVs). These were single rockets that could carry multiple nuclear warheads, each one targeted on a different location. The advent of radar-evading cruise missiles and neutron bombs that were capable of killing people without damaging physical infrastructure also increased levels of uncertainty. When President Reagan proposed building an elaborate nuclear defense system, called "star wars" by its critics, Gorbachev vigorously objected on the grounds that the proposed shield would actually increase the

likelihood that a nation in possession of such technology would be more apt to consider a first strike.
The Soviet leader was also concerned about the enormous cost involved in trying to match any potential
American "star wars" system.

Both Reagan and Gorbachev had much to gain
from improved bilateral relations, and in their early
meetings a surprising level of trust developed that enabled them to move forward.
In 1988 the two leaders were able to reach an agreement on reducing the number of
nuclear weapons deployed in Europe. Gorbachev also shrunk the size of the armed
forces and agreed to withdraw troops stationed in Eastern Europe. Many Europeans
had long feared that a nuclear exchange between the United States and the Soviet
Union might begin in Europe, where the West's conventional forces were thought to

Mikhail Gorbachev and Ronald Reagan   The diplomacy between the Soviet and American leaders helped
to ease Cold War tensions and reduce the threat of nuclear war. Gorbachev's reforms also contributed to
the demise of Communist rule in Eastern Europe as well as the Soviet Union.

be inferior to Warsaw Pact capabilities. Gorbachev also withdrew Soviet support for communist regimes in the Third World and canceled further nuclear weapons tests. By 1991, the United States and the Soviet Union agreed to reduce their nuclear and conventional forces. The Cold War was over, and the specter of nuclear annihilation resulting from a superpower confrontation receded.

All of these actions made Gorbachev immensely popular in the West, but at home he was viewed less favorably. The Soviet government planned to shift some of the anticipated savings from military cutbacks to the domestic sector, but as the media were now free to report, evidence of substantive change in the economy was hard to detect by the late 1980s. Persistent economic stagnation, mismanagement, shortages of consumer goods, and rising unemployment persuaded some Russians that *glasnost* was a failure. Some were nostalgic for the days of empire and guaranteed employment, and even for the era of Stalin and Brezhnev.

Peaceful Revolutions in Eastern Europe

Greater openness in Moscow shook the regimes in its Eastern European satellite states, which suffered from the same economic hardships that hampered the Soviet Union. The communist leaders of these countries came under enormous popular pressure to institute democratic political and economic reforms. When Gorbachev indicated that the Soviet Union would no longer interfere in their internal affairs, the political floodgates opened across the Eastern Bloc.

Poland was the first country to jettison its hidebound communist leadership. In 1980 a noncommunist union of shipyard workers had been formed under the name **Solidarity.** The following year the government began a harsh crackdown, banning Solidarity and arresting its leader, Lech Walesa (b. 1943). As the Polish economy continued to deteriorate during the 1980s, however, the Communist Party felt obliged to reopen discussions with the union. In 1989 Solidarity was legalized; with the approval of the Soviet Union, nationwide elections were called. The influential Roman Catholic Church threw its support behind reform efforts, and Solidarity candidates won a stunning victory in the elections. Unwilling to use force against his own people, the communist Polish president, General Wojciech Jaruzelski (b. 1923), asked the victors to form a new government. The following year, the once-jailed Walesa was elected president of democratic Poland.

Anticommunist reformers in Hungary were the next to take action against the Iron Curtain status quo. The Soviets had intervened once before in Hungary (in 1956), but Moscow took no action in the fall of 1989 as a multiparty political system emerged and free elections were held. Janos Kadar (1912–1989), the communist leader whom the Soviets had installed in 1956, was forced to step down. In neighboring Czechoslovakia, also the scene of a brutal Soviet crackdown in 1968, student and worker demonstrators filled the streets night after night demanding greater political and personal freedoms. In December the communist government suddenly resigned, and the noted playwright (and dissident) Vaclav Havel (b. 1936), together with the leader of the 1968 movement for reform, Alexander Dubcek (1921–1992), emerged as the new leaders of the country.

Similar events occurred in East Germany where demonstrations against the government began in October 1989. Once again the communist government

View the **Closer Look**

Collapse of the Berlin Wall

on **MyHistoryLab.com**

The Fall of the Berlin Wall The collapse of the Berlin Wall was the most dramatic moment during the disintegration of Eastern Europe's communist systems. Thousands of demonstrators from East and West Berlin converged on the Wall on November 9, 1989, and began to dismantle this hated symbol of European and German division.

capitulated. In November the East German authorities ordered that the Berlin Wall, long the symbol of Cold War and divided Europe, be opened. Civilians from both sides of the divided city began to dismantle it brick by brick. In 1990 East and West Germany united, ending 45 years of Cold War division.

The remaining communist states in Eastern Europe quickly followed the lead of their neighbors. Bulgarian dissidents ousted their aging Stalinist head of state without violence, but in Romania Nicholae Ceausescu (1918–1989) was the one communist dictator who refused to go peacefully. Although he ordered troops to fire on unarmed demonstrators, he lost the support of the army, and fierce fighting broke out in the capital Bucharest. Ceausescu and his wife fled but were captured and executed in December 1989. Further south, communist Yugoslavia adopted a multiparty political system in January 1990. By this date, in just over one year, all of Eastern Europe had freed itself from Soviet control, formed democratic governments after holding free and open elections, and started to make the difficult transition from command economies to free markets.

The Soviet Union Implodes None of the historic events in Eastern Europe could have taken place without the acquiescence of Soviet authorities. Gorbachev was convinced that reform in the Soviet Union was best served by permitting the satellite states to pursue their own political futures. After enabling these states to break free from Soviet control, he then called for ending the Communist Party's monopoly of power at home. He sincerely believed that by embracing political pluralism, the communists would strengthen their mandate to rule in a period of rapid economic change. It did not work out that way. After 1990, Gorbachev faced a number of serious challenges. Proponents of rapid democratization, led by Boris Yeltsin (1931–2007), the president of the Russian Republic, pushed Gorbachev to accelerate the transition to a market economy and loosen central government control over the Soviet Union's constituent republics. Communist hard-liners wanted to restore the dictatorial supremacy of the Communist Party. Finally, nationalism was growing rapidly in a number of the Soviet republics, in particular the Baltic states of Latvia, Lithuania, and Estonia. They had never acknowledged their absorption by Stalin in 1940, and they demanded independence. When further unrest occurred in some of the Islamic republics of central Asia, Gorbachev was forced to negotiate new arrangements between Moscow and the constituent republics.

These negotiations were ongoing when in August 1991 hard-line communist members of the government who had been appointed by Gorbachev ordered the armed forces to occupy Moscow. Gorbachev was arrested and detained in the Crimea. However, Yeltsin defied the plotters, and after two days the coup collapsed. Russia's pro-democracy forces had achieved a crucial victory. The coup attempt had totally discredited the Communist Party. Even Gorbachev rejected it. The coup also doomed the Soviet Union. In December 1991 a new **Commonwealth of Independent States** replaced it, and Gorbachev was out of office (see Map 26–1).

Continued Russian Reforms   The chief heir of Soviet power was Boris Yeltsin's Russia, which began a rapid but difficult transition to democratic government and free-market capitalism. His government had some important successes, particularly

MAP 26-1 The End of the Soviet Union   At the end of 1991, the Soviet Union dissolved into 15 separate republics. The experiment in communist rule had failed to provide Soviet citizens with a standard of living remotely comparable to that enjoyed in Western Europe.

QUESTION: Can the breakup of the Soviet Union be considered a form of decolonization?

Read the **Document**

Scientists Examine Russia's Economy and Environment, 1991–1993

on **MyHistoryLab.com**

in the area of disarmament. The member states of the new Commonwealth of Independent States turned over their nuclear stockpiles to Russia. The United States pledged to assist the Russians in handling and decommissioning these stockpiles, and by the mid-1990s both nations agreed to stop targeting each other. But developments on the domestic front were not reassuring. Skyrocketing prices placed most consumer goods beyond the reach of the average citizen. As inefficient government factories were closed, unemployment rates climbed. A 1993 standoff between Yeltsin and his hard-line communist opponents led Yeltsin to authorize a military assault on the Russian parliament building. The president was able to consolidate his power after Russians elected a new Parliament in December 1993, but subsequent government reform efforts were compromised by the outbreak of war between the central government and the predominantly Muslim province of Chechnya in the south.

An ailing Yeltsin managed to win reelection as president in 1996, but his popularity continued to slump in the face of deepening economic problems and charges of political corruption at the local and national levels. A large black-market economy developed in Russia's cities, crime rates escalated, and many Russians began to lose hope that political democracy would lead to economic betterment. Increasing levels of alcohol and drug abuse were but two indicators of a larger disquiet afflicting post-Soviet Russian society. For many citizens in democratic Russia, newly secured freedoms included the freedom to fail, to be unemployed, and to be without much hope for the future. Vladimir Putin was elected president in 2000, and while his administration continued to endorse free-market reforms and closer relations with the United States, Putin began to emphasize Russian nationalism and the need for greater state control in the face of escalating terrorism by Chechen separatists. By 2007, diplomatic relations with Europe and the United States began to cool, with President Bush expressing public concern over the erosion of personal freedoms in Russia, and with President Putin taking strong exception to plans by the Bush administration to place a missile defense system in former East Bloc countries. Putin even suggested that implementation of the plans would lead to a new arms race. By 2010, American President Barak Obama and Russian President Demitri Medvedev worked to defuse tensions and stress common values, but it had become clear to many observers that the bilateral relationship had become more complicated.

The Fate of Communism   A few states—North Korea, Vietnam, Laos, China, and Cuba—retained their official commitment to Marxism after the swift collapse of the Soviet Union. However, in reality, most of them had degenerated into cynical dictatorships or oligarchies long before Gorbachev came to power. With the collapse of the Soviet Union, Fidel Castro lost his main financial backer, and the Cuban economy nose-dived. The secretive North Korean state spiraled toward economic collapse in the 1990s, and famine or its prospect became a constant of everyday life there. North Korea was reduced to blackmailing the West; it repeatedly threatened to begin producing nuclear weapons unless the United States

Read the **Document**

Famine in North Korea

on **MyHistoryLab.com**

provided it with energy assistance and food. By 2007 the secretive North Korean leadership agreed in principle to end its nuclear program in return for massive economic assistance and food imports, but the pledge was never carried out. In 2010 the North was again provoking its southern neighbor, sinking a South Korean warship and firing artillery shells at a South Korean island.

In Communist China, the Party leadership under Deng Xiaoping (1905–1997) used military force to suppress a student-led democracy movement in 1989 in Beijing. Yet Deng's government nonetheless introduced market reforms that mirrored practices in the capitalist West. Inefficient industries were closed down, Western companies invested in China, and a widespread push for economic modernization informed all aspects of government policy. Deng and his successors worked skillfully to preserve the Communist Party's exclusive hold on political power while fostering a Western-oriented economic order. By 2010 China had emerged as a global economic powerhouse and a major consumer of nonrenewable natural resources like oil, but economic liberalization had not led to significant political liberalization.

> 📖 Read the Document
>
> *Deng Xiaoping, on* Introducing Capitalist Principles to China
>
> on **MyHistoryLab.com**

Repression   Despite the pursuit of market-based economic reforms in the 1980s and 1990s, China's authoritarian communist government has maintained its monopoly over political power. A student-led democracy movement was crushed in May 1989. Here a lone protester defies a row of tanks in Beijing.

Even with the Chinese exception, at the start of the twenty-first century some political theorists in the West declared that liberal democracy and free-market capitalism were about to triumph around the globe, unchallenged by any other social, economic, or political systems. Marxist claims about the inevitable collapse of capitalism seemed discredited, while a new enthusiasm for free-market principles and pluralistic democracy spread across the globe. Capitalist Hong Kong continued to flourish one decade after its reintegration into China in 1997, communist Vietnam slowly opened up its economy to Western companies, and, despite a sharp economic downturn in the late 1990s, Asia's "economic tigers"—Singapore, Thailand, Hong Kong, Malaysia, Taiwan, South Korea, and Japan—continued to serve as models for developing states throughout Asia. Western models seemed to be defining *globalization* on the political and economic fronts.

United Europe?

Strength in Unity   The end of the global conflict in 1945 presented war-torn Western European nation-states with an opportunity to lower some of the political, economic, and ideological divisions that had divided peoples for centuries. Now that the era of colonialism was coming to a close, European leaders began to entertain the prospect that a wider European union, absent since the fall of Rome in the fifth century, might facilitate the recovery of the entire continent and promote the movement of goods, capital, and labor over a wide geographical area.

Democracy and the Welfare State   Multiparty democratic government was quickly restored across Western Europe after the defeat of Nazism. Thirteen billion dollars of Marshall Plan assistance boosted economic recovery efforts, and governments took control of key industries and services, including transportation, utilities, and some financial institutions. With economic recovery well underway by the early 1950s, the promise of a better life under democratically elected governments captured the imagination of millions. Citizens who had become familiar with widespread government direction of the economy during wartime expected the anticipated benefits of peace to be distributed more equitably. Social services were expanded in almost every Western European country after the war as governments struggled to insulate their respective populations from acute material hardship. The "**welfare state**" offered its citizens health-care benefits, more generous unemployment and accident insurance, housing subsidies, and expanded educational opportunities. Among Western countries, only the United States resisted the trend toward "cradle to grave" assistance, remaining wary of the high tax requirements of these innovative programs.

Employment opportunities remained abundant during a long period of unparalleled growth that moderated only after 1973. In Western Europe, gross domestic product per capita increased dramatically in the half-century after the war while the average hours worked per year declined, allowing a growing middle class additional leisure time and greater opportunity for holiday travel. In general Europeans at the start of the twenty-first century were better off in terms of income and the material quality of life than at any earlier time in history. The longer the prosperity continued,

Innovations in Health Care   Polio was a viral illness that afflicted humans since ancient times. An extensive outbreak occurred in the first half of the twentieth century, until a vaccination created by Jonas Salk became widely available in the West in 1955. Its containment is an example of advances made in public health with the support of governments in Western Europe and the United States. This photograph from 1955 shows mothers and children in London waiting in line for the newly developed vaccine.

the more typical it became for them to take such growth as normative rather than exceptional. People invested in their homes, in their children's education, and most readily in all manner of durable goods. Women entered the workforce in large numbers, while younger adults were more apt to relocate and change jobs repeatedly in search of professional advancement. A general mood of optimism, even in the face of the Cold War insecurities, characterized the domestic scene.

European Integration   From an American perspective, one key objective of the Marshall Plan was to initiate greater economic cooperation *among* European nations. In particular, a German state that was dependent upon economic contacts with its immediate neighbors would be unlikely to pose another threat to the stability of the continent. In 1950 West Germany and France took the first steps on the long road to economic union when a joint coal and steel authority was formed with the goal of eliminating tariff barriers while streamlining mineral extraction and industrial production. Two years later four additional countries (Italy, Luxembourg, Belgium, and the Netherlands) joined the alliance, known as

Read the Document

A Common Market and European Integration (1960)

on **MyHistoryLab.com**

the European Coal and Steel Authority. In 1957 the member states signed the much broader Treaty of Rome, an agreement that established the European Economic Community (EEC) or **Common Market.** In addition to ending discriminatory national tariffs, the EEC abolished restrictions on the movement of labor and capital across international borders.

As productivity and trade increased during the prosperous 1950s, supporters of the economic union looked forward to the day when the emerging European community would stand as an economic, military, and political rival to the American and Soviet superpowers. This projected autonomy won additional support after a French and British military intervention in Egypt was condemned by both the Soviets and the Americans. The Suez Crisis of 1956 proved a great humiliation for the French and British and strengthened the case for political and economic union. In 1948 through 1949 a multistate forum for the exchange of ideas on common problems had been organized as the Council for Europe. While this body had no enforcement powers, it served as an early clearinghouse for crossborder political dialogue.

By 1967 a host of smaller cooperative bodies joined with the EEC to form the European Community (EC), an umbrella organization dedicated to the establishment of a free-trade zone embracing all member states. An executive headquarters was located in Brussels, and a European Parliament was established with over 500 members elected for five-year terms. While not superseding the sovereign lawmaking authority of the member states, the European Parliament represented an incipient legislative assembly for the community. Soon after the breakup of the Soviet Union in 1991, the 12 member states of the European Economic Community (EEC) redefined themselves as the **European Union.** They voted to create an inclusive free-trade zone and to permit their nationals to live and work in any member nation. By the end of the decade, the majority of EU countries had adopted a common currency, the Euro, and established a central bank to oversee the transition to a transnational financial system. Eastern European countries like Poland, the Czech Republic, Hungary, Romania, and Bulgaria were welcomed into the European Union, and additional countries applied for membership (see Map 26–2). By 2000, Europe had become the most affluent region of the world after the United States.

Read the **Document**

Treaty on European Union
on **MyHistoryLab.com**

Read the **Document**

François Mitterrand, Speech to the United Nations, 1990
on **MyHistoryLab.com**

View the **Closer Look**

The Copenhagen Opera House
on **MyHistoryLab.com**

Europeans also demonstrated greater cooperation in military affairs. The U.S.-led North Atlantic Treaty Organization (NATO) had been established after World War II to defend Western Europe against potential Soviet aggression. After the Cold War, NATO was promoted as a Europe-wide security umbrella. In 1999 Poland, the Czech Republic, and Hungary joined NATO, although this caused great consternation in Russia. After the Europeans joined forces with their North American NATO allies in a military campaign against Serbia in 1999, the possibility of a joint European

MAP 26-2 The Growth of the European Union After the devastation of two world wars, Europeans were determined to reduce the threats of nationalism and competition. Beginning in 1957, European governments formed a succession of political and economic alliances, leading to the establishment of the European Union (EU).

QUESTION: How does the eastward expansion of the European Union affect its relations with Russia?

Union military establishment of over 50,000 troops moved closer to reality. A few countries, especially Great Britain, expressed reservations over the potential loss of national identity and fiscal autonomy implied by these steps, but overall most states welcomed concrete plans designed to eclipse centuries of rivalry, suspicion, and conflict in Europe.

Preserving National Identities   Chancellor Helmut Kohl (b. 1930) of the West German government pledged to improve living standards in the former communist East Germany after unification, and under his leadership Germany launched a costly renewal effort in former communist-controlled areas. Inefficient state-owned industries were privatized, the nation's capital was moved from Bonn to Berlin, and infrastructure and social services were improved. United Germany, with over 80 million inhabitants, became Europe's most populous country and its leading economic power in the 1990s. While economic downturns have led to the reappearance of neo-Nazi elements, both Kohl and his successors, Gerhard Schröder (b. 1944) and Angela Merkel (b. 1954), worked to assimilate refugees and new immigrants. They also strengthened Germany's relationship with France, recognizing the value of strong bilateral relations with the continent's largest state.

France, with a population of just over 50 million, supported the European Union while at the same time emphasizing the dangers of cultural homogenization. Of all the Western European states, France remained the most skeptical about the projection of American political and military power worldwide. Under the leadership of Presidents François Mitterrand (1916–1996) and Jacques Chirac (b. 1932), France maintained a relatively strong economy despite periods of high unemployment. The French, like the Germans, experienced challenges from right-wing political movements, but in national elections these extremist movements, most often associated with anti-immigrant sentiment, have only received nominal support. In the 2007 presidential race, conservative Nicholas Sarkozy (b. 1955) campaigned on a platform of economic renewal, and his election signaled the rise of a new generation of national leaders born after World War II.

In Britain both the Conservative governments of Margaret Thatcher (b. 1925) and John Major (b. 1944) and the Labour-led governments of Tony Blair (b. 1953) and Gordon Brown (b. 1951) were much more supportive of America in the international arena. The Labour Party moved to the center of the political spectrum during the 1990s, deemphasizing its socialist roots and adopting pro-business economic policies. Blair's government devolved political authority onto newly created regional legislative assemblies in Scotland and Wales. The Labour Party also returned considerable political power to local authorities in Northern Ireland, forwarding the peace process between Catholic and Protestant communities in that troubled region. Although generally supportive of European economic cooperation, Britain has not adopted the Euro currency, and Euro-skeptics, including those in the current Conservative government of David Cameron, continue to play an important role in politics.

While each of Europe's major states has taken strides to balance national sovereignty with the proven benefits of greater integration, Europe as a whole has not wielded the same level of international influence that the United States has since the end of the Cold War. Europe's economy, while unquestionably stronger under a single market, also faces challenges ranging from the high cost of labor and benefits to the rise of multinationals that enjoy access to cheap labor markets in developing countries. The emergence of the global economy has the potential of undermining consumer confidence at home as more jobs are relocated overseas. A major economic downturn beginning in 2008 obliged some EU member states, including Greece, Ireland and Portugal, to request major financial assistance from the Union. In the wake of the economic crisis, Europe's earlier enthusiasm for the spread of the global economy has been tempered.

Housing Development, Dublin   Beginning in the 1980s, the Irish economy enjoyed unprecedented growth, spurred in part by foreign investment from such high-tech firms as Dell and Google. For decades, the country had been a net exporter of people, but during the boom period the country became a destination for many immigrants from Africa and Eastern Europe. The success of the "Celtic tiger" also radically altered the Irish landscape. New housing developments like this one emerged during a speculative mania that came to an end in 2008. With the collapse in the housing market and mounting national debt, Ireland's youth are again emigrating for opportunities abroad.

Private Lives and Consumer Culture   The quality of life for most residents of Western Europe improved dramatically during the final decades of the twentieth century. Birth rates boomed after World War II, perhaps one measure of the resilience of humans in the aftermath of the most horrific conflict in history. From approximately 250 million in 1945, Europe's population climbed to over 300 million before the economic recession of the 1970s. Birth rates then began to decline, and today Europe's population is barely at replacement level (defined as 2.3 children per mother) with women and men electing to have fewer children while focusing on professional and leisure activities outside of the home. Divorce rates have continued to increase, and the role of organized religion has waned, but the family has remained a valued unit of social, emotional, and economic order. Single-parent households became more commonplace throughout the Western world, and many children often spent time in formal day-care programs, since there was no longer a caregiver at home during business hours. Once at home, family members placed a premium on private space, and new construction increasingly featured separate rooms for sleeping, entertainment, and meals.

Housing stock expanded in most Europeans countries, but increasing numbers of workers followed the American pattern of suburban living and long commutes on congested motorways and public transport. Cities continued to attract rural migrants, while retailing lost its regional and personal flavor. Where once the homemaker shopped in locally owned stores on the high street, by the 1980s new suburban shopping centers anchored by large conglomerate retailers had become the norm. Standardized sizes and product lines replaced items made by craftspeople for individual clients. By the start of the twenty-first century the Internet internationalized the buying experience with online or e-commerce vendors, blurring regional and national distinctions. In Western Europe, as in North America, the consumer service sector grew as jobs in traditional manufacturing areas migrated to cheaper labor markets in the developing world. Many educated professionals in the services industry found themselves reduced to "blue collar" wages, while top managers were paid high salaries and lucrative bonuses on the basis of their ability to impose new efficiencies.

On the broader consumer front, reservations about the increasing "Americanization" of Europe's national cultures grew sharply during the final quarter of the twentieth century. Before the fall of the Berlin Wall, American youth culture was seen by authorities in the East as an imminent threat to socialist values. The reservations expressed in the West were more subtle, focusing on topics like the dangers of homogenization and planned obsolescence in product development. Youth culture became increasingly product-oriented across Europe, with American movies, computer software, music, and fashion all setting the benchmarks for standardization. The controversial opening of a Disney theme park outside of Paris in the mid-1990s highlighted the omnipresence of American leisure entertainment in Europe. Getting and spending became an end in itself, a lifestyle that was aggressively promoted by advertisers with advanced university degrees in applied subjects such as marketing and "entrepreneurship." These trends were lamented by a number of journalists, artists, and intellectuals, inspiring new forms of dissent that challenged widely held assumptions in the dominant culture. A severe economic downturn in 2008 and the failure of a number of major financial institutions in Europe and America affirmed for many the fragility of market-based economic systems.

The Fear of Terrorism   Perhaps an even greater threat to the security of Western democracies at the start of the twenty-first century came from international terrorist groups, especially those associated with radical Islamist movements. Carefully planned terrorist attacks against the United States on September 11, 2001, led to a broad-based international response against the Islamist Taliban regime in Afghanistan. A military coalition led by the United States ousted the Taliban, but the terrorist leader (and Saudi national) Osama bin Laden eluded capture for a decade before being killed by American forces in the spring of 2011.

□●├ **Read** the **Document**

*America Enters a New
Century with Terror, 2001*

on **MyHistoryLab.com**

The early fight against international terrorists enhanced cooperation among countries as ideologically diverse as China and the United States. Unfortunately, the spirit of cooperation did not last. Soon after the establishment of a new government in Afghanistan, the administration of George W. Bush turned its attention to Iraq, whose leader Saddam Hussein was thought to be producing weapons of mass destruction. Inspectors from the United Nations had been assigned to Iraq after the Gulf War of 1991, but Hussein's regime was reluctant to cooperate with the inspectors, who were eventually withdrawn from the country. In the spring of 2003, American and British forces invaded Iraq and ousted Hussein, but the occupying troops found no evidence of weapons of mass destruction. Subsequent reports and Congressional inquiries revealed that the administration had acted on deeply flawed "intelligence" information. The invasion had not been endorsed by the United Nations, and many of America's strongest allies in the fight against terrorism criticized the military action in Iraq. Much of the sympathy and support that America received after the tragedy of September 11th evaporated in the lead-up to the Iraq war.

Contrary to the optimistic predictions of the Bush administration, the postwar occupation of Iraq showed few signs that a beacon of Arab democracy in the Middle East would be established at any time in the near future. A civil war in all but name, the divisions between Iraq's Shiite majority and the Sunni minority were deep and lasting. Thousands of civilians lost their lives in sectarian bloodletting after 2003, while hundreds of thousands of additional Iraqis fled the violence, becoming long-term refugees in neighboring Arab states.

Read the Document

Statement from Chancellor Schröder on the Iraq Crisis

on **MyHistoryLab.com**

Europeans turned against the American-led occupation, and in Britain, Prime Minister Tony Blair left office in the summer of 2007 with his reputation much diminished because of his support of the Bush administration's policies in Iraq.

Many experts argued that the type of state-sponsored terrorism alleged against Iraq was not the principal threat facing the West at the start of the new century. Instead, the danger was much more insidious precisely because it could not be identified with a state. Most of the September 11th suicide hijackers, not to mention bin Laden, were Saudi nationals who were as contemptuous of the Saudi monarchy as they were of America. A 2005 terrorist attack in London's underground was organized and carried out by British-born Muslim youths and in December 2009 a Nigerian national attempted to detonate a bomb aboard an American airliner as it prepared to land in Detroit. Fears that well-armed terrorist cells might secure materials to construct and plant a "dirty" nuclear bomb in a major city led to a heightened emphasis in the West on espionage and intelligence gathering. Difficult as it has been to prevent nuclear escalation at the state level, it may be even more difficult to keep nuclear, chemical, and biological weapons out of the hands of shadowy but well-financed terrorist groups who are determined to inflict as much harm as possible on the West. The fight has obliged Western democracies to reevaluate their commitment to civil liberties. Just as democratic states abridged freedoms during the two world wars, they found it difficult after September 11th to establish an acceptable balance between the need for enhanced domestic security and the preservation of personal autonomy. Reports of secret CIA detention centers in Eastern Europe, where suspects were held without charge for long periods, exacerbated the growing divide between Europe and the United States over the appropriate response to terrorist threats.

War in Afghanistan   In the aftermath of the September 11, 2001, terrorist attacks, the United States led a NATO invasion of Afghanistan, ousting the Taliban regime, which had sheltered al-Qaeda. One decade later, a resurgent Taliban poses a serious threat and Western hopes for the emergence of a democratic Afghanistan have faded. Here, a Turkish soldier in a NATO unit patrols the capital city of Kabul.

Science, Technology, and the Environment

Innovation and Health   Like residents of every developed country, Europeans benefited from a wide range of advances in the applied sciences. During the war years, basic laboratory research assumed a level of strategic importance equal to military operations in the field. Specialists in physics, engineering, biology, chemistry, metallurgy, and electronics were encouraged—and fully funded—to take risks and to innovate. The solitary genius or inventor of an earlier age was displaced by the collaborative team working in large research institutes and corporations. National governments continued their role as the principal patrons of scientific research during the Cold War, citing national security priorities and partnering with leading universities and private institutes to develop new technologies.

The output was impressive. Beginning in the 1950s, wartime research into radar navigation and jet aircraft engines transformed the civilian aeronautics industry. The collaboration of American, British, and German refugee scientists on atomic weapons set the stage for the commercialization of nuclear power for peaceful purposes. By the 1960s Europe's nuclear power stations had become key to the electricity generation industry. Transistors replaced unreliable vacuum tubes in the early 1950s, inaugurating the age of miniaturization and anticipating the computer age. The latter technology, while again a spin-off from wartime research, reached its full commercial potential with the advent of the personal desktop computer in the 1980s.

The health services offered broader state-funded programs as part of the postwar promise to enhance the lives of all citizens. Government stressed the importance of prevention, health education, and infant care, and specialist doctors worked closely with researchers to better treat patients. Improved housing, sanitation, and rules of cleanliness reduced the incidence of disease, but the advent of "killer bacterias" played an even greater role in extending life. During the 1930s scientists recognized that sulfa drugs were effective against a range of infectious diseases. Plant research at Oxford University, for example, led to the discovery of the plant mold penicillin in 1941, which was used effectively during and after the war to treat the onset of septicemia. The scourge of polio was eradicated in the 1950s through new vaccines, and a measles vaccine in the 1960s eliminated a recurring epidemic that had been most dangerous for young children. An expanding range of new antibiotic drugs was made commercially available after the war, and by the 1970s traditional scourges like tuberculosis and smallpox had been eliminated. At the turn of the twenty-first century infectious communicable diseases had ceased to be the leading cause of death in the developed world.

Physicians and researchers then turned their attention to the treatment of chronic noncommunicable organ disease. New surgical procedures and chemical interventions reduced cancer and cardiovascular mortality. Organ and bone marrow transplants, together with heart bypass operations, became commonplace at major hospitals. New machines for diagnosis and treatment, including ultrasound, dialysis, and MRI (magnetic resonance imaging) machines, offered doctors additional life-saving tools. Even patients suffering from chronic psychiatric conditions were helped by the advent of new psychotropic drugs. In genetics, the structure of DNA (deoxyribonucleic acid) was discovered in 1953 by the British research team of Francis Crick and James Watson. By the final decade of the century scientists were beginning to clone animal and plant products and organs, prompting medical ethicists to debate the implications of this research for human culture. Overall the medical breakthroughs were welcome, but by the close of the century the escalating cost of treatment and professional services placed enormous strains on national health systems and the governments that funded them.

Environmental Challenges   Before the outbreak of World War I in 1914, few people in the West thought in terms of common global problems or threats whose resolution was of interest to governments and people everywhere on Earth. At the end of the twentieth century, a wide array of challenges had global implications, from resource use to **global warming** to pollution. The unprecedented mastery of nature that has been one of the signal features of Western civilization over the past 200 years may have improved the quality of life for the inhabitants of industrially advanced nations, but it has also

◉—Watch the Video
British Petroleum Oil Spill—Environmental Disasters
on **MyHistoryLab.com**

led to serious and perhaps irreversible environmental degradation on a global scale. As developing nations raced to "catch up" with the West, the pace of degradation accelerated.

Global Warming   Protests at U.N. Climate Change Conference, Montreal, December 2005. Global warming has emerged as a major environmental issue and political challenge in recent years.

Overgrazing on land, soil exhaustion resulting from intensive agriculture, deforestation on every continent, disposal of nuclear waste, and the exhaustion of fisheries all contributed to an emerging ecological crisis that transcended national borders. When coupled with the reckless discharge of industrial waste leading to contamination of water resources and air pollution from coal-burning factories and the ubiquitous automobile, the planet's ability to accommodate the needs of the world's rising population was cast into doubt. The burning of fossil fuels greatly increased the carbon dioxide in the atmosphere, and many scientists claimed that the resultant global warming increased average temperatures around the world. It is feared that this may cause ocean levels to rise, which would flood low-lying coastal areas, increase the number of destructive storms, and cause havoc with world agriculture. Since many people in the developing world understandably aspire to a "Western" quality of life, the current indulgent path to modernization may accelerate harmful processes.

International Meetings   Since the impact of environmental degradation reaches well beyond the borders of the nation-state, addressing the problem requires international cooperation. In 1992 the United Nations hosted an international earth summit in Rio de Janeiro. However, it quickly became obvious that it would be extremely difficult to convince developed nations in Western Europe, Asia, and North America to take measures that might adversely affect the lifestyles of their citizens and reduce the levels of resources they consumed. Nor did developing nations wish to accept restraints on their modernization plans, especially since the West had reached its industrial primacy absent any restraints.

In 1997 the United Nations hosted another important meeting, this time on global warming, in Kyoto, Japan. Again, leading industrial states were reluctant to commit to enforcing the recommendations that emerged from the meeting. Despite recent successes in lowering harmful emissions levels from automobiles and factories, the strength of modern industrial economies continued to depend on the ever-increasing consumption of nonrenewable resources. The nuclear power alternative to fossil fuels, briefly back in favor at the start of the new century, suddenly lost its appeal after a devastating earthquake in Japan in the spring of 2011 crippled a major installation, sending dangerous levels of radioactive materials into the atmosphere.

North Versus South   The image of a North-South divide is based on the fact that most of the world's wealthiest nations and regions (the United States, Japan, Europe, Canada) are situated north of the equator, while the poorest regions (sub-Saharan Africa, South Asia, Latin America) are in the south-

◉─⌐Watch the Video

Africa as an Urban, Not Rural, Place

on **MyHistoryLab.com**

ern hemisphere. The northern hemisphere contains about one-quarter of the world's population, but most of the world's goods and services originate here. In the United States, approximately 300 million people (4.5 percent of the world's total) consume over a quarter of the world's resources.

The problem of global economic inequality, of rich nations growing richer and consuming more and more of Earth's resources while poor nations continue to struggle with overpopulation, poor health care, lack of education, economic underdevelopment, and political instability, has become *the* great global challenge of the early twenty-first century. It is also the problem with the most serious ethical implications for the modern West. In 1800, just as the Industrial Revolution was beginning to spread from England to North America, the world's richest societies (all in the West) were about twice as affluent as the poorest. Two centuries later, the gap had widened considerably. The richest countries are now perhaps 100 times better off than the poorest. Income disparities between the richest and the poorest nations continue to expand even as the world's economy becomes more integrated and interdependent. Thanks to modern electronic communications, many of the poor have instant access to the sounds and images of Western affluence. Radio, television, and the Internet have transformed expectations. The more than one billion people (20 percent of the world's population) who live on less than $500 per year are well aware of lifestyles in the West and Japan (see Map 26–3).

Population Growth   When World War I started in 1914, there were just under two billion people on Earth. At the beginning of the twenty-first century, that number skyrocketed to just over six billion. Much of the growth was made possible by the spread of Western medical technology, especially in disease prevention and nutrition. In the industrialized West, population levels are either stagnant or declining, whereas in the world's poorest nations, rapid growth is the norm. During the twenty-first century, the peoples of China, South Asia, and Africa will make

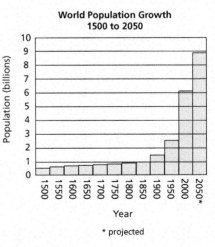

World Population Growth 1500 to 2050

x-axis: Year (1500, 1550, 1600, 1650, 1700, 1750, 1800, 1850, 1900, 1950, 2000, 2050*)
y-axis: Population (billions), 0 to 10

* projected

Figure 26-1

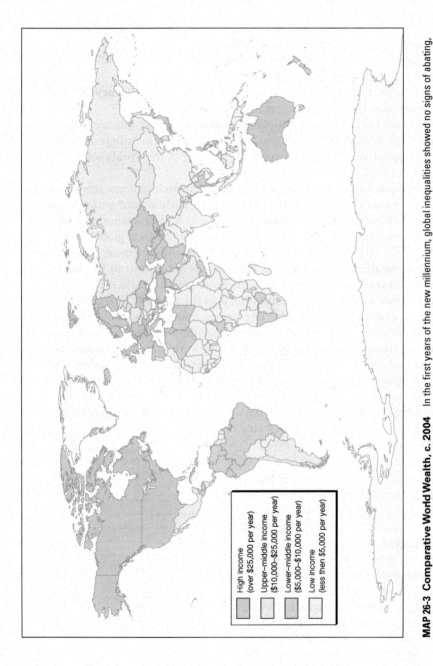

MAP 26-3 Comparative World Wealth, c. 2004 In the first years of the new millennium, global inequalities showed no signs of abating, as many poor countries found themselves trapped in a cycle of debt and underdevelopment.

QUESTION: What factors might help explain the disparity in wealth between the northern and southern hemispheres?

Legend:

- High income (over $25,000 per year)
- Upper–middle income ($10,000–$25,000 per year)
- Lower–middle income ($5,000–$10,000 per year)
- Low income (less then $5,000 per year)

up an ever-increasing percentage of the global population. If current demographic trends continue, many of these people will live in sprawling urban concentrations. Mexico City, with almost 16 million residents, and Mumbai (Bombay) in India, with 14 million, are examples of cities whose governments struggle mightily with housing and sanitation challenges. Still, internal migrants continue to relocate to urban centers around the world in ever-larger numbers, hoping for adequate employment and a better standard of living.

The South Seeks Redress   Global inequality became a contentious political issue during the final three decades of the twentieth century. Industrial producers in the West were exporting vast quantities of goods to developing countries, but as these countries fell deeper into debt, Western lending institutions began to lose faith in the ability of government leaders in the southern hemisphere to manage their economies. In the mid-1980s, for example, 80 percent of Sudan's total export earnings were being used merely to pay interest on the country's foreign debt. The leaders of many postcolonial states had the misfortune of attempting to raise living standards and provide jobs for a public that was well aware of conditions in the modern West.

Beginning in the 1970s, developing nations sought to win a series of concessions from the advanced industrialized countries through the United Nations. In this international forum, political leaders from the southern hemisphere argued that decades of imperialism and colonial domination had facilitated Europe's head start in the process of modernization. Calling for a **New International Economic Order** (NIEO), countries that had recently achieved political independence from Europe demanded substantive economic concessions from the northern hemisphere. These concessions would take the form of lower tariffs on goods imported from developing countries, and prices for their exports that were indexed to the cost of exports from developed nations. In this way, developing nations hoped to close the enormous and ever-widening gap between industrial capacity in the northern and southern hemispheres. Poor states also called for a more generous foreign aid formula. The United Nations had set a standard of 0.7 percent of gross national product as the benchmark for annual foreign aid contribution, but in the early 1980s only a handful of northern hemisphere states had met this minimum. Finally, developing countries requested a larger voice in international financial agencies like the World Bank and the International Monetary Fund, where decisions typically reflected the interests of the northern hemisphere, and especially the United States.

The North Dissents   Proponents of NIEO hoped to redistribute wealth through structured policies endorsed by the United Nations. Economic decision making would shift from strict market criteria into the hands of an international body where all nations would have an equal vote. Not surprisingly, developed nations, particularly those in the West, resented the implication that their success was due to centuries of exploitation and unfair trade policies carried out during the colonial era. In rebuttal, the Western industrialized democracies claimed that most of the economic problems of postcolonial states were due to internal domestic failings: fiscal mismanagement, poor planning, and political corruption. In the late 1980s and early 1990s successful examples of development in countries like South Korea and Malaysia seemed to prove that a country's previous colonial status was not a barrier to economic health. The shattered Japanese economy of 1945 had by the early 1980s become one of the world's leaders, and Japan's gross domestic product was second only to that of the United States. Even communist China experienced record economic growth starting in the 1990s. In India, despite ongoing poverty for the majority, a vibrant middle class of between 100 and 200 million suggested that under competent governments, market-based economics could transform the lives of millions.

Oil Shocks   The only instance of rapid postwar development in the southern hemisphere during the 1970s occurred in the oil-rich nations of the Middle East. When member states of the Organization of Petroleum Exporting Countries (OPEC) quadrupled the price of oil in 1973, Western industrialized economies suffered a severe economic shock, with recession, high levels of unemployment, and inflation causing significant distress. In the years following the original spike in oil prices, the biggest and fastest transfer of wealth in history took place. Some oil-producing states, particularly Saudi Arabia, began modernizing their economies on the strength of exceptional export earnings. Because of their new affluence, Arab leaders were reluctant to support the NIEO call for radical adjustments to the market economy.

Women and the Struggle for Equality

The rebuilding of Western Europe after the catastrophe of World War II had important consequences for the women's movement. The United Nations **Universal Declaration of Human Rights,** set forth as a nonbinding resolution in 1948, set a high standard for all of the signatory states, many of whom continued to exclude women from full civil equality. In Western Europe universal suffrage was finally realized after the war. However, women's access to equality in education and employment remained unrealized. The early hope that voting rights would lead swiftly to the implementation of civil and personal equality through the power of the ballot box was not realized.

☐●┤Read the Document

The United Nations,
Universal Declaration of
Human Rights, *1948*

on **MyHistoryLab.com**

During the 1960s, the women's movement assumed a more determined stance across Western Europe and North America. Although political rights had been secured, women continued to shoulder responsibilities that narrowed their opportunities outside of the home. Still regarded as the principal caregiver in the family, responsible for household and children, feminists like Betty Friedan (1921–2006) in the United States and Simone de Beauvior (1908–1986) in France called for a reconceptualization of gender roles. For those women in the West who did manage to secure an education and entry into the professions, inequalities in compensation and access to promotion (the so-called glass ceiling) demonstrated that the quest for equality had to be fought on a large number of fronts against considerable,

☐●┤Read the Document

Betty Friedan, The Problem
That Has No Name, *1963*

on **MyHistoryLab.com**

and sometimes subtle, opposition. By the mid-1990s, women's participation in paid employment outside of the household exceeded 70 percent in Britain, 66 percent in Germany, and over 85 percent in Sweden, but percentages of women in supervisory positions remained minimal.

The Role of the United Nations   One of the most difficult challenges facing Western feminists during the late twentieth century involved the tension between the ideals of universality and cultural diversity. In 1967 the United Nations adopted a **Universal Declaration of Women's Rights** that was heavily influenced by European and American standards. Many of the specific freedoms included in the Declaration, such as "equal rights with men during marriage and at its dissolution," were alien to cultures outside the West. For example, in Western Europe and the United States, the postwar feminist movement placed great emphasis on women's right to choose to work, breaking the "cult of domesticity" that had been imposed on middle-class women in the nineteenth century. This agenda was irrelevant to most women outside of the West, where women worked out of necessity and where most of that work was in the agricultural sector. Again, the West seemed to be defining the process of globalization.

Both the U.N. declarations of Human Rights and of Women's Rights embraced the Enlightenment conviction that certain human values can and must be shared irrespective of cultural claims. Many political leaders in non-Western settings rejected this position, especially in the Muslim world. In the oil-rich Arab states, for example, where the infusion of export revenues in the 1970s supported extensive infrastructure development, the new affluence did little to alter the status of women. Some Muslim women even defended strict Islamic codes as a way to express their dissent from the harmful effects of Western popular culture. In India the ancient tradition of dowry, where the bride's family would pay an agreed sum to the family of the groom, continued despite having been outlawed by the national government. Critics of dowry have argued persuasively that the practice leads to the devaluation of female children, and in extreme cases to infanticide, by impoverished families who cannot afford to pay.

Western Values?   Authoritarian and absolutist regimes around the globe continued to restrict women to the domestic sphere at the close of the century, often appropriating the language of cultural diversity to legitimize their policies. Two important measures of the status of women, access to education and to contraception, indicate that the gap between the West and the developing world remains immense. By the mid-1990s, enrollment levels for boys and girls in primary schools were equal in Western Europe, North America, and the former Soviet Union, but opportunities for boys were greater in Africa, South Asia, and the Middle East. Almost three-quarters of women of childbearing age in the West were using contraception, whereas the figure was only two-fifths in South Asia, the Middle East, and North Africa. Access to contraception was lowest in sub-Saharan Africa. At the start of the twenty-first century, prospects were not good that the core elements of the U.N. Declaration of Women's Rights would be adopted outside of the industrialized West.

PEOPLE IN CONTEXT   Simone de Beauvoir

Simone de Beauvoir (1908–1986) was raised in a middle-class Roman Catholic household and completed a degree in philosophy in 1929. While in college at the Sorbonne, she fell in love with the existentialist philosopher Jean-Paul Sartre. Although they rejected conventional marriage, they remained together for the next 50 years. During the 1930s, de Beauvoir taught high school and generally avoided politics. During the Nazi occupation of France, she lived in Paris and dedicated herself to full-time writing. In 1949 she published *The Second Sex,* a groundbreaking study of the condition of women in the modern West. It quickly became a foundational text for the women's movement.

The Second Sex argues that women are not biologically predetermined to serve solely as mothers and wives, but instead are free to determine their own fate in the world. "No biological, psychological, or economic fate determines the figure that the human female presents in society; it is civilization as a whole that determines this creature." For too long women had been culturally defined by men as "the other." *The Second Sex* called upon women to reject all views that attempted to define their essential nature. The book had a wide readership in the West; in the United States, Betty Friedan's *The Feminine Mystique,* first published in 1963, drew many of its ideas from de Beauvoir.

Simone de Beauvoir avoided active involvement in the women's movement during the 1950s and 1960s. She thought that the advance of socialism throughout the West would have a greater impact in advancing the goal of human equality. She was a strong

Simone de Beauvoir   In the 1970s Beauvoir became active in France's women's liberation movement. In 1972 she signed the Manifesto of the 343, a list of famous women who claimed, mostly falsely, to have had an abortion. In this photo, de Beauvoir is arriving for the famous 1972 trial in Bobigny of a woman and her friend who were accused of performing an abortion on the woman's 16-year old daughter. The minor was acquitted; the two adults were fined and given suspended sentences.

opponent of colonialism and criticized France's efforts to retain control over Vietnam and Algeria. During the last 15 years of her life, her growing disillusionment with socialism led her to take a more active role in the women's movement. She served as president of the French League of Women Voters and became involved in a number of journals dedicated to women's issues. ■

QUESTION: Is feminism a uniquely Western phenomenon?

Religious Divides and Ethnic Nationalism

The Fate of Christianity In the aftermath of global war, the Holocaust, and the use of atomic weapons, many Europeans lost faith in centuries-old traditional forms of Christianity. Church attendance decreased and the authority once exercised by priests and pastors was called into question. In response, some influential Protestant thinkers turned away from the reliance upon reason that had characterized mainstream religious thought since the late nineteenth century. The Swiss theologian Karl Barth (1886–1968) was the leader of a neo-orthodox movement within Protestantism that emphasized humankind's inability to know God through reason. Barth unapologetically returned to traditional concepts of original sin, the Trinity, and the transformative power of the Resurrection. The German-born theologian Paul Tillich (1886–1965), who had served as an army chaplain during World War I but who fled Nazi Germany for the United States in 1933, insisted in his post–World War II writings that human existence was meaningless without God. One must make the "leap of faith" to escape from the banality and cruelty of modern existence. The German-Jewish religious philosopher Martin Buber (1878–1965), himself a 1938 refugee from Nazi Germany, authored a groundbreaking work titled *I and Thou* in 1923 that continued to influence Western thought after 1945. Buber, who became a leading intellectual in the new state of Israel, maintained that the relationship between the individual and God, characterized by mutuality and trust, must also direct human-to-human relations. Too often humans adopt an I–It relationship with each other, treating fellow humans as objects for their own use and advancement.

Within the Roman Catholic tradition, Pope John XXIII (r. 1958–1963) launched an important reform movement that was subsequently carried forward by the Second Vatican Council between 1962 and 1965. The Church approved the use of vernacular languages in the mass, extended opportunities for lay participation in religious services, and, most importantly, reached out to non-Catholic denominations in an effort to build ecumenical bridges. The Catholic Church also worked to improve its relationship with the Jewish community, acknowledging and repudiating a tragic history of anti-Semitism and coercion. Perhaps most significantly, the spirit of Vatican II began to transform the relationship between the Catholic Church and the conservative political establishment in Latin America. A new **liberation theology** inspired clergy to champion the right of poor people and linked the Christian message with calls for greater social and economic justice. Pope John Paul II (r. 1978–2005) championed efforts to end Soviet control over Eastern Europe, but he was wary of liberation

Pentecostals in Brazil Evangelical Christianity has won millions of new converts in impoverished regions of Latin America and Africa in recent years. Pentecostalism has proven especially popular among poor urban dwellers.

theology and warned priests against taking too great a role in political activities at the national level. The reputation of the Roman Catholic Church also suffered at the start of the new century as charges of pedophilia dominated the news in more developed countries. Massive victim compensation packages placed enormous strain on the fiscal resources of more than a few influential Roman Catholic dioceses. In the worldwide Anglican communion, debates over the propriety of female priests, same-sex marriages, and the ordination of homosexuals pitted the more conservative African episcopate against bishops in the more liberal European and North American churches.

[▶]Read the Document

Camilo Torres and Liberation Theology (1950s)

on **MyHistoryLab.com**

Militant Islam   One-fifth of the world's population was Muslim at the end of the twentieth century, and Islam continues to attract new converts. Living in countries around the globe, Muslims, like believers in the other great world religions, hold a wide range of political views. But during the final three decades of the twentieth century, a new form of militant politicized Islam, known as **Islamism** began to win converts from North Africa to Southeast Asia. Angered by Western (particularly American) support for Israel, by the painful memory of colonial rule, and by the growing influence of Western cultural forms, new antidemocratic leaders in countries like Libya, Syria, Iraq, and Iran called for Muslim unity and vigorous resistance to all manifestations of Western culture. More recently, Islamic fundamentalism has become a serious challenge to the Western-dominated process of globalization.

In addition to militant Muslim political leaders, a more popular, grassroots Islamic fundamentalism developed in a number of regions. These Islamists decried Western secularism and commercialism and called for a return to traditional Islamic cultural and religious forms, including the imposition of harsh restrictions on women. In 1979 militant fundamentalists overthrew the American-backed Shah Reza Pahlavi (1919–1980) of Iran. The Shah had sponsored a program of rapid economic modernization, but his repressive monarchy cracked down hard on all forms of dissent.

Iranian Revolution   The emergence of Ayatollah Ruholla Khomeini (1900–1989), who was living in exile in France, as the de facto ruler of Iran symbolized the rejection of Western values and cultural influence at the heart of the Islamist movement. Ironically, however, Khomeini's return from exile and successful rise to power would have been impossible without the aid of Western technology. While still living in France, he was able to foster dissent against the Iranian monarchy by smuggling audiotapes of his sermons into Iran. Once in power, Khomeini employed the same brutal methods of repression and torture against his opponents that the Shah had used (but now on "religious" grounds). Khomeini built and maintained his regime around the idea of opposition to the United States, "the Great Satan," while simultaneously employing all of the technologies developed first in the West in order to strengthen his hold on power.

> ◉⊣Watch the Video
>
> *The 1979 Islamic Revolution in Iran: A Turning Point for the Middle East and the World*
>
> on **MyHistoryLab.com**

Islamic Fundamentalism   Three decades after the 1979 Iranian revolution, the country is split between advocates of reform and supporters of a strict, repressive interpretation of Islam imposed by the country's conservative clerics and "supreme leaders" of the country, Ayatollah Ali Khamenei (left) who currently is in power, and Ayatollah Ruhollah Khomeini (right), the father of the revolution.

The success of the Islamic political revolution in Iran inspired opponents of moderate Muslim regimes throughout the Middle East. In November 1979, some 400 radical Muslims seized the Grand Mosque in Mecca, Saudi Arabia, and declared the end of the Saudi monarchy. It took the embarrassed Saudi government three weeks to reestablish control over Islam's holiest site. In 1981 Egyptian fundamentalists opposed to normalized relations with Israel assassinated President Anwar Sadat (1917–1981). His successor, Hosni Mubarak (b. 1928) ruled in an autocratic manner for three decades, using the threat of Islamic radicalism as an excuse for repression and arbitrary arrests. The Mubarak regime was finally toppled by a popular democratic movement in the spring of 2011. Islamic fundamentalists' view of Israel as a product of Western imperialism and the ongoing Israeli-Palestinian dispute continues to serve as a rallying point for radicals who wish to reclaim the Middle East for Islam.

Western powers have grown deeply suspicious of governments that are committed to fundamentalist Islam. In 1991, for example, France and the United States supported the Algerian army's decision to suspend democratic elections in that former French colony to prevent the anticipated victory of a militantly Islamic government, an event that sparked terrorist killings in France and contributed to wholesale slaughter of civilians in Algeria. More recently, Europe joined with the United States in demanding the government of Iran open its nuclear research program to a comprehensive U.N. inspections protocol. European leaders strongly suspected that Iran was trying to develop nuclear weapons, something that the Iranian government vehemently denied. Some observers in the West saw Islamic fundamentalism taking the place of communism as the chief global challenge to liberal democracy. When, in the spring of 2011 a number of popular and ostensibly democratic revolts broke out across North Africa, the Middle East and Iran against long-standing repressive regimes, Europe and the United States offered both moral and in some cases material support, seeing in the movements a salutary alternative to Islamic fundamentalism.

Ethnic Cleansing in Yugoslavia   One of the key features of globalization at the close of the twentieth century was the emphasis of international economic cooperation and the irrelevance of national borders when it came to the production and distribution of goods. By the close of the twentieth century, Poland, Hungary, and the Czech Republic had made a successful transition to democracy and economic reform despite the hardships involved when inefficient industries were shut down. They had been granted NATO membership, and they had applied for membership in the expanding European Union. In rural Bulgaria, Romania, and Albania, the transition was more difficult, but democratic political institutions continued to function. Further south in the Balkans, the decade of the 1990s was filled with horror and destruction. Here, just as Western Europe moved toward greater economic integration in the 1990s, heightened nationalism, ethnic tension, and war marked every aspect of daily life.

Yugoslavia was established immediately after World War I, but the new country was, like the pre–World War I Austrian Empire, a multiethnic and multilingual territorial entity. Over the centuries, there had been little love lost among the Serbs, Croatians, Slovenes, Montenegrins, Bosnians, Albanians, and Macedonians who now made up Yugoslavia. The greatest tensions were those between Orthodox Christian Serbs and Roman Catholic Croats, and between both of these groups and Muslims.

While each ethnic and religious group had a particular region as its homeland, the population of Yugoslavia was mixed, with members of each group living in lands dominated by another group.

Marshal Josef Tito (1892–1980) had managed to repress ethnic rivalries during his 35 years as leader of Yugoslavia, but after his death in 1980, tensions increased in the wake of a downturn in the economy. In particular, the strident nationalist leader of Serbia, Slobodan Milošević (1941–2006), alleged that Serbs residing in regions where they were in the minority were discriminated against by their neighbors. In the summer of 1990, less than one year after the collapse of communism in Eastern Europe, predominantly Catholic Slovenia and Croatia withdrew from the Yugoslav federation and were quickly recognized by the member states of the European Community.

The Serb leadership, responding to appeals from the Serb minority in Croatia, attacked Croatia in 1991 in an effort to preserve a Serb-dominated Yugoslav state. When the fighting spread to Bosnia and Herzegovina in the following year, Serb forces began a policy of "ethnic cleansing" aimed at the Muslim inhabitants of Bosnia. Muslim civilians were attacked, raped, and killed, and Serbs also established a series of concentration camps to house (and starve) those Bosnians who were captured in the fighting. The city of Sarajevo, host city of the 1984 Winter Olympics, was bombed incessantly by Serbian artillery. Finally, in 1994 NATO forces threatened retaliation unless the Serbs withdrew from their positions around the city. The opposing sides met in Dayton, Ohio, in 1995 to work out a complicated peace agreement. However, the end of hostilities in Bosnia did not mean the end of the suffering for civilians elsewhere in the former Yugoslavia.

Ethnic Nationalism   The Bosnian capital of Sarajevo was repeatedly bombed by Serbian forces in the early 1990s. The remains of a Roman Catholic Church highlight the fact that civilians were often the victims of ethnic hatred in the Balkans.

Beginning in 1999, Milošević ordered Serb troops to drive mostly Muslim ethnic Albanians from their homes in the southern province of Kosovo. After reports of mass killings of unarmed civilians, NATO responded with an intensive bombing campaign against Serbian targets. It was the largest military campaign in Europe since the end of World War II, and it succeeded in forcing the Serbians out of Kosovo. Milošević was later arrested and sent to the International Court in the Hague to stand trial for human rights violations. Thousands died during these conflicts. While American and European military and political cooperation in the face of Serbian aggression affirmed the trend toward international cooperation, ethnic nationalism in the Balkans pointed in the opposite direction. Conflict in the Balkans belied the trend toward global understanding and cooperation across borders. Instead, it pointed toward a future where ethnicity and religion became tragic pretexts for political division and bloodshed.

Ethnic Nationalism in Russia   The Commonwealth of Independent States (CIS) had replaced the defunct Soviet Union in 1991, but within many of the successor states religious and ethnic minorities began to call for greater autonomy. Russians living in independent Ukraine and the Baltic states remained restive, while ethnic minorities in Armenia and Georgia threatened the stability of those fledgling governments. The most serious challenge to the Russian Republic was centered in the Caucasus, where insurgents in the Muslim-dominated region of Chechnya clashed with Russian authorities in the mid-1990s. Russian military forces withdrew from the region in 1996 without settling the issue of Chechnya's independence. However, Russian President Vladimir Putin (b. 1948) resumed military operations in 1999 after a series of terrorist attacks against apartment buildings in central Moscow were blamed on Chechen rebels. Almost a quarter of a million refugees fled the region in the wake of intensive Russian air strikes. Although initially condemned by the West, Russian actions in Chechnya were viewed with greater tolerance by some European and American political leaders after the September 2001 terrorist attacks against the United States.

The Postindustrial West

By the final decade of the twentieth century it was becoming clear that the West's manufacturing age was nearing an end; it was not for lack of skill, but simply a matter of making things cheaper elsewhere. New economic trends, fueled by rapidly changing technology, positioned the world's first industrial countries to assume a new profile. Where once there were large factories, labor unions, and long careers for men with a single company that offered a generous pension program, now there was the "information age" and the "knowledge economy." Financial and consumer services, health care, information technology, all twinned with short-term, project-oriented contracts, absence of defined benefits, and maximum mobility across the EU, had become the new growth sectors in professional employment. Women as well as men entered these "white collar" professions, and for married couples the advent of two incomes made the attractions of consumer life possible. Birth rates in the developed countries are now at or below replacement levels, and advanced birth control procedures allow couples to delay or avoid the responsibilities of childbearing while they pursue professional goals.

Low wage and low skill jobs still existed, of course, but they were increasingly relegated to newcomers from abroad fleeing even greater economic hardship in their home countries. Some arrived illegally from former Soviet Bloc countries like Ukraine and Moldova; others were smuggled into the EU from China by unscrupulous entrepreneurs. Many of the legal immigrants worked in the agricultural sector, where mechanization, together with improved fertilizers and seed, made possible huge surpluses. Still others lived in substandard housing and formed segregated communities on the outskirts of major cities. Few enjoyed access to proper medical care or employer-provided benefits. The "Three D" jobs—dull, dirty, and dangerous—were assumed by society's "others," at the very time when the presence of immigrant communities heightened anxiety about the impact of growing multiculturalism on national identity. Europe and the United States had yet to come to terms with changing demographics. Both a traditional sending area (Europe) and a traditional receiving area (United States) were equally reluctant to embrace newcomers who were essential to the postindustrial economy.

Europe and the United States were also committed, in principle at least, to strengthening international cooperation, consultation, and economic interdependence. This had been the goal of postwar rebuilding efforts from the Marshall Plan forward, and the accomplishments had been significant. In terms of fundamental social, political, and economic values, the West continued to serve as a bulwark of individual freedoms. How those freedoms were best protected and extended, however, were matters of considerable friction in the wake of the 2003 Iraq invasion. The trans-Atlantic unity that was so much in evidence in the months after September 11th unraveled precipitously once the American-led war against terrorism shifted into an unprecedented preemptive mode. There was little sympathy in Europe for the "with us or against us" tone of rhetoric that emanated from the Bush White House, especially after it was demonstrated that there was no connection between al-Qaeda and the oppressive regime of Saddam Hussein.

The postindustrial West continued to dominate the global economy in the early years of the twenty-first century. Non-Western states aspired to comparable levels of prosperity, but as the chasm between rich and poor areas of the world grew larger, resentment and frustration intensified. Immigrants sought to redress the balance on the micro level by relocating to the affluent states. Others lashed out against the Western powers, the old colonial masters, by denouncing the capitalist and secularized states, and by appealing to the disaffected to attack these states by whatever means possible. Many in the West recognized that the problem of terrorism would never be addressed effectively by military means alone. In a globalizing world, the images of affluence were available instantly through the wonders of electronic communications in all of its forms.

⊙─Watch the Video

The Great Contradictions of the Twentieth Century

on **MyHistoryLab.com**

Extending a modicum of that affluence to others, while simultaneously protecting a fragile natural environment, demanded much more than force of arms and blueprints for the export of Western-style democracy.

KEY
QUESTION
REVISITED

Has the West
defined the process of
globalization?

The defense of cultural pluralism has become one of the principal rallying points for critics of modern Western civilization and globalization at the start of the twenty-first century. The criticism takes many forms, but three approaches stand out. In the postcolonial age, it is argued, the omnipresence of Western values, tastes, products, and popular culture undermine the cultural integrity of peoples and societies around the world. Western technology—movies, television, radio, the Internet, and especially social media—floods world markets with the overriding idea that consumption represents the highest human good. The world has been overwhelmed with consumer-oriented capitalist ideology, a monolithic cultural perspective that can tolerate no rivals. Having abandoned the old imperialism of territorial control and no longer facing a hostile Soviet Union, the West has fashioned a new and more insidious form of domination. Instead of forcing colonial peoples to abandon their traditional social and religious patterns, Western technology lures them to cast off their traditions for the environmentally fatal attractions of capitalist consumer culture.

Religious critics argue that modern Western civilization has marginalized faith traditions for an emotionally and intellectually sterile form of secular rationalism. The focus in the West has turned away from consideration of the transcendent. According to these critics, the focus is now on the production of goods and services, efficiency, competition with one's neighbor, and development and mastery of the physical environment without proper consideration of long-term consequences. The end of the Cold War has afforded the West a precious opportunity to put its enormous material resources at the service of higher moral standards; instead, the end of superpower rivalry has led to the acceleration of cultural trends that satisfy narrow material interests absent any reference to a spiritual compass. In part, the rise of Islamic fundamentalism is due to this perception that Western culture has repudiated its former concern with religious values.

Finally, early twenty-first century criticism of Western civilization from within the academic community emphasizes the West's association with various forms of exploitation. Slavery, racism, sexism, imperialism, degradation of the natural environment, and class conflict have all been a part of the West's rise to economic and military primacy over the past three centuries. Western achievements were made possible through the exploitation of indigenous peoples, women, the poor, and the enslaved. Western capitalist culture, with its emphasis on rationality and efficiency, continues to strengthen inequalities while buttressing the power of traditional elites.

While the debate over the impact of Western culture in a global context is valuable, criticism of Western civilization runs the risk of forgetting that change and reform have also been at the heart of Western culture. The Enlightenment tradition, anchored in the rationalist heritage of ancient Greece and the equalitarian assumptions at the core of Jewish and Christian thought, provided the intellectual underpinning for the West's critical approach to life. From antislavery to women's rights, in the struggle for political democracy and in the establishment of free universal education, Western civilization at its best has been self-reflective and tolerant, open to change, and committed to the dignity of the individual. This is the type of civilization celebrated by Vaclav Havel at the opening of this chapter.

As the values of democracy and freedom find voice around the world in the twenty-first century, it is crucial, as Havel reminds us, to preserve the richness and diversity of cultural expression. Those who protest the globalization of culture provide timely reminders that no single world view can satisfy the human quest for meaning in existence. Creative expression, scientific ingenuity, moral inquiry, and spiritual exploration all remained vibrant in diverse settings despite the spread of Western cultural forms. Cultural isolation has diminished thanks to modern communications and travel, but pluralism has survived, assuring that new solutions to future problems will originate out of a rich variety of intellectual contexts.

Key Terms

globalization, *p. 772*
perestroika, *p. 773*
Solidarity, *p. 775*

European Union, *p. 782*
global warming, *p. 789*

liberation theology, *p. 797*
Islamism, *p. 798*

Activities

1. Why did Mikhail Gorbachev permit the Soviet satellites in Eastern Europe to break away from Soviet rule?

2. Describe how the nuclear dilemma has changed since the end of the Cold War.

3. Is Western-style capitalism's focus on consumption and growth sustainable?

4. Why did ethnic conflict grip the former Yugoslavia during the 1990s, and how did Europe respond?

5. Outline the key components of global culture, and explain why many Muslims reject them.

6. Can Europe's post–World War II recovery be replicated in the developing world? What, in your view, does the northern hemisphere owe the southern hemisphere?

7. Describe how the role of women and the family changed in the postmodern world, and comment on its consequences.

Further Reading

Jeremy Black, *Europe since 1990* (2009), a highly readable examination of the very recent past.

John Robert McNeill, *Something New Under the Sun: An Environmental History of the Twentieth Century* 2001, a comprehensive and balanced survey.

Graham Fuller, *The Future of Political Islam* (2003), a introductory overview by a former government officer involved in information gathering.

T. R. Reid, *The United States of Europe: The New Superpower and the End of American Supremacy* (2004), a respected journalist's account of the emerging influence of the European Union.

Jeffry Frieden, *Global Capitalism: Its Fall and Rise in the Twentieth Century* (2007), looks at developments in market-based economies.

MyHistoryLab Connections

Visit **MyHistoryLab.com** *for a customized Study Plan that will help you build your knowledge of* Western Civilization and the Global Community.

Questions for Analysis

1. How is the British Petroleum oil spill similar to other environmental disasters in recent history?

◉─[Watch the Video British Petroleum Oil Spill—Environmental Disasters, p. 789

2. According to the video, what are some of the characteristics that make African cities cosmopolitan?

◉─[Watch the Video Africa as an Urban, Not Rural, Place, p. 791

3. Did Betty Friedan speak for the majority of women in the United States in the late 1950s and early 1960s and, if not, whom did she overlook and what problems did they tend to face?

[◉─[Read the Document Betty Friedan, *The Problem That Has No Name,* 1963, p. 794

4. What are some of the things that led to the 1979 Islamic revolution in Iran and why is this event viewed as a turning point for both the Middle East and for the world?

◉─[Watch the Video The 1979 Islamic Revolution in Iran: A Turning Point for the Middle East and the World, p. 799

5. What are some of the contradictions of the twentieth century and how might historians reconcile these contradictions?

◉─[Watch the Video The Great Contradictions of the Twentieth Century, p. 803

Other Resources from This Chapter

[◉─[Read the Document Vaclav Havel, "The Need for Transcendence in the Postmodern World," p. 771

[◉─[Read the Document Ronald Reagan, Speech at the Brandenburg Gate (1987), p. 773

[◉─[Read the Document Mikhail Gorbachev on the Need for Economic Reform (1987), p. 773

Read the Document *An Explanation of Space-based Nuclear Defense*, Bill Chappell, p. 774

View the Closer Look Collapse of the Berlin Wall, p. 775

Read the Document Scientists Examine Russia's Economy and Environment, 1991–1993, p. 778

Read the Document Famine in North Korea, p. 778

Read the Document Deng Xiaoping, on *Introducing Capitalist Principles to China*, p. 779

Read the Document A Common Market and European Integration (1960), p. 781

Read the Document Treaty on European Union, p. 782

Read the Document François Mitterrand, Speech to the United Nations, 1990, p. 782

View the Closer Look The Copenhagen Opera House, p. 782

Read the Document America Enters a New Century with Terror, 2001, p. 786

Read the Document Statement from Chancellor Schröder on the Iraq Crisis, p. 787

Read the Document The United Nations, *Universal Declaration of Human Rights*, 1948, p. 794

Read the Document Camillo Torres and Liberation Theology (1950s), p. 798

GLOSSARY

Absolutism A form of government in the seventeenth and eighteenth centuries in which the ruler possessed complete and unrivalled power.

Act of Supremacy Act passed by the English Parliament in 1534 that severed England's ties with the papacy and established the king as the head of the Church in England.

Anti-Semitism Prejudice, hostility, or legal discrimination against Jews.

Appeasement British diplomatic and financial efforts to stabilize Germany in the 1920s and 1930s in hopes of avoiding a second world war.

Articles of Confederation The first constitution of the new national government of the United States, 1781–1789.

Balfour Declaration A 1917 British commitment to support the creation of a Jewish homeland in the Middle East after the conclusion of World War I, while simultaneously committing to respect Palestinian claims in the region.

Bill of Rights The first ten amendments to the United States Constitution of 1789 were informed by fears of too much power being concentrated in the hands of a distant central government.

Boxer Rebellion An effort by Chinese nationals to expel Westerners from China in 1900. A combined American, European and Japanese force defeated the rebels.

Commonwealthmen Eighteenth-century British political writers who claimed that Britain was the only state in Europe not controlled by an absolute monarch.

Condottiere Commander of an army of mercenaries; when hired to defend one of Italy's towns, the risk was that he would use his soldiers to take over and make his power permanent.

Congress of Vienna A conference of the major powers of Europe in 1814 to 1815 to establish a new balance of power at the end of the Napoleonic wars.

Continental Congress Leading opponents of British policy in North America gathered in Philadelphia in 1774 and again in 1775 to frame a coordinated political and military response to perceived British aggression.

Council of Trent A church council, meeting from 1545 to 1563, that was charged with the responsibility of strengthening the Roman Catholic Church to equip it to respond to the challenge of the Protestant Reformation.

Decolonization Withdrawal of Western nations from colonies in Africa and Asia after World War II.

Deism Seventeenth- and eighteenth-century belief that God created the universe and established immutable laws of nature but did not subsequently intervene in the operation of nature or in human affairs.

Diet A German political assembly.

Divine Right Political theory that held the institution of monarchy had divine origin and that the monarch functioned as God's representative on Earth.

Dreyfus Affair The trials of Captain Alfred Dreyfus on treason charges, which dominated French political life in the decade after 1894 and revealed fundamental divisions in French society.

Dutch East India Company Chartered in 1602 and granted a monopoly over trade with Asia by the States-General of the Netherlands, this multinational organization generated strong revenues for its stockholders and acted as a quasi-governmental agency, waging war, negotiating treaties, and establishing overseas colonies.

Edict of Nantes A decree that King Henry IV issued in 1598 that established places in France where Protestants could legally worship.

Enlightened Despots The term assigned to absolute monarchs who initiated a series of legal and political reforms in an effort to realize the goals of the Enlightenment.

Enlightenment An international intellectual movement of the eighteenth century that emphasized the use of reason and the application of the laws of nature to human society.

Entente Cordial The pre–World War I defensive understanding of France, Russia, and Great Britain designed to restrain German territorial ambitions in Europe and overseas.

European Union A successor organization to the EEC; the organization attempted to integrate European political, economic, cultural, and military structures and policies.

Existentialism Twentieth-century philosophy that emerged in the interwar era and influenced many thinkers and artists after World War II. Existentialism emphasizes individual freedom in a world devoid of meaning or coherence.

Fair A regularly scheduled time for merchants and customers to gather at a particular place for the purpose of conducting business; frequently corresponded with a holiday (a *feria*, "feast day").

Fascism Twentieth-century political ideology that rejected the existing alternatives of conservatism, communism, socialism, and liberalism. Fascists stressed the authoritarian power of the state, the efficacy of violent action, the need to build national community, and the use of new technologies of influence and control.

Five-Year Plans Stalin's effort to set ambitious production targets and force peasants, workers into a collectivized economy.

Fronde A series of popular uprisings against the French crown between 1649 and 1653. The clashes threatened the government of the new king, Louis XIV, but were ultimately unsuccessful.

Global Warming An increase in the average temperature of the Earth's atmosphere, especially a sustained increase great enough to cause changes in the global climate. The present warming is generally attributed to an increase in the greenhouse effect, brought about by increased levels of greenhouse gases, largely due to the effects of human activity.

Globalization The tendency of capital and trade flows to move beyond domestic and national markets to other markets around the globe, thereby increasing the interconnectedness of these flows. Globalization also refers to the increasing interconnectedness of culture, music, art, food, dress, and ideas that has been increasing in recent times.

Grand Alliance Wartime alliance, begun in 1941, involving the Soviet Union, Britain, and the United States and committed to the defeat of the Nazi regime and its allies.

Great Depression Calamitous drop in prices, reduction in trade, and rise in unemployment that devastated the global economy beginning in 1929.

Great Reform Bill Parliamentary legislation in 1932 that opened up voting rights to middle-class males in Britain. The bill was the first in a series of reforms that would extend the franchise to the working class by the end of the nineteenth century.

Guild A medieval union or corporation that monopolized the production of a product with the intent of sustaining a healthy market.

Hanseatic League An alliance of cities in northern Germany (established in 1359) that enabled them to dominate commerce in the Baltic and North Seas.

Holocaust Adolf Hitler's effort to murder all the Jews in Europe during World War II.

Indulgence A papal dispensation from the obligation to perform a penance.

Industrial Revolution Sustained period of economic growth and change brought on by technological innovations in the process of manufacturing; began in Britain in the mid-eighteenth century.

Inquisition A church court established by the papacy to root out heresy in Catholic countries.

Internal Combustion Engine Lighter and more portable than the stream engine, the new technology was powered by liquid petroleum and led to the advent of the automobile age by the end of the nineteenth century.

Islamism Islamic radicalism or *jihadism*, this ideology insists that Islam demands a rejection of Western values and that violence in this struggle against the West is justified.

Jacobins A French political party supporting a democratic republic that found support in political clubs throughout the country and dominated the National Convention from 1792 until 1794.

Kulturkampf An attack on the power and autonomy of the Roman Catholic Church in Germany during the chancellorship of Otto von Bismarck. The campaign included the expulsion of the Jesuit order from Germany and the advancement of state schools over religious institutions.

Laws of Nature Simple, rational and comprehensible principles governing the physical, moral, and religious realms. Faith in the existence of laws of nature was strong during the Enlightenment.

League of Nations International body founded after World War I and designed to resolve future international disagreements through peaceful means.

Lend-Lease Program President Roosevelt's effort in early 1941 to provide Britain with essential war material, including warships, despite America's official noninvolvement in World War II.

Liberation Theology The effort by certain Roman Catholic theologians to combine Marxism with traditional Christian concern for the poor.

Line of Demarcation A longitudinal line decreed by the pope in 1494 to divide territories in the western hemisphere between Spain and Portugal.

Marshall Plan The use of U.S. economic aid to restore stability to Europe after World War II and to undercut the appeal of communist ideology.

Marxism The theory of Karl Marx (1818–1883) and Friedrich Engels (1820–1895) that stated history is the result of class conflict, which will end in the inevitable triumph of the industrial proletariat over the bourgeoisie and the abolition of private property and social class.

Meiji Restoration A reorganization of the Japanese government in 1867 that marked the beginning of an intense campaign of Westernization and modernization.

Modern Devotion A religious revival originating in northern Europe during the fourteenth and fifteenth centuries that promoted education and charitable work.

Modernism Term applied to artistic and literary movement from the late nineteenth century through the 1950s. Modernists sought to create new aesthetic forms and values.

Mufti A specialist in the interpretation of Islamic religious law.

Munich Agreement British and French agreement with Hitler in 1938 to partition Czechoslovakia and allow German control over the Sudetenland in the expectation that this would be Hitler's final demand for territory.

Nationalism The belief that the people who form a nation should have their own political institutions and that the interests of the nation should be defended and promoted at all costs.

NATO (North Atlantic Treaty Organization) is the defensive anti-Soviet alliance of the United States, Canada, and the nations of Western Europe established in 1949.

Nazism Twentieth-century political ideology associated with Adolf Hitler that adopted many Fascist ideas but with a central focus on racism and particularly anti-Semitism.

New Economic Policy Lenin's 1921 policy of allowing Soviet farmers and small business to operate in a market economy. The policy was designed to jump-start the economy after years of civil war and internal revolution.

New Imperialism The third phase of modern European imperialism, which occurred in the late nineteenth and early twentieth centuries and extended Western control over almost all of Africa and much of Asia.

New Model Army A Protestant military organization established by Oliver Cromwell in 1645 that enabled the English Parliament to depose King Charles I and govern England as a Puritan republic.

Oratory of Divine Love An organization of Catholic clergy and laity that was established in the sixteenth century to work for religious renewal.

Peace of Augsburg A truce that was declared between Protestant and Catholic factions in Germany in 1555 and which prevented religious conflict in Germany until 1618.

Peace of Westphalia The international agreement concluded in 1648 that ended the Thirty Years' War and resolved numerous boundary disputes.

Perestroika "Restructuring." The attempt in the 1980s to reform the Soviet government and economy.

Perspective The techniques developed by painters during the era of the Renaissance to create the illusion of three-dimensional space on a flat surface.

Peterloo Massacre Government attack on civilian protesters in Manchester, England, in 1819 that came to symbolize opposition to popular calls for change during periods of economic distress.

Philosophes The writers and thinkers of the Enlightenment, especially in France.

Podestà A neutral stranger who was brought in to rule and mediate among factions when conflict caused the government of an Italian town to break down.

Pragmatic Sanction of Bourges An agreement in 1438 between the king of France and the pope that extended the authority of the French monarchy over the Catholic Church in France.

Predestination Belief, primarily associated with the Swiss theologian John Calvin, that the absolute sovereignty of God implies that a person's conduct cannot alter God's decision about his or her ultimate fate.

Proletariat An unskilled industrial worker who was entirely dependent on wage labor for his/her survival. According to many nineteenth-century social theorists, including Karl Marx, the proletariat faced constant exploitation by the owners of the means of production.

Puritan Name for a radical Protestant faction that drew its inspiration from the Swiss Reformation. It temporarily overthrew the monarchy and established a Republican government in England.

Racism The pseudoscientific theory that biological features of race determine human character and worth.

Realpolitik The "power politics" approach to international relations pioneered by German Chancellor Otto von Bismarck during the third quarter of the nineteenth century.

Reform (Calvinist Protestantism) Protestant churches that trace their origin less to Martin Luther and Germany than to the work of the Swiss reformers Ulrich Zwingli and John Calvin.

Reign of Terror A purging of alleged enemies of the French state between 1793 and 1794, organized by the Committee of Public Safety, that resulted in the execution of 17,000 people.

Republicanism A political theory first developed by the ancient Greeks, especially the philosopher Plato, but elaborated on by the ancient Romans and rediscovered during the Italian Renaissance. The fundamental principle of Republicanism as developed during the Italian Renaissance was that government officials should be elected by the people or a portion of the people.

Romanticism An artistic and literary movement of the late eighteenth and nineteenth centuries that involved a protest against classicism, appealed to the passions rather than the intellect, and emphasized the beauty and power of nature.

Russian Revolution Revolution in Russia in 1917 that overthrew the tsar and eventually brought the Bolsheviks, a Communist party led by Lenin, to power.

Sansculottes Literally, "those without knee-britches"; working-class revolutionaries who initiated the radical stage of the French Revolution in 1792.

Scientific Revolution In the sixteenth and seventeenth centuries, a period of new scientific inquiry, experimentation, and discovery that resulted in a new understanding of the universe based on mathematical principles and led to the creation of the modern sciences, particularly astronomy and physics.

Serfs During the Middle Ages, serfs were agricultural laborers who worked and lived on a plot of land granted to them by a lord to whom they owed a certain portion of their crops. They could not leave the land, but they had certain legal rights that were denied to slaves.

Skepticism During the Enlightenment, skepticism involved the systematic questioning of all alleged truths and a rigorous assessment of truth claims using empirical evidence and rational thinking.

Solidarity Trade union and political party in Poland that led an unsuccessful effort to reform the Polish communist state in the early 1980s; it survived state persecution to lead Poland's first non-communist government since World War II in 1989.

Spanish Armada The great fleet that Philip II launched in 1588 in what proved to be a futile attempt to conquer England and subdue Protestant resistance in the Netherlands.

St. Bartholomew's Day Massacre A surprise attack that the French monarchy launched (August 24, 1572) on Protestants who had gathered in Paris to celebrate the wedding of a daughter of queen regent Catherine de Medicis to Henry of Navarre, a Protestant leader.

Stalin's Purges (or Great Terror) Period of mass arrests and executions particularly aimed at Communist Party members. Lasting from 1934 to 1938, the Great Purge enabled Stalin to consolidate his one-man rule over the Soviet Union.

State Socialism Government provision of worker benefits, including accident, sickness, and old age insurance pioneered in Germany under Otto von Bismarck in an effort to undermine the appeal of Marxism.

Steam Engine Developed by James Watt in the 1760s, the steam engine made nonhuman productive power portable, launching the railroad age and allowing manufacturing to develop in urban areas first in Britain and then across Europe.

Studia humanitas The mission of the intellectual leaders of Italy's Renaissance, a search for methods to discover and realize the potentials of human nature.

Survival of the Fittest A term coined by Herbert Spencer who applied evolutionary theory to social and economic change to argue against state assistance to the poor and disadvantaged.

Tabula Rasa John Locke claimed that every person was born without any inborn or innate ideas but instead the mind at birth was a blank slate. The tabula rasa theory had enormous implications for the power of education to shape human personality.

Thirty Years' War A devastating war fought on German territory from 1618 to 1648; originating as a conflict between Germany's Protestants and Catholics, concern for the balance of power ultimately encouraged French and Scandinavian monarchs to intervene.

Treaty of Brest-Litovsk A punitive peace imposed by the victorious Germans on Russia and signed by the Bolshevik government in 1917.

Treaty of Versailles Peace settlement with Germany at the end of World War I; included the War Guilt Clause fixing blame on Germany for the war and requiring massive reparations.

Trench Warfare Warfare marked by slow wearing down of the opposing forces and piecemeal gains at heavy cost. The term applies especially to World War I.

Triple Alliance The defensive military alliance of Germany, Austria-Hungary, and Italy brokered by German Chancellor Bismarck in the 1880s.

Urbanization The social process whereby cities grow and societies become more urban.

Warsaw Pact The military alliance of the Soviet Union and its Eastern European satellite states in the Cold War era.

Working Class People who work for wages, especially low wages, including unskilled and semiskilled laborers and their families.

Yalta A resort city in Crimea in the southern Ukraine on the Black Seas that was the site of the Allied conference between Roosevelt, Stalin, and Churchill in February 1945.

SUGGESTED RESOURCES

Introduction

The increasing interconnectedness of the modern world has produced numerous reflections on the nature of history and the importance of understanding the interrelatedness of global peoples.

J. M. Hobson, *The Eastern Origins of Western Civilization* (2004); D. Landes, *The Wealth and Poverty of Nations* (1998); R. Royal, "Who Put the West in Western Civilization?" *The Intercollegiate Review* (Spring 1998); William Hallo and Klaas Dijkstra, *Origins: The Ancient Near-Eastern Background of Some Modern Western Institutions* (1996); F. Fukuyama, *The End of History and the Last Man* (1993); J. Roberts, *The Triumph of the West* (1985).

Chapter 12

Europe's Renaissance and Age of Exploration mark a turning point in global history. Many of the key developments that have shaped life in the modern world can be traced to this era: mass literacy, global exchanges of goods and cultures, widening divergence of Christian and Muslim peoples, and the resurgence of influences from the ancient phase in Western civilization.

C. L. Frommel, *The Architecture of the Italian Renaissance* (2007); R. Jacoff, *The Cambridge Companion to Dante* (2007); N. R. Havely, *Dante* (2007); K. A. Simon Eliot, *A Companion to the History of the Book* (2007); E. Enenkel, *Petrarch and His Readers in the Renaissance* (2006); L. Fusco, *Leonardo de' Medici* (2006); R. Crum, *Renaissance Florence: A Social History* (2006); H. Kamen, *Spain, 1469–1714: A Society in Conflict* (2005); J. Reston, *Dogs of God: Columbus, the Inquisition, and the Defeat of the Moors* (2005); S. Füssel, *Gutenberg and the Impact of Printing* (2005); J. Snyder, *Northern Renaissance Art* (2005); R. Mackenney, *Renaissances: The Cultures of Italy, c. 1300–1600* (2005); H. Thomas, *Rivers of Gold: The Rise of the Spanish Empire, from Columbus to Magellan* (2004); J. C. Smith, *The Northern Renaissance* (2004); J. Najemy, *Italy in the Age of the Renaissance, 1300–1550* (2004); J. Edwards, *Ferdinand and Isabella* (2004); P. Strathern, *The Medicis: Godfathers of the Renaissance* (2003); B. Lewis, *What Went Wrong? Western Impact and Middle Eastern Response* (2002); H. Beinart, *The Expulsion of the Jews from Spain* (2002); P. Russell, *Prince Henry "the Navigator": A Life* (2000); S. Bemrose, *A New Life of Dante* (2000); M. Greene, *A Shared World: Christians and Muslims in the Early Modern Mediterranean* (2000); P. Johnson, *The Renaissance: A Short History* (2000); P. Dollinger, *The German Hansa* (1999); P. Burke, *The European Renaissance: Centers and Peripheries* (1998); B. Thompson, *Humanists and Reformers* (1996); L. Jardine, *Worldly Goods: A New History of the Renaissance* (1996); C. G. Nauert, *Humanism and the Culture of the Renaissance* (1995); B. G. Kohl & A. A. Smith, *Major Problems in the History of the Italian Renaissance* (1995); J. Hale, *The Civilization of Europe in the Renaissance* (1994); J. Huizinga, *The Autumn of the Middle Ages* (1924/1996); G. Holmes, *Renaissance* (1996); F. Fernandez-Armesto, *Columbus* (1991); M. L. King, *Women of the Renaissance* (1991); G. V. Scammell, *The First Imperial Age: European Overseas Expansion, c. 1400–1715* (1989); L. Martins, *Power and Imagination: City-States in Renaissance Italy* (1989); A. W. Crosby, *The Biological Expansion of Europe* (1986); J. N. Hillgarth, *The Spanish Kingdoms, 1250–1516* (1978); E. L. Eisenstein, *The Printing Press as an Agent of Change* (1978); G. Leff, *The Dissolution of the Medieval Outlook, an Essay on Intellectual and Spiritual Change in the Fourteenth Century* (1976); H. Inalcik, *The Ottoman Empire: The Classical Age, 1300–1600* (1973); D. Waley, *The Italian City Republics* (1969); B. Lewis, *Istanbul and the Civilization of the Ottoman Empire* (1963).

Chapter 13

Despite the confident predictions of some secularists, religion has not faded as a significant factor influencing the behavior of modern peoples and states. The history of the era of Europe's Reformation and religious wars may, therefore, be of special interest to students of current world affairs. It is also important for the study of American history, for the religious ideologies that emerged at this time were transplanted to America and shaped the American way of life.

Frank Tallett & D. J. B. Trim, *European Warfare, 1350–1750* (2010); Michael Braddick, *God's Fury, England's Fire: A New History of the English Civil Wars* (2009); Hans Hillerbrand, *The Division of Christendom: Christianity in the Sixteenth Century* (2007); R. Shaughnessy, *The Cambridge Companion to Shakespeare and Popular Culture* (2007); S. Ronald, *The Pirate Queen: Queen Elizabeth I, Her Pirate Adventurers, and the Dawn of Empire* (2007); R. Rex, *Henry VIII and the English Reformation* (2006); M. Bennett, *Oliver Cromwell* (2006); G. W. Bernard, *The King's Reformation: Henry VIII and the Remaking of the English Church* (2005); P. Oswald, *Mary Stuart* (2005); L. DeLisle, *After Elizabeth: The Rise of James of Scotland and the Struggle for the Throne of England* (2005); M. Holt, *The French Wars of Religion, 1562–1629* (2005); C. V. Wedgwood, *The Thirty Years' War* (2005); L. Picard, *Elizabeth's London: Everyday Life in Elizabethan London* (2004); H. Kleinschmidt, *Charles V: The World Emperor* (2004); H. Kamen, *Golden Age Spain* (2004); P. Collinson, *The Reformation: A History* (2004); M. Mullett, *Martin Luther* (2004); D. McKim, *The Cambridge Companion to Martin Luther* (2003); C. Levin, *Elizabeth I, Always Her Own Free Woman* (2003); B. Pursell, *The Winter King: Frederick V of the Palatinate and the Coming of the Thirty Years' War* (2003); L. Frieda, *Catherine de Medici, Renaissance Queen of France* (2003); Susan Brigden, *New Worlds, Lost Worlds: The Rule of the Tudors* (2002); A. Levi, *Renaissance and Reformation: The Intellectual Genesis* (2002); G. Parker, *Philip II* (2002); M. Kitchen, *The Cambridge Illustrated History of Germany* (2000); R. J. Knechy, *Catherine de' Medici* (1998); C. Haigh, *Elizabeth I*, 2nd ed. (1998); S. Greenblatt, Ed., *The Norton Shakespeare* (1997); B. Thompson, *Humanists and Reformers: A History of Renaissance and Reformation* (1996); P. Gaunt, *Oliver Cromwell* (1996); C. Lindberg, *The European Reformations* (1996); M. P. Holt, *The French Wars of Religion, 1562–1629* (1995); R. Ashton, *Counter-Revolution: The Second Civil War and Its Origin, 1646–1648* (1995); W. P. Stephens, *Zwingli* (1994); A. McGrath, *Reformation Thought: An Introduction*, 2nd ed. (1993); G. H. Williams, *The Radical Reformation*, 2nd ed. (1992); H. A. Oberman, *Luther* (1992); S. Ozment, *Protestants: The Birth of a Revolution* (1992); J. Wormald, *Mary Queen of Scots: A Study in Failure* (1991); J. McConica, *Erasmus* (1991); H. Kamen, *Spain 1469–1714: A Society of Conflict*, 2nd ed. (1991); S. J. Lee, *The Thirty Years' War* (1991); E. Cameron, *The European Reformation* (1991); R. Bonney, *The European Dynastic States, 1494–1660* (1991); A. McGrath, *A Life of John Calvin: A Study in the Shaping of Western Culture* (1990); P. Caravan, *Ignatius Loyola: A Biography of the Founder of the Jesuits* (1990); A. G. Dickens, *The English Reformation*, 2nd ed. (1989); W. J. Bouwsma, *John Calvin: A Sixteenth-Century Portrait* (1988); P. Collinson, *The Religion of Protestants: The Church in English Society, 1559–1625* (1982); S. Ozment, *The Age of Reform, 1250–1550: An Intellectual and Religious History of Late Medieval and Reformation Europe* (1980); R. S. Dunn, *The Age of Religious Wars, 1559–1715*, 2nd ed. (1979); F. Braudel, *The Mediterranean and the Mediterranean World in the Age of Philip II*, 2 vols. (1976); M. R. O'Connell, *The Counter Reformation, 1559–1610* (1974); P. Gay & R. K. Webb, *Modern Europe to 1815* (1973); A. Wandruszka, *The House of Habsburg* (1965).

Chapter 14

The sixteenth-century Reformation set the stage for the formation of strong centralized states in Europe. No longer competing with church authorities for the allegiance of their subjects, state sovereignty and dynastic power reached new heights during the seventeenth and eighteenth centuries. Recent scholarly literature has focused on the limits of absolutism during this period, highlighting the importance of economic and political checks on the power of monarchs who claimed to rule by divine right, and contrasting European monarchical power with its more absolutist forms in non-Western civilizations.

M. S. Anderson, *Europe in the Eighteenth Century, 1713–1783* (1987); J. Black, *Eighteenth-Century Europe, 1700–1789* (1990); J. Black, *European Warfare, 1660–1815* (1994); T. Blanning, *The Pursuit of Glory: Europe 1648–1815* (2007); J. Blum, *The End of the Old Order in Rural Europe* (1978); F. Braudel, *The Structures of Everyday Life* (1982); J. Brewer, *The Sinews of Power: War, Money and the English State, 1688–1783* (1989); G. Burgess, *Absolute Monarchy and the Stuart Constitution* (1996); J. C. D. Clark, *English Society, 1688–1832* (1985); I. Madariaga, *Catherine the Great: A Short History* (1990); W. Doyle, *The Old European Order* (1992); M. W. Flinn, *The European Demographic System, 1500–1820* (1981); P. Goubert, *The Ancient Regime: French Society, 1600–1750* (1974); L. Hughs, *Russia in the Age of Peter the Great* (1998); J. I. Israel, *The Dutch Republic: Its Rise, Greatness, and Fall, 1477–1806* (1995); D. McKay & H. M. Scott, *The Rise of the Great Powers, 1648–1815* (1983); A. Pagden, *Lords of All the World: Ideologies of Empire in Spain, Britain and France, 1492–1830* (1995); G. Parker, *The Military Revolution: Military Innovation and the Rise of the West, 1500–1800* (1998); D. J. Sturdy, *Louis XIV* (1998).

For primary sources illustrating the theory and practice of absolutism, see:
http://lcweb.loc.gov/exhibits/bnf/bnf0005.html

Chapter 15

The Scientific Revolution of the sixteenth and seventeenth centuries provided an important backdrop to the Enlightenment. Traditionally, the advance of scientific inquiry has been interpreted in terms of expanding human rationality and a knowable deity who was also a supreme architect. More recently, historians have emphasized the importance of an earlier magical and alchemical tradition to scientific inquiry. Scholars have also worked to highlight the limits of reason during these centuries by examining the persistence of religious intolerance and the persecution of women accused of witchcraft.

H. Butterfield, *The Origins of Modern Science* (1949); C. M. Cipolla, *Before the Industrial Revolution: European Society and Economy, 100–1700*, 2nd ed. (1980); P. Dear, *Revolutionizing the Sciences: European Knowledge and Its Ambitions, 1500–1700* (2001); R. Hall, *Scientific Revolution, 1500–1800* (1945); K. J. Howell, *God's Two Books: Copernican Cosmology and Biblical Interpretation in Early Modern Science* (2003); M. Jacob, *The Cultural Meaning of the Scientific Revolution* (1988); H. Kearney, *Science and Change, 1500–1700* (1971); T. S. Kuhn, *The Copernican Revolution* (1957); L. Schiebinger, *The Mind Has No Sex? Women in the Origins of Modern Science* (1990); W. M. Spellman, *John Locke* (1997); W. M. Spellman, *European Political Thought, 1600–1700* (1998); R. S. Westfall, *Never at Rest: A Biography of Isaac Newton* (1981); R. S. Westman, *The Copernican Achievement* (1975); B. Willey, *The Seventeenth Century Background* (1949); M. E. Wiesner, *Women and Gender in Early Modern Europe* (1994); P. Zagorin, *Francis Bacon* (1998).

For sources on the life and work of Galileo, see the Galileo Project at:
http://galileo.rice.edu/lib/catalog.html

Oxford's Museum of the History of Science offers online exhibits at:
http://www.mhs.ox.ac.uk

Chapter 16

Most studies of the European Enlightenment concentrate on the ideas of a small intellectual elite. While it is important to recognize the significance of the many social, political, and religious reform efforts that emerged during the eighteenth century, it is also useful to acknowledge the practical limits of the Enlightenment. Studies of slavery, the condition of women, and the lives of common people during this era have increased dramatically. This new scholarship has alerted us to the complexity and variety of eighteenth-century thought and lived experience.

C. Becker, *The Heavenly City of the Eighteenth-Century Philosophers* (1935); G. Cragg, *The Church and the Age of Reason* (1966); L. Crocker, *An Age of Crisis: Man and World in Eighteenth-Century French Thought* (1959); R. Darnton, *The Business of Enlightenment: A Publishing History of the Encyclopedia* (1979); P. Gay, *The Enlightenment: An Interpretation*, 2 vols. (1969); S. Gaukroger, *Francis Bacon and the Transformation of Early Modern Philosophy* (2001); N. Hampson, *A Cultural History of the Enlightenment* (1968); P. Hazard, *The European Mind, 1680–1715* (1935); R. Houston, *Social Change in the Age of the Enlightenment* (1995); M. Jacob, *The Radical Enlightenment: Pantheists, Freemasons and Republicans* (1980); L. Krieger, *An Essay on the Theory of Enlightened Despotism* (1975); J. Lough, *The Encyclopedia* (1971); F. Manuel, *The Eighteenth Century Confronts the Gods* (1959); G. Ritter, *Frederick the Great: A Historical Profile* (1968); H. Scott, *Enlightened Absolutism* (1990); R. Shackleton, *Montesquieu: A Critical Biography* (1961); J. Shklar, *Men and Citizens: A Study of Rousseau's Social Theory* (1969); S. Spencer, Ed., *French Women and the Age of Enlightenment* (1984); I. Wade, *The Intellectual Origins of the French Enlightenment* (1957); P. Zagorin, *How the Idea of Religious Toleration Came to the West* (2003).

For documents on the Enlightenment and additional web links, see:
http://www.fordham.edu/halsall/mod/modsbook10.html

Chapter 17

The institutions and values of Old Regime Europe, including monarchy, aristocracy, and legal inequality, were challenged and overturned during the final quarter of the eighteenth century. The changes brought about by the American Revolution were modest in comparison with the events that began in Paris in 1789. On the American side, the break from Britain was comparatively bloodless, and the prerevolutionary social structure remained in place after independence.

In France, however, fundamental restructuring took place during the 1790s and the rise of Napoleon Bonaparte to power signaled the extension of revolutionary principles across Europe. Some recent studies have emphasized the social implications of the French Revolutions for all of Europe.

D. Armitage, *The Declaration of Independence: A Global History* (2007); B. Bailyn, *The Ideological Origins of the American Revolution* (1967); D. Bell, *The First Total War: Napoleon's Europe and the Birth of Warfare as We Know It* (2007); R. Cobb, *The People's Armies* (1987); F. Furet, *Interpreting the French Revolution* (1981); P. Gay, *The Enlightenment*, 2 vols., (1978); J. Godechot, *The Counter-Revolution: Doctrine and Action* (1971); J. Landes, *Women and the Public Sphere in the Age of the French Revolution* (1988); G. Lefebvre, *The Coming of the French Revolution*, trans. R. R. Palmer (1947); M. Lyons, *Napoleon Bonaparte and the Legacy of the French Revolution* (1994); R. Middlekauff, *The Glorious Cause: The American Revolution, 1763–1789* (1982); E. Morgan, *The Stamp Act Crisis* (1953); R. R. Palmer, *The Age of Democratic Revolution*, 2 vols. (1941); C. Robbins, *The Eighteenth-Century Commonwealthmen* (1959); D. G. Sutherland, *France, 1789–1815: Revolution and Counterrevolution* (1986); B. Stone, *The Genesis of the French Revolution* (1994); W. Stinchcombe, *The American Revolution and the French Alliance* (1969); G. Wood, *The Radicalism of the American Revolution* (1990).

For scholarly essays and additional texts on the American Revolution, see:
http://odur.let.rug.nl/~usa/

For scholarly essays, images, maps, and documents on the French Revolution, see:
http://chnm.gmu.edu/revolution/

Chapter 18

The factory age began in Britain during the late eighteenth century and spread rapidly to Western Europe and North America during the first half of the nineteenth century. Industrialization had a major impact on social and economic life. The impact of the factory on the natural environment was not a major concern of early industrialists, most of whom equated the advanced machine technology and urbanization with human progress. However, the social and environmental costs of industrialization are now part of the large body of scholarship on this broad topic.

C. Chinn, *Poverty Amidst Prosperity: The Urban Poor in England, 1834–1914* (1995); P. Deane, *The First Industrial Revolution* (1965); G. Himmelfarb, *The Idea of Poverty: England in the Early Industrial Age* (1983); D. Landes, *The Unbound Prometheus: Technological Change and Industrial Development in Western Europe from 1750 to the Present* (1969); P. Mathias, *The First Industrial Revolution* (1983); K. Morgan, *The Birth of Industrial Britain: Social Change, 1750–1850* (2004); C. Nardinelli, *Child Labor and the Industrial Revolution* (1990); I. Pinchbeck, *Women Workers and the Industrial Revolution, 1750–1850* (1930, reprinted 1969); S. Pollard, *Peaceful Conquest: The Industrialization of Europe, 1760–1970* (1981); E. P. Thompson, *The Making of the English Working Class* (1964); P. Stearns, *The Industrial Revolution in World History* (1993); L. Tilly & J. Scott, *Women, Work and Family* (1978).

For additional sources on the Industrial Revolution, see:
http://history.evansville.net/industry.html

Chapter 19

The defeat of Napoleon meant the end of French domination of Europe, but the ideas of the French Revolution could not be extinguished. Conservative regimes attempted to restore the prerevolutionary political and social order in the West, but liberal reformers, spurred by the changes introduced by the early stages of industrialization, pushed for constitutional, representative government and the inclusion of the middle class in the political process. At the same time, the plight of the new urban working class was championed by socialist and Marxist thinkers.

B. Anderson, *Imagined Communities: Reflections on the Origin and Spread of Nationalism* (1991); A. Arblaster, *The Rise and Decline of Western Liberalism* (1984); C. A. Bayly, *The Birth of the Modern*

World, 1780–1914 (2004); A. Briggs, *The Making of Modern England* (1959); M. Brock, *The Great Reform Act* (1974); I. Deak, *The Lawful Revolution: Louis Kossuth and the Hungarians, 1848–1849* (1979); J. Droz, *Europe Between Revolutions, 1815–1848* (1967); J. Elster, *An Introduction to Karl Marx* (1985); J. F. C. Harrison, *Quest for the New Moral World: Robert Owen and the Owenites in Britain and America* (1969); E. J. Hobsbawm, *The Age of Revolution, 1789–1848* (1962); R. Porter & M. Teich, Eds., *Romanticism in National Context* (1999); R. Price, *The Revolutions of 1848* (1989); J. Sperber, *The European Revolutions, 1848–1851* (1994); D. Thompson, *The Chartists: Popular Politics in the Industrial Revolution* (1984).

The Yale Law School Avalon Project provides additional documents at:
http://www.yale.edu/lawweb/avalon/19th.htm

Chapter 20

The American and French revolutionaries skillfully appealed to the ideas of citizenship, equality before the law, and the rights of man as central components of national identity. Initially, nationalism was situated within the broader context of human freedom. By the second half of the nineteenth century, however, nationalism had become an exclusive rather than an inclusive phenomenon. New nation-states emerged, with leaders accentuating the unique cultural features of the citizenry. Historians have emphasized the role played by conservatives in redefining nationalism in this more parochial manner.

R. F. Bensel, *Yankee Leviathan: The Origins of Central State Authority in America* (1990); D. Blackbourn, *The Long Nineteenth Century: A History of Germany, 1780–1918* (1998); G. Chapman, *The Dreyfus Affair: A Reassessment* (1955); F. J. Coppa, *The Wars of Italian Independence* (1992); G. Craig, *Germany, 1866–1945* (1978); S. Elwitt, *The Making of the Third Republic: Class and Politics in France, 1868–1884* (1975); R. A. Kann, *The Multinational Empire, 1875–1914* (1950); W. B. Lincoln, *The Great Reforms: Autocracy, Bureaucracy, and the Politics of Change in Imperial Russia* (1990); G. Mosse, *The Crisis of German Ideology* (1964); B. F. Pauley, *The Habsburg Legacy, 1867–1939* (1972);

O. Pflanze, *Bismarck and the Development of Germany,* 3 vols. (1990); H. Rogger, *Russia in the Age of Modernization and Revolution, 1881–1917* (1983); A. Sked, *The Decline and Fall of the Habsburg Empire, 1815–1918* (1989); D. M. Smith, *The Making of Italy, 1796–1870* (1968); N. Stone, *Europe Transformed* (1984); J. P. Taylor, *The Struggle for Mastery in Europe, 1848–1918* (1974); G. Wawro, *Warfare and Society in Europe, 1792–1914* (2000); T. Zeldin, *France, 1848–1945,* 2 vols. (1973, 1977).

Helpful scholarly analysis of the Victorian era is available at:
http://www.victoriandatabase.com

Chapter 21

The imperial expansion of the West during the late nineteenth century sharply accelerated a process that began just prior to 1500. Europe's industrial power facilitated the new age of empire in Africa and Asia, while Western cultural developments, especially ideas concerning race, strengthened arguments in favor of empire. The impact of Western ideas in a global setting, and the incongruity between European democratic politics and colonial administration, are topics that have interested scholars of this period.

D. Abernethy, *The Dynamics of Global Dominance: European Overseas Empires, 1415–1980* (2000); C. Allen, *The Human Christ: The Search for the Historical Jesus* (1998); F. Baumer, *Modern European Thought* (1977); P. Bowler, *Evolution: The History of an Idea* (1989); J. Burrow, *The Crisis of Reason: European Thought, 1848–1914* (2000); O. Chadwick, *The Secularization of the European Mind in the Nineteenth Century* (1975); A. Danto, *Nietzsche as Philosopher* (1965); M. Doyle, *Empires* (1986); A. Desmond & J. Moore, *Darwin* (1992); B. Farrington, *What Darwin Really Said* (1966); G. Fredrickson, *Racism: A Short History* (2003); P. Gay, *Freud: A Life for Our Time* (1988); J. C. Greene, *The Death of Adam* (1961); E. Hobsbawm, *The Age of Empire, 1875–1914* (1987); T. Pakenham, *The Scramble for Africa* (1991); A. Hochschild, *King Leopold's Ghost: A Story of Greed, Terror, and Heroism in Colonial Africa* (1999); P. Roazen, *Freud's Political and Social Thought* (1968); R. Stromberg,

European Intellectual History Since 1789 (1986); N. Wilson, *God's Funeral* (1999).

Primary sources from the age of imperialism can be found at:
http://www.fordham.edu/halsall/mod/modsbook36.html

Chapter 22

Western Europe's global dominance was short-lived. At the start of the twentieth century Europe's great powers afforded their citizens a quality of life that could scarcely be imagined one century earlier. However, four years of devastating warfare shattered the self-confidence of the West, undermining economic security and calling into question many of the optimistic assumptions about human rationality first articulated during the Enlightenment.

I. Beckett, *The Great War, 1914–1918* (2001); J. Black, *The Great War and the Making of the Modern World* (2011); V. Dedijer, *The Road to Sarajevo* (1966); N. Ferguson, *The Pity of War: Explaining World War I* (2000); F. Fischer, *Germany's Aims in the First World War* (1967); S. Fitzpatrick, *The Russia Revolution, 1917–1932* (1994); P. Fussell, *The Great War and Modern Memory* (1975); M. Gilbert, *The First World War* (1994); Elisabeth Glaser, *The Treaty of Versailles: A Reassessment After 75 Years* (1998); O. Hale, *The Great Illusion, 1900–1914* (1971); L. Hart, *The Real War, 1914–1918* (1964); H. Holborn, *The Political Collapse of Europe* (1951); J. Jole, *The Origins of the First World War* (1984); J. Keegan, *The First World War* (1999); J. Keynes, *The Economic Consequences of the Peace* (1920); L. Lafore, *The Long Fuse* (1971); A. Mayer, *The Politics and Diplomacy of Peacemaking* (1967); H. Nicholson, *Peacemaking* (1965); K. Robbins, *The First World War* (1984); D. Stevenson, *The First World War and International Politics* (1988); A. Walworth, *Wilson and His Peacemakers* (1986); J. Williams, *The Homefronts: Britain, France, and Germany, 1914–1918* (1972); J. Winter, *The Experience of World War I* (1988).

Chapter 23

The democratic liberal tradition was placed squarely on the defensive during the years between World War I and World War II. A successful communist revolution in Russia, the emergence of authoritarian rule in Spain and Japan, and the ominous rise of Fascism in Italy and Germany challenged the viability of responsible self-government around the world. Scholars have examined the crisis of Western liberal values during these years in a variety of studies that range from the more traditional fields of diplomatic and political history, to more recent efforts in cultural and social studies.

B. Bosworth, *Mussolini's Italy: Life Under the Fascist Dictatorship* (2007); K. D. Bracher, *The German Dictatorship* (1970); R. J. P. Clavin, *The Great Depression in Europe, 1929–1939* (2000); D. Cohen, *The War Come Home: Disabled Veterans in Britain and Germany* (2001); R. Conquest, *The Great Terror: Stalin's Purges of the Thirties* (1968); I. Deutscher, *Stalin: A Political Biography* (1967); G. Eley, *Forging Democracy: The History of the Left in Europe* (2002); R. Evans, *The Coming of the Third Reich* (2004); S. Fitzpatrick, *Stalin's Peasants: Resistance and Survival in the Russian Village After Collectivization* (1994); K. Galbraith, *The Great Crash* (1979); N. Greene, *From Versailles to Vichy: The Third Republic, 1919–1940* (1970); R. Hamilton, *Who Voted for Hitler?* (1982); M. Jackson, *Fallen Sparrows: The International Brigades in the Spanish Civil War* (1994); B. Kent, *The Spoils of War: The Politics, Economics, and Diplomacy of Reparations, 1918–1932* (1993); I. Kershaw, *Hitler: 1889–1936 Hubris* (1998) and *Hitler: 1936–1945 Nemesis* (2000); C. Kindleberger, *The World in Depression, 1929–1939* (1986); M. Kitchen, *Europe Between the Wars: A Political History* (1988); E. Nolte, *Three Faces of Fascism* (1965); S. Payne, *A History of Fascism, 1914–1945* (1995); D. Peukert, *Inside Nazi Germany: Conformity, Opposition, and Racism in Everyday Life* (1987); D. P. Silverman, *Reconstructing Europe After the Great War* (1982); D. M. Smith, *Mussolini* (1982); R. J. Sontag, *A Broken World, 1919–1939* (1971); R. Tucker, *Stalin in Power* (1990); E. G. Walters, *The Other Europe: Eastern Europe to 1945* (1988);

J. Winter, *Sites of Memory, Sites of Mourning: The Great War in European Cultural History* (1998).

Documents related to the rise of Fascism can be found at:
http://www.lib.byu.edu/~rdh/eurodocs/germ/1945.html

Chapter 24

The massive destruction of World War II effectively put an end to Europe's position of global dominance. Shattered economies, demoralized civilian populations, and the moral turpitude of the Holocaust left Europe in a state of dependency in 1945. Yet the war also marked the triumph of liberal democratic principles over a hate-filled Nazi world-view. On the home front, the war transformed the role of women in the workplace, energized whole populations around a broad set of humane values associated with the Enlightenment tradition, and fostered a strong movement in favor of international cooperation.

R. Adams, *British Politics and Foreign Policy in the Age of Appeasement, 1935–1939* (1993); A. Beevor, *The Battle for Spain: The Spanish Civil War 1936–1939* (2006); P. Bell, *The Origins of the Second World War in Europe* (1986); C. Browning, *The Origins of the Final Solution* (2004); B. Calber, *The Battle of Britain* (1962); B. Collier, *The War in the Far East* (1970); T. Des Pres, *The Survivors* (1976); H. Feis, *Churchill, Roosevelt, Stalin* (1957); M Geyer, *Shattered Past: Reconstructing German Histories* (2003); H. Liddell Hart, *History of the Second World War* (1970); A. Iriye, *Power and Culture: The Japanese-American War, 1941–1945* (1981); J. Keegan, *The Second World War* (1989); M. Knox, *Mussolini Unleashed* (1982); M. Marrus, *The Holocaust in History* (1987); R.J. Overy, *War and Economy in the Third Reich* (1995); R. Overy, *Why the Allies Won* (1995); J. Remak, *The Origins of the Second World War* (1976); W. Rock, *British Appeasement in the 1930s* (1977); M. Sherwin, *A World Destroyed: The Atomic Bomb and the Grand Alliance* (1975); D. Watts, *How War Came* (1989); G. Weinberg, *A World at Arms: A Global History of World War II* (1994); G. Weinberg, *The*

Foreign Policy of Hitler's Germany, 2 vols. (1970, 1979); G. Wright, *The Ordeal of Total War, 1939–1945* (1968); E. Wiesel, *Night* (1958).

Primary sources from World War II are available at:
http://www.yale.edu/lawweb/wwii/wwii.htm

Chapter 25

The Grand Alliance of the United States, Great Britain, and the Soviet Union during World War II raised expectations that a new international order might be realized after the defeat of Nazi Germany and imperial Japan. However, despite the fact that a new international organization, the United Nations, was established in 1945, deep ideological differences between the world's two "superpowers" led to the emergence of a "Cold War" that lasted until the late 1980s. While European decolonization led to the emergence of new nation-states around the globe, many of these states were alternately courted and coerced by the superpowers into joining the Cold War struggle. Recent scholarship has examined the overall cost of this rivalry in terms of lost opportunities in the areas of education, medicine, food production, environmental protection, and balanced economic development in the non-Western world.

M. Beschloss, *The Crisis Years: Kennedy and Khrushchev, 1960–1963* (1991); D. Caute, *The Dancer Defects: The Struggle for Cultural Supremacy During the Cold War* (2003); L. Davis, *The Cold War Begins* (1974); A. DePorte, *Europe Between the Superpowers* (1979); L. Freedman, *The Evolution of Nuclear Strategy* (1989); J. Gaddis, *The United States and the Origins of the Cold War, 1941–1947* (1972); J. Gaddis, *We Know Now: Rethinking the Cold War* (1998); J. L. Gaddis, *The Cold War: A New History* (2005); R. Garthoff, *The Great Transition: American-Soviet Relations and the End of the Cold War* (1994); J. Gimbel, *The Origins of the Marshall Plan* (1976); L. Halle, *The Cold War as History* (1967); E. J. Hobsbawm, *The Age of Extremes: A History of the World, 1914–1991* (2001); T. Judt, *Postwar: A History of Europe Since 1945* (2005); S. Karnow, *Vietnam: A History* (1984); P. Kenez, *A History of the Soviet Union from the Beginning to the End* (1999); W. LaFeber, *America, Russia, and the Cold War* (1976); G. Partos, *The World That Came in from the Cold* (1993); A. Rubenstein, *Soviet Foreign Policy Since World War II* (1981); M. Walker, *The Cold War* (1993); O. A. Westad, *The Global Cold War: Third World Interventions and the Making of Our Times* (2005); M. Young, *The Vietnam Wars 1945–1990* (1991).

Cold War documents and an additional bibliography are available at:
http://wwics.si.edu/index.
cfm?fuseaction=topics_id=1409

Chapter 26

Despite being eclipsed by the United States and the Soviet Union after World War II, Western Europe rebounded quickly thanks to massive economic aid from the United States. Economic stagnation in Soviet-controlled areas contrasted sharply with high standards of living in the democratic West. The end of the Soviet Union and the reintegration of Europe have raised the prospect of greater economic, military, and political union in Europe. Europe stands poised as one of the world's great economic powerhouses. During the last decade, an abundance of literature has emerged on the New Europe.

J. Black, *Europe Since 1990* (2009); E. Bottome, *The Balance of Terror: Nuclear Weapons and the Illusions of Security, 1945–1985* (1986); A. Brown, *The Gorbachev Factor* (1996); J. Chafetz & A. Dworkin, *Female Revolt: Women's Movement in World Historical Perspective* (1986); Colin Crouch, *Social Change in Western Europe* (1999); D. Hiro, *Holy Wars: The Rise of Islamic Fundamentalism* (1989); L. Johnson, *Central Europe: Enemies and Neighbors and Friends* (1996); J. Keep, *Last of the Empires: A History of the Soviet Union, 1945–1991* (1995); P. Kennedy, *Preparing for the Twenty-First Century* (1993); P. Kenney, *A Carnival of Revolution: Central Europe 1989* (2002); R. Khalidi, *Resurrecting Empire: Western Footprints and America's Perilous Path in the Middle East* (2004); M. Klare, *Blood and Oil* (2004); M. Milani, *The Making of Iran's Islamic Revolution* (1994); J. Newhouse,

Europe Adrift (1997); R. Pells, Not Like Us: How Europeans Have Loved, Hated, and Transformed American Culture Since World War II (1997); A. Rashid, The Taliban: Militant Islam, Oil and Fundamentalism in Central Asia (2000); D. Remnick, Lenin's Tomb (1993); D. Sassoon, The Culture of the Europeans (2006); L. Silber & A. Little, Yugoslavia: Death of a Nation (1996); A. Slaughter, A New World Order (2005); G. Stokes, The Walls Came Tumbling Down: The Collapse of Communism in Eastern Europe (1993); H. Turner, Germany from Partition to Reunification (1992); S. Weart, Nuclear Fear: A History of Images (1988); D. Yergin, The Prize: The Epic Quest for Oil, Money, and Power (1992).

For recent scholarly articles on the European Union, see:
http://www.mtholyoke.edu/acad/intrel/eu.htm

PHOTO CREDITS

Part 6: xii and 528: The Art Gallery Collection/ Alamy

Chapter 18: 530: Hulton Archive/Getty Images; **536:** Walker Art Gallery, National Museums, Liverpool/The Bridgeman Art Library; **538:** Chicago Historical Society; **540:** The Granger Collection, NYC; **542:** Art Resource/The Metropolitan Museum of Art; **547:** Historical Picture Archive/Corbis; **548:** Image Asset Management Ltd./SuperStock; **549:** The Granger Collection, NYC; **551:** Guttmann/ Getty Images

Chapter 19: 558: *Solidiers disperse demonstrating crowds in front of the Lower Autrian Diet in Vienna on March 13, 1848,* J. Albrecht. Colored lithograph, 31.5 × 23 cm. Inv. 20.107. Wien Museum Karlsplatz, Vienna, Austria/Erich Lessing/Art Resource; **561:** Bildarchiv der Osterreichische Nationalbibliothek; *Liberty Leading the People, July 28, 1830* (1830), Eugene Delacroix. Oil on canvas, 260 × 325 cm. RF129. Hervé Lewandowski. Louvre, Paris, France. Réunion des Musées Nationaux/Art Resource, NY; **571:** Private Collection/Alinari/The Bridgeman Art Library; **572:** Alinari/Art Resource, NY; **575:** North Wind Picture Archives/Alamy; **576:** Museum of London; **578:** Blake, William (1757–1827). Yale Center for British Art, Paul Mellon Collection, USA/The Bridgeman Art Library; **582:** The Granger Collection, NYC

Chapter 20: 586: The Print Collector/Alamy; **591:** Prince Otto von Bismarck in Uniform with Prussian Helmet, Franz von Lenbach. Kunsthistorisches Museum, Vienna, Austria. Erich Lessing/Art Resource, NY; **596:** Mary Evans Picture Library/Weimar Archive; **600:** Henry Guttmann/Getty Images; **605:** *Lunch of the District Administration - the farmers wait patiently* (1872), Grigoriy Grigoryevich Myasoyedov. bpk, Berlin/Tretyakov Gallery, Moscow, Russia/Art Resource, NY; **608:** Hulton Archive/Getty Images; **611:** Bettmann/Corbis; **612:** Bettmann/Corbis; **613:** Interfoto/ Personalities/Alamy

Chapter 21: 618: Reproduced by permission of the Syndics of Cambridge University Library;

622: Wellcome Trust Medical Photographic Library; **626:** The Granger Collection, NYC; **628:** North Wind Picture Archives/Alamy; **630:** North Wind Picture Archives/Alamy; **633:** Private Collection/The Bridgeman Art Library; **635:** Pictorial Press Ltd/Alamy; **639:** The Granger Collection, NYC; **641:** *Night Café (Le Café de nuit)* (1888), Vincent van Gogh. Oil on canvas, 28-1/2 × 36-1/4 in. 1961.18.34. Yale University Art Gallery, New Haven, Connecticut, U.S.A./Art Resource, NY

Part 7: xiii and 646: *Guernica* (1937), Pablo Picasso. Oil on canvas, 350 × 782 cm. © 2011 Estate of Pablo Picasso / Artists Rights Society (ARS), New York/John Bigelow Taylor/Art Resource, NY

Chapter 22: 648: "Women of Britain Say - Go!", recruitment poster, 1915 (litho), Kealey, E.P. (20th century)/Private Collection/Photo © Bonhams, London, UK/The Bridgeman Art Library; **651:** Bettmann/Corbis; **656:** National Archives and Records Administration; **659:** Alice Schalek/Three Lions/Getty Images; **661:** Library of Congress; **663:** Brown Brothers; **666:** Hulton Archive/Keystone/Getty Images; **667:** Russian propaganda poster celebrating 1st May (colour litho), Russian School, (20th century)/ Museum of the Revolution, Moscow, Russia/ The Bridgeman Art Library International; **668:** Bettmann/Corbis; **672:** Bettmann/Corbis

Chapter 23: 678: Library of Congress; **682:** Library of Congress; **684:** View of the technical school wing (1926–1927). Gropius, Walter (1883–1969). Bauhaus School in Dessau, Germany.
© 2011 Artists Rights Society (ARS), New York/ VG Bild-Kunst, Bonn/Vanni/Art Resource, NY; **685:** The Granger Collection, NYC; **689:** Bettmann/Corbis; **692:** Bettmann/Corbis; **695:** Library of Congress; **696:** Library of Congress; **700:** David King Collection

Chapter 24: 706: Hulton-Deutsch Collection/ Corbis; **713:** Disentangled German on Champs-Elysees. Paris, France, September, 1940. LAP-67 Roger-Viollet/The Image Works; **716:** Oasis/ Photos 12/Alamy; **718:** Dmitri Baltermants/The Dmitri Baltermants Collection/Corbis; **721:** Corbis; **722:** Swim Ink 2, LLC/Corbis; **723:**

Bettmann/Corbis; **728:** Keystone/Hulton Archive/Getty Images; **729:** Archive Holdings Inc/Archive Photos/Getty Images

Part 8: xv and 737: Atlantide Phototravel/ Corbis

Chapter 25: 738: Bettmann/Corbis; **740:** RDA/ Central Press/Hulton Archive/Getty Images; **745:** Bettmann/Corbis; **746:** Everett Collection Inc/ Alamy; **750:** Bettmann/Corbis; **751:** Intense autumn cleaning (decolonisation), from 'Ludas Matyi', 6th October 1960 (colour litho), Gizi, Szego (20th century)/Private Collection/Archives

Charmet/The Bridgeman Art Library; **753:** Jules Motte/SIPA Press; **757:** David King Collection; **761:** Owen/Black Star; **764:** Library of Congress

Chapter 26: 770: Anthony Vizard/Eye Ubiquitous/Corbis; **774:** White House/CNP/ Corbis; **776:** David Brauchli/Reuters/Corbis; **779:** Thomson Reuters; **781:** Hulton Archive/ Getty Image; **785:** Destinations/Corbis; **788:** Ahmad Masood/Reuters/Corbis; **790:** Christine Muschi/Reuters/Corbis; **796:** Alain Dejean/ Sygma/Corbis; **798:** Ricardo Azoury/Corbis; **799:** Abedin Taherkenareh/epa/Corbis; **801:** Corbis

INDEX

Note: Page numbers ending in "f" refer to figures. Page numbers ending in "m" refer to maps. Page numbers ending in "t" refer to tables.

A

Abdul Hamid II (Ottoman Empire), 606, 608f
absolutism
  France, 427, 429–434
  Prussia, 421
  Russia, 439
Abyssinia, 591
Academie des Sciences, 455
Act of Supremacy (England, 1534), 396
Adams, Abigail, 475, 489–490
Adams, John, 475, 489–490, 506
administration. *See* bureaucracy
Adoration of the Lamb (van Eyck), 357f
The Advancement of Learning (Bacon), 460
Afghanistan, 652, 773, 786–787, 788f
Africa. *See also specific countries*
  Berlin Conference on African affairs (1884), 624–626
  decolonization of, 751–752, 751f
  new imperialism and, 620–627, 625m, 630f, 631
  Portuguese exploration of, 369
  postcolonial migrations from, 753, 754, 755m
  slave trade in, 490
African soldiers, in World War I, 658
Africa (poem, Petrarch), 348
Afrika Korps, 714, 726
afterlife. *See* death/mortality
Agadir, 652
Against the Robbing and Murdering Hordes of Peasants (Luther), 385–386
Age of Reason. *See* Enlightenment
Age of Religious Wars, 379
agriculture
  early modern era, 423–425
  Enlightenment, 484
  Europe (medieval), 367–368
  famines (*See* famines)
  Great Depression, 686
  Industrial Revolution and, 535–537
  Scientific Revolution and, 461–462
  slave trade, 490, 492
  Soviet Union, 699
  World War I, 663
agronomy, 462–463
Albania/Albanians, 608, 653, 691, 714, 800
Albert of Brandenburg, 381
Alberti, Leon Battista, 340, 351f
Alembert, Jean le Rond d', 480
Alexander I (Hungary), 691
Alexander III (Russia), 604
Alexander II (Russia), 604, 614

Alexander I (Russia), 519, 560, 561, 563
Alexander VI (pope), 392
Alexandra (wife of Nicholas II), 664–665
Algeria/Algerians, 658, 717, 726, 751, 754, 800
Alighieri, Dante, 347–348
Alliance system, in World War I, 650–653
al Qaeda, 803
Alsace, 598, 671
Americanization, 610–611
American Revolution, 499–527
Americas, slave trade in, 492. *See also* Latin America; *specific countries*
Amish, 389
Amritsar, 659–660
Anabaptists, 388–389, 405
Anatolia, 672. *See also* Turkey
Andropov, Yuri, 773
anesthetics, 538
Anglican Church (Church of England)
  Charles II and, 414
  civil war and, 410, 411, 435
  conservatives vs. liberals, 798
  creation of, 397
  early Stuarts and, 434
  end of monopoly of, 601
  Scientific Revolution and, 466
Anne of Cleves, 397
anomie (anxiety), 637
Anschluss (Nazi unification with Austria), 709
anthropology, 636
antiballistic missiles (ABMs), 765
antibiotics, 789
anti-Semitism. *See also* Holocaust
  German nationalism and, 612
  Hitler's, 691
  Nazi Germany, 688, 693, 696–697
  Poland, 443–444
  Third French Republic, 599, 600
antiseptics, 538
ANZUS, 759
apocalyptic preaching, 385
appeasement (1933–1939), 708–711
Aquinas, Thomas, 453
Arab Spring (2011), 800
Aragon, 444
archaeology, 636
archetypes, 636
architecture. *See also* infrastructure; *specific buildings and types of architecture*
  Bauhaus School, 684, 684f
  Enlightenment, 494
  Renaissance, 350, 351–353, 359
Arden, Mary, 406
Aristarchus of Samos, 456
aristocracy. *See also* hereditary succession; *specific nobles and dynasties*
  Europe (early modern era), 422–423

French Revolution and, 510
aristocratic *salons*, 481
Aristotle, 454, 458
Arkwright, Richard, 540
Armenia, 608
armies. *See* war/militarization
arms race. *See* nuclear arms race
Arouet, Francois Marie. *See* Voltaire
Arthur (English prince), 395–396
Articles of Confederation, 505
artillery, 363
Artois, count of, 511
arts. *See also* culture and society
  Bauhaus School, 684, 684f
  Enlightenment, 493–495
  Italian Renaissance, 345–357, 356f
  Medici family and, 344
  modern art and music, 640–642
  modernism, 638–640
  Northern Renaissance, 358–361
  "socialist realism," 701
  Spanish Golden Age, 403
  transformation in, 638–642
Asia. *See also specific countries*
  Cold War events and issues in, 754–761
  decolonization of, 748, 750–751
  new imperialism and, 620, 626–631, 629m
  World War II, 723–725
assassinations
  Alexander I (Hungary), 691
  Alexander II (Russia), 604, 614
  Ferdinand, Francis, 651, 653
  Henry III (France), 404
  Henry IV (France), 429
  Sadat, Anwar, 800
  William of Orange, 400
assignats (government bonds), 511
astronomy, 456–460
Atlantic, battle of (World War II), 726
Atlantic exploration, 367–373
Atlee, Clement, 742
atomic bombs, 636, 739. *See also* nuclear arms race
Augustine of Hippo, 339
Auschwitz, 719
ausgleich (compromise), 603
Australia, 658, 659, 725, 759
Austria
  Cold War and, 754
  Nazi Germany and, 709
  Treaty of Versailles and, 670–671
Austrian Empire (Habsburg Empire). *See also* World War I
  anti-Semitism in, 612
  Catherine the Great and, 441
  Charles V and, 387
  Congress System and, 560–563
  decline of, 602–603, 603m
  dual monarchy, 602–603
  early modern era, 446
  French absolutism and, 433–434
  French Revolution and, 511, 513
  German Confederation and, 602–603